COVID-19 Pandemic, Geospatial Information, and Community Resilience

Global Applications and Lessons

COVID-19 Pandemic, Geospatial Information, and Community Resilience

Global Applications and Lessons

Abbas Rajabifard

Greg Foliente

Daniel Paez

CRC Press
Taylor & Francis Group
Boca Raton London New York

CRC Press is an imprint of the
Taylor & Francis Group, an **informa** business

First edition published 2021
by CRC Press
6000 Broken Sound Parkway NW, Suite 300, Boca Raton, FL 33487-2742

and by CRC Press
2 Park Square, Milton Park, Abingdon, Oxon, OX14 4RN

© 2021 Taylor & Francis Group, LLC

CRC Press is an imprint of Taylor & Francis Group, LLC

Library of Congress Cataloging-in-Publication Data

ISBN: 978-0-367-77531-5 (hbk)
ISBN: 978-1-032-02045-7 (pbk)
ISBN:978-1-003-18159-0 (ebk)

Typeset in CMR9
by KnowledgeWorks Global Ltd.

Contents

Foreword

The COVID-19 pandemic has left no country untouched, with governments and all sectors of society impacted. As a consequence, our world is now being forced to rapidly adapt to confronting social and economic changes and challenges, from local to global levels, across all industries and sectors, and in all areas of supply and demand. However, the pandemic also presents us with a chance to rise from the challenges we face as a global community and identify new opportunities in which we can grow and build resilient and sustainable communities.

COVID-19 has reinforced the unprecedented need for data, geospatial information, enabling technologies, and insights for governments and citizens across the globe, to not only enable decision-makers to inform policies and planning, but to also minimize the risk to people, especially the most vulnerable population groups. As it continues, the pandemic has not only exacerbated our world's vulnerabilities within and among countries, it has reinforced pre-existing obstacles to realizing the SDGs – structural inequalities, socio-economic gaps, and systemic challenges and risks.

In response, and strategically led by the UN-GGIM Academic Network, this timely book brings together expertise from all around the world, presenting advanced research and case studies that raise awareness and provide valuable insights on the critical role of geospatial information and enabling technologies to better respond to and manage the global crisis we continue to face.

While COVID-19 is an unprecedented challenge, we also live in a time of unprecedented access to data, innovation and technology. This gives us the opportunity to facilitate geospatial data sharing on a scale as never before, making a real impact for all citizens of the world through delivering decision-ready solutions that not only aids decision-making during the pandemic, but creates a framework and structure that will remain in place as we recover and increase our global resilience.

Looking beyond the devastation that has occurred, we can see the truly interconnected nature of our world, further highlighting the United Nations notion that no one is safe until everyone is safe. It is imperative that at this time, we act in solidarity with our communities all around the world, particularly the most vulnerable, in order to grow our sense of humanity and build a more sustainable and resilient future.

The ideas, research and solutions shared in this book will no doubt aid in the global effort to better understand the current pandemic as we continue together to create a better future for all.

Dr. Greg Scott
UN-GGIM Secretariat
United Nations Statistics Division
Department of Economic and Social Affairs

Acknowledgments

This book brought together the expertise of more than 120 leading professionals, practitioners and academic from more than 30 countries in different related fields for managing pandemic, in particular experts in the field of geospatial industry, and policy-makers and their perspectives to share their experiences and approaches to respond to CIVID-19 pandemic to improve community resilience.

The book is the result of a collaborative initiative of the United Nations Global Geospatial Information Management (UN-GGIM) Academic Network, its members and Centre for Spatial Data Infrastructures and Land Administration (CSDILA) and Centre for Disaster Management and Public Safety (CDMPS) at the University of Melbourne, Australia. Similarly, FIG Commission 7 has been another instrumental entity for the development of this book, especially in demonstrating the critical role of the geospatial community in the fight against the pandemic. The book has drawn upon the advanced research and methods implemented that aid the global effort to better understand and respond to the COVID-19 pandemic and its devastating impacts.

The editors have been privileged to have been involved with the UN-GGIM Academic Network in a leadership role, enjoying the support of the Academic Network members and a vast number of researchers, practitioners and policy makers and geospatial engineers throughout the journey for the preparation of this book.

We would like to acknowledge and thank the contribution of all chapter authors and other contributors. In particular, we would like to thank the support of Dr. Greg Scott from UN-GGIM Secretariat Team for his support and contribution.

We are grateful to the CRC Press, Taylor and Francis Group, for their support and arrangement to publish this work as Open Access, which allows all to use the experiences and research presented in this book to their own best advantage. In particular, we would like to express our sincere thanks to Ms. Irma Britton, Senior Editor, Environmental Sciences, GIS & Remote Sensing CRC Press – Taylor & Francis Group for her contribution, continuous support, and facilitation for publishing this book. We also like to thank Ms. Rebecca Pringle and the rest of the T&F publishing team for their professionalism during the preparation and publication of this book.

Finally, we would like to thank the Department of Infrastructure Engineering and the research team at the CSDILA for their support, and in particular special thanks to Dr. Farhad Laylavi, Ms. Negar Naderpajouh, Dr. Ida Jazayeri and Ms. Jemma Brewster from the CSDILA Centre for their outstanding editorial assistance in preparation of this publication.

We hope this book can contribute to the global response to the COVID-19 pandemic where we can share invaluable tools and insights and work together to not only overcome the unprecedented challenges we face but also aid in the creation of a stronger and more resilient future for all.

Abbas Rajabifard, Greg Foliente and Daniel Páez
Editors

Editors

Prof. Abbas Rajabifard

Professor Abbas Rajabifard is Director of Smart and Sustainable Development and Director of Centre for SDIs and Land Administration, Faculty of Engineering and Information Technology, the University of Melbourne. He is an active leader in land and geospatial modernisation, disaster resilience, sustainability, digital twin, and urban analytics, and his passion is in the field of research and innovation to serve global community. He has spent his career researching, developing, applying and teaching land administration and geospatial information to deliver benefits to both governments and wider society. Prof. Abbas is also Discipline Leader Geomatics, at University of Melbourne. He is Chair of the UN Global Geospatial Information Management Academic Network (a strategic research and training arm for member states to address Sustainability Development Goals). Further details at: https://findanexpert.unimelb.edu.au/profile/6142-abbas-rajabifard

Prof. Greg Foliente

Prof. Greg Foliente is Enterprise Professor in the Faculty of Engineering and Information Technology and Deputy Director of the University of Melbourne's Centre for Disaster Management and Public Safety (CDMPS). He leads interdisciplinary and transdisciplinary research, education, consulting and collaboration initiatives that advance innovation in the urban systems and built environment sectors, focussing on improved sustainability, liveability and resilience. Greg is also the Founder and Director of nBLue Pty Ltd, an international consulting practice on system sustainability and resilience. He previously worked for over 20 years at Australia's national science agency, the CSIRO, where he led numerous international and national research programs. Further details at: https://www.linkedin.com/in/foliente/

Dr. Daniel Paez

Daniel Paez is a qualified Civil Engineer with a PhD in Geomatics from the University of Melbourne and with several years of experience in management consulting, academic research, project management and policy development. He currently works as a senior land and spatial analysis consultant based in Sydney, Australia. Dr. Paez is an associate researcher in universities in Colombia and Australia and a world expert in strategic planning, geospatial analysis and complex system models for urban development. Daniel has applied this expertise in a wide range of projects and public policies including land administration, GIS, Spatial data infrastructures, land use planning, sustainable transportation and stakeholder management. As an international consultant, he has worked in over 13 countries in many regions of the world including North Africa, Latin-America and South East Asia. More recently he has been working closely with international organizations including UN-habitat and the World Bank on developing better strategies to involve the social and private sectors as partners in development projects. He also participated in the development of the UN urban-rural land linkage framework as a mechanism to achieve the Sustainable Development Goals (SDGs). Further details at: https://www.linkedin.com/in/daniel-paez-11bb546/

List of Contributors

Nadia Abbaszadeh Tehrani (Chapter 22)
Aerospace Research Institute, Ministry of Science, Research, and Technology – Iran

David Abbott (Chapter 26)
Data Analysis and Dissemination, Statistics for Development Division – Pacific Community

Eva Alisic (Chapter 27)
Melbourne School of Population and Global Health, The University of Melbourne – Australia

Mark Allan (Chapter 42)
Infrastructure Engineering Department, The University of Melbourne – Australia

Khlood Ghalib Alrasheedi (Chapter 25)
RMIT University – Australia

Arturo Ardila-Gomez (Chapter 46)
World Bank – USA

Lesley Arnold (Chapters 12 & 24)
Surveying and Spatial Sciences Institute (SSSI) – Australia

Kathryn A. Arnold (Chapter 23)
Smart Places, Council for Scientific and Industrial Research (CSIR) – South Africa

Mohd. Ammar Ashraf (Chapter 14)
Indian Institute of Remote Sensing, Indian Space Research Organisation – India

Orhun Aydin (Chapter 9)
Environmental Systems Research Institute (ESRI) & Spatial Sciences Institute, University of Southern California – USA

Sultana Nasrin Baby (Chapter 25)
City of Whittlesea Council, Victoria – Australia

Efthimios Bakogiannis (Chapter 39)
National Technical University of Athens – Greece

Michael Batty (Chapter 18)
Centre for Advanced Spatial Analysis (CASA), University College London – UK

Keith Clifford Bell (Chapter 2)
World Bank (WB) – Thailand

Jiri Bouchal (Chapter 30)
Laboratory on Geoinformatics and Cartography, Department of Geography, Faculty of Science, Masaryk University – Czech Republic

Phil Bright (Chapter 26)
GIS, Innovation and Dissemination Lead, Statistics for Development Division – Pacific Community

Maria Antonia Brovelli (Chapter 3)
Department of Civil and Environmental Engineering, Politecnico di Milano – Italy

Malcolm Campbell (Chapter 41)
GeoHealth Laboratory & School of Earth and Environment & Geospatial Research Institute, University of Canterbury – New Zealand

Lauren Carpenter (Chapter 27)
Melbourne School of Population and Global Health, The University of Melbourne – Australia

Nathaniel Carpenter (Chapter 45)
Department of Computing and Information Systems, The University of Melbourne – Australia

Rosario Casanova (Chapter 19)
Academic Network UNGGIM Americas, University of Republic – Uruguay

Katitza Marinkovic Chavez (Chapter 27)
Melbourne School of Population and Global Health, The University of Melbourne – Australia

Yiqun Chen (Chapter 16)
Centre for Spatial Data Infrastructures and Land Administration, The University of Melbourne – Australia

Serena Coetzee (Chapters 3 & 13)
Department of Geography, Geoinformatics and Meteorology, University of Pretoria – South Africa

David J. Coleman (Chapter 29)
Department of Geodesy and Geomatics Engineering, University of New Brunswick – Canada

Antony K. Cooper (Chapter 23)
Smart Places, Council for Scientific and Industrial Research (CSIR) – South Africa

Anna Dabrowski (Chapter 45)
International Education and Development, Australian Council for Educational Research (ACER) – Australia

Vladimir V. Evtimov (Chapter 2)
Food and Agriculture Organization of the United Nations (FAO) – Italy

Inger Fabris-Rotelli (Chapter 8)
Department of Statistics, University of Pretoria – South Africa

Farinaz Farhanj (Chapter 22)
Aerospace Research Institute, Ministry of Science, Research, and Technology – Iran

Mariana Flores (Chapter 28)
University of Seville – Mexico

Greg Foliente (Chapters 1, 6 & 47)
Centre for Disaster Management and Public Safety, The University of Melbourne – Australia

Frank Friesecke (Chapter 36)
DVW e.V. – Gesellschaft für Geodäsie, Geoinformation und Landmanagement Rotkreuzstr – Germany

Amir Gholami (Chapter 17)
Geomatics Department, Marand Technical Faculty, University of Tabriz – Iran

Lisa Gibbs (Chapter 27)
Melbourne School of Population and Global Health, The University of Melbourne – Australia

Branislava Godic (Chapter 10)
Transport, Health and Urban Design Research Lab, Melbourne School of Design, The University of Melbourne – Australia

Paloma Merodio Gómez (Chapter 19)
UNGGIM Americas, National Institute of Statistics and Geography (INEGI) – Mexico

David R. Green (Chapter 5)
UAV/UAS Centre for Environmental Monitoring and Mapping (UCEMM), University of Aberdeen – Scotland, UK

Billy J. Gregory (Chapter 5)
UAV/UAS Centre for Environmental Monitoring and Mapping (UCEMM), University of Aberdeen/DroneLite – Scotland, UK

A. Yair Grinberger (Chapter 13)
Department of Geography, The Hebrew University of Jerusalem – Israel

Lukas Herman (Chapter 30)
Laboratory on Geoinformatics and Cartography, Department of Geography, Faculty of Science, Masaryk University – Czech Republic

Álvaro Monett Hernández (Chapter 19)
Economic Commission for Latin America and the Caribbean (ECLAC) – Chile

Jiri Hladik (Chapter 30)
Laboratory on Geoinformatics and Cartography, Department of Geography, Faculty of Science, Masaryk University – Czech Republic

Thanh Ho (Chapter 10)
Transport, Health and Urban Design Research Lab, Melbourne School of Design, The University of Melbourne – Australia

Matthew Hobbs (Chapter 41)
GeoHealth Laboratory & School of Earth and Environment & Geospatial Research Institute,University of Canterbury – New Zealand

Felicia N. Huang (Chapter 11)
Lee Kuan Yew Centre for Innovative Cities, Singapore University of Technology and Design – Singapore

Hishmi Jamil Husain (Chapter 40)
TATA Steel Ltd. & Institute of Rural Management Anand – India

Iacopo Iacopini (Chapter 18)
Centre for Advanced Spatial Analysis (CASA), University College London – UK

Milad Janalipour (Chapter 22)
Aerospace Research Institute, Ministry of Science, Research, and Technology – Iran

Bola Michelle Ju (Chapter 24)
World Bank – South Korea

Levente Juhasz (Chapter 13)
GIS Center, Florida International University – USA

Neda Kaffash Charandabi (Chapter 17)
Geomatics Department, Marand Technical Faculty, University of Tabriz – Iran

Alex R. Karachok (Chapter 5)
UAV/UAS Centre for Environmental Monitoring and Mapping (UCEMM), University of Aberdeen/DroneLite – Scotland, UK

Kathrine Kelm (Chapter 24)
World Bank – USA

Alice Kesminas (Chapter 35)
Department of Infrastructure Engineering, The University of Melbourne – Australia

Hassan M. Khormi (Chapter 43)
Department of Social Sciences, Jazan University Main Campus – Saudi Arabia

Simon Kingham (Chapter 41)
GeoHealth Laboratory & School of Earth and Environment & Geospatial Research Institute,University of Canterbury – New Zealand

Pravin Kokane (Chapter 14)
Department of Geography, University of Mumbai – India

Milan Konecny (Chapter 30)
Laboratory on Geoinformatics and Cartography, Department of Geography, Faculty of Science, Masaryk University – Czech Republic

Menno-Jan Kraak (Chapter 34)
Department of Geoinformation Processing, University of Twente – Netherlands

Charalampos Kyriakidis (Chapter 39)
National Technical University of Athens – Greece

Farhad Laylavi (Chapter 7)
Centre for Spatial Data Infrastructures and Land Administration, The University of Melbourne – Australia

Alize Le Roux (Chapter 22)
Smart Places, Council for Scientific and Industrial Research (CSIR) – South Africa

Jamie Leach (Chapter 33)
Open Data Australia – Australia

Kelly Lim (Chapter 11)
Lee Kuan Yew Centre for Innovative Cities, Singapore University of Technology and Design – Singapore

Marije Louwsma (Chapter 20)
Commission 8, International Federation of Surveyors (FIG) – Netherlands

Chantel Ludick (Chapter 23)
Smart Places, Council for Scientific and Industrial Research (CSIR) – South Africa

Colin MacDougall (Chapter 27)
Melbourne School of Population and Global Health, The University of Melbourne – Australia

Gerbrand Mans (Chapter 23)
Smart Places, Council for Scientific and Industrial Research (CSIR) – South Africa

Lukas Marek (Chapter 41)
GeoHealth Laboratory & School of Earth and Environment & Geospatial Research Institute, University of Canterbury – New Zealand

Raul Marino (Chapter 28)
Bucaramanga City Planning Department – Colombia

Carmen Martin (Chapter 31)
University of Toulouse – France

James M. McCaw (Chapter 27)
Melbourne School of Population and Global Health, The University of Melbourne – Australia

Niamh Meagher (Chapter 27)
Doherty Institute for Infection and Immunity, The Royal Melbourne Hospital – Australia

Richard Milton (Chapter 18)
Centre for Advanced Spatial Analysis (CASA), University College London – UK

Marco Minghini (Chapter 13)
European Commission, Joint Research Centre (JRC) – Italy

Mohammad Reza Mobasheri (Chapter 4)
Remote Sensing Laboratory, Remote Sensing & Data Management Knowledge-Based Co. – Iran

Zaffar Sadiq Mohamed-Ghouse (Chapter 12)
Surveying and Spatial Sciences Institute (SSSI) – Australia

Hossein Mokhtarzadeh (Chapter 37)
Department of Biomedical Engineering, Melbourne School of Engineering, The University of Melbourne – Australia

Abolfazl Mollalo (Chapter 22)
Department of Public Health and Prevention Sciences, School of Health Sciences, Baldwin Wallace University – USA

Peter Mooney (Chapter 13)
Department of Computer Science, Maynooth University – Ireland

Hartmut Müller (Chapter 20)
Commission 3, International Federation of Surveyors (FIG) – Germany

Roberto Murcio (Chapter 18)
Centre for Advanced Spatial Analysis (CASA), University College London – UK

Adrian Murone (Chapter 25)
City of Whittlesea Council, Victoria – Australia

Gaspar Mora-Navarro (Chapter 44)
Department of Cartographic Engineering, Geodesy and Photogrammetry, Universitat Politècnica de València – Spain

Daniel Paez (Chapters 1 & 47)
Commission 7, International Federation of Surveyors (FIG) – Australia

Nooshin Pahlevanzadeh (Chapter 22)
Aerospace Research Institute, Ministry of Science, Research, and Technology – Iran

François Pérès (Chapter 31)
University of Toulouse – France

Saied Pirasteh (Chapter 40)
GeoAI Smarter Map and LiDAR Lab, Faculty of Geosciences and Environmental Engineering, Southwest Jiaotong University – China

Alana Pirrone (Chapter 27)
Melbourne School of Population and Global Health, The University of Melbourne – Australia

Chryssy Potsiou (Chapters 15 & 39)
National Technical University of Athens – Greece

Katie Potts (Chapter 16)
Centre for Spatial Data Infrastructures and Land Administration, The University of Melbourne – Australia

David J. Price (Chapter 27)
Melbourne School of Population and Global Health, The University of Melbourne – Australia

Phoebe Quinn (Chapter 27)
Melbourne School of Population and Global Health, The University of Melbourne – Australia

Shuddhasattwa Rafiq (Chapter 25)
The Department of Economics at Deakin Business School – Australia

Abbas Rajabifard (Chapters 1, 16 &47)
Centre for Spatial Data Infrastructures and Land Administration, The University of Melbourne – Australia

Tammineni Rajitha (Chapter 40)
TATA Steel Ltd., India & Institute of Rural Management Anand – India

Tomas Reznik (Chapter 30)
Laboratory on Geoinformatics and Cartography, Department of Geography, Faculty of Science, Masaryk University – Czech Republic

Carmen Femenia-Ribera (Chapter 44)
Department of Cartographic Engineering, Geodesy and Photogrammetry. Universitat Politècnica de València – Spain

Kirsikka Riekkinen (Chapter 38)
Department of Built Environment, School of Engineering, Aalto University & National Land Survey – Finland

Inger Fabris-Rotelli (Chapter 8)
Department of Statistics, University of Pretoria – South Africa

Andrea Ramírez Santiago (Chapter 19)
National Institute of Statistics and Geography (INEGI) – Mexico

Freya M. Shearer (Chapter 27)
Melbourne School of Population and Global Health, The University of Melbourne – Australia

Vinita Shinkar (Chapter 14)
Indian Institute of Remote Sensing, Indian Space Research Organization Dehradun – India

Prashant Shukle (Chapter 29)
Global Geospatial Group – Canada

Evan Sidhi (Chapter 11)
Lee Kuan Yew Centre for Innovative Cities, Singapore University of Technology and Design – Singapore

Richard Simpson (Chapter 32)
Meta Moto & University of Melbourne – Australia

Steve Snow (Chapter 9)
Environmental Systems Research Institute (ESRI) – USA

Mark Stevenson (Chapter 10)
Transport, Health and Urban Design Research Lab, Melbourne School of Design, The University of Melbourne – Australia

Renate Thiede (Chapter 8)
Department of Statistics, University of Pretoria – South Africa

Jason Thompson (Chapter 10)
Transport, Health and Urban Design Research Lab, Melbourne School of Design, The University of Melbourne – Australia

Rafael Ponce Urbina (Chapter 9)
Environmental Systems Research Institute (ESRI) – USA

Maarten Vanhoof (Chapter 18)
Centre for Advanced Spatial Analysis (CASA), University College London – UK

Elkin Vargas (Chapter 28)
BuroDAP Colombia – Colombia

Piret Veeroja (Chapter 6)
Melbourne School of Design, The University of Melbourne & Centre for Urban Transitions, Swinburne University of Technology – Australia

Tony Wheeler (Chapter 12)
Surveying and Spatial Sciences Institute (SSSI) – Australia

Jesse Wiki (Chapter 41)
GeoHealth Laboratory & School of Earth and Environment & Geospatial Research Institute, University of Canterbury – New Zealand

Matthew Wilson (Chapter 41)
GeoHealth Laboratory & School of Earth and Environment & Geospatial Research Institute, University of Canterbury – New Zealand

Zhixuan Yang (Chapter 21)
Dongbei University of Finance and Economics – China

Godwin Yeboah (Chapter 13)
Institute for Global Sustainable Development, University of Warwick – UK

Belinda Yuen (Chapter 11)
Lee Kuan Yew Centre for Innovative Cities, Singapore University of Technology and Design – Singapore

Yibo Zhang (Chapter 16)
Centre for Spatial Data Infrastructures and Land Administration, The University of Melbourne – Australia

Part I

Setting the Scene

1

The Role and Value of Geospatial Information and Technology in a Pandemic

Abbas Rajabifard, Daniel Paez and Greg Foliente

1.1 Introduction

The coronavirus COVID-19 pandemic is the defining global crisis of our time and the most devastating challenge the world has faced since World War II, having a profoundly deep impact on the way we perceive our world and our everyday lives. While beginning as a health crisis, it has grown fast in just over few months to be an unprecedented socio-economic and environmental crisis that has spread to every continent and country. As a result, the world has been facing unprecedented social and economic changes and challenges, across all industries and sectors, at every scale (from local, to national and to global level). The COVID-19 virus is a global pandemic, as all our societies are connected, in which no country or jurisdiction is left unscathed as a result of this situation.

This book aims at covering these disciplinary intersections that happen when Geographic Information Systems (GIS) and location intelligence are used in action to respond to the crises and plans for recovery. The experiences and the information included in this book will be a learning tool for communities to being prepared, making the right decisions, and keeping informed to be able to improve community resilience and respond to future crisis.

During a pandemic political borders mean nothing, and every society has been impacted in some way. In June 2020, the World Bank forecast that global gross domestic product (GDP) would shrink by 5.2% [1] in 2020, with recessions in both advanced and emerging market economies. The devastating effects on the global economy will take years to overcome, as governments around the world grapple with the situation and make impossible decisions that aim to meet both the health and economic wars faced as a result of the virus in an attempt to save lives but also limit the financial distress faced by the global economy.

We are now living with a new norm of practice, and as each day passes, people all over the world are not only losing their lives and their health, but also employment, their livelihoods, connections with their friends and family, with no real sense of when life will return to a familiar normality. In this context, good data and statistics, in particular location information and related attributes are key for our resilience and data infrastructure for sustainable future. These data are crucial as they make essential contributions to our strategic pathways on our wider public safety. In a global crisis, our leaders and decision-makers require the fast delivery of information that is accessible and reliable, so urgent and effective responds to COVID-19 are available to make the right choices, manage the complexity and uncertainty and thus lead the world to a more resilient and sustainable future.

From a location information (location intelligence) perspective, the COVID-19 pandemic has highlighted to the world the unequivocal importance and need for geospatial information, enabling technologies, and clear and concise information for governments that enable decision-makers to keep their citizens safe, plan for the future and protect the most vulnerable in our communities.

So much of managing a pandemic is inherently a geographic and location issue. In order to manage outbreaks, perform contact-tracing and enable a robust community response to stop the spread, spatial information is required, and location information is paramount. The social and environmental factors, including population density and age, employment and lifestyle, all influence patterns of disease occurrence and prevalence.

As such, location information, mapping and related analytical tools such as GIS tools are widely used by health departments, safety and emergency management authorities and wider professionals around the world for gathering and analysing data to support informed decisions. The use of location intelligence and GIS for understanding this outbreak and its relationship to infrastructure, population, businesses and other location-based information requires both a clear understanding of the relevant geospatial principles and the relevant aspects of data monitoring, planning and mapping.

1.2   Critical Role of Location Information

The COVID-19 pandemic is proving a need for a collaborative geospatial infrastructure that will help us better understand the crisis at hand at both a local and global scale, as well as better prepare us for future pandemics worldwide. There is a growing need for real-time maps, and location information to track and share location data, and as such, a geospatial-enabled platform, along with data analytics tools and solutions play a critical role in assisting the pandemic's front lines and keeping the general public informed and prepared.

GIS for example has always been a tool in managing the response to large-scale disasters by using location technology that helps to understand the situation at hand, develop a response and prepare a road to recovery. A spatial team is of paramount importance to help create the maps, data, apps, analysis and dashboards that are required for emergency management and resource allocation.

Early in 2020, there was an extraordinary effort around the globe where GIS practitioners in every country began to work together, sharing information that helped us all grasp the situation at hand and also enabled the decision-makers in their response to the virus at local, national and global levels. The Johns Hopkins Coronavirus Dashboard, based on Esri software, was originally built by a handful of people but has evidently grown into the primary tool used to track and monitor the virus, being viewed "nearly a trillion times only a few months into the pandemic" as stated by Esri CEO, Jack Dangermond.

Location information plays a critical role managing the spread of the virus and protecting our communities by providing the tools required in collecting vital data, mapping the current crisis, simulating the results from modelling response variables, contact tracing and determining hot spots, managing high-risk locations and distributing help where it is needed most. Spatial experts around the world have come together and shared critical information that has transpired into an unprecedented effort to manage the COVID-19 pandemic in a way that has not been evident in our history. This effort has been on a global scale and as such we have evolved into a world that supports a connected and global GIS. In our new interconnected world, we all benefit from this phenomenal transformation that impacts every government, industry and citizen, where we can make better and more informed decisions about our future.

1.3   Impact of COVID-19 on the Sustainable Development Goals (SDGs)

The Sustainable Development Goals (SDGs), as outlined by the United Nations as part the global plan to create a better future for all, now play an even more critical role in providing a framework tool that puts health and prosperity at the core of the road to recovery for all nations and all people around the globe. The COVID-19 pandemic has emphasised the challenges facing governments from taking the extraordinary steps needed to attain the SDGs. The vulnerabilities and obstacles that exist in different countries when working towards achieving the SDGs are even more prominent now, including socio-economic gaps, structural inequalities, systemic challenges and risks, as well as a lack of timely fundamental data and enabling technologies to measure and monitor what is happening where, when and how (UN-GGIM White paper, COVID-19). The United Nations Committee of Experts on Global Geospatial Information Management (UN-GGIM) has been taking steps to explore how geospatial information has been used to support national response efforts, and the influence and impact of the geospatial data ecosystem in responding to the global COVID-19 pandemic.

This unprecedented time has also been the first time where geospatial data location intelligence from all around the world has been collected, visualised and made available from local to global levels, through numerous dashboards, including from the WHO and Johns Hopkins University to name a few. These geospatial visualizations clearly communicate the situation and guide decision-making, all through location-based data, and demonstrate that when the geographic dimension is considered, information can be communicated in a clearer, more effective manner, not only to governments but to every individual citizen on the globe.

Of significant importance, contact tracing applications have demonstrated hope by identifying outbreak hotspots, providing those in power with a means to identify, inform and subsequently treat those infected, limiting the spread of the pandemic among the population. In order to achieve successful contact tracing, there needs to be high-level access to geospatial information, which can be queried and classified by age, gender, demography and geography, at every level.

There is an urgent need for the work and issues raised by the UN-GGIM to be addressed and made available across the globe, including data availability, core reference data, interoperability, common geographies, integration of statistics and geography, privacy and confidentiality, the relevance of the Integrated Geospatial Information Framework (IGIF).

With the Integrated Geospatial Information Framework (IGIF) at its core, the UN-GGIM has published findings on what components are required to respond to the COVID-19 crisis, such as leadership, governance, legal and policy, data and technology. The work demonstrates that a clear connection to the IGIF will enable countries to respond in a more timely manner in a crisis where time is critical. Through its initiatives, the UN-GGIM aims to bring the international geospatial community together, along with the the the statistical, public health, and development sectors to fight the current pandemic and to build a more resilient and robust global community.

As the IGIF provides a holistic and inclusive Framework, applicable to all countries and in all situations, it is able to be applied to the global COVID-19 pandemic. As an example, the IGIF is highly beneficial in disaster response, where data sharing and geospatial information are critical. Similarly, the response to COVID-19 also requires the ability to share integrated geospatial information in real-time. This ensures that the same information will be delivered to all the key players of the response at the same time. This is also critical in the responding to the aftermath of any disaster, where geospatial determines what happens next and where actions are needed. Outlined in the UN-GGIM white paper publications, the IGIF focuses on geospatial information that is integrated with any other meaningful data to solve societal and environmental problems, acts as a catalyst for economic growth and opportunity, and to provide understanding and benefit from a countries development priorities and the SDGs. While the IGIF has anchored the geospatial response to COVID-19, it is important to note that it was not developed as a response to COVID-19, only as an enabling mechanism to achieve the ambitious targets set by the SDGs. However, its usefulness has provided countries with a basis for leveraging geospatial information, either to integrate existing capacity, or through developing new capability. As a result, the IGIF has demonstrably enabled countries to determine their national geospatial response to COVID-19. The IGIF has nine strategic pathways, influenced by Governance, Technology and People, that work together as a basis and guide for developing, integrating, strengthening and maximizing geospatial information management and related resources in all countries, resulting in tangibly enabled countries to leverage geospatial information in their COVID-19 response.

The most vulnerable countries around the world that have faced the greatest challenges with achieving the SDGs, now face the greatest challenges with the COVID-19 pandemic. Collecting high-quality geospatial information as well as producing, analysing and using timely and reliable location-based data is often not possible, and in many countries where may exist in some form somewhere, it is often not discoverable, structured, interoperable or standardized. It cannot be readily accessed, shared, and more importantly, integrated with other data for decision-making.

Both in attaining SDGs and responding to the pandemic, geospatial information is the key integrator that enables informed decision-making, as well as enabling visualisation and analysis required to communicate key data to decision-makers and the general public. As such, the past few months have been a testament to the importance of collectively developing mechanisms, mobilizing resources and strengthening the global capacity of geospatial information. In this way we can then meet the challenges of COVID-19, and work to build back a stronger path forward on the road to meet the needs of the SDGs in the future.

The UN-GGIM has provided a platform for the global geospatial community and demonstrated its importance to respond to the challenge of COVID- 19. It has become evident how urgent and critical it is to have a multifaceted system that mobilises resources and ensures that all agencies, including government and the private sectors, have access to geospatial information in order to best manage the pandemic, and work towards the SDGs. Implementing the IGIF has been an important step in developing dashboards and communicating the spread and developments of COVID-19.

There is no denying that the pandemic has been a setback in achieving the SDGs around the globe, however it is also a time of great opportunity and growth as there has never been a time in history where people from every corner of the world are working together to bring solutions and advancements to better our health, our communities, our environment and the economy. This particularly effects developing countries, which may for the first time have access to geospatial data and tools that will not only benefit the management of the pandemic in such countries, but also provide their agencies with digital data for challenges that lie ahead.

1.4 Digital Innovation During a Pandemic

In times of great pressure that require solutions to distinct challenges, scientists and engineers are required to fast develop methods, technologies and innovation, and create new good practices. The pandemic has illustrated that novel innovations including dashboards and entirely new processes can be fast tracked and implemented, in a matter of weeks, rather than years. As a result, governments are able to make better and more informed decisions by understanding where the risks exist. Emerging technologies such as Artificial Intelligence (AI) help to expedite the development of a vaccine, and predict the most effective public health measures through simulation and help move much of our lives to an online environment, where we can maintain our economic and education systems to continue employment and schooling as well as our connection to one another.

This also highlights the gap across various social groups in digitally isolated countries and regions. The COVID-19 crisis reminds us that we should nurture the socially beneficial applications of digital technologies and work to improve accessibility and usage in the countries and areas which require the greatest leverage and aid. There are many examples of digital innovation across the globe including in the United Nations Educational, Scientific and Cultural Organization (UNESCO) and the International Business Machines Corporation (IBM) that support the development and deployment of public health mobile applications to help manage the pandemic by providing informed data-driven decisions and social distancing measures. There is also a push to enhance access to the Internet across the globe through UNESCO that aims to foster collaboration and partnership in developing countries.

Governments around the world are also now spending record funding (US$10.5t [2] and rising) to manage the COVID-19 pandemic which means there is a real opportunity for partnerships with businesses to emerge and fast track innovations that lead an advancement in technologies, and how we manage public health as well as how we restore the environment.

However, governments, businesses and the financial services sector need to ensure that investments in innovation create opportunities, reduce inequality and lead to net gains in employment. And governments can do more than just fund innovation; they can ensure learning is plugged back into the state. Digitalization lessons from industry, for example, can be applied to public sector services to deliver better and more effective access, while preserving provision in the face of budget deficits.

1.5   Collaboration and Engagement

Throughout the pandemic, we've seen the development of extraordinary models of collaboration that have resulted in the largest exchange of scientific data in history. It has been remarkable to see competitors work together in joint initiatives. And although there have been some level of disagreement amongst governments and international agencies, we have also observed efficient and effective collaborations between the state and private sectors to deliver technological and medical solutions at speed. This time during the pandemic has been an example of just how much we can achieve as international citizens, when we all focus on a common goal.

There has, however, been indications of an increase in the social divides, similar to the aftermath of the global financial crisis (GFC), where the recovery of many markets were uneven and the people who struggled the most fell further into crisis. The impact on jobs around the world has been dire: the International Labor Organization (ILO) estimates a decline in global working hours in the second quarter of 2020 of around 10.7% (equivalent to 305 million full-time jobs) relative to the last quarter of 2019 [3]. And the workers in poorly paid jobs, casual contracts or who are self-employed are increasing in numbers making them more vulnerable to layoffs during the economic downturn and with less access to social security safety nets. An inequality in healthcare, including access to medical attention, testing availability, access to intensive care and medication, has also been one of the crucial issues of the pandemic observed around the world. Further to this, the recent occurrence of protests that has spread from the United States across Europe to Australia demonstrates the urgent need for inequality to be addressed.

There is also the likelihood that another pandemic may happen in the future, and as such, building a close coordination between central government and local governments, and ensuring closer international collaboration, together with the sharing of digital innovation and technological advancements are of increasing importance for a sustainable future.

1.6   Opportunities Emerging from the Pandemic

Our wider society through governments, the private and the public sectors have a unique and strategic opportunity to shape the recovery and the future economy in such a way that will ensure a more sustainable and more equitable outlook for all. There is now a chance to reframe the future by building a fairer, more prosperous society founded on greener, more resilient, productive economies. While every country and region will have different priorities and starting points, the starting principle for all governments should seek to build more resilient economies while also tackling the climate change challenges and social inequalities.

Social equity is a priority that underpins sustainable economic prosperity. The opportunity to address social inequality, improve outcomes for all citizens, including fairer access to employment is an opportunity during this time that should not be missed. A sustainable recovery is not just about creating jobs; it's about creating high-quality, accessible jobs that improve peoples' lives, which in turn creates more stable societies. The pandemic has also forced the adoption of new ways of working. Organizations must reframe their work and the role of offices in creating safe, productive and enjoyable jobs and lives for employees.

The environmental opportunities in the pandemic that promote a green recovery is clear. The vast majority of the world's total GDP is moderately or highly dependent on a stable environment and is therefore susceptible to disruption due to climate change [4]. Without action to address climate change, an additional 100 million people could be pushed into poverty by 2030 and 143 million in just three regions could be displaced [5]. In the wake of COVID-19, governments and companies have an opportunity to plot greener, fairer and more sustainable days ahead. The pandemic has also raised environmental fears to the public too, as the enforced pause on industrial pollution and travel has resulted in cleaner air where CO_2 emissions are now predicted to be at the lowest level in 14 years [6]. United Nations studies also now estimate that a move to low-carbon, resilient economies could possibly create 65 million new jobs between now and 2030 [7].

1.7 Moving Forward from the Pandemic

With the lessons that we are all learning from this pandemic, our leaders in the public and private sectors, in academia must look to rise from the challenges we face and identify opportunities, in which we can find new ways to keep growing and building resilient and sustainable communities, and infrastructure.

Through the devastation, the COVID-19 pandemic has also demonstrated the interconnected nature of our world and communities, and further highlights the United Nations notion, that no one is safe until everyone is safe. We must act in solidarity with our communities all around the world, in order to save lives and overcome the devastating impacts that this virus has, not just to our health, but socially and from an economic standpoint. By demonstrating strong partnerships, we can grow our sense of humanity and inspire all generations to hope for a healthier and more prosperous future for all, where we learn from navigating through this challenging journey and work together to build greater resilience in every community.

1.8 This Book, Objectives, Chapter Outline

This book brings together the expertise of leading professionals, practitioners and academics in different related fields for managing pandemic, in particular experts in the field of geospatial industry, and policy-makers and their perspectives to share their experiences and approaches to respond to the COVID-19 pandemic, and they share their lessons for any similar pandemic in future in order to improve community resilience. The themes and objectives of the book are in line with the critical challenges that our global community is facing. It is also in line with challenges, gaps, and the work plan of the UN-GGIM Academic Network.

Over 120 authors from regions all around the world contributed to the production of this book, including contributions from more than 30 countries and country case studies.

FIGURE 1.1

Contributions and country case studies

The authors have shared their observations, research and best practices in their jurisdictions and organizations that are relevant to professional lines of work or supporting training and teaching modules focusing on COVID-19 applications. This will provide the foundation that would help to reassess the field, affirm successful approaches and point to future possibilities.

The book brought together two types of contributions, scientific chapters, and industry and practitioner observations, structured into 47 chapters in 5 parts. The authors have worked together in hope of taking steps towards achieving more sustainable, safe and resilient future. In doing so, the book will address the following objectives:

- Review foundational aspects of geospatial sciences and technologies for supporting intelligent decision-making for pandemic management.

- Identify a coherent set of tools, guidelines or standards to help researchers, data producers and practitioners and authorities utilize geospatial information for decision-making during various pandemic phases.

- Provide a resource on current best practices for utilizing location intelligence for local, regional, national and global level pandemic management.

- Reflect on the lessons learnt from COVID-19 pandemic, and present a forward-looking collection of ongoing research, development and practice, with an emphasis on the role of location and geospatial science, that can improve the resilience of community, society, economy and environment.

- Provide a medium for presenting the challenges, solutions, opinions and insights from different stakeholders regarding their experience through the pandemic.

The beginning chapters of this book provide an overview of the principles and foundations for geospatial science and technologies, followed by an outline of current approaches for pandemic management and reflections for ongoing development and future prospects for geospatial data in building a more resilient community, society, economy and environment. This book is unique in that it contains observations from various countries and industries, including the challenges they faced, the solutions they came across, the opinions and insights they had during this crisis. It will help build tight bonding between industries and academics and drive more industry-oriented research opportunities.

In Chapter 2, Keith Clifford Bell and Vladimir V. Evtimov draw from the experience of the World Bank and the Food and Agriculture Organization (FAO) to discuss a way forward to ensure the resilience of countries, cities and communities through authoritative geospatial information and land administration. Maria Antonia Brovelli and Serena Coetzee explore open geospatial data for responding to the COVID-19 challenge in Chapter 3, by examining what data is useful when studying the spatio-temporal spread of the virus and investigating the availability of such open data. In Chapter 4, Mohammad Reza Mobasheri reports on the role of remote sensing in the detection, evaluation and mapping factors relating to public health. The chapter focuses on an introduction to the importance and use of remote sensing through an examination of successful remote sensing applications.

David Green et al. explore the potential of drone technology during pandemics in Chapter 5. The study includes an overview of current drone technology and future developments, as well as investigation into the issues facing successful mainstream implementation of the use of drones for such applications, and the problems that need to be overcome to allow this technology to become mainstream. In Chapter 6, Piret Veeroja and Greg Foliente look at the role of social and built environments on social interactions in Melbourne prior to, and during, the COVID-19 pandemic and discuss possible social and built environment interventions to increase social interactions.

Farhad Laylavi reports on a study in Chapter 7, which aims to contextualise social vulnerability to pandemic situations. The study presents the preliminary indicators of social vulnerability and presents a discussion of the implications, limitations and future work. In Chapter 8, Renate Thiede and Inger Fabris-Rotelli present an algorithm for detecting informally developed roads in satellite images and quantify the uncertainty associated with the results. Such roads play an important role in the development of COVID-19 response strategies in developing countries.

In Chapter 9, Rafael Ponce Urbina et al. showcase a holistic view of the uses of GIS to monitor, analyse and disseminate knowledge pertaining to maritime geospatial data during the COVID-19 pandemic. Mark Stevenson et al. outline recent research in city design and the transmission of COVID-19 in Chapter 10. The chapter highlights the role of city design in virus transmission, particularly in high-density road networks and public transit.

In Chapter 11, Felicia N. Huang et al. discuss social media use and community resilience development during the COVID-19 pandemic in Singapore. Lesley Arnold, Zaffar Sadiq Mohamed-Ghouse and Tony Wheeler report on the role of professional bodies during a pandemic in Chapter 12, with a focus on the role of the Surveying and Spatial Sciences Institute (SSSI) in Australia. In Chapter 13, Peter Mooney et al. explore OpenStreetMap (OSM) data use cases during the early months of the pandemic. The chapter contributes to the knowledge on how volunteered geographic information (VGI) initiatives such as OSM respond and are used or accessed during a global crisis such as COVID-19.

In Chapter 14, Pravin Kokane et al. explore the utilisation of geospatial network analysis techniques for optimal route planning during the pandemic. Chryssy Potsiou discusses the critical issue of formalising informal settlements to empower residents against COVID-19 and other disasters in Chapter 15. The chapter reports on how geospatial experts can provide the means to support governments to identify and empower those most vulnerable to the pandemic, and the measures that have taken place. Abbas Rajabifard et al. provide a discussion around spatially enabled platform supporting managing pandemic, and also review of the applications and systems in place for such a spatially enabled COVID-19 in Chapter 16.

In Chapter 17, Neda Kaffash Charandabi and Amir Gholami propose a global model to help determine the important periods of each country, predict confirmed cases and to discover spatio-temporal hot/cold spots based on wavelet and neural networks. In Chapter 18, Michael Batty et al. give a report on London in Lockdown, discussing the issues of mobility in the pandemic city.

Rosario Casanova et al. in Chapter 19 discuss the Americas geospatial response to COVID-19 through an overview and analysis of the implementation of UN-GGIM global frameworks, as well as a discussion of the gaps and challenges faced. In Chapter 20, Marije Louwsma and Hartmut Müller explores spatio-temporal information management to control the pandemic in Europe. Zhixuan (Jenny) Yang reports on online higher education in Chapter 21, with a focus on how online education facilitated by Information and Communication Technology (ICT) in China has been implemented during the COVID-19 pandemic. The chapter analyses the experience of online education, and uses a case study to evaluate the critical elements involved.

In Chapter 22, Nadia Abbaszadeh Tehrani et al. provide a time-series analysis of COVID-19 in Iran, from a remote sensing (RS) perspective. The chapter discusses the novel approach that utilises remote sensing data to monitor the pandemic at a national level, as well as examining the applicability of RS coupled with time-series analysis for the study area. Alize le Roux et al. present the COVID-19 Vulnerability Dashboard for South Africa in Chapter 23, which maps out the vulnerability to the pandemic across the whole of South Africa. The study aims at helping local authorities and other stakeholders with disaster risk reduction and evidence-based decision-making.

Bola Michelle Ju et al. describe the rapid development of location-based apps in Chapter 24, focusing on the seven applications which saved lives during the pandemic in South Korea. In Chapter 25, Sultana Nasrin Baby et al. report on a spatial analysis of urban parkland and COVID-19 in the City of Whittlesea, in Victoria, Australia. Phil Bright and David Abbott describe the impact of COVID-19 to the Pacific Island Countries and Territories (PICTs) in Chapter 26.

In Chapter 27, Freya M. Shearer et al. present evidence to inform evolving COVID-19 response planning by analysing how Australians were thinking, feeling and behaving in response to the so-called "first wave" of the COVID-19 epidemic and the associated public health measures. Raul Marino et al. present the results of an investigation relating to the lack of access to public space and social interactions in three Latin-American cities in Chapter 28. David J. Coleman and Prashant Shukle provide a case study in Chapter 29 on how geospatial information and technologies were used in Canada. They highlight observations made in the early stages of Canada's response to the pandemic and provide a critical discussion and opportunities for future development and cooperation.

Milan Konecny et al. discuss the roles of geospatial intelligence in addressing COVID-19 challenges in Czechia in Chapter 30. They present three approaches to improving response to COVID-19, including visual analytics; Tracking and analysis solutions; and decision support systems. Carmen Martin and François Pérès provide an observation and analysis of COVID-19 in France in Chapter 31, with a focus on the multi-phase and multidimensional approach to a complex societal imbalance.

In Chapter 32, Richard Simpson explores the importance of a worldwide infrastructure when managing complex pandemic scenarios. He investigates the challenges faced with uncoordinated international cohesion and the accumulative crisis humanity faces as a result. In Chapter 33, Jamie Leach as an observation explores the Open Data Pandemic, and discusses the issues that arise in data sharing around the globe.

In Chapter 34, Menno-Jan Kraak addresses the challenges of mapping COVID-19, and addresses two issues including the professional cartographic design challenges and the most common cartographic mistakes witnessed in the media. In Chapter 35, Alice Kesminas also provides an observation by discussing the importance of engagement to build smarter and more resilient communities. She addresses the role that geospatial information and technology play in building community resilience and discusses the challenges faced to successfully plan and manage resilient communities.

In Chapter 36, Frank Friesecke investigates how the coronavirus could change urban planning. The study explores the changes in how we operate schools, retail, work environments and presents a first vision of the direction in which the city of the future could develop towards in light of COVID-19 and other potential pandemics in the future. In Chapter 37, Hossein Mokhtarzadeh shared his view and investigates the move towards agile strategies during the pandemic. This chapter reports on a observational study completed through a number of interviews with experts discussing how they cope with a global crisis.

Kirsikka Riekkinen provides observations from Finland in Chapter 38, with a focus on the opportunities for digitalisation, and the use of geographic information in the Finnish context. Efthimios Bakogiannis et al. report on the possible future of Greek cities in Chapter 39, with a focus on what the cities will look like after the pandemic period with a case study review analysis and best practice assessment.

Saied Pirasteh et al. explore the COVID-19 pandemic challenges and impacts on the Sustainable Development Goals 2030 in Chapter 40. The chapter discusses an understanding of the pandemic and its influences on SDGs 2030, from an Indian perspective. Malcolm Campbell et al. discuss the value of a policy-response research model in Chapter 41. The authors discuss the GeoHealth Laboratory (GHL) research model that is based on a relationship contract funding model in New Zealand.

Mark Allan outlines the lessons learned from management of the Melbourne COVID-19 pandemic in Chapter 42. His contribution chapter presents some observations made and discusses a future of co-existence with the virus.

In Chapter 43, Hassan M. Khormi explores spatial modelling concepts in Saudi Arabia as an observation. The study reports on how the Saudi authorities implement GIS concepts in controlling the spatial risks of the pandemic. Carmen Femenia-Ribera and Gaspar Mora-Navarro examine COVID-19 in Spain with a focus on the use of geospatial information in Chapter 44. Nathaniel Carpenter and Anna Dabrowski discuss the lessons learned from the COVIDSafe app in Chapter 45, a track and trace technology designed for the Australian context. The chapter focuses on understanding conditions for successful implementation of track and trace technologies. Arturo Ardila-Gomez explores sustainable transport as a key pillar to community resilience during the COVID-19 pandemic in Chapter 46.

The book then concludes in Chapter 47, with synthesis of key lessons and future work to improve our planning and preparation for the next pandemic, focusing on geospatial information and related techno-social innovations for enhanced community resilience.

References

[1] https://www.worldbank.org/en/publication/global-economic-prospects

[2] https://blogs.imf.org/2020/05/20/tracking-the-9-trillion-global-fiscal-support-to-fight-covid-19/

[3] ILO Monitor: COVID-19 and the world of work. Fourth edition. https://www.ilo.org/global/about-the-ilo/newsroom/news/WCMS_743036/lang--en/index.htm

[4] World Economic Forum. (2020). Nature Risk Rising: Why the Crisis Engulfing Nature Matters for Business and the Economy.

[5] https://www.worldbank.org/en/topic/climatechange/overview

[6] https://www.msn.com/en-gb/news/world/coronavirus-tracked-global-co2-emissions-fell-to-lowest-level-in-14-years-during-lockdowns/ar-BB14mRZY

[7] https://news.un.org/en/story/2018/09/1019472

Part II

Technical and Techno-Social Solutions

2

Land Administration and Authoritative Geospatial Information: Lessons from Disasters to Support Building Resilience to Pandemics

Keith Clifford Bell and Vladimir V. Evtimov

Throughout 2020, much has been written advocating investment in geospatial information and land administration systems as solutions to pandemic resilience, but closer analyses may suggest a lack of rigor and even a tendency for hype. Resilience of countries, cities and communities in the context of land administration and geospatial information is best achieved through sustainable, authoritative, geospatial information under the framework of National Spatial Data Infrastructure (NSDI) and comprehensive and secure Land Administration Systems (LAS). However, it is becoming increasingly clear that the pandemic has severely impacted progress towards all the SDGs under the 2030 Agenda. Responding to disasters and pandemics does not afford the luxury of extended templated diagnostic assessments, economic and financial analyses and cost-benefit studies of investing in LAS and NSDI. Drawing on the experiences of the WB-FAO partnership, the Chapter discusses good practices of rapid assessments of the resilience and resilience impact of authoritative NSDI and LAS.

2.1   Introduction

"The COVID-19 crisis threatens to reverse much of the development progress made in recent years and throw hundreds of millions of people back into poverty. It has required countries to respond rapidly and decisively to major disruptions of their healthcare systems, their economies and the livelihoods of their citizens. I have been inspired by the World Bank Group's response – mobilizing fast to deliver urgent support to countries to minimize loss of life, mitigate severe economic hardship, protect hard-earned development gains, and protect the poorest and most vulnerable".
David Malpass, President of the World Bank.[1]

The COVID-19 pandemic has triggered the deepest global recession in decades, and this is well reported by both the World Bank [1] and the International Monetary Fund (IMF). This is the first recession since 1870 to be triggered solely by a pandemic. After more than a decade of uninterrupted growth, the global economy came to a sudden halt because of the pandemic. The debate continues as to how deep it will be; its duration; and how far its impacts will reach. The pandemic has

---

[1]World Bank President's end of year address to staff townhall, July 2, 2020.

caused contractions across the vast majority of emerging market and developing economies as well as advanced economies. Lasting damage to labor productivity and potential output are already well identified. Across the world it would seem there is strong consensus for immediate policy priorities of alleviation of the human costs and attenuation of the short-term economic losses. Thereafter, once the crisis abates, there is also consensus that it will be necessary to reaffirm a credible commitment to policies to support long-term sustainable development. The COVID-19 recession's speed and depth with which it has struck suggests the possibility of a sluggish recovery. For many emerging market and developing countries, however, effective financial support and mitigation measures are particularly hard to achieve because a substantial share of employment is in informal sectors. The speed with which countries can overcome the pandemic health crisis and pave the way for economic recovery remains to be seen.

The COVID-19 pandemic is not the first global pandemic and it will not be the last, may almost be cliché now. Countries, especially low- and middle-income countries (LIC and MIC), are at the time of writing, fully focused on dealing with the severe health and economic crises. Generally, immediate priorities are budgetary support, health and food security. Beyond recovery, all nations, and development partners, must turn their respective foci to future preparedness to ensure that nations can better withstand the shocks of any future pandemic, with the impacts minimized to the greatest extent possible and recovery enabled in the shortest possible timeframe. However, no degree of preparedness can prevent future pandemics or disasters. Preparedness should include investment in land administration systems (LAS) and national spatial data infrastructures (NSDI).

The WB and the Food and Agriculture Organization (FAO) have partnered in many countries to promote the fundamental roles of LAS and NSDI to support the 2030 Agenda for Sustainable Development and also for improving disaster resilience at the national, city and community levels, in line with the Voluntary Guidelines on the Responsible Governance of Tenure (VGGT) [2] and the Sendai Framework for Disaster Risk Reduction 2015-30 [3].

2.2   Emergencies – Disasters and Pandemics

There are some similarities between the impacts of shocks created by a natural disaster and those created by disease – but only some. No country, regardless of its level of social and economic development is immune from the increasing frequency and severity of emergencies caused by disasters and pandemics. The World Health Organization ([4], p. 22) has prepared a very comprehensive Classification of Hazards, covering disasters, pandemics, conflicts and environmental degradation. From the disaster perspective it has consistency with the Sendai Framework, which sets out the case for all development to be risk-informed in order to be sustainable.

The Disaster Management Cycle, which originates from the United States Federal Emergency Management Agency (FEMA)[2] is widely utilized. Over the past decade, the Disaster Management Cycle, has been interpreted, modified and adopted by many agencies around the world. Recently, with health crises, including the current pandemic, even WHO has adopted an equivalent 4-phase cycle [4] – Preparation, Response, Recovery and Mitigation. Understanding the cycle, enables a better appreciation of where geospatial information and land administration can be effectively applied in terms of response and building resilience, which is discussed later in this Chapter.

2.3   Economic and Financial Impacts of Disasters and Pandemics

Direct economic losses from disasters have increased by more than 150 percent over the past 20 years, with losses disproportionately borne by vulnerable developing countries. The bill from

---

[2]Noted by [5].

natural disasters had reached around US$200 billion per year, an increase of 4 times since the 1980s. However, it is estimated that this has now risen to around US$300 billion per year. Cumulatively, over the past 30-year period, disasters have cost nearly US$4 trillion and caused around 2.5 million deaths. Two-thirds of these losses are due to extreme storms, floods and drought [4].

WHO has advised that over the previous 30 years, more than 80 percent of deaths from natural disasters occurred in LIC and MIC and that the disaster impacts on GDP was on average 20 times higher in LIC than high-income countries (HIC). Further, and from the health perspective, WHO reported that during 2012-17, there were 1,200 health outbreaks in 168 countries, including those due to new or re-emerging infectious diseases. In 2018, a further 352 infectious disease events, including the Middle East respiratory syndrome coronavirus (MERS-CoV) and the Ebola virus disease. Estimated losses from infectious diseases, through their effects on productivity, trade and travel, have been calculated at about US$500 billion or 6 percent of global income per year [4].

The WB [6] has identified critical impacts of the current pandemic. These are summarized as follows, with specific implications for land administration and geospatial information identified by the authors of this Chapter:

- Disrupting billions of lives and livelihoods, the COVID-19 pandemic threatens decades of hard-won development gains and demands an urgent, exceptional response. The severity of the pandemic is challenging the world's health systems, while associated lockdowns and travel restrictions have upended normal life for most people – even as lockdowns ease in some countries. The pandemic is spurring changes in behaviors and trends likely to transform the post-COVID-19 world. Lockdowns require resolving homelessness and unhealthy, crowded slums.

- The range of growth outcomes in 2020-21 remains exceptionally uncertain, and recovery is highly dependent on global progress in containing and mitigating the pandemic. In a base case scenario, the global economy could shrink by 5.2 percent in 2020 before rebounding in 2021; in the downside scenario of prolonged shutdowns, world output could contract by almost 8 percent in 2020 (roughly equivalent to the combined GDP of France, Italy, and Spain). The recession in advanced economies is hitting developing countries hard, and the WB now projects negative growth for over 150 countries in 2020. The emerging food crisis could intensify, and food insecurity could spread much more widely. Can governments afford to invest in LAS and NSDI to build resilience to future disaster and epidemic impacts? In the short-term, especially for LIC, the answer is likely to be no, without international development assistance.

- Billions of jobs are under threat worldwide. Nearly 80 percent of the world's informal economy workers, around 1.6 billion, have now experienced COVID-19 lockdowns and slowdowns in hard-hit industries including wholesale and retail, food and hospitality, tourism, transport and manufacturing. With 740 million women globally in informal employment and a majority employed in services, women are particularly hard hit by the crisis. Remittance flows are a key source of revenues for many developing economies, and expected to fall by one-fifth in 2020. Tourism is another area hard hit. Many countries across East and South Asia are especially dependent on both tourism and remittances to a combined level of 20-30 percent of GDP. Loss of jobs places many people, renters and those with mortgages, at high risk of defaulting and subsequent eviction. Evictions create opportunities for property speculation and land grabbing, as well as governance challenges for land administration.

- The COVID-19 crisis is exacting a massive toll on the poor and vulnerable. Millions of people will fall into extreme poverty, while millions of existing poor will experience even deeper deprivation, the first increase in global poverty since 1998. This will mean an estimated additional 18 million extremely poor people in Fragile and Conflict-affected States (FCS), and the pandemic is deepening existing sources of fragility and exacerbating instability in Fragility, Conflict and Violence (FCV) settings. Land conflicts are major issues in FCS and can have long-term consequences as displaced people flee. Already the pandemic has manifested as a critical risk for refugee and resettlement camps. Homeless people are at high risk of contracting and spreading the virus and are not subjected to effective screening. Safe social distancing is largely not possible. Contact tracing of the homeless is also very difficult. Homelessness through eviction of insolvent renters is straining LIC, MIC and HIC alike.

- The scale of the financing challenge for developing countries is measured in trillions of US dollars. The sudden reversal of capital flows has helped finance the exceptional fiscal packages in the advanced economies but has left emerging market and developing economies exposed. The additional financing needs for developing countries arising from the crisis remain uncertain, but they will be exceptionally high and likely to persist over the medium term. Pandemic-related external financing gaps for active International Development Association (IDA)[3] countries could be in the range of US$25-100 billion per year – assuming that incremental financing needs arising from the crisis are in the range of 2-10 percent of GDP and that only half of these can be met internally. For WB International Bank for Reconstruction and Development (IBRD)[4] borrowers (representing approximately one-third of MIC GDP), the equivalent range is US$150-600 billion annually. This has serious implications for countries needing financing of resilience requiring investments in LAS and NSDI.

The pandemic has highlighted the urgent need for policy action to cushion its consequences, protect vulnerable populations, and improve countries' capacity to cope with similar future events. It is also critical to address the challenges posed by informality and limited safety nets and undertake reforms that enable strong, inclusive and sustainable growth. However, the pandemic's rapid global economic impacts highlight the fragility of the sustainability of SDG Goal 1, extreme poverty alleviation [1].

2.4   Overview of WB-FAO Partnership

Since 1964, the Cooperative Programme (CP) between FAO and the WB has continued to support reforms concerned with secure access to land and other natural resources, reinforced national food security and nutrition, mainstreaming responsible land governance and sustainable economic development. Rapid penetration of innovative hi-tech geomatics accelerated digitalization of LAS and advancement of e-government have naturally expanded the FAO-WB investment partnership in the land sector to encompass NSDI. The body of experiences, good practices and lessons learned during such land sector investments supported by international development partners have duly informed, and are integrated in the VGGT. In general, poor tenure security, non-recognition of legitimate land rights and interests, or lack of land and geospatial records on access rights reduce the resilience of people to natural disasters and to climate change effects. Mindful of the resilience impact of LAS and NSDI, and triggered by various recent hazards, several joint interventions of the WB and FAO pay special attention to resilience building, and/or use resilience as an entry point for investing in land sector reforms.

The WB and FAO have partnered to promote the fundamental role of LAS and NSDI infrastructure for improving disaster resilience at the community and national levels, in line with the VGGT and the Sendai Framework. The recent CP experiences have highlighted good practice rapid assessments of the resilience and resilience impact of national land administration and geospatial information systems, which are relevant to the pandemic context, over several countries, which are discussed in this Chapter.

---

[3]IDA is part of the World Bank Group. IDA offers concessional loans and grants to the world's poorest developing countries.

[4]IBRD is part of the World Bank Group. The IBRD offers loans to middle-income developing countries.

2.5   Resilience Enablement Through LAS and NSDI

Comprehensive and authoritative LAS and NSDI are of strategic importance for economic prosperity and inclusive growth, sustainable development, responsible governance of natural resources, and resilience – due to their potential to facilitate information synergy across multitudinous thematic domains and thus support efficient and effective decision making, as well as leveraging land as a fundamental economic factor and original source of all material wealth. In the context of national and community resilience, LAS and geospatial information are critically significant for systemic and institutional preparedness to enable the country, government and communities to mitigate hazards, adapt and recover from shocks or stresses. Such preparedness, adaption and recovery should be without compromising long-term development prospects of communities, cities, localities, regions and countries. That means digital information, secure data storage of land administration information and an NSDI providing geospatial information that is accessible, authoritative and sustainable. These are activities which must be led by the government for the benefit of all, with civil society, community, private sector professionals, investors and academic participation.

Resilience, be it for disasters or pandemics, requires a high degree of geospatial preparedness, which is best achieved through NSDI. For NSDI, countries require: (i) an agreed common geospatial framework with defined horizontal and vertical reference systems; (ii) standards, data sharing protocols and data access; (iii) fundamental mapping or geospatial datasets; (iv) an agreed lead agency mandate for the overall coordination of the NSDI and designated lead agencies for the production and maintenance of fundamental geospatial data themes; (v) communications; security; and (vi) human, technical and financial capacity to sustain the systems. In the context of a pandemic, further geospatial-related requirements may include: (i) access to mobility data from telecommunication networks, video-surveillance, urban and other sensors; (ii) tools to analyze the influx of near real-time data; (iii) spatially-enabled systems to support public health surveillance; and (iv) policies for balancing the protection of personal data privacy and confidentiality with ensuring the public good.

Many countries, especially LIC, may have very limited digital geospatial information and immature NSDI, limiting, or inhibiting, their preparedness for disasters or pandemics. For some LIC and MIC, recent wars or civil conflict have further left legacies of weak geospatial preparedness. Also, a legacy of conflict is often that LAS are either non-existent or in very poor shape due to the destruction of land records and other evidence of rights. For such countries, preparing any NSDI investment should be preceded by an assessment or stocktake of the existing systems. There is undoubtedly a geospatial preparedness inequity between countries, especially LIC, which places them at a severe disadvantage in developing resilience that requires geospatial information.

A major impediment to pandemic preparedness is often the weak street and postal addressing systems which precludes effective emergency response, contact tracing and monitoring of families and individuals for medical testing and follow-ups, vaccination programs, reliable reporting statistics, delivery and access to social benefits and so forth. For homeless people, even in advanced economies with well-developed address systems, the lack of access to an address is a major limitation and poses health risks especially where such people are mobile. Indigenous, customary and communal tenure systems are also especially vulnerable during pandemics where lack of formal records, geospatially referenced land parcels fabric and an addressing system leave inhabitants vulnerable.

As the world endures the pandemic and moves to the new norms, governments, often with international development assistance, will need to: (i) review how existing systems worked or failed during the pandemic; (ii) assess the effectiveness of geospatial information's and LAS contributions to surveillance and tracking; (iii) identify whether any non-traditional land and geospatial data sources (e.g. crowd-source data) may have government response to the pandemic; (iv) examine the effectiveness of measures used in the property markets, including valuation and government guarantee of tenure rights, addressing both ownership, leaseholds and rentals, to mitigate financial and economic downturns and ensure good governance; (v) review the impacts of land-indigence, landlessness and homelessness on the spread of the virus; (vi) study the impacts of regulated spatial planning on controlling the spread of the coronavirus and other future pandemics and health crises.

Authoritative geospatial information plays critical roles in all phases of disaster management: disaster prediction, prevention, preparedness and mitigation, emergency response, evacuation planning, search and rescue, shelter operations, and the post-disaster restoration and monitoring. Reliable and comprehensive land administration information, including land records are critical for many of the phases of disaster management including preparedness, recovery and reconstruction. Especially important for the pandemic context, is address information to enable reliable contact tracing and even social distancing. LAS and NSDI underpin economic and social recovering, supporting the minimization of the shocks of disasters and pandemics and enabling quicker recovery to return to normal.

Assessing the likely impact of disaster events requires detailed inventory of real estate assets, buildings, housing, crops, and infrastructure, including specific location-based information such as street address, and other horizontal and vertical positioning referencing data. Although, pandemics don't damage or destroy such items a spatial inventory of housing and occupancy would be expected to be beneficial.

Secure tenure is the key to reducing disaster vulnerability and risks. The more secure, formal and reconcilable the rights and systems are, the less vulnerable land users are to eviction or loss of livelihoods in the case of a disaster, and the more likely they are to receive compensation for losses sustained. Secure tenure increases investments in dwellings, which reduces risks and improves resilience through better siting and construction of buildings. Better quality housing in terms of space, ventilation, access, amongst other factors is conducive to supporting good social distancing and enhancing pandemic resilience.

Land administration and geospatial information needs to be accurate, reflect reality on the ground, and be up to date if it is to contribute to disaster preparedness and risk mitigation, and responses to disaster events. In many countries this is not the case, making them vulnerable to disasters. Street addressing transcends both land administration and geospatial information and is vital for both disaster and pandemic resilience.

Sharing land and geospatial information with disaster risk management agencies and enabling them to harness these valuable data in their planning and operations enhances the overall process and supports government-wide agendas, but often there are disconnects between a number of these key elements and a lack of interoperability. NSDI are essential to overcoming these issues. Improving interoperability means overcoming technical, capacity, legal, and cultural impediments.

LAS and NSDI can only perform their roles if they are themselves resilient – which means they must also be sustainable. Yet often LAS records are paper-based and are vulnerable to destruction. Remote storage of electronic data offers greater protection providing such data are properly secured. The organizations responsible for LAS and NSDI geospatial systems need to have business recovery plans which are regularly tested. These organizations need to be adequately resourced in terms of finances, trained personnel, equipment and facilities at all times. However, data must also be accessible. LAS and NSDI that are not able to deliver reliable, accessible information when there is no disaster or pandemic, cannot be expected to deliver during the times of disaster or pandemic.

Governance issues play an important role in the effectiveness of LAS and NSDI. Corrupt or ineffective town planning, land management, or building control systems enhance the risks from disaster events and impede recovery and reconstruction. Stakeholder involvement is needed so that all parties know the parts they must play in the event of a disaster event. Those responsible for disaster planning and mitigation and for reconstruction and recovery should be accountable to the population and respect human rights. Governance will be tested after any disaster. It is too early to assess any governance challenges from the COVID-19 pandemic, but in the near future such studies should be undertaken.

In light of the above, Table 2.1 summarizes applications for land administration and geospatial information in the emergency contexts of disasters and pandemics.

TABLE 2.1

Land Administration and Geospatial Information Uses for Disasters and Pandemics

PHASE	DISASTER		PANDEMIC	
	Geospatial	**Land Administration**	**Geospatial**	**Land Administration**
Preparation	Needs assessment Planning and response: • evacuation • communications • medical support • stockpiling resources location • logistics planning Prediction & Warning: • monitoring • forecasting • early warning • exercising Street addressing	Spatial planning Security of tenure Security of records Security of occupancy Street addressing	Needs assessment Planning and response: • evacuation • communications • medical support • stockpiling resources location • logistics planning Prediction & Warning: • monitoring • forecasting • early warning • exercising Street addressing	Spatial planning Security of tenure Security of occupancy Street addressing
Response	Coordination Situation Analysis – Appreciation Crisis maps Emergency aid - Search and rescue, Evacuation & shelters, Medical, Food, water Emergency resources dispatch Early damage assessment	Early damage assessment	Epidemiological surveillance support systems Contact tracing Situation Analysis – Appreciation Pandemic mapping Cases and deaths distribution, monitoring Testing coordination and monitoring Emergency resources dispatch Streamlining supply chains – delivery medical and food Targeting community investments to reduce risk of contagion and minimizing negative economic impacts	
Recovery	Recovery Reconstruction Rehabilitation: • coordination • damage assessment review • monitoring and evaluation Tenure security location Housing Spatial Planning Transport & infrastructure Utilities Communications and ICT Agriculture Livelihoods	Rights identification Tenure security Housing Spatial Planning Land re-allocation	Epidemiological surveillance support systems Contact tracing Pandemic mapping Cases and deaths distribution, monitoring Testing coordination and monitoring Emergency resources dispatch Streamlining supply chains – delivery medical and food Targeting community investments to reduce risk of contagion and minimizing negative economic impacts	Spatial planning Formalization of rights
Prevention and Mitigation	Hazard risk analysis Simulation & modelling Risk mapping Building & asset inventory Public awareness raising Training & capacity building	Land records digitization Data security Secure, safe facilities Online services Spatial planning Land re-allocation	Spatial planning Street addressing	Spatial planning Security of tenure

2.6   COVID-19: Specific Challenges

The pandemic has created land-tenure related and spatial challenges that have never been experienced before. These include, but are not limited to:

- Lockdown – requires a secure, serviceable, habitable place to live (dwelling) that is accessible to emergency services, power, water, sanitation. Homeless people and slum dwellers are especially at risk of contracting and spreading the virus

- Social distancing – sufficient space between people when they live and reside – again, homeless people and slum dwellers are especially at risk of contracting and spreading the virus

- Contact tracing – requires physical address – homeless people and slum dwellers are unlikely to have an address

- Privacy of personal information.

In response to the COVID-19 pandemic, many countries requested their citizens to practice social-distancing, stay-at-home and to stay safe. This has created significant challenges to implement, given the vast numbers of homeless people in both developed and developing nations. Also, for many countries housing conditions and density of informal settlements often do not allow residents to follow basic hygienic measures or to keep the minimum social distance to reduce spreading the virus. Much is being reported on the need to undertake *"formalization or regularization of slums and illegal settlements"*. However, that may secure rights, but it does not improve safety, well-being, services, or quality of life.

Gender is also being reported as a specific COVID-19 challenge. Men have sustained a greater death toll from the pandemic than women. In April 2020, men accounted for 65 percent of deaths [7]. Stanley and Prettitore [8] specifically cite the gender experiences with tenure security of Aceh and North Sumatra following the December 2004 tsunami. It is well reported that in times of disasters and conflicts women may be especially vulnerable regarding tenure security and access to land rights [9]. In the longer term, reforming inheritance laws and marital property regimes will be key to improving the implementation and enforcement of women's rights to housing land and property rights, as well as ensuring that social and cultural norms also change. Titles or other rights instruments are not sufficient to bring about change and ensure the rights of women.

However, are women more vulnerable to the tenure-related shocks of the pandemic? Although Stanley and Prettitore [8] advise that women are more vulnerable, this Chapter suggests that it is probably far too soon to draw firm conclusions, but as more research and analysis is undertaken, it may also better highlight the vulnerabilities of women under a pandemic crisis. Nonetheless the tenure rights of everyone must be respected and the challenges are always there.

"Experience from post-disaster land activities in Aceh, Indonesia, and from post-conflict land restitution programs in Colombia have shown that with willingness and a focus on women's particular barriers, we can make a difference. It's time we break down the barriers to women's access to land around the world, and make sure to protect women's rights while the pandemic places them in a precarious situation" [8].

The United Nations Economic Commission for Europe (UNECE) Working Party on Land Administration and the International Federation of Surveyors (FIG) have admirably worked together to examine the situation of informal settlements in the pan-European region and have identified ways to formalize informal developments. The result has been the "Guidelines for the Formalization of Informal Constructions" [10], which provides a practical guide, explaining how to structure a program for the formalization of informal constructions. The Guidelines would seem to have the potential to be considered globally to assist countries in post-COVID-19 recovery. Benefits from formalizing informal settlements could contribute to economic recovery by integrating them into land markets, with clear ownership titles and registration. Security of tenure, ownership of land and property provides access to credit, and environmental, planning, construction, and utility-provision improvements can be initiated to a standard where people can live in adequate and healthy homes. The authors of this chapter would suggest that the Guidelines may have gone much further in terms of actual technical content especially regarding implications for construction, infrastructure service and utilities. Notwithstanding, these UNECE and FIG Guidelines are a useful reference for any country or jurisdiction seeking to address formalization of informal tenure. Commendably, UNECE has always been proactive when it comes to guidelines, especially in terms of improving land administration systems information in the region. Most notably, the UNECE [11] "Guidelines on Land Administration" have been referred to widely, not only in the European region, but globally.

It is well-reported that there are at least one billion urban dwellers currently living in informal settlements, which has increased from a 1996 estimate of around three-quarters of a billion. It will no doubt continue to grow as the world's urban population continues to grow. The importance of tackling this issue is undeniable and measured under several United Nations Sustainable Development Goals (SDGs). SDG target 1.4 stresses that governments should ensure that all men and women, particularly the poor and vulnerable, have equal rights to economic resources, as well as access to basic services, ownership and control over land and other forms of property and inheritance. SDG 11 stresses that cities and human settlements should be inclusive, safe, resilient and sustainable. The growth and magnitude of natural disasters around the world, of all types, have clearly identified the need for building resilience. Informal settlements have been built outside the formal system of laws and regulations that ensure tenure, legal ownership and safe, resilient structures. Informal development is not a new issue. However, over the last 30 years, informal development has become an increasingly urgent matter. UNECE reported in 2007 that more than 50 million people lived in informal settlements in 20 member-states of the UNECE region. Europe has experienced a rise of urban dwellers who cannot afford to pay rent, with housing costs rising particularly rapidly in the more prosperous large cities. This is especially the case for the Southern and Eastern parts of the region, while Western European countries are said to have more than 6 percent of their urban dwellers living in insecure housing conditions.

Slums are especially vulnerable due to:

- High population densities contribute to rapid and broader spread of infection which accelerates transmission

- Household overcrowding makes behaviors like social distancing difficult

- Poor living conditions exacerbate transmission slowing behavior

- Limited access to health services

- Reliance on crowded transport services increases contagion risk

- Working in the informal sector poses risks [12].

Renters, tenants, lessees and mortgagees are vulnerable to the economic impacts of the pandemic. All too often renters, tenants and lessees are forgotten in discussions of tenure security, as they do not hold absolute ownership rights. Rather, their tenure rights would be expected to be covered under contracts. However, often such tenure rights are not automatically inheritable, plus their security is generally subject to payment of rent, therefore they may be forfeited when rent payment defaults, leading to eviction. Similarly, mortgagees who are unable to defray mortgage repayments to the financier, may lose tenure rights and face foreclosure and eviction. Such problems are experienced globally, in both developed and developing economies. Notably some countries legislated relief periods for rents and mortgages – but periods of several months are already proving to be insufficient to people who have lost income and assets.

As the COVID-19 pandemic spreads across the globe, lives, livelihoods, food supplies and food security are being severely disrupted. In the face of this crisis, investment in agriculture and food systems provide an important way to support communities' resilience against crises and ensure robust food supply chains. This has very profound implication for land and tenure security as land is a critical factor in agriculture. Investment in the sector is crucial now more than ever, but experience shows that focusing only on more investments is not enough. The "Principles for Responsible Investment in Agriculture and Food Systems" (RAI) by the Committee on World Food Security

[13] are the main global instrument to provide guidance in this regard. The RAI have heavily drawn from guiding frameworks such as the Principles for Responsible Agricultural Investment that respects rights, livelihoods, and resources (PRAI) by FAO, International Fund for Agricultural Development (IFAD), United Nations Conference on Trade and Development (UNCTAD), and the WB, and also build on the VGGT [14].

Location of citizens has been highlighted as a very important element of managing and responding to COVID-19 cases and transmissions. In public health, contact tracing has dual roles. Firstly, contact tracing is undertaken to find all infected persons and those who have been in contact with infected persons. It has been a very effective pillar of the control of communicable diseases, e.g. contact tracing was primarily responsible for small pox eradication, rather than universal immunization. Secondly, contact tracing may be undertaken to learn more about the disease characteristics, especially the spatial context including infection clusters, locations of secondary and subsequent infection waves/spikes.[5] At the time of writing this Chapter, it has been reported that with the escalation of new cases in the USA, at around 50,000 new cases per day, contact tracing may no longer be viable.[6]

The pandemic has brought a global re-thinking of the confidentiality of personal information to better manage spread of the disease. Arguably, when the greater good is public health, new approaches to privacy of personal information are necessary. However, risks of abuse are being raised globally. In April 2020, the EU produced its "Commission Recommendation of 8.4.2020 on a common Union toolbox for the use of technology and data to combat and exit from the COVID-19 crisis, in particular concerning mobile applications and the use of anonymized mobility data". Also, in April 2020, the EU produced "Guidelines 04/2020 on the use of location data and contact tracing tools in the context of the COVID-19 outbreak". Both publications provide very useful guidance to any country or jurisdiction seeking to address personal information and also contact tracing through policy and regulatory means. Commendably, the EU has continued to be progressive in promoting sound policy with information and also NSDI. In 2007, the EU issued Directive 2007/2/EC for establishing an Infrastructure for Spatial Information in the European Community (INSPIRE). In 2016, the General Data Protection Regulation (EU)2016/679 (GDPR) was approved by the European Parliament as a regulation in EU law for data protection and privacy throughout the EU, and member countries are required to comply.

In the COVID-19 context, vulnerable communities around the world are expected to face increased land grabs, migration, displacement, corruption, and evictions. For many countries, especially LIC and MIC, it is unlikely they have sufficient capacity and resources to fully address these challenges. Technology will undoubtedly play key roles, as already has been demonstrated with smart phone applications for contact tracing. At this time, there are many questions, and clarity may only come with time:

- Can LIC and MIC afford to fund LAS and NSDI investments at sufficient levels to rebound from the pandemic in order to return society to normal, when all countries have suffered huge economic losses?

- Articulating the benefits of funding land services, protecting the land claims of vulnerable populations, and accelerating the pace of securing land and property tenure is very important. Advocating for significant investments in technology, and ensuring political support to digital transformation at a time when there may be greater financial priories, is a huge challenge. How are we seeing technology and land data playing a role in COVID-19 planning and response and perhaps more importantly, what role can it play in post-pandemic response to better prepare us for the long-term?

- What successful technology-based approaches to land governance (including land administration, land development and land use planning) and lessons learned during COVID-19 can be continued? Evidence-based advocacy, rather than rhetoric and evidence from the land sector is required. Already there is an abundance of blogs, webinars and lobbying of governments and

---

[5]https://en.wikipedia.org/wiki/Contact-tracing

[6]https://www.docwirenews.com/docwire-pick/hem-onc-picks/the-covid-19-pandemic-close-to-12-million-world-cases-contact-tracing-no-longer-possible-in-us-south-and-more/

international finance institutions to fund technical interventions – often claiming pandemic recovery will be quicker through quickly deploying technologies that can be used to collect and manage land and geospatial data – such as smartphones, tablets, computers, handheld GPS/GNSS, and drones to name a few – how are they being used to equitably and inclusively accelerate land administration processes?

Building resilience, through sustainable LAS and NSDI requires investment – both for the development and implementation as well as ongoing maintenance, further development and continuous improvement. It very much should remind everyone why the word "infrastructure" was included in the term NSDI – which was to ensure that soft infrastructure is funded in a similar manner to hard infrastructure. The recession and financial challenges of governments around the globe, especially in LIC and MIC, creates opportunities for alternative service delivery including public-private partnerships (PPP). Bell [15] raised opportunities such as the provision of information technology (IT) infrastructure and services, positioning infrastructure and services including Continuously Operating Reference Stations (CORS) and customer service delivery as potential areas, subject to necessary safeguarding. Loss of capacity and governance concerns may also create openings for PPP modalities to support resilience investments in LAS and NSDI. However, any such investments, must be rigorously safeguarded by government oversight to ensure reliability, sustainability, good governance, public access and affordability.

2.7   Pragmatic Rapid Assessment of LAS and NSDI Maturity in Resilience Contexts

Countries cooperate with development partners to assess their respective land and geospatial information sectors and get advice on policy, legal, institutional, capacity and technology reforms aiming to boost sustainable socio-economic growth and natural resources management, enhance resilience to adversities, and safeguard the environment. The WB and FAO have frequently partnering through their CP to respond to such requests, promoting also the fundamental role of LAS and NSDI infrastructure for improving disaster resilience at the community and national levels, in line with the VGGT and the Sendai Framework. A rapid LAS and NSDI assessment approach has shaped up through the CP and collaboration with members and others, mostly driven by pragmatic considerations and restrictions imposed by funding modalities. The recent partnership experiences have highlighted good practice rapid assessments of the resilience and resilience impact of national land administration and geospatial information systems, over several countries including Nepal, Myanmar, Lebanon, Kyrgyzstan, and Uzbekistan. The same pragmatic rapid assessment approach was also used unilaterally by the WB in Kerala, Punjab, the Solomon Islands, Lao People's Democratic Republic (see Table 2.2).

TABLE 2.2

Experiences with Pragmatic Rapid Assessment of LAS and NSDI Maturity in Resilience Contexts within Selected Countries

Country	Tailored focus	Major findings in resilience context	Advantages / benefits
Kyrgyzstan[a]	» Next generation land governance and geospatial information services › *building NSDI and geospatial data and services* › strengthening public land management › strengthening property valuation and taxation › strengthening land tenure and access to encourage investment » **LAS and NSDI as a game-changer** for: › development › integrated planning, taxation, and sustainable resource management › *disaster risk management (DRM)* › *climate resilience* › private sector investment support	» Hindrances for DRM /climate resilience identified: › limited access due to geospatial data secrecy › no obligation for data sharing or exchange › shortage of authoritative digital datasets › poor geospatial capacity across stakeholders › departmental silo culture	» highly participatory » local trust / consensus » full country ownership » use national sources » optimal speed » affordability » flexibility » recommends strategy
Myanmar[b]	» Land sector needs assessment › land policy and regulatory framework › forestland administration and management › land administration › *geospatial infrastructure and services* › property valuation and taxation » **LAS and NSDI with core geospatial datasets as a public good** underpin: › *peace building* › food security › poverty eradication › sustainable economic development › *disaster and climate resilience* › land use policy implementation › e-governance advancement	» Resilience suffers from immature LAS and NSDI: › relevant legal frame still under development › *One Map* policy initiative still not ripe › poor governance informatization / digitalization › wanting capacity, technological innovation › restrictions on access to geospatial data	» highly participatory » local trust / consensus » full country ownership » use national sources » fits absorption capacity » monitoring benchmark » recommends strategy » remedy problems » realize opportunities » pro-poor » SDG achievement in disaster risk reduction[c]
Kerala[d] India	» **Rebuild Kerala Initiative** targeting: › prepare better for future disasters › *more resilient, green, inclusive and vibrant* vision for the future › generate revenue from property taxation and value capture › prioritize *resurvey and update of land records* › unified *on-line Land Information Management System* › *interlinked digital databases*	» Weaknesses in the land and geospatial systems exacerbated the impact of natural disasters › missing *right information at the right time* › unplanned land uses and encroachments › fragmented, outdated, inconsistent land records › outdated / historical paper mapping › vulnerability of land records to destruction › insufficient local revenue from land » Poor and social underclasses are at serious risk from disasters due to lack of formal rights and poor spatial planning	» highly participatory » local trust / consensus » full state ownership » use state sources » optimal speed » affordability » fits absorption capacity » pro-poor » recommends action

TABLE 2.2

Continued – Experiences with Pragmatic Rapid Assessment of LAS and NSDI Maturity in Resilience Contexts within Selected Countries

Country	Tailored focus	Major findings in resilience context	Advantages / benefits
Nepal[e]	» Modernized, transparent and **resilient LAS and NSDI to improve national and community resilience to disasters** › *policy and legal framework for LAS and NSDI* › land registration and *LAS* › *NSDI and related systems* › land and property valuation › information and communications technologies › education & training for surveying, geospatial sciences and LAS › social review	» Resilience is best supported through a sustainable, digital LAS and an authoritative NSDI, receiving necessary budget, operational and development requirements: › review land laws; draft consolidated land code › mandate NSDI as national priority › ensure whole-of-government coordination › lead agency and data custodian designations › foundation data sets › funding › data standards › protocols for access and sharing » National DRM strategy did not consider holistically LAS or NSDI – but just for hazard risk mapping » No national coordination for NSDI » The impact of civil war 1996-2016 on the LAS were greater than the 2015 earthquake. Civil war destroyed land offiices and all land records in many districts – not yet recovered, and thus leaving communities very vulnerable. The earthquake damaged records in multiple districts, but there was no loss of services » Social underclasses are at serious risk from disasters due to lack of formal rights and poor spatial planning	» highly participatory » local trust / consensus » full country ownership » use national sources » optimal speed » affordability » flexibility » fits absorption capacity » pro-poor » recommends action
Punjab[f]	» Build a **unified land records management system** including *increased resilience to disasters* needs to: › assess legislation with consideration of the resilience angle › assess disaster resilience with land and geospatial systems	» To increase resilience to disasters, one should: › improve community resilience through enhancing tenure security › leverage the use of geospatial data » Poor and social underclasses are at serious risk from disasters due to lack of formal rights and poor spatial planning	» participatory » local trust / consensus » local ownership » optimal speed » affordability » pro-poor » recommends action

TABLE 2.2

Continued – Experiences with Pragmatic Rapid Assessment of LAS and NSDI Maturity in Resilience Contexts within Selected Countries

Country	Tailored focus	Major findings in resilience context	Advantages / benefits
Solomon	» **Land and geospatial system resilience needs assessment** › diagnosis of LAS and geospatial information system, their infrastructure and resilience impact › design *improvements for resilience* › emphasise on access to land for development › develop *LAS and NSDI investment plan*	» Resilience of land, real property and the people to land relationships requires: › community desire for better land management › register customary rights – critical for resilience › universal base map for all the Solomon Islands › share public geospatial datasets via geoportal	» participatory » local trust / consensus » local ownership » optimal speed » affordability » recommends action
Lao PDR[h]	» **Geospatial prioritization** tool to: › geographically target systematic land registration › determine geographical distribution of *natural disaster vulnerabilities* and *tenure security risks* › identify hotspots wherein interventions can achieve maximum impact › support projects design and implementation	» Natural disaster vulnerabilities must be a factor in enhancing tenure security at the local level, to: › ensure effectiveness and efficiency › reaching those who need tenure security most	» participatory » local trust / consensus » local ownership » optimal speed » affordability » recommends action

[a] World Bank (2017) Kyrgyz Republic: Next Generation Land Administration and Management Services – non lending technical assistance (P158348), Bishkek, 2017

[b] World Bank (2018) Myanmar: Towards a Sustainable Land Administration and Management System – land sector needs assessment technical assistance (P157559), Nay Pyi Taw, 2018

[c] http://www.fao.org/myanmar/news/detail-events/en/c/1033174/

[d] World Bank (2020) Solid Ground: Increasing community resilience through improved land administration and geospatial geospatial information systems, Washington DC, 2020, p. 33

[e] World Bank (2020) Nepal: Technical Assistance to Develop the Land Administration and Geospatial Information Systems (*Resilience and Resilience Impact of the Land and Geospatial Systems*, P165271), Kathmandu, 2020

[f] World Bank (2020) Improving Resilience and the Resilience Impact of National Land and Geospatial Systems - Phase II implementation support, Washington DC, 2020, pp. 7-53

[g] World Bank (2020) Improving Resilience and the Resilience Impact of National Land and Geospatial Systems - Phase II implementation support, Washington DC, 2020, pp. 54-87

[h] World Bank (2020) Improving Resilience and the Resilience Impact of National Land and Geospatial Systems - Phase II implementation support, Washington DC, 2020, p. 4

The pragmatic rapid approach allows to produce targeted outputs within a short term (a couple of weeks) and with modest workload (around a man-month of expert input per topic). The approach relies on: strong ownership by, and participation of stakeholders – coupled with international expertise knowledgeable of good practices;[7] expert analysis by brief desk review of web-sources, published documents, research, articles and statistics relying on local sources; gathering hands-on information in a limited series of face-to-face, profiling and cross-cutting technical discussions and field visits – during a short mission facilitated by the beneficiary; intensive home-based synthesis of outputs; and verification of findings and recommendations by key stakeholders. This good practice, – based on long-term WB and FAO expertise and experience – proves relevant and is appreciated by beneficiaries, since it is, among others: inherently focused on leaving no one behind, in line with good practices,[8] and endeavoring to reach the furthest behind first; affordable; very adaptable to

---

[7] viz. VGGT and the Sendai Framework.

[8] Land-indigence refers to land holders whose land is: (i) too small or otherwise inadequate to support healthy living, social distancing during pandemics or other health crises; and/or (ii) insufficient for a livelihood in the context of rural small farmers.

country specificity; participatory – thus capacitating in-country stakeholders; matching the needs – as its emphases, depth and detail can be tailored to the topical reform agenda; and producing outputs within tight time frames.

In assessing LAS and NSDI requirements the WB and FAO look at various tools to support and inform the work including a range of geomaturity and SDI-readiness[9] instruments, considering and evaluating also other available tools for geomaturity and NSDI-readiness, including the Integrated Geospatial Information Framework (IGIF) developed under the United Nations Initiative on Global Geospatial Information Management (UN-GGIM). UN-GGIM is currently drafting a Framework for Effective Land Administration (FELA), as reference for developing, reforming, renewing, strengthening or modernizing land administration and management systems. Early discussions with selected WB client countries suggest that there are parallels with IGIF. That is, rather than implement another costly and time-consuming framework, simply consider its key elements during the rapid assessment. FAO has communicated its doubts regarding FELA's added value in the context of other existing UN instruments. Within WB, similar doubts are shared. Experience with IGIF's NSDI diagnostic, alignment to policy drivers, socio-economic assessment, and action planning, as piloted for example in Guyana[10] (2018-19) – helps to draw parallels and inform the approaches elsewhere. However, after evaluation, it is often agreed with the governments that the pragmatic rapid approach is more suited to the resilience context especially as it is cheaper and quicker.

2.8   Build Back Better

Following a disaster event, it is not sufficient just for reconstruction to take place, but construction and land administration and geospatial information should be enhanced through building back better, so that there is greater resilience to future disaster events [1, 6]. Disaster events often reoccur so that just undertaking recovery work is an inadequate response, as it is likely to be destroyed by the next disaster event. Only by building back better can communities be protected in the future. Investment in doing so produces substantial returns on the capital employed. Similarly, following a pandemic, building back better principles should also be adopted.

Rebuilding after disaster events requires reliable, accurate geospatial data, at the appropriate levels of precision to enable engineering and construction works to be undertaken, something that volunteer geographic information cannot achieve. Following the pandemic, reliable, accurate geospatial information is also required, especially to support rehabilitation of slums and areas of homelessness to ensure they are appropriately planned and serviced to ensure health and well-being.

From the historical perspective, the concept of "Build Back Better" (BBB) was probably first coined in Indonesia in 2005 in discussions between WB, the UN Special Envoy for Tsunami (Bill Clinton) and officials of the government's reconstruction agency (WB, 2005).[11] The original concept was very much focused on physically building back better in terms of engineering of structures, assets and infrastructure, better planning, community safety, early warning as well as land rights, and gender equality. However, in the context of the pandemic, BBB has taken on broader roles including low carbon, climate change, green growth, the digital economy, addressing inequality, amongst other topics [16]. Investment in NSDI and LAS have much to contribute to this new view of BBB. Apropos SDGs 13 and 14, in the post-COVID-19 world, there is good reason to be optimistic that these and other long-standing global and regional issues will be addressed. LAS and NSDI have critical roles in contributing significantly to the solutions.

---

[9]Spatial-Data-Infrastructure readiness.

[10]FAO (2018), Mainstreaming Sustainable Land Development and Management in Guyana (project GCP/GUY/003/GRI).

[11]Attribution of this term's origin has been incorrectly attributed to the Sendai Framework, wherein it is reported that the term: *"was firstly defined and used officially in the UN Sendai Framework for Disaster Risk Reduction 2015-2030, which was agreed at the Third UN World Conference on Disaster Risk Reduction 14-18 March 2015, which was held in Sendai Japan, and this document was adopted by the UN General Assembly on 3 June 2015"*.

2.9   Concluding Remarks

All countries, inter-governmental coordination bodies, development agencies, civil society organizations and professional bodies such as FIG have a role to play in promoting resilience through LAS and NSDI. The less hype and the more evidence-based approaches to support resilience, the better prepared communities will be to withstand the shocks of the next disaster or pandemic. Fit-for-purpose investments, that can be incrementally improved over time, which require sustainable LAS and NSDI, will enable resilience and ensure that legacy systems are not barriers to recovery after any shock. The partnership between the WB and FAO to promote the VGGT, will continue to play a leading global role in supporting the resilience of countries, cities and communities.

For the land sector, the outbreak again brings to light the very intimate, spatial relationships between land, people and communities – and how the shocks of any disaster or pandemic disrupts life and livelihoods.

The land sector can better promote the adaption of relevant technologies. There is evidence that fit-for-purpose approaches to land administration can reduce costs and promote greater transparency and accountability in the building of complete LAS, given the growing availability and reach of technologies that can be used to collect and manage data, – such as smartphones, tablets, computers, handheld GPS/GNSS, and drones to name a few. However, technology is never a solution, rather it is an enabler. Using technology to overcome development challenges is not a new phenomenon. This is particularly true in the land sector, where tools for collecting and managing data relating to land use and rights have advanced considerably in recent decades. In the post-pandemic recovery, technology is likely to prove even more critical for the collection and management of land-related data to advance land rights and tenure security for millions of people left out of formal land systems. Mere formalization of rights in over-populated, unhealthy slums, will not build resilience unless there is spatial planning.

For those working in international development, the pandemic has brought almost everything to a complete standstill. Development agency priorities are generally committed to the higher priorities of governments dealing with the economic meltdowns as well as addressing health demands and urgent needs for survival of society including food security. These priorities may see deferments of new investment projects for LAS and NSDI. Most land sector interventions take considerable time to implement and political will is paramount. The post-pandemic world presents opportunities for significant progress with carbon emission reduction, climate change, green growth and PROBLUE. LAS and NSDI have key roles to play in the resilience of the post-pandemic world by Building Back Better.

"Adversity has the effect of eliciting talents, which in prosperous circumstances would have lain dormant".
Horace, Latin Philosopher (65-8 BC).

References

[1] World Bank. Global Economic Prospects, A World Bank Group Flagship Report. Washington, D.C., 2020.

[2] FAO·CFS. Voluntary Guidelines on the Responsible Governance of Tenure of Land, Fisheries and Forests in the Context of National Food Security. Rome, Italy, 2012.

[3] UNDRR. *Sendai framework for disaster risk reduction 2015–2030*. United Nations Office for Disaster Risk Reduction. New York, 2015.

[4] WHO. Health Emergency and Disaster Risk Management Framework, World Health Organization. Switzerland, 2019.

[5] Bell K.C. Post-Disaster Recovery and Reconstruction from an International Development Perspective: Impact and Challenges for Land and Geospatial Professionals, keynote presentation to the 78th FIG Working Week 2016, "Recovery from Disaster", Christchurch. New Zealand, 2016.

[6] World Bank. Saving Lives, Scaling-up Impact and Getting Back on Track: World Bank Group COVID-19 Crisis Response Approach Paper. Washington, D.C., 2020.

[7] World Bank. Gender Dimensions of the COVID-19 Pandemic, Policy Note. World Bank, Washington, D.C., 2020.

[8] V. Stanley and P. Prettitore. How COVID-19 puts Women's Housing, Land, and Property Rights at Risk, World Bank blog "Sustainable Cities". Washington, D.C., 2020. URL `https://blogs.worldbank.org/sustainablecities/how-covid-19-puts-womens-housing-land-and-property-rights-risk?CID=WBW_AL_BlogNotification_EN_EXT`.

[9] World Bank Government of Japan and FAO. The Voluntary Guidelines and the World Bank: Increasing Women's Access to Land, Approaches that Work, A Good Practices Brief, Brief No. 1. World Bank, Washington, D.C., 2015.

[10] UNECE and FIG. Guidelines for the Formalization of Informal Constructions, Report No. ECE/HBP/196, a Joint Publication of the United Nations Economic Commission for Europe (UNECE) and the International Federation of Surveyors. New York, USA, 2020.

[11] UNECE. Land Administration Guidelines: With Special Reference to Countries in Transition, United Nations and Economic Commission for Europe. *New York & Geneva*, 1996.

[12] World Bank. Global Responses to COVID 19 in Slums and Cities: Practices from around the World, GSG Urban Poverty and Housing, Working Document. Washington, D.C., 2020.

[13] FAO·CFS. Principles for Responsible Investment in Agriculture and Food Systems, Food and Agriculture Organization of the United Nations Committee on World Food Security. 2014.

[14] FAO. Ensuring Resilient Communities and Food Supply in the Face of the COVID-19 Pandemic with Investments Guided by the CFS-RAI. 2020. URL `http://www.fao.org/in-action/responsible-agricultural-investments/news/detail/en/c/1279359/`.

[15] Bell K.C. Global Experiences with Public Private Partnerships for Land Registry Services: A Critical Review, in Coordinates, Vol XV, Issue 11, November 2019, Vol XV, Issue 12, December 2019, Vol XVI, Issue 1. 2019 and 2020.

[16] Cliffe S. Building Back Better in the Response to COVID–19: Action on Political Cohesion, Climate Change, and Inequality, CIC blog. *Center on International Cooperation*, New York University, 2020. URL `https://cic.nyu.edu/blog/building-back-better-COVID-19`.

3

Open Geospatial Data for Responding to the COVID-19 Challenge

Maria Antonia Brovelli and Serena Coetzee

The period after the appearance of the SARS-CoV-2 virus has seen a flourishing of dynamic online maps and dashboards useful for communicating the spread of the disease, but not for the in-depth study of the phenomenon. The speed at which the disease is disseminated calls for rapid analysis and action. Data that is readily available, such as open data, or rapidly collected, e.g. by citizens, can make a significant contribution to modelling, understanding and containing the spread of a disease. This chapter explores open geospatial data responding to the COVID-19 challenge: What data is useful for studying the spatio-temporal spread of the virus? What is the availability of such open data? The chapter wants to answer these questions critically, also providing useful information to all those who want to support research, not only linked to this zoonosis, but more generally future epidemics and pandemics for which we should be better prepared.

3.1 Introduction

The globalized society of today is challenged by various emerging diseases, in many cases, zoonoses, such as the Ebola Virus Disease (EVD), bird flu, swine flu, SARS-CoV and MERS-CoV, and these are often related to climate change. Coronavirus disease (COVID-19) caused by the severe acute respiratory syndrome coronavirus 2 (SARS-CoV-2), is a classical example. COVID-19 is a communicable disease where infections are transmitted from one person to another through little droplets, emitted when someone talks or coughs. A person can be infected through direct contact with the droplets, or by touching droplets that have settled on a surface or object and touching their face afterwards [1]. COVID-19 is therefore often transmitted when people are in close contact with each other (within 1 m) or in places that are frequented by many people. It also seems that certain demographics, e.g. older people, are more often severely affected by the disease.

On 11 March 2020, the World Health Organization (WHO) declared the COVID-19 epidemic a pandemic, and by October 2020, there were close to 35 million confirmed cases and more than a million deaths reported [2]. Governments have always had to respond to natural disasters and outbreaks of infectious diseases, the cause of loss of life and the devastation of both the environment and national economies.

The current viral epidemic is of colossal proportions and the rate of infection multiplies rapidly, favored by our densely populated urban centers and an interconnected global economy. Moreover this is not an isolated occurrence, as we have been experiencing similar situations with Ebola, HIV, dengue, SARS, MERS, Zika and West Nile. Researchers estimate [3] that zoonotic diseases account for 75% of all new or emerging diseases in humans.

The recent and dramatic evolution of the COVID-19 pandemic has highlighted and accelerated some developments that were already taking place in the scientific world and in society in general. If digitization is what immediately catches the attention, a second aspect which deserves great attention, is the use of maps in the communication of information relating to the virus spread. Our daily lives have been pervaded by dashboards with maps, a key source of information about the status of the pandemic (from the beginning of the epidemic until today), ranging in scale from hotspots in cities to provinces in a country and countries on a world map.

These dashboards, however, show only simple data visualizations (e.g. number of infections per administrative area, such as country or province), which represents, even in its powerful effectiveness, only a small part of the value of geospatial information applied to health-related information. Georeferenced data, in fact, could play a crucial role in the analysis of the phenomenon itself, leading, for example, to the production of vulnerability and resilience maps, which can help, if not to eradicate the virus, at least to study its spread, evaluate appropriate containment measures for different areas, and thus reduce its impact. Generally, geospatial information constitutes potentially decisive support for offering and making accessible a multidimensional and scalable approach, necessary for the rethinking and reorganization of our entire society in a spatial perspective. Furthermore, the UN GGIM's Strategic Framework on Geospatial Information and Services for Disasters recommends that geospatial information provided by Member States and the international community "shall be openly accessible to the disaster risk management community, as appropriate" [4].

Since the problem we are facing affects the whole world, this chapter focuses on open data with global coverage. Open geospatial data with global coverage has the advantage that anyone anywhere in the world can use the data in the same way for their specific part of the world [5]. It can therefore provide a homogeneous framework to scholars and decision makers for analysing the multifaceted aspects related to the pandemic. The Open Knowledge Foundation [6] lists three key features of open data and content: 1) availability and access at a reasonable cost and in convenient and modifiable form; 2) licence that allows reuse and distribution in machine-readable form; and 3) universal participation without discrimination against fields of endeavour (e.g. commercial or non-commercial) or against persons or groups. The notion of data being "open" is not only associated with free and unrestricted access to the data, but also with transparent and inclusive consensus-based decision-making [7]. [8] identified three different kinds of open geospatial data. Firstly, there is data collected by volunteers who organize themselves into communities, e.g. OpenStreetMap. Secondly, some open geospatial data is collected by authorities and published in the spirit of freedom of access to information legislation. Thirdly, open geospatial data is also collected and published by researchers to encourage reuse of the data. Another kind of data is provided by commercial organizations for humanitarian purposes, specifically in the fight against COVID-19. This chapter provides examples of these four kinds of data. Geospatial data is useful for addressing many different humanitarian and socio-economic challenges, however, in this paper, we focus only on pandemics.

This paper should not be considered to be the final milestone nor does it claim to be complete and exhaustive, but rather a path that leads to identifying what is openly available to support the activities of experts who do not belong to the geospatial domain and who need these data to contextualize and enrich their analyses with meaning. A second aspect, addressed instead at geospatial experts, is the definition of the deficiencies in the data and information that we make openly and freely available, so that anyone can acquire a direct and immediate advantage in easily using spatio-temporal products. In the next section we describe what geospatial data is useful in the case of disasters, such as the COVID-19 pandemic. Subsequently, we present and discuss several sources of relevant open geospatial data. The chapter is concluded with an assessment of the availability and suitability of open geospatial data for responding to the COVID-19 challenge.

3.2 What Data Is Useful for Responding to the COVID-19 Challenge?

Epidemics and pandemics are disasters that cause significant damage to humans, physical structures, the economy or the environment. Risks associated with a disaster are reduced by following a risk management approach that identifies, assesses and reduces risks. Depending on the stage of the disaster, risks are managed by prediction, prevention, mitigation preparedness, response, recovery and rehabilitation [9]. To reduce risks associated with COVID-19, geospatial data can be used in many ways, e.g.

- to predict how the disease will spread, e.g. by identifying and analysing places or routes frequented by many people in close proximity to each other;

- to prevent the spread of the disease, e.g. by identifying vulnerable areas based on population density, demographics (age) and/or income, and protecting them;

- to mitigate the spread of the disease, e.g. by tracing people who visited the same locations as an infected person;

- to strengthen preparedness, e.g. by adjusting the number of planned surgical procedures in relation to the number of infections in a hospital's catchment area;

- to respond to the disease, e.g. by working out optimal routes for testing or awareness campaigns; and

- to monitor and communicate the spread of the disease at different scales, e.g. infections by country or province, or more fine-grained by street block, event or building and even location of an infected individual.

Table 3.1 matches different kinds of geospatial data to the different aspects of risk reduction. The remainder of this section elaborates on how these datasets can be used to identify, assess and reduce COVID-19-related risks.

TABLE 3.1
Geospatial data for risk management in disasters (A = Prediction, B = Prevention, C = Mitigation, D = Preparedness, E = Response, F = Monitor and Communication).

Geospatial data	A	B	C	D	E	F
COVID-19 infections	X		X		X	X
Reference information	X	X	X	X	X	X
Places frequented by many people	X	X	X	X		X
Travel networks and mobility	X	X	X	X		X
Land cover	X	X		X		
Address data	X		X		X	
Demographic data	X	X		X	X	
Air pollution	X	X		X		
Water sources	X	X	X	X	X	
Health facilities				X	X	X

Based on knowledge at the time of writing, the COVID-19 disease is mainly transmitted through close physical contact and respiratory droplets. Contamination happens either through direct contact with respiratory droplets or through droplets that have settled on a surface or object. Transmission happens when a contaminated hand touches the mouth, nose or eyes [1]. Therefore, places frequented by many people or where people are in close proximity to each other present a higher risk of transmissions. Because transmission happens through respiratory droplets emitted by people, tracking the locations visited by contaminated people and closing them for a period of time can help to contain the spread.

Geospatial information about locations and routes that are frequented by many people is of specific relevance when studying COVID-19. Examples are networks of public transport and travel by air; capacity and occupation of places or buildings where people may gather in large groups, such as socio-sanitary and social structures, educational institutions, recreational, cultural, sporting structures, penitentiary institutions, structures of social marginality, accommodation in general; places characterised by large concentrations of people, e.g. related to agriculture (e.g. markets), commerce (e.g. shopping centres) and industry (e.g. factories); and in poorer communities, communal toilets and water taps may pose a risk to COVID-19 transmission.

It has been observed that the risk of zoonosis, i.e. a pathogen such as a virus or a parasite moving from animal to humans, is higher when there are significant ecological changes in an area [10]. In such cases, humans may come into close contact with animals that previously lived far away from any human activity. Land cover datasets provide information about such ecological changes and can help with identifying areas at risk of zoonosis.

In order to study and understand the actual spread of the disease, location-based information about the infected people and the places they visited is required. Information about such locations is often provided in the form of a residential address that has to be converted into coordinates through geocoding based on geo-referenced address data. However, to protect the personal information of individuals, the information is usually published in an aggregated form, e.g. by administrative or statistical boundary. Administrative areas, place names and address data are also relevant when determining and reporting who may be affected by the predicted spread of the disease.

Older people (above 60 years) and those with underlying medical conditions, such as cardiovascular disease, chronic respiratory disease, diabetes and cancer, are at a higher risk of complications or the disease being fatal [1]. Therefore locations where these people receive care, such as old age homes, hospitals and long term care facilities, need special protection. The nature of the household may also present a vulnerability. When different generations live together in the same household, it may be difficult to isolate the older generation from the rest of the household. Similarly, when many people share the same room or ablutions, e.g. in dormitories or large families, physical distancing measures to avoid contamination may be difficult. To identify vulnerable areas that need protection, demographic and population data play an important role, including geospatial data about the socio-economic status, age, health conditions, lifestyle, household size and population density.

Another vulnerable part of the population lives in slums and informal settlements, or is displaced and lives in camps and camp-like settings. Such communities are often neglected or stigmatized and without access to health care services that are otherwise available to the general population. Satellite imagery can be used to detect such settlements, if they are not yet reflected in datasets of authorities. Satellite imagery and data contributed by volunteers, e.g. through the OpenStreetMap ecosystem, is also essential for understanding these settlements so that control measures and interventions amenable to the spatial characteristics of the settlement can be planned and implemented, e.g. routes for community health workers involved in testing campaigns or access points for delivering food parcels.

Frequent and thorough hand hygiene is one of the most important measures to prevent the spread of COVID-19 [11]. Unfortunately, a large part of the world's population does not have access to a basic hand washing facility with soap and water in their home. In 2017, three billion people were without such a facility [12]. These people are vulnerable to the COVID-19 disease and any information about access to safe drinking water can help to identify those without such access.

Other examples of vulnerabilities are non-communicable diseases, such as hypertension, diabetes and chronic respiratory disease, e.g. linked to air pollution [13]. Environmental datasets about the concentration of air pollution and data about the prevalence and spatial distribution of non-communicable diseases can help with identifying parts of the population vulnerable to COVID-19.

In the WHO's interim guidance on critical, readiness and response actions, objectives for controlling and slowing down COVID-19 infections include rapidly finding (e.g. through testing) and isolating cases, and tracing their contacts; suppressing community infections by implementing control measures at locations at risk; and reducing mortality by ensuring continuity of essential social and health services [14]. Geo-referenced address data can help with locating cases and their contacts, e.g. through geocoding, while other geospatial data layers identify locations at risk (see above) where control measures have to be implemented. Spatial accessibility and capacity of health services in response to the disease can be assessed with geospatial data about hospital locations, their available equipment (e.g. intensive care units and ventilators) and occupation (e.g. availability of beds in general wards). Additionally, the locations and capacity of places collecting and treating medical and hazardous waste, e.g. infected masks, gloves and other personal protection equipment (PPE), can be identified and assessed.

Citizen science projects involving geospatial data present the opportunity to strengthen preparedness and responses. For example, volunteers can contribute data that provides geospatial reference, such as the road network, landmarks and health facilities. They can further enhance this data by adding opening times of health facilities, such as pharmacies, in their local communities.

In summary, location-based data that helps to answer the following questions is useful for responding to the COVID-19 challenge:

- Where are locations with high risk of transmission?

- Where are the vulnerable people?

- Where are the infected people, and where were they in the past few weeks?

- Where are the healthcare facilities that can support infected people?

To communicate the answers to these questions, a base map is required for context and orientation. The base map shows reference information, such as landmarks, place names, transportation routes, administrative areas or an aerial photo as backdrop. These help the map reader with determining and orienting the location of the map. Depending on the purpose of the map, the reference information may differ; in some cases satellite imagery or aerial photography is used.

3.3 What is the Availability of such Open Data With Global Coverage?

In this section we present and discuss several sources of open geospatial data with global coverage identified as useful for responding to the COVID-19 challenge in the previous section. The link in the Annex lists URLs for datasets discussed in this section, together with the formats and licenses in which they are published.

3.3.1 COVID-19 Infections

The first datasets we have to deal with are those related to the virus evolution in time and space. The global coverage of available open data is good enough because almost all countries are included but the resolution is very poor. Data are generally available per country and not with any more detail. The first and main source of information is the dataset made freely available for non-profit public health, educational, and academic research purposes in a GitHub repository [15] by the Center for Systems Science and Engineering (CSSE) at the Johns Hopkins University (JHU). Data sources are many and various, mainly the different national agencies, and the great value of the JHU dataset is that, after their manual and automatic pre-processing, data are available in a standard format.

The folders contain daily case reports of confirmed cases (C), deaths (D), recovered cases (R) and active cases (A), where A = C-R-D.

Moreover, some computed indexes are also available, such as the Case Fatality Ratio (CFR), which allows immediate comparison between data from different countries, as well as the creation of thematic maps , e.g. choropleth, as it is the relative value of confirmed cases per 100,000 persons.

For the sake of comparing data between different countries, the European Centre for Disease Prevention and Control [16] provides new total cases and deaths day by day, as well as the population count in 2018. This data is ready for studying differences in the evolution of the virus because curves, e.g. by shifting it in such a way that all sets have the same starting outbreak point (for instance, corresponding to a certain percentage of the affected population).

The United Nations Statistics Division, in partnership with Esri, makes the layers of JHU available in various formats, including KML, GeoJSON and shapefile. The data is also accessible through an API and Geoservices [2].

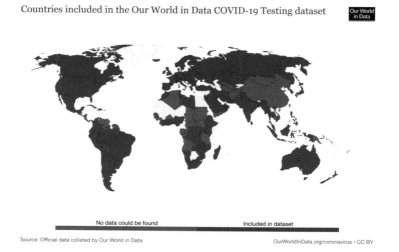

Countries included in the Our World in Data COVID-19 Testing dataset

No data could be found   Included in dataset

Source: Official data collated by Our World in Data   OurWorldInData.org/coronavirus · CC BY

FIGURE 3.1
Countries included in the Our World in Data COVID-19 Testing Dataset (Source: Official data collated by Our World in Data [17])

Finally, information about COVID-19 testing, collected by Our World in Data [18], is published as open data. The testing dataset is updated around twice a week. The dataset includes, for the countries visible in Figure 3.1, a detailed description of how the country's data is collected [17]. Some ancillary information, such as hand washing facilities (from the United Nations Statistics Division) and hospital beds per 1,000 people (from many documented sources) are also available.

3.3.2 Reference Information

When information is communicated via a map, reference information provides context and orientation. For a thematic map, reference is usually provided by a small set of layers, e.g. country or state boundaries and their names. Depending on the scale, more (e.g. thematic map of a city) or less (e.g. thematic map of the world) reference information can be provided. Other types of maps, e.g. one that displays locations of health care services in a specific city or suburb requires much more reference information, including such features as addresses, streets, public transportation and landmarks. In some cases, an aerial photo or satellite image of the area can be useful. While data discussed in other subsections can also be used as reference information on maps (e.g. the travel network in 3.3.4), in this section we focus on base maps, imagery, place names and administrative areas.

3.3.2.1 Base Maps

OpenStreetMap is a crowdsourced dataset to which a global community of mappers contributes geospatial information and maintains it. OpenStreetMap was inspired by Wikipedia and started in the UK in 2004 as an alternative to proprietary map data with restrictions on the availability and use of data. It is maintained through an ecosystem of software, servers, tools, users, and contributors

[8]. In many parts of the world, the quality, and specifically the completeness, of OpenStreetMap data is as good as that of authoritative datasets, if not better [19], and if the quality is not good enough, the OpenStreetMap ecosystem makes it very simple for anyone to add or improve the data. In this context, OpenStreetMap has been used very successfully during disasters and humanitarian initiatives, including the COVID-19 pandemic, where volunteers added data remotely in areas where data are scarce or non-existent [20]. A large number of mapping tasks, e.g. including Peru and Botswana, were published on the task manager of the Humanitarian OpenStreetMap Team (HOT) during the COVID-19 pandemic. Volunteers from all over the world contributed map data that could subsequently be used by health workers.

The OpenStreetMap ecosystem presents another advantage: a range of tools are available for collection, maintenance, processing and visualization of data. OpenStreetMap is widely used as a basemap in COVID-19 dashboards (see e.g. [21], [22], [23], [24]) and also on websites that show emerging hotspots of infections (e.g. [25], [26]). Many of these sites were built with one of the tools in the OpenStreetMap ecosystem, such as mapbox and Leaflet.

Wikimapia is another example of a crowdsourced map with global coverage, where anyone can add geospatial features and annotate them. It was started in 2006 by two Russian Internet entrepreneurs, inspired by Wikipedia. Wikimapia is open data, but it is derived largely from aerial imagery provided by Google Maps. Copyright related to such derived data is sometimes unclear and dependent on the area of jurisdiction (country or region). Some owners of aerial photography provide licenses for the use of the data but retain the exclusive right to derive geospatial data from it. While Google has not initiated any legal court battles over this, their terms and conditions prohibit derivations without a license from Google [27].

Natural Earth is maintained by a community of volunteers, supported by the North American Cartographic Information Society. In contrast to the previous two datasets, it also includes raster data (e.g. for shaded relief and bathymetry), and some layers specifically useful for small scale maps, e.g. graticules and geographic lines (polar circles, tropical circles, the equator and the International Date Line). The data can be downloaded at scales of 1:10 m, 1:50 m, and 1:110 million, which is not as detailed as OpenStreetMap and Wikimapia, but nevertheless suitable for maps of the world or specific countries and regions. At the time of writing, the latest version (v4.1.0) was announced in 2018, therefore the data is also not as recent as the previous two datasets, however, at the available scales, the data is not likely to change frequently [28].

3.3.2.2 Imagery

A rich dataset of free and open satellite imagery, with different spatial and temporal resolutions and useful for studying different parameters, is available. Specific licenses depend on the agencies which are providing the data. Formats also depend on the satellites and, in some cases, images are available in more than one format. The best way for finding imagery is to browse portals (see relevant examples in Table 3.2), which make this satellite imagery available and often also tools for their basic processing [29].

TABLE 3.2
Portals with access to free and open satellite data

Portal	URL
USGS Earth Explorer	https://earthexplorer.usgs.gov
LANDVIEWER	https://eos.com/landviewer/
COPERNICUS OPEN ACCESS HUB	https://scihub.copernicus.eu
SENTINEL HUB	http://apps.sentinel-hub.com/eo-browser, http://apps.sentinel-hub.com/sentinel-playground
NASA EARTHDATA SEARCH	https://search.earthdata.nasa.gov
REMOTE PIXEL	https://search.remotepixel.ca
INPE IMAGE CATALOG	http://www.dgi.inpe.br/catalogo

Another interesting portal is that of OpenAerialMap [30], where one can find, apart from some openly licensed satellite imagery, also imagery from unmanned aerial vehicles (UAVs). All imagery is made available through the Humanitarian OpenStreetMap Team's Open Imagery Network (OIN) Node. The images are available for tracing in OpenStreetMap.

3.3.2.3   Place Names

GeoNames is a global database of more than 25 million names for 11 million geographical features, classified into nine categories (e.g. administrative areas, water features, parks, etc.), and further classified into 645 different feature codes. At the time of writing, GeoNames included 4.8 million populated places. GeoNames integrates data from various sources. The quality of the data depends on the source that contributed the data, therefore a wiki interface allows users to improve the quality by editing, correcting or adding new names through a wiki interface.

The GEOnet Names Server (GNS) is the official repository of standard spellings of geographic names outside the United States, sanctioned by the United States Board on Geographic Names (US BGN). At the time of writing, it included 12 million names for 7 million features, each feature described by its feature class, location, administrative division, and quality. The data can be downloaded as text files (per country or feature class or the entire dataset), or accessed through web services [31]. For a global dataset, place names in the US and Antarctica can be added by downloading them from the US BGN geographic names information system [32].

In the above sources features are represented by a point. These are useful as labels on maps or to search for a place. However, sometimes boundaries (polygons) are needed. Quattroshapes is a gazetteer of non-overlapping polygons, distinguishing it from gazetteers with simple point geometries. The gazetteer is based on data from GeoNames, Yahoo GeoPlanet, Flickr geotagged photos and EuroGeoGraphics [33].

3.3.2.4   Administrative Areas

Thematic maps show information about a specific theme, e.g. about COVID-19 infections. Such information is often displayed per administrative area, such as country, state, province, city, municipality, suburb or ward.

The World Bank publishes a dataset with administrative boundaries approved by the organization. The dataset includes international (country) boundaries, disputed areas, coastlines and lakes [34]. Sub-national boundaries for individual countries can be downloaded from the Humanitarian Data Exchange of the United Nations Office for the Coordination of Humanitarian Affairs (OCHA) [35].

For lower level administrative boundaries, GADM, a global dataset of administrative areas at all levels of sub-division, is available [36]. The GADM project sourced data for many countries from their national governments, from NGOs, and/or from maps and lists of names available on the Internet (e.g. from Wikipedia) [37]. This dataset is convenient to use because it is available as a single global layer, however, care should be taken, as it is not necessarily based on the latest authoritative sources (the website provides limited information).

Administrative boundaries are also included in some other datasets, such as Natural Earth and OpenStreetMap. Once again, care should be taken because these are not necessarily based on authoritative sources.

3.3.3   Places Frequented by many People

Because COVID-19 is mainly transmitted through close physical contact and respiratory droplets, places frequented by many people or where people are in close proximity to each other present a higher risk of transmissions. A first indicator for areas containing places frequented by many people would be data about settlement and population density. Locations of refugee camps are another way of identifying places frequented by many people. They are typically densely populated and have been identified to be COVID-19 vulnerable by the WHO. A list of refugee camps from 2014 is available in [38]. An online world map, as well as maps and statistics published as PDFs, are available on the UNHCR operational portal for refugee situations [39]. However, despite our extensive searches, including the UNHCR portal, we could not find downloadable location-based data about refugee camps.

Once areas with high settlement or population densities have been identified, data about specific places frequented by many people in these areas are useful for risk management at a larger scale. A plethora of different kinds of places could be relevant, ranging from supermarkets, restaurants, shopping centres to fitness centres, stations, schools and universities. On maps and in geospatial data, these are often referred to as points of interest.

While completeness of data in different countries and regions varies, OpenStreetMap includes an extensive set of points of interest (close to 33 million points), each identified with the "amenity" tag. At the time of writing, there were at least 71 different kinds of amenities in seven different categories: sustenance, education, transportation, financial, healthcare, entertainment, arts & culture, and others. Several tools and scripts are available for extracting points of interest from the OpenStreetMap dataset [40]. Wikimapia is another crowdsourced geospatial dataset. At the time of writing it included close to 24 million points of interest in 94 different categories [41].

Points of interest datasets are widely used, not only on maps, but also for a wide range of location-based services, e.g. for reviewing or recommending points of interest. Studies specifically about the quality of points of interest in OpenStreetMap and Wikimapia have not been conducted at a global scale; they have however been included in studies about the quality of OpenStreetMap generally. Barriers for assessing the quality of points of interest generally include the fact that no reference datasets exist against which one can compare them (apart from comparing OpenStreetMap to Wikimapia), they cannot be assessed against satellite imagery, which is possible for many other kinds of features (e.g. building and roads), and ground truthing at a global scale is just too expensive. Nevertheless, OpenStreetMap and Wikimapia are often the only available open datasets for points of interest and therefore useful. The quality of individual classes of points of interest, for which reference datasets exist, can however be assessed e.g. for transportation or health facilities. See also sections 3.3.4 and 3.3.10 in this regard.

3.3.4 Travel Networks and Mobility

The official global reference dataset for transport networks is Global Roads, version 1 (gROADSv1), based on the combination of the available, and topologically correct, road data at national level. The common data model is that of the United Nations Spatial Data Infrastructure Service (UNSDI-T). The data were collected, harmonized and homogenized over an extensive period of time, spanning a few decades. This means that updating the data and spatial accuracy may vary greatly from country to country [42].

The second dataset of interest is OpenStreetMap. The project was initiated specifically for collecting data about streets, not only their geometry, but also any features related to transportation networks. The main features related to travel networks are: arialways, aeroways, highways, public transport, railways, routes and waterways. The many different typologies and the many attributes used for the description of the features make this dataset an invaluable source of detailed information [43].

Despite its heterogeneity in spatial and semantic distribution, the dataset is rich and accurate in many developed regions [19], [44], [45] and richer than gROADSv1 in (at least some) developing countries [46] compared OpenStreetMap against gROADSv1 in Tanzania, Uganda and Kenya, finding that the former shows less roads in the ratio of 5.6, 6.5 and 2.5 respectively. Moreover, the mean spatial accuracy is 35 m for OpenStreetMap and 600 m for gROADSv1.

About mobility, recently, data was made available by Google (open data) and Facebook (upon agreement). Google trends [18] aim to provide insight into what has changed in response to policies aimed at combating COVID-19. They are based on anonymized data collected by apps such as Google Maps when the user turns on the Location History setting (which is off by default). Data are not absolute values, but rather the changes in time referred to a baseline day, which is the median value from the 5-week period between 3 January and 6 February 2020. Data are aggregated per day (starting from 16 February) and per country (where available), and represent the change in the number of visitors to specific types of location: grocery stores, pharmacies, parks, train stations, retail, recreation, and workplaces; and the duration in case of the residential category. Data per region (second administrative level) is available at [47].

In response to the COVID-19 pandemic, Facebook launched an initiative within Facebook Data for Good [48], and made available, for researchers and non-profit operators who have signed data license agreements, different typologies of maps and geospatial data: co-location maps, trends and staying at home maps, movement maps, network coverage maps and maps of the Social Connectedness Index, which measures the strength of connectedness between two geographic areas as measured by Facebook friendship ties.

Data are provided by Facebook as CSV files upon request, starting from the day of the request, on a grid that follows the Bing Tile System [49]. For the spatial resolution, in principle, the smallest allowed size guaranteeing privacy protections is Bing Tile Level 16, which is equivalent to roughly 600m near the equator, but the resolution of the requested dataset is computed on the base of the time needed for its periodical update. The calculation of the movement data is much heavier, from the computational point of view (cross matrix of calculations between all the panes) than the population count, and this is the reason why the spatial resolution of the movement datasets is coarser than that of the population density (see later section 3.3.7) and depends strongly on the size of the area of interest. As examples, in the case of Italy and the Lombardy region within Italy, pixel sizes are respectively about 7.5 km (Bing Tile Level 4 - 9.8 km at the equator) and 3.5 km (Bing Tile Level 5 - 4.9 km at the equator). Lombardy covers approximately 8% of the whole Italian territory, with 16.7% of its population (mean density equal to 422 inhabitants/km^2). The temporal resolution is 8 hours.

Apart from the above, two datasets are available to everyone: the "Change in Movement", which compares the movement of people with respect to a baseline period; and the "Stay Put", which provides information on the fraction of the population that appears to stay within a small area surrounding their home for an entire day. The Movement Range data is available as a CSV file only for some countries. All the maps are based on data collected from Facebook users.

3.3.5   Global High-resolution Land Cover Maps

The anthropization of the environment (deforestation, habitat degradation and fragmentation, intensification of agriculture and climate change) facilitates the passage of pathogens from animals to humans. To study the extent of these effects, the basic maps to start from are land cover maps. Thanks to the availability of open satellite images in ever increasing resolution, in recent years we have witnessed the creation of various maps that can be a valuable tools for researchers from different environmental disciplines. Some of these maps are multiclass, such as GlobeLand30 and FROM-GLC. Others represent specific elements of interest, such as urbanized areas (Global Urban Footprint and Global Human Settlement Layer), water resources (Global Surface Water) and forested areas (Forest/Non-Forest map and Global forest cover gain/loss). Some characteristics of the land cover maps can be seen in Table 3.3.

Apart from these datasets, as for the other features of interest, OpenStreetMap can be a good source of data. Specifically, in OpenStreetMap the detail of land use is reported. Therefore, from the point of view of knowledge about an area, the information is also richer than basic land cover data, even if the limitation is that it is not homogeneously distributed across the globe, because the amount of data in an area depends on the activity and contributions of volunteers in that area.

3.3.6   Address Data

Addresses are essential for locating infected cases, to trace contacts after someone tests positive, to accurately identify and respond to emerging clusters of COVID-19, and to determine households at risk as a result of these clusters. Addresses are typically maintained by local authorities [50], however, a global uniform open dataset facilitates the development of tools that can leverage economies of scale. The Universal Postal Union (UPU) [51] supports countries to develop and improve their addressing systems. The aim is to improve the coverage of addressing infrastructures globally. However, the UPU does not publish open address data.

TABLE 3.3
Global high-resolution land cover maps

	Res(m)	Year(s)	Producer
GlobeLand30 (GL30)	30	2000, 2010, 2020	National Geomatics Center of China
FROM-GLC	30	2010, 2015, 2017	Tsinghua University
Global Urban Footprint	12	2011	German Aerospace Center (DLR)
Global Human Settlement Layer (GHS BUILT-UP GRID S1)	20	2016	Joint Research Center (JRC)
Global Surface Water	30	1984-2018, every year	Joint Research Center (JRC)
Forest/Non-Forest map	25	2007-2010, 2015-2017, every year	Japan Aerospace Exploration Agency (JAXA)
Global forest cover gain	30	2000-2012, (one map for the whole period)	Hansen/UMD/Google/ USGS/NASA
Global forest cover loss	30	2001-2019, every year	Hansen/UMD/Google/ USGS/NASA

An alternative is the OpenAddresses.io initiative [52]. Data is collected from authorities all over the world, integrated into a uniform data model, and made available for downloads. Data sources can be added or improved through a GitHub site. In 2020, OpenAddresses consisted of more than 475 million addresses integrated from thousands of sources from all over the world. Figure 3.2 shows the coverage on 4 October 2020.

FIGURE 3.2
Global coverage of OpenAddresses.io on 4 October 2020 [52]

Addresses in OpenAddresses.io follow a rather restrictive data model, essentially comprising a number, street, city, postcode, district, region, and an additional attribute called "unit" for uniquely identifying different units at the same address. Each address has a unique identifier and a coordinate associated with it. One can specify the type (e.g. industrial or residential) of the address and add notes. The data model does not specifically cater for local variations, such as addresses without street names or addresses requiring both a suburb and a city or municipality name [53]. Following an international data model, such as that specified in ISO 19160-1 [54], would resolve this. Apart from improving issues that arise when address data is converted from source model to the OpenAddresses.io model, there are no quality checks on the address data *per se*, as this is the responsibility of the authority from where the data is sourced.

Addresses in OpenStreetMap are tagged with "addr:housenumber". Addresses can be a feature on their own or they are associated with a building, site or other area. In some parts of the world, address ranges are available, i.e. a line (called "way" in OpenStreetMap) tagged as "addr:interpolation" runs parallel to the street. The start and end nodes of the line are tagged with the numbers of the addresses closest to them. Address ranges do not provide individual address records, but in the absence of other address data, such ranges are very useful for routing and geocoding because the location of addresses with numbers between those at the start and end nodes can be interpolated along the line. Early in October 2020, there were just over 106 million "addr:housenumber" tags in OpenStreetMap, and close to 100 million fewer "addr:street" tags [55]. Challenges with the way in which addresses are represented in OpenStreetMap have been noted and improvements have been proposed [56]. Address data can be extracted and downloaded in the same way as any other OpenStreetMap data.

A single source of uniform address data across the world makes it possible to develop geocoding tools and services that can be used anywhere in the world for locating infected patients and their contacts. For example, a geocoding service based on OpenStreetMap data is available at `https://nominatim.openstreetmap.org`. Some geocoding services, such as `https://geocode.earth/sources`, are based on multiples data sources including OpenStreetMap and OpenAddresses.

3.3.7 Demographic Data

Demographics is a huge field, encompassing characteristics of the population in terms of population density, age, gender, socio-economic, health conditions, presence of vulnerable population, lifestyle, etc. General data sources, to be considered for our purposes, include open data published by the World Bank [57] and the Organisation for Economic Co-operation and Development (OECD) [58]. In the former, data are available in various formats, with various temporal extensions, and there is a special section related to COVID-19. The latter contains data of OECD countries and some non-OECD economies. The temporal coverage consists of different years, depending on the specific parameter under consideration; the most recent year is generally 2018.

Among the various characteristics of the population, the population age and its density were considered by the authors as examples, because of their importance with respect to COVID-19: the older population has more severe symptoms and density of the population is inversely related with social or physical distancing required to combat the virus.

About age, classes for population ranges 0-14 [59]; 15-64 [60]; and above 65 [61], considering male, female, total, absolute number and percentage per country were estimated by the World Bank based on the World Bank's total population and age/sex distributions of the United Nations Population Division's World Population Prospects: The 2019 Revision [62], [63]. The temporal coverage is from 1960 to 2018. If interested in the population with a certain age or within a certain age interval, these data can be found, for OECD countries and some non OECD economies, in the OECD's statistics. The temporal coverage is again from 1960 to 2018.

For population density, three global high resolution global datasets are available. The Gridded Population of the World, most recent version is GPWv4.11 [64], is a set of raster layers with the estimates of the count and density of people per 30 arc-second (around 1 km) grid cell for each of the five years: 2000, 2005, 2010, 2015 and 2020, consistent with national censuses and population registers. All estimates of population counts and population density have also been nationally adjusted to population totals from the United Nation Population Division's World Population Prospects: The 2015 Revision [65]. Data is downloadable in ASCII (text), GeoTiff and netCDF format. In addition, rasters are available for basic demographic characteristics (age and sex), geographic characteristics (land and water areas) and data quality indicators [64].

An interesting dataset, even if limited for now to 169 countries, is provided by CIESIN and the Connectivity Lab at Facebook [66]. The name of this dataset, computed for 2015, is the High Resolution Settlement Layer (HRSL) and its resolution is of 1 arc-second (approximately 30 m). The population estimates are based on recent census data and high-resolution (0.5 m) satellite imagery from DigitalGlobe.

The second global dataset is GHS_POP Global population grids at epochs 1975, 1990, 2000, 2015 and with resolution of 250 m, 1 km, 9 arcsec, 30 arcsec.

The third source of data is WorldPop [67]. Different datasets are provided, based on different methodologies [68]. Data can be downloaded per country at a resolution of 3 and 30 arc-seconds (approximately 100 m and 1 km at the equator, respectively).

The last dataset worth mentioning is a dynamic one and is available within the already mentioned initiative of Facebook Data for Good. Data about population density (more precisely, Facebook user density) has a temporal resolution of 8 hours and a spatial resolution varying on the region of interest, following the same rule seen in section 3.3.4 for mobility data. In the case of population density, the resolution is better because the time of computation for the updated data is lower. Considering the previous examples, the pixel size is that of a tile at Bing Tile Level 5 for Italy (around 3.5 km at the equator) and of Bing Tile Level 7 for Lombardy (around 1.2 km at the equator).

3.3.8   Concentration of Air Pollutants

Air pollution is one of the world's largest health and environmental problems. Even if there has been a general decrease in air pollution in rich countries in comparison to the threatening concentration of some decades ago, localised high values still remain in some areas, and in middle-income countries the death rates due to air pollution are the highest. Moreover, persistent exposure to air pollution weakens the respiratory system, creating a continuous irritation. There are two different typologies of pollution: outdoor and indoor (household).

Global data about outdoor air pollution are generally available per country. An example is the 1990-2016 series of concentrations of particulate matter with a size of less than 2.5 μm (PM2.5) and ozone (O_3), downloadable from [69]. A remarkable source of global open data for monitoring the temporal evolution of air quality is available in satellite data. Table 3.4 lists satellites, sensors and relative spatial and temporal resolution.

TABLE 3.4

Satellites, sensors for air quality monitoring, spatial and temporal resolutions (source: [70])

Satellite	Sensor	Spatial resolution	Temporal resolution
Aqua	Atmospheric Infrared Sounder (AIRS) Level 2 and 3 products	$1^\circ x1^\circ$	daily, 8-day, monthly
Terra and Aqua	Moderate Resolution Imaging Spectroradiometer (MODIS)	250 m, 500 m, 1 km	1-2 days
Terra	Measurement of Pollution in the Troposphere (MOPITT)	$1^\circ x1^\circ$	daily, monthly
Aura	Ozone Monitoring Instrument (OMI)	13 km x 24 km	daily
Suomi-NPP	Ozone Mapping and Profiler Suite (OMPS)	50 km x 50 km	101 minutes, daily
Sentinel 5-P	TROPOspheric Monitoring Instrument (TROPOMI)	7 km x 3.5 km	daily
Suomi-NPP	Visible Infrared Imaging Radiometer Suite (VIIRS)	375-750 m	1-2 days

The most recent satellite of this family is represented by Sentinel 5P, launched in 2017 by the European Space Agency within the Copernicus Initiative. The onboard TROPOMI (TROPOspheric Monitoring Instrument) spectrometer allows the monitoring of ozone (O_3), methane (CH_4), formaldehyde (HCHO), aerosol, carbon monoxide (CO), Nitrogen dioxide (NO_2) and Sulfur dioxide (SO_2). TROPOMI takes measurements every second covering an area of approximately 2600 km wide and 7 km long in a resolution of 7×7 km. Data can be freely downloaded upon registration. The first data were released in July 2018.

Using data from the Copernicus Sentinel-5P it was possible to analyse, for instance, the decline of air pollution, specifically NO_2 concentrations, in some areas of the world as a consequence of the lockdown that was implemented to prevent the spread of the coronavirus. The maps in Figure 3.3 show the NO_2 concentration over Italy before and during the lockdown.

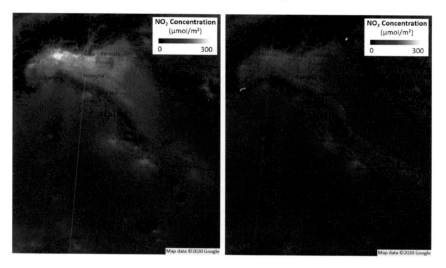

FIGURE 3.3

Concentration of NO_2 over Italy before the lockdown (average value in January 2020) and during the lockdown (average value from 9 March to 9 April 2020)

Indoor air pollution is caused mainly by the use of solid fuels for cooking. While indoor air pollution has been on the decrease since the 1990s, 40% of the world population still does not have access to clean air cooking fuels. Death rates from air pollution are highest in low-income countries. A selection of indicators about indoor air pollution are available in visualizations (maps and graphs), and also for download from [71]. Indicators are provided at the country level, and were sourced from the World Bank and from the Global Health Data Exchange.

3.3.9   Water Sources

Referring to water and sanitation, indicators for the United Nations Sustainable Development Goal (SDG) 6 are available, but again, at country scale. Maps, charts and data can be found on the UN Water geoportal [72]. Figure 3.4 is an example, showing the proportion of the population in a country using safely managed sanitation services.

The local alternative, as seen before, is to consider the features related to water available in OpenStreetMap. By using overpass turbo (`http://overpass-turbo.eu`) and browsing to the area of interest, the simple query:

```
node
 [amenity=drinking_water]
 ({{bbox}});
Out;
```

allows us, i.e. to obtain the map and data corresponding to points where drinkable water is available. The result of the query in a portion of Dar Es Salaam is shown in Figure 3.5.

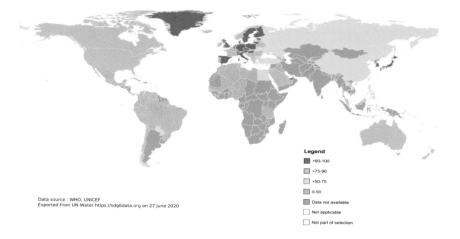

FIGURE 3.4

Proportion of population using safely managed sanitation services (Source: UN Water [73])

FIGURE 3.5

Drinking water locations in a portion of Dar Es Salaam (Source: OpenStreetMap contributors [74])

3.3.10   Health Facilities

General data about the health condition of the population (again at country level) can be found on the WHO website. The Global Health Observatory (GHO) [75] provides access to data and analyses for over 30 health themes ranging from health systems to disease-specific themes, as well as direct access to the full database. The same database archives data about the density of hospitals per 100,000 people (district/rural hospitals, health centres, health posts, provincial hospitals, specialized hospitals, hospitals as a whole), hospital beds (per 10,000 people), pharmacists, medical doctors, nurses and midwives (both absolute number, per 10,000 people, and density for 1,000 people). Some of this data can also be downloaded in cartographic format from the already mentioned website of the United Nations Statistics Division, in the "Healthcare Resources" section of the portal.

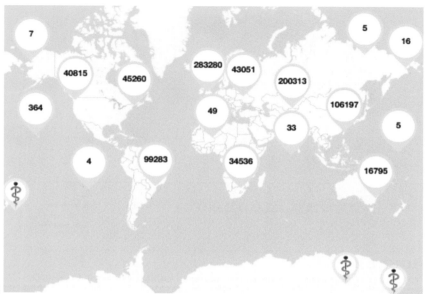

healthsites io.png

FIGURE 3.6
Location of health sites on 4 October 2020 (Source: HealthSites.io [76])

healthsites io graphs.png

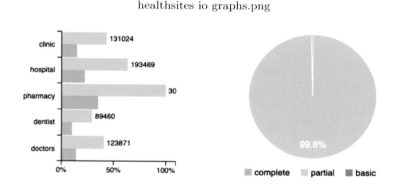

FIGURE 3.7
Number of heath sites per type (on the left) and completeness of attributes (on the right) on 4 October 2020 (Source: HealthSites.io [76])

Unfortunately, none of these datasets have local data. If one requires data at such granularity, the Global Healthsites Mapping Project [77], which is based on the OpenStreetMap data model, is a good starting point for finding locations and contact details of health facilities (clinics, doctors, hospitals, dentists, pharmacies, etc). It is a collaborative project and a long list of partners are contributing based on a citizen science or VGI (volunteered geographic information) approach. The Global Healthsites Mapping Project provides a domain specific view of OpenStreetMap data, focusing on the needs of those working with health facility data. The Heathsites.io platform [76] does not require users to be experts in the general OpenStreetMap data model and allows them to be more focused specifically on the health domain, even if the same data can be accessed from the general OpenStreetMap database and platform in various ways, e.g. with Overpass Turbo [78] or via the QuickOSM QGIS plugin [79]. Currently, 820,244 health sites are mapped (Figure 3.6), however, their descriptions are far from complete (Figure 3.7).

FIGURE 3.8
Locations of health sites in Europe on 4 October 2020 (Source: Eurostat [80])

Another interesting source of data, unfortunately only for Europe, is shared by Eurostat [80]. The dataset, which will be improved progressively, integrates the location of European healthcare services extracted from official national registers. By now it contains almost 15,000 features (Figure 3.8). When available, the capacity in terms of number of beds, rooms and practitioners and whether the healthcare site provides emergency medical services is archived. The dataset is not homogeneous neither in the level of detail nor in timeliness and update frequency. Nevertheless, it is well known that "reliable pan-European geospatial datasets for EU institutions are required to further develop GI capacities at EU level, and an important step in reducing inequalities across the EU" [81].

Global information about intensive care or ventilators is not available in any dataset. Similarly, location-based information about capacity of (and places for) collecting and treating medical and hazardous waste could not be found. To be precise, there is no data related to waste generally and again, the only source, however quite fragmented, is OpenStreetMap [82].

3.4 Discussion and Conclusion

Our study shows that global open datasets are available for many aspects of risk management before, during and after a pandemic. However, it is not always easy to find these datasets. Some of them can only be found via a (geo)portal, which often makes them inaccessible to web crawlers that search and index content for general purpose web search engines. Search engines specifically developed for datasets, such as Google's dataset search (https://datasetsearch.research.google.com), which crawls and indexes metadata about datasets in schema.org format, can improve the situation. Another challenge lies in finding the license terms and conditions for using open data. For some datasets that we discussed in this paper, the licensing information was readily available and simple to understand (e.g. standardized Creative Commons licenses). For others, we struggled to locate the licensing information or, when datasets are compiled from many different sources, different licenses may apply to different parts of the dataset (see for example, OpenAddresses.io).

The UN GGIM has identified a set of 14 global fundamental geospatial data themes, amongst others, in support of the 2030 Sustainable Development Agenda and its 17 Sustainable Development Goals (SDGs). These datasets are considered to be "the minimum primary sets of data that cannot be derived from other data sets, and that are required to spatially represent phenomena, objects, or themes important for the realisation of economic, social, and environmental benefits consistently" [83]. There is considerable overlap between nine of the UN GGIM fundamental geospatial datasets and the list of datasets that we identified as useful in the case of a global pandemic: Addresses, Buildings & Settlements, Functional Areas (includes administrative areas), Geographical Names, Land Cover & Land Use, Physical Infrastructure (includes schools and hospitals), Population Distribution, Transport Networks and Water. The list of fundamental geospatial data themes presents a foundation for global geospatial information management. As a next step, detailed regional specifications are being developed. Eventually, these will lead to improved geospatial information at the national level, which can then be integrated into global datasets.

The biggest concern with the global open datasets discussed in this chapter is that many of them are not available with sufficient granularity. Fine-grained data is particularly critical in the case of a global threat, such as the current pandemic. We live in a hyper-connected world and therefore, while taking into account local differences, many challenges need to be addressed at a global level. Therefore global analyses are required, based on data with much more detail than currently provided (e.g. mostly by country). There is a definite and urgent need to move towards providing high resolution global data.

Some government agencies are already moving in this direction, for example, ESA provides satellite imagery globally down to 10 m resolution (Sentinel 2) as open data. This makes global analyses possible that were previously unthinkable. Some private companies are also moving in this direction. Consider, for example, the case of Facebook which, with the Facebook Data for Good initiative, makes many dynamic data of interest for humanitarian purposes freely available to nonprofits and universities that have signed data license agreements.

Another fundamental move towards fine-grained data is exhibited by the many initiatives related to OpenStreetMap. OpenStreetMap has been confirmed as one of the most important geospatial data projects in the last 20 years. The quality of OpenStreetMap data is often the subject to criticism. However, the wider OpenStreetMap community, which includes other communities, such as HOT, Missing Maps, Healthsites, Geochicas, etc., has equipped itself with tools and procedures that allow a solid first validation of the data. For example, during the pandemic, HOT created at least 199 projects covering approximately 124,000 km^2, many of which had been mapped and validated by the time of writing this chapter. It is in the communities' own best interest to provide the best possible data, not only because they will use their own data, but also because there is awareness among volunteers that the data will be used for humanitarian purposes and therefore the better it is, the more effective it can be. Many scientific publications have examined the quality of OpenStreetMap data in various case studies. The results are generally comforting because where OpenStreetMap communities are more developed and mature, the comparison with authoritative data [84], [85], [86] is very favourable. Where OpenStreetMap data are scarce, it is often not possible to make comparisons with reference data because these data simply do not exist or are not available [46].

Academics have approached OpenStreetMap with slowness, gathering some momentum in recent years, not only on aspects of general interest, that is the collaborative collection of data, but also the educational perspective of such an experience. In 2014, the academic community developed YouthMappers [88] to explicitly bring together and nurture the student communities and their faculty that operate within and together with the broader set of OpenStreetMap communities around youth-based identities. Founded by faculty from Texas Tech University, the George Washington University, and West Virginia University, with support from the US Agency for International Development's GeoCenter, and now administered by Arizona State University,

FIGURE 3.9
Locations of YouthMappers Chapters in October 2020 (Source: YouthMappers [87])

YouthMappers organize as chapters on university campuses, run by student leadership under the guidance of university professor mentors. By October 2020, the network had grown (Figure 3.9) to 222 campus chapters in 50 countries, linking more than 5,000 OpenStreetMap students volunteers [87]. YouthMappers' motto is "We don't just build maps. We build mappers", emphasizing the importance of mapping the world in order to get to know it better. This experience should, in the opinion of the authors of the chapter, become the heritage of all schools and universities because it would be an enrichment of global knowledge of the world and, at the same time, an enrichment of the skills of young people. Governments should encourage and support these initiatives, taking the advantage of having more detailed maps and more geographically aware young citizens. University networks, such as the UN GGIM Academic Network, could become sounding boards for the initiative itself and contribute both to its dissemination and to the design and development of procedures for data assessment, which would therefore become the heritage of all humanity.

Annex: List of datasets

The list of datasets is available at https://docs.google.com/spreadsheets/d/19amm6CbDOTOPObA8xcZ-8itdCMaOPXSu3OqUVuDQr4s/edit#gid=0.

References

[1] World Health Organization. Advice on the use of masks in the context of COVID-19. Interim guidance WHO/2019-nCov/IPC_Masks/2020.4, World Health Organization, June 2020. URL https://apps.who.int/iris/handle/10665/332293.

[2] United Nations, Department of Economic and Social Affairs, Statistics. UN COVID-19 Data Hub, 2020. URL https://covid-19-data.unstatshub.org/. Library Catalog: covid-19-data.unstatshub.org.

[3] Centers for Disease Control and Prevention. Zoonotic Diseases, July 2017. URL https://www.cdc.gov/onehealth/basics/zoonotic-diseases.html. Library Catalog: www.cdc.gov.

[4] UN-GGIM Working Group on Geospatial Information and Services for Disasters (WG-GISD). Strategic Framework on Geospatial Information and Services for Disasters. Technical report, United Nations Committee of Experts on Global Geospatial Information Management, August 2017. URL http://ggim.un.org/UN-GGIM-publications/.

[5] Codrina Maria Ilie, Maria Antonia Brovelli, and Serena Coetzee. Monitoring SDG 9 with global open data and open software: A case study from rural Tanzania. *ISPRS - International Archives of the Photogrammetry, Remote Sensing and Spatial Information Sciences*, XLII-2/W13:1551–1558, June 2019. ISSN 2194-9034. doi: 10.5194/isprs-archives-XLII-2-W13-1551-2019. URL https://www.int-arch-photogramm-remote-sens-spatial-inf-sci.net/XLII-2-W13/1551/2019/.

[6] Open Knowledge Foundation. What is open?, 2020. URL https://okfn.org. Library Catalog: okfn.org.

[7] Maria Antonia Brovelli, Codrina Maria Ilie, and Serena Coetzee. Openness and Community Geospatial Science for Monitoring SDGs: An Example From Tanzania. In Abbas Rajabifard, editor, *Sustainable Development Goals Connectivity Dilemma: Land and Geospatial Information for Urban and Rural Resilience*, pages 313–324. CRC Press, Boca Raton, 1 edition, August 2019. ISBN 978-0-429-29062-6. doi: 10.1201/9780429290626. URL https://www.taylorfrancis.com/books/9781000690682.

[8] Serena Coetzee, Ivana Ivánová, Helena Mitasova, and Maria Brovelli. Open Geospatial Software and Data: A Review of the Current State and A Perspective into the Future. *ISPRS International Journal of Geo-Information*, 9(2):90, February 2020. ISSN 2220-9964. doi: 10.3390/ijgi9020090. URL https://www.mdpi.com/2220-9964/9/2/90.

[9] United Nations Office for Disaster Risk Reduction. Sendai Framework for Disaster Risk Reduction 2015 - 2030. Technical report, United Nations, New York, 2015. URL https://www.undrr.org/publication/sendai-framework-disaster-risk-reduction-2015-2030.

[10] Organisation for Economic Co-operation and Development (OECD). Environmental health and strengthening resilience to pandemics. Technical report, Organisation for Economic Co-operation and Development (OECD), 2020. URL https://read.oecd-ilibrary.org/view/?ref=129_129937-jm4ul2jun9&title=Environmental-health-and-strengthening-resilience-to-pandemics.

[11] World Health Organization. Recommendations to Member States to improve hand hygiene practices to help prevent the transmission of the COVID-19 virus. Interim guidance WHO/2019-nCov/Hand_Hygiene_Stations/2020.1, World Health Organization, April 2020. URL https://www.who.int/publications/i/item/recommendations-to-member-states-to-improve-hand-hygiene-practices-to-help-prevent-the-transmission-of-the-covid-19-virus.

[12] United Nations, Department of Economic and Social Affairs, Sustainable Development. Goal 6 | Department of Economic and Social Affairs, 2020. URL https://sdgs.un.org/goals/goal6.

[13] Markus Amann, Mike Holland, Rob Maas, Bert Saveyn, and Toon Vandyck. Costs, benefits and economic impacts of the EU Clean Air Strategy and their implications on innovation and competitiveness. Technical report, IIASA, 2017. URL http://gains.iiasa.ac.at.

[14] World Health Organization. Critical preparedness, readiness and response actions for COVID-19. Interim guidance WHO/COVID-19/Community_Actions/2020.4, World Health Organization, June 2020. URL https://www.who.int/publications/i/item/critical-preparedness-readiness-and-response-actions-for-covid-19.

[15] CSSEGISandData. CSSEGISandData/COVID-19, July 2020. URL https://github.com/CSSEGISandData/COVID-19. original-date: 2020-02-04T22:03:53Z.

[16] European Centre for Disease Prevention and Control (ECDC). Download today's data on the geographic distribution of COVID-19 cases worldwide, July 2020. URL https://www.ecdc.europa.eu/en/publications-data/download-todays-data-geographic-distribution-covid-19-cases-worldwide. Library Catalog: www.ecdc.europa.eu.

[17] Max Roser, Hannah Ritchie, Esteban Ortiz-Ospina, and Joe Hasell. Coronavirus Pandemic (COVID-19). *Our World in Data*, March 2020. URL https://ourworldindata.org/coronavirus.

[18] Hannah Ritchie. Google Mobility Trends: How has the pandemic changed the movement of people around the world?, June 2020. URL https://ourworldindata.org/covid-mobility-trends. Library Catalog: ourworldindata.org.

[19] Mordechai Haklay. How Good is Volunteered Geographical Information? A Comparative Study of OpenStreetMap and Ordnance Survey Datasets. *Environment and Planning B: Planning and Design*, 37(4):682–703, 2010. doi: 10.1068/b35097. URL https://doi.org/10.1068/b35097. _eprint: https://doi.org/10.1068/b35097.

[20] Humanitarian OpenStreetMap Team (HOT). HOT COVID-19 RESPONSE, 2020. URL `https://www.hotosm.org/projects/hot-covid-19-response/`.

[21] The Awareness Company. COVID-19 Awareness, 2020. URL `https://health.hydra.africa/#/`. Library Catalog: health.hydra.africa.

[22] HealthMap. Novel Coronavirus (COVID-19), 2020. URL `https://www.healthmap.org/covid-19/`.

[23] RCMRD. RCMRD Covid-19 Open Data Hub, 2020. URL `http://covid19.rcmrd.org/`. Library Catalog: covid19.rcmrd.org.

[24] NSF Spatiotemporal Innovation Center,. COVID-19 Spatiotemporal Rapid Response Gateway, 2020. URL `https://covid-19.stcenter.net/index.php/covid19-livemap/`.

[25] NAVER Corporation. Coronamap site, 2020. URL `https://coronamap.site/`. Library Catalog: coronamap.site.

[26] geo-spatial.org. Coronavirus COVID-19 România, 2020. URL `https://covid19.geo-spatial.org/`.

[27] OpenStreetMap Wiki Contributors. Wikimapia, June 2019. URL `https://wiki.openstreetmap.org/wiki/Wikimapia`.

[28] Natural Earth. Natural Earth, 2020. URL `https://www.naturalearthdata.com/`. Library Catalog: www.naturalearthdata.com.

[29] Earth Observing System. 7 Top Free Satellite Imagery Sources in 2019, 2020. URL `https://eos.com/blog/7-top-free-satellite-imagery-sources-in-2019/`.

[30] HOT partners and community. OpenAerialMap, 2020. URL `http://openaerialmap.org/`. Library Catalog: openaerialmap.org.

[31] United States Board on Geographic Names. NGA GEOnet Names Server (GNS), 2020. URL `https://geonames.nga.mil/gns/html/index.html`.

[32] US Board on Geographic Names. Domestic Names, 2020. URL `https://www.usgs.gov/core-science-systems/ngp/board-on-geographic-names`.

[33] foursquare. Quattroshapes by foursquare, 2020. URL `http://quattroshapes.com/`.

[34] World Bank. World Bank Official Boundaries, 2020. URL `https://datacatalog.worldbank.org/dataset/world-bank-official-boundaries`.

[35] United Nations Office for the Coordination of Humanitarian Affairs (OCHA). Humanitarian Data Exchange, 2020. URL `https://data.humdata.org/`. Library Catalog: data.humdata.org.

[36] GADM. GADM website, 2020. URL `https://www.gadm.org/`.

[37] Wikipedia contributors. GADM, March 2019. URL `https://en.wikipedia.org/w/index.php?title=GADM&oldid=888438996`. Page Version ID: 888438996.

[38] Wikipedia contributors. Refugee camp, June 2020. URL `https://en.wikipedia.org/w/index.php?title=Refugee_camp&oldid=965048407`. Page Version ID: 965048407.

[39] UNHCR, The UN Refugee Agency. Operational Portal - Refugee Situations, 2020. URL `https://data2.unhcr.org/en/situations`.

[40] OpenStreetMap Wiki Contributors. Points of interest, April 2020. URL `https://wiki.openstreetmap.org/wiki/Points_of_interest`.

[41] Wikimapia. Wikimapia - Let's describe the whole world!, 2020. URL `http://wikimapia.org/#lang=en&lat=-29.000000&lon=24.000000&z=12&m=w`.

[42] Center for International Earth Science Information Network - CIESIN - Columbia University, and Information Technology Outreach Services - ITOS - University of Georgia. Global Roads Open Access Data Set, Version 1 (gROADSv1), 2013. URL `https://sedac.ciesin.columbia.edu/data/set/groads-global-roads-open-access-v1`.

[43] OpenStreetMap Wiki Contributors. Map Features, July 2019. URL `https://wiki.openstreetmap.org/wiki/Map_Features`.

[44] Maria Brovelli, Marco Minghini, Monia Molinari, and Peter Mooney. A FOSS4G-based procedure to compare OpenStreetMap and authoritative road network datasets. In *Geomatics Workbooks No 12*, Como, Italy, 2015.

[45] Maria Brovelli, Marco Minghini, Monia Molinari, and Peter Mooney. Towards an Automated Comparison of OpenStreetMap with Authoritative Road Datasets. *Transactions in GIS*, 21(2):191–206, 2017. doi: 10.1111/tgis.12182.

[46] Stefan Jovanovic, Dina Jovanovic, Gorica Bratic, and Maria Antonia Brovelli. Analysis of free road data in Tanzania, Ugana and Kenya using free and open source software. *ISPRS - International Archives of the Photogrammetry, Remote Sensing and Spatial Information Sciences*, XLII-2/W13:1567–1572, 2019. doi: 10.5194/isprs-archives-XLII-2-W13-1567-2019. URL https://www.int-arch-photogramm-remote-sens-spatial-inf-sci.net/XLII-2-W13/1567/2019/.

[47] Google LLC. COVID-19 Community Mobility Report, 2020. URL https://www.google.com/covid19/mobility?hl=en. Library Catalog: www.google.com.

[48] Facebook. Facebook Data for Good, 2020. URL https://dataforgood.fb.com/. Library Catalog: dataforgood.fb.com.

[49] Joe Schwartz. Bing Maps Tile System - Bing Maps, 2018. URL https://docs.microsoft.com/en-us/bingmaps/articles/bing-maps-tile-system. Library Catalog: docs.microsoft.com.

[50] Serena Coetzee, Martijn Odijk, Bastiaan van Loenen, Janette Storm, and Jantien Stoter. Stakeholder analysis of the governance framework of a national SDI dataset – whose needs are met in the buildings and address register of the Netherlands? *International Journal of Digital Earth*, 13(3):355–373, March 2020. ISSN 1753-8947, 1753-8955. doi: 10.1080/17538947.2018.1520930. URL https://www.tandfonline.com/doi/full/10.1080/17538947.2018.1520930.

[51] Universal Postal Union. About addressing, 2020. URL http://www.upu.int/en/activities/addressing/about-addressing.html.

[52] OpenAddresses.io. About openaddresses.io, 2020. URL https://openaddresses.io/.

[53] Serena Coetzee and Antony K Cooper. What is an address in South Africa? *South African Journal of Science*, 103:10, 2007.

[54] International Organization for Standardization (ISO). ISO 19160-1:2015, Addressing — Part 1: Conceptual model. Technical report, International Organization for Standardization (ISO), Geneva, 2015. URL https://www.iso.org/obp/ui/#iso:std:iso:19160:-1:ed-1:v1:en.

[55] OpenStreetMap Contributors. OpenStreetMap Taginfo, 2020. URL https://taginfo.openstreetmap.org/.

[56] OpenStreetMap Wiki Contributors. Address Improvement, May 2019. URL https://wiki.openstreetmap.org/wiki/Address_Improvement.

[57] World Bank. World Bank Open Data, 2020. URL https://data.worldbank.org/.

[58] Organisation for Economic Co-operation and Development (OECD). OECD Statistics, 2020. URL https://stats.oecd.org/#.

[59] World Bank. Population ages 0-14 (% of total population), 2020. URL https://data.worldbank.org/indicator/SP.POP.0014.TO.ZS.

[60] World Bank. Population ages 15-64 (% of total population), 2020. URL https://data.worldbank.org/indicator/SP.POP.1564.TO.ZS.

[61] World Bank. Population ages 65 and above (% of total population), 2020. URL https://data.worldbank.org/indicator/SP.POP.65UP.TO.ZS.

[62] United Nations, Department of Economic and Social Affairs, Population Division. *World population prospects 2019. Volume I: Comprehensive Tables (ST/ESA/SER.A/426)*. United Nations, New York, 2019. ISBN 978-92-1-148327-7. URL https://population.un.org/wpp/Publications/Files/WPP2019_Volume-I_Comprehensive-Tables.pdf. OCLC: 1130546520.

[63] United Nations, Department of Economic and Social Affairs, Population Division. *World Population Prospects 2019. Volume II: Demographic Profiles (ST/ESA/SER.A/427)*. United Nations, New York, 2019. ISBN 978-92-1-004643-5. doi: 10.18356/7707d011-en. URL https://www.un-ilibrary.org/population-and-demography/world-population-prospects-2019-volume-ii-demographic-profiles_7707d011-en.

[64] Center For International Earth Science Information Network-CIESIN-Columbia University. Gridded Population of the World, Version 4 (GPWv4): Population Density, Revision 11, 2018. URL https://sedac.ciesin.columbia.edu/data/set/gpw-v4-population-density-rev11. type: dataset.

[65] United Nations, Department of Economic and Social Affairs, Population Division. World Population Prospect - The 2015 revision. Key findings and advance tables. Technical Report ESA/P/WP.241, United Nations, New York, 2015. URL https://www.un.org/en/development/desa/publications/world-population-prospects-2015-revision.html.

[66] Facebook Connectivity Lab and Center for International Earth Science Information Network - CIESIN - Columbia University. High Resolution Settlement Layer (HRSL). Source imagery for HRSL © 2016 DigitalGlobe., 2016. URL https://www.ciesin.columbia.edu/data/hrsl/#data.

[67] WorldPop. Open Spatial Demographic Data and Research, 2020. URL https://www.worldpop.org/.

[68] Andrew J. Tatem. WorldPop, open data for spatial demography. *Scientific Data*, 4(1):1–4, December 2017. ISSN 2052-4463. doi: 10.1038/sdata.2017.4. URL http://www.nature.com/articles/sdata20174.

[69] Hannah Ritchie and Max Roser. Outdoor Air Pollution. *Our World in Data*, November 2019. URL https://ourworldindata.org/outdoor-air-pollution.

[70] NASA EarthData. Health and Air Quality Data Pathfinder | Earthdata, May 2020. URL https://earthdata.nasa.gov/learn/pathfinders/health-and-air-quality-data-pathfinder.

[71] Hannah Ritchie and Max Roser. Indoor Air Pollution. *Our World in Data*, November 2019. URL https://ourworldindata.org/indoor-air-pollution.

[72] UN-Water. UN-Water SDG 6 Data Portal, 2020. URL https://sdg6data.org/.

[73] UN Water. Un water maps, 2020. URL https://sdg6data.org/maps.

[74] OpenStreetMap Contributors. OpenStreetMap, 2020. URL https://openstreetmap.org/.

[75] World Health Organization. The Global Health Observatory, 2020. URL https://www.who.int/data/gho/data/indicators.

[76] healthsites.io. About healthsites.io, 2020. URL https://healthsites.io/.

[77] OpenStreetMap Wiki Contributors. Global Healthsites Mapping Project, 2020. URL https://wiki.openstreetmap.org/w/index.php?title=Global_Healthsites_Mapping_Project&oldid=1971053.

[78] OpenStreetMap Wiki Contributors. Overpass turbo, February 2020. URL https://wiki.openstreetmap.org/wiki/Overpass_turbo.

[79] QGIS project. 10.2. Lesson: Useful QGIS Plugins — QGIS Documentation documentation, 2020. URL https://docs.qgis.org/3.10/en/docs/training_manual/qgis_plugins/plugin_examples.html.

[80] Eurostat. Healthcare services, 2020. URL https://ec.europa.eu/eurostat/web/gisco/geodata/reference-data/healthcare-services.

[81] Eurostat. Healthcare services in Europe, 2020. URL https://gisco-services.ec.europa.eu/pub/healthcare/metadata.pdf.

[82] OpenStreetMap Wiki Contributors. Waste Processing, July 2020. URL https://wiki.openstreetmap.org/wiki/Waste_Processing.

[83] United Nations Committee of Experts on Global Geospatial Information Management. The Global Fundamental Geospatial Data Themes, 2019. URL https://ggim.un.org/documents/Fundamental%20Data%20Publication.pdf.

[84] Maria Antonia Brovelli, MArco Minghini, and Monia Elisa Molinari. An automated GRASS-based procedure to assss the geometrical accuracy of the OpenStreetMap Paris road network. *ISPRS - International Archives of the Photogrammetry, Remote Sensing and Spatial Information Sciences*, XLI-B7:919–925, 2016. doi: 10.5194/isprs-archives-XLI-B7-919-2016. URL https://www.int-arch-photogramm-remote-sens-spatial-inf-sci.net/XLI-B7/919/2016/.

[85] M. A. Brovelli, M. Minghini, M. E. Molinari, and G. Zamboni. Positional accuracy assessment of the OpenStreetMap Buildings layer through automatic homologous pairs detection: the method and a case study. *ISPRS - International Archives of the Photogrammetry, Remote Sensing and Spatial Information Sciences*, XLI-B2:615–620, 2016. doi: 10.5194/isprs-archives-XLI-B2-615-2016. URL https://www.int-arch-photogramm-remote-sens-spatial-inf-sci.net/XLI-B2/615/2016/.

[86] Maria Brovelli and Giorgio Zamboni. A New Method for the Assessment of Spatial Accuracy and Completeness of OpenStreetMap Building Footprints. *ISPRS International Journal of Geo-Information*, 7(8):289, July 2018. ISSN 2220-9964. doi: 10.3390/ijgi7080289. URL http://www.mdpi.com/2220-9964/7/8/289.

[87] YouthMappers. YouthMappers Chapter Profiles, 2020. URL https://www.youthmappers.org/chapters. Library Catalog: www.youthmappers.org.

[88] Patricia Solís, Brent McCusker, Nwasinachi Menkiti, Nuala Cowan, and Chad Blevins. Engaging global youth in participatory spatial data creation for the UN sustainable development goals: The case of open mapping for malaria prevention. *Applied Geography*, 98:143–155, 2018. doi: 10.1016/j.apgeog.2018.07.013.

4

Remote Sensing and Computational Epidemiology

Mohammad Reza Mobasheri

Remote sensing techniques have been developed over the past five decades and formed an important part of an interdisciplinary approach for many interdisciplinary science including health, environment, disease monitoring, biodiversity, and determination of habitat and ambient parameters. This new approach is based on the capability of looking at multispectral views of the environment at multiple spatial and temporal scales. This new interdisciplinary ideas of remote-sensing approach, have emerged for the detection, evaluation, and mapping of factors affecting public health. Such applications have helped to achieve considerable advancement in knowledge and insight for the environmental and public health administrations to work together in teams. This synergy has enabled them to explore solutions to previously unsolved environmental issues and managerial problems. Demand for talented researchers in remote sensing, GIS, and spatial modeling are continuously increasing. This includes environmental scientists, conservation, monitoring, and assessment experts. Perhaps it is not too much to hope that we can change our view of life and justify our habits to prevent what has happened during pandemic COVID-19 again. This book chapter is written with this hope in mind. Many scientists and resource managers already recognized the importance of adopting an approach in prediction of epidemics and pandemics before their occurrences.

4.1 Introduction

Remote sensing techniques have been developed over the past five decades and formed an important part of an interdisciplinary approach for many sciences including health, environment, disease monitoring, biodiversity, and determination of habitat and ambient parameters. The remote sensing technology is based on the capability of looking at multispectral views of the environment at multiple spatial and temporal scales. The information collected through this technology is readily integrated with other forms of data, including a global positioning system (GPS), geographical information system (GIS), and field observational data. This information is essential to prepare a foundation for species-specific models to map the habitat of any creatures as small as a virus and as large as an elephant. This may include testable predictions of their population dynamics and the development of biodiversity indicators and species-environment characteristics.

Interdisciplinary remote sensing consists of concepts, methodology, technology, and innovation. These elements when integrated may provide a unique opportunity to implement novel solutions to the problems that exist at the leading edge of environmental science and management. These problems are among the most complex issues of our time.

This interdisciplinary approach of remote-sensing has emerged for the detection, evaluation, and mapping of factors affecting public health. Such applications have helped to achieve considerable advancement in knowledge and insight for the environmental and public health administrations, enabling them to work together. This synergy has also enabled them to explore solutions to previously unsolved environmental issues and managerial problems.

There are increasing belief and evidence that the health of human being and other species is adversely affected by human activities and landscape change [1–3]. Perhaps it is not too much to hope that we can change our view of life and justify our habits to prevent what has happened during pandemic COVID-19 again.

Interdisciplinary researches to understanding the environmental factors for the insects to be prepared for breeding and extraction of these factors from satellite images have shown the power of remote sensing in monitoring environmental issues. Of course not sufficient mainstream remote-sensing research texts have dealt with this emerging approach in detail to help the growing collaboration among those specializing in remote sensing, health management, and ecosystem scientists, in critical decision making and efforts on the ground. This book chapter is written with this hope in mind. Many scientists and resource managers have already recognized the importance of adopting an approach in prediction of epidemics and pandemics before their occurrences [4, 5], and in parallel with this recognition, the use of remote sensing and GIS approaches have noticeably increased [6, 7]. For example, research carried by Ahmadian et al. [4], regarding Malaria outbreak, has proved the potential of remote sensing and GIS. A section of this chapter is assigned to this work. Also, a section is assigned to Cholera epidemic prediction. Finally, an approach to the prediction of COVID-19 epidemic occurrence using remote sensing and surface data is suggested.

4.2   Remote Sensing and Health

In what follows, remote sensing technology is discussed. This is followed by an explanation on how this technology is related to the virus and some other vector disease.

4.2.1   What is a Virus?

A virus is a submicroscopic infectious agent that replicates itself only inside the living cells of an organism. Viruses can infect all types of life forms, from animals and plants to microorganisms, including bacteria and archaea [8]. Viruses are found in almost every ecosystem on Earth and are the most numerous type of biological entity [9, 10]. When infected, a host cell is forced to rapidly produce thousands of identical copies of the original virus. Most virus species have virions too small to be seen with an optical microscope as they are one hundredth the size of most bacteria.

Viruses spread in many ways. One transmission pathway is through disease-bearing organisms known as vectors: for example, viruses are often transmitted from plant to plant by insects that feed on plant sap, such as aphids; and viruses in animals can be carried by blood-sucking insects and vampire bats. The infectious dose required to produce infection in humans is less than 100 particles in Influenza viruses [11, 12] and to some extent in COVID-19. The variety of host cells that a virus can infect is called its "host range". This can be narrow or broad, meaning a virus is capable of infecting only few species, or infecting many.

Viral infections in animals provoke an immune response that usually eliminates the infecting virus. Immune responses can also be produced by vaccines, which confer an artificially acquired immunity to the specific viral infection. Some viruses, including those that cause AIDS, HPV infection, viral hepatitis, and COVID-19 evade these immune responses and result in chronic infections.

4.2.2   How is a Virus related to Remote Sensing?

In this section, the relation between different respiratory diseases (including COVID-19) and the atmospheric and environmental parameters that are investigated by different workers will be discussed. All these atmospheric and environmental parameters can be assessed by and extracted from images acquired by different sensors on board of different satellites.

Many researchers have observed a connection between the occurrence of respiratory diseases such as influenza (A and B) and COVID-19 and climatic parameters such as air temperature, air moisture content, relative humidity, wind speed, and amount of precipitation [12, 13]. Although the outbreak and epidemic, contagious on person to person, the weather conditions may play a key role in making some regions potentially suitable for the virus to be activated (Ianevski et al. 2019). This is the case for many other epidemic diseases such as Malaria and Cholera. In what follows, a few of these researches will be introduced.

Peci et al. [13], claimed that the occasion of incidence of influenza increases during rainy seasons in tropical climates and during the dry, cold months of winter in temperate climates. They found that the seasonality of influenza A and B viruses is different in most temperate climates. A negative association of both absolute humidity and temperature with influenza A and B viruses was observed.

Guo et al. [12] found an association between mean temperature, relative humidity (RH), and the atmospheric pressure with influenza cases for children between 0-17 years old. They claimed that the relative risks increase as the temperature falls below $20°C$, RH lower than 50%, or higher than 80%. Also, the risk of influenza increased with rising atmospheric pressure with 1,005 hPa as the breakpoint. They found that the effect of coldness, humidity, dryness, high-pressure, and low-pressure showed statistical significance both in females and males. The cold effect increases with age while the humidity affected all ages of children, whereas, dryness mainly affects ages 4-14 years. High-pressure mainly affected the age of 0-3, whereas the low-pressure affects preschool children aged 0-6 years old.

Ianevski et al. [14] investigated the effects of meteorological parameters such as temperature, UV index, humidity, wind speed, atmospheric pressure, and precipitation (all acquirable by remote sensing technique) on IV activity in Norway, Sweden, Finland, Estonia, Latvia, and Lithuania during 2010-2018 in Influenza virus epidemics while considering the pace of global warming. They deployed correlation and machine learning analysis techniques and found that low temperature and UV radiation can preserve Influenza virus infectivity. The researchers believe that low temperature and UV index were the most suitable predictive indexes among other meteorological factors in Northern Europe. Of course, their in-vitro experiments confirmed that low temperature and UV radiation preserved Influenza virus infectivity.

Most recently, Wang et al. [15] have researched the ongoing global pandemic of COVID-19. Their aim was to predict the effect of the upcoming summer in the northern hemisphere and expected to have a reduction of the transmission intensity of COVID-19 with increasing humidity and temperature. They used data from the cases with symptom-onset dates from January 19 to February 10, 2020, for 100 Chinese cities, and cases with confirmed dates from March 15 to April 25 for 1,005 U.S. counties. The relationship between the transmissibility of COVID-19 and the temperature/humidity was assessed. They found a similar influence of the temperature and relative humidity on effective reproductive number (R values) of COVID-19 for both China and the U.S. before lockdown in both countries. There was the reduction of reproduction by increasing temperature and humidity. This reduction of transmission was not further continued until July when the temperature and humidity had risen.

In an unpublished work of Xu et al. [16], the impact of environmental factors including pollution contaminants on COVID-19 transmission was investigated. They studied the relative risk of COVID-19 due to weather conditions and ambient air pollution. In this work, the daily reproduction at 3,739 global locations was controlled for the delay between infection and detection. After that they associated these with local weather conditions and ambient air pollution. They observed a negative relationship between the estimated reproduction number and temperatures above $25°C$, and a U-shaped relationship with outdoor ultraviolet exposure, with a weaker positive association with air pressure, wind speed, precipitation, diurnal temperature, SO_2, and ozone.

This was followed by a projection of the relative risk of COVID-19 transmission due to environmental factors in 1,072 global cities. The findings showed that warmer temperature and moderate outdoor ultraviolet exposure may offer a modest reduction in transmission.

Scafetta [17] investigated about COVID-19 and its possible relation to specific weather conditions. The findings showed that the 2020 winter weather in the region of Wuhan (Hubei,

Central China) – where the virus first showed up in December 2019 and spread widely from January to February 2020 was very similar to that of the Northern Italian provinces of Milan, Brescia, and Bergamo, where the pandemic has been very severe from February to March 2020. According to this study such similarity may suggest the worsening of the pandemic under weather temperatures between 4°C and 11°C. Based on this result, Scafetta [17] prepared maps of world-specific isotherm to locate, month by month, the world regions that share similar temperature ranges. The analysis showed that this isotherm zone extended mostly from Central China toward Iran, Turkey, West-Mediterranean Europe (Italy, Spain, and France) up to the United State of America from January to March 2020, and coinciding with the geographic regions most affected by the pandemic in the same period. He predicted that in Autumn of the Northern hemisphere, the pandemic could return and affect the same regions again. Scafetta [17] believes that the Tropical Zone and the entire Southern Hemisphere, but in restricted southern regions, could avoid a strong pandemic because of the sufficiently warm weather during the entire year.

In a study, Njifon et al. [18] investigated the role of meteorological parameters in the seasonality of influenza viruses in tropical and subtropical regions particularly in Northern Cameroon, a region characterized by high temperatures. The researchers focused on the effect of temperature, humidity, and rainfall from January 2014 to December 2016. Their results and conclusion analysis showed that there was a statistically profound association between overall influenza activity and influenza A activity for average relative humidity. They noticed a lag between humidity rise and Influenza activity where a unit increase in humidity within a given month leads to more than 85% rise in overall influenza and influenza A activity two months later. However, they believed that none of the three meteorological variables could explain the influenza B activity.

Besides the dependence of Influenza and COVID-19 to the weather parameters, there are other vector-borne diseases such as Malaria, Cholera, Ebola, and Dengue that all proved to be dependent on some weather parameters and environmental conditions. Ahmadian et al. [4], conducted a research for the determination of high potential region for Malaria outbreak using satellite images. The findings of this research showed that the insect begins breeding when the temperature is between 25C and 35°C, relative humidity between 50 to 80%, presence of vegetation cover, and presence of water pools. All these factors were supplied using Landsat images and overlaid to find the risk potential area. The results were compared with the number of registered patients in all sentinels around within the study area. Details of the methodology are presented in the following section.

4.3   Remote Sensing Methods to Predict Health-related Outbreaks

This section is assigned to the remote sensing methods by which disease epidemic and outbreaks regions can be predicted. Numerous research has so far been conducted to predict time and regions where a disease outbreak or epidemic occurs.

4.3.1   Malaria Case Study

Based on WHO [19], in 2017, an estimated 219 million cases of malaria occurred worldwide, compared with 239 million cases in 2010 and 217 million cases in 2016. Although there were an estimated 20 million fewer malaria cases in 2017 than in 2010, data for the period 2015-2017 highlight that no significant progress in reducing global malaria cases was made in this time frame. Most malaria cases in 2017 were in the WHO African Region (200 million or 92%), followed by the WHO South-East Asia Region with 5% of the cases and the WHO Eastern Mediterranean Region with 2%.

Malaria is an infectious disease that is being transferred by the female mosquito of the species Anopheles. Out of four malaria parasites responsible for disease outbreak, Plasmodium falciparum is the most important one. The life cycle of the malaria parasite develops in the anopheline and in the human body [20, 21].

These parasites require suitable environmental parameters to complete their development cycle within the mosquito. These parameters are temperature, humidity, vegetation, and water [4]. The cycle begins when the anopheline sucks human blood usually during the night time. After two to three days the mosquito starts breeding. The breeding sites are usually water, preferably swamps or slow-flowing water bodies. In the dry and semi-dry regions, these water bodies can appear after the occurrence of heavy seasonal rain in the region. Depending on the parasite species and availability of suitable humidity and air temperature, it takes 8 to 30 days for the parasite to develop in the mosquito after which the parasitic will be ready to transmit to humans through mosquito stings.

The influence of the temperature on the feeding behavior of the mosquito, its survival, and the length of the cycle that the parasite needs to develop in the mosquito before it can be infective to humans is immense. For instance, the main mosquito species responsible for Plasmodium falciparum infections feed every second day at 25°C and every third day at lower temperatures [21].

The chance of mosquito survival is low at extreme temperatures i.e. the temperatures below 5°C and temperatures above 40°C (in some reports 35°C) are deadly for the mosquito. In this regard, the optimum mosquito survival chance is found at 32°C [21].

The environmental vulnerability of the disease is mainly determined by the effects that climatic factors can have on the abundance of malaria vectors. The population of vectors depends critically upon elements of the weather and land-use all achievable using remote sensing data [22–24]. Then epidemiological and demographic models can be deployed to relate these data to estimate the distribution of humans and parasites at a high spatial resolution [22]. Such models can in turn help in providing an empirical basis for defining the disease burden of polyparasitism and the potential health impact of removing or reducing disease risk.

In summary, a temperature range of 25°C to 35°C and a relative humidity range of 50 to 80 percent is suitable for developing malaria outbreaks. In a study conducted by Ahmadian et al. [4], a methodology for extracting temperature, humidity, water bodies, and vegetated area all from satellite images is presented and details of which are as follows.

4.3.2   Materials and Methods

In the work of Ahmadian et al. [4], when needed, weather data collected in nearby synoptic stations were used as ground truth. Also the synoptic station reports were used to select the proper satellite images after raining occurrence. Analysis of the weather stability and visibility for estimation of the severity of the atmospheric effects on the satellite images were two other important aspects of using weather data.

The Satellite images used in this work were selected upon these criteria:

- The image should contain regions where the malaria outbreaks occur

- The image should contain regions where a considerable amount of raining has happened in one to a few days before the date of image acquisition

- The visibility in the regions covered by the image scene should be greater than 10 kilometers

- The region should contain a minimum amount of cloud cover

- The image acquisition date should be between August to November and between February to May when most of the raining in the region happens

- The sensors having thermal bands were used for LST calculation

- The availability of malaria statistics for the period of the study

Taking all these conditions into account, only Landsat and ASTER images were found suitable where the former images were available. Out of five Landsat images from November 2000 to August 2005, the image of April 19, 2003 was found the most suitable one for this study. Noting that all Landsat images with acquisition dates beyond April 2003 were defected due to the malfunctioning of the 7ETM+ Scan Line Corrector [22, 25].

Geo-referencing, Radiometric calibration (Atmospheric corrections), and DN to radiance and then reflectance conversion for the visible and SWIR and DN to radiance for thermal bands were the processing steps that were taken. These images were used for producing the following products.

4.3.3   Study area

The study area was two districts located in the south of Iran right at the north of Hormuz straight in the Persian Gulf (Figure 4.1). The two districts are Minab and Kahnooj. Minab is situated between 26, 7'N and 27, 26'N and 56, 48'E and 57, 50'E with an altitude of 27m from mean sea level and approximately 104 kilometers from the Persian Gulf. Kahnooj on the other hand is located between 27, 50'N and 28, 59'N and 56, 45'E to 57, 53'E with an altitude of 469m from mean sea level approximately 330 kilometers inland. The malaria outbreaks data for these two districts were collected from the related Health and Hygiene Bureau (Table 4.1).

TABLE 4.1
Number of affected people in monthly malaria outbreaks for the period of 2003-2004

Month	Apr	May	Jun	Jul	Aug	Sep	Oct	Nov	Dec	Jan	Feb	Mar
Minab	3	17	27	15	6	380	1020	339	95	17	1	8
Kahnooj	13	40	23	45	35	20	11	28	5	0	4	4

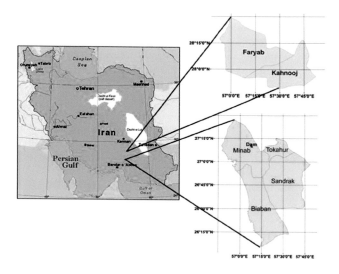

FIGURE 4.1
Location of the study area

4.3.4   Malaria Distribution Maps for Incidence Factors

Usually, three indices of Prevalence, API, and Incidence are being used in malaria outbreak investigations where the Incidence index is used in this research. The reason for this selection is the short duration required for the calculation of this index [4]. This index can be calculated using equation (4.1):

$$Incidence = \frac{M}{P_{month}} \times k \qquad (4.1)$$

where M is the number of positive cases in a few months, P is the average population in the region for those months, and k is a scale factor equal to 1,000. Table 4.2 shows the health centers, region population, and calculated Incidence index for Minab and Kahnooj region respectively.

TABLE 4.2
Health centers, region population, and calculated Incidence index for Minab (left) and Kahnooj (right)

Health Center	2003 Population	*Incidence* April to June	Health Center	2003 Population	*Incidence* April to June
Darpahn	6,702	0.149	City Zone 1	12,452	2.811
Sandark	13,429	0.074	City Zone 2	11,677	2.569
Sareni	11,481	0	City Zone 3	13,048	0.077
Hashtbandi	11,481	0.087	Sahlavar	5,340	0.187
Karian	13,665	0.073	Chah Morid	5,217	0.575
Banzark	25,190	0.198	Hoorani	16,455	0.425
Sirik	12,439	0.241	Faryab	11,631	2.493
Bemani	21,450	0	Dehpish	5,065	0.395
Hakami	14,305	0.070			
Tiab	10,787	0.185			
Haj Khademi	64,807	0.015			
Minab City	62,652	0.303			

4.4   Vegetated Area Mapping

To map the vegetated area in the images, usually vegetation indices such as Normalized Difference Vegetation Index (NDVI), Simple Ratio (SR), and Enhanced Vegetation Index (EVI) or modified version of them is being used. The index used in this work was NDVI where the threshold value of 0.2 was used. This threshold was tested using ground data and other vegetation indices. A detailed discussion regarding uncertainties involved with this threshold value will be presented in the discussion and analysis section. The NDVI index takes advantage of the red edge effect in the vegetation spectral reflectance curve i.e. low reflectance in the red ρ_R and very high reflectance in near-infrared ρ_{NIR}. The reflectance difference in these two spectral bands can be normalized to 1 using the following equation:

$$NDVI = \frac{\rho_{NIR} - \rho_R}{\rho_{NIR} + \rho_R} \tag{4.2}$$

NDVI varies between -1 and +1 where its value for vegetated pixels is generally greater than 0.2, with values exceeding 0.65 indicating dense vegetation. Taking a flying range of mosquitoes into account a two kilometers distance around any vegetated point is considered.

4.5   Water Body Mapping

There are different methods and approaches for mapping patches of water bodies in the scenes where Normalized Difference Water Index (NDWI) and Tasselled Cap Transformation (TC) are two appropriate ones. Using field data, they found TC more appropriate for this work. This transformation takes advantage of 6 bands of 7ETM+ sensor and is of the form [26]:

$$
\begin{bmatrix} Brightness \\ Greenness \\ Wetness \end{bmatrix} = \begin{bmatrix} b1 & b2 & b3 & b4 & b5 & b7 \\ g1 & g2 & g3 & g4 & g5 & g7 \\ w1 & w2 & w3 & w4 & w5 & w7 \end{bmatrix} \times \begin{bmatrix} CH1 \\ CH2 \\ CH3 \\ CH4 \\ CH5 \\ CH7 \end{bmatrix} \tag{4.3}
$$

where CH1 to CH7 stands for reflectance in bands 1 to 7 (excluding band 6 which is thermal). bi, gi, and wi are coefficients of transformation for brightness, greenness, and wetness respectively, and are shown in Table 4.3.

TABLE 4.3
Tasseled cap transformation coefficients for 7ETM+ sensor

Bands	1	2	3	4	5	7
bi	0.3561	0.3972	0.3904	0.6966	0.2286	0.1596
gi	-0.3344	-0.3544	-0.4556	0.6966	-0.0242	-0.2630
wi	0.2626	0.2144	0.0926	0.0656	-0.7629	0.5388

For the regions containing patches of the water body, wetness takes a value of greater than -0.0710. Applying this threshold to the image and again taking 2 kilometers flight zone for the mosquitoes around water bodies, figures 8 and 9 for Minab and Kahnooj were produced respectively. The detected water bodies in the Kahnooj image were as small as a pixel and consequently cannot be detected visually in the figure.

4.6   Land Surface Temperature

To calculate LST, the following equation suggested by the Landsat team is used:

$$
T_s = \frac{k_2}{Ln\left(\frac{\varepsilon_{NB}k_1}{R_c} + 1\right)} \tag{4.4}
$$

where R_c is the corrected spectral flux density that reaches the sensor (W/m^2/μm), ε_{NB} is the surface narrow-band emissivity, k_1 and k_2 are constants equal to 666.09 (Kelvin) and 1282.71 (W/m^2/μm) respectively [27]. Applying equation (4.4) to the channel 6 radiance image, the surface temperature for Minab and Kahnooj was calculated.

4.7   Air Temperature

To calculate air temperature, the Surface Energy Balance Algorithm for Land (SEBAL) is used [28]. This algorithm consists of 25 modules where a combination of empirical formulas, synoptic data from nearby weather stations, and image extracted data (such as surface temperature) are being processed in these modules. Detail of this algorithm can be found in [28]. The SEBAL algorithm output maps for air temperature for Minab and Kahnooj are shown while the temperature range of 25°C to 35°C is imposed on the image (Figure 4.2). It can be seen that except in very small areas, the other parts of the region have temperature within the 25°C to 35°C zone.

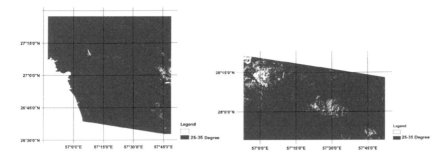

FIGURE 4.2
Satellite extracted maps of air temperature between 25°C and 35°C for Minab (left) and Kahnooj (right)

4.8 Relative Humidity

Using the calculated air temperature image in the previous step one can calculate the saturated partial water vapor pressure using the following equation [4]:

$$e_s = 6.1121 \times exp[(17.502 \times T_a)(240.97 + T_a)^{-1}] \tag{4.5}$$

where e_s is saturated partial water vapor pressure in millibar and T_a is the air temperature in degrees of Celsius. Then using partial vapor pressure e calculated from measured synoptic station data and assuming negligible horizontal gradient in e for the time of image acquisition, the relative humidity RH in the selected scene can be calculated using equation (4.6) below:

$$RH = e \times 100 \tag{4.6}$$

They produced maps of relative humidity (for 50% to 80% range).

4.9 Results and Analysis

Now all maps of parameters necessary for high-risk region determination are prepared. Since these parameters do not affect the mosquito's survival equally, then a simple overlying of these layers of information would not be appropriate and parameters such as temperature, humidity, water body, and vegetation must have different weighting coefficients. An unpublished work of suggested weighing coefficients of 0.35, 0.25, 0.25, and 0.15 for temperature, humidity, water body, and vegetation respectively. Having overlaid these layers using appropriate weighing coefficients, the resulted high-risk map is shown in Figure 4.3 where number 10 shows the highest risk.

Combining the incidence indices (Section 4.3.4) and Figure 4.3 helps compare between different calculated risk regions and calculated incidence index using field data (Figure 4.4). As can be seen, the highest risk regions can only be found in Minab. This degree of risk cannot be seen in Kahnooj mostly due to the lack of suitable humidity conditions.

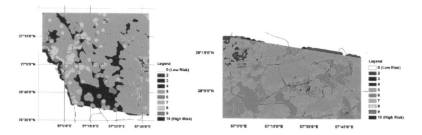

FIGURE 4.3

High-risk maps of Minab (left) and Kahnooj (right). Higher numbers represent higher risk regions

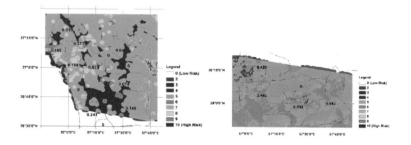

FIGURE 4.4

Comparison of different calculated risk regions (Figure 4.3) and calculated incidence index using field data. The zeros in the image are due to the lack of information for those regions.

4.10   Discussion

There are sources of uncertainties with the extraction of any layers of information from satellite images. The amount of uncertainties compared to the field data differ for different parameters. The uncertainties are due to the unknown surface emissivity values for LST extraction of up to $2°C$, uncertainties in relative humidity of up to 3% due to the assumption of uniformity for partial vapor pressure throughout the sub-scene, and the uncertainty in the air temperature. The uncertainties in vegetation and water bodies mapping are of the second order of importance because these uncertainties can be included in the 2 kilometers flying zone already considered in the maps. Adding the uncertainties in LST and relative humidity to the lower and upper limits of temperature and humidity, the effect found was a small expansion around the potential area. Since this research aimed to show the high-risk potential area to the local manager for deputing mosquitoes exterminating group to these regions, a few meters away from the high-risk region will not make much difference.

It is found that one can predict the malaria outbreak by extracting environmental parameters necessary for mosquito's parasite life cycle. These parameters were temperature ($25°C$ to $35°C$), relative humidity (50% to 80%), patches of water, and vegetation covers. Regarding 10 degrees in temperature range and 30% in humidity range, as well as 2 kilometers flying zone for the mosquito, any intrinsic uncertainties in the extraction of these parameters from satellite images due to their resolutions and intervening atmosphere - which were the sources of concern for many satellite approaches - did not affect the results seriously. A weighed overlying of the four layers of information i.e. air temperature, relative humidity, patches of water bodies, and vegetated area showed acceptable agreements with the field-collected data. Of course, there are still some uncertainties involved with the weighing coefficients for these layers which call for further investigation. Also, there are other parameters such as shadows, manmade pools, pots of water, and many other factors that may help and affect the outbreaks which each must be considered separately. However, the satellite ability in the detection of high-risk potential regions may provide non-expensive information on a routine basis not only in malaria but for other epidemics as well, where studies in those areas are the aims of these authors.

4.11   Cholera Case Study

Vibrio Cholerae (VC), a bacterium autochthonous to the aquatic environment, is the agent causing Cholera, a severe aquatic, life-threatening diarrheal disease occurring mostly in developing countries. VC has many different types of serogroups, only two of which can cause epidemic cholera. Those two serogroups are called serogroups O1 and serogroups O139 (O139 is found only in Asia) and can cause epidemic cholera if they also produce the cholera toxin. VC, including both serogroups O1 and O139, is found in association with crustacean zooplankton, mainly copepods, and notably in ponds, rivers, estuarine, and coastal region globally. Cholera bacteria attach to zooplanktons (copepods), form thin biofilms in the brackish water especially in coastal regions. Since copepods feed on phytoplankton, the proliferation of phytoplankton increases the number of cholera bacteria. (Shafiqul Islam), a member of an interdisciplinary research team from Tufts University and National Oceanic and Atmospheric Administration, US. The incidence of cholera and the occurrence of pathogenic VC strains with zooplankton were studied in many areas.

If one can measure the density of chlorophyll and track the blooming of phytoplankton, the prediction of Cholera outbreak (mostly in endemic regions) seems possible. The satellite data on chlorophyll concentration could be used to routinely monitor coastal processes and track cholera outbreaks. The privilege of using satellite data is its suitable spatial and temporal coverage as well as low expenses.

Rahimi-Doab [5] conducted research on Cholera endemic regions. He claimed that the bloom or the flowering of phytoplankton, and as a result, the flourishing of the zooplankton and feeding are closely correlated with the temperature at the sea surface (SST). The SST can be continuously monitored through thermal channels of satellite sensors. By monitoring SST and measuring the seawater chlorophyll as a sign of plankton flourishing and knowing the amount of rainfall as an agent for the transfer of micronutrient materials from shore to sea, Rahimi-Doab (2018) could predict the disease outbreak one month in advance. However, the disease has its trend in each region and the peak of the disease in each region was different in terms of time and number of patients. This requires calibrating the suggested model for each region. In Rahimi-Doab's [5] work, the statistical analysis of the log-linear Poisson Generalized Linear Model (GLM) was used to predict the appropriate time for the growth of VC in the sea and its subsequent outbreak. For this purpose, the effects of three environmental factors i.e. SST, chlorophyll concentration of seawater extracted from the products of MODIS onboard of Aqua platform, and the rainfall data supplied by TRMM satellite, were all taken as independent variables and investigated. The case study region was the 2011 outbreak in Benin, Africa and the results showed that these factors were correlated to the disease outbreak in that endemic region.

Finally, the model was applied to the outbreak cases in the southern coastal regions of Iran. The model could predict the occurrence of the outbreak, one month in advance. Although the output of the model tells us the number of patients however, this number depends on the suitability of each of the three environmental factors, which are included as independent variables in the model.

4.12   Conclusions

The two aforementioned case studies showed that the environmental factors and parameters are playing a key role in the occurrence of outbreak and/or epidemic in many cases. This includes vector-borne diseases as well as viruses including COVID-19. All these environmental parameters are acquirable from satellite images. As mentioned in previous sections, COVID-19 and other similar viruses have shown some dependencies on some environmental parameters but, the main issue in these kinds of epidemics is the behavior of the patients affected or those who carry the viruses and spread it in the ambient. Our preliminary studies show that we might be able to classify different parts of the city based on the temperature, humidity, wind speed and direction, surface cover, height, and air pressure, and some other factors and compare these classes with the results of the affected people's population in those regions. The equation that could be the basis of this investigation can be of the form of equation (4.7):

$$COVID - CF = f(Ta, LST, RH, P, Vs, Vd, SC, H) \qquad (4.7)$$

Where $COVID - CF, Ta, LST, RH, P, Vs, Vd, SC$, and H are COVID-19 Contagious Factor, air temperature at 2m height, Land Surface Temperature, Relative Humidity, air pressure, wind speed, wind direction, Surface Cover, and Height of the land on that region, respectively.

The work which is currently undergoing showed the dependence of the Influenza and to some extent COVID-19 outbreaks to the air temperature, humidity, wind speed and direction, and density of the population. The results, which will be published separately, may help to highlight the hotspots and inform the people regularly.

References

[1] P. Daszak, A.A. Cunningham, and A.D. Hyatt. Anthropogenic environmental change and the emergence of infectious diseases in wildlife. *Acta Tropica*, 78(2):103 – 116, 2001. ISSN 0001-706X. doi: https://doi.org/10.1016/S0001-706X(00)00179-0.

[2] S.K. Majumdar. *Wildlife Diseases: Landscape Epidemiology, Spatial Distribution and Utilization of Remote Sensing Technology*. Book publications of the Pennsylvania Academy of Science. Pennsylvania Academy of Science, 2005. ISBN 9780945809197.

[3] Daniel B. Botkin, Henrik Saxe, Miguel B. Araújo, Richard Betts, Richard H. W. Bradshaw, Tomas Cedhagen, Peter Chesson, Terry P. Dawson, Julie R. Etterson, Daniel P. Faith, Simon Ferrier, Antoine Guisan, Anja Skjoldborg Hansen, David W. Hilbert, Craig Loehle, Chris Margules, Mark New, Matthew J. Sobel, and David R. B. Stockwell. Forecasting the Effects of Global Warming on Biodiversity. *BioScience*, 57(3): 227–236, 03 2007. ISSN 0006-3568. doi: 10.1641/B570306.

[4] A. Ahmadian Marj, M. R. Mobasheri, M. J. Valadan Zoej, Y. Rezaei, and M. R. Abaei. Exploring the use of satellite images in the estimation of potential malaria outbreak regions. *Environmental Hazards*, 8(2): 89–100, 2009. doi: 10.3763/ehaz.2009.0003.

[5] M Rahimi-Doab. Cholera Outbreak Potential Region Determination Using Satellite Images. Master's thesis, Khavaran Institute of Higher Education, 2018.

[6] R.I. Miller. *Mapping the Diversity of Nature*. Springer Netherlands, 1994. ISBN 9780412455100.

[7] Woody Turner, Sacha Spector, Ned Gardiner, Matthew Fladeland, Eleanor Sterling, and Marc Steininger. Remote sensing for biodiversity science and conservation. *Trends in Ecology & Evolution*, 18(6):306–314, 2003. ISSN 0169-5347. doi: https://doi.org/10.1016/S0169-5347(03)00070-3.

[8] Eugene V. Koonin, Tatiana G. Senkevich, and Valerian V. Dolja. The ancient virus world and evolution of cells. *Biology Direct*, 1:29–29, Sep 2006. ISSN 1745-6150. doi: 10.1186/1745-6150-1-29.

[9] C. Martin Lawrence, Smita Menon, Brian J. Eilers, Brian Bothner, Reza Khayat, Trevor Douglas, and Mark J. Young. Structural and functional studies of archaeal viruses. *The Journal of biological chemistry*, 284(19): 12599–12603, May 2009. ISSN 0021-9258. doi: 10.1074/jbc.R800078200.

[10] Robert A Edwards and Forest Rohwer. Viral metagenomics. 3(6):504–510, June 2005. doi: 10.1038/nrmicro1163.

[11] Elizabeth Robilotti, Stan Deresinski, and Benjamin A. Pinsky. Norovirus. *Clinical Microbiology Reviews*, 28 (1):134–164, Jan 2015. ISSN 1098-6618. doi: 10.1128/CMR.00075-14.

[12] Qiaozhi Guo, Zhiqiang Dong, Weilin Zeng, Wenjun Ma, Danyang Zhao, Xin Sun, Sitang Gong, Jianpeng Xiao, Tiegang Li, and Wensui Hu. The effects of meteorological factors on influenza among children in guangzhou, china. *Influenza and other Respiratory Viruses*, 13(2):166–175, Mar 2019. ISSN 1750-2659. doi: 10.1111/irv.12617.

[13] Adriana Peci, Anne-Luise Winter, Ye Li, Saravanamuttu Gnaneshan, Juan Liu, Samira Mubareka, and Jonathan B. Gubbay. Effects of Absolute Humidity, Relative Humidity, Temperature, and Wind Speed on Influenza Activity in Toronto, Ontario, Canada. *Applied and Environmental Microbiology*, 85(6):e02426–18, Mar 2019. ISSN 1098-5336. doi: 10.1128/AEM.02426-18.

[14] Aleksandr Ianevski, Eva Zusinaite, Nastassia Shtaida, Hannimari Kallio-Kokko, Miia Valkonen, Anu Kantele, Kaidi Telling, Irja Lutsar, Pille Letjuka, Natalja Metelitsa, Valentyn Oksenych, Uga Dumpis, Astra Vitkauskiene, Kestutis Stašaitis, Christina Öhrmalm, Käre Bondeson, Anders Bergqvist, Rebecca J. Cox, Tanel Tenson, Andres Merits, and Denis E. Kainov. Low temperature and low uv indexes correlated with peaks of influenza virus activity in northern europe during 2010-2018. *Viruses*, 11(3):207, Mar 2019. ISSN 1999-4915. doi: 10.3390/v11030207.

[15] Jingyuan Wang, Ke Tang, Kai Feng, and Weifeng Lv. High temperature and high humidity reduce the transmission of covid-19. *SSRN Electronic Journal*, 2020. doi: 10.2139/ssrn.3551767.

[16] Ran Xu, Hazhir Rahmandad, Marichi Gupta, Catherine Digennaro, Navid Ghaffarzadegan, Heresh Amini, and Mohammad S. Jalali. The Modest Impact of Weather and Air Pollution on COVID-19 Transmission. *SSRN Electronic Journal*, 2020. doi: 10.2139/ssrn.3593879.

[17] Nicola Scafetta. A Proposal for Isotherm World Maps to Forecast the Seasonal Evolution of the SARS-CoV-2 Pandemic. *Preprints*, (2020040063), 2020. doi: 10.20944/preprints202004.0063.v1.

[18] Hermann Landry Munshili Njifon, Chavely Gwladys Monamele, Cyprien Kengne Nde, Marie-Astrid Vernet, Gake Bouba, Serges Tchatchouang, Mohamadou Ripa Njankouo, Raphaël Tapondjou, Louis Deweerdt, Wilfred Mbacham, and Richard Njouom. Influence of meteorological parameters in the seasonality of influenza viruses circulating in northern cameroon. *Influenza and other Respiratory Viruses*, 13(2):158–165, Mar 2019. ISSN 1750-2659. doi: 10.1111/irv.12612.

[19] World Health Organization (WHO). *World malaria report*. 2018. ISBN 978-92-4-156565-3.

[20] Frank C Tanser, Brian Sharp, and David le Sueur. Potential effect of climate change on malaria transmission in Africa. *The Lancet*, 362(9398):1792 – 1798, 2003. ISSN 0140-6736. doi: https://doi.org/10.1016/S0140-6736(03)14898-2.

[21] Hector Caraballo and Kevin King. Emergency department management of mosquito-borne illness: malaria, dengue, and west nile virus. *Emergency medicine practice*, 16(5):1–23, 2014.

[22] Jonathan A. Patz and Sarah H. Olson. Malaria risk and temperature: influences from global climate change and local land use practices. *Proceedings of the National Academy of Sciences of the United States of America*, 103(15):5635–5636, Apr 2006. ISSN 0027-8424. doi: 10.1073/pnas.0601493103.

[23] David J. Rogers, Sarah E. Randolph, Robert W. Snow, and Simon I. Hay. Satellite imagery in the study and forecast of malaria. *Nature*, 415(6872):710–715, Feb 2002. ISSN 0028-0836. doi: 10.1038/415710a.

[24] S. I. Hay, C. J. Tucker, D. J. Rogers, and M. J. Packer. Remotely sensed surrogates of meteorological data for the study of the distribution and abundance of arthropod vectors of disease. *Annals of Tropical Medicine & Parasitology*, 90(1):1–19, 1996. doi: 10.1080/00034983.1996.11813021.

[25] Naoko Nihei, Yoshihiko Hashida, Mutsuo Kobayashi, and Akira Ishii. Analysis of malaria endemic areas on the indochina peninsula using remote sensing. *Japanese Journal of Infectious Diseases*, 55(5):160–166, Oct 2002. ISSN 1344-6304.

[26] Mohammadreza Mobasheri and A. Sadeghi Naeini. Using IRS products to recover 7ETM+ defective images. *American Journal of Applied Sciences*, 5(6):618–625, 2007. doi: 10.3844/ajassp.2008.618.625.

[27] S. Liang. *Quantitative Remote Sensing of Land Surfaces*. Wiley Series in Remote Sensing and Image Processing. Wiley, 2004. ISBN 9780471723714.

[28] W.G.M. Bastiaanssen, H. Pelgrum, J. Wang, Y. Ma, J.F. Moreno, G.J. Roerink, and T. van der Wal. A remote sensing surface energy balance algorithm for land (SEBAL).: Part 2: Validation. *Journal of Hydrology*, 212-213:213–229, 1998. ISSN 0022-1694. doi: https://doi.org/10.1016/S0022-1694(98)00254-6. URL http://www.sciencedirect.com/science/article/pii/S0022169498002546.

5

The Potential of Drone Technology in Pandemics

David R. Green, Alex R. Karachok and Billy J. Gregory

In recent years, drones or Unmanned Airborne Vehicles (UAVs) have become associated with aerial data and image acquisition for many environmental applications. Unexpectedly, the COVID-19 pandemic in 2020 has led to new opportunities for drones in many new application areas, with and without the use of remote sensing imaging technology. Many unique applications have already been proposed within a short period of time, some building on existing pre-COVID-19 demonstrations and ideas, to exploring new possibilities for use. Whilst drone technology is well-established, there are still factors requiring further investigation to fully exploit drones. These include: allocation, management and control of drone air space, operation Beyond Visual Line of Sight (BVLOS), the role of existing and new telecommunication networks, safe operation in built-up areas, and societal approval and acceptance. This chapter presents an overview of current drone technology and future developments and the exploration of some existing and proposed applications. The chapter will examine the issues facing successful mainstream implementation of the use of drones for these applications, and the problems that need to be overcome to allow this technology to mature and become mainstream.

5.1 Introduction

Drones or UAVs first became popular about six years ago when Parrot, 3DR, and DJI began to market their off-the-shelf platforms to the public. Categorised mainly as 'toys' at first these low-cost multi-rotor aircraft rapidly became very popular for recreational flying. Their widespread appeal soon grew as they became easier to fly and could carry small cameras. The addition of GoPro Hero cameras and DJI Zenmuse gimbals helped to facilitate and reveal the potential of these small airborne platforms and sensors for aerial photography and videography.

Although the future potential of drones for applications outside remote sensing and the derived photogrammetric and visualisation products we have become so familiar with were already under consideration prior to COVID-19, the widespread impact of the pandemic has triggered a rapid escalation in interest in the role of drone technology. Already the COVID-19 pandemic has provided a new opportunity to explore the potential role of drones in other application areas, both with and without the use of remote sensing technology. Many unique applications have already been proposed within a short period of time, some capitalising on existing demonstrations and ideas, to those exploring new possibilities.

Two streams of application have been considered: (1) delivering essential goods and services, and (2) battling the spread of coronavirus. Some examples already under development and testing include: the delivery of parcels, medical supplies, and information e.g. broadcasts; personal, health and environmental monitoring, enforcing social distancing, mapping, and spraying to disinfect.

Whilst drone technology is already well-established, there are still many factors that currently require further investigation to allow this proposed potential to be fully exploited. These include the allocation, management and control of drone air space, operation Beyond the Visual Line of Sight (BVLOS), the use of new telecommunications networks, safe operation considerations in built-up areas, as well as social acceptance. With this context in mind some of the existing and proposed applications that are either already under development or being developed will be explored. This will include an overview of current drone technology and future developments. The chapter will then look at the issues facing successful implementation of the use of drones for these applications, and the problems that need to be overcome to allow this technology to become mainstream in the future.

5.2   Developments in Drone Technology

Today there are a wide range of UAV and drone platforms which include multi-rotors (quadcopter (4), hexacopter (6), and octacopter (8)), fixed wing, and Vertical Takeoff and Landing (VTOLs). In addition, some small-scale helicopters have also been used for remote sensing. High quality gimbals now support a wide range of DSLR cameras of varying different sizes, and additional camera-based sensors, such as NIR and NDVI cameras. Larger cameras and sensors can be carried by bigger drones with the required lift and battery capacity.

There are now many more options for sensors that can be mounted on small aerial platforms. Whilst RGB cameras are generally still in widespread common use, the demand for other sensors, both non-imaging and imaging, and low-cost, higher resolution systems has seen many other types of cameras/sensors become available. These include modified GoPro cameras and similar types of miniaturised cameras that can be filtered to sense the Near Infrared (NIR) and other portions of the Electromagnetic Spectrum (EMS). Examples include the range marketed by MapIR [1] and IR-Pro in the USA. Alongside these have been developments in small multi-spectral sensors specifically aimed at agricultural, horticultural crop and forest canopy monitoring. The Parrot Sequoia 5-band multi-spectral camera is one such example [2]. A larger version of this sensor, is the MicaSense RedEdge [3]. These provide the opportunity to acquire five (5) bands of imagery, and also to generate NDVI images. Other companies such as Sentera (www.sentera.com) also provide NDVI cameras based on different spectral wavelengths.

More advanced sensors are now also available to take greater advantage of the information content of the electromagnetic spectrum including thermal, hyperspectral, and Lidar instruments. Many drone manufacturers offer thermal camera-ready platforms with either their own thermal cameras e.g. Yuneec [4] and DJI [5] or ones made by a thermal camera manufacturer e.g. FLIR. Hyperspectral cameras are available for drones from a number of different manufacturers e.g. Headwall [6]. These can be useful in many applications because of the number of wavelengths that can be sensed (e.g. up to 255 channels) greatly increasing the dimensionality of the spectral dataset and resulting in the potential acquisition of more information of interest. These are expensive, often need specialist aerial platforms, and require more training to use and to extract the information. Another common sensor is Lidar (both terrestrial and bathymetric versions) which can be mounted on a number of specialist UAV platforms e.g. Riegl [7]. Terrestrial lidar has the potential to see through a vegetation canopy. Bathymetric lidar sensors can be mounted on small aerial platforms and have the capability to generate depth information in water 20-40m deep providing the water is clear and not too turbulent e.g. Riegl's Bathycopter [8]. These also have the capability to generate 3D information of underwater surfaces.

Radar systems have also been integrated into large UAV systems for navigation and image acquisition. More recently, studies have revealed success with the development of small, low-cost, high-resolution radar systems specifically designed for operation on small unmanned aerial vehicles [9–11].

In a very short period of time, drone technology has evolved from being quite basic to very advanced and increasingly customised for specific environmental applications. Several key developments in the technology have facilitated this transformation.

One of the major constraints of early platforms was the available battery technology. Early batteries provided a limited power source often only giving 6-8 minutes of flight time. This was not a major drawback for short recreational flights, but when including considerations such as operation in colder air, wind strength, and take-off, return to home, and landing requirements, the actual flight duration time was reduced quite considerably. Within a few years, however, these basic batteries have evolved into smart batteries that not only provide longer flight times e.g. 20-25 minutes, but also supply information to the controller and operator about battery status and remaining flight time. Within a few years these batteries have also become more compact and the average flight time has now increased to around 30 minutes. Considerable effort is now being put into improving the quality and battery life, as well as the development of new types of batteries [12], especially for multi-rotors. Fixed-wing aircraft by contrast typically already have longer flight times, ranging from 45 to 55 minutes, as they are lighter and offer less resistance in flight, making them more suitable for larger area coverage.

Early UAVs were usually flown manually by the pilot, often without an First Person View (FPV) device, and stereo-imagery was acquired through skilled flying by the drone pilot where overlapping flight-lines were visually assessed to provide the required stereo-imagery for generating photo-mosaics and 3D models. Today sophisticated phone and tablet Apps for both Android and iPhone operating systems, either provided by the drone companies (e.g. DJI Go4) or third party companies (e.g. Litchi [13], and Pix4D [14]), allow for varying levels of autonomous flight to be planned and executed. The phone and tablet Apps now available allow for either very basic simple autonomous flight (Litchi) or more sophisticated grid pattern flightpaths (Pix4D) to be conducted that allow the pilot to customise the overflight pattern e.g. straight line or grid, the camera tilt, speed, and the flying height of the aircraft amongst other things. Over time, the data/image capture task has now become a one-button 'push' for take-off and one for landing. The technology has therefore made it much easier to conduct repeat flights of the same area to gather multi-temporal imagery of a site. Nearly all modern drones now have autonomous flight capability, and this in turn allows them to be used for more advanced aerial survey tasks.

Additionally, some drones (e.g. the DJI Mavic Air 2) now come equipped with the new AirSense technology utilising ADS-B aviation technology for receiving signals from nearby airplanes and helicopters and displaying their locations on the on-screen map on the DJI Fly App [15].

Not surprisingly the growing number of different UAVs and the range of applications is already beginning to raise concerns about the availability and safe use of air space particularly where other industry areas will also be affected by competition for the existing air space. This will ultimately require legislation. UAV communication with the ground control system (GCS), for example, requires radio frequencies with sufficient band width. As recently as 2008, the International Telecommunication Union (ITU) had not allocated bandwidth to UAVs meaning that they have to use different radio frequencies in every country [16], something that needs to be taken into account by international operators and manufacturers.

Several drone capture methods have also been developed either to physically capture drones in a net or through 'drone snatching' using another drone in situations where illegal flights are being conducted or in emergency situations [17, 18]. All weather drone operation is now being developed and delivery drones are already able to safely operate in heavy rain and high winds [19].

5.3 The Impact of COVID-19

Prior to the COVID-19 pandemic, although drone technology was already well-established with many professional applications worldwide there were already a number of new ideas emerging for their use in a wider range of imaging and non-imaging applications.

At the time, drones were also increasingly coming under scrutiny because of the increasing occurrence of operational incidents. Though not all were substantiated, some accidents nevertheless began to have a negative impact on the perception of this technology leading to alienation of the public from supporting the continued growth of this industry. In part this was a direct result of the rapid growth in uncontrolled use of both commercial and recreational drones, with a lack of pilot training and enforcement of regulations. However, responses to concerns about privacy and safety also had many positive developments leading to improved technology, education and awareness raising, training, best practice guidelines and tighter regulations that have since helped to allay some public concern.

The COVID-19 pandemic, however, rather suddenly and unexpectedly triggered growing recognition and a new level of acceptance of drone technology, driven not so much by the increase in commercial uses prior to the outbreak of COVID-19, but by the timely emergence of new ideas that have highlighted drone technology as an important way to help deal with and, possibly even overcome, the constraints and health emergencies imposed on society by the virus in early 2020. In addition, the collection of higher resolution data that can be processed and integrated with other information for planning and decision-making.

Two new streams of application have been pursued: (1) delivering essential goods and services, and (2) battling the spread of coronavirus. Some examples already under development and being tested include: the delivery of parcels, food, medical supplies, and information e.g. broadcasts; personal, health and environmental monitoring, enforcing social distancing, mapping, and spraying to disinfect contaminated areas. These are explored below.

5.3.1   Delivering Essential Goods and Services

Prior to the arrival of COVID-19, numerous articles and press releases revealed a growing commercial interest in the use of so-called 'delivery drones' for the delivery of parcels, supplies, food. and drink. It has been predicted that by 2030 the drone package delivery market will be worth £21bn [20]. Similar forecasts have been made by others about the impact of this technology e.g. by 2026, more than a million drones could be carrying out retail deliveries, up from 20,000 today, according to new analysis from Gartner [21].

Amazon and a number of other companies were originally at the forefront of promoting these ideas, and successful demonstrations had already been carried out as proof of concept. Prime-Air, for example, was first trialled by Amazon in 2016 to demonstrate parcel delivery within a 30 minute timeframe [22]. Prime-Air development centres were set up in the United States, the United Kingdom, Austria, France and Israel. Research studies showed that drone platforms already available – albeit larger than some of the more familiar recreational drones – could easily be adapted and modified to carry small boxes and containers. Coupled with new autonomous flight capability it has since been shown possible to programme a drone to carry a cup of coffee or a meal from point A to point B. Larger platforms were also shown to be capable of carrying larger payloads such as parcels. DHL also launched drone operation tests in urban areas in China to test the so-called 'last-mile' delivery challenges being considered. Compared to road transport, the benefits of autonomous drone services were found to be significant and included a reduction in delivery times, and provided cost savings, reduced energy consumption, and a lower carbon footprint [21]. In addition, such drones were able to provide faster delivery for customers with the added benefit of giving consumers more control over the time and location of a delivery [19].

The capability of larger drones to carry boxes also opened up the possibility of carrying supplies to remote and inaccessible locations (e.g. in the event of an emergency or for delivering medical supplies) where timing is often important. Several trials have been undertaken and revealed the potential to expand drone-based deliveries to more applications. For example, in Canada, they have been delivering supplies, including medical supplies, to native communities in places where there are a lot of small, remote reserves far from resource hubs [23].

However, despite the potential there are many drone-related issues that require early solutions to allow for the practical realisation of these ideas in the future e.g. the establishment of an air traffic management system. In addition, there have been some concerns that drones maybe the target of 'hackers' who may be able to take control of a drone and steal the goods being carried.

Meantime, on a more positive note these ideas and developments have also begun to find favour with roles that might be useful to help deal with the actual and perceived impact of the COVID-19 pandemic.

The collection of high-resolution spatio-temporal data can provide the means to generate real-time information e.g. images, maps, and surveys at the community level to assist in planning and decision-making, as well as for use in an emergency response both during and after an event.

A recent report in 2020 highlights the opinion that the pandemic will be 'a catalyst for accelerating the viability and acceptance of commercial drone deliveries' [24]. 53 per cent of companies who took part in a recent survey believe commercial drone deliveries will be commonplace by 2023, helped by the public and private sector actively seeking to develop safe ways to guarantee services whilst containing the spread of any viruses [24].

Drone delivery has the potential to provide people with low-cost and near instant access to vital medical supplies, regardless of whether they live in a city or a rural community. Benefits arising will be in helping to manage chronic health conditions, enabling more home-based acute care, and reducing the number of hospitalisations and trips to accident and emergency rooms [19].

Drones have been used to deliver medical supplies in the Dominican Republic [25].

5.3.2   Battling the Spread of Coronavirus

Aside from using drones being used to carry goods, many drones are also equipped with cameras, microphones and speakers and so can be used for monitoring and to both gather and deliver information. In this respect they will utilise existing functionality that has not necessarily been used in this way before.

An area of application where there is now immense potential for drone use lies with personal, health and environmental monitoring, enforcing social distancing, mapping, and spraying to disinfect. These are all ways where drones may help to reduce the spread of the corona virus. As drones typically carry cameras - whether RGB colour or thermal - they can be used both indoors and outdoors as a remote monitoring platform.

The growing use of custom-built drone platforms carrying thermal cameras to monitor heat loss from buildings, for firefighting applications, and is also being proposed (and has already been used) to help monitor the health of people where temperature can be used as an indicator of possible infection from the corona virus. The benefit of having an airborne platform is obviously that it is in the air, far from contacting humans and can still return accurate results [26].

In Canada, Draganfly is adapting scanning technology for drones to combine thermal imaging systems and a computer program with learning algorithms to monitor temperature, heart and respiratory rate at a distance to aid in the detection of someone sneezing or coughing, and can be used for screening [27].

This is basically an extension of the more traditional use of cameras for remote sensing of surfaces that provides imagery for automated or manual interpretation. Some commercial drones (e.g. the DJI Mavic Enterprise) also carry loudspeakers that can be used to communicate information to individuals on the ground with one application being the provision of messages to help enforce social distancing in public spaces. The use of drones to communicate information and messages can also be used in many other environmental monitoring or situation scenarios. Having a remote video platform that can both record and broadcast live is a much better alternative than putting someone at risk to film by hand. You also get a more holistic picture, and can easily document dangerous gatherings from a distance without having to get close to people who are violating the pandemic regulations.

The capability to carry a larger payload also allows drones to carry other materials and equipment. One example, which is an extension of the application of drones for spraying crops, is the use of drones to carry disinfectant and spray equipment to disinfect environmental locations or internal rooms. Cities have also been using Drones such as DJI's agricultural drones to spray disinfectant on an area, which is a lot more cost-efficient than employing a team of workers using expensive and equipment to spread disinfectant by hand on the ground [28, 29]. In Scotland, a UK company Droneports has recently demonstrated the capability of drones being used to support the NHS by delivering COVID-19 test kits and medical supplies to an island off the coast of the

Scottish mainland. The demonstration showed how supplies could be delivered more quickly to the island than the normal route used by road and ferry [30].

Similar trials, which are now being fast-tracked in light of the pandemic, have also been reported in other parts of the UK [31].

During the COVID-19 crisis, drones have already been used to deliver medication and test samples in other remote locations in Ghana, Rwanda, and Chile. In Charlotte, North Caroline, USA, drones have been used to deliver personal protective equipment and supplies to frontline medical teams. This initiative was part of the North Carolina Department of Transportation's (NCDOT's) Unmanned Aircraft System Integration Pilot Program (IPP).

Unmanned aerial vehicles have also been used in several cities around the world to monitor compliance with virus-related safety measures as well as to spray disinfectant e.g. in India and China [21]. China was in fact one of the first countries to use drones in response to COVID-19 and as early as February 2020, Antwork - part of the Japanese group Terra Drone - used a drone to transport test samples and medical supplies from a local hospital in Zhejiang province to a nearby disease control centre. In 2019, Antwork were the first urban drone delivery company to obtain a license from the Civil Aviation Administration of China (CAAC). Some of the benefits arising from this demonstration were that the transport time was halved, and this in turn was found to relieve stress on medical staff.

In April 2020, Manna Aero were approved by Ireland's aviation authority to deliver medication and critical supplies to roughly a dozen households under confinement. In Switzerland, Matternet - a US company - had already been cleared to carry out autonomous, beyond-the-line-of-sight flights for the transport of blood samples between hospitals in the city of Lugarno. Another US-based drone operator, Zipline supported Ghanaian authorities by providing a 'contactless drone delivery' service to collect Coronavirus test samples from 1000 rural health facilities and to deliver them to laboratories in Accra and Kumasi [32]. These are just a few of the practical demonstrations that have already been developed to highlight the potential of autonomous aerial technology to assist in emergencies.

Other mentioned uses of drones include the delivery of non-medical products such as groceries and other food supplies to people and communities, and to extend the already well-tried data acquisition role that they have been demonstrating in the field of mapping, which sees drones providing real time imagery for emergency response and near real time mapping. The extension of the mapping role to areas that have not been mapped at certain scales also has potential in the context of COVID-19.

(a) (b) (c)

FIGURE 5.1
a) A Quadcopter Drone Lifting a Bag (Billy J. Gregory - DroneLite); b) Monitoring urban areas during lockdown (Alex R. Karachok - UCEMM); c) A thermal camera image (Billy J. Gregory - DroneLite)

5.4   Summary and Conclusions

Drones began as recreational toys, a modern-day, updated radio-controlled model aircraft but with the added benefits provided by the evolution of the technology. Recognition of their potential for many commercial applications soon raised the public profile of drones and their many uses. However, various incidents with drones involved in injuries and near misses with civilian aircraft have somewhat dented the positive perception of drone technology with the public threatening to derail future growth of the market.

With the sudden and very significant impact of COVID-19 worldwide and the need for monitoring, mapping, and social distancing to minimise contact between people and to help reduce the spread of infections, robotic technologies were soon recognised as one way by which many aspects of the pandemic could be monitored and assisted. As a direct result of this, drone technology is gradually beginning to find growing support although it is still true to say that a number of issues are still a cause for concern.

The practical experience gained so far during the COVID-19 pandemic has been both stimulating and has undoubtedly paved the way for developments needed to make better use of drone applications in the future. Furthermore, lessons learned during the crisis and from examining the use-cases that have proved to be of societal benefit during the corona virus crisis will very likely encourage updates to drone regulations that go beyond the use of drones in times of crisis enabling the wider use of drone technologies in the future.

The ability to enhance the collection of up-to-date high resolution data over both space and time using drones (aerial, terrestrial, or waterborne) will provide a basis for more detailed information that can help emergency response and planning teams in the context of building community resilience frameworks in the future.

However, significant developments in the technology are still needed to overcome some of the public concerns and to allow drone applications to reach their full potential. This includes major advances in existing telecommunications, air traffic management systems, and regulations amongst a number of other things.

Being at a stage when we are now already able to successfully utilise and adapt current drone technology to conduct numerous activities safely and remotely has been very timely in light of the COVID-19 pandemic.

The progress made during this pandemic will undoubtedly help society to function more safely and more effectively during times of crisis in the future whereby drone technology will be able to provide the data and information needed to assist in an emergency response, whilst also being able to assist communities to build future resilience.

References

[1] MAPIR. Mapir cameras, 2020. URL https://www.mapir.camera/. Accessed on 27 September 2020.

[2] Parrot. Parrot drones sequoia camera, 2020. URL https://www.parrot.com/uk/shop/accessories-spare-parts/other-drones/sequoia. Accessed on 27 September 2020.

[3] MicaSense. Micasense rededge sensor, 2020. URL https://micasense.com/rededge-mx/. Accessed on 27 September 2020.

[4] Yuneec. Yuneec drones, 2020. URL https://www.yuneec.com. Accessed on 27 September 2020.

[5] DJI. Dji drones, 2020. URL https://www.dji.com. Accessed on 27 September 2020.

[6] Headwall Photonics. Headwall sensor drone integration, 2020. URL https://www.headwallphotonics.com/uav-integration. Accessed on 27 September 2020.

[7] Riegl. Riegl laser management systems, 2020. URL http://www.riegl.com/. Accessed on 27 September 2020.

[8] Riegl. Riegl bathycopter, 2020. URL http://www.riegl.com/products/unmanned-scanning/bathycopter/. Accessed on 27 September 2020.

[9] Li, CJ and Ling, H. Synthetic aperture radar imaging using a small consumer drone. In *International Symposium on Antennas and Propagation & USNC/URSI National Radio Science Meeting*, pages 3–9. IEEE, 2015.

[10] Scannapieco, AF, Renga, A, Fasano, G, and Moccia, A. Ultralight Radar for Small and Micro-UAV Navigation. In *International Archives of the Photogrammetry, Remote Sensing and Spatial Information Sciences, International Conference on Unmanned Aerial Vehicles in Geomatics*, volume XLII-2/W6, pages 333–338. IEEE, 2017.

[11] Ball, M. High-resolution sar imagery captured with small uas. unmanned systems technology, 2019. URL https://www.unmannedsystemstechnology.com/2019/02/high-resolution-sar-imagery-captured-with-small-uas/. Accessed on 27 September 2020.

[12] Unifly. Breakthrough in new type of battery for drones, 2020. URL https://www.unifly.aero/news/breakthrough-in-new-type-of-battery-for-drones. Accessed on 27 September 2020.

[13] Litchi. Litchi software, 2020. URL https://flylitchi.com/. Accessed on 27 September 2020.

[14] Pix4D. Pix4d software, 2020. URL https://www.pix4d.com/. Accessed on 27 September 2020.

[15] Abbott, J. Dji mavic air 2 review - the best drone around for beginners and hobbyists, 2020. URL https://www.techradar.com/uk/reviews/dji-mavic-air-2-review. Accessed on 27 September 2020.

[16] Everaerts, J. The Use of Unmanned Aerial Vehicles (UAVs) for Remote Sensing and Mapping. *Proceedings of The International Archives of the Photogrammetry, Remote Sensing and Spatial Information Sciences*, XXXVII Part B1:1187–1191, 2008.

[17] Skitmore, A. *Launch and Recovery System for Improved Fixed-Wing UAV Deployment in Complex Environments.* Unpublished Masters Thesis. Department of Maritime and Mechanical Engineering. Liverpool John Moores University, 2018.

[18] Skitmore, A. *Launch and Recovery System for Improved Fixed-Wing UAV Deployment in Complex Environments.* Chapter 18. In, Green, DR, Gregory, BJ, and Karachok, AR, 2020 (Eds.). Unmanned Aerial Remote Sensing: UAS for Environmental Applications, CRC Press. 324p, 2020.

[19] McKinsey & Company. Debate: Will delivery uavs scales by 2030, 2020. URL `https://www.mckinsey.com/industries/capital-projects-and-infrastructure/our-insights/debate-will-delivery-uavs-scale-by-2030`. Accessed on 27 September 2020.

[20] Ford, J. Skyports join 'beyond visual line of sight' uav trials, 2020. URL `https://www.theengineer.co.uk/skyports-bvlos-uav-caa-sandpit/`. Accessed on 27 September 2020.

[21] Wray, S. Cities should prepare for an increase in delivery drones, 2020. URL `https://cities-today.com/cities-should-prepare-for-an-increase-in-delivery-drones/`. Accessed on 27 September 2020.

[22] Amazon Prime Air. First prime air delivery, 2020. URL `https://www.amazon.com/Amazon-Prime-Air/b?ie=UTF8&node=8037720011`. Accessed on 27 September 2020.

[23] D'Sa, P. Drones will deliver covid-19 supplies to remote beausoleil first nation, 2020. URL `https://www.google.com/amp/s/m.huffingtonpost.ca/amp/entry/drone-covid-first-nation_ca_5edea533c5b6fd8a1a2912a0/`. Accessed on 27 September 2020.

[24] The Engineer. Covid-19 catalyst for commercial drone deliveries, 2020. URL `https://www.theengineer.co.uk/commercial-drone-deliveries-protolabs-report/`. Accessed on 27 September 2020.

[25] DJI. Dji - delivering the future of healthcare, 2020. URL `https://youtu.be/TnXySwo8g7M`. Accessed on 27 September 2020.

[26] Kiro7. Drones detecting body temperature being used in covid-19 response, 2020. URL `https://www.kiro7.com/news/local/drones-detecting-body-temperature-being-used-covid-19-response/CAGP3UM2IRCI7HMXPZMOL7OOXY/`. Accessed on 27 September 2020.

[27] Burke, D. New reality: a revolution in infectious disease testing could be just overhead, 2020. URL `https://www.cbc.ca/news/canada/nova-scotia/drones-covid-19-detection-computers-pandemic-technology-1.5534104`. Accessed on 27 September 2020.

[28] Reagan, J. Eaglehawk deploys disnfectant drones to sanitize facilities, 2020. URL `https://www.google.com/amp/s/dronelife.com/2020/05/05/disinfectant-drones-eaglehawk/amp/`. Accessed on 27 September 2020.

[29] Syracuse. Syracuse company develops coronavirus-killing drone for arenas and stadiums, 2020. URL `https://www.syracuse.com/coronavirus/2020/05/syracuse-company-develops-coronavirus-killing-drone-for-arenas-and-stadiums.html`. Accessed on 27 September 2020.

[30] Press Association 2020. Covid-19 test kit delivery drones receive funding boost, 2020. URL `https://www.eastlothiancourier.com/news/national-news/18573416.covid-19-test-kit-delivery-drones-receive-funding-boost`. Accessed on 27 September 2020.

[31] Mee, E. Drones will deliver medical supplies in trial, transport secretary says, 2020. URL `https://news.sky.com/story/coronavirus-drones-will-deliver-medical-supplies-in-trial-transport-secretary-says-11978376`. Accessed on 27 September 2020.

[32] International Transport Forum. Drones in the era of coronavirus, 2020. URL `https://www.itf-oecd.org/sites/default/files/drones-covid-19.pdf`. Accessed on 27 September 2020.

6

The Role of Neighbourhood Social and Built Environments on Social Interactions and Community Wellbeing Through the COVID-19 Pandemic

Piret Veeroja and Greg Foliente

This chapter looks at the role of social and built environments on social interactions in Melbourne prior to, and during, the COVID-19 pandemic and discuss possible social and built environment interventions to increase social interactions. Melbournians have experienced two COVID-19 waves of infection and two lockdowns since March 2020 and faced severe physical and social distancing restrictions. These have increased the importance of local amenities and neighbourhoods, but also the need and skills to use telecommunication services for different social (and work related) purposes. Lockdown periods provide an opportunity to upskill peoples' technical skills that can be used after the pandemic to access more resources and create balance between online and face-to-face social environments. Possibilities in urban planning to repurpose the built environment and use technology to utilise local neighbourhoods are discussed. These proposed changes in social and built environments may be beneficial in dealing with future pandemics.

6.1 Introduction

Studies show that social interactions improve people's wellbeing, satisfaction with life [1], happiness [1], mental health [2], physical health [3], longevity [4] and reduce psychological distress such as anxiety [5, 6]. Social interactions contribute to increased sense of purpose, belonging and self-worth [2, 7]. These kinds of contributions motivate people and encourage them to take better care of themselves (e.g. to engage in physical activity or reduce alcohol intake) which lead to improved mental health [2]. Lack of social interactions, on the other hand, has been found to reduce quality of life, wellbeing, mood ([8, 9] and health outcomes (such as insomnia, depression, dementia and suicide) and increase unhealthy behaviours (such as smoking, drinking alcohol, having unhealthy diet) [10].

As soon as the World Health Organisation (WHO) [11] announced that COVID-19 is a public health emergency of international concern, in response, many countries imposed restrictions such as social distancing, isolation and stay-at-home requirements. These types of restrictions may lead to loneliness and boredom [12]. Social isolation is opposite to social connectedness and has found to be related to psychological distress, such as anxiety [6, 13], depression, stress [6, 13] and loneliness [13]. Indeed, quarantine during the SARS outbreak in 2003 ([14], as cited in [13]) and the swine flu outbreak in 2009 ([15], as cited in [13]) was associated with increased depression and anxiety. Tull et al. [13] studied stay-at home restrictions and daily changed routines due to COVID-19 pandemic with mental health outcomes (n=500) in the United States. They concluded that the restrictions were associated with health related anxiety, financial worry and loneliness. Smith et al. [6] investigated the relationship between social isolation and mental health outcomes during COVID-19 pandemic (n=278) in the Unites States. They found statistical relationships between the two and concluded that higher psychological flexibility and ability to accept difficult experiences helped to reduce the negative effects of social isolation [6].

Social capital, which is formed by strong and weak social networks, is found to be necessary in effective crisis response and recovery [16]. McCrea et al. [17] found that social and amenity dimensions were the main contributors of community wellbeing, that in turn, contributed towards community resilience. Communities with higher level of social capital, for example, were found to recover faster and in a more satisfactory and sustainable fashion from earthquakes than communities with lower social capital levels [16, 18].

This chapter aims to look at the role of social and built environments on social interactions in Melbourne prior to, and during, the COVID-19 pandemic and discuss about possible social and built environment interventions during and after the pandemic to increase social interactions. The discussions follow the main phases of COVID-19, as shown in Figure 6.1 for Victoria, Australia.

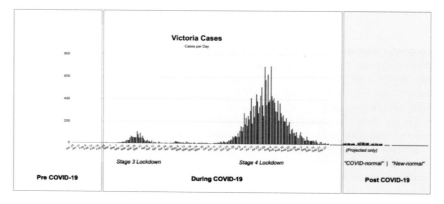

FIGURE 6.1
The Main Phases of COVID-19 Cases in the State of Victoria, Australia (Main data plot from: https://www.dhhs.vic.gov.au/victorian-coronavirus-covid-19-data)

6.2   Pre COVID-19

A previous study found that perceived social environment and especially feeling of belonging, sense of community and participation in community activities were more important to older Melbournians' (aged 55 years or above, n=476) local social interactions frequency than perceived and objective built environment measures [19]. Additionally, the importance of some types of perceived destinations for local social interactions were distinguished, such as cafes, bars and restaurants and footpaths. Looking at local social interaction satisfaction, the results were similar. Social interactions frequency, feeling of belonging and sense of community were social environment elements that contributed to older adults' local social interactions satisfaction. Perceived importance of local services for social interactions, however had a negative relationship with social interactions satisfaction [19].

Socioemotional selectivity theory explains that peoples' social networks are changing over time [20]. Younger people's social interactions are claimed to be future-oriented with the aim of gaining information, experiences and new social contacts [21]. Older people, on the other hand, have been found to prefer smaller, but emotionally meaningful and satisfying contacts [21]. It is thus expected that the importance of social and built environments in social interactions frequency and satisfaction is different in different age groups. Therefore, a follow up study that included younger, middle aged and older Melburnians were carried out. Surprisingly, the study reached similar conclusions across different age groups [22].

6.3 During COVID-19

6.3.1 Social and Physical Distancing Restrictions in Melbourne

The Victorian premier announced a State of Emergency in mid-March 2020, and on 30 March, Victoria entered a Stage 3 lockdown (see Figure 6.1). This meant that Victorians had only four reasons to leave home: shopping for food and supplies, (essential) work or education, exercising or caregiving. Restaurants, bars and coffees were allowed to be open for take-away only; beauty, personal services, entertainment, culture and sporting venues were closed. These restrictions started to ease in the beginning of June. Shortly after the ease of restrictions, the number of COVID-19 cases rose and in the beginning of August Victoria entered a Stage 4 lockdown (Figure 6.1). Additional social and physical distancing measures were introduced in this stage: curfew from 8PM–5AM (unless seeking or giving care or essential work), Victorians were allowed to shop (once a day, one person per household) and exercise one hour per day (maximum two people) in 5 km radius from their home. By the time of writing this chapter, Regional Victoria has entered to Stage 3 lockdown and some of the Stage 4 restrictions have eased for Metropolitan Melbourne (e.g. curfew is lifted) [23].

Previous studies have found that destinations (such as parks and nature strips, shops, services, cafes/bars/restaurants and community places) encourage peoples' local social interactions [24–26]. The Stage 3 and Stage 4 restrictions in Metropolitan Melbourne (and in the rest of the Victoria) have increased the importance of local destinations (especially after applying the five-km rule). People are more than ever dependent on their neighbourhoods and presence of local amenities. For instance, inhabitants who live in a close proximity to a park (or any other type of natural environment) or are able to access footpaths that are continuous and have even surface may be better off in terms of physical and mental health than those who are not able to access these types of amenities.

6.3.2 Social Interactions During the Pandemic

The COVID-19 pandemic may have adverse personal impacts, such as worrying about catching the virus, experiencing partial or full loss of income, worrying about job or housing security, uncertainty, home schooling, increased risk of family violence, and other mental, physical and social pressures caused by the lockdown and the resulting isolation. All these factors combined can lead to mental health crisis that in turn may lead to long-term problems in wellbeing, productivity and healthcare costs [27]. Social contact and support from family and friends and community are especially important in times like these. In May 2020, the United Nations (UN) warned that the COVID-19 might turn into mental health crisis [28] and reported an increase in levels of distress that causes misery due to the COVID-19 virus and emphasised the importance of the international community to support peoples' mental health during the pandemic [29]. A study of three cities in different countries in Latin America (n=650) found that about one third of the participants missed face-to-face social interactions the most, when asked about the activities people miss due to the COVID-19 restrictions [30].

Fisher et al. [31] found that about a quarter of Australians experienced mild to moderate depressive symptoms or anxiety on the first month of COVID-19 restrictions. In 2020, there has been 66% increase in lifeline support calls compared to the previous year and two third of the calls were made by Victorians [32]. Alfred Hospital Crisis Assessment and Treatment Team have faced 50% increase in callouts after the first lockdown in March 2020 [33].

The Australian Government has provided an additional $500 million in mental health and suicide prevention funding to assist in coping with the COVID-19 pandemic since January 2020. The Government provides several free-of-charge or low-cost telephone and telehealth services, such as Lifeline, Kids Helpline, Beyond Blue, Suicide Call-Back Service, MensLine Australia, Open Arms – Veterans and Families counselling, and HeadtoHealth services for Victorians. Citizens and permanent residents can access 10 additional subsidised psychological sessions to face mental issues caused by the pandemic. For older Australians, the Government has established the Older Persons COVID-19 Support Line (phone support) and Community Visitors Scheme (telephone or online). The latter connects older adults with volunteers who spend time with them during the pandemic; but face-to-face visits are replaced with telephone or online contacts [23].

Direct face-to-face social interactions and the use of neighbourhood social and built environments (and amenities) were minimised during the first lockdown and further restricted during the second lockdown in Melbourne (Figure 6.1). During the second lockdown, the majority of Melbournians were allowed to have face-to-face contacts with people from their own households (and other neighbourhood contacts such as when grocery shopping or ordering take-away coffee when adhering social and physical distancing rules). Therefore, the importance of virtual social environment was more important than ever before.

Telehealth services, however, can only be accessed when people have the ability and opportunity to use the technologies. The less skilled Internet users may become increasingly disconnected from the society and miss out on the digital support sources [34]. More than 2.5 million Australians are not online [35]. Digital inclusion requires access to high quality and affordable Internet service, hardware and sufficient data allowance, and ability and skills to use the technology. The Australian Digital Inclusion Index [36] shows, for example, that Australians with lower income, education, and employment levels; and adults aged 65 years or older are less digitally included [35]. Moreover, about 2.7 million (34%) Australians aged 50 years or older have low digital skills or they don' t use the technology or the Internet [36]. More than half (57%) of people aged 70 years or older have low digital skills and 74% of them do not use the Internet [36].

Gorenko et al. [37] recommended considering older adults' (and other socio-demographic groups) personal preferred remote communication methods and pre-pandemic technological literacy skills when providing interventions and improving technology using skills. These could include using technology that older adults are comfortable with (e.g. telephone), providing print materials with instructions, reminders and tips, and/or involving a household member or caretaker to explain/help to set up, use and/or troubleshoot the technology [37].

The internet, social media and other mobile applications are replacing traditional media and have both positive and negative effects [38]. The use of social media and the Internet may contribute to 'infodemic', which is information overload [12]. Banerjee and Rai [12] for example, describe COVID-19 as 'digital epidemic' where all sorts of information (including false information) about the virus travels faster than the virus itself. They recommend practicing social media distancing [12]. This means that while it is crucial to increase technical literacy in different age and demographic groups, then it is necessary to include information about where to find and how to control reliability of information/sources and understand the ethics or values underpinning specific artificial intelligence (AI) applications.

Another way to increase peoples' social interactions during the pandemic could be to set up virtual physical health programs that accommodate for different physical abilities and help people to stay active; provide online courses and classes; encourage volunteering in different programs [36, 39] or send out letters and greeting cards for those who are not technologically advanced [36, 39]. Mariana Atkins and Baldassar [36] proposed to establish a buddy system where (older) adults can regularly check in and communicate with volunteers, or those with good technological literacy skills can help to set up and teach others' who are less skilled. This sort of volunteering enables people to feel they are helping others and may help to reduce their own feeling of isolation [39]. Office et al. [40], for example, investigated a phone outreach program (n=14 volunteers, 25 calls) where medical students called to older Americans during the COVID-19 pandemic. The volunteers described the calls as impactful for the students and call recipients [40]. Community and religious groups could set up regular online/telephone meetings to share information and explain it, give health and mobility tips [36].

Gehl [41] observed changes in using public spaces during the pandemic in Denmark. They found that downtown activities were dropped, but the use of public spaces is similar as before the pandemic and places that offer activities (e.g. playgrounds) were used more than ever before [41]. This differs from the Melbourne context, because the use of public spaces (e.g. playgrounds, benches) was restricted. After easing some of the restrictions, small groups of people were allowed to have picnics in Melbourne. Inspired by the New York 'social distancing circles', similar circles were drawn on the grounds of some popular parks in Melbourne, so the groups who use the park are able to stay further than 1.5m from other groups [42].

6.4   Post COVID-19

It is important to learn from the current pandemic and keep upskilling peoples' technological literacy and provide access to sufficient and affordable technology. This helps to ensure that people are able to access virtual social environment if the COVID-19 virus lingers on in the community or a similar situation occurs again in the future. Virtual social environment does not replace face-to-face community social interactions, but it may open an opportunity for members of society to be more effective, knowledgeable, resourceful and participatory in events that happen in physically distant locations. Some scholars propose that partially transforming to telehealth (e.g. mental and physical health issues, support group meetings for substance users, therapy sessions with councillors, outpatient programs, medication management programs) may be beneficial for patients and clinicians [27]. The future community social interactions may be a combination of face-to-face community social environment and virtual social environments (more accessible than it was before the pandemic). A future study could investigate the best ways to balance these modes of communication to ensure the best health and wellbeing outcomes.

Florida et al. [43] argued that historically, pandemics (e.g. Hispanic flue, plague) have always spread in cities (New York, London, Paris) and discussed about the ability of cities to bounce back after the virus. He argued that vulnerable people and families may be moving to suburbs, but cities will attract job seekers with higher number of jobs and salaries, and with more affordable rents than before the pandemic [43]. Joel Kotkin [43] added that cities may need to change crowded public transport with safer options (such as utilising autonomous vehicles), and it is critical to develop suburbs that produce lower emissions, provide working-from home opportunities, and lower commuting times. The provision of a metro-wide network of dedicated bicycle lanes has also attracted the attention/interest of many urban stakeholders.

The importance of the built physical environment may increase after the pandemic, and it might have a huge role to play in adjusting to the new 'COVID-19 normal' environment (Figure 6.1). Since the beginning of the pandemic, people have been asked to physically distance themselves from others. This means that urban planners need to think how to increase the amenities and infrastructure and decrease car-dependence [44]. Some urban planners and architects, however, see the opportunity in reduced use of city spaces due to COVID-19. This situation could be a turning point in how we use and think about cities. Jonathan et al. [45] see it as an opportunity to repurpose city streets for people to promote walking and cycling and create safe and attractive streets and cities or to convert street parking lots to places for street socialising. The restrictions have also further encouraged and strengthened discussions around 20-minute/15-minute cities. The concept has been proposed in Plan Melbourne [46]. These concepts refer to an idea that cities are polycentric and residents are able to access everything they need (e.g. employment, education, shopping, recreation) within 20 (or 15) minute walk, bike ride or via safe public transport from their home [47]. This sort of development, however, may mean more high-rise buildings in the areas, which may not be desirable in the future when planning for pandemic, as inhabitants would need to share lifts and common areas [48].

Chen et al. [49] propose that robotics (drones, driverless vehicles and service robots) and AI may be more useful than ever before. They concluded that facial-recognition software may offer new ways for aerial, ground and checkpoint territorial control, while admitting the possible problems with public safety, privacy and control [49]. Autonomous goods deliveries, drone transports, access to places via QR (or similar) codes and biometric screening to identify residents with high temperatures may be future solutions in urban environments if a similar pandemic occurs [49]. But these technologies require strong social acceptance and robust regulatory frameworks.

6.5   Concluding Comments

Social interactions with family, friends and the broader community are especially important for positive mental health outcomes, personal and community wellbeing during a pandemic. The use of social and built environments (and especially local destinations and amenities) have changed due to the COVID-19 pandemic. Telephone and Internet services are crucial to provide satisfying social environment, maintain social relationships with family, friends and community, and exchange information during these times. People with low income, education and employment levels and older adults, however, may not have enough means and/or skills to access these. Targeted or alternative solutions are needed, such as upskilling these societal groups to use the technology and provide affordable access to the Internet and technology during and post pandemic times. Finally, it is important to consider possibilities to repurpose and/or adapt existing built environment, better plan new ones and introduce more accessible technological innovations. Improved social and built environments may function as an opportunity for urban neighbourhood communities to recover faster via building local social capital and improved resilience when dealing with future pandemics.

References

[1] J. F. Helliwell and R. D. Putnam. The social context of well-being. *Philosophical Transactions of the Royal Society of London Series B-Biological Sciences*, 359(1449):1435–46, 2004. doi: 10.1098/rstb.2004.1522.

[2] Ichiro Kawachi and Lisa F Berkman. Social ties and mental health. *Journal of Urban health*, 78(3):458–467, 2001.

[3] Julia Sander, Jürgen Schupp, and David Richter. Getting together: Social contact frequency across the life span. *Developmental Psychology*, 53(8):1571, 2017.

[4] Eran Shor and David J Roelfs. Social contact frequency and all-cause mortality: A meta-analysis and meta-regression. *Social Science & Medicine*, 128:76–86, 2015.

[5] L. Gibbs. Promoting resilience while preventing disease transmission: An Australian COVID-19 study. In A. Rajabifard, D. Páez, I. Britton, & G. Foliente (Eds.), *Pandemics Geospatial Information and Community Resilience*. 2020.

[6] Brooke M Smith, Alexander J Twohy, and Gregory S Smith. Psychological inflexibility and intolerance of uncertainty moderate the relationship between social isolation and mental health outcomes during COVID-19. *Journal of Contextual Behavioral Science*, 2020. doi: https://doi.org/10.1016/j.jcbs.2020.09.005.

[7] Sheldon Cohen, Lynn G Underwood, and Benjamin H Gottlieb. *Social support measurement and intervention: A guide for health and social scientists*. Oxford University Press, 2000.

[8] J. T. Cacioppo, L. C. Hawkley, and R. A. Thisted. Perceived social isolation makes me sad: 5-year cross-lagged analyses of loneliness and depressive symptomatology in the Chicago Health, Aging, and Social Relations Study. *Psychology and Aging*, 25(2): 453–463. doi: 10.1037/a0017216.

[9] Jeannette Golden, Ronán M Conroy, Irene Bruce, Aisling Denihan, Elaine Greene, Michael Kirby, and Brian A Lawlor. Loneliness, social support networks, mood and wellbeing in community-dwelling elderly. *International Journal of Geriatric Psychiatry*, 24(7):694–700, 2009. doi: 10.1002/gps.2181.

[10] Kimberly A Van Orden, Emily Bower, Julie Lutz, Caroline Silva, Autumn M Gallegos, Carol A Podgorski, Elizabeth J Santos, and Yeates Conwell. Strategies to Promote Social Connections Among Older Adults During 'Social Distancing'Restrictions. *The American Journal of Geriatric Psychiatry*, 2020. doi: https://doi.org/10.1016/j.jagp.2020.05.004.

[11] World Health Organisation. WHO Director-General's statement on IHR Emergency Committee on Novel Coronavirus (2019-nCoV). 2020. URL https://www.who.int/dg/speeches/detail/who-director-general-s-statement-on-ihr-emergency-committee-on-novel-coronavirus-(2019-ncov).

[12] Debanjan Banerjee and Mayank Rai. Social isolation in Covid-19: The impact of loneliness. *International Journal of Social Psychiatry*, 66(6): 525-527, 2020. doi: 10.1177/0020764020922269.

[13] Matthew T Tull, Keith A Edmonds, Kayla Scamaldo, Julia R Richmond, Jason P Rose, and Kim L Gratz. Psychological outcomes associated with stay-at-home orders and the perceived impact of covid-19 on daily life. *Psychiatry research*, pages 289, 113098, 2020. doi: https://doi.org/10.1016/j.psychres.2020.113098.

[14] L. Hawryluck, W. L. Gold, S. Robinson, S. Pogorski, S. Galea, and R. Styra. SARS control and psychological effects of quarantine, Toronto, Canada. *Emerging Infectious Diseases*, 10(7): 1206-1212, 2004. doi: 10.3201/eid1007.030703.

[15] Michael G Wheaton, Jonathan S Abramowitz, Noah C Berman, Laura E Fabricant, and Bunmi O Olatunji. Psychological predictors of anxiety in response to the H1N1 (swine flu) pandemic. *Cognitive Therapy and Research*, 36(3):210–218, 2012. doi: 10.1007/s10608-011-9353-3.

[16] Nicholas Pitas and Colin Ehmer. Social capital in the response to covid-19. *American Journal of Health Promotion*, 0(0), page 0890117120924531, 2020. doi: 10.1177/0890117120924531.

[17] R. McCrea, A. Walton, and R. Leonard. Developing a model of community wellbeing and resilience in response to change. *Social Indicators Research*, 129(1), 195-214, 2016.

[18] D. P. Aldrich. Building resilience: Social capital in post-disaster recovery. *University of Chicago Press*, 2012.

[19] P. Veeroja. The role of social and built environments in supporting older adults social interaction (Doctorial dissertation). *The University of Melbourne*, 2019.

[20] Laura L Carstensen, Derek M Isaacowitz, and Susan T Charles. Taking time seriously: A theory of socioemotional selectivity. *American Psychologist*, 54(3):165, 1999.

[21] Kevin B Wright and Brian R Patterson. Socioemotional selectivity theory and the macrodynamics of friendship: The role of friendship style and communication in friendship across the lifespan. *Communication Research Reports*, 23(3):163–170, 2006.

[22] P. Veeroja, G. Foliente, R. McCrea, H. Badland, C. Pettit, and J. Day. How neighbourhood social and built environments influence social interactions: Differences between life stages. In R.W. Marans, R. Stimson, & N. Webster (Eds.), *Handbook of Quality of Life Research: Place and Space Perspectives*. Northampton, MA, USA (submitted, under review): Edward Elgar Publishing Inc.

[23] Department of Health and Human Services. Coronavirus (COVID-19) resources for the general public. 2020. URL https://www.health.gov.au/resources/collections/novel-coronavirus-2019-ncov-resources.

[24] Paula J Gardner. Natural neighborhood networks—Important social networks in the lives of older adults aging in place. *Journal of aging studies*, 25(3):263–271, 2011. doi: https://doi.org/10.1016/j.jaging.2011.03.007.

[25] Paul Hickman. "Third places" and social interaction in deprived neighbourhoods in Great Britain. *Journal of Housing and the Built Environment*, 28(2):221–236, 2013. doi: 10.1007/s10901-012-9306-5.

[26] H. J. Lee. Older adults third places and perceived social connectedness. (Doctor of Philosophy). *Texas A&M University*, 2015. URL http://oaktrust.library.tamu.edu/bitstream/handle/1969.1/155291/LEE-DISSERTATION-2015.pdf?sequence=1.

[27] S. Noori and I. Rosenthal. Mental Health after COVID-19. In the wake of the pandemic, there will be an even greater need for help in the face of loss, isolation and trauma. *Scientific American*, 2020. URL https://www.scientificamerican.com/article/mental-health-after-covid-19/.

[28] United Nations. Policy Brief: COVID-19 and the Need for Action on Mental Health. 2020. URL https://www.un.org/sites/un2.un.org/files/un_policy_brief-covid_and_mental_health_final.pdf.

[29] United Nations. N leads call to protect most vulnerable from mental health crisis during and after COVID-19. 2020. URL https://news.un.org/en/story/2020/05/1063882.

[30] R. Marino, E. Vargas, and M. Flores. Impacts of COVID-19 lockdown restrictions on housing and public space use and adaptation: Urban proximity, public health, and vulnerability in three Latin American cities. In A. Rajabifard, D. Páez, I. Britton, & G. Foliente (Eds.), COVID – 19. *Geospatial Information and Community Resilience*. Taylor & Francis Group, 2020.

[31] Jane RW Fisher, Thach Duc Tran, Karin Hammarberg, Jayagowri Sastry, Hau Nguyen, Heather Rowe, Sally Popplestone, Ruby Stocker, Claire Stubber, and Maggie Kirkman. Mental health of people in australia in the first month of covid-19 restrictions: a national survey. *The Medical Journal of Australia*, page 1, 2020.

[32] J. Blakkarly. With Melbourne under lockdown and the Victorian government announcing much-needed funding for mental health services, we asked your questions about what support is actually available. *SBS News*, 2020. URL https://www.sbs.com.au/news/we-put-your-questions-about-mental-health-support-during-the-pandemic-to-the-experts.

[33] J. Longbottom. On the frontline with a mental health emergency team as they respond to the dark reality of the coronavirus crisis. *ABC News*, 2020. URL https://www.abc.net.au/news/2020-07-05/coronavirus-mental-health-crisis-response-team-during-covid-19/12402370.

[34] Minh Hao Nguyen, Jonathan Gruber, Jaelle Fuchs, Will Marler, Amanda Hunsaker, and Eszter Hargittai. Changes in Digital Communication During the COVID-19 Global Pandemic: Implications for Digital Inequality and Future Research. *Social Media+ Society*, 6(3):2056305120948255, 2020. doi: 10.1177/2056305120948255.

[35] J. Barraket and C. Wilson. Digital inclusion and COVID-19. *CSI Response*, 2020. URL https://www.csi.edu.au/media/uploads/csi-covid_factsheet_digitalinclusion.pdf.

[36] L Atkins, & Baldassar. COVID-19, social isolation and ageing. CSI Response. 2020. URL https://www.csi.edu.au/media/uploads/csi_fact_sheet_social_covid-19_social_isolation_and_ageing.pdf.

[37] Julie A Gorenko, Chelsea Moran, Michelle Flynn, Keith Dobson, and Candace Konnert. Social Isolation and Psychological Distress Among Older Adults Related to COVID-19: A Narrative Review of Remotely-Delivered Interventions and Recommendations. *Journal of Applied Gerontology*, page 0733464820958550, 2020. doi: 10.1177/0733464820958550.

[38] Creighton Connolly, S Harris Ali, and Roger Keil. On the relationships between covid-19 and extended urbanization. *Dialogues in Human Geography*, 10(2):213–216, 2020. doi: 10.1177/2043820620934209.

[39] Annie T Chen, Shaoqing Ge, Susie Cho, Andrew K Teng, Frances Chu, George Demiris, and Oleg Zaslavsky. Reactions to covid-19, information and technology use, and social connectedness among older adults with pre-frailty and frailty. *Geriatric nursing (New York, N.Y.)*, *S0197-4572(0120)30245-30247*, 2020. doi: 10.1016/j.gerinurse.2020.08.001.

[40] Marissa S Rodenstein, Tazim S Merchant, Tricia Rae Pendergrast, Lee A Lindquist, et al. Reducing Social Isolation of Seniors during COVID-19 through Medical Student Telephone Contact. *Journal of the American Medical Directors Association*, 21(7):948–950, 2020. URL https://doi.org/10.1016/j.jamda.2020.06.003.

[41] J. Gehl. Public Space & Public Life during COVID 19. 2020. URL https://covid19.gehlpeople.com/files/report.pdf.

[42] R. Russo. Social circles have been drawn in this Melbourne park to help with social distancing. *Timeout*, 2020. URL https://www.timeout.com/melbourne/news/social-circles-have-been-drawn-in-this-melbourne-park-to-help-with-social-distancing-093020.

[43] R. Florida, E. Glaeser, M. M. Sharif, K. Bedi, T. J. Campanella, C. H. Chee, and J. . . . Sadik-Khan. How Life in Our Cities Will Look After the Coronavirus Pandemic. *Foreign Policy*, 2020. URL https://foreignpolicy.com/2020/05/01/future-of-cities-urban-life-after-coronavirus-pandemic/.

[44] B. Michael, F. Geoffrey, H. Jim, S. Mike, T. Steve, C. Maxine, and P. . . . Stephen. Growing Pains. The Crisis in Growth Area Planning. 2020. URL https://www.charter29.com/s/Charter-29-Report-200904-as-printed-and-mailed.pdf.

[45] D. Jonathan, D. Kim, and S. Quentin. We can't let coronavirus kill our cities. Here's how we can save urban life. 2020. URL https://www.architectureanddesign.com.au/features/features-articles/we-can-t-let-coronavirus-kill-our-cities#.

[46] Victoria State Government. Plan Melbourne 2017-2050. 2017. URL http://www.planmelbourne.vic.gov.au/.

[47] D. L. Boucher. Local Living, Rise of 20 Minute Cities Post-Covid. 2020. URL https://theurbandeveloper.com/articles/local-living-rise-of-20-minute-cities-post-covid.

[48] B. Hall. 'Generational catastrophe': How COVID-19 could reshape Melbourne. 2020. URL https://www.theage.com.au/national/victoria/generational-catastrophe-how-covid-19-could-reshape-melbourne-20200715-p55c7b.html.

[49] B. Chen, S. Marvin, and A. While. Containing COVID-19 in China: AI and the robotic restructuring of future cities. *Dialogues in Human Geography*, 10(2): 238–241, 2020. doi: 10.1177/2043820620934267.

7

Social Vulnerability to COVID-19: Preliminary Indicators and Research Agenda

Farhad Laylavi

Disease outbreaks and epidemics, similar to natural hazards, affect different socioeconomic groups in different ways. Understanding the varying degrees of vulnerability across socioeconomic groups, commonly referred to as social vulnerability, can lead to enhanced decision making and better resource allocation in a pandemic situation like COVID-19. This chapter reports on a study which aims to contextualise social vulnerability to pandemic situations in the wake of the COVID-19 pandemic. By building upon the existing literature and novel observations made during the pandemic, the study attempts to identify the preliminary indicators of social vulnerability to pandemics. Consequently, three main components of social vulnerability to pandemics are identified: societal determinants, built environment determinants, and individual characteristics. The latter two are discussed in detail. The chapter ends with a discussion of the implications and limitations of the study and outlines a research agenda for further work.

7.1 Introduction

Though not as frequent as natural hazards, disease outbreaks and epidemics do occur and leave behind a trail of death, destruction, and devastation. In that sense, epidemics can be thought of as natural hazards, posing public health threats and causing emergencies in the same way as earthquakes or hurricanes [1]. However, biological hazards and pandemics seem to recognise no boundaries, no particular groups, and no exceptions. Pandemics, as evidenced by the recent COVID-19 outbreak, lead to significant and long-lasting disruptive and traumatic consequences of a different nature, dynamic, and severity, compared to those of non-biological hazards. For instance, while disasters such as earthquakes and floods can inflict substantial immediate loss of life and harm the economy, mainly due to physical and infrastructural damage, epidemics cause no direct physical damage to structures or property. Instead, they pose enormous threats to humanity in terms of public health, morbidity, and mortality, as well as multifaceted socioeconomic losses due to the resultant confinement, social isolation, and suspension of economic activities.

Like natural hazards and environmental shocks, epidemics are likely to affect various demographic groups disproportionately. Lessons learned from past disasters around the world demonstrate that one's personal, social, and contextual attributes play an essential role in how one prepares for, responds to, and recovers from hazards and disasters [2–4]. The notion that the same disaster is experienced in different ways by different socioeconomic and demographic groups is generally regarded in the disaster literature as "social vulnerability" [5–7]. The development of methods and indicators to identify groups that are more susceptible to complications from health pandemics can result in better prioritisation of the response strategies, and effective resource allocation by the government and health authorities.

While the use of the term "social vulnerability" in the scientific literature can be traced back to the 1970s (e.g. [8]), it was after the mid-1990s that the concept came to be widely used in the disaster management domain [3, 5, 9]. This means that most of the systematic attempts to conceptualise, define, and measure social vulnerability in a disaster context are relatively new in many ways and are still in their conceptual or methodological adolescence. Moreover, the vast majority of the studies conducted in this area are primarily concerned with social vulnerability to natural and environmental hazards, and, to the best of the author's knowledge, little systematic attention has been paid to the assessment of social vulnerability to disease outbreaks and epidemics.

This chapter, first and foremost, intends to contextualise social vulnerability to pandemic situations in the wake of the COVID-19 crisis. To achieve this, Section 7.2 sets the scene and provides the context for social vulnerability relating to pandemics and disease outbreaks. Section 7.3 identifies preliminary indicators of social vulnerability to pandemics. Finally, implications, limitations, and an agenda for further research are discussed in Section 7.4.

7.2   Social Vulnerability and Pandemics

The scientific use of the term "vulnerability" draws its roots from geography and natural hazards literature, but it is also used in different fields, referring to diverse settings and situations [10]. "Vulnerability", in general, refers to susceptibility to threat scenarios, which can manifest itself in various ways, such as harm, powerlessness, and marginality of both physical and social systems [11, 12]. The available literature suggests that vulnerability is a broad and multifaceted concept encompassing an array of causes and contexts, such as physical, social, economic, political, and environmental.

The multi-dimensional nature of the concept of vulnerability is widely recognised and endorsed by the United Nations Office for Disaster Risk Reduction (UNDRR), where social, economic, and infrastructural vulnerabilities are considered as the constituent dimensions of the vulnerability of a specific region to hazards [13, 14]. According to UNDRR [14], infrastructural vulnerability refers to the basic infrastructures required for the production of goods and sustainability of livelihoods; economic vulnerability is associated with the economic status of individuals and communities, and social vulnerability accounts for the inability of people and society to cope with, or recover from, the devastating impacts of disasters.

Social vulnerability, among other types of vulnerability, is relatively more challenging to observe, define, and quantify [15–17]. This explains why socially created vulnerabilities are ignored or overlooked in both emergency decision-making and loss estimation reports in favour of more quantifiable factors such as human casualties and property loss [6]. The complexity surrounding the social dimension becomes even more significant during health crises like the COVID-19 pandemic. During pandemics, high levels of uncertainty and novel problems, coupled with environment-specific factors, lead to greater social, economic, and environmental complexity [18]. These all point to a need to adapt social vulnerabilities in the pandemic's context and recognise their role in coping and resource management strategies.

Although social vulnerability to pandemics has not been fully characterised, the reports from previous pandemics in 1918 and 2009 imply a link between socioeconomic factors and pandemic outcomes [19–21]. During the 1918 influenza pandemic, mortality rates in high-income countries were relatively lower than those in low-income countries. For example, in country-level analyses, the mortality rate in India was 40 times higher than in Denmark [22], and the mortality rates in some Central and South American countries were up to 20 times higher than in European countries [23].

Similar results were also found at city and community levels. Studies on the 1918 pandemic detected a considerable link between disease transmissibility and population density, illiteracy, and unemployment in Chicago [24]. Likewise, Rutter et al. [25] found an association between deprivation and the mortality rate for the 1918 pandemic in England. The results of these studies show that marginalised and disadvantaged social groups may be at greater risk from disease outbreaks. Thus, the explicit identification of populations vulnerable to disease outbreaks can be of great use in devoting attention to the groups most at risk during pandemics and their aftermath. Such a precise identification can be determined through the empirical analysis of precise indicators and variables.

The next section of this chapter is devoted to social vulnerability indicators in the context of the COVID-19 pandemic.

7.3 Social Vulnerability Indicators

Herein, social vulnerability refers to the combinations of social, cultural, economic, political, and institutional factors that account for the inability of society to cope with or withstand the impact of disasters and large-scale crises [14, 26]. There is broad agreement over the key defining factors of social vulnerability itself. Examples of such factors include [5–7, 11, 27–29]:

- poverty and economic marginalisation,

- lack of, or limited access to, resources and lifelines,

- ethnic and language minorities,

- community connectedness,

- household structure and housing conditions, and

- age and general health status.

However, as Cutter et al. [6] and Kuhlicke et al. [30] have also pointed out, there are discrepancies in specific indicators and variables representing the broader factors and the techniques used for the quantification of social vulnerability.

Despite disagreements over the indicators and variables, quantitative and statistical methods are widely used in the quantification of social vulnerabilities. Two examples are the Social Vulnerability Index (SoVI) developed in 2003 at the University of South Carolina, and the Social Vulnerability Index (SVI) developed in 2011 at the US Centres for Disease Control and Prevention (CDC). The SoVI is a place-specific and quantitative method which provides an empirically-based comparative tool to measure the capacity of social groups to cope with or recover from environmental hazards [6]. The SVI is also a well-recognised approach to facilitate the location-based quantification and comparison of social vulnerabilities to disasters [7]. Quantitative methods similar to SoVI and SVI focus on the identification of social vulnerability components associated with the specific context of the study. They then apply location-based and statistical models to the census data or other available information corresponding to the identified components.

Thus, the identification of the components of social vulnerability relating to COVID-19 could be considered as the first step towards formulating a reliable model. The rest of this chapter will be concerned with this step. Meaningful and relevant indicators are the building blocks of quantitative and empirical analysis. This study aims to identify the key social vulnerability indicators in the COVID-19 pandemic context. First of all, the preliminary indicators will be extracted from the literature or the author's observations and research during the development of the COVID-19 situation in Australia. After that, the proposed indicators will be assessed and validated by a group of emergency management and public safety experts.

It seems that COVID-19 related vulnerabilities generally arise from both the viral infection itself and the response measures, such as restrictions on the movement of people, business closures, and the subsequent economic downturn. The elderly population and people with underlying medical conditions are at higher risk if they are infected with the COVID-19 virus[1] [31]. However, the entire community appears to be more impacted by the indirect effects of COVID-19, namely, the response measures and their negative well-being and socioeconomic outcomes. To simplify the concept, this chapter will explore social vulnerability to COVID-19 as a whole without differentiating between the direct and indirect impacts of COVID-19.

Building upon the previous literature (e.g., [2, 6, 7, 32–34]), this chapter identifies three main components of social vulnerability to pandemics, namely, individual characteristics, built environment determinants, and societal determinants (Figure 7.1). Identification of the indicators associated with each component should be a prerequisite to any attempt at quantification. However, due to the time limitations, and given the intrinsic complexity of societal determinants, this chapter will focus on individual characteristics and built environment determinants. Societal determinants will be left for future work.

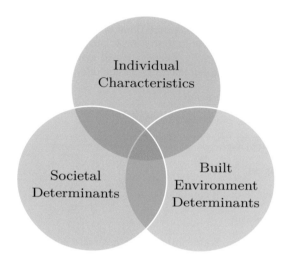

FIGURE 7.1
Main components of social vulnerability to COVID-19

7.3.1 Individual Characteristics

Individual characteristics refer to the personal attributes that may have a determinate role in an individual's susceptibility and capacity to tolerate the impacts of pandemics in general, and COVID-19 in particular. Examples of such characteristics include age, gender, ethnicity, education, disability, family conditions, and household circumstances.

7.3.1.1 Age

Those at both ends of the age spectrum are referred to as potentially more vulnerable when exposed to environmental hazards [2, 5–7, 29, 32, 35]. While people of all ages can be infected with the COVID-19 virus, older people appear to be more susceptible to it. Also, a compromised immune system or pre-existing medical condition, which can increase the severity of the infection is more common in the elderly population. Apart from the risk of exposure itself, older people are especially vulnerable to loneliness, which is the typical outcome of COVID-19 restrictions and social distancing measures. Moreover, given the prevalence of negative stereotyping of older people and age-based

---

[1]According to the Australian Government Department of Health, people aged 70 years and over, people aged 65 years and over with chronic medical conditions, people with compromised immune systems, and Aboriginal and Torres Strait Islander people over the age of 50, are at greater risk of more serious illness if they are infected with coronavirus (https://bit.ly/2YuIw47).

discrimination, and their potential increase during public health emergencies, the older population can face various kinds of mistreatment and barriers in accessing health care and support services.

7.3.1.2 Gender

Gender-based vulnerabilities to environmental hazards are extensively discussed in the existing literature [29, 36, 37]. In the context of the COVID-19 pandemic, early studies indicate a tendency towards higher mortality in men than women in confirmed COVID-19 cases across the world [38, 39]. Women, on the other hand, seem to be more susceptible to the socioeconomic consequences of the pandemic. Also, there are several reports of increases in the frequency and intensity of violence against women, and a significant rise in reporting of first-time family violence by women in Australia and across the world [40, 41]. This newly emerging phenomenon is referred to as "shadow pandemic" by UN Women [42]. The United Nations Population Fund (UNFPA) projections predicted that for every three months of the lockdown, 15 million cases of gender-based violence could occur globally [43].

7.3.1.3 Minority Status and Language

Race, ethnicity, religion, and language proficiency are among the factors contributing to social vulnerability to natural hazards [6, 7, 29, 44–46]. These factors can signify unequal or uncertain access to livelihood resources and health services during a pandemic and can lead to various forms of discrimination in the allocation of welfare and relief packages. Also, the author's observations and published records [47, 48] reveal a further amplification of ethnic inequality arising from a dramatic rise in racism and racially motivated attacks towards people of specific racial origins. As a result, some population groups can turn inwards and may experience a greater sense of isolation and exclusion at a time when staying connected matters most.

7.3.1.4 Family and Household Structure

Family structure refers to different forms of family or household settings, such as single-person household, shared living with non-family, a married or cohabiting couple (with or without children), single-parent families, and extended families. Previous studies suggest that overcrowded families, single-person households, and single-parent households are more vulnerable to natural hazards [6, 30, 44]. For example, according to Holand et al. [16], two-parent families can better manage the different responsibilities faced before, during, and after a hazard.

Within the context of CODIV-19, family structure can also be associated with the allocation of in-house spaces and utilities, which, if required, is critical for effective self-isolation and minimising the risk of within-household transmission [49, 50]. This issue can be more severe in families with children or in extended families where special needs such as remote schooling of children or nursing care of older adults may increase the demand for space in a house.

7.3.1.5 Disabilities and Health Conditions

In general, people with physical or mental disabilities and those suffering from chronic health conditions are considered the most vulnerable groups in society, and disasters increase this vulnerability even further [3, 5]. Also, disabled groups are less likely to receive support or benefit from disaster relief programs [30]. In addition, as outlined previously, people with a suppressed immune system or a pre-existing health condition (e.g. heart-related issues, diabetes, chronic respiratory disease, or cancer) are more likely to progress to severe forms of COVID-19.

7.3.1.6 Education

An overview of previous studies suggests that people with higher education are more resilient to the impacts of disasters. Groups with higher education have better access to the necessary information and resources and can secure government financial assistance more than those with lower education [6, 29, 51, 52]. Given the complexity of the COVID-19 pandemic and its rapid development, higher education can increase awareness of resources, facilitate access to critical information, and maximise compliance with response protocols. Moreover, people with higher education levels are expected to have higher computer competency and digital communication skills, which have proved to be crucial for staying connected, seeking practical help, online shopping, remote working, and online training.

7.3.1.7 Employment and Occupation

Employment plays a crucial role in financial security, access to resources and the overall well-being of individuals, families, and communities. It is recognised that disasters cause high levels of unemployment, especially in the short term [53, 54]. Employment instability during a disaster could decrease coping capacity and increase dependency on external financial support. For example, early studies in Australia show that casual workers and the self-employed, especially young people working in the food, hospitality and retail sectors, are likely to be disproportionately impacted by the pandemic-created economic downturn [55, 56]. Occupations with less dependency on physical movement and remote-friendly jobs appear to be more resilient during situations similar to COVID-19.

7.3.1.8 Financial Status

Financial status is a notion encompassing various financial factors such as income, expenses, assets, savings, and debts. Financial status is believed to have a significant impact on the overall health of a person or household, their social status and connectedness, and their ability to deal with and recover from crises [57, 58]. Previous studies have reported a strong tie between financial status and social vulnerability to disasters [5, 6, 29, 32, 44]. For instance, while financial commitments such as mortgages can make people more vulnerable in times of crisis, people with reasonably large savings can show better resilience to shocks from crises. Moreover, observations made during the COVID-19 pandemic indicate that better financial status can be considered as a positive factor in people's adherence to the public health guidelines and government pandemic protocols.

7.3.1.9 Insurance Coverage

Adequate insurance coverage (whether it be health insurance, income protection, life insurance, or trauma cover) can decrease susceptibility to the adverse consequences of disasters [33, 59, 60]. For example, private health cover enhances the choice of providers and improves access to timely and effective health care services and management [61, 62]. Income protection insurance or trauma cover can help families ease or avoid financial stresses caused by the COVID-19 economic downturn.

7.3.1.10 Ownership Status

Ownership status refers to the ownership of property and motor vehicles. Various studies emphasise the role of house and car ownership in reducing the negative consequences of environmental hazards [6, 7, 32]. Regarding the COVID-19 pandemic situation, it is believed that car and house ownership, especially with no significant mortgage or car loans in place, can significantly reduce the financial stress and mental pressure caused by the pandemic's economic effects. Car ownership can provide families with better and safer commuting options and reduce their reliance on public transport – where the risk of infection is greater.

7.3.2 Built Environment Determinants

The built environment refers to the physical form of communities [63]. Some studies have demonstrated that built environment factors are significantly associated with health outcomes [33, 64]. Previous studies in the field of natural hazards attempted to measure built environment vulnerability by factors such as population density, quality of urban infrastructure, and road network density [16, 32]. Given the unique nature of the COVID-19 pandemic, this section identifies the following preliminary indicators as the pandemic's built environment determinants.

7.3.2.1 Spatial Accessibility

Spatial accessibility refers to the proximity and ease of access to essential urban services, civic amenities, and public infrastructure. Proximity to essential services and amenities such as hospitals, pharmacies, supermarkets, and parks can be a valuable resource, especially when there are limitations imposed on the movement of people and goods to prevent the spread of a virus. Studies show that people residing in inner metropolitan areas have better access to civic amenities than the residents of the outer metropolitan areas [65]. A proximity analysis conducted by the author within the state of Victoria, Australia shows that the number of essential amenities drops significantly as one moves away from the CBD (Figure 7.2). For example, the average number of essential services in a 5 km radius in the inner metropolitan suburbs of Melbourne is three times more than those in the middle metropolitan suburbs. The analysis suggests that the classification of residential areas based on their distance from the CBD can be a reliable indicator of spatial accessibility.

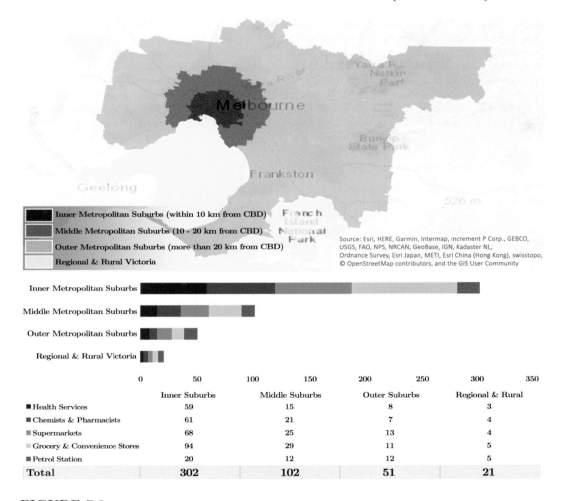

	Inner Suburbs	Middle Suburbs	Outer Suburbs	Regional & Rural
■ Health Services	59	15	8	3
■ Chemists & Pharmacists	61	21	7	4
■ Supermarkets	68	25	13	4
Grocery & Convenience Stores	94	29	11	5
■ Petrol Station	20	12	12	5
Total	**302**	**102**	**51**	**21**

FIGURE 7.2
Average number of essential amenities within 5 km radius of residential addresses

In order to perform the analysis, Victoria's suburbs have been classified into four zones: inner metropolitan suburbs (located within 10 km from the Melbourne CBD), middle metropolitan suburbs (located between 10 to 20 km from the Melbourne CBD), outer metropolitan suburbs (located more than 20 km from the Melbourne CBD), and regional and rural areas (suburbs located outside of the Melbourne metropolitan area). Then, the average number of accessible services is calculated, based on the mean of the number of selected essential services falling within 5 km radius of 10 random residential addresses in each zone. The analysis was produced using ArcGIS Pro 2.5.0 and data downloaded from OpenStreetMap,[2] Victoria's Department of Health and Human Services,[3] and the Australian Bureau of Statistics.[4]

7.3.2.2   Urban Infrastructure

Networks of robust urban infrastructure and essential utility systems (e.g., sewage and water networks, telecommunications, electricity, gas, road network, and public transport) play a vital role in protecting public health and the environment. The role of urban infrastructure becomes more crucial during disasters and public health emergencies, and the COVID-19 pandemic is no different. The continuity and quality of urban infrastructure and essential utility services during large-scale pandemics can provide a more convenient means for accessing essential services, complying with the stay-at-home orders, and staying connected with families, friends, and professional peers.

Evidence from previous health emergencies like the cholera epidemics during the 1800s suggests that, in some cases, contaminated water and sewage networks can contribute to the spread of disease [66]. Although this is not the case for the COVID-19 virus at the moment, some studies imply that the potential spread of COVID-19 via sewage networks must not be neglected [67]. Also, many countries have started monitoring wastewater for traces of the COVID-19 virus, and some found evidence of the virus days or even weeks before the first official case was declared [68]. It is possible, therefore, that ongoing surveillance of sewage and water systems can provide early warning of impending outbreaks and help contain the spread of contagious diseases in the early stages.

7.3.2.3   Population Density

Population density is a measurement of the population per unit area and is recognised as a key determinant of vulnerability to natural and environmental hazards [28, 29, 69]. Studies have investigated the role of population density in both the 1918 influenza pandemic [24] and the present COVID-19 pandemic [70, 71], and suggest that in cities with greater population density, the virus spreads faster than in less crowded cities, due to more frequent contacts among people.

7.3.2.4   Walkability

Walkability refers to the extent to which the built environment can provide safe and friendly conditions for walking and cycling [72, 73]. A considerable volume of published studies describes the role of walking and cycling in promoting good physical and mental health and achieving greater social equality [74–76]. With the multi-directional effects of COVID-19 on most outdoor facilities and activities, a walkable neighbourhood can greatly encourage walking, cycling, and physical activity. Recent studies like Mattioli et al. [77] and McDougall et al. [78] suggest that physical activities can play a significant role in mitigating the physical and mental health challenges presented by COVID-19.

7.4   Discussion and Conclusion Remarks

COVID-19 has created unprecedented challenges across the globe and is expected to have lasting impacts in the years to come. Understanding how pandemics influence the lives of various socioeconomic groups can help decision-makers develop a clearer perception of the situation and direct resources to where they will have the most significant effect. As outlined earlier in this

---

[2]https://www.openstreetmap.org/
[3]https://www.dhhs.vic.gov.au/
[4]https://www.abs.gov.au/

chapter, a large body of literature under the umbrella concept of social vulnerability is devoted to understanding how different socioeconomic groups experience crises differently. However, due to the rarity of pandemics in recent history, little work has been done on social vulnerability in the context of disease outbreaks and pandemics.

This study is an early attempt to understand social vulnerability to disease outbreaks, learning from the COVID-19 pandemic and its socioeconomic ramifications on society. Borrowing from the literature, this chapter has elaborated on the concept of social vulnerability to the COVID-19 pandemic, which was later followed by the identification of social vulnerability components in pandemic settings. Three main components have been recognised: individual characteristics, built environment determinants, and societal determinants, the first two of which have been further divided into indicators to provide a more detailed description of their role in social vulnerability to pandemics.

It should be noted that this chapter is neither an attempt to define social vulnerability to pandemics on a global scale nor to provide an exhaustive list of its indicators. The study presents several inherent limitations that should be noted before future research directions are discussed. The first limitation comes from the highly-complex nature and rapidly changing and still unfolding implications of the COVID-19 pandemic. No doubt establishing a thorough understanding of the multi-dimensional impact of the ongoing pandemic will take years. The second limitation concerns the time constraints, which restricted the study to investigate selected components of social vulnerability to pandemics and leave the detailed investigation of the societal components for future work. The third limitation originates from the jurisdiction in which this study takes place. Some of the justifications in this chapter are made through careful observations of the COVID-19 situation in Australia and may not be generalisable to other countries because of different socioeconomic or cultural circumstances.

Future directions of this study include further expansion of the concept by a detailed investigation of the societal determinants of social vulnerability to COVID-19, as well as the external validation of the outcomes through focus groups or interviews. This will be followed by studying the relationship between the indicators and the morbidity and mortality caused by the pandemic using the actual COVID-19 data, which can lead to a more thorough validation of the work. Future extensions of this study will also explore potential biases or preconceived assumptions associated with the various indicators as well as the interplay between them. For example, while high population density can contribute to pandemic-related vulnerabilities, densely populated areas are likely to have better urban infrastructure networks. Similarly, people with higher education or better financial status are expected to be less vulnerable to pandemics, but the prevalence of international and long-distance mobility in such groups may also place them on the list of highly exposed and primary long-distance carriers of disease, especially in the early stages of a pandemic. It is expected the ultimate outcomes of this ongoing research will enhance the overall awareness of pandemics and will be of considerable value in drafting future pandemic preparedness plans.

References

[1] John McConnell. Pandemic influenza: learning from the present. *Public health*, 124(1):3, 2010.

[2] Shirley Laska and Betty Hearn Morrow. Social vulnerabilities and hurricane katrina: an unnatural disaster in new orleans. *Marine technology society journal*, 40(4):16–26, 2006.

[3] Betty Hearn Morrow. Identifying and mapping community vulnerability. *Disasters*, 23(1):1–18, 1999.

[4] Deborah S.K. Thomas, Brenda D. Phillips, William E. Lovekamp, and Alice Fothergill, editors. *Social Vulnerability to Disasters*. CRC Press, may 2013. ISBN 9780429253683. doi: 10.1201/b14854.

[5] Piers Blaikie, Terry Cannon, Ian Davis, and Ben Wisner. *At Risk: Natural Hazards, People's Vulnerability and Disaster*. Routledge, 2nd edition, 2004. ISBN 9780415252157.

[6] Susan L. Cutter, Bryan J. Boruff, and W. Lynn Shirley. Social vulnerability to environmental hazards. *Social Science Quarterly*, 84(2):242–261, 2003. doi: 10.1111/1540-6237.8402002.

[7] Barry E. Flanagan, Edward W. Gregory, Elaine J Hallisey, Janet L. Heitgerd, and Brian Lewis. A social vulnerability index for disaster management. *Journal of Homeland Security and Emergency Management*, 8(1), 2011. doi: 10.2202/1547-7355.1792.

[8] Richard J. Estes and John S. Morgan. World social welfare analysis: a theoretical model. *International Social Work*, 19(2):29–41, 1976. doi: 10.1177/002087287601900207.

[9] Susan L Cutter. Vulnerability to environmental hazards. *Progress in Human Geography*, 20(4):529–539, 1996. doi: 10.1177/030913259602000407.

[10] Hans-Martin Füssel. Vulnerability: A generally applicable conceptual framework for climate change research. *Global Environmental Change*, 17(2):155–167, 2007. doi: 10.1016/j.gloenvcha.2006.05.002.

[11] W. Neil Adger. Vulnerability. *Global Environmental Change*, 16(3):268–281, 2006. doi: 10.1016/j.gloenvcha. 2006.02.006.

[12] Barry Charles Ezell. Infrastructure vulnerability assessment model (i-vam). *Risk Analysis*, 27(3):571–583, 2007. doi: 10.1111/j.1539-6924.2007.00907.x.

[13] UN Inter-Agency Secretariat of the International Strategy for Disaster Reduction (UN/ISDR). *Living With Risk: A Global Review of Disaster Reduction Initiatives*, volume 1. United Nations Publications, 2004. ISBN 9211010640. URL https://www.undrr.org/publication/living-risk-global-review-disaster-reduction-initiatives.

[14] United Nations Office for Disaster Risk Reduction (UNDRR). *United Nations Global Assessment Report on Disaster Risk Reduction (GAR2019)*. United Nations Publications, 2019. ISBN 978-92-1-004180-5. URL https://www.undrr.org/publication/global-assessment-report-disaster-risk-reduction-2019.

[15] Alexander Fekete. Validation of a social vulnerability index in context to river-floods in germany. *Natural Hazards and Earth System Sciences*, 9(3) 2009. doi: 10.5194/nhess-9-393-2009.

[16] Ivar S Holand, Päivi Lujala, and Jan Ketil Rød. Social vulnerability assessment for norway: A quantitative approach. *Norsk Geografisk Tidsskrift-Norwegian Journal of Geography*, 65(1):1–17, 2011. doi: 10.1080/00291951.2010.550167.

[17] Eric Tate. Social vulnerability indices: A comparative assessment using uncertainty and sensitivity analysis. *Natural Hazards*, 63(2):325–347, 2012. doi: 10.1007/s11069-012-0152-2.

[18] Mohammad Ghaderi. Public health interventions in the face of pandemics: network structure, social distancing, and heterogeneity. Economics Working Papers 1732, Department of Economics and Business, Universitat Pompeu Fabra, Jun 2020. URL https://ideas.repec.org/p/upf/upfgen/1732.html.

[19] Tommy Bengtsson, Martin Dribe, and Björn Eriksson. Social class and excess mortality in sweden during the 1918 influenza pandemic. *American Journal of Epidemiology*, 187(12):2568–2576, 2018. doi: 10.1093/aje/kwy151.

[20] Svenn-Erik Mamelund, Clare Shelley-Egan, and Ole Rogeberg. The association between socioeconomic status and pandemic influenza: protocol for a systematic review and meta-analysis. *Systematic Reviews*, 8(1):5, 2019. doi: 10.1186/s13643-018-0931-2.

[21] Lori Uscher-Pines, Patrick S. Duggan, Joshua P. Garoon, Ruth A. Karron, and Ruth R. Faden. Planning for an influenza pandemic: Social justice and disadvantaged groups. *Hastings Center Report*, 37(4):32–39, 2007. doi: 10.1353/hcr.2007.0064.

[22] Christopher JL Murray, Alan D Lopez, Brian Chin, Dennis Feehan, and Kenneth H Hill. Estimation of potential global pandemic influenza mortality on the basis of vital registry data from the 1918-20 pandemic: a quantitative analysis. *Lancet*, 368(9554):2211–2218, 2006. doi: 10.1016/S0140-6736(06)69895-4.

[23] Lone Simonsen, Peter Spreeuwenberg, Roger Lustig, Robert J. Taylor, Douglas M. Fleming, Madelon Kroneman, Maria D. Van Kerkhove, Anthony W. Mounts, and W. John Paget. Global mortality estimates for the 2009 influenza pandemic from the glamor project: A modeling study. *PLoS Medicine*, 10(11):e1001558, 2013. doi: 10.1371/journal.pmed.1001558.

[24] Kyra H. Grantz, Madhura S. Rane, Henrik Salje, Gregory E. Glass, Stephen E. Schachterle, and Derek A.T. Cummings. Disparities in influenza mortality and transmission related to sociodemographic factors within chicago in the pandemic of 1918. *Proceedings of the National Academy of Sciences of the United States of America*, 113(48):13839–13844, 2016. doi: 10.1073/pnas.1612838113.

[25] Paul D. Rutter, Oliver T. Mytton, Matthew Mak, and Liam J. Donaldson. Socio-economic disparities in mortality due to pandemic influenza in england. *International Journal of Public Health*, 57(4):745–750, 2012. doi: 10.1007/s00038-012-0337-1.

[26] Seth E. Spielman, Joseph Tuccillo, David C. Folch, Amy Schweikert, Rebecca Davies, Nathan Wood, and Eric Tate. Evaluating social vulnerability indicators: criteria and their application to the Social Vulnerability Index. *Natural Hazards*, 100(1):417–436, 2020. doi: 10.1007/s11069-019-03820-z.

[27] W. Neil Adger and P. Mick Kelly. Social vulnerability to climate change and the architecture of entitlements. *Mitigation and Adaptation Strategies for Global Change*, 4(3-4):253–266, 1999. doi: 10.1023/a:1009601904210.

[28] Jose Manuel De Oliveira Mendes. Social vulnerability indexes as planning tools: Beyond the preparedness paradigm. *Journal of Risk Research*, 12(1):43–58, 2009. doi: 10.1080/13669870802447962.

[29] Farin Fatemi, Ali Ardalan, Benigno Aguirre, Nabiollah Mansouri, and Iraj Mohammadfam. Social vulnerability indicators in disasters: Findings from a systematic review. *International Journal of Disaster Risk Reduction*, 22:219–227, 2017. doi: 10.1016/j.ijdrr.2016.09.006.

[30] Christian Kuhlicke, Anna Scolobig, Sue Tapsell, Annett Steinführer, and Bruna de Marchi. Contextualizing social vulnerability: Findings from case studies across Europe. *Natural Hazards*, 58(2):789–810, 2011. doi: 10.1007/s11069-011-9751-6.

[31] Australian Government Department of Health (DoH). Coronavirus (COVID-19) Health Alert, 2020. URL https://www.health.gov.au/news/health-alerts/novel-coronavirus-2019-ncov-health-alert. Accessed on 20 August 2020.

[32] Anita Dwyer, Christopher Zoppou, Ole Nielsen, Susan Day, and Stephen Roberts. Quantifying social vulnerability : A methodology for identifying those at risk to natural hazards. *Geoscience Australia*, 2004. ISBN:1920871098.

[33] Chia Yuan Yu, Ayoung Woo, Christopher T. Emrich, and Biyuan Wang. Social vulnerability index and obesity: An empirical study in the US. *Cities*, 97(September 2019), 2020. doi: 10.1016/j.cities.2019.102531.

[34] Australian Institute of Health and Welfare. Australia's Health 2016. 2016. doi: 10.25816/5ec1e4cd2547f. URL https://www.aihw.gov.au/reports/australias-health/australias-health-2016. Accessed on 15 July 2020.

[35] Yung Jaan Lee. Social vulnerability indicators as a sustainable planning tool. *Environmental Impact Assessment Review*, 44:31–42, 2014. doi: 10.1016/j.eiar.2013.08.002.

[36] Susan L. Cutter. The forgotten casualties redux: Women, children, and disaster risk. *Global Environmental Change*, 42:117–121, 2017. doi: 10.1016/j.gloenvcha.2016.12.010.

[37] Elaine Enarson and P G Dhar Chakrabarti, editors. *Women, Gender and Disaster: Global Issues and Initiatives*. SAGE Publications India Pvt Ltd, New Delhi, 2009. doi: 10.4135/9788132108078.

[38] Jian-Min Jin, Peng Bai, Wei He, Fei Wu, Xiao-Fang Liu, De-Min Han, Shi Liu, and Jin-Kui Yang. Gender differences in patients with covid-19: Focus on severity and mortality. *Frontiers in Public Health*, 8:152, 2020. doi: 10.3389/fpubh.2020.00152.

[39] Garima Sharma, Annabelle Santos Volgman, and Erin D. Michos. Sex Differences in Mortality From COVID-19 Pandemic. *JACC: Case Reports*, 2(9):1407–1410, 2020. doi: 10.1016/j.jaccas.2020.04.027.

[40] Naomi Pfitzner, Kate Fitz-Gibbon, and Jacqui True. Responding to the 'shadow pandemic': practitioner views on the nature of and responses to violence against women in Victoria, Australia during the COVID-19 restrictions. *Bridges Monash University*, 2020. doi: 10.26180/5ed9d5198497c. Accessed on 25 August 2020.

[41] Kim Usher, Navjot Bhullar, Joanne Durkin, Naomi Gyamfi, and Debra Jackson. Family violence and COVID-19: Increased vulnerability and reduced options for support. *International Journal of Mental Health Nursing*, 29(4):549–552, 2020. doi: 10.1111/inm.12735.

[42] Phumzile Mlambo-Ngcuka. Violence against women and girls: the shadow pandemic. *UN Women*, 2020. URL https://bit.ly/35ZOvSU. Accessed on 24 September 2020.

[43] The United Nations Population Fund (UNFPA). New unfpa projections predict calamitous impact on women's health as covid-19 pandemic continues, 2020. URL https://bit.ly/329KfxK. Accessed on 13 August 2020.

[44] Wenfang Chen, Susan L. Cutter, Christopher T. Emrich, and Peijun Shi. Measuring social vulnerability to natural hazards in the Yangtze River Delta region, China. *International Journal of Disaster Risk Science*, 4(4):169–181, 2013. doi: 10.1007/s13753-013-0018-6.

[45] Mathew C. Schmidtlein, Roland C. Deutsch, Walter W. Piegorsch, and Susan L. Cutter. A sensitivity analysis of the social vulnerability index. *Risk Analysis*, 28(4):1099–1114, 2008. doi: 10.1111/j.1539-6924.2008.01072.x.

[46] Keith Wailoo, Karen M. O'Neill, Jeffrey Dowd, and Roland Anglin, editors. *Katrina's Imprint: Race and Vulnerability in America*. Rutgers University Press, 2010. ISBN 978-0-8135-4978-1.

[47] Victor Sojo and Hari Bapuji. The Toxic Spread of COVID-19 Racism. *The University of Melbourne's Pursuit*, 2020. URL https://pursuit.unimelb.edu.au/articles/the-toxic-spread-of-covid-19-racism. Accessed on 16 August 2020.

[48] Ben Schneiders and Clay Lucas. Asian-Australian groups report surge in racist abuse, assaults during pandemic. *The Age*, 2020. URL https://bit.ly/2R7A4U7. Accessed on 2 August 2020.

[49] Bernard Ekumah, Frederick Ato Armah, David Oscar Yawson, Reginald Quansah, Florence Esi Nyieku, Samuel Asiedu Owusu, Justice Odoiquaye Odoi, and Abdul-Rahaman Afitiri. Disparate on-site access to water, sanitation, and food storage heighten the risk of COVID-19 spread in Sub-Saharan Africa. *Environmental Research*, 189, 2020. doi: 10.1016/j.envres.2020.109936.

[50] Lucinda Platt and Ross Warwick. Are some ethnic groups more vulnerable to COVID-19 than others? *The Institute for Fiscal Studies*, 2020. URL https://www.ifs.org.uk/inequality/?p=1074. Accessed on 5 August 2020.

[51] Raya Muttarak and Wolfgang Lutz. Is education a key to reducing vulnerability to natural disasters and hence unavoidable climate change? *Ecology and Society*, 19(October):1–8, 2017.

[52] Nathan J. Wood, Christopher G. Burton, and Susan L. Cutter. Community variations in social vulnerability to Cascadia-related tsunamis in the U.S. Pacific Northwest. *Natural Hazards*, 52(2):369–389, 2010. doi: 10.1007/s11069-009-9376-1.

[53] Christopher G. Burton. Social vulnerability and hurricane impact modeling. *Natural Hazards Review*, 11(2): 58–68, 2010. doi: 10.1061/(ASCE)1527-6988(2010)11:2(58).

[54] Yu Xiao and Edward Feser. The unemployment impact of the 1993 US midwest flood: a quasi-experimental structural break point analysis. *Environmental Hazards*, 13(2):93–113, 2014. doi: 10.1080/17477891.2013. 777892.

[55] Stefanie Dimov, Tania King, Marissa Shields, and Anne Kavanagh. The Young Australians Hit Hard During COVID-19. *The University of Melbourne's Pursuit*, 2020. URL https://pursuit.unimelb.edu.au/articles/the-young-australians-hit-hard-during-covid-19. Accessed on 9 August 2020.

[56] Geoff Gilfillan. COVID-19 : Impacts on casual workers in Australia — a statistical snapshot. Research paper series, Parliament of Australia, 2020.

[57] Nancy E. Adler and Judith Stewart. Health disparities across the lifespan: Meaning, methods, and mechanisms. *Annals of the New York Academy of Sciences*, 1186:5–23, 2010. doi: 10.1111/j.1749-6632.2009.05337.x.

[58] Andrew D Pinto, Monica Da Ponte, Madeleine Bondy, Amy Craig-Neil, Kathleen Murphy, Suhal Ahmed, Pratik Nair, Alyssa Swartz, and Samantha Green. Addressing financial strain through a peer-to-peer intervention in primary care. *Family Practice*, 37(4), 2020. ISSN 1460-2229. doi: 10.1093/fampra/cmaa046.

[59] Lakshita Boora and Gordhan K. Saini. Infusing Disaster Management Through Social Marketing: A Case Study of New Delhi, India. *Asian Journal of Environment and Disaster Management*, 5(1):1, 2013. doi: 10.3850/s179392402013001981.

[60] Ehren B. Ngo. When disasters and age collide: Reviewing vulnerability of the elderly. *Natural Hazards Review*, 2(2):80–89, 2001. doi: 10.1061/(ASCE)1527-6988(2001)2:2(80).

[61] Jill Bernstein, Deborah Chollet, and Stephanie Peterson. How Does Insurance Coverage Improve Health Outcomes? *Mathematica Policy Research, Inc.*, pages 1–5, 2010.

[62] Francesca Colombo and Nicole Tapay. Private Health Insurance in Australia: A case study. *OECD Health Working Paper*, 2003. doi: 10.1787/478608584171.

[63] Ross C. Brownson, Christine M. Hoehner, Kristen Day, Ann Forsyth, and James F. Sallis. Measuring the Built Environment for Physical Activity. *American Journal of Preventive Medicine*, 36(4):99–123, 2009. doi: 10.1016/j.amepre.2009.01.005.

[64] Daniel D Reidpath, Cate Burns, Jan Garrard, Mary Mahoney, and Mardie Townsend. An ecological study of the relationship between social and environmental determinants of obesity. *Health & Place*, 8(2):141–145, 2002. doi: 10.1016/S1353-8292(01)00028-4.

[65] Australian Government Department of Health. Review of Australian Government Health Workforce Programs, 2013. URL https://bit.ly/3ifcd0b. Accessed on 10 July 2020.

[66] Mary Dobson. *Disease: the extraordinary stories behind history's deadliest killers*. Metro Books, London, 2013. ISBN 1435151666.

[67] University of Stirling. Sewage poses potential COVID-19 transmission risk, experts warn, 2020. URL https://www.sciencedaily.com/releases/2020/05/200506133603.htm. Accessed on 24 August 2020.

[68] Gemma Chavarria-Miró, Eduard Anfruns-Estrada, Susana Guix, Miquel Paraira, Belén Galofré, Gloria Sáanchez, Rosa Pintó, and Albert Bosch. Sentinel surveillance of SARS-CoV-2 in wastewater anticipates the occurrence of COVID-19 cases. *medRxiv*, page 2020.06.13.20129627, 2020. doi: 10.1101/2020.06.13.20129627. URL http://medrxiv.org/content/early/2020/06/13/2020.06.13.20129627.abstract.

[69] Sammy Zahran, Samuel D. Brody, Walter Gillis Peacock, Arnold Vedlitz, and Himanshu Grover. Social vulnerability and the natural and built environment: A model of flood casualties in Texas. *Disasters*, 32(4): 537–560, 2008. doi: 10.1111/j.1467-7717.2008.01054.x.

[70] Mohsen Ahmadi, Abbas Sharifi, Shadi Dorosti, Saeid Jafarzadeh Ghoushchi, and Negar Ghanbari. Investigation of effective climatology parameters on covid-19 outbreak in iran. *Science of The Total Environment*, 729:138705, 2020. doi: 10.1016/j.scitotenv.2020.138705.

[71] Jingyuan Wang, Ke Tang, Kai Feng, and Weifeng Lv. High Temperature and High Humidity Reduce the Transmission of COVID-19. *SSRN Electronic Journal*, 2020. doi: 10.2139/ssrn.3551767.

[72] L. D. Frank, J. F. Sallis, B. E. Saelens, L. Leary, L. Cain, T. L. Conway, and P. M. Hess. The development of a walkability index: Application to the neighborhood quality of life study. *British Journal of Sports Medicine*, 44(13):924–933, 2010. doi: 10.1136/bjsm.2009.058701.

[73] Wonho Suh, Bo Sung, and Youngjin Yurk. Walkability Assessment for Elderly Citizens and People with Disabilities. *International Journal of Engineering and Technology*, 9(4):346–349, 2017. doi: 10.7763/ijet. 2017.v9.995.

[74] Kim Dovey and Elek Pafka. What is walkability? The urban DMA. *Urban Studies*, 57(1):93–108, 2020. doi: 10.1177/0042098018819727.

[75] Richard Sennett. *Building and dwelling: ethics for the city.* Farrar, Straus and Giroux, 2018. ISBN 0374200335.

[76] Mark Stevenson, Jason Thompson, Thiago Hérick de Sá, Reid Ewing, Dinesh Mohan, Rod McClure, Ian Roberts, Geetam Tiwari, Billie Giles-Corti, Xiaoduan Sun, Mark Wallace, and James Woodcock. Land use, transport, and population health: estimating the health benefits of compact cities. *The Lancet*, 388(10062): 2925–2935, 2016. doi: 10.1016/S0140-6736(16)30067-8.

[77] Anna Vittoria Mattioli, Matteo Ballerini Puviani, Milena Nasi, and Alberto Farinetti. COVID-19 pandemic: the effects of quarantine on cardiovascular risk. *European Journal of Clinical Nutrition*, 74(6):852–855, 2020. doi: 10.1038/s41430-020-0646-z.

[78] Craig W. McDougall, Caroline Brown, Craig Thomson, Nick Hanley, Mark A. Tully, Richard S. Quilliam, Phil J. Bartie, Lesley Gibson, and David M. Oliver. From one pandemic to another: emerging lessons from COVID-19 for tackling physical inactivity in cities. *Cities & Health*, pages 1–4, 2020. doi: 10.1080/23748834. 2020.1785165.

8

Informal Road Detection and Uncertainty in Remote Sensing

Renate Thiede and Inger Fabris-Rotelli

This chapter presents an algorithm for detecting informally developed roads in satellite images, and quantifying the uncertainty associated with the results. Informal unpaved roads are common in developing countries, and arise naturally through human movement, typically in conjunction with informal housing. These roads are not authorised nor maintained by government, nor recorded in official databases or online maps. Consequently, information on their location and extent is not available to official decision-makers, severely limiting on the development of COVID-19 response strategies. This information is critical for planning the placement of testing centers and clinics, the navigation of emergency medical services, and studying the movements of the population for contact tracing and mobility purposes. The algorithm obtains these roads in a fast and efficient manner using freely available software, making it a viable solution for developing countries. The uncertainty metrics provide a measure of the reliability of the information. The algorithm is demonstrated on areas in South Africa, a developing country with one of the highest number of COVID-19 cases globally.

8.1 Introduction

Currently, the Worldometer[1] reports that South Africa is in the top ten countries worldwide for total COVID-19 cases and among the top fifteen for total deaths. Eight of the countries in the top fifteen, both for cases and deaths, are in the developing world. The Google mobility index[2] indicates that mobility generally decreased in all sectors except the residential sector, compared to a baseline day before the start of the pandemic. In South Africa, mobility in the residential sector increased by 14% compared to baseline data for the country, while the increase in Brazil and India were 10% and 14%, respectively. This highlights the need for modelling mobility within residential areas. However, much of the movement within residential areas, particularly in informal settlements, is developed by residents without government approval. These settlements arise when rapid urbanisation in developing countries leaves governments unable to meet infrastructure needs. Two-thirds of the population of the global south lives in informally developed settlements [1]. In South Africa, this population is growing at a faster rate than the population living in government-registered formal settlements [1].

---

[1]https://www.worldometers.info/coronavirus/#countries accessed on 28 September 2020.
[2]www.google.com/covid19/mobility/

Informal roads herein refer to any roads created by residents without government approval. These roads occur in and around a variety of settlements, which may be formal, traditional or informal. They arise naturally through human movement on foot and by vehicle, and are not authorised or maintained by government, nor commonly recorded in official databases or online maps.

The current COVID-19 pandemic highlights the need for such road data to be obtainable at short notice. The location and extent of informal roads provide crucial information regarding citizens' transport opportunities and possibilities for movement, required for government monitoring of cases. The South African government acknowledges that contact tracing is important for the COVID-19 pandemic.[3] Although the University of Cape Town in South Africa has developed a contact tracing app,[4] the population uptake of the app is unlikely to reach the requirement due to limited access to smart phones and cellular services. At this stage, they do not provide a comprehensive solution for South Africa.

The World Health Organisation[5] provides detailed advice on contact tracing which involves, for example, managing and monitoring contacts daily and direct monitoring by a contact tracing team. The knowledge of roads in informal settings are thus essential for navigation by such teams, as well as medical personnel checking on isolating cases. In addition, roads provide accessibility to services. During COVID-19 it is essential that all citizens have access to facilities such as hospitals, within a certain travel distance or travel time from their homes. Knowledge of the roads assists decision makers in optimal placing of additional emergency testing and support facilities. The same holds for other essential services such as banks and grocery stores.

In order to obtain informal-road information, remote sensing data can be utilised to provide such data rapidly, at no health or safety risk, and at low cost, as satellite images provide a comprehensive overview of settlements and infrastructure. This avoids the infection risk, as well as crime-related security risks[6] associated with land surveying. The question then becomes how to extract the information from remote sensing data. Manual digitisation of informal roads from satellite imagery is a time-consuming and complex process [2], leading to delays in data availability. An automatic or semi-automatic method for extracting informal roads from satellite imagery is therefore required. Developing such an extraction method must take into account the unique challenges posed by informal roads. Due to their unplanned nature, informal roads often occur in irregular networks, and may not have clear boundaries or centrelines. Their unpaved surfaces exhibit heterogeneous colour and fade into their surroundings, and road width may change abruptly. This contradicts many of the assumptions made by traditional formal-road extraction methods [3–5]. Furthermore, since information on these roads does not typically exist in any database, accuracy cannot be assessed using reference data. An informal-road extraction method must therefore preferably provide a measure of extraction uncertainty that does not rely on a comparison with ground truth.

This chapter presents a novel approach to extract informal unpaved roads from remote sensing images along with an associated uncertainty measure, and provides an overview of uncertainty measurement approaches. The presented approach is tailored for the unique characteristics and circumstances of informal roads. Uncertainty is quantified for each distinct road object by assessing its linearity, where more linear shapes are considered more certain to be roads. The approach is demonstrated for areas in the South African provinces of Gauteng and North West. It may be implemented using only open source software, making it ideal for the developing world.

This technique was previously presented as an unpublished Masters thesis in [6]. Here we give a broader overview of the problem, particularly with relation to the COVID-19 pandemic. Approaches for assessing uncertainty are discussed in the absence of ground truth, and sources of uncertainty around informal roads are investigated.

---

[3] www.sacoronavirus.co.za, 23 May 2020 Contact Tracing Toolkit; accessed on 8 July 2020.
[4] https://www.news.uct.ac.za/article/-2020-03-27-coviid-new-app-to-avoid-future-lockdowns
[5] www.who.int, Contact Tracing in the Context of COVID-19, 10 May 2020.
[6] South Africa ranks third in the world. www.numbeo.com/crime/ranking_by_country.jsp

8.2 Literature

There is limited research on informal-road extraction because of the unique challenges of informal roads, such as geometric inconsistencies of the width of roads, visually unclear road boundaries and heterogeneous surface reflectance.

Several comprehensive overviews of formal-road extraction techniques are available in the literature [7–9]. Methodologies include morphological methods [10–12], dynamic programming [13], multi-scale and multi-resolution analyses [14], and segmentation and classification [15, 16] knowledge- and logic-based techniques [17], fuzzy modeling and fuzzy logic [18], and spatial reasoning.

Deep learning approaches have become popular for road extraction in recent years. Abdollahi et al. [19] provide an overview, stating that there are four main types of deep learning used for road extraction. These are generative adversarial networks (GANs) [20], deconvolutional networks [21, 22], fully convolutional neural networks (FCNs) [23–25], and patch-based convolutional neural network (CNN) models [26]. However, deep learning methods typically require large datasets for model or network training, complex training, or large amounts of storage and memory [19]. This makes such methods infeasible for the financially constrained situations of the developing world.

The above methods were proposed to detect formal roads. The only approach in the literature developed for informal roads is that of [3], which detects roads in informal settlements in São Paolo, Brazil. Several challenges were experienced therein, such as misclassifying buildings as roads, difficulty in detecting dirty or muddy roads, and errors caused by the presence of cars and other objects on roads. There is therefore a need for further research in this area. In addition, the method in [3] requires the use of proprietary software, namely eCognition.[7] It can therefore not be implemented freely or in financially constrained situations, which may occur in the developing world.

In [27], the formal-road extraction method of [28] was able to detect some informal roads, however, this method also relied on proprietary eCognition software.

As highlighted in [3], informal roads differ from formal roads in some key characteristics. Formal roads tend to appear as long linear objects of constant width, either straight lines or regular curved shapes. Informal roads are of varying lengths and widths [3], often exhibiting sharp changes in road width. Formal, planned roads are generally laid out in regular patterns, and connect to other roads at planned junctions. Informal roads may exhibit irregular patterns [3], as their locations are influenced by convenience and environmental factors, rather than pre-planned design. They may also exhibit discontinuities. Formal roads are in general designed to be suitable for automobile navigation, and must adhere to specific standards, such as those specified by the South African National Road Traffic Act.[8] Informal roads are created ad-hoc. Their structure depends on their function, such as narrow roads being suitable for small vehicles and foot traffic, or broad roads for larger vehicles. These properties may change abruptly along the same road, depending on the way in which different stretches of the road are travelled. Formal roads are generally paved or clearly delineated, separated from their surroundings by boundaries or sidewalks. Informal roads often do not possess clearly visible boundaries, and may have similar reflectance as their surroundings, including bare soil areas and yards, or buildings with roofs made from local soil. Informal roads may exhibit heterogeneous colouring, such as brighter, harder soil on well-travelled parts of the road, or darker soil on wet or muddy patches. In the context of informal settlements, land cover may be highly heterogeneous at the scale of roads, which [3] mentions as a particular challenge for informal-road extraction.

Any approach for detecting informal roads must be able to rely on the characteristics possessed by informal roads and take their circumstances into account. The Normalised Difference Vegetation Index (NDVI) will herein be used to isolate bare soil areas.

Spectral information alone is not sufficient for informal roads. Traditional dwellings, made from

---

[7]https://geospatial.trimble.com/products-and-solutions/ecognition

[8]South African Legal Information Institute, National Road Traffic Act, 1996 [No. 93 of 1996] - G 17603. Available online: http://www.saflii.org/za/legis/num act/nrta1996189/

local materials, may appear spectrally similar to bare soil or vegetation, while open bare soil areas that are not roads will be spectrally identical to informal roads. Furthermore, informal roads exhibit heterogeneous reflectance across the road surface, so that uniform colour cannot be assumed as in some formal-road extraction methods [5]. Incorporating geometric and structural properties decreases the risk of confusing roads with spectrally similar areas and objects [4, 29]. Since roads are linear structures, measuring linearity will provide a way of detecting the presence of roads, even where their boundaries are not clearly visible. Detecting the linearity of roads that are not straight has proved a challenge in the past [15]. Informal roads are not necessarily straight, but may be visually erratic or winding, as determined by the navigational needs and environmental constraints from which the roads have arisen. Measuring the compactness and elongation of objects [30] allows for detecting curvilinear objects, that are linear but not straight. These measures were employed in [28] to determine whether or not image objects were roads.

Image objects appear differently at different scales [31]. The scale at which an image is analysed determines what objects will be identified [32]. Since informal roads differ in length and width, and roads of varying sizes may appear in the same area, searching for informal road segments at a single scale is not suitable. The Discrete Pulse Transform (DPT) [33] provides a multi-scale decomposition of an image by recursive application of the LULU operators [34]. It is used to find and analyse image objects of any scale. It is straightforward to extend the working of the DPT to find pulses of a certain shape, in particular linear shapes, defined by their compactness and elongation. This is efficient in terms of both computation time and simplicity. In the approach presented herein, colour and reflectance information are utilised to isolate bare soil areas, which are then further analysed using the DPT. In this way, size and shape information available in satellite imagery are combined to effectively detect unpaved informal roads of various sizes, exhibiting heterogeneous colour and irregular shapes. The only requirement is that the roads should be linear.

Aside from measuing linearity, compactness and elongation provide an additional advantage which is critical for decision-making, namely, they are used to provide a measure of certainty related to the extracted objects [28]. This is crucial in the case where road information may be used as input to a larger process, such as mobility monitoring for COVID-19 response. Many studies have focused on assessing the accuracy of the results of road extraction algorithms [35–37]. However, such uncertainty analyses are usually conducted in separate studies and not included as part of the road extraction process.

This chapter presents a practical solution to the problem of detecting informal roads and assessing their associated uncertainty. This is critical for improving mobility modelling, contact tracing and service provision during the COVID-19 pandemic. The algorithm described herein may be implemented using free open-source software, and can therefore be used in financially challenged situations, such as in developing countries. Additionally, the algorithm provides measures of certainty related to the identified road objects, rather than hard binary classification.

8.3   Uncertainty Measures in Remote Sensing

In order to gauge the reliability of the results of a road extraction algorithm, some form of accuracy assessment or uncertainty evaluation is required. This is particularly important when the output of the extraction is used in further decision-making, such as mobility tracking for COVID-19 response. Informed decisions can only be made on the basis of well-understood, reliable data.

Uncertainty quantification and accuracy assessment are usually done as separate processes external to the road extraction. Methods including uncertainty measures as part of the extraction algorithm output are rare in the literature, as noted nearly twenty years ago [38]. While a wide array of accuracy assessment techniques have become available, little has changed in terms of built-in uncertainty quantification that provides uncertainty measures as part of the algorithm output.

Firstly, it is necessary to differentiate between accuracy and uncertainty. Herein, accuracy will refer to a measurement that compares the results of an extraction algorithm with some reference data that is assumed to be true [36]. Accuracy assessment gives an indication of how well the extraction approach can be expected to perform. However, it does not provide direct information about the reliability of the results on any given dataset for which no reference data is available. Uncertainty, on the other hand, is an inherent property of the extraction, resulting from intrinsic ambiguity in the data and particular extraction algorithm. Uncertainty quantifies the confidence we have in the extraction results [39]. This is of particular importance in the case of informal roads, which exhibit unique characteristics and sources of uncertainty that differ from the challenges faced by formal roads [3, 40].

A variety of specific methods is aimed at quantifying the uncertainty in remote sensing applications [41]. These methods may provide a nuanced understanding of the sources of uncertainty. While these are worth considering, the focus of this research is not to comprehensively quantify all uncertainty, but rather to present a road extraction algorithm which is coupled with its uncertainty.

Uncertainty arises from ambiguities inherent to the data and approach. It may not be possible to quantify all sources of uncertainty [42], therefore, any uncertainty measurement will exhibit some form of subjectivity. The more sources considered, the more comprehensive the uncertainty measures will be. However, this may lead to a very complicated uncertainty quantification process. Balcaen et al. [42] state that it is impossible to separate all possible sources of uncertainty present in a physical measurement. It is therefore necessary to consider sources of uncertainty, and ways of quantifying their influence, that are appropriate to the purpose and structure of the algorithm. The way in which uncertainty quantification may be incorporated into the algorithm depends on the steps followed. Fuzzy and probabilistic classification techniques provide advantages to model and quantify uncertainty [43]. Classification and feature extraction methods using Bayesian solutions tend to quantify parameter uncertainty via Markov Chain Monte Carlo approaches [44, 45], while deep learning methods such as [46] can use Monte Carlo dropout. Other approaches include the use of additional data or knowledge, such as the feature extraction approach of [47], which compares multiple images of the same places at similar times. Expert knowledge may also be used, as in [48] for assessing the uncertainty of slum boundaries, or the shoreline change detection approach of [49].

Herein, we balance the complexity of uncertainty quantification with simplicity of calculation and interpretation. We measure uncertainty based on certain physical characteristics of roads, namely their linearity, calculated via compactness and elongation, as in [50] and [28]. This is measured during the final steps of the algorithm. Uncertainty during data collection and earlier steps of the algorithm necessarily propagate and influence the final results [51]. These sources are not directly measured, but will be discussed.

Sources of uncertainty for this approach are summarised in Figure 8.1. Uncertainty may be caused by extraneous factors, including image capturing technology and circumstances on the ground. Image capturing is limited by physical factors such as atmospheric disturbance, very bright reflectance when the sun directly hits a tin roof or other reflective surface, the number of wavelengths captured by the satellite, and limited spatial resolution. This could lead to mixed pixels, caused by land cover heterogeneity or irregular road boundaries at a level too small to be captured by the pixels. Circumstances on the ground include road characteristics such as irregular networks, unclear boundaries, heterogeneous reflectance, and occlusion by trees and shadows [3, 40]. Uncertainty is also caused by parameter choices and the working of the algorithm itself. This is true for all extraction algorithms, though the exact way in which uncertainty is inherent to the algorithm, depends on the steps followed. Herein, uncertainty may arise from a loss of information during adaptive median smoothing, conversion of colour to greyscale information, adaptive thresholding, morphological opening, filtering by linearity and size, identification of image objects by the DPT, and adaptive dilation. While the process was developed to remove noise while preserving relevant detail, uncertainty is nonetheless present. The methodology is explained in the next section.

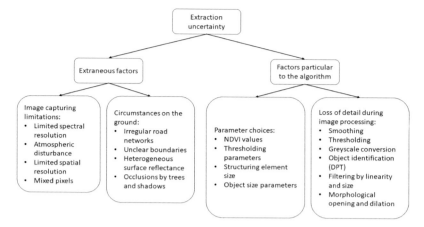

FIGURE 8.1
An overview of the sources of extraction uncertainty.

8.4   Road Extraction Algorithm

This section presents an overview of the algorithm methodology, summarised in Figure 8.2. Interested readers may refer to [6] for an in-depth discussion of the algorithm development.

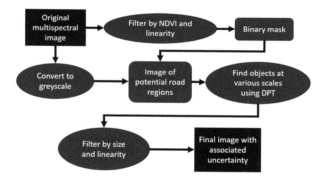

FIGURE 8.2
An overview of the road extraction algorithm.

The input to the algorithm is a multispectral satellite image with four bands, namely RGB and NIR. The NDVI is calculated from the red and NIR information, which is then used to isolate bare soil areas. A lower bound of 0.1 removes shadows and paved surfaces, while an upper bound of 0.3 removes dense vegetation. According to [52], grasslands and shrubs exhibit NDVI values in the interval [0.2,0.3], therefore, this is a lenient upper bound that allows for the inclusion of grassy paths and narrow roads bordered by grass. Optimal NDVI values for effective removal of unwanted areas may change slightly based on the individual image characteristics. This step results in a thresholded binary image containing bare soil areas. These areas are then filtered by linearity, where linearity is defined by compactness and elongation.

$$\text{Compactness} = \frac{2(\sqrt{\pi a})}{p}$$

$$\text{Elongation} = \frac{a}{\text{len}^2}$$

where a is the area of the region, p is the perimeter of the region, and len is the length of the region. Length is measured as the major axis of the smallest ellipse enclosing the region. Objects with compactness below 0.3 and elongation below 0.2 are considered potential roads [28].

The result of this filtering is a binary mask containing potential road areas. The original image is converted to greyscale and multiplied by this mask, resulting in a greyscale image containing the full grey intensity information of only those areas which are potential roads. This is done because the Discrete Pulse Transform (DPT) operates on greyscale input.

The DPT is applied to this image to extract image objects at various scales. These objects are filtered by size, elongation and compactness to identify linear pulses with a road-like shape. This requires the specification of parameters related to the size, elongation and compactness. The size parameters vary depending on the spatial resolution of the image, as well as the typical sizes of roads and objects in the image. User input is therefore required for the size parameters. The parameters used for compactness and elongation are 0.3 and 0.2 as mentioned above.

Certainty is quantified using the compactness and elongation measures, as in the method of [50], also used in [28]. For each image object, the necessity of the object being a road is calculated. The necessity specifies the degree to which it is certain that an object is a road [50], and may also be used to evaluate certainty [53]. This measure is based on compactness and elongation, used as inputs to a Z-shaped fuzzy membership function f.

$$f(x; a, b) = \begin{cases} 1 & x \leq a \\ 1 - 2(\frac{x-a}{b-a})^2 & a \leq x \leq \frac{a+b}{2} \\ 2(\frac{x-b}{b-a})^2 & \frac{a+b}{2} \leq x \leq b \\ 0 & x \geq b \end{cases} \tag{8.1}$$

This results in the measures $\mu_c = f(c_x, a_c, b_c)$, based on compactness, and $\mu_e = f(e_x, a_e, b_e)$, based on elongation, where c_x and e_x are the compactness and elongation, respectively, of an image object x. The parameters a_c and a_e are lower bounds for the compactness and elongation respectively, while b_c and b_e are upper bounds. A lower bound of 0 is used for both compactness and elongation. Since the compactness of a road object must be less than 0.3, an upper bound of $b_c = 0.6 = 2 \times 0.3$ is used. The elongation of a road object is less than 0.2, therefore an upper bound of $b_e = 0.4 = 2 \times 0.2$ is used. The necessity, or certainty that the object is a road, is quantified as follows.

$$\text{Certainty} = 1 - \max(1 - \mu_c, 1 - \mu_e)$$

Image objects with lower compactness and elongation are more likely to be roads, therefore they have a higher associated certainty, and vice versa. The ultimate output of the algorithm is the final road objects along with their associated certainty. The certainty measure is of utmost importance as it gives an indication of the reliability of the extraction inherent to a given dataset, without the need for comparison to reference data. This makes this technique highly relevant for the informal road problem, since reference data on informal roads are not generally available in official records.

8.5   Accuracy Assessment

Accuracy assessment is performed by comparing the extracted roads with a reference, assumed to represent the truth. A variety of methods exist in the literature for assessing the accuracy of the results of road extraction algorithms [35–37]. The work of [37] is seminal in assessing the accuracy of automatic road extraction. Therein, the length of roads in the extraction is compared with the length of roads in the reference. This approach has been widely used throughout the literature, either directly or as the basis of other evaluation methods [54–56]. The above-mentioned method of [35] was adapted from [37], considering edges instead of centrelines. However, since informal roads may not have clearly visible boundaries, relying on a purely edge-based approach is not suitable. In order to determine how closely the edges and centrelines, respectively, of the extraction and reference are positionally aligned, Pratt's Figure of Merit (PFOM) is calculated separately on the road edges and centrelines, providing a measure based on the distance between the extracted and reference centres.

Per-pixel measures are calculated by comparing each pixel of the extraction with each pixel of the reference. A true positive (TP) occurs when the extraction classifies a pixel as a road, and the corresponding pixel in the reference is also a road. A true negative (TN) occurs when the pixel is non-road in both the extraction and the reference. A false positive (FP) is a pixel that is classified as road in the extraction, but is non-road in the reference, while a false negative (FN) is detected as non-road by the extraction but is a road pixel in the reference. Based on the true positive, false positive and false negative counts, the completeness, correctness and quality are calculated as follows:

$$\text{Completeness} = \frac{TP}{TP + FN}$$

$$\text{Correctness} = \frac{TP}{TP + FP}$$

$$\text{Quality} = \frac{TP}{TP + FP + FN}$$

$$= \frac{\text{Compl.} \times \text{Corr.}}{\text{Compl.} + \text{Corr.} - \text{Compl.} \times \text{Corr.}}$$

These measures all range between 0 and 1, where higher values indicate higher accuracy. A higher completeness indicates that fewer false negatives were observed, while a higher correctness indicate that fewer false positives were observed. Quality does not include extra information that the above present in completeness and correctness, but is useful for summarising the accuracy with a single measure for the sake of making comparisons.

The above measures give an estimate of the overall accuracy of the algorithm. However, they do not distinguish between possible sources of error as caused by road characteristics. Pratt's Figure of Merit (PFOM) presents a way to compare the accuracy based on road edges, with that based on road centrelines. The formula is

$$PFOM = \frac{1}{\max\{N_R, N_E\}} \sum_{i=1}^{N_E} \frac{1}{1 + \alpha + \delta_i^2}$$

where N_R is the number of pixels of the reference edges, N_E is the number of pixels of the extracted edges, α is a scaling constant usually set equal to $\frac{1}{9}$, δ_i is the Euclidean distance between the ith detected pixel and the nearest reference pixel. For a perfect match, $PFOM = 100\%$.

Herein, PFOM is calculated in two different ways. It is firstly calculated on the edges of the reference and extraction. The edges are calculated using the Laplace gradient [35]. This edge-based PFOM assesses how precisely the boundaries of objects are captured. Secondly, PFOM is calculated on the reference and extraction skeletons. The formula above is not altered, but the reference and extracted skeletons are used as the reference and extracted image, respectively. This therefore measures the distance between the centrelines. The centrelines are obtained via skeletonisation of the full road objects. The calculation of centrelines depends on the full extent of the objects, including their edges. Therefore, the edge-based and skeleton-based PFOM measures are not independent, but may be interpreted to measure different aspects of the extraction.

The accuracy assessment methods used herein are pixel-based, i.e. the extraction and reference data are compared in raster form. This choice was made for computational simplicity, as the algorithm outputs raster results. Object-based methods have become increasingly popular along with the rise of object-based image analysis [57, 58]. This requires the data to be in vector form, namely the roads are considered as polygons. Radoux et al. [59] provide an overview of some object-based accuracy assessment measures. Many of the same concepts hold as in the pixel-based case. Metrics such as completeness, correctness, quality are calculated based on the number of road objects correctly identified, rather than the number of pixels. The distinction is made between count-based and area-based approaches. For pixel-based assessment, these concepts are equivalent, given that pixels all have the same area. The number of pixels correctly classified is then equal to the area of the image that is correctly classified [59]. MacLean et al. [60] recommend the use of area-based accuracy assessment in the case where the results of an algorithm are in vector form, and incorporates the area of the polygons into the classification matrix. Object-based accuracy assessment allows for a versatile range of measures. Möller et al. [61] compare the geometric properties of extracted and reference objects [61]. Lizarazo [58] presents similarity indices which can be used to evaluate the accuracy of an extraction with regards to various aspects, namely shape, position and edges. Maxwell and Warner [62] propose a centre-weighted approach to accuracy assessment, which allows for fuzzy boundaries between objects of different classes. An object-based accuracy assessment method could be enlightening regarding potential sources of error and hence uncertainty, and could address the problem of unclear road boundaries. Performing object-based assessment on the results of this algorithm is the subject of current extended research.

8.6 Application

This section gives results of the algorithm for images of informal roads in South Africa. To demonstrate the accuracy of the algorithm, the final extracted roads are compared with reference data in this case, which were obtained via manual digitisation. The algorithm is demonstrated to be useful for extracting informal roads with associated uncertainty. This is a critical step for obtaining comprehensive information on the mobility of residents with a view on understanding and planning government response to the spread of COVID-19.

8.6.1 Study Area and Data

The three study areas considered are shown in Figure 8.3. These exhibit roads that are good candidates for formalisation. The datasets are taken from a multispectral VHR Pléiades-1B image with an estimated azimuth angle of $65°$ and a spatial resolution of $0.5\,m$.[9] The study areas are situated in the north-western parts of Gauteng Province and the south-eastern parts of North West Province, South Africa. The informal settlements in these areas are in many cases starting to formalise and the informal roads are beginning to take on a grid-like structure.

Figure 8.4 shows possible challenges for road extraction. The roads in area 1 are of a light colour set in dark surroundings. Challenges for this area include roads occluded by trees, circled in green, grassy roads, circled in blue, as well as light-coloured patches of sand, circled in yellow. Areas 2 and 3 both exhibit narrow roads in a semi-rural setting, lined with open yards of similar colour to the roads. Both areas also contain some paved roads, which should not be detected by the algorithm. Some of the roads in area 3 are partly vegetated, which may lead to false negatives. The trees occluding parts of the roads may lead to false negatives, while sandy patches may cause false positives. The footpaths in area 3 (circled in grey) are of particular note. Road extraction algorithms do not generally consider footpaths to be roads, and footpaths are indeed not likely to be officially recognised as roads. However, they remain conduits for travel, and may provide important information regarding mobility, especially between residential areas.

---

[9]Data provided by and used with permission from the CSIR.

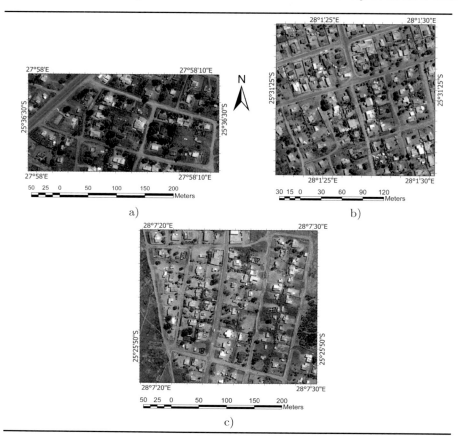

FIGURE 8.3
Areas to which the algorithm was applied. a) Hoekfontein, North West Province; b) Mabopane, North West Province; c) Soshanguve, Gauteng Province

8.6.2   Demonstration for Area 1

The process is demonstrated for area 1 (Figure 8.3 (a)). This area is characterised by narrow roads of a bright colour relative to their surroundings. There is also a paved road present in the image, which should not be detected by the algorithm.

Figure 8.5 shows the first processing steps. The original image is in (a). The image is thresholded by NDVI value in (b), and filtered by linearity in (c). This binary image is multiplied with the greyscale version of the original image, resulting in the image of potential road regions in (d).

The DPT is now applied to the image of potential road regions. This obtains image structures, or pulses, at various scales, as illustrated in Figure 8.6. At small scales, such as in (a), pulses are detected that correspond to all the larger image objects. However, pulses corresponding to unwanted non-road objects are also detected. At large scales (e.g. Figure 8.6(d)), those parts of the road network that are joined, are detected. However, roads smaller than that scale are not detected. This suggests the necessity of combining the results of the DPT at smaller and larger scales. Therefore, those pulses smaller than a given threshold, are intersected with the pulses larger than that threshold. The goal of this intersection is to remove noise and small pulses that are not part of road objects, while preserving image pulses that form part of larger objects, which may potentially be roads. The results of this step are shown in Figure 8.7. Noise and undesirable smaller objects are removed, while larger areas that might contain roads are preserved.

Lastly, any object that does not satisfy the compactness and elongation requirements is removed.

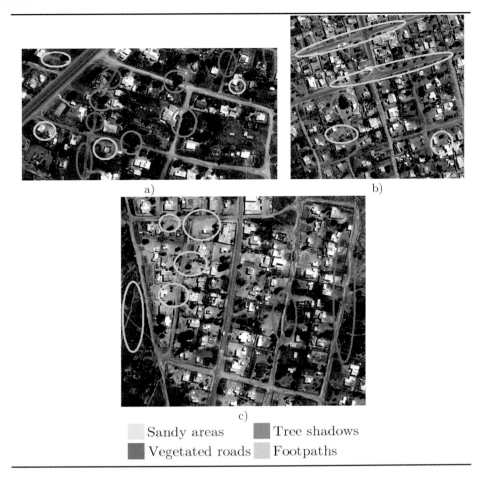

a)

b)

c)

| Sandy areas | Tree shadows |
| Vegetated roads | Footpaths |

FIGURE 8.4

Possible sources of error for areas 1-3 shown in (a)-(c) respectively.

The final results are given in Figure 8.8 (a), and overlaid with the original image in (b) for illustrative purposes.

TABLE 8.1

Certainty measures for area 1.

	Minimum	Mean	Maximum	% Objects with Certainty $> 50\%$
Certainty	60.35%	79.36%	95.80%	100.00%

The certainty associated with the extracted road objects is quantified via the certainty measure defined in Section 8.4, based on the compactness and elongation of the road objects. Figure 8.9(a) illustrates the certainty. Lighter road objects are more certain to be roads based on their compactness and elongation, while darker objects are less certain. The results are given in Table

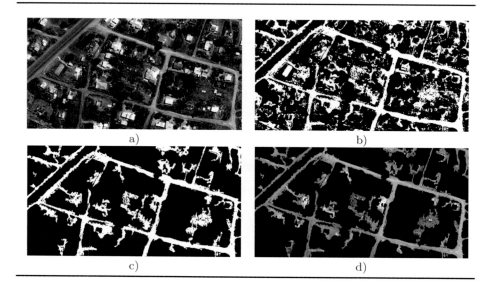

FIGURE 8.5

First steps for area 1. a) The original image. b) Areas with an NDVI below 0.1 or above 0.3 are removed, thereby isolating bare-soil areas. c) The results on the image in (b) after filtering by linearity. d) The mask in (c) overlaid with the greyscale image contains potential road regions.

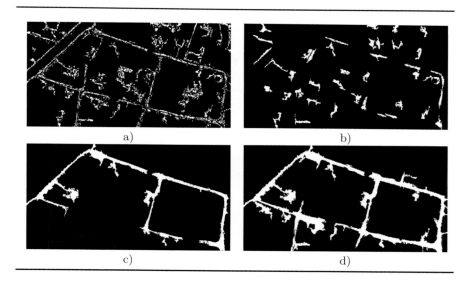

FIGURE 8.6

Image pulses of various sizes extracted using the DPT. a) Pulse sizes 0-100. b) 300-400. c) 8 000-9 000. d) 15 000-16 000.

8.1. The average certainty per image object was 79%. All road objects were more than 50% certain to be roads. The minimum certainty observed was 60%, while the maximum was 96%.

To quantify the extraction accuracy, extracted roads are compared to reference data, which was obtained via manual digitisation. Figure 8.10(a) and (b) show the extracted results and the

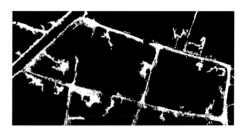

FIGURE 8.7
Pulses intersected by size.

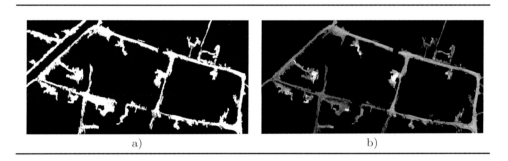

a) b)

FIGURE 8.8
Results of the process. a) The binary image is the final output. b) The resulting image overlaid with the original image for illustrative purposes.

0 1

FIGURE 8.9
Certainty associated with extracted road objects. The lighter the colour of the image object, the more certain it is to be a road, as measured its by compactness and elongation.

reference roads, respectively, overlaid with the original image for illustration. The binary images are compared at pixel-level to obtain completeness, correctness and quality metrics, and at edge level and at centreline level using PFOM. The results are discussed in Section 8.6.3.

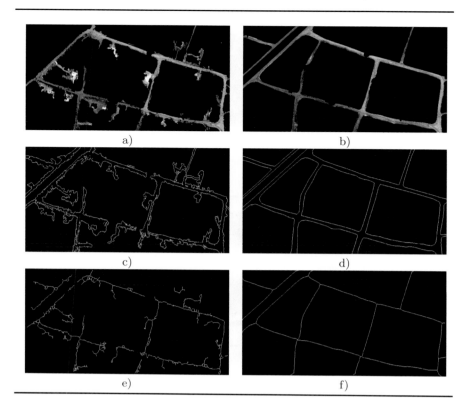

FIGURE 8.10
Comparison of results and reference. a) Extracted road objects (overlaid with the original image for illustrative purposes). b) Reference roads. c) Extracted road edges. d) Reference road edges. e) Skeleton of the extracted roads. f) Skeleton of the reference.

8.6.3   Results for All Areas

The results of the algorithm are displayed in Figure 8.11. These show which parts of the roads were detected correctly, as well as false positives and false negatives. The results the pixel-based accuracy and Pratt's Figure of Merit (PFOM) are given in Tables 8.2 and 8.3 respectively.

The pixel-based measures, quantifying accuracy in terms of overall extent, are given Table 8.2. For area 1, the completeness figure of 66.93% indicates that over two-thirds of the road pixels were accurately captured by the algorithm. The completeness was not much lower for areas 2 and 3, being above 60% in both cases. This indicates that not too many false negatives were observed. The correctness measures for areas 1, 2 and 3 were 57%, 43.33% and 38% respectively, indicating that false positives presented a greater challenge, especially in area 3. For areas 1 and 2, the per-pixel quality corresponds closely to the PFOM metric based on road edges, indicating that the extent was captured with approximately 45% accuracy for area 1, and with 34% for area 2. Area 3 experienced a 4% difference in pixel-based quality and edge-based PFOM, with a higher accuracy according to edge-based PFOM. The PFOM metrics based on road skeletons measure the alignment of extracted and reference centrelines. This gives a value of 47.60% for area 1, 33.50% for area 2 and 32% for area 3. While the presence of roads was therefore generally detected correctly, challenges were experienced at the edges. This is to be expected given the imprecise boundaries of unpaved roads and bare soil areas adjacent to roads. The skeletons-based PFOM was higher than the edge-based PFOM for areas 1 and 2, which was expected, but surprisingly the edge-based

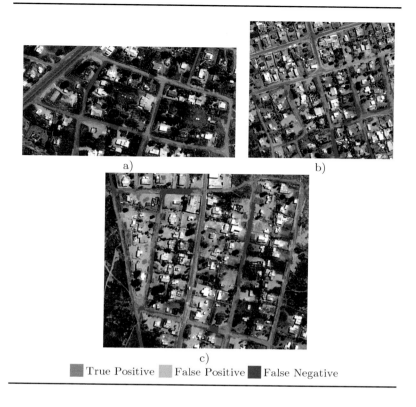

c)

■ True Positive   ■ False Positive   ■ False Negative

FIGURE 8.11
Results of the algorithm for areas 1-3 shown in a)-c) respectively.

TABLE 8.2
Per-pixel accuracy measures.

Area	1	2	3
Completeness	66.93%	61.56%	60.56%
Correctness	57.00%	43.33%	38.00%
Quality	44.48%	34.11%	30.46%

measure was higher for area 3. This may be due to the large number of false positives in area 3, as the centrelines of these regions would not correspond to the centrelines of any roads in the reference. This explanation also accounts for the greater similarity between the measures for area 2 as opposed to area 1, since area 2 contained more false positives than area 1. The results indicate that area 3 experienced the most false positives and negatives, while area 1 experienced the least. It is of note that area 3 outperformed area 2 in the edge-based PFOM measurement. However, the measures were low for both areas, indicating that road edges remain a challenge.

Figure 8.12 shows the certainty associated with the extracted road segments. Table 8.4 gives relevant statistics. Area 3 generally had the lowest certainty scores, except for the maximum, where the lowest was experienced by area 2. All areas had maxima of over 87%, and all means were over 75%. The highest variance was only 1.47% (area 1).

TABLE 8.3
Pratt's Figure of Merit.

PFOM based on:	Area		
	1	2	3
Edges	45.33%	33.86%	34.72%
Skeletons	47.60%	33.50%	32.00%

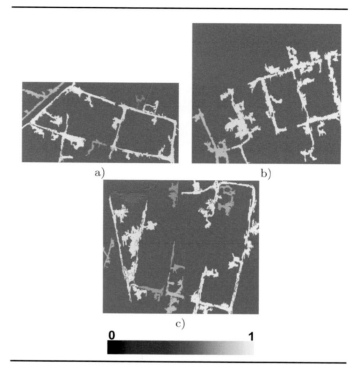

a)   b)

c)

0   1

FIGURE 8.12
Certainty associated with extracted road objects. The lighter the colour of the image object, the more certain it is to be a road, as measured its by compactness and elongation. a)-c) show results for areas 1-3 respectively.

TABLE 8.4
Certainty statistics for all areas, calculated on all extracted road objects.

Area	1	2	3
Mean	79.36%	89.22%	76.58%
Minimum	60.35%	82.35%	57.65%
Maximum	95.80%	93.46%	95.63%
Percent > 50%	100.00%	100.00%	100.00%
Variance	1.47%	0.19%	1.40%

8.7   Discussion

The results indicate that the algorithm successfully detects the presence of informal roads in a variety of circumstances and for various road characteristics. Significantly, the presence of curved roads was detected accurately. Footpaths were also detected, which provide valuable information regarding the movement of people in residential areas. Improvement is needed to determine road boundaries and reduce errors, especially false positives.

Various sources of uncertainty are identified. Figure 8.13 illustrates road characteristics and environmental circumstances that led to false positives and negatives in the analysis. This is compared to the possible causes of error that were identified a priori in Figure 8.4, namely occlusions by trees, narrow and vegetated roads, road-adjacent open areas of similar colour to roads, and dusty paved roads.

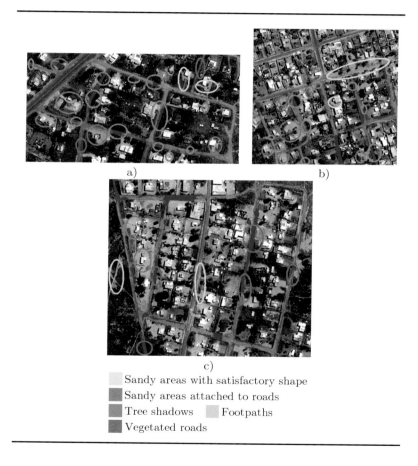

a)   b)

c)

   Sandy areas with satisfactory shape
   Sandy areas attached to roads
   Tree shadows   Footpaths
   Vegetated roads

FIGURE 8.13
Results of the algorithm for areas 1-3 shown in a)-c) respectively.

Trees and tree shadows contributed to false negatives in areas 1 and 2, as shown by the areas circled in green in Figure 8.13(a) and (b). In areas 1 and 3, some roads were not detected since they were partly overgrown. This is illustrated by the areas circled in magenta and cyan, respectively, in Figure 8.13(a) and (c). Area 3 experienced the greatest challenges with false negatives, while area 1 experienced the least. Despite some sources of false negatives, most roads were detected, as indicated visually and also by the relatively high completeness for all areas.

False positives presented a greater challenge, as evidenced by the lower correctness scores. This is confirmed visually. In area 1 (Figure 8.13(a)), some buildings were not eliminated in the NDVI thresholding step, and contributed to the false positives detected. It is possible that these roofs were made from clay tiles or some substance that was spectrally similar to bare soil. This is a challenge that should be kept in mind for future applications, especially in areas with traditional housing, where the roofs are made of local clay or grass. False positives were also caused by unpaved areas with road-like linearity. These can be seen in all areas, circled in yellow. In area 1, these non-road areas with road-like characteristics are clearly navigable and used for transport, however, they were not considered roads in the reference due to their short length and the fact that they terminate in yards. This contrasts with the shoulders of the paved road in area 1, which were captured in the reference due to their width, visual clarity, and the fact that they connect to other informal roads, implying that they are used for transport. In area 2 (Figure 8.13(b)), a high number of false positives was caused by the large section of formal road that was falsely detected as road. The road was not removed by the thresholding step due to the layer of dust over the road. In all areas, unpaved areas attached to roads caused false positives. Due to being connected with the unpaved roads, the algorithm considered them to be part of the same image object, thereby including them with the detected roads.

The footpaths in area 3 are of particular importance. These were detected as roads. From the perspective of detecting roads to monitor mobility, this is a desirable result, since footpaths are used to move within and between residential areas. Detecting footpaths is therefore relevant for understanding population mobility patterns, especially in the residential sector.

8.8   Conclusion and Future Work

The algorithm generally works well for detecting the presence of informal roads. It additionally detects road shoulders, footpaths, and elongated navigable stretches, all of which can be used for transport. Non-road areas that are connected to roads provide challenges in terms of false positives. False negatives were caused by trees, shadows, and narrow and vegetated roads. The detection of precise extents and edges of roads presented a significant challenge. At this stage, the algorithm can be used to identify the location of informal roads. It also compares favourably to other extraction algorithms, as discussed in detail in [6].

Further refinement to the algorithm is needed to reduce false positives and refine road edges. Future research could also incorporate information on the presence, orientation and connectivity of paved roads. Additional data could be used, for instance, images could be compared over time. Informal roads that broaden over time are in use, and therefore considered important by the community, while informal roads that are not in use will diminish over time. Additional covariates could also be used to predict where roads will appear, based on convenient navigability of the area under investigation. Covariates could also be included to assist in uncertainty quantification. However, incorporating information additional to the multispectral satellite image will increase the data requirement. This should be done with caution, as the goal of the algorithm is to be implemented within the constraints of the processing ability and data availability in a developing world context. Another avenue of future research is the development of comprehensive uncertainty measures, which could be integrated with road extraction methodology. Evaluating this algorithm using object-based accuracy assessment is the subject of current research. This aims to address the problem of unclear road boundaries. In the future, we aim to expand the uncertainty quantification to allow for fuzzy or indeterminate road boundaries.

Informal-road extraction provides much-needed data on informal roads that is otherwise unavailable to government and modellers. This data is critical for obtaining a comprehensive view of mobility within residential areas, and hence for mobility modelling, contact tracing and service provision. Further development of uncertainty analysis will be beneficial as understanding the uncertainty associated with this data will help decision-makers to better evaluate the reliability of the data used in planning COVID-19 response. As COVID-19 data becomes more accessible in South Africa, merging of this work with case location data will provide further insights into the spread of the disease. Such a direction is vital for a virus that will affect those most vulnerable in communities, leaving a scar on society for years to come.

References

[1] Simon Runsten, Francesco Fuso Nerini, and Louise Tait. Energy provision in South African informal urban settlements - a multi-criteria sustainability analysis. *Energy Strategy Reviews*, 19:76–84, 2018.

[2] Peter Haunold and Werner Kuhn. A keystroke level analysis of manual map digitizing. In *European Conference on Spatial Information Theory*, pages 406–420. Springer, 1993.

[3] RAA. Nobrega, CG. O'Hara, and JA. Quintanilha. Detecting road in informal settlements surrounding Sao Paulo City by using object-based classification. In *1st International Conference on Object-based Image Analysis*, 2006.

[4] Runsheng Li and Fanzhi Cao. Road network extraction from high-resolution remote sensing image using homogenous property and shape feature. *Journal of the Indian Society of Remote Sensing*, 46(1):51–58, 2018. doi: 10.1007/s12524-017-0678-6.

[5] Abolfazl Abdollahi, Hamid Reza Riyahi Bakhtiari, and Mojgan Pashaei Nejad. Investigation of SVM and level set interactive methods for road extraction from Google Earth images. *Journal of the Indian Society of Remote Sensing*, 46(3):423–430, 2017. doi: 10.1007/s12524-017-0702-x.

[6] Renate Thiede. Statistical accuracy of an extraction algorithm for linear image objects. Master's thesis, University of Pretoria, 2019.

[7] Juan B Mena. State of the art on automatic road extraction for GIS update: a novel classification. *Pattern Recognition Letters*, 24(16):3037–3058, 2003.

[8] Weixing Wang, Nan Yang, Yi Zhang, Fengping Wang, Ting Cao, and Patrik Eklund. A review of road extraction from remote sensing images. *Journal of Traffic and Transportation Engineering*, 3(3):271–282, 2016. doi: 10.1016/j.jtte.2016.05.005.

[9] I Kahraman, I Karas, and A Akay. Road extraction techniques from remote sensing images: A review. *International Archives of Photogrammetry Remote Sensing and Spatial Information Sciences*, 42:339–342, 2018.

[10] Chunsun Zhang, Shunji Murai, and Emmanuel Baltsavias. Road network detection by mathematical morphology. In *ISPRS Workshop on 3DGeospatial Data Production: Meeting Application Requirements*, pages 185–200, 1999. doi: 10.3929/ethz-a-004334280.

[11] Silvia Valero, Jocelyn Chanussot, Jon Atli Benediktsson, Hugues Talbot, and Björn Waske. Advanced directional mathematical morphology for the detection of the road network in very high resolution remote sensing images. *Pattern Recognition Letters*, 31(10):1120–1127, 2010. doi: 10.1016/j.patrec.2009.12.018.

[12] C Zhu, W Shi, M Pesaresi, L Liu, X Chen, and B King. The recognition of road network from high-resolution satellite remotely sensed data using image morphological characteristics. *International Journal of Remote Sensing*, 26(24):5493–5508, 2005.

[13] Sahar Movaghati, Alireza Moghaddamjoo, and Ahad Tavakoli. Road extraction from satellite images using particle filtering and extended Kalman filtering. *IEEE Transactions on Geoscience and Remote Sensing*, 48(7):2807–2817, 2010.

[14] Christian Heipke, Carsten T Steger, and R Multhammer. Hierarchical approach to automatic road extraction from aerial imagery. In *Integrating Photogrammetric Techniques with Scene Analysis and Machine Vision II*, volume 2486, pages 222–231. International Society for Optics and Photonics, 1995.

[15] J Amini, MR Saradjian, JAR Blais, C Lucas, and A Azizi. Automatic road-side extraction from large scale imagemaps. *International Journal of Applied Earth Observation and Geoinformation*, 4(2):95–107, 2002. doi: 10.1016/s0303-2434(02)00004-1.

[16] JB Mena and JA Malpica. Color image segmentation using the Dempster-Shafer theory of evidence for the fusion of texture. *International Archives of Photogrammetry Remote Sensing and Spatial Information Sciences*, 34(3/W8):139–144, 2003.

[17] Jiuxiang Hu, Anshuman Razdan, John C Femiani, Ming Cui, and Peter Wonka. Road network extraction and intersection detection from aerial images by tracking road footprints. *IEEE Transactions on Geoscience and Remote Sensing*, 45(12):4144–4157, 2007.

[18] Lizy Abraham and M Sasikumar. A fuzzy based road network extraction from degraded satellite images. In *2013 International Conference on Advances in Computing, Communications and Informatics (ICACCI)*, pages 2032–2036. IEEE, 2013.

[19] Abolfazl Abdollahi, Biswajeet Pradhan, Nagesh Shukla, Subrata Chakraborty, and Abdullah Alamri. Deep learning approaches applied to remote sensing datasets for road extraction: A state-of-the-art review. *Remote Sensing*, 12(9):1444, 2020.

[20] Xiangrong Zhang, Xiao Han, Chen Li, Xu Tang, Huiyu Zhou, and Licheng Jiao. Aerial image road extraction based on an improved generative adversarial network. *Remote Sensing*, 11(8):930, 2019.

[21] Jun Wang, Jingwei Song, Mingquan Chen, and Zhi Yang. Road network extraction: A neural-dynamic framework based on deep learning and a finite state machine. *International Journal of Remote Sensing*, 36 (12):3144–3169, 2015.

[22] Teerapong Panboonyuen, Peerapon Vateekul, Kulsawasd Jitkajornwanich, and Siam Lawawirojwong. An enhanced deep convolutional encoder-decoder network for road segmentation on aerial imagery. In *International Conference on Computing and Information Technology*, pages 191–201. Springer, 2017.

[23] Jonathan Long, Evan Shelhamer, and Trevor Darrell. Fully convolutional networks for semantic segmentation. In *Proceedings of the IEEE Conference on Computer Vision and Pattern Recognition*, pages 3431–3440, 2015.

[24] Emmanuel Maggiori, Yuliya Tarabalka, Guillaume Charpiat, and Pierre Alliez. Fully convolutional neural networks for remote sensing image classification. In *2016 IEEE International Geoscience and Remote Sensing Symposium (IGARSS)*, pages 5071–5074. IEEE, 2016.

[25] Alexander Buslaev, Selim S Seferbekov, Vladimir Iglovikov, and Alexey Shvets. Fully convolutional network for automatic road extraction from satellite imagery. In *CVPR Workshops*, pages 207–210, 2018.

[26] Yanan Wei, Zulin Wang, and Mai Xu. Road structure refined CNN for road extraction in aerial image. *IEEE Geoscience and Remote Sensing Letters*, 14(5):709–713, 2017.

[27] RN Thiede, IN Fabris-Rotelli, A Stein, P Debba, and M Li. Road extraction in remote sensing images of South African informal settlements. Honours research project, 2017.

[28] Mengmeng Li, Alfred Stein, Wietske Bijker, and Qingming Zhan. Region-based urban road extraction from VHR satellite images using binary partition tree. *International Journal of Applied Earth Observation and Geoinformation*, 44:217–225, 2016. doi: 10.1016/j.jag.2015.09.005.

[29] Weifeng Liu, Zhenqing Zhang, Shuying Li, and Dapeng Tao. Road detection by using a generalized Hough transform. *Remote Sensing*, 9(6):590, 2017. doi: 10.3390/rs9060590.

[30] Mourad Bouziani, Kalifa Goita, and Dong-Chen He. Rule-based classification of a very high resolution image in an urban environment using multispectral segmentation guided by cartographic data. *IEEE Transactions on Geoscience and Remote Sensing*, 48(8):3198–3211, 2010.

[31] Michael Bock, Panteleimon Xofis, Jonathan Mitchley, Godela Rossner, and Michael Wissen. Object-oriented methods for habitat mapping at multiple scales-Case studies from Northern Germany and Wye Downs, UK. *Journal for Nature Conservation*, 13(2-3):75–89, 2005.

[32] Silvia Valero, Philippe Salembier, Jocelyn Chanussot, and Carles M Cuadras. Improved binary partition tree construction for hyperspectral images: application to object detection. In *IEEE International Geoscience and Remote Sensing Symposium*, pages 2515–2518. IEEE, 2011. doi: 10.1109/igarss.2011.6049723.

[33] CH Rohwer and DP Laurie. The discrete pulse transform. *SIAM Journal on Mathematical Analysis*, 38(3): 1012–1034, 2006.

[34] CH Rohwer and LM Toerien. Locally monotone robust approximation of sequences. *Journal of Computational and Applied Mathematics*, 36(3):399–408, 1991.

[35] Guilherme Pina Cardim, EA Silva, and Maurício Araújo Dias. Algorithm development for analysis of statistical accuracy of the extraction of cartographic features in digital images. *Transactions on Machine Learning and Artificial Intelligence*, 2(2):32–47, 2014.

[36] Christian Wiedemann. External evaluation of road networks. *International Archives of Photogrammetry Remote Sensing and Spatial Information Sciences*, 34(3/W8):93–98, 2003.

[37] Christian Heipke, H Mayer, C Wiedemann, and O Jamet. Evaluation of automatic road extraction. *International Archives of Photogrammetry and Remote Sensing*, 32(3 SECT 4W2):151–160, 1997.

[38] Stefan Hinz, Christian Wiedemann, and Heinrich Ebner. Self-diagnosis within automatic road network extraction. *International Archives of Photogrammetry Remote Sensing and Spatial Information Sciences*, 34(2):185–192, 2002.

[39] Konstantin Osypov, Yi Yang, Aimé Fournier, Natalia Ivanova, Ran Bachrach, Can Evren Yarman, Yu You, Dave Nichols, and Marta Woodward. Model-uncertainty quantification in seismic tomography: method and applications. *Geophysical Prospecting*, 61(Challenges of Seismic Imaging and Inversion Devoted to Goldin): 1114–1134, 2013.

[40] R. N. Thiede, I. N. Fabris-Rotelli, A. Stein, P. Debba, and M. Li. Uncertainty quantification for the extraction of informal roads from remote sensing images of South Africa. *South African Geographical Journal*, 0(0): 1–24, 2019. doi: 10.1080/03736245.2019.1685404. URL https://doi.org/10.1080/03736245.2019.1685404.

[41] Guangxing Wang, George Z Gertner, Shoufan Fang, and Alan B Anderson. A methodology for spatial uncertainty analysis of remote sensing and GIS products. *Photogrammetric Engineering & Remote Sensing*, 71(12):1423–1432, 2005.

[42] Ruben Balcaen, PL Reu, Pascal Lava, and Dimitri Debruyne. Stereo-DIC uncertainty quantification based on simulated images. *Experimental Mechanics*, 57(6):939–951, 2017.

[43] Arko Lucieer, Alfred Stein, and Peter Fisher. Multivariate texture-based segmentation of remotely sensed imagery for extraction of objects and their uncertainty. *International Journal of Remote Sensing*, 26(14): 2917–2936, 2005.

[44] Kasper Cockx, Tim Van de Voorde, and Frank Canters. Quantifying uncertainty in remote sensing-based urban land-use mapping. *International Journal of Applied Earth Observation and Geoinformation*, 31: 154–166, 2014.

[45] Daniel Schraik, Petri Varvia, Lauri Korhonen, and Miina Rautiainen. Bayesian inversion of a forest reflectance model using sentinel-2 and landsat 8 satellite images. *Journal of Quantitative Spectroscopy and Radiative Transfer*, 233:1–12, 2019.

[46] Michael Kampffmeyer, Arnt-Borre Salberg, and Robert Jenssen. Semantic segmentation of small objects and modeling of uncertainty in urban remote sensing images using deep convolutional neural networks. In *Proceedings of the IEEE Conference on Computer Vision and Pattern Recognition Workshops*, pages 1–9, 2016.

[47] Brian P Salmon, Waldo Kleynhans, J Corné Olivier, and Colin P Schwegmann. Improving features used for hyper-temporal land cover change detection by reducing the uncertainty in the feature extraction method. In *2017 IEEE International Geoscience and Remote Sensing Symposium (IGARSS)*, pages 1740–1743. IEEE, 2017.

[48] Divyani Kohli, Richard Sliuzas, Norman Kerle, and Alfred Stein. An ontology of slums for image-based classification. *Computers, Environment and Urban Systems*, 36(2):154–163, 2012.

[49] Phillipe Wernette, Ashton Shortridge, David P Lusch, and Alan F Arbogast. Accounting for positional uncertainty in historical shoreline change analysis without ground reference information. *International Journal of Remote Sensing*, 38(13):3906–3922, 2017.

[50] Imane Sebari and Dong-Chen He. Automatic fuzzy object-based analysis of VHSR images for urban objects extraction. *ISPRS Journal of Photogrammetry and Remote Sensing*, 79:171–184, 2013. doi: 10.1016/j.isprsjprs.2013.02.006.

[51] Qi Zhang and Penglin Zhang. An uncertainty descriptor for quantitative measurement of the uncertainty of remote sensing images. *Remote Sensing*, 11(13):1560, 2019.

[52] AK Bhandari, A Kumar, and GK Singh. Feature extraction using Normalized Difference Vegetation Index (NDVI): A case study of Jabalpur city. *Procedia Technology*, 6:612–621, 2012.

[53] Bernadette Bouchon-Meunier, Radko Mesiar, Christophe Marsala, and Maria Rifqi. Compositional rule of inference as an analogical scheme. *Fuzzy Sets and Systems*, 138(1):53–65, 2003.

[54] Guilherme Cardim, Erivaldo Silva, Mauricio Dias, Ignácio Bravo, and Alfredo Gardel. Statistical evaluation and analysis of road extraction methodologies using a unique dataset from remote sensing. *Remote Sensing*, 10(4):620, 2018.

[55] KS Sim, YY Kho, Chih Ping Tso, ME Nia, and HY Ting. A contrast stretching bilateral closing top-hat Otsu threshold technique for crack detection in images. *Scanning*, 35(2):75–87, 2013.

[56] Moslem Ouled Sghaier and Richard Lepage. Road extraction from very high resolution remote sensing optical images based on texture analysis and beamlet transform. *IEEE Journal of Selected Topics in Applied Earth Observations and Remote Sensing*, 9(5):1946–1958, 2015.

[57] Thomas Blaschke, Geoffrey J Hay, Maggi Kelly, Stefan Lang, Peter Hofmann, Elisabeth Addink, Raul Queiroz Feitosa, Freek Van der Meer, Harald Van der Werff, Frieke Van Coillie, and D Tiede. Geographic object-based image analysis–towards a new paradigm. *ISPRS Journal of Photogrammetry and Remote Sensing*, 87: 180–191, 2014.

[58] Ivan Lizarazo. Accuracy assessment of object-based image classification: another STEP. *International Journal of Remote Sensing*, 35(16):6135–6156, 2014.

[59] Julien Radoux and Patrick Bogaert. Good practices for object-based accuracy assessment. *Remote Sensing*, 9(7):646, 2017.

[60] Meghan Graham MacLean and Russell G Congalton. Map accuracy assessment issues when using an object-oriented approach. In *Proceedings of the American Society for Photogrammetry and Remote Sensing 2012 Annual Conference, Sacramento, CA, USA*, pages 19–23, 2012.

[61] Markus Möller, Jens Birger, Anthony Gidudu, and Cornelia Gläßer. A framework for the geometric accuracy assessment of classified objects. *International Journal of Remote Sensing*, 34(24):8685–8698, 2013.

[62] Aaron E Maxwell and Timothy A Warner. Thematic classification accuracy assessment with inherently uncertain boundaries: An argument for center-weighted accuracy assessment metrics. *Remote Sensing*, 12 (12):1905, 2020.

9

Management and Analysis of Maritime Geospatial Data During COVID-19: Case Studies, Opportunities and Challenges

Rafael Ponce Urbina, Orhun Aydin and Steve Snow

This chapter presents a holistic view of the uses of GIS to monitor, analyze and disseminate knowledge pertaining to maritime geospatial data during the COVID-19 pandemic are showcased. The challenges pertaining to authoritative data production during a pandemic are identified. Challenges faced by national hydrographic offices and International Maritime Organization (IMO) members to provide the most up to date information for the Safety of Life at Sea (SOLAS) during the pandemic is discussed. The value brought by analyzing and mapping such data during the pandemic is demonstrated with case studies on tracking the impacts of pandemic on maritime supply chains, continuity of operations for business and ports, and maintaining status of ship fleets. This chapter is concluded with public-facing analytical products that serve and analyze maritime data.

9.1 Introduction

COVID-19 pandemic has been disrupting human movement, travel and trade patterns on air, land and sea. Impacts of the current pandemic on maritime traffic offers challenges and opportunities to quantify the level of supply chain disruption, delineate high-risk sea routes and provide a proxy for the intercontinental spread of COVID-19.

Disruptions to maritime industry have significant consequences for the local and global economy that rely on transport and trade of goods [1]. Understanding long and short term impacts of COVID-19 on the maritime supply line disruptions is required to increase the resilience of maritime transportation systems to future pandemics, and hasten the recovery period of the maritime ecosystem.

Geographic accuracy is essential in detecting and responding to any infectious disease outbreak [2], whether is a pandemic [3], a seasonal influenza [3], or a local outbreak of food-borne illness [4]. Based on experience of GIS use supporting many health-related agencies at all levels of government, critical areas in which geospatial information is critical are summarized below:

- Assessing risks
- Evaluating threats
- Tracking outbreaks
- Maintaining situational awareness

- Documenting disparity
- Ensuring the focused allocation of resources
- Notifying communities
- Minimizing the disruption caused by necessary community health intervention

Minimizing the impacts of the COVID-19 pandemic on the maritime ecosystem can only be possible via continuous geospatial data feeds, impactful analysis and enabling artificial intelligence systems, and disseminating data and knowledge in an effective manner. We discuss the multifaceted impacts of COVID-19 maritime industry within the context of GIS.

9.1.1 The Use of Geospatial Data and Systems

Location information is critical to decision making associated with large outbreaks, determining the origins of the infection, spread (speed and direction) and measures to isolate it, how to respond to it and how to organize the work force to minimize disruption as much as possible [5].

Location intelligence becomes even more critical when the outbreak can no longer be contained through contact tracing and quarantine [6]. Location-based information can be used to inform multiple, specific community interventions and activities [7]. Using common types of GIS analysis, such as mapping where things are, mapping the "most" and "least", mapping disease density, finding "what's inside" or "what's nearby", and mapping change, authorities can prioritize interventions and re-organize their resources [8]. Time is another crucial dimension that is naturally represented inside GIS [9]. Temporal and spatio-temporal analysis of geo-enabled data pertaining to COVID-19 is essential understanding current trade delays and supply line disruptions [10].

The maritime community, especially the shipping industry and port authorities, need geospatial information to safeguard the integrity of the logistic chain to maintain the essential goods supply during the pandemic. [11].

9.1.2 Impacts on the Maritime Community

The maritime community is wide and includes many different sectors, all connected in one way or another, and all suffering the impacts of the COVID-19 pandemic [12]. In an attempt to simplify this complex ecosystem, we have divided it into those sectors that affect the so called blue economy, with two large branches: shipping and ports. In this classification, we exclude fisheries and tourism (leisure yachting) despite their importance to local and global economy. Local and partial data pertinent to fisheries and tourism makes it cumbersome to evaluate the global challenges pertinent to and the use of maritime geospatial data during the COVID-19 pandemic.

The shipping industry has been significantly impacted by the pandemic. Broadly, we can divide this impact in three main categories:

- Cargo or goods (containers and bulk)
- Oil and gas (tankers)
- Passengers (cruise liners)

The transport of goods and hydrocarbons appear to have been operating consistently, which is true in some respects. That and the global economic downturn are presenting unprecedented challenges that can cause disruptions in the supply chain. Some estimates by the International Monetary Fund estimate global GDP growth will fall 3% in 2020 [13, 14], and the World Trade Organization (WTO) expects a fall in trade between 13% and 32% [15]. Depending on the duration of the outbreak and how governments deal with it, there could be a partial recovery in 2021 [14].

According to the WTO the most affected sectors in Q2 2020 have been automobiles and containers and have seen a weak demand for goods in general as well as some constraints in the supply chain [14]. The largest container company in the world, Moller-Maersk has stated that container volumes could be around 25% lower in Q2 2020 [14].

Because of countries reducing the risk of infection of COVID-19, ship traffic has been reduced by approximately 25% in the first half of 2020. The pandemic has resulted in less demand for imports and exports of cargo between countries. Many goods that cannot store for 14 days cannot be shipped due to 14 day waiting periods in quarantine. Because of the reduced demand for cargo many companies have become bankrupt due to the pandemic.

In the oil and gas sector, besides the common impacts to navigation, ship's maintenance and crew rotation, specific situations such as the floating oil storage can be significantly affected. Because of the drop in oil prices due to high production with low demand, the need for floating storage has skyrocketed. According to S&P Global Platts, in May of 2020 there were more than 200 million barrels of oil and derived products on floating storage in tankers, which is around 5% of the global carrying capacity. These tankers will need maintenance and to fulfill contractual requirements. Many tankers are at anchor or idling near major ports around the world with the risk of getting exposed to extreme weather conditions, potential piracy activities and in some cases, to political conflict. The longer these tankers stay at sea fully loaded, the bigger the risk of cargo degradation or loss because of the extended time or worse, the risk of accidents and environmental pollution.

As per the cruise industry, it generates an estimated $150 billions in global economic activity, supporting more than one million jobs worldwide [16]. This sector is perhaps the one that is most impacted by the pandemic, with almost no activities due to several COVID-19 outbreaks on board, travel restrictions, port closures and prohibition to sail from the US Center for Disease Control (CDC) since March of 2020 [17]. With around 95 % of the global cruise fleet in lay-up, there are concerns on risks for both, ship owners and insurance companies due to the Atlantic hurricane season, considering that almost half of those ships are in and around the Americas. Similarly, for the typhoon season in the Pacific. Other important impacts are the costs of having these ships laid-up for an extended period of time, which is estimated between $1 million and $3 million per month and the costs of bringing them back to service.

Those above are perhaps the most evident impacts to the shipping industry, but there are other less visible and equally important aspects that are being impacted, such as disruptions on machinery maintenance and repairs, ship owners risk delays on scheduled maintenance and services, disruption in the supply of spare parts and other essentials such as lube-oil and hydraulic oils and travel restrictions for specialist engineers to access the ship to provide maintenance or repairs. Engines can also be damaged by delays in the analysis of sulphur emissions, because of the cap on sulphur emissions under International Maritime Organization (IMO) 2020, vessels have been using blended low-sulphur fuels, which in order to avoid engine damage, require analysis prior to be used by the ship's engines. This requires the dispatch of fuel samples to shore-based laboratories and with COVID-19 restrictions, it may not be possible to do in time. There are manuals that detail how to proceed with on board testing kits and there is the possibility to use distillate fuels as an alternative, but the normal procedures are disrupted. There are several other areas of the shipping business impacted by the COVID-19, the examples above, are meant to give a sense of the deep effects this pandemic has in the industry. The maritime ports sector has seen a reduction in containers volumes, quarantine of vessels by ports for 14 days, port closures, and port operations in general.

Reduced operations and personnel have an impact on possible cargo damage, which if stored in high risk areas without the appropriate security controls can run the risk of losses from fire or extreme weather conditions and delay in the supply chain can also result in cargo damage, mainly to perishable or temperature-sensitive goods. With vessels being quarantined and ports being quarantined cargo movement is delayed. This will also have an impact on the insurance industry, with a potential increase of claims.

9.1.3 Significance of Machine Learning for Maritime During COVID-19

Problems pertaining to every subsystem in the maritime ecosystem rely on accurate data and reproducible analysis that result in data products. In addition, maritime data has the potential to serve as a proxy for COVID-19's impact on global trade [18]. The availability and density of maritime data require scalable deployment of artifical intelligence to extract patterns [19], find anomalies [20] and forecast disruptions [21]. Live maritime data has the potential to be an early warning sign for supply line disruptions due to COVID-19 [22].

Shipping and maritime data, depending on the source, can be represented one of three ways:

1. Track/movement analysis

2. Spatio-temporal analysis

3. Time-series analysis

Depending on the aims of the maritime community all approaches have the potential to answer important questions pertinent to supply chain and trade activity during the COVID-19 pandemic. Movement prediction is another useful data product obtained from track-level analysis of vessel movement [23]. Anomalies and movement prediction are important components for maritime community to ensure safe navigation, an ever important topic during a pandemic and associated supply line disruption [22]. Spatial analysis of maritime data has provided proxies for secondary sources of information on ship movement that is not available publicly in real time. In particular, satellite imagery from ship emissions and ship wakes are used to reconstruct ship tracts which in turn can be used for further analysis [24]. Track and movement analysis for maritime data is performed at the agent level and movement anomaly detection methods are frequently used to identify unexpected movement of vessels [25].

Spatio-temporal analysis of ship traffic using Getis-Ord statistic [26] has shown to effectively detect bottlenecks of ship traffic at natural and artificial confinements, such as ports and straits [27]. In addition, space-time analysis of ship tracks from AIS feeds has been found useful for delineating areas where shipping volume is observed to drop unexpectedly. Despite differences in their formulation and uses, operationalizing artificial intelligence during the COVID-19 pandemic requires uninterrupted data streams, near real-time data curation and resilient analysis networks to ensure information flow on issues of vital importance to communities on supply-line disruption.

9.1.4 The Maritime Ecosystem's Needs for Data & Challenges

As discussed above, maritime transport is more important than ever, ships must keep moving, ports need to stay open and cross-border trade flowing. Besides the challenges in maintaining the supply chain, there is a human factor that is no less important. The shipping industry normally replaces crews every certain time, this operation is becoming very difficult. The International Maritime Organization (IMO) has promoted the key role seafarers play during the pandemic and the need to recognize them as key or essential workers, by identifying the dangers they face while doing their jobs.

This pandemic has created an unprecedented crisis for ship crews, with the difficulties to travel and restrictions imposed by governments and port authorities, the normal crew change that periodically has to happen has been interrupted and in many cases seafarers are stuck at sea way passed the due time, creating health risks and safety issues.

Normally more than 100,000 seafarers must be changed monthly in order to comply with international regulations for crew welfare and safe working hours. In the current situation, it is estimated that around 400,000 seafarers are being impacted by the COVID-19 restrictions.

The International Transport Workers' Federation (ITF), that represents about 1.4 million seafarers, has decided not to celebrate the 2020 Day of the Seafarer, due to the humanitarian crisis that the travel restrictions have created at sea. The global supply chain could be at risk.

The IMO together with the United Nations Conference on Trade and Development (UNCTAD) are encouraging governments and maritime industry stakeholders to take a pragmatic approach, such as granting exceptions and waivers where they are appropriate. Also, the use of technology and electronic means for communications between ships and shore, encouraging governments and maritime industry stakeholders to take a pragmatic approach, such as granting exceptions and waivers where they are appropriate. Here is where the use of Geospatial Information in the application of IMO e-Navigation principles should be used in order to provide maritime services that facilitate and expedite administrative, commercial and operational activities. E-Navigation is a way to systematically ensure "berth-to-berth navigation", improving efficiency when a ship is approaching the port.

In this sense, the "Single Window" concept, at least for some of the most important activities should be implemented. The e-Navigation concept for a "single window" is where a ship (or a shipping company) can access a series of services from registered service providers before arriving the Port.

In this topic there are important geospatial aspects to consider from another organization, the International Association of Marine Aids to Navigation and Lighthouse Authorities (IALA), which standards such as the IHO S-200 series and organizations like the PortCDM Council (Collaborative Decision Making) will contribute in improving efficiency coming in to and going out of a port.

The International Hydrographic Organization (IHO) is the entity in charge of developing standards and specifications to be applied to products and services used in the maritime world. They have developed the S-100 standard, officially called the Universal Hydrographic Data Model, from which many new product specifications are being developed. Most if not all national hydrographic offices around the world follow IHO standards in one way or another. As per the COVID-19 pandemic, IHO has not emitted any specific guidelines or recommendations to its members, but they have suspended all in person meetings and activities, including the General Assembly meeting that did not take place in 2020 as scheduled.

While normally the bulk of the organization's work happens by correspondence, there is important work that occurs during technical working group physical meetings, that has the advantage of isolating themselves from the day to day work for one week to make significant advancements in developing standards and make key decisions with all the relevant stakeholders present in the same room. These on-site meetings have been replaced with webcasts in an effort to continue with their working plans and minimize the effects of the pandemic on their work.

National hydrographic offices are the authoritative government agencies, equivalent to national mapping agencies on land, in charge of producing navigational charts and other complementary information products for safety of navigation. Some of these agencies in general have experienced challenges for keeping up with their regular production and updating services, and they have been adapting to the pandemic circumstances in different ways. As we will see in the NOAA use case below, some agencies have implemented enterprise systems that allow them to work remotely and continue with their regular activities as close as possible to the normal times.

Hydrographic surveying activities in general cannot be performed in the office, there are many phases of this type of surveys that need to be performed on the field, and sometimes physical distancing between hydrographers is almost not possible, if we consider a small hydrographic survey boat with two or three hydrographers on board collecting data together for long periods of time or a larger hydrographic survey ship at sea with crew confined in small compartments for several weeks in a row.

Similar situation and risks are being experienced by land surveyors, and many governments around the world have implemented guidelines to increase safety of their workers while in the field. Although these measures and guidelines are often generic and not specific to surveyors, much less to hydrographic surveyors.

Oftentimes hydrographic surveys are not on the top of the list of priorities during a pandemic, but the need to keep the navigational routes mapped and up to date is as important as keeping the shipping fleets moving. There is no hard evidence that the hydrographic surveying activities around the world have diminished to the point to consider them in crisis, but there are signs of some reduction of activities, this is true for both government and private organizations. Because a pandemic is not the same as a meteorological phenomenon such as a hurricane or typhoon, the characteristics of coastal waters haven't been affected, then there is not an immediate or emergency need and surveying activities can be planned carefully following all the appropriate measures.

On the other hand, nautical chart and related information production are activities that can be done remotely or from home. Many national hydrographic offices around the world have implemented telework measures in order to keep up with the necessary production updates and distribution of digital publications. Thus, nautical data products can be effectively served with the exception of some activities that require onsite labor such as the distribution of printed nautical charts and other paper nautical publications.

9.1.5   Challenges Faced by Information Product Providers

The standards related to the S-100 Universal Hydrographic Data Model [28], are geospatial data standards that can support a wide variety of hydrographic-related digital data sources. S-100 is fully aligned with mainstream international geospatial standards, specifically the ISO 19000 series of geographic standards. This alignment enables easier integration of hydrographic data and applications into geospatial solutions. S-100 is more flexible than the old S-57 and enables the use of imagery and gridded data types, enhanced metadata and many encoding formats. It also provides a flexible and dynamic maintenance regime for features, their attributes and portrayal through a dedicated Registry online. One can think of S-100 as a framework of components that provides instructions for building standardized Product Specifications for hydrographic data, enabling true interoperability between different data standards and systems.

The IMO e-Navigation [29] is defined as the harmonized collection of marine information, its integration and exchange for "presentation and analysis both on board, and ashore by electronic means to enhance berth to berth navigation and related services for safety and security at sea and protection of the marine environment" [30].

The term "Single Window" can be understood as the point of contact for communication in relation to ship-to-shore and shore-to-ship. In this sense, it's mentioned in the IMO resolution A.950(23) "Maritime Assistance Service" (MAS) adopted on 05 December 2003. "Single Window" can also mean a service or institution on land that collects all information related to safety of navigation before sending them to ships, as defined in IMO documents on e-Navigation. The information products and services to be provided by the IMO e-Navigation single window concept should be based on standards that would allow them to be used anywhere in the world. In this sense, the IHO S-100 series are perhaps the most important one.

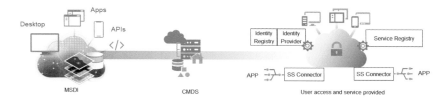

FIGURE 9.1
Geospatial Information to the e-Nav "Single Window" concept (Source: https://www.esri.com/)

By adopting S-100 standards, there are new products and services that can be provided following the e-Navigation concept from which the Maritime Service Portfolios (MSPs) can be developed and shared through a Common Maritime Data Structure (CMDS), which could be considered a derivation or extension of a Marine Spatial Data Infrastructure (MSDI). The Hydrospatial Agency not necessarily has to create the CMDS, but the MSDI should provide the "connectors" to feed a CMDS with their products and services.

The role is not anymore constrained to producing nautical charts (and in some cases Sailing Directions, Notice to Mariners, Tide Tables and related information), through this type of infrastructure, authorities and service providers can go beyond that. Bathymetric Surfaces, Near Real Time Tides and Currents, Under the Keel Clearance Management, Marine Protected Areas, and more necessary information can be provided through MSPs. Port Authorities and Administrations will benefit from this, Port Pilots, Dredging Operations, Port Security, Port Services, Port Logistics, will certainly be improved through these MSPs.

The right side of the graphic above shows the e-Nav concept for a "single window" where a ship (or a shipping company) can access these services from registered service providers before arriving the Port. The PortCDM Council (Collaborative Decision Making) has taken the role of developing the S-200 series of standards for IALA, being the first one developed the S-211 standard for Port Call Messages, standardizing sharing of data on Intentions and Outcomes of Movements, Services and Administrative events.

All the above mentioned systems are an integral part of what is commonly known as "Port

Community Systems" (PCS), which are open and neutral platforms that can connect multiple systems together with the purpose to provide intelligent and secure exchange of information between different organizations that participate in a seaport community, such as agents and shipping lines, customs and excise, logistics providers, terminal and warehouse operators. A PCS can integrate into a national single window or act as a national single window.

9.1.6   Working Remotely and Disconnected

The COVID-19 outbreak has made maritime organizations and geospatial authorities rethink how the modern workplace can operate during major disruptions.

Maritime software, such as ArcGIS will support the management and production of maritime data that is compliant with the International Hydrographic Organization's (IHO) S-4, S-57 and S-100 series of standards.

With the COVID-19 crisis engulfing and disrupting businesses, it has become necessary for our national mapping agencies and industry leaders and experts, to reevaluate ways for maintaining successful business continuity.

As the workforce adapted the organization's senior leadership team implemented powerful operational tools that ensured production was maintained and tracked across environments. Two actions that were taken were

1. Enablement of virtual and disconnected environments

2. Automated apps and dashboards that optimized the organizations' communication responsiveness.

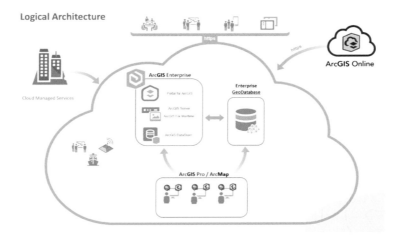

FIGURE 9.2
Leveraging Virtual, Disconnected, and Cloud Environments with ArcGIS (Source: https://www. esri.com/)

First action requires leveraging virtual environments and disconnected editing. This offered GIS users the advantage of working remotely with large amounts of geospatial information including maps, statistics, imagery, and other forms of remotely sensed data which exists across multiple distributed networks or in the cloud. This was done using via virtualization and disconnected work loads. Virtualization allows remotely connecting to a server GIS (such as ArcGIS Enterprise) with desktop virtualization. This provides the ability to collaborate directly with colleagues in a multi-user environment. Disconnectedness enables completing tasks, projects, and production. Reconnect later to synchronize work with the larger workforce.

The second action requires leveraging automated templates for apps and dashboards that optimize communication and workflows. Organization are now driven to adapt to unexpected yet urgent catastrophes like the COVID-19 pandemic, with accurate ready-to-use apps and dashboards, for building and reporting critical information to stakeholders, constituents and at-risk groups. Customized (COTS) out of the box Operations Dashboards, tools, GIS software, predesigned templates, libraries of reusable widgets and applications like the WebApp Builder give instant ability for performing time-sensitive decision making and building optimized workflow communication strategies.

9.2   Case Studies

The importance of maritime data acquisition, analysis via machine learning and AI and data product dissemination is elaborated with three case studies, one from NOAA and two from ESRI, respectively.

9.2.1   National Oceanic and Atmospheric Administration – Office of Coast Survey

The pandemic has forced the NOAA Office of Coast Survey (US National Hydrographic Office) to re-organize the way they conduct business. The safety of navigation in US waters is one of Coast Survey's main responsibilities and updating navigational charts is one of their most essential functions. Prior to the COVID-19, Coast Survey's Marine Chart Division (MCS) had developed an on-site sever-based system that allowed their staff and contractors to work remotely when needed, so when the pandemic struck and the need to establish physical distance for everyone, they could quickly shift one hundred percent of its workforce (more than 100 cartographers) to a work-from-home status. During this period the Division has continued to apply updates to nautical charts and has made progress on its effort to rescheme the suite of nautical charts in the United States according to their cartographic plan.

The MCD system relies on Citrix, allowing users to connect to a virtual server or desktop application remotely, so there is no need for a program to be installed on the local or physical system. MCD cartographers connect to their IT services from home via internet connection. Security is ensured by using VPN and a single sign-on (SSO) and advanced security controls. Using an application called XenApp, that facilitates the installation of applications on a server that can be accessed without having to install anything on the client machine, except for the Citrix client software, cartographers access the ArcGIS-based enterprise chart production system, called "Nautical Chart System II" (NCPSII).

In this way, all the processing happens on the server, through mouse clicks and keystrokes from the client that feels like if the production software is running locally, and the client screen refreshes from the responses to the server through a remote display protocol called "Independent Computing Architecture" (ICA).

The configuration of Citrix, together with the ArcGIS-based NCSII, was a key step in preparing the workforce to work remotely. However, a very important factor might be the general willingness of the users and management to work remotely before the pandemic started. NOAA OCS had already set up infrastructure - hardware, software and the user's understanding of how to work from home. Every staff member was provided with a laptop with the appropriate software installed to enable them to work remotely even if they were not currently teleworking.

They also benefit from robust virtual meeting capabilities that allow system administrators to work directly with the users to run upgrades and troubleshoot problems. This enabled OCS to keep the virtual convenience of working shoulder to shoulder.

With this arrangement, the Marine Chart Division has kept up with their usual production activities. They have been updating charting products and have been applying all critical (dangers to navigation) corrections to their products. In addition, MCD has also reschemed 259 ENCs during

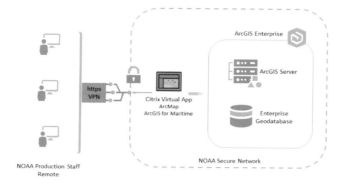

FIGURE 9.3
NOAA's Nautical Chart System for remote work diagram (Source: https://www.esri.com/)

the work from home period, continuing with their modernization plans that include retiring paper nautical charts.

Working remotely has been a positive experience, thanks to the NCPSII platform capabilities and flexibility, the overall productivity has not been affected, these results are causing OCS to consider the possibility to increasing their flexibility with regard to telework, although there is no official guidance for the post-pandemic activities.

9.2.2 Space-Time Analytics for Quantying Impacts of COVID-19 on Shipping Trade

Restrictions due to COVID-19 measures impact maritime traffic and all sectors of the economy that rely on maritime transport of goods. Live space-time data plays an essential role to for modeling and pattern mining studies to quantify current status of traffic restrictions, expected delays of transported goods and changes to port activity.

We use time series clusters and space-time patterns in the Oxford COVID-19 Government Response Tracker's (OxCGRT) stringency index which quantifies the extent to which governments take actions to restrict day to day activities [31]. The index is the average of 17 selected mitigation and suppression measures employed by different countries [31].

Daily stringency index mapped at the county-level is aggregated into a space-time structure, the space-time cube. Space-time patterns of the stringency index are mined by classfying the local changes to the Getis-Ord Statistics, namely the G_i^* statistics (Getis and Ord, 1992). The G_i^* tatistic is a z-score where extreme values imply significantly high (hot-spot) or significantly low (cold-spot) in a spatial neighborhood compared to the global average of stringency index. G_i^* values close to zero implies stringency index in the area is similar to the global average at a given time.

Stringency index space-time patterns are depicted in Figure 9.4. Space-time patterns indicate Russia and parts of South America as Oscillating Hot-Spot. This pattern means these countries and their neighbors oscillate around global average for stringency for extended periods of time and go above the global average for short periods of time. Locations that are classified as sporadic hot spots go above the global average for stringency at certain times and fall back to the average. Majority of Europe exhibits oscillating cold spot which indicates stringency is lower than global average at certain times.

Space-time patterns of stringency informs the expected maritime opening and closures of an entire region using data from neighboring countries. This space-time metric gives a clear idea of how regions of the world may open up over time and which regions are still under high stringency measures.

We also performed a time-series analysis of stringency per country to assess when maritime traffic may return back to normal as stringency measures are lifted at the country level.

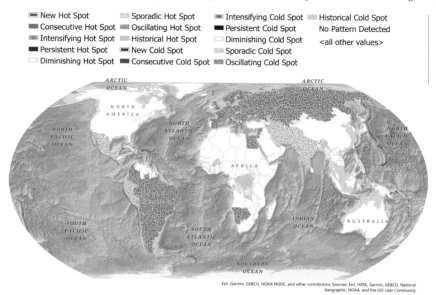

FIGURE 9.4

Emerging Hot Spot Classes of Oxford's COVID-19 Government Response Tracker (OxCGRT) Stringency Index (Display variable)

Three clusters identified in Figure 9.5 indicate change of stringency of countries over time. Blue time series clusters show a high rate of increase in the stringency index, this can imply reduced ship traffic from these countries. Red cluster indicates countries that started their stringency measures later on increase at a higher rate. Green countries are the ones with stabilizing and a lower level of stringency.

FIGURE 9.5

Time-Series Clusters of Oxford's COVID-19 Government Response Tracker (OxCGRT) Stringency Index (Display variable)

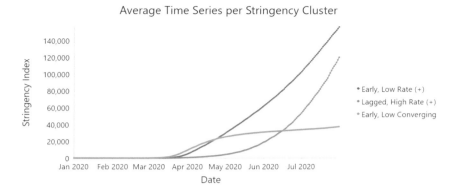

FIGURE 9.6
Time Series Clusters (same coloring scheme as Figure 9.5 of Oxford's COVID-19 Government Response Tracker (OxCGRT) Stringency Index (Display variable)

Figure 9.6 demonstrates the challenges awaiting the maritime industry due to COVID-19 as some countries are getting ready to resume regular daily activities and others deeper into the pandemic with strict measures. Three distinct time series are labelled with respect to when stringency measures were imposed and the rate of increase in their stringency measures over times. Note that countries symbolized with blue in Figure 9.5 started stringency measures earlier and their measures have been increasing ever since. Red group countries started lock-downs later but they have been ramping up efforts at a high rate. Green countries have a converging profile for their stringency measures which are not extensive as the countries in blue and red groups.

The spatial heterogeneity of imposed lock-downs and reductions to business activity indicate that even after the pandemic is declared to be over, a significant lag is to be expected for supply chains to return back to normal. Countries marked with green in Figure 9.5 are expected to ramp up their trade activities as the pandemic is under control, however countries with large trade volumes such as United States and China that fall under the blue category will need more time for their maritime operations to go back to normal.

9.2.3 Disseminating Live Traffic Data During the Pandemic: ESRI Ireland

One threat to maritime was the occurrence of outbreaks on vessels. The effects of such outbreaks had a major impact on economic and trade activities. In 2018 the cruise ship industry was estimated to be worth over $29.4 billion dollars and it is predicted to carry over 19 million passengers annually. An important tool used to monitor and measure global vessel movement is the Automatic Identification System (AIS). AIS uses ship transponders and satellite communications which feed into Vessel Traffic Services (VTS). From these data feed ships with known outbreaks were tracked and monitored.

In early 2020, COVID-19 hit the leisure cruise ship industry which resulted in many issues of quarantine and the need to provide medical assistance to those in dire need. In Europe, ESRI Ireland created a web-based Global Vessel Dashboard dashboard using vessel traffic from the AISHub to monitor the situation. The AIS hub collates and shares vessel data collected from approximately 750 tracking stations run by the AISHub community. ESRI Ireland enriched the raw vessel data with information on cruise ships that reported COVID-19 outbreaks using public data.

FIGURE 9.7
ESRI Ireland's Maritime Dashboard for Vessel Traffic in Europe

9.3   Conclusions

By leveraging geospatial technology using existing GIS capabilities, national mapping agencies and geospatial authorities can address continuity of operations, leverage virtual and disconnected environments, and optimize communications and workflows. These approaches can be used individually or collectively to ensure mission and business success during a time of crisis. NOAA's work on implementing data standards and virtualization is a representative example of opportunities in maritime for operationalizing geospatial servers that leverage maritime data conforming to international standards. It is important to note that the remote infrastructure for data collection, mapping and dissemination has resulted in positive outcomes for the scale that is required by a large organization such as NOAA. ESRI Ireland's data dissemination method through dashboards shows the value of geospatial maritime data visualization and interactive data dissemination during the COVID-19 pandemic.

Challenges with respect to changing type of work environment and establishing uninterrupted data streams during the pandemic are important to quantify the impact of the pandemic on maritime activity and global trade in general. Our showcase of the importance of AI and machine learning as it pertains to stringency index demonstrates spatiotemporal heterogeneity in factors that impact maritime traffic and supply lines. The stringency as a proxy for maritime activity shows that vessel activity between countries may not go back to normal immediately after the pandemic due to different levels of stringency measures throughout the world. Thus, concerted efforts taken by international organizations are required to restore the maritime traffic and intercontinental supply lines. As prolonged supply line disruptions are expected to cause major alterations to supply routes and trade deals, COVID-19 serves the latest pandemic of the digital age, where live maritime data and remote work can keep organizations and country levels afloat during time of crisis. A better understanding of the logistical chain and identification of weak points along the way as well as prioritization of essential goods will be key. This extends to terrestrial transportation, warehousing and distribution centers. The crew change system has to be reviewed and adapted to the circumstances based on how the pandemic is being addressed and controlled around the world, and the recognition of ship's crew as essential workers is also very important in maintaining operations.

References

[1] Mayada Omer, Ali Mostashari, Roshanak Nilchiani, and Mo Mansouri. A framework for assessing resiliency of maritime transportation systems. *Maritime Policy & Management*, 39(7):685–703, 2012.

[2] Michio Hongo, Yutaka Nagasaki, and Tomotaka Shoji. Epidemiology of esophageal cancer: Orient to occident. effects of chronology, geography and ethnicity. *Journal of Gastroenterology and Hepatology*, 24(5):729–735, 2009.

[3] K David Patterson and Gerald F Pyle. The geography and mortality of the 1918 influenza pandemic. *Bulletin of the History of Medicine*, 65(1):4–21, 1991.

[4] Jonathan D Mayer. Geography, ecology and emerging infectious diseases. *Social Science & Medicine*, 50 (7-8):937–952, 2000.

[5] Diansheng Guo. Visual analytics of spatial interaction patterns for pandemic decision support. *International Journal of Geographical Information Science*, 21(8):859–877, 2007.

[6] Maged N Kamel Boulos and Estella M Geraghty. Geographical tracking and mapping of coronavirus disease covid-19/severe acute respiratory syndrome coronavirus 2 (sars-cov-2) epidemic and associated events around the world: how 21st century gis technologies are supporting the global fight against outbreaks and epidemics, 2020.

[7] Geovanna Villacreses, Gabriel Gaona, Javier Martinez-Gomez, and Diego Juan Jijon. Wind farms suitability location using geographical information system (gis), based on multi-criteria decision making (mcdm) methods: The case of continental ecuador. *Renewable Energy*, 109:275–286, 2017.

[8] Timothy P Robinson. Spatial statistics and geographical information systems in epidemiology and public health. *Advances in Parasitology*, 47:81–128, 2000.

[9] Donna J Peuquet. Time in gis and geographical databases. *Geographical Information Systems*, 1:91–103, 1999.

[10] Padam Bahadur Poudel, Mukti Ram Poudel, Aasish Gautam, Samiksha Phuyal, Chiran Krishna Tiwari, Nisha Bashyal, and Shila Bashyal. Covid-19 and its global impact on food and agriculture.

[11] Christophe Claramunt, Thomas Devogele, Sebastien Fournier, Valerie Noyon, Mathieu Petit, and Cyril Ray. Maritime gis: from monitoring to simulation systems. In *Information Fusion and Geographic Information Systems*, pages 34–44. Springer, 2007.

[12] Daniel Depellegrin, Mauro Bastianini, Amedeo Fadini, and Stefano Menegon. The effects of covid-19 induced lockdown measures on maritime settings of a coastal region. *Science of The Total Environment*, page 140123, 2020.

[13] Chang Woon Nam et al. World economic outlook for 2020 and 2021. In *CESifo Forum*, volume 21, pages 58–59. Cesifo Institute-Leibniz Institute for Economic Research at the University of Munich, 2020.

[14] World Trade Organization (WTO). Trade set to plunge as COVID-19 pandemic upends global economy. Press release, 2020. URL https://www.wto.org/english/news_e/pres20_e/pr855_e.htm.

[15] World Trade Organization (WTO). *Press Release*. Information and Media Relations Division of the World Trade Organization, 2020.

[16] Hong Wang, Jianyong Shi, and Junqing Mei. Research on the development of the world's cruise industry during 2017–2018: Strong demands stimulate the sustainable high growth. In *Report on the Development of Cruise Industry in China (2018)*, pages 3–35. Springer, 2019.

[17] Hirohito Ito, Shinya Hanaoka, and Tomoya Kawasaki. The cruise industry and the covid-19 outbreak. *Transportation Research Interdisciplinary Perspectives*, page 100136, 2020.

[18] Ziaul Haque Munim, Mariia Dushenko, Veronica Jaramillo Jimenez, Mohammad Hassan Shakil, and Marius Imset. Big data and artificial intelligence in the maritime industry: a bibliometric review and future research directions. *Maritime Policy & Management*, pages 1–21, 2020.

[19] Bradley J Rhodes, Neil A Bomberger, and Majid Zandipour. Probabilistic associative learning of vessel motion patterns at multiple spatial scales for maritime situation awareness. In *2007 10th International Conference on Information Fusion*, pages 1–8. IEEE, 2007.

[20] Ines Obradović, Mario Miličević, and Krunoslav Žubrinić. Machine learning approaches to maritime anomaly detection. *Naše more: znanstveni časopis za more i pomorstvo*, 61(5-6):96–101, 2014.

[21] Gökçe Çiçek Ceyhun. Recent developments of artificial intelligence in business logistics: A maritime industry case. In *Digital Business Strategies in Blockchain Ecosystems*, pages 343–353. Springer, 2020.

[22] Dmitry Ivanov. Predicting the impacts of epidemic outbreaks on global supply chains: A simulation-based analysis on the coronavirus outbreak (covid-19/sars-cov-2) case. *Transportation Research Part E: Logistics and Transportation Review*, 136:101922, 2020.

[23] Branko Ristic, Barbara La Scala, Mark Morelande, and Neil Gordon. Statistical analysis of motion patterns in ais data: Anomaly detection and motion prediction. In *2008 11th International Conference on Information Fusion*, pages 1–7. IEEE, 2008.

[24] James D Lyden, Robert R Hammond, David R Lyzenga, and RA Shuchman. Synthetic aperture radar imaging of surface ship wakes. *Journal of Geophysical Research: Oceans*, 93(C10):12293–12303, 1988.

[25] Virginia Fernandez Arguedas, Giuliana Pallotta, and Michele Vespe. Automatic generation of geographical networks for maritime traffic surveillance. In *17th international conference on information fusion (FUSION)*, pages 1–8. IEEE, 2014.

[26] Arthur Getis and J Keith Ord. The analysis of spatial association by use of distance statistics. In *Perspectives on spatial data analysis*, pages 127–145. Springer, 2010.

[27] Liye Zhang, Qiang Meng, and Tien Fang Fwa. Big ais data based spatial-temporal analyses of ship traffic in singapore port waters. *Transportation Research Part E: Logistics and Transportation Review*, 129:287–304, 2019.

[28] Robert Ward, Lee Alexander, Barrie Greenslade, and Anthony Pharaoh. IHO S-100: The New Hydrographic Geospatial Standard for Marine Data and Information. Canadian Hydrographic Conference, British Columbia, Canada, 2008.

[29] Adam Weintrit. Development of the imo e-navigation concept–common maritime data structure. In *International Conference on Transport Systems Telematics*, pages 151–163. Springer, 2011.

[30] International Maritime Organization (IMO). Draft e-Navigation strategy implementation plan. Report, 2014. URL http://www.imo.org/en/OurWork/Safety/Navigation/Pages/eNavigation.aspx.

[31] Thomas Hale, Samuel Webster, Anna Petherick, Toby Phillips, and Beatriz Kira. Oxford covid-19 government response tracker. *Blavatnik School of Government*, 25, 2020.

10

City Design and the Transmission of COVID-19

Mark Stevenson, Jason Thompson, Branislava Godic and Thanh Ho

We outline recent research in which Google maps were acquired for cities from across the globe. Using unique methods including convolutional neural networks and graph-based approaches, nine city designs were identified based on land-use characteristics such as road networks, public transit, green space and blue space. In this chapter, we assess the influence of these land-use characteristics in each of the city designs on the transmission of COVID-19 and hence the number of positive cases of COVID-19. The chapter highlights the role of city design with respect to the transmission of COVID-19 and particularly, on transmission of the virus in cities identified with high density road networks and public transit. The chapter concludes by discussing the potential policy implications arising from certain city designs and infectious disease out-breaks.

10.1 The Pandemic that is COVID-19

Between November and December 2019 numerous patients presented to hospitals in the city of Wuhan (Hubei Province, China) with severe respiratory symptoms due to a virial infection. By January 2020, officials in agencies such as the World Health Organisation were aware of the onset of what has become the COVID-19 pandemic. To complicate the onset of the epidemic, the observed infections coincided with the Chinese Lunar New Year holiday where an estimated 3 billion trips are undertaken during the month-long holiday period [1]. Movement of large populations, facilitated by China's established transport system, was a significant challenge during the early stages of the outbreak, just as it was one hundred years earlier where transmission of the Spanish Flu, was exacerbated via the various transport modes carrying returning soldiers from World War 1 [2]. China moved quickly to mitigate the spread of COVID-19 by closing-down its extensive transport system [3]. There is considerable evidence pointing to the value of such measures with Tian et al [4] estimating 37% fewer cases of COVID-19 in cities in which the transport systems were closed-down.

The travel restriction on January 23, 2020, in Wuhan City and the following lock-down in the whole Hubei Province and nearby cities managed to slow the transmission of the virus in China. However, by January 31, 2020, an estimated 1.5 infected air travellers who had departed China, were transmitting the virus each day across the globe [5]. The hyper-mobility and interconnectedness of 21st century transport networks, including high-speed and high-capacity rail and intercontinental air travel have enabled the virus to spread rapidly [6].

Over the ensuing 8 months, COVID-19 cases (or specifically SARS-CoV-2 infections) have been reported in every country other than a few island states such as Cayman Island, Mauritius, Guernsey, Fiji and Dominica [7]. As of 14 August 2020, there were more than 20.7 million cases of COVID-19 in more than 188 countries and territories, resulting in more than 750,000 deaths [7].

As observed in Figure 10.1, there is considerable country variation in the number of COVID-19 cases. One explanation for the variation between countries is the differences in government

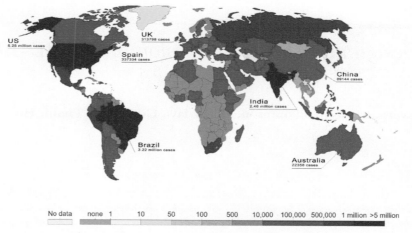

FIGURE 10.1
Global Variation in COVID-19 Cases

response to managing the pandemic. Recent research [8] has mapped a country's response to the pandemic by the timeliness to implement efficacious public health responses. Responses such as, the implementation of physical distancing strategies, remaining at home other than for essential purposes, ongoing enhancements of the health system, extensive travel restrictions, extensive contact-tracing and quarantining of infected individuals and social and economic provisions to assist individuals with the impact of closing-down much of a country's economy in an effort to minimise transmission. As observed in Figure 10.2, two months after the first notification of COVID-19, individual government response to the pending pandemic varied with countries reporting cases of COVID-19 implementing many of the public health responses described above whilst other countries being much slower to respond, presumably associated with no or few cases being reported. Responding quickly to the pandemic, however, did not confer a rapid reduction in infections. As highlighted by the dark brown colour in Figure 10.2, countries such as China, the United States of America (US) and Brazil instituted many public health responses by March 22, 2020 and at the time of writing (August 2020) both the US and Brazil have not suppressed the transmission of COVID-19. It should be noted, however, that implementation of 'stay at home' orders in countries such as the United States were not implemented on a country-wide level, but rather on a state or region-by-region basis that followed the progression of new COVID-19 cases across the country.

Not only is there is considerable variation in COVID-19 cases between countries there is also considerable variation between regions and cities within countries. Figure 10.3 highlights the considerable variation observed in COVID-19 cases within the US and the United Kingdom.

The variation within countries observed in Figures 10.3 is not easily explained as it likely reflects a multitude of factors ranging from governance structures, a poor safety culture within the country, lack of resources (including the ability to institute quarantine measures), inadequate health resources, and poor communication with the public, to name a few [9]. Importantly, the influence of a city's urban design and the variation of such designs between cities in a country may also be an important factor influencing the transmission of COVID-19. Only recently, has the research literature explored a number of these designs with respect to health outcomes (specifically road trauma) [10] and certainly not with respect to COVID-19.

In the remainder of this chapter we describe how city designs can be classified based on land-use characteristics such as road networks, public transit, green space and blue space (e.g., water bodies). Once a classification system is identified for specific city designs, we will assess whether specific city designs are associated with the reported cases of COVID-19.

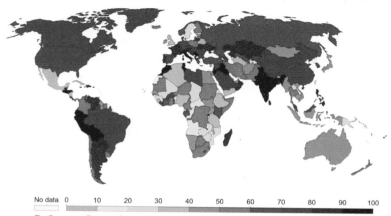

FIGURE 10.2
Country Variation in Government Response to COVID-19 as of March 22, 2020

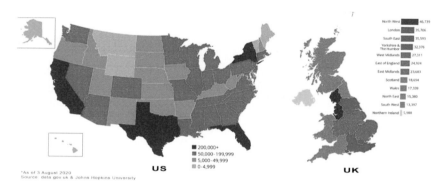

FIGURE 10.3
Variation in COVID-19 Cases in the US and the United Kingdom

10.2 Using Spatial Data to Identify Global City Design

To assess whether specific city design elements could be classified into discrete categories, we used the Google maps API to analyse a set of 1000 stylised maps for every city listed in the 2018 United Nations world population prospect report [11] with a population exceeding 300,000. A total of 1667 cities across the globe were identified. Using a convolutional neural network (CNN) modelling approach based on 'Inception V3' architecture [12], we identified whether cities could be correctly classified as being from their actual (ground truth) location. Each map was of approximately 400m x 400m size and contained representation of road networks, public transport networks, green space (e.g., parks and reserves) and blue space (water bodies). Details of the approach including the calibration of the stages are described in Thompson et al [10].

Once classification of cities to their ground truth location was completed, a graph of the confusion matrix produced by the CNN was created that represented nodes (cities) connected by vertices that represented cities occasionally mistaken for one another in the CNN process. A modularity analysis (similar to a cluster analysis) was then performed on the graph to isolate groups of cities among the 1667 that were regularly misclassified (i.e., confused for one another). This process produced a set of nine major city design types. Table 10.1 describes the nine city designs, a brief description of the design and lists the proportion of cities that fall within the respective city designs. The majority (64%) of low- and middle-income countries and their respective cities, fall within the city design Informal and Irregular; city designs with informal road infrastructure and limited public transit. In contrast, many cities from high income countries were classified under city designs described as either the Motor City and or Intense city design characterised either by high capacity road networks or high-density road networks and high public transit (see Figure 10.4).

Clearly not all cities in a country have the same design. Figure 10.5 illustrates the variation in city design within a country. The proportion of city design types within a country are based on the results of the convolutional neural network analysis. It is evident there is considerable variation in city designs within some countries and absolutely no variation in other countries. For example, there is considerable variation among cities in Vietnam with 4 city designs identified and similarly in China. In contrast, cities within Sweden, Switzerland, Norway, Ireland and Denmark only fall within one city design namely, the High Transit city design, which reflects urban form that is medium density with high capacity formal road networks and high public transport.

The opportunity to classify cities using objective data from standardised maps highlights the utility of spatial data. Such data provides insights on urban form not previously reported. However, the classification of nine city designs is limited to the four land use characteristics that could be systematically attained from the google maps. Nonetheless, these characteristics are important elements particularly in the context of pandemics whereby highly integrated public transit systems can escalate the transmission of infectious diseases.

TABLE 10.1

Types of city design and the proportion of cities classified under each design

Type of City Design	Description	Cities classified in the design (%, N)
Informal	Sparse, low capacity informal road infrastructure, limited rail transport, low formal green space	23% (365 cities)
Irregular	High green space, mixed formal and informal infrastructure, few high capacity road networks, limited mass transit	21% (311 cities)
Large Blocks	Medium density, formal low and high capacity road networks, medium railed transport	9% (146 cities)
Cul-de-sac	Very high density, low capacity mixed formal and informal road networks, low mass transit.	1% (26 cities)
High-Transit	Medium density, high capacity, formal road networks, high public transport	10% (163 cities)
Motor city	Medium to low density, high capacity, grid-based, road networks, medium railed transport	10% (158 cities)
Chequerboard	High density, medium capacity mixed formal and informal road networks, medium public transport	16% (257 cities)
Intense	Very high density, mixed formal high capacity and informal road networks, high public transport	1% (22 cities)
Sparse	Low capacity, low density formal and informal road networks, low public transport	9% (142 cities)

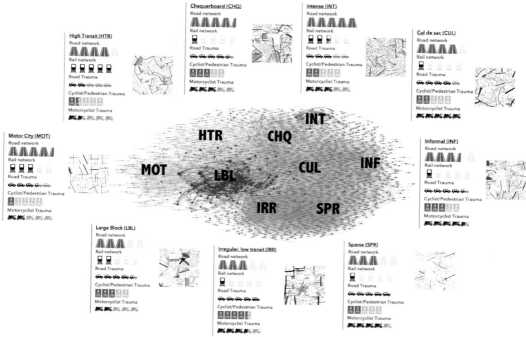

Figure showing each city design's road and public transport characteristics, sample map images and the relationship between each city type and road trauma outcomes.

FIGURE 10.4

Confusion Matrix Produced by the Convolutional Neural Network

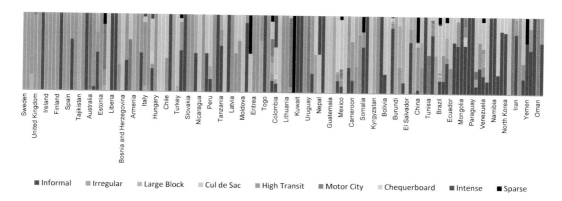

FIGURE 10.5

Proportions of city design types identified in each country

10.3   Relationship Between City Design and COVID-19

As the COVID-19 pandemic enters its 9 month and many countries such as Australia are grappling with a second wave of outbreaks, important public health responses to mitigate the transmission particularly managing public transit and boarder control both between cities and countries are of increasing importance. Understanding which city designs (if any) are likely to increase the propensity to mitigate transmission is of utmost importance. Given the characteristics of the nine city designs, one might expect that cities that are categorised under the following designs as particularly vulnerable for increased transmission especially if the government response is not proactive namely; *Large Block, High Transit, Chequerboard* and *Intense* city designs; these designs have higher population densities along with greater density of road and public transit.

While the relationship of city designs that include reference to road and public transport networks bears a logical relationship to rates of road trauma across countries, the extent to which city design contributes to communicable disease is less certain. It could be hypothesised that a higher proportion of public transit infrastructure and consequent use might lead to greater likelihood of close contact between individuals and person-to-person transmission. Alternatively, the proportion of public transit may be less important than population density in the city, which could determine how close citizens may be forced together on any given day. Finally, it may be these factors are ultimately less important than the timing and intensity of public health and social policies (e.g., stay at home orders) that promote social distancing and limit the potential negative impact of features associated with compact city design – features we have increasingly come to associate with good rather than poor health [13].

To investigate the relationship between city design features and COVID-19, we took an available subset of cities and assessed, up to the time that initial 'stay at home' orders were implemented, an array of factors against the mean growth in COVID-19 cases for each city. We considered the following factors: i) the proportion of each city's land-area dedicated to railed public transit, ii) the proportion of each city's land-area dedicated to road networks, iii) the recorded population density of each city in persons per km^2, iv) the mean block size of each city, v) the regularity of each city's blocks (e.g., how 'square' they are), and vi) the timing of implementation of initial 'stay-at home' orders for each city. This last factor is important to consider alongside the characteristics of city design in order to understand the growth (or decline) in COVID-19 cases under a relatively 'natural' or unmitigated scenario, before the implementation of stringent public health policy measures that might otherwise restrict the free movement and interaction of city residents.

A total of 220 cities from the original list of 1667 were selected. This was the total number of cities for which individual daily cases for COVID-19 data were available at the time of writing. Given the reduced number of cities available for analysis across city designs we restricted our analysis to the measured characteristics of images from within these cities as described above, rather than describing associations with city design types.

Across the selected cities, sixty-three cities were excluded due to missing data across one or more of the factors described above hence, a total of 157 cities were analysed. The findings from the analysis highlighted that a city's design across public transit infrastructure, road infrastructure, block size, and block regularity were not associated with the rates of COVID-19 case growth. Importantly, the findings pointed to a city's population density as significantly associated with case growth albeit, a negative relationship indicating that cities with higher population densities were associated with lower reported case growth from the time the initial case was reported to the first stay-at-home orders. Similarly, days taken between initial case identification and stay-at-home orders were also negatively associated with mean case growth over time.

Focusing on individual cities and regions included in this analysis provides some insight into why both population density and extended delays to the instigation of stay-at-home orders appear negatively associated with the cases of COVID-19. Many cities with high population density are located within countries that also had long delays between identification of their first COVID-19 case and the instigation of stay-at-home orders including those in Japan, Vietnam, Thailand and the city-state of Singapore (see Figure 10.6). This delay does not infer increased transmission as these countries have touted effective control of COVID-19 infections through means other than economic and stay-at-home orders including mass testing, mask-wearing, hygiene promotion, and rapid contact tracing.

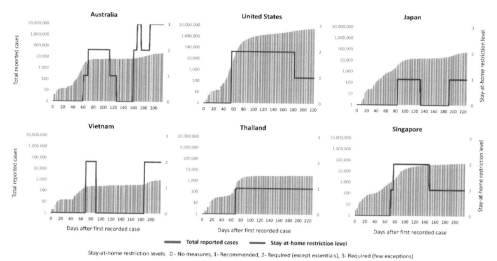

FIGURE 10.6
Total reported cases vs stay-at-home restriction levels, days after first recorded case

As a consequence, our assumption that city designs that reflect extensive road infrastructure, public transit systems and high population densities might exacerbate the transmission of COVID-19, does not hold in its entirety. It appears, that only high population density is associated with COVID-19 cases although it highlights that the densely populated cities have reduced cases of COVID-19. From this cursory analysis, the threat posed by extensive transport systems and highly populated cities is less than first imagined and, is at least not as important factor as the public health orders deployed by city and government institutions to mitigate transmission of COVID-19.

10.4   Conclusion

As highlighted in the chapter, in the early stages of the pandemic, a comprehensive public health response including closing-down the transport systems in response to the rising cases of infection was necessary; this was certainly the situation in China. Similar responses were instituted across the globe albeit at varying time periods. In this chapter we explored, using mapping techniques, the role of city designs in the transmission of COVID-19 with the likelihood of cities with extensive public transit and high densities (described in this chapter as *High Transit* cities) having an increase propensity for transmission.

Despite being able to classify cities into distinct designs based on a combination of spatial characteristics and methods of artificial intelligence, when the city designs were assessed against the number of COVID-19 cases, the design of the city was not associated with the likely number of COVID-19 cases observed but rather high population densities and longer times to initiate stay-at-home orders reduced the COVID-19 cases observed.

What the findings in this chapter points to is that whatever the potential threats posed by cities with high population densities, extensive public transit or smaller block sizes with respect to the transmission of COVID-19, their effects are not dominant over the comprehensive implementation of social or public health interventions. This is not to say that living conditions in individual neighbourhoods, highly utilised public transit networks, or other city features might not provide circumstances for more ready transmission of communicable disease between individuals, but rather, that the evidence is not strong that city design is the primary driver. One alternate explanation to what is observed here is that what we are seeing reflects community resilience. Community resilience is the ability of communities/cities to respond positively to crises such as the pandemic. Countries/cities that responded comprehensively (and not necessarily promptly) to the threat of COVID-19 by instituting appropriate public health responses (as described in this chapter), see rapid declines in the rate of infections. This points to the role that good governance and community resilience can play when faced with emergencies such as a pandemic.

References

[1] Simiao Chen, Juntao Yang, Weizhong Yang, Chen Wang, and Till Bärnighausen. Covid-19 control in china during mass population movements at new year. *The Lancet*, 395(10226):764–766, Mar 2020. ISSN 0140-6736. doi: 10.1016/S0140-6736(20)30421-9. URL https://doi.org/10.1016/S0140-6736(20)30421-9.

[2] John Mathews. World war one's role in the worst ever flu pandemic. *The Conversation*, 2014. URL https://bit.ly/2S14Bn8. Accessed on 13 August 2020.

[3] Nature. 2020. URL https://go.nature.com/2S45NGj. Accessed on 13 August 2020.

[4] Huaiyu Tian, Yonghong Liu, Yidan Li, Chieh-Hsi Wu, Bin Chen, Moritz U. G. Kraemer, Bingying Li, Jun Cai, Bo Xu, Qiqi Yang, Ben Wang, Peng Yang, Yujun Cui, Yimeng Song, Pai Zheng, Quanyi Wang, Ottar N Bjornstad, Ruifu Yang, Bryan Grenfell, Oliver Pybus, and Christopher Dye. The impact of transmission control measures during the first 50 days of the covid-19 epidemic in china. *medRxiv*, 2020. doi: 10.1101/2020.01.30.20019844. URL https://www.medrxiv.org/content/early/2020/03/10/2020.01.30.20019844.

[5] Christopher A Mouton, Russell Hanson, Adam R Grissom, and John P Godges. COVID-19 Air Traffic Visualization: By January 31, 2020, at Least 1.5 Daily Infected Passengers Were Originating in China. *RAND Corporation*, 2020. URL https://www.rand.org/pubs/research_reports/RRA248-2.html.

[6] Lucy Budd and Stephen Ison. Responsible transport: A post-covid agenda for transport policy and practice. *Transportation Research Interdisciplinary Perspectives*, 6:100151, 2020. doi: 10.1016/j.trip.2020.100151.

[7] Our World in Data. 2020. URL https://bit.ly/3i8Arci. Accessed on 13 August 2020.

[8] Thomas Hale, Noam Angrist, Beatriz Kira, Anna Petherick, Toby Phillips, and Samuel Webster. Variation in government responses to covid-19. version 6.0. *Blavatnik School of Government Working Paper*, 2020. URL https://www.bsg.ox.ac.uk/covidtracke. Accessed on 14 August 2020.

[9] Annayath Maqbool and Noor Zaman Khan. Analyzing barriers for implementation of public health and social measures to prevent the transmission of covid-19 disease using dematel method. *Diabetes & Metabolic Syndrome: Clinical Research & Reviews*, 14(5):887–892, 2020. ISSN 1871-4021. doi: https://doi.org/10.1016/j.dsx.2020.06.024.

[10] Jason Thompson, Mark Stevenson, Jasper S Wijnands, Kerry A Nice, Gideon Dpa Aschwanden, Jeremy Silver, Mark Nieuwenhuijsen, Peter Rayner, Robyn Schofield, Rohit Hariharan, et al. A global analysis of urban design types and road transport injury: an image processing study. *The Lancet Planetary Health*, 4 (1):e32–e42, 2020.

[11] United Nations, Department of Economic and Social Affairs, Population Division . World Urbanization Prospects: The 2014 Revision, Highlights (ST/ESA/SER.A/352). 2014.

[12] Christian Szegedy, Vincent Vanhoucke, Sergey Ioffe, Jon Shlens, and Zbigniew Wojna. Rethinking the inception architecture for computer vision. In *Proceedings of the IEEE conference on computer vision and pattern recognition*, pages 2818–26, 2016.

[13] Mark Stevenson, Jason Thompson, Thiago Hérick de Sá, Reid Ewing, Dinesh Mohan, Rod McClure, Ian Roberts, Geetam Tiwari, Billie Giles-Corti, Xiaoduan Sun, Mark Wallace, and James Woodcock. Land use, transport, and population health: estimating the health benefits of compact cities. *The Lancet*, 388(10062): 2925–2935, Dec 2016. ISSN 0140-6736. doi: 10.1016/S0140-6736(16)30067-8.

11

Sensing Community Resilience Using Social Media

Felicia N. Huang, Kelly Lim, Evan Sidhi and Belinda Yuen

This chapter discusses social media use and community resilience development during the COVID-19 pandemic in Singapore. Although around one in four Singapore residents are Twitter users, little is known about their attitudes and sentiments or the roles that social media fulfils in supporting community resilience during a pandemic. The chapter investigates how social media affects citizens' self-resilience capacities during various stages of the COVID-19 pandemic evolution, in particular, in terms of information gathering, information dissemination, information exchange, collaborative problem-solving, coping and promotion of connectedness in order to derive opportunities and challenges for community resilience building. More than a tool for collaborative problem-solving, Twitter is used to coordinate top-down community response and promote connectedness. Geo-tagged data analysis suggests that different regional characteristics do not lead to difference in community resilience efforts across Singapore. Singapore, as a nation, works together as a community in fighting the pandemic.

11.1 Introduction

The COVID-19 pandemic has unleashed unprecedented disruption to economy and society. In its wake, COVID-19 related posts on social media platforms such as Facebook, Twitter, and YouTube have increased. Publicly accessible data posted on social media platforms by users around the world are increasingly used by researchers to quickly identify the main thoughts, attitudes, and feelings surrounding COVID-19 [1]. The scientific community has reported the potential effects of mass isolation on an individual's well-being, and mental health [2, 3]. Yet, there is little or no discussion on the use of social media to sense community resilience during the COVID-19 pandemic.

This study aims to fill this knowledge gap and sense community resilience during the COVID-19 pandemic in Singapore by examining tweets with the *SGUnited* hashtag. This study validates the use of #SGUnited tweets to study how community resilience evolves during the COVID-19 pandemic in Singapore. Additionally, it demonstrates the importance of the Singaporean online community, especially the grassroot communities, to spread community resilience. Results reveal that pandemic increases community resilience, especially in the prelude and the aftermath of a severe lockdown. During a strict lockdown, community resilience is high, but an opposing current of negativities, anxieties, and self-concerns is also high, with potential to undermine group unity if not addressed well. Geographical characteristics of different regions in Singapore are reflected into the content of the tweets. Analysis shows that regional characteristics do not lead to differences in community resilience efforts across Singapore, perhaps because of its small land area (721 sq km) and high population density (7821 persons per sq km).

11.2   Previous Research

11.2.1   Community Resilience During Disasters

Much has been written about the definition of community resilience [4]. Suffice to summarise that community resilience is the ability of a society to cope with and rebound in the face of adverse events or crisis [5, 6]. Understandably, communities with high resilience are usually able to bounce back quickly from adversity and building resilience is often connected with building strong communities [7]. Even though state institutions are important, a community's citizens and public awareness of and responsibility for managing local disaster are critical to sustaining and increasing national resilience in disasters.

In response to the COVID-19 pandemic, the scientific community has increasingly reported on individual well-being, including the potential effects of mass isolation on mental health [2, 3]. Prime, Wade, and Browne [8] discuss the literature on past adversities that have affected populations, such as natural and man-made disasters and recessions, to illustrate numerous aspects in which the well-being of children and families can be at risk during COVID-19.

While resilience exists at the individual and family level, it also occurs at societal level. Vinkers et al. [9] discuss the importance of resilience at both the individual and societal level during the COVID-19 pandemic. Kimhi et al. [10] explore the contribution of community resilience towards decreasing or enhancing anxiety and depression during the pandemic among members of Israel's Jewish and Arab communities.

11.2.2   Community Resilience and Social Media

Social media has become an integral part of many people's everyday lives. It is not surprising that social media is widely used in emergency scenarios. Social networking can influence citizens' self-reliance in the event of a crisis by providing avenues for getting quick and reliable information that reduces uncertainty [11]. Other studies suggest that the public rely on a mix of formal and informal information sources to seek information when using social media during disasters [12, 13]. More specifically, research on the use of Twitter in an emergency context reveals emergency information diffusion of retweets and private messages [14, 15], and information sharing behaviours on Twitter during disasters [16, 17].

Riding on the rapid growth of COVID-19 content on social media, researchers have been using social media to identify the main thoughts, attitudes, and feelings surrounding COVID-19. Li et al. [18] sampled and analysed Weibo posts to explore the impacts of COVID-19 on people's mental health. Su et al. [19] accessed Weibo and Twitter posts to examine and compare the impact of COVID-19 lockdown on individuals' psychological states in China and Italy. Park et al. [20] investigated information transmission networks and news-sharing behaviours regarding COVID-19 on Twitter in Korea. Budhwani and Sun [21] assessed if there was an increase in the prevalence and frequency of the phrases 'Chinese virus' and 'China virus' on Twitter after the 16 March 2020 US presidential reference of this term.

Aside from country-specific studies, others have interrogated worldwide trends. Lwin et al. [22] examined worldwide trends of four emotions—fear, anger, sadness, and joy—and the narratives underlying those emotions during the COVID-19 pandemic. Abd-Alrazaq et al. [1] identified the main topics posted by Twitter users globally during the COVID-19 pandemic, from 2 February to 15 March 2020. They observed the need for proactive social media monitoring to address the spread of fake news and misinformation on social media.

Social media is not just popular among the community. Rufai and Bunce [23] explored the role of Twitter as used by the Group of Seven (G7) world leaders in response to COVID-19. Chen, Lerman, and Ferrara [24] developed a multilingual COVID-19 Twitter dataset that other researchers can use while Mackey et al. [25] detected and characterized user-generated conversations that could be associated with COVID-19-related symptoms. So far, however, no existing study has used social media to explore community resilience during the pandemic. In the pages that follow, we will use Twitter data to sense community resilience in Singapore during the COVID-19 pandemic.

11.2.3 Singapore Community Resilience During COVID-19 Pandemic

Singapore won praise from the World Health Organisation for its early response to dealing with COVID-19 pandemic without the need for enforced lockdowns [26]. Even after the migrant worker dormitory cases emerged and circuit breaker (lockdown) enforced, Singapore's COVID-19 pandemic response has been swift and fatality is generally low [27]. Singapore's success is, however, not unique.

Epidemiologists universally acknowledge that communities in Asia including Hong Kong SAR, South Korea, Taiwan, and Vietnam have been more successful than the United States and most European countries in 'flattening the curve' and limiting the spread of the COVID-19 virus among its populations [28]. Some have attributed this to cultural traits such as the collectivist Confucian mindset internalized among Asian societies that prioritise social unity, group goals and greater good of the community over individual desires [28]. Creating social cohesion is important to community resilience [29].

In February 2020, Singapore has launched SGUnited campaign to encourage the population to work together and overcome the challenges arising from the pandemic. The clarion call is to 'stay safe, stay strong and stay united'. In early February 2020, the prime minister and other members of the government advocated using #SGUnited, that soon gained traction in the social media. The timeline of how the COVID-19 outbreak in Singapore had evolved from 1 January to 30 June 2020 is summarised:

- **Imported Phase** (1 January – 3 February 2020). During the imported phase, imported COVID-19 cases increasingly entered Singapore. The first confirmed case was reported on 23 January, a tourist from Wuhan [30]. The first confirmed case involving a Singaporean was confirmed on 31 January, a Singaporean returning from Wuhan [31].

- **Early Local Cluster Phase** (4 February – 23 March 2020). During this phase, local clusters and transmission developed. The first cluster of local transmission was reported on 4 February at Yong Thai Hang, a shop that mainly served Chinese tourists [32].

- **Stronger Measure Phase** (24 March – 6 April 2020). During this phase, the number of cases began to rise exponentially around the world. Singaporean overseas were encouraged to return [33], causing a spike in imported cases. This spike signalled a new phase in Singapore's fight against COVID-19. Various safe distancing measures and travel restrictions were introduced. Singapore registered 1,000 cases on 1 April [34].

- **Circuit Breaker (Lockdown) Initial Phase** (7 April – 20 April 2020). During this phase, the government of Singapore introduced the Circuit Breaker, an elevated set of safe distancing measure to pre-empt the trend of increasing local transmission of COVID-19 [35]. The exponential increase was caused by infection among migrant workers living in dormitories. The first dormitory cluster was identified on 30 March, with four infections at S11 dormitory [36]. Cases quickly ballooned to 4,427 on 16 April, 60% of which were migrant workers [34].

- **Circuit Breaker Tightened Phase** (21 April – 11 May 2020). The exponential increase in cases did not slow down. On 21 April, the prime minister announced tighter measures to the Circuit Breaker period, to further reduce the transmission of COVID-19. He also announced that the Circuit Breaker period would be extended by another four weeks until 1 June 2020 [37].

- **Circuit Breaker Relaxed Phase** (12 May – 1 June 2020). On 2 May, the Multi-Ministry COVID-19 Taskforce announced that it would ease some of the tighter circuit breaker measures in the coming weeks. Particularly from 12 May, a significant number of retail and businesses were allowed to resume operation [38].

- **Safe Reopening Phase NG Phase** (2 June – 30 June 2020). As the daily number of new community cases had declined significantly and the dormitory situation had stabilized, Singapore exited the Circuit Breaker on 1 June 2020 [39].

11.3   Methods

11.3.1   Data Collection

#SGUnited was used as a proxy for resilience tweets. Tweets with the #SGUnited were collected using the Twitter Standard Search API from the start of the project, in mid-April to 30 June 2020. Twitter users' information were extracted from the tweets collected. Overall, there were 5,784 users. Their tweets since 1 January 2020 were then scraped using the Twitter Timeline API. The Twitter Timeline API was less restrictive than the Twitter Standard Search API. Finally, all the tweets with #SGUnited were filtered. We collected 17,367 tweets from 1 January 2020 to 30 June 2020, of which 1,011 were geolocated tweets.

11.3.2   Data Pre-Processing

Punctuation marks and stop words such as 'an' and 'the' were removed from the tweets. Furthermore, various forms of the same word (e.g. travels, traveling, and travel's) were lemmatized by converting them to the main word (e.g. travel) using the *WordNetLemmatizer* module of the Natural Language Toolkit Python library. Following the terms and conditions, terms of use, and privacy policies of Twitter, all data were anonymized and were not reported verbatim to any third party.

11.3.3   Data Analysis

Five types of analysis were performed on the tweets to understand different aspects of resilience: (a) frequency count and analysis of popular information sources, (b) topic extraction, (c) sentiment analysis, (d) pronoun analysis, and (e) geospatial analysis.

The frequency of #SGUnited tweets and retweets was analysed according to the earlier mentioned COVID-19 evolution timeline. Then, popular users and influencers were extracted from two popularity measures. The first popularity measure was based on the number of tweets a user posted that were retweeted by others. The second popularity measure was based on the number of retweets that a user received for his/her tweets.

Sentiment and pronoun analyses were performed to discover how and when tweets were used to create a venue for collaborative problem solving and promotion of connectedness. Pronouns were calculated by listing them and finding them in the tweets. First person singular pronouns included 'I', 'me', 'my', and 'mine'. First person plural pronouns included 'we', 'us', 'our', 'ours'. Second person pronouns included 'you', 'your', and 'yours'. Third person singular pronouns were 'he', 'him', 'his', 'she', 'her', 'hers', 'it', 'its'. Lastly, third person plural pronouns were 'they', 'them', 'theirs'. Sentiment scores (ascription of positive or negative emotional valence) were given to tweets using *Vader* library in Python.

Topic modelling technique, specifically the *TwitterLDA* [40], was used to extract topics from tweets. Topic distribution in a day would identify popular topics from the tweets. The topics were visualized using R library *LDAViz* [41]. Tableau was used for visualization of other graphs.

There were 1,011 geolocated tweets. Eliminating the ones that were in other countries, and that were too generic (i.e. only mention Singapore), 840 tweets remained for analysis. Of these, 442 tweets had geocoordinate points, whereas the rest only had polygon coordinates that showed in which of the five Singapore regions they belonged to: North, East, West, North East, or Central. Topics of the tweets of each region were extracted to discover the topics discussed at each region.

11.4 Results

The examination of how social media affects citizens' self-resilience capacities during various stages of the COVID-19 pandemic evolution involved three areas: (1) how social media affected self-resilience in terms of information gathering, dissemination, and exchange; (2) how social media affected self-resilience in terms of collaborative problem solving, coping, and promotion of connectedness; and (3) whether social media showed any regional-specific community resilience.

11.4.1 Information Gathering, Dissemination, and Exchange During the COVID-19 Pandemic

According to Bruns and Liang [42], Twitter is particularly suitable for crisis communication. With its flat and flexible communicative structures, any visitor can access public tweets. Such communicative structure facilitates fast, and large-scale collection of information [43]. Particularly during major events, the follower-followee relationships can lead to emergent social properties at a macro-scale, which are driven by a bottom-up self-organization of information [44], thus providing unique access to information deemed important by the community. Additionally, Twitter is a persistent source of data about individual responses to a disaster within a community, establishing Twitter as a valuable tool for measuring disaster resilience across communities [45]. The exploration into how Twitter, as a medium of information gathering, dissemination, and exchange, affects the capacities of community resilience in Singapore during the COVID-19 pandemic involves reviewing the intensity of information gathering and dissemination at various stages of the pandemic, the topic of information exchanged, and popular information sources.

11.4.1.1 Tweets Intensity at Various Stages of the Pandemic

Social media provides clear opportunities for two-way crisis communication between authorities, media and citizens [46]. This two-way communication helps to build community resilience by providing emergency information and facilitating community response and recovery [47]. Intensity of tweets during various stages of pandemic is analysed to discover at which stages are the crisis communication information exchanges among Singaporeans most prevalent.

The number of tweets, and retweets appears to follow closely the COVID-19 phases in Singapore (Table 11.1). Intensity of tweets gained momentum during the implementation of stronger measure when the global and national infected cases increased (Figure 11.1). The intensity reached its peak during the Circuit Breaker tightened measure period following the emergence of dormitory clusters in Singapore that created an upsurge of national infected cases. As the number of cases stabilized, the government relaxed the lockdown measures and the number of tweets also seemed to decline.

TABLE 11.1
The number of tweets and retweets across different phases of COVID-19

Phase	Date	No. of Tweets	No. of Retweets	Sum SG Daily Infected
Imported	1 Jan – 3 Feb	6	0	18
Early local clusters	4 Feb – 12 Mar	563	683	492
Stronger measure	13 Mar – 6 Apr	4,241	1,226	866
Circuit Breaker initial	7 Apr – 20 Apr	2,575	1,069	6,649
Circuit Breaker tightened	21 Apr – 11 May	6,102	3,670	15,808
Circuit Breaker relaxed	12 May – 1 Jun	2,930	1,457	11,505
Safe reopening	2 Jun – 30 Jun	2,516	1,236	8,884

The results follow previous studies of Twitter showing that during natural hazards, there is a gradual increase in tweet intensity with hazard proximity [46]. The suggestion is that Twitter presents a disaster communication platform that provides essential information during crucial times throughout the COVID-19 pandemic in Singapore. But unlike natural disaster, where there is an objective definition of hazard during a pandemic. In our results, hazard is equated with strict lockdown, and the highest number of infected cases. But the current pandemic is protracted with no cure insight yet, the "strict lockdown" definition may not be the same for all countries, and no one can really predict whether the number of infected cases has reached a tipping point. Future studies can investigate whether hazard during a pandemic has a universally accepted objective measure.

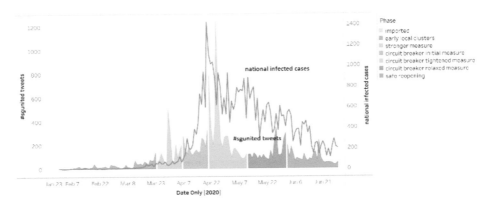

FIGURE 11.1
Community resilience tweets by phase and number of national infected cases, 1 January to 30 June 2020

11.4.1.2   Popular Topics and Tweets

Disasters are inherent with a high degree of uncertainty and the perception of severe threat [48]. The central characteristics, functions, and applications of social media in disaster relate to social convergence to provide support and information sharing to reduce uncertainty [11]. On Twitter, people spread information that they feel or know to be newsworthy through retweeting notwithstanding the possibility of fake news [44].

In Table 11.2, the top two topics in #SGUnited tweets are listed; topic definition can be found on Table 11.3. Here's how the table should be read. For example, during the imported phase, topic 24 (lifestyle and leisure) becomes the most discussed topic for three days, and topic 10 (COVID transmission and test) is the most discussed topic for a day. In total, during the imported phase, there are four days where tweets with #SGUnited are found. During the period, topic 11 (estate economy) is the second most discussed topic for two days, while topic 24 (lifestyle and leisure), and topic 0 (youth, global, and national unity) are the second most discussed topic for a day.

For Singapore, during the COVID-19 pandemic, the community seemed to focus on accessing Twitter to get and exchange information relating to lifestyle and leisure (Table 11.2). For most of the days throughout the six-month period, topic 24 (lifestyle and leisure) was the first or second most discussed topic. Topic 24 communicated information exchange about lifestyle changes that were crucial to curb the pandemic spread, e.g. promotional message of online products that were advertised to help fight viruses, different new safeguarding efforts on travel in public transport, guidelines for the wearing of masks, and introduction to the 'soaper 5'. Singapore introduced the concept of soaper 5 (Wipe Up Wilson, Super Soaper Soffy, Virus Screener Varun, Hands Down Hana, and Mask Up Mei Mei) to help little children build a new lifestyle habit in the midst of the pandemic.

Besides being a tool to promote new lifestyle changes, Twitter was also a popular platform to promote positivity, and connectedness. For example, during the Stronger Measure phase, the ClapforSGUnited event on 30 March 2020 [49] was accompanied with an increase in topic 2 (appreciation for frontliners) and topic 18 (appreciation for healthcare workers) including retweets (Figure 11.2). These topics became the second most discussed topic for a few days during the Stronger Measure phase. Similarly, during the Circuit Breaker tightened phase, SingforSG event saw an increase in topic 0 (youth, national, and global unity), and topic 2 (appreciation for frontliners) discussion on Twitter. SingforSg event was created by MediaCorp (a media and entertainment group), inviting Singaporeans to take part in a nationwide singalong to promote unity during COVID-19. The results highlighted the importance of large-scale fun events at the national level to promote a sense of community unity on Twitter. Not only did these events create an increase in retweets during the event days, but also a few days following the event.

TABLE 11.2
Top two most discussed topics during COVID-19

Phase	Date	Topic	No. of Days the Topic was the $1^{st}/2^{nd}$ Most Discussed Topic
The first most discussed topic			
Imported	1 Jan – 3 Feb	24, 10	3, 1
Early local clusters	4 Feb – 12 Mar	24, 0, 10, 4, 7, 14, 15, 2, 3, 8, 20, 21	19, 2, 2, 2, 2, 2, 2, 1, 1, 1, 1, 1
Stronger measure	13 Mar – 6 Apr	24, 19, 22, 5, 2, 15, 11, 18, 17	15, 2, 2, 1, 1, 1, 1, 1, 1
Circuit Breaker initial	7 Apr – 20 Apr	24, 9, 8, 19	10, 2, 1, 1
Circuit Breaker tightened	21 Apr – 11 May	24, 5, 21, 0, 7, 10, 15, 4, 2	10, 2, 2, 2, 1, 1, 1, 1, 1
Circuit Breaker relaxed	12 May – 1 Jun	24, 3, 16, 1, 13, 11	13, 3, 2, 1, 1, 1
Safe reopening	2 Jun – 30 Jun	24, 1, 5, 10, 13, 0, 6, 17, 21, 22	15, 2, 2, 2, 2, 1, 1, 1, 1, 1
The second most discussed topic			
Imported	1 Jan – 3 Feb	11, 24, 0	2, 1, 1
Early local clusters	4 Feb – 12 Mar	24, 21, 7, 5, 10, 2, 0, 15, 3, 8, 11, 1, 18, 19	12, 5, 4, 3, 2, 2, 1, 1, 1, 1, 1, 1, 1, 1
Stronger measure	13 Mar – 6 Apr	24, 18, 5, 7, 2, 17, 19, 11, 0, 4	6, 5, 3, 3, 2, 2, 1, 1, 1, 1
Circuit Breaker initial	7 Apr – 20 Apr	24, 21, 9, 19, 8, 5, 17, 15	4, 4, 1, 1, 1, 1, 1, 1
Circuit Breaker tightened	21 Apr – 11 May	24, 21, 12, 23, 5, 7, 3, 9	7, 6, 2, 2, 1, 1, 1, 1
Circuit Breaker relaxed	12 May – 1 Jun	21, 19, 24, 14, 16, 1, 5, 15, 4, 22, 17	5, 4, 3, 2, 1, 1, 1, 1, 1, 1, 1
Safe reopening	2 Jun – 30 Jun	24, 6, 22, 5, 21, 17, 19, 7, 10, 14, 12, 20	7, 4, 3, 2, 2, 2, 2, 2, 1, 1, 1, 1

Note: Refer to Table 11.3 for topic definition.

TABLE 11.3

LDA generated topics

Topic 0	youth, national, and global unity	Topic 12	COVID-19 cases
Topic 1	tourism, and daily entertainment	Topic 13	safe reopening
Topic 2	frontliners appreciation for	Topic 14	food delivery and cooking
Topic 3	stay-home stay-home and cooking	Topic 15	webinar, and digital tech
Topic 4	live updates and livestream	Topic 16	religious celebration and Brompton bike
Topic 5	jobs, companies, and industries	Topic 17	dengue, and Malay words
Topic 6	fitness and health	Topic 18	appreciation for healthcare workers
Topic 7	education and job training	Topic 19	video and radio broadcast
Topic 8	domestic life and foreign worker	Topic 20	stay positive
Topic 9	circuit breaker and lockdown	Topic 21	public holiday nature, and relaxing
Topic 10	COVID-19 transmission and test	Topic 22	art, innovation, and nation rebuilding
Topic 11	estate economy	Topic 23	Ramadhan
		Topic 24	lifestyle, and leisure

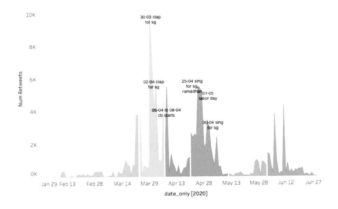

FIGURE 11.2

Number of retweets

Similar to the discovery by Vicari et al. [43] for disaster, our data showed that Twitter was primarily used as a means to disseminate warnings and behaviour guidelines during the pandemic. On Table 11.2, topic 9 (Circuit Breaker) became the most discussed topic on Twitter for a few days during the Circuit Breaker initial phase. This topic contributed to a high number of retweets (See Figure 11.2). Two weeks into the Circuit Breaker, on 21 April, the prime minister announced the extension of the Circuit Breaker. This announcement circulated widely on Twitter (Figure 11.2). The circuit breaker extension caused topic 9 (Circuit Breaker) to appear as the second highest ranked topic for a day during the Circuit Breaker Tightened phase (Table 11.2). During important milestones of the pandemic, Twitter provided an additional channel (besides traditional media like newspaper, radio and television) to announce important measures, specifically the Circuit Breaker.

By posting circuit breaker announcements on Twitter, #SGUnited tweets and retweets offered a glimpse into how social media could provide emergency intelligence through crowdsourcing, and boost the coordination of community response and recovery, lending evidence to how social media could be used to help build community resilience [47].

Festivals and national holidays also contributed to an increase in information dissemination on Twitter, i.e. retweets, during the pandemic. During the Circuit Breaker tightened period, Muslims in Singapore started their month of fasting. The event created an increase in retweets on 25 April (Figure 11.2) and topic 23 (Ramadhan, the fasting month and related activities) also became the second most discussed topic for a few days during the Circuit Breaker tightened period (Table 11.2). On 1 May, tweets about Labour Day (a public holiday) celebration spread widely on Twitter, inducing an increase in retweets (Figure 11.2). In consequence, topic 21 (public holiday, and relaxing activities) became the most discussed topics for a few days during the Circuit Breaker tightened period (Table 11.2). Besides expressing happiness during public holidays, messages during those days were also accompanied with resilience messages, such as encouraging words, a call for fundraising, and volunteerism. Festivals nurture community resilience through the sharing of values, interests, and traditions central to the host community [50]. The finding suggests that national holidays and festivals could be utilized to spread positive messages on social media as community cohesion increases during those days.

Our topic results seemed to be quite different from previous research. Abd-Alrazaq et al. [1] in their study of COVID-19-related tweets between 2 February and 15 March 2020 discovered that the five most discussed topics were deaths, fear, travel bans, economic losses, and panic buying. Generally, these tweets were largely negative. Currently, there was no previous research that specifically addressed the most discussed topics about COVID-19 in Singapore. Our analysis on tweets with #SGUnited revealed that the COVID-19 and related tweets were mostly positive and concentrated on introducing measures and lifestyle changes. This could be due to the content of postings introduced on #SGUnited. For example, during the stronger measure phase of the COVID-19, travel ban and advisory were introduced by the Singapore government but, the tweets with #SGUnited that were most widely disseminated during that phase were not about travel ban, but about encouragement, the Clap for SG activity.

Previous research on the use of Twitter for nurturing community resilience is usually focused on natural disaster. In these studies, Twitter mostly works as an early warning system [11, 43–45]. Requests for help and information on disaster recovery are also posted on Twitter, improving the lines of communication, thus enhancing self-resilience of citizens [11]. The community resilience fingerprints during natural disasters are largely related to ecological and infrastructure categories [45]. But, COVID-19 pandemic appears to have a different pathway from natural disaster.

Unlike natural disaster, the COVID-19 pandemic is protracted. Local communities need to be ready for the next waves, as long as there is no cure yet for the pandemic and the incidence and deaths related to COVID-19 continue to rise within the global community. In Singapore, through #SGUnited, Twitter is being used as an early warning system for the pandemic as well as for introducing and encouraging lifestyle changes in the community, which are important to sustaining the care and safety of the community. In consequence, lifestyle topic takes the majority of conversations on Twitter.

11.4.1.3 Popular Information Sources

Influential actors including heroes, and role models are important stakeholders during a disaster [43]. They can play an active role in nurturing community resilience through social media. Table 11.4 lists the top 20 popular users who were retweeted. They include government representatives, citizens, influencers, and private entities.

The most widely retweeted users appeared to be citizens while other entities (e.g. mainstream journalism) appeared to be the most likely retweeted users (Table 11.4). Postings from government entities are likely to be retweeted, and they are widely retweeted as well. Since citizens are more widely retweeted, the importance of building community resilience at the grassroots level should not be underestimated. That is, bottom-up activism is as equally important as a top-down directive in responding to the pandemic. Additionally, other non-governmental entities, especially online news portals, as the most likely retweeted users offer great options to encourage the implementation of top-down directives as their messages are highly likely to gain traction. In sum, official information dissemination by the government agencies though important, may not be sufficient on its own during a pandemic; the process could be complemented by both citizens and other entities like mainstream journalism to further support information exchange and promote connectedness.

TABLE 11.4

Top 20 popular users by popularity measure and user category

User Category	Popularity Measure Based on how widely they are retweeted	Based on how likely they get retweeted
Government (government departments and individuals like prime minister and ministers)	6	6
Other Entities (e.g. mainstream journalism business and private sector)	5	9
Citizens	8	4
Influencer (e.g. individuals with social media following)	1	1
	20	20

11.4.2   Promotion of Connectedness and Collaborative Problem Solving

Singaporeans generally appeared positive during the pandemic. There were more positive tweets than negative tweets (Figure 11.3). Nevertheless, a handful of negative tweets still existed. Their frequency generally did not fluctuate and remained low, and flat throughout. One exception was seen during the Circuit Breaker tightening phase where there was a surge of negative tweets alongside the positive tweets. Negative tweets could erode the promotion of connectedness during the pandemic. Most of the negative tweets were complaints about government institutes and government-imposed measures. Some of the tweets expressed dissatisfaction with how the government handled the COVID-19 situation. Some of the tweets complained about having to wear mask on the mass rapid transit system. There were also tweets that complained about racism.

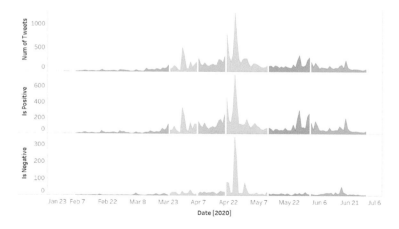

FIGURE 11.3

Positive and negative tweets from 1 January to 30 June 2020

The results of the pronouns analysis agreed with the results of the sentiment analysis. As shown on Table 11.5 and Figure 11.4, during the Circuit Breaker tightened phase, although there was a prevalence of the first-person plural pronoun ('we'), first-person singular pronouns ('I') also increased a lot as compared to other periods. The first-person singular pronoun suggested selfishness and attention to the self [51]. Yet, during the circuit breaker initial phase, and safe reopening phase, the number of first-person plural pronoun ('we') were significantly higher than first-person singular pronoun ('I'). The results seemed to indicate that during the prelude and the aftermath of a hazard (lockdown), community unity was higher than individual concern. However, during the lockdown, community unity was accompanied by negative emotions and individual concerns. The implication is that the city and community need to be very vigilant during the lockdown (a hazard) because individual anger, exasperation, and selfishness could easily build up and spread. Top-down directives and bottom-up activism could be employed to boost positivity, hope, and bonding during such times.

TABLE 11.5
Total number of different pronouns

Pronoun	Total
First Person Singular	3,592
First Person Plural	12,581
Second Person	5,182
Third Person Singular	3,348
Third Person Plural	2,188

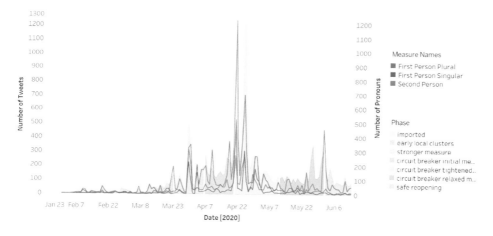

FIGURE 11.4
Number of tweets and different pronouns throughout different phases of the pandemic

As first-person plural pronoun ('we') in a sentence indicates unity [51], 119 tweets with the highest number of first-person plural pronoun ('we') were further analysed to discover the types of collaborative problem solving and promotion of connectedness done through Twitter. The top three messages with the highest community unity markers (the word 'we'), were about the promotion of connectedness (64%), namely, expressing appreciation for healthcare workers, urging fellow citizens to follow COVID-19 preventive measures, and sharing positivity and words of encouragement (Table 11.6). Our results agree with previous research that social media is useful to offer help, ask for help, and aid in recovery services [11]. During the pandemic when job losses, wage cuts and economic contraction are being experienced by many citizens, Twitter users used the platform to request for donation, sharing new job and volunteer opportunities. For example, crowd wisdom provided solutions for unemployed persons and small businesses by posting job opportunities and rallying people to help and support small businesses.

The ability of social media to connect people through time and space enhances collaborative problem-solving and citizens' ability to cope and make sense of the situation, particularly in a highly ambiguous social context [11, 52]. However, collaborative problem-solving occupies less than 50% of the communication on Twitter. Mostly, the bulk of the communication revolves around the promotion of connectedness including spreading positivity and urging fellow citizens to follow rules.

TABLE 11.6
Tweets with high number of first-person plural pronouns

Category	Total	Percentage
Appreciation for frontline, and healthcare workers	32	27%
Urging fellow citizens to strictly follow measures	27	23%
Sharing positivity	17	14%
Sharing information	16	13%
Selling product/service	10	8%
Requesting donation or other support	8	7%
New COVID-related job opportunities	4	3%
Encouraging citizens to support small businesses	3	3%
Volunteer opportunities	1	1%
Complains about government measures	1	1%

11.4.3   Regional-Specific Community Resilience

Community resilience concepts apply best to place-based communities, i.e. a community that is bound together by a place [53]. Singapore, as a nation, has given place-based planning a particular emphasis in the country's long-term development plan with much focus on place identity [54]. Place and urban spatial structure exert a powerful influence on people's everyday activities [55]. This section explores whether regional characteristics lead to regional-specific community resilience. The number of tweets and the top five topics across the five regions of Singapore are tabulated in Table 11.7.

TABLE 11.7
Distribution of topics and tweets across Singapore's five regions

Region	Number of Tweets	Top 3 Topics	Topic[1] %1
Central Region	479 (0.57)	21, 24, 0	42%, 30%, 4%
North Region	74 (0.09)	24, 21, 0	43%, 20%, 4%
North East Region	78 (0.09)	24, 21, 0	32%, 14%, 9%
West Region	166 (0.20)	24, 5, 21	47%, 33%, 4%
East Region	43 (0.05)	21, 24, 0	35%, 26%, 7%
Total	840		

Note: [1] shows percentage of topic in Top 3 Topics in sequence.

The most popular topics for all regions are topic 24 (lifestyle and leisure), topic 21 (public holiday, nature, and relaxing), and topic 0 (youth, national, and global unity). Nevertheless, there is an aberration in the West Region where there is a relatively high number of topic 5 (jobs, companies, and industries). One may quickly conjecture that the West Region, as the industrial region of Singapore, becomes the main source of jobs topic. However, looking deeper into the tweets, all tweets from the West region that talks about topic 5, come only from one user, MukundanAP, a data scientist and motivational speaker who shares business leadership quotes daily.

The analysis seems to suggest that regional differences in Singapore are not big enough to warrant a difference in community resilience across regions during the COVID-19 pandemic. This could be due to the small land size, high population density, compact urban development and coherent policy response in Singapore. Unlike in the United States where people of different states can take different responses to wearing a mask to reduce COVID-19 transmission, the COVID-19 policy responses are implemented uniformly nationwide in Singapore.

Furthermore, people-place relationship in community resilience is often based on the assumption that different communities within geographically defined space have different levels of vulnerability and resilience, the result of different sense of community and ideals as well as attachment to place [56, 57]. In Singapore, where land is small, transportation is convenient, and government directives are strictly imposed, regional difference does not create different vulnerabilities. For example, during the water shortages in 1961 and 1963, regions near the reservoirs do not have advantages because water is rationed evenly across the nation [58]. Ethnic integration policy in Singapore's housing programme that mixes different races in public housing estates where 80% of resident population live, has strengthened social cohesion [59]. As a result, from what is shown by the tweets, different region in Singapore does not show different community resilience effort.

Berkes and Ross [56] identified two different strands of community resilience studies. The first strand treats community resilience as a social-ecological system strongly affected by geographical locations. The second strand treats community resilience as a social entity affected by personal development, social connections, and mental health. Perhaps, for the case of Singapore, the resilience of a community as a social entity is more relevant than the resilience of a community as a geographical unit.

Singapore has two different COVID-19 clusters, that are geographically unseparated, but socially separated, i.e. the dormitory cluster, and the community cluster. A stark difference in the living condition of the two clusters produces different infection rate. Dormitory cluster infection rate has been very high, even when community cluster infection rate remains moderate. The difference in social classes in Singapore has created different vulnerabilities to the pandemic.

11.5   Conclusion

In this study, #SGUnited tweets were analysed to sense community resilience in Singapore during the COVID-19 pandemic. Various analyses were performed on the tweets to understand different aspects of resilience tweets: (a) frequency count, and popular users analysis, (b) topic extraction, (c) sentiment analysis, (d) pronoun analysis, and (e) geospatial analysis. Frequency count shows that resilience tweets follow different phases of government measures in curbing the pandemic. During the time when strict lockdown is imposed, resilience tweets are high, and during relaxed measures, resilience tweets are low. Popular user analysis reveals the importance of citizens in popularizing tweets while topic extraction indicates that although the 'lifestyle and leisure' topic takes the bulk of the conversation on Twitter, it rarely gains traction. Other topics, such as Circuit Breaker, and appreciation for healthcare front-liners, are more likely to get popular during a health pandemic.

Sentiment and pronoun analysis show that #SGUnited tweets are generally positive and contain a lot of first personal plural pronouns ('we'), indicating group unity. Tweets with the highest number of group unit markers ('we'), are mostly about the promotion of connectedness, and community response coordination than about collaborative problem solving. It would appear that Twitter is mostly used in Singapore as a tool to promote connectedness and coordinate top-down government directives during the pandemic. Perhaps because of this effort towards connectedness, the geospatial analysis does not show much regional differences. Instead, the indication is that Singapore works as one community to fight the pandemic even though there might be differences in infection rate among population groups. Overall, our study illustrates the use of social media as a population-level sensor for community resilience during the pandemic; it provides a promising data source for understanding user attitudes, thoughts and feelings towards the unprecedented health epidemic. Central to strengthening community resilience is partnership and a coordinated approach that informs and engages all stakeholders including the people themselves, to mobilise collective efforts and practise social responsibility.

Acknowledgements

This research is supported by the Lee Li Ming Programme in Ageing Urbanism at the Lee Kuan Yew Centre for Innovative Cities, Singapore University of Technology and Design.

References

[1] Alaa Abd-Alrazaq, Dari Alhuwail, Mowafa Househ, Mounir Hamdi, and Zubair Shah. Top concerns of tweeters during the COVID-19 pandemic: infoveillance study. *Journal of medical Internet research*, 22(4): 1–9, 2020.

[2] L. Lades, K. Laffan, M. Daly, and L. Delaney. Daily emotional well-being during the COVID-19 pandemic. *British Journal of Health Psychology, Brief Report COVID-19*, 1–10, 2020.

[3] Samantha K Brooks, Rebecca K Webster, Louise E Smith, Lisa Woodland, Simon Wessely, Neil Greenberg, and Gideon James Rubin. The psychological impact of quarantine and how to reduce it: rapid review of the evidence. *The Lancet*, 395(10227) 2020.

[4] Rod McCrea, Andrea Walton, and Rosemary Leonard. Developing a model of community wellbeing and resilience in response to change. *Social Indicators Research*, 129(1):195–214, 2016.

[5] W Neil Adger. Social and ecological resilience: are they related? *Progress in human geography*, 24(3):347–364, 2000.

[6] Sonny S Patel, M Brooke Rogers, Richard Amlôt, and G James Rubin. What do we mean by'community resilience'? A systematic literature review of how it is defined in the literature. *PLoS currents*, 9, 2017.

[7] Rockerfeller Foundation. 100 Resilient Cities. 2017.

[8] Heather Prime, Mark Wade, and Dillon T Browne. Risk and resilience in family well-being during the COVID-19 pandemic. *American Psychologist*, 75(5): 631–643, 2020.

[9] Christiaan H Vinkers, Therese van Amelsvoort, Jonathan I Bisson, Igor Branchi, John F Cryan, Katharina Domschke, Mirko Manchia, Luisa Pinto, Dominique de Quervain, Mathias V Schmidt, et al. Stress resilience during the coronavirus pandemic. *European Neuropsychopharmacology*, 35: 12–16, 2020.

[10] Shaul Kimhi, Yohanan Eshel, Hadas Marciano, and Bruria Adini. Distress and Resilience in the Days of COVID-19: Comparing Two Ethnicities. *International Journal of Environmental Research and Public Health*, 17(11):3956, 2020.

[11] Manon Jurgens and Ira Helsloot. The effect of social media on the dynamics of (self) resilience during disasters: A literature review. *Journal of Contingencies and Crisis Management*, 26(1):79–88, 2018.

[12] Mel Taylor, Garrett Wells, Gwyneth Howell, Beverley Raphael, et al. The role of social media as psychological first aid as a support to community resilience building. *The Australian Journal of Emergency Management*, 27(1):20–26, 2012.

[13] Christian Reuter and Thomas Spielhofer. Towards social resilience: A quantitative and qualitative survey on citizens' perception of social media in emergencies in europe. *Technological Forecasting and Social Change*, 121:168–180, 2017.

[14] Masaharu Tsubokura, Yosuke Onoue, Hiroyuki A. Torii, Saori Suda, Kohei Mori, Yoshitaka Nishikawa, Akihiko Ozaki, and Kazuko Uno. Twitter use in scientific communication revealed by visualization of information spreading by influencers within half a year after the Fukushima Daiichi nuclear power plant accident. *PloS one*, 13(9):1–14, 2018.

[15] Jeannette Sutton, Emma S. Spiro, Britta Johnson, Sean Fitzhugh, Ben Gibson, and Carter T. Butts. Warning tweets: Serial transmission of messages during the warning phase of a disaster event. *Information, Communication & Society*, 17(6):765–787, 2014.

[16] Fujio Toriumi, Takeshi Sakaki, Kosuke Shinoda, Kazuhiro Kazama, Satoshi Kurihara, and Itsuki Noda. Information sharing on twitter during the 2011 catastrophic earthquake. In *Proceedings of the 22nd International Conference on World Wide Web*, pp. 1025–1028, 2013.

[17] M. Mendoza, B. Poblete, and C. Castillo. Twitter under crisis: Can we trust what we RT? *In Proceedings of the first workshop on social media analytics*, pp. 71–79, 2010.

[18] Sijia Li, Yilin Wang, Jia Xue, Nan Zhao, and Tingshao Zhu. The impact of COVID-19 epidemic declaration on psychological consequences: a study on active Weibo users. *International journal of environmental research and public health, pp. 1-9,* 17:2032, 2020.

[19] Yue Su, Jia Xue, Xiaoqian Liu, Peijing Wu, Junxiang Chen, Chen Chen, Tianli Liu, Weigang Gong, and Tingshao Zhu. Examining the impact of COVID-19 lockdown in Wuhan and Lombardy: a psycholinguistic analysis on Weibo and Twitter. *International Journal of Environmental Research and Public Health, pp. 1-10,* 17:4552, 2020.

[20] Han Woo Park, Sejung Park, and Miyoung Chong. Conversations and medical news frames on twitter: Infodemiological study on covid-19 in south korea. *Journal of Medical Internet Research,* 22(5) 1–11, 2020.

[21] Henna Budhwani and Ruoyan Sun. Creating COVID-19 Stigma by Referencing the Novel Coronavirus as the "Chinese virus" on Twitter: Quantitative Analysis of Social Media Data. *Journal of Medical Internet Research,* 22(5): 1–7, 2020.

[22] May Oo Lwin, Jiahui Lu, Anita Sheldenkar, Peter Johannes Schulz, Wonsun Shin, Raj Gupta, and Yinping Yang. Global sentiments surrounding the COVID-19 pandemic on Twitter: analysis of Twitter trends. *JMIR public health and surveillance,* 6(2): 1–4, 2020.

[23] Sohaib R Rufai and Catey Bunce. World leaders' usage of Twitter in response to the COVID-19 pandemic: a content analysis. *Journal of Public Health,* 42(3), 1–7 2020.

[24] Emily Chen, Kristina Lerman, and Emilio Ferrara. Tracking Social Media Discourse About the COVID-19 Pandemic: Development of a Public Coronavirus Twitter Data Set. *JMIR Public Health and Surveillance,* 6(2): 1–9, 2020.

[25] Tim Mackey, Vidya Purushothaman, Jiawei Li, Neal Shah, Matthew Nali, Cortni Bardier, Bryan Liang, Mingxiang Cai, and Raphael Cuomo. Machine Learning to Detect Self-Reporting of Symptoms, Testing Access, and Recovery Associated With COVID-19 on Twitter: Retrospective Big Data Infoveillance Study. *JMIR Public Health and Surveillance,* 6(2): 1–9, 2020.

[26] I. Togoh. Singapore, Praised For Its Initial Coronavirus Response, Closes Schools And Offices To Prevent Second Wave Of Infections. *[online] Forbes,* 2020. URL https://www.forbes.com/sites/isabeltogoh/2020/04/03/singapore-praised-for-its-initial-coronavirus-response-closes-schools-and-offices-to-prevent-second-wave-of-infections/#1902e26a73f0. Accessed on 15 September 2020.

[27] D. Sim and X. Kok. Coronavirus: Why so few deaths among Singapore's 14,000 Covid-19 infections? *South China Morning Post,* 2020. URL https://www.scmp.com/week-asia/health-environment/article/3081772/coronavirus-why-so-few-deaths-among-singapores-14000. Accessed on 17 September 2020.

[28] Victor Cha. Asia's covid-19 lessons for the west: Public goods, privacy, and social tagging. *The Washington Quarterly, pp. 1–18,* 2020.

[29] Ivan Townshend, Olu Awosoga, Judith Kulig, and HaiYan Fan. Social cohesion and resilience across communities that have experienced a disaster. *Natural Hazards,* 76(2):913–938, 2015.

[30] Z. Abdullah and H. Salamat. Singapore Confirms First Case Of Wuhan Virus. *[online] Channel News Asia,* 2020. URL https://www.channelnewsasia.com/news/singapore/wuhan-virus-pneumonia-singapore-confirms-first-case-12312860. Accessed on 15 September 2020.

[31] T. Goh. Wuhan Virus: First Singaporean Case Confirmed; She Was On Scoot Flight From Wuhan. *[online] The Straits Times,* 2020. URL https://www.straitstimes.com/singapore/health/wuhan-virus-first-singaporean-confirmed-to-have-virus-she-was-on-scoot-flight-from. Accessed on 15 September 2020.

[32] A. Chang. Coronavirus: S'pore Reports First Cases Of Local Transmission; 4 Out Of 6 New Cases Did Not Travel To China. *The Straits Times,* 2020. URL https://www.straitstimes.com/singapore/coronavirus-spore-reports-first-cases-of-local-transmission-4-out-of-6-new-cases-did-not. Accessed on 15 September 2020.

[33] Ministry of Health Singapore. Tighter Measures To Minimise Further Spread Of Covid-19. *Ministry of Health Singapore News Highlight,* 2020. URL https://www.moh.gov.sg/news-highlights/details/tighter-measures-to-minimise-further-spread-of-covid-19. Accessed on 15 September 2020.

[34] D. Sim and X. Kok. How Did Migrant Worker Dorms Become Singapore's Biggest Covid-19 Cluster? *South China Morning Post,* 2020. URL https://www.scmp.com/week-asia/explained/article/3080466/how-did-migrant-worker-dormitories-become-singapores-biggest. Accessed on 15 September 2020.

[35] Ministry of Health Singapore News Highlight. Circuit Breaker To Minimise Further Spread Of Covid-19. 2020. URL https://www.moh.gov.sg/news-highlights/details/circuit-breaker-to-minimise-further-spread-of-covid-19. Accessed on 15 September 2020.

[36] A. Kamil. Covid-19: 35 New Cases Reported; 3 New Clusters Emerge, Including 1 At A Live Music Bar On Circular Road. *[online] TODAYonline,* 2020. URL https://www.straitstimes.com/singapore/health/wuhan-virus-first-singaporean-confirmed-to-have-virus-she-was-on-scoot-flight-fromhttps://www.todayonline.com/singapore/covid-19-35-new-cases-reported-3-new-clusters-emerge-including-1-live-music-bar-circular. Accessed on 15 September 2020.

[37] Singapore Government Agency. Circuit Breaker Extension And Tighter Measures: What You Need To Know. *Singapore Government Agency Website*, 2020. URL https://www.gov.sg/article/circuit-breaker-extension-and-tighter-measures-what-you-need-to-know. Accessed on 15 September 2020.

[38] Ministry of Health Singapore. Easing The Tighter Circuit Breaker Measures, Preparing For Gradual Resumption Of Activity After 1 June. *Ministry of Health Singapore News Highlights*, 2020. URL https://www.moh.gov.sg/news-highlights/details/easing-the-tighter-circuit-breaker-measures-preparing-for-gradual-resumption-of-activity-after-1-June. Accessed on 15 September 2020.

[39] Singapore Government Agency. Safe Re-Opening: How Singapore Will Resume Activities After The Circuit Breaker. *Singapore Government Agency Website*, 2020. URL https://www.gov.sg/article/safe-re-opening-how-singapore-will-resume-activities-after-the-circuit-breaker. Accessed on 15 September 2020.

[40] Wayne Xin Zhao, Jing Jiang, Jianshu Weng, Jing He, Ee-Peng Lim, Hongfei Yan, and Xiaoming Li. Comparing twitter and traditional media using topic models. In *European conference on information retrieval*, pp. 338–349. Springer, Berlin, Heidelberg, 2011.

[41] Carson Sievert and Kenneth Shirley. LDAvis: A method for visualizing and interpreting topics. In *Proceedings of the workshop on interactive language learning, visualization, and interfaces*, pp. 63–70, 2014.

[42] Axel Bruns and Yuxian Eugene Liang. Tools and methods for capturing Twitter data during natural disasters. *First Monday*, 17(4), 2012.

[43] Rosa Vicari, Ioulia Tchiguirinskaia, Bruno Tisserand, and Daniel Schertzer. Climate risks, digital media, and big data: following communication trails to investigate urban communities' resilience. *Natural Hazards & Earth System Sciences*, 19(7): 1485–1498, 2019.

[44] Kate Starbird, Leysia Palen, Amanda L Hughes, and Sarah Vieweg. Chatter on the red: what hazards threat reveals about the social life of microblogged information. In *Proceedings of the 2010 ACM conference on Computer supported cooperative work*, pp. 241–250, 2010.

[45] Benjamin A Rachunok, Jackson B Bennett, and Roshanak Nateghi. Twitter and disasters: a social resilience fingerprint. *IEEE Access*, 7:58495–58506, 2019.

[46] Teun Terpstra, Richard Stronkman, Arnout de Vries, and Geerte L Paradies. Towards a realtime Twitter analysis during crises for operational crisis management. *In Proceedings of the 9th International ISCRAM Conference*, pp. 1–9, 2012.

[47] Neil Dufty. Using social media to build community disaster resilience. *The Australian journal of emergency management*, 27(1):40–45, 2012.

[48] Centers for Disease Control and Prevention. Crisis and Emergency Risk Communication. 2012.

[49] O. Ho. Coronavirus: Claps For Front-Line Fighters From Windows, Balconies. *The Straits Times*, 2020. URL https://www.straitstimes.com/singapore/claps-for-front-line-fighters-from-windows-balconies. Accessed on 15 September 2020.

[50] J. Ali-Knight, M. Robertson, A. Fyall, and A. Ladkin. International perspectives of festivals and events: paradigms of analysis. *Elsevier*, 2008.

[51] Cindy Chung and James W Pennebaker. The psychological functions of function words. *Social Communication*, 1:343–359, 2007.

[52] Thomas Heverin and Lisl Zach. Use of microblogging for collective sense-making during violent crises: A study of three campus shootings. *Journal of the Association for Information Science and Technology*, 63 (1):34–47, 2012.

[53] C.A. Maida. Sustainability and communities of place. *New York, NY: Berghahn*, 2007.

[54] B. Yuen. Searching for place identity in Singapore. *Habitat International*, 29(2): 197–214, 2005.

[55] P. Naess. Urban Structure Matters. *London: Routledge*, 2006.

[56] Fikret Berkes and Helen Ross. Community resilience: toward an integrated approach. *Society & Natural Resources*, 26(1):5–20, 2013.

[57] L.J. Vale and T.J. Campanella. The resilient city: how modern cities recover from disaster. *Oxford University Press*, 2005.

[58] Centre for Liveable Cities Singapore. Water Shortages And Rationing In Singapore. *Oxford University Press*, 2005. URL https://eresources.nlb.gov.sg/infopedia/articles/SIP_2020-02-20_192848.html. Accessed on 23 September 2020.

[59] Singapore Government Agency Website. HDB'S Ethnic Integration Policy: Why It Still Matters. *www.gov.sg.*, 2020. URL https://www.gov.sg/article/hdbs-ethnic-integration-policy-why-it-still-matters. Accessed on 23 September 2020.

12

Role of the Professional Body in a Pandemic

Lesley Arnold, Zaffar Sadiq Mohamed-Ghouse and Tony Wheeler

Surveying and spatial sciences professional bodies are highly conscious of the impact that the novel coronavirus COVID-19 is having on Members and sustaining partners. This awareness has seen member services and activities repackaged across the globe accordingly. This chapter gives an Australian perspective of the role of the professional body during the pandemic: from ensuring the continued availability of professional development events, advocating on behalf of Members and industry, and maintaining professional networking opportunities.

12.1   Introduction

The COVID-19 pandemic has created a public health emergency that has had a massive impact on society and economies worldwide. Almost everyone is being impacted in some way by the unprecedented enforced business closures, border lockdowns and social distancing measures enacted to reduce the spread of the virus.

This disruption has, and continues to have, an impact on professional bodies and their members. Members are faced with the fear of unemployment, having to come to grips with home schooling and social isolation, sifting through misinformation to stay on top of evolving pandemic-related policy and regulations, and confronting a new way of life where health concerns and the wellbeing of family are the highest priority.

Understanding how the professional body can provide value during these unprecedented times is not clear cut. Like governments and businesses, the Surveying and Spatial Sciences Institute (SSSI) Australia, is grappling with the question 'What are the impacts and consequences of the COVID-19 pandemic on our members and industry?' – and, as a voice for our members, 'What are some of the services and solutions we can offer Members to boost opportunities for continued learning, networking and career development - in a time when job security, financial markets and economies are so uncertain'?

To answer these questions, SSSI conducted a COVID-19 Member Survey in April 2020 to gauge Member concerns and understand their needs. The responses received were encouraging - SSSI was on the right track, but with scope for improvement in six areas explained in this Chapter, namely:

1. **Advocacy**: Advocate on behalf of the surveying and spatial sciences as an essential service during the pandemic.

2. **CPD**: Continue to provide opportunities for Continuing Professional Development (CDP) but in an online format across all disciplines – surveying, hydrographic, engineering and mine surveying, spatial information and cartography, and remote sensing and photogrammetry.

3. **Member Connect**: Provide opportunities for Members to connect including channels where

they can seek support and advice on professional matters from other Members, while working from home environments.

4. **Job Opportunities**: A National 'Jobs Board' and support for curriculum vitae/resume writing.

5. **Member Services**: Adapt member processes to align with COVID-19 restrictions, such as removing the need for face-to-face communications.

6. **Economic Sensitivity**: Review the cost of services and hardship guidelines to align with economic uncertainties faced by Members.

For many Associations [1], the COVID-19 pandemic has created more work. Keeping members up-to-date with information updates, increased advocacy on behalf of members (including liaison with government, industry and other associations), moving professional development and member meetings online, and increasing webinar and digital content production, has had a substantial impact on workloads. According to the COVID-19 Impact Survey 'Finding Opportunity in Crisis' conducted by the Australian Society of Association Executives (AuSAE), 'through this disruption, associations have been working tirelessly to collect, curate and disseminate information, advocate to government to assist in the formation and impact of policy, and provided support and assistance for the professions and industries they represent'.

This Chapter discusses the role of the Surveying and Spatial Sciences Institute (SSSI), Australia during the COVID-19 pandemic. Results from the COVID-19 Member Survey are discussed, along with how the Institute is responding to Member feedback.

The lessons learned have application to similar industry associations and professional bodies, looking for ways to respond to Member's needs during these extraordinary times, as well as providing pathways for Members to apply their unique surveying and spatial sciences skillsets to help communities better manage infectious disease outbreaks.

12.2 Serving Surveying and Spatial Science Professionals

The Surveying and Spatial Sciences Institute (SSSI) is Australia's peak body representing the interests of surveying and spatial science professionals. SSSI combines the disciplines of land surveying, engineering and mining surveying, cartography, hydrography, remote sensing and spatial information science.

SSSI Members work in diverse roles across various sectors (health, transport, energy, planning, security, resources, education, property, etc.) including academia, government and private businesses throughout Australia and New Zealand, as well as overseas nations.

SSSI gives a voice to Members of the surveying and spatial sciences community, building upon the traditions, values and history of the surveying and spatial sciences profession, as well as fostering and empowering Members to achieve excellence and make positive contributions to the global community through learning programs that showcase innovative technological developments in both the national and international arena. SSSI recognises and showcases the excellence achieved by surveying and spatial sciences practitioners and the significant contributions they make to the wellbeing of communities.

While SSSI conducts ongoing reviews of Members services, the challenges posed to Members and developments in the profession itself have been fast-paced during the pandemic. One of the biggest impacts by far, has been the lockdown restrictions as these have prevented face-to-face meetings, Continuing Professional Development (CPD) events, and networking opportunities. These challenges are not unique to SSSI. The International Federation of Surveyors[1] (FIG) notes

[1]International Federation of Surveyors (FIG) a United Nations and World Bank recognised non-governmental organisation of national member associations, cadastral and mapping agencies and ministries, universities and corporates from over 120 countries

significant developments in surveying professional education due to the COVID-19 restrictions and the need to adapt to online learning and teaching. According to Associate Professor David Mitchell, Chair of FIG Commission 2 FIG, this has presented a range of challenges including which learning management system and video communications platforms to use, how to reach those students without adequate internet connection or with poor ICT quality, and how to teach those tasks that are heavily based around face-to-face contact, such as practical field projects, computer lab sessions and cartographic design projects. The result of these considerations has revealed some valuable lessons for blended learning opportunities [2].

12.3   COVID-19 Member Survey

To better understand how Members are faring during the COVID-19 Pandemic, SSSI issued a survey early April 2020 to Members asking them how SSSI can support their professional needs during this difficult time. There were seven questions. The results are summarised below and addressed in the following sections:

1. **Are you currently concerned about achieving your CPD points to maintain your professional and/or certified status?** (50% No; 38% Yes; and 12% Undecided)

2. **What type of CPD are you most interested in participating in?** Respondents could choose more than one option. (67% Surveying; 47% Geospatial; 28% Data Science; 27% Business Practices; 14% Project Reviews; and 39% Soft Skills)

3. **Are you aware that SSSI offers a program of online live webinars and recorded eCPD events, to assist you to maintain CPD?** (92% answered Yes; and 8% answered No)

4. **Have you participated in a SSSI webinar?** (19% answered No; and 44% answered Yes)

5. **What has prevented you from participating?** (19% said topic was not of interest; 34% said time not convenient; 22% said the cost was too high; 8% were not comfortable with the technology; and 41% said they did not have the time)

6. **How has COVID-19 impacted your work life?** (3% Made redundant; 16% Work hours reduced; 5% partner/spouse made redundant; 48% Working as normal; 42% Working as normal but from home; 13% Juggling work and home schooling; 15% Other – e.g. retired)

7. **Are you interested in participating in online social events with other surveying and spatial professionals, for example afternoon virtual drinks, online quiz nights?** (36% answered Yes; and 66% answered No)

The survey was completed by 362 Members. This low response rate told its own story – that Members were faced with other more pressing issues during the onset of the pandemic.

Nonetheless, the results were revealing and the feedback has helped SSSI respond differently in terms of advocacy, CPD, Member Connect (networking), job prospects, member services, financial sensitivities and volunteer opportunities.

12.3.1   Advocacy

SSSI has been encouraging growth and increasing the level of the understanding of the surveying and spatial profession across allied professions and the wider community over many years. This is typically done through incentives to support education in schools, informative articles, blogs and white papers on topics of critical relevance to the industry, as well as building the relevance of surveying and spatial sciences in government policy and, more recently facilitating online panel discussions.

In recent years, the focus for SSSI has been advocating on Australia's Services Export Plan [3], 2026 Spatial Industry Transformation and Growth Agenda [4], Diversity and Inclusion [5], Asia Pacific Capacity Development [6], Square Kilometre Array [7], mentoring for young professionals [8], geospatial in schools [9], Australia's Decadal Plan for Geography [10], and Australia's Spatial and Space Road Map, and so forth.

With the COVID-19 Pandemic, policy positions are evolving rapidly, and SSSI is now advocating alongside other industry associations – calling on all Australian Governments to ensure that responses to COVID-19 include dedicated strategies and take all necessary measures to protect and support people.

SSSI is also helping our professionals to be heard – advocating for surveying to be classified as an essential service for the community during the pandemic. Hydrographic surveyors are essential to maintaining the safety of our ports, engineering and mine surveyors are crucial to mining operations, and cadastral surveyors are essential to construction projects. All these services have ramped up as the government increases mining and construction to buoy up the economy. GIS professionals have also been busier than usual, particularly in the health sector where the crucial need for mapping services, COVID-19 dashboards and spatial analysis have increased as outbreaks have escalated. And yet, surveying and professionals are struggling to meet higher than usual demands due COVID-19 restrictions, for example:

- Surveyors costs have increased due to survey teams travelling in individual vehicles to worksites to maintain social distancing.

- Intrastate border lockdowns, such as those between regions in Western Australia, have prevented surveyors travelling to worksites, as travel permits only apply to recognised essential services.

- Engineering and Mine Surveyors are struggling to get to mine sites, because of the lack of local flights and restrictions on seating allocations.

While the methods of advocacy remain largely the same (policy statements, newsletters, telephone communications, opinion pieces) during the pandemic, the topics have undergone a considerable change – creating new 'advocacy territory' for SSSI and likeminded organisations. With this new environment, brings the need to engage more often with Members in order to respond on their behalf and in a time-sensitive manner.

12.3.2   Continuing Professional Development

SSSI offers members a Continuing Professional Development (CPD) Program designed to complement the busy professional wishing to undertake activities to further their current skills and experience within the workplace.

Given the cancellation of face-to-face events to comply with social distancing measures, it was surprising that the majority of survey respondents were not concerned about achieving their CPD accreditation for the year. Their optimism was buoyed by the increase in webinars and the ability to participate in monthly CPD meetings online.

As the COVID-19 outbreak unfolded, the ability to respond quickly with online CPD webinars was enabled through the support of Member volunteers, government, private industry and regional associations. SSSI held regular communications with cooperating regional associations – ASEAN Federation of Land Surveying and Geomatics[2] (AFLAG), Pacific Geospatial and Surveying Council[3] (PGSC) and Surveying & Spatial New Zealand[4] (S+SNZ). The outcome of these

---

[2] ASEAN Federation of Land Surveying and Geomatics (AFLAG), is the professional association duly accredited by the ASEAN Secretariat based in Jakarta, Indonesia representing the Geodetic Engineers, Surveyors and Geomatics practitioners in the region).

[3] Pacific Geospatial and Surveying Council (PGSC) vision is to focus on sustainable development in the Pacific Islands region enabled by world-class geospatial information and surveying services.

[4] Surveying & Spatial New Zealand (S+SNZ) is the professional body representing survey and spatial

discussions was the addition of jointly supported online events to provide mutual CPD opportunities for members of respective organisations.

The SSSI has been proactive in establishing Memorandums of Understandings (MOUs) and reciprocating arrangements with several likeminded professional associations and not for profit organisations including Open Geospatial Consortium[5] (OGC), Urban and Regional Information Systems Association[6] (URISA), FIG and International Society for Photogrammetry and Remote Sensing (ISPRS). These collaborations are proving crucial during the pandemic, particularly as the appetite for learning programs has increased, as they foster shared resourcing opportunities and knowledge-sharing. Collaboration is ongoing, and there has been a high-degree of information sharing through online panel discussions, to explore mutually beneficial opportunities for Members. The SSSI continues to monitor webinar activities globally for relevant content and opportunities for Members, and conversely, is also recording attendance levels to see if webinar fatigue sets in, to see if other opportunities need to be considered.

12.3.3 Member Connect

One of the primary roles of a professional body is enabling networking opportunities for members, locally, nationally and internationally. SSSI supports a network of strategic partners across all levels of government, Not-for-profit (NFP) and the private sector. The aim is to proliferate influence and broaden the support base to increase the reach and benefits for the membership.

Before the pandemic, SSSI provided a dedicated series of network building opportunities. For many Members this network helps to build careers, stay connected with peers, and to share experiences and learn from each other. At the local level, the regional committees customise networking events that have local interest to Members; at a National level, events are coordinated by the National Events Manager, and international events are typically organised through a steering committee, made up of interested parties.

With face-to-face events cancelled, SSSI has had to find creative ways to enable Members to connect. For example, the Locate 20 conference was reinvented as Locate Connect[7] – a virtual series bringing experts together to present on location-based topics and contribute to Q&A panel sessions.

While socialising has been difficult during the pandemic, survey respondents indicated that they were not especially looking for virtual social events from their professional body. People cited being 'time poor' as the main drawback, while others noted they happy to wait for face-to-face socialising to return.

Nonetheless, amidst the COVID-19 pandemic, SSSI went virtual for the annual Oceanic Asia-Pacific Spatial Excellence Awards (APSEA), held 28 May 2020. These awards recognise the achievements of enterprises and individuals in the surveying and spatial sciences industry. While it wasn't the gala dinner evening that Members are accustomed to, it still provided the opportunity to congratulate those that have contributed extensively to the four pillars of the profession – academia, government, research and the private sector. APSEA has been a highlight for 2020 and given the industry an opportunity to celebrate excellence.

The SSSI adopted a ChatApp to enable participants of the Bushfire recovery Map-a-thon[8] to connect. The App was rated a huge success, as it brought people together to share knowledge and ask questions of those who understand surveying and spatial sciences matter. At one point during the map-a-thon, there were over 200 participants logged in to the chat channel. It was an ideal way for the Map-a-thon community to network with each other and not feel isolated when working

---

professionals who work collaboratively to strengthen and celebrate the knowledge, capability and innovation within this exciting sector for the benefit of society.

[5]Open Geospatial Consortium (OGC) Global Resource for Information and Standards.

[6]Urban and Regional Information Systems Association (URISA) a non-profit association that provides education and training, a vibrant and connected community, advocacy for geospatial challenges and issues, and essential resources for GIS professionals throughout their careers.

[7]Locate Connect is a program of Locate Conferences Australia which SSSI is 50% shareholder and contributor https://www.locateconference.com/2021/locate-connect-program/

[8]OpenStreetMap is a collaborative project to create a free editable map of the world, accessible at https://wiki.openstreetmap.org/wiki/Mapathon

from home locations. In addition, organisers could make announcements to assist mappers, and supporters, such as Nearmap and OpenStreetMap (OSM), were able to participate and solve any technical issues immediately. Even after the map-a-thon, participants were still engaging on the chat channel, and it was exciting to see our international participants log-in during the day to get feedback before they started mapping.

SSSI is currently testing the method to enable professionals to keep in-touch during pandemic. The Chat channel includes conversations to share information on (1) spatial technologies being used to Tackle COVID-19; (2) privacy and sensitivity issues around data usage, particularly for contact tracing Apps; (3) impacts to business resulting from lockdowns and social distancing requirements; and (4) general announcements about events and Webinars.

12.3.4   Job Prospects

A common thread among survey respondents was the future of the profession, job prospects, and support for job seekers. Currently, SSSIs provides services that enable Members to maintain professional industry standards. This is achieved through certification programs that are relevant to current and emerging industry requirements. The certification essentially recognises that a person has demonstrated that he or she has the necessary knowledge and experience to competently work in their area of expertise.

Government organisations are increasingly adding certification as a criterion for businesses responding to tenders. This is because certification affords insurance of currency and knowledge. Since the COVID-19 outbreak there has been increased interest from regional associations to leverage these internationally accredited certification processes locally to increase job prospects for their Members. SSSI is also the authorised assessing authority for surveying and spatial sciences professionals emigrating to Australia. This experience of Migration Skills Assessment could be utilised by other countries to setup a similar process in their region and train assessors.

As a consequence of the pandemic, Members are now faced with work redundancies and the need to upskill to find new opportunities. The pandemic has highlighted that SSSI has a broader role in assisting Members to be 'Job Ready'. In addition, to CPD and certification to enhance career progression, survey respondents are keen to have support for professional curriculum vitae/resume writing, and notifications of job openings and scholarship opportunities in the surveying and spatial sciences field. Job application writing, interview training, presentation skills and a 'jobs board' are new areas for the SSSI to focus on.

12.3.5   Member Services

Magazines, journals and bulletins provide the most effective method for keeping Members up-to-date. The majority of these communiques are now online. However, for SSSI, some processes were still tied to the postal service and that created some concern due to delayed services, brought about by the increase postal traffic during the pandemic as people moved to online shopping delivery. For this reason, newsletters and renewal notifications were moved to online/email-only transactions. Members have been quick to approve the change – noting a reduced environmental footprint.

COVID-19 has resulted in several process improvements. To become a Member, applicants were required to meet a Justice of the Peace in person to have original academic records certified. Due to social distancing requirements, this requirement has been removed and the process to become a Member is now far more streamlined.

Cash payments for renewals are also no longer acceptable to Members during the pandemic. As a result, SSSI had to fast-track more flexible payment options for events, professional certification, membership renewals and re-joining fees – with BPay, PayPal and credit card options now available to Members in addition to the existing cheque and Electronic Funds Transfer (EFT).

SSSI regional committees also had to rethink how they engaged with Members and provided services. The SSSI Board, regional committees, and other interest groups moved to online platforms to continue their important work and socialise.

The pandemic has also fast-tracked the need to consider other process improvements, such as speaking with businesses and surveyors' boards to better understand the pain points for Members and employers alike. According to [11], now is the time to reimagine business models, confront challenges and position for future opportunities; this includes recovering revenue, rebuilding operations, rethinking the organisation and accelerating the adoption of digital solutions.

12.3.6 Economic Sensitivity

Both associations and Members are facing economic setbacks during the pandemic, and this is posing a conundrum. The cancellation of conferences and face-to-face events has removed an income stream for Professional bodies, and this revenue is required to keep Member fees down. Yet, increasing Member fees is not a palatable option. Members are also facing hardship due to reduced household incomes resulting from redundancies. This poses a dilemma for the professional body faced with having to spend additional resources (without receiving additional revenue) to be able to provide new services.

Professional bodies survive by being able to achieve sustainable 'economies of scale'. As the number of Members increase, services become more cost effective, for example the unit cost of printing a publication is reduced as the number of copies increases. This means that retaining Members and increasing Member numbers has a direct effect on the number and quality services offered, and the price-point for Members.

Interestingly, the AuSEA noted that 'Through this crisis Associations have reported increased member engagement and in some cases growth in membership as they became a trusted source of truth for their members and communities' [1].

However, the question remains, 'what can the Professional Body do to address the current economic sensitives brought on by the pandemic'?

SSSI Members are our most important asset, and providing 'value for money' to Members has never been more crucial than during the pandemic. The new financial year provided the opportunity to consider new member services, renewal options and renewal incentives.

SSSI introduced the **MemberOne Program**, essentially an incentive scheme for existing members to introduce new members to SSSI. The more members referred, the greater discount the Member receives to their SSSI membership fee – a substantial saving during these uncertain times. The program outline is as follows:

- Introduce one new person that becomes a financial member during 20/21FY and receive 20% discount off your membership fee in 21/22FY.

- Introduce two new people that become financial members during 20/21FY and receive 25% discount off your membership fee in 21/22FY.

- Introduce three new people that become financial members during 20/21FY and receive 30% discount off your membership fee in 21/22FY.

In addition, SSSI has introduced monthly payment options to assist those facing hardship. Members can choose to pay monthly instead of paying an annual upfront fee. Also, SSSI has reviewed the Membership Policy to ensure the guidelines for hardship applications are applicable to pandemic situations and are simplified so as not to exacerbate the circumstances generating the hardship. While it is not possible to list all the possible circumstances, the 'Hardship Application' exempts annual subscriptions for:

- extended illness that results in a member being on extended sick leave from their work place; and

- a period of extended unemployment.

From 1 July 2020, SSSI made all webinars free to Members. This action was in response to Members' survey feedback. SSSI Webinars offer value for money when considered part of Membership fees. In addition, when SSSI does return to face to face events, that aim is to ensure that event pricing is reflective of a significant financial advantage to SSSI members over non-members. This will be important, as the financial impacts of the pandemic are expected to last for some time to come.

12.4   Moving Back to Normality

There is a general perception that there is no returning to normal after COVID-19, but professional bodies do need a pathway forward. The world is likely to recover at differing speeds, and the speed will vary depending on the type of industry.

Professional bodies require a strategic decision-making framework that is a staged approach to assessing needs and priorities – one that looks beyond the current disruptions to reposition Member services to suit a post-pandemic society. This is the next big challenge for the professional body.

The pandemic affords the opportunity to step back and reposition Member services so that when life starts to get back to normal, whatever this may look like, there are new initiatives, hopes and opportunities for Members to look forward to.

12.5   Conclusion

During a pandemic, the professional body has an important role to play in supporting its Members and the profession it represents. This paper has presented a case study of the challenges faced by the Surveying and Spatial Science Institute (SSSI) Australia, and its Members. Through the COVID-19 Membership Survey, SSSI has been progressively responding to Members suggestions and concerns in the areas of advocacy, CPD, Member connect, Job Prospects, Member services, economic sensitivity, and opportunities for volunteering.

The next big challenge for the professional body is to look beyond the COVID-19 disruptions, and reposition Member services to suit a post-pandemic society. This will require a strategic and staged approach to implementation, and consideration of the lessons learned during the pandemic. In summary, the major lessons learned have been to:

- Vastly increase the amount of content that Members can access online, including an ambitious plan for online CPD and learning, that has since been well publicised, recognised and respected. The current climate has provided an opportunity for some Members to upskill, progress qualifications and learn new skills such as programming and latest software developments. For those Members that are 'time poor' content is available and can be downloaded after the live events.

- Establishing strong networks with other likeminded associations and organisations. The opportunity to think globally and act locally, by leveraging national and international exclusive partner agreements, has enabled SSSI to provide members with the best possible content for them to improve and grow their knowledge and competitive edge.

- Adopt a mindset of 'process improvement'. During the COVID-19 pandemic, SSSI took the opportunity to streamline processes across the business, particularly around membership applications, renewals and flexible payment options, as well as removing the need for face-to-face communications – no longer appropriate during the pandemic.

- Enhance Certification Programs. SSSI, through its Engineering Mine Surveying Commission volunteers, has enhanced the Engineering and Mine Surveying Certification process – providing Members with an additional incentive to learn, and have that learning recognised.

- Maximise value for Members by opening up communication channels in times of crisis. The SSSI connected with Members via the COVD-19 Member Survey. The feedback has enabled SSSI to makes decisions that create value for money for members including free Webinars and opportunities to enhance job prospects; as well as consider the financial constraints on Members and their families during this difficult time.

References

[1] AuSAE (Australian Society for Association Executives), 2020.

[2] David Mitchell. COVID-19 responses and FIG2020: lessons for Surveying Education, FIG Commission 2: Professional Education, 2020. URL https://fig.net/fig2020/articles/FIG2020_2_professional_education. htm.

[3] Surveying and Spatial Sciences Institute. Launch of Action Plan for Australia's Export Services, 2019. URL https://sssi.org.au/knowledge-hub/news/launch-of-action-plan-for-australia-s-export-servi.

[4] 2026 Agenda. 2026 Spatial Industry Transformation and Growth Agenda, 2019. URL https://2026agenda. com/.

[5] 2026 Agenda. Diversity and Inclusion, 2019. URL https://2026agenda.com/diversity-and-inclusion/.

[6] Surveying and Spatial Sciences Institute. Asia Pacific Capacity Development Network, 2019. URL https: //sssi.org.au/knowledge-hub/news/asia-pacific-capacity-development-network-report.

[7] Surveying and Spatial Sciences Institute. Steps taken on SKA quest, 2019. URL https://sssi.org.au/ knowledge-hub/news/steps-taken-on-ska-quest.

[8] Surveying and Spatial Sciences Institute. National YP Mentoring Program, 2019. URL https://sssi.org.au/ sssi-community/special-interest-groups/young-professionals/national-yp-mentoring-program.

[9] Surveying and Spatial Sciences Institute. Geospatial Schools Competition - Winners Announced!, 2019. URL https://sssi.org.au/knowledge-hub/news/geospatial-schools-competition-winners-announced.

[10] Surveying and Spatial Sciences Institute. Australia's Decadal (strategic) Plan for Geography launched 22 November 2018, 2018. URL https://sssi.org.au/knowledge-hub/news/australia-s-decadal-strategic-plan-for-geography.

[11] McKinsey. From surviving to thriving: Reimagining the post-COVID-19 return, 2020. URL https://www.mckinsey.com/featured-insights/future-of-work/from-surviving-to-thriving-reimagining-the-post-covid-19-return#.

13

OpenStreetMap Data Use Cases During the Early Months of the COVID-19 Pandemic

Peter Mooney, A. Yair Grinberger, Marco Minghini, Serena Coetzee, Levente Juhasz and Godwin Yeboah

Created by volunteers since 2004, OpenStreetMap (OSM) is a global geographic database available under an open access license and currently used by a multitude of actors worldwide. This chapter describes the role played by OSM during the early months (from January to July 2020) of the ongoing COVID-19 pandemic, which - in contrast to past disasters and epidemics - is a global event impacting both developed and developing countries. A large number of COVID-19-related OSM use cases were collected and grouped into a number of research frameworks which are analyzed separately: dashboards and services simply using OSM as a basemap, applications using raw OSM data, initiatives to collect new OSM data, imports of authoritative data into OSM, and traditional academic research on OSM in the COVID-19 response. The wealth of examples provided in the chapter, including an analysis of OSM tile usage in two countries (Italy and China) deeply affected in the earliest months of 2020, prove that OSM has been and still is heavily used to address the COVID-19 crisis, although with types and mechanisms that are often different depending on the affected area or country and the related communities.

13.1   Introduction

The OpenStreetMap (OSM) project was started in University College London in 2004 and has subsequently grown to be arguably the largest and most popular Volunteered Geographic Information (VGI) and open geographic data project in the world today [1]. The data within the OSM database is completely open and is available under an Open Database License (ODbL). The contributors of geographic data to OSM are predominantly citizens not specifically connected to the professional production or management of geographic data. However, in recent years, governments and commercial companies have become involved in the contribution of data to OSM and the editing and maintenance of the existing data. Mooney and Minghini [2] provide an extensive description of the users and uses of OSM data. Many people who encounter OSM mistakenly consider the online maps and associated digital cartographic products from OSM as the entire OSM project. This is incorrect. OSM is primarily a very large spatial database of geographic data. Online maps and other services such as routing or information services are derived products and could not exist without the underlying OSM database. The data model used within the OSM database is simple to understand but is powerful enough to prove capable of expressing the complex geographical relationships and topologies encountered in real world environments such as road networks, commercial and industrial settings, landuse features such as lakes and rivers, and residential buildings.

The data model expresses three object types: nodes (or points), polygons and polylines (collectively called ways). Relations are a logical object expressing a collection of these objects to represent complex compound geographic features such as railway stations, airports, transport routes, etc. Every object (except those nodes making up ways) must have at least one descriptive attribute associated with it. These attributes are called tags and are stored as key-value pairs. Very detailed guidance on the available tags, acceptable values for specific keys, and usage examples are provided on the Map Features page in the OSM Wiki [3] and often within software. However, the application and use of tags on objects in OSM is not strictly enforced and follows a folksonomy approach allowing contributors to choose tags as they see appropriate. This approach has led to many criticisms of the quality of OSM data over the years [4]. One unique aspect of the OSM database is the ability for anyone to access the entire contribution and editing history of the data within the database. This allows researchers to study the evolution of the OSM data in specific areas, study contribution patterns over time, analyse how the OSM database grows with influence from external events such as natural or humanitarian disasters.

There are a number of methods which support contribution or insertion of geographic data into the OSM database. These methods are supplemented by a myriad of software tools and services available with the entire OSM ecosystem. Field survey, implying a physical knowledge of the area under survey, using GPS tools, cameras and other software is supported widely. Social events called "mapping parties" often involve people meeting up at group events to undertake field mapping of a specific area ([5, 6]). However, the most commonly used approach is remote mapping using web-based interfaces such as the popular iD editor allowing contributors to remotely map an area by digitizing data on top of satellite imagery. Contributors using this approach are urged to have some knowledge of the area being mapped and at minimum consult the extensive documentation and guidance on the OSM wiki on how to map properly. "Mapathons" are popular events where people, even located in different parts of the world, meet virtually and do remote mapping on the same area. Finally, the software-automated import of existing geographic datasets and databases is also possible and has been used widely in OSM to import datasets such as road networks and buildings. Automated imports are complex database operations and those undertaking such imports are strongly encouraged to seek the approval of the local OSM community in the geographic area of the import before proceeding. Imports should also be clearly documented in the OSM wiki.

Previous to the COVID-19 pandemic OSM had been used in many humanitarian and environmental disaster situations where access to up-to-date and accurate geographic data was immediately required and remote mapping and field mapping exercises could quickly generate geographic data for an area if none existed. This chapter will analyse and understand how OSM has been used during the early months of the COVID-19 pandemic. By early months we are referring to the period between January 2020 and July 2020. In January 2020 the World Health Organization (WHO) announced the COVID-19 epidemic, a public health emergency of international concern. The coronavirus disease 2019 (COVID-19) has subsequently become a global pandemic and has imposed unprecedented change all over the world in how we interact as humans, in our working practices, and how medical professionals carry out their work. Most countries in the world have experienced many COVID-19 related deaths and high rates of COVID-19 spread amongst their populations. This chapter will be a strong and defined contribution to the knowledge on how VGI initiatives such as OSM respond and are used or accessed during a global crisis such as the COVID-19 pandemic. The novel aspect of this work is that this critical assessment is being delivered during this unfolding and unprecedented event rather than from an a posteriori position. Furthermore, we believe that this work will produce knowledge about humanitarian mapping in a context never studied before - a global event with significant impacts in developed regions.

The remainder of the chapter is organized as follows. In Section 13.2 we provide a discussion of background and related work. Section 13.3 provides an overview of the methodology and research employed in this work. In Section 13.4 we discuss the use of OSM data in the COVID-19 response, while section 13.5 discusses the collection of new OSM data for COVID-19 responses. Section 13.6 briefly discusses current academic research with OSM during the COVID-19 response. In section 13.7 we make some conclusions and outline some future work.

13.2 Background and Related Work

The potential of OSM for supporting humanitarian efforts during crisis situations was noticed as early as 2010 after a magnitude 7.0 earthquake struck Haiti. Volunteers across the world supported humanitarian efforts through mapping activities across multiple platforms, including OSM contributors who produced much data using available aerial imagery within only a few weeks [7]. These efforts have led to the formation of the Humanitarian OpenStreetMap Team (HOT), an international charitable organization which organizes and oversees open mapping in humanitarian contexts [8]. Since then, HOT was involved in initiating and coordinating mapping efforts in multiple cases, including following the 2013 Yolanda Typhoon in the Philippines [9] and the 2015 Nepal Earthquake [10]. The open source Tasking Manager (TM) software [11], developed by HOT and aimed at coordinated collaborative mapping, was also re-used by several communities worldwide, such as the Italian one to coordinate mapping after the 2016 earthquake [12]. Today, digital humanitarianism in OSM goes beyond disaster response with the organization of activities that aim at supporting vulnerable communities to increase their resilience [13–15]. Furthermore, the richness of OSM data facilitates further applications, frequently including the development of third party tools that utilize OSM data for creating additional data or carrying geographic analyses. For example, efforts after the 2010 Haitian earthquake also included the application of an Emergency Route Service relying on up-to-date OSM data [16]; OSM data was also used as a baseline for the Flooded Streets tool used to produce a crowdsourced map of flooded streets in Chennai, India during a 2015 flooding event [17].

One issue that is also being considered within this context is the management of health crises and the possible contributions of OSM to managing health crises and monitoring epidemics. Mooney et al. [18], when discussing the role of VGI in pervasive health applications, identify OSM as a potential "virtual audit instrument" describing local environments. Accordingly, much effort is being put into collecting information required for monitoring health-related outcomes, e.g. mapping settlements and buildings to assist malaria prevention in Kenya and Mozambique [19], health facilities[20], and other critical infrastructure [21], while other works strive to utilize existing data to mitigate health effects and assess accessibility to medical facilities [22–25]. The response to the 2014-2016 Ebola outbreak in West Africa, which turned from a local response to an extended international effort [26] presents a relevant and unique example. During the breakout, HOT volunteers mapped large portions of the infected regions, providing support for on-the-ground teams of the Médecins Sans Frontières and facilitating the production of epidemiological maps [27, 28]. Additionally, an OSM-based navigation service (OSM Automated Navigation Directions - OsmAnd) was used to support data collection activities by locals [29]. The studies surveyed above present crisis relief and disaster response as a multi-dimensional framework. The support of relief efforts may begin with providing reliable basemaps but extends even beyond the production of the information that these maps require into the development of new products and services, based on OSM data, for the benefit of responders and the general population.

In the following sections we use this to survey and analyse the different dimensions through which the OSM community has responded to the COVID-19 crisis. Bearing in mind the cross-boundary effects of the pandemic, we also consider the formation of inter-regional collaborations, as in the case of the Ebola outbreak discussed above.

13.3 Methodology and Research Approach

To survey and analyse the different dimensions through which the OSM community has responded to the COVID-19 crisis we considered the following *OSM Response Frameworks* (our terminology) as follows:

- **OSM usage as a cartographic basemap in COVID-19 related applications** which can indicate the project's maturity and ability to compete as an alternative to commercial and authoritative mapping service providers;

- **COVID-19 related applications or services using OSM data** (such as points of interest, road networks, building data such as hospitals or medical facilities);

- **Initiatives or applications aimed at the collection of new OSM data** immediately relevant to the COVID-19 pandemic response or management;

- **COVID-19 influenced imports of authoritative geospatial data into OSM** where there are gaps in the OSM database for a particular country or region; and,

- **Academic research about the role of OSM in the COVID-19 response**.

The proposed methodology for understanding the role played in each of the OSM Response Frameworks is comprised of a number of research tasks which are summarised as follows:

- traditional literature review focused on standard academic sources, web searches of social media, and research of available gray literature such as multimedia, reports, presentations and mailing lists;

- analysis of OSM map tile access and usage on a global scale, including comparison with the pre-COVID-19 situation to find out whether the pandemic has generated more OSM tile access and usage than pre-COVID-19 situation.

While most readers will be familiar with traditional literature reviews, the tiled web map system requires some explanation. The tiled web map system divides the earth into a set of regular tiles corresponding to different zoom levels. Web-based maps usually display geographic information by loading map image tiles (or lately, vector tiles) corresponding to a geographic area and stitching them together to a visually seamless map experience. A description of tiled web maps is found in Juhasz and Hochmair [30]. OSM tiles can be displayed on any map free of charge if adhering to the tile usage policy [31]. We extracted OSM tile usage statistics from Planet OSM [32] for affected areas in Italy (Lombardy) and China (Wuhan) along with control areas within the same country (Sicily and Beijing, respectively) to reveal whether COVID-19 increases tile usage. Our detailed methodology and technical details can be found in Figure 13.1. We choose zoom level 13, in which details correspond to the regional level with one tile covering 23.9 km^2 (Figure 13.1) and compare usage between pre-COVID-19 (January 1 - 21) and affected times (February 5 - 25 in China and March 11 - 31 in Italy).

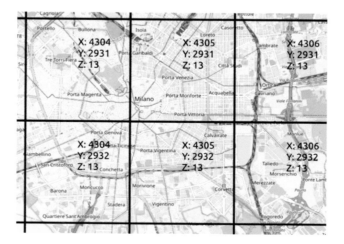

FIGURE 13.1
Illustration of web map tiles in zoom level 13 in the area of Milan, Italy.

13.4   Use of OSM Data for COVID-19

We searched for websites offering web maps and geospatial services related to the COVID-19 pandemic. The bulleted list below (at the end of this Section 13.4) presents a typology of the websites with references to prominent examples. We identified two major types of websites - visualizations of COVID-19 data and geospatial services. The most prominent example of data visualizations are dashboards which simply overlay OSM data with other types of data, i.e. OSM was used as a basemap only (see some examples in Figure 13.2 and Figure 13.3). Online dashboards are typically driven by open data on the pandemic released by governments and/or other organizations (e.g. the popular dataset from the Center for Systems Science and Engineering at Johns Hopkins University [33]) and communicate numbers and statistics, usually updated on a regular basis, through tables, graphs and thematic maps. These dashboards serve to inform experts, decision makers and the general public. Many of the dashboards designed by national governments, research organizations and volunteers use OSM as the basemap. A subtype within this group of websites are websites presenting dynamic visualizations of the spread of the virus. It seems that most of the dashboards featuring OSM basemaps are also realized with open source mapping software and designed by volunteers, and research or not-for-profit organizations and businesses. Dashboards produced by governments (which show the same COVID-19 data) seemed instead to rely more heavily on proprietary technology and basemaps.

The geospatial services group includes three subtypes. The first provides more types of geospatial information, extending beyond contagion patterns. The information content in these websites is very diverse, ranging from general information on issues such as resilience and support measures for enterprises to practical information, e.g. locations for testing for COVID-19 and on the availability of masks in pharmacies. The second subtype extends this approach (and hence there is some overlap between the two subtypes), allowing users to contribute data themselves, i.e. become "produsers" [34]. Notice that these are platform-specific data (e.g. where masks are 3-d printed) and not data that are fed back into OSM. The third subtype facilitates more complex spatial queries, e.g. by comparing users' location history to assess their exposure to COVID-19 or when identifying areas allowed for travel in the vicinity of users' homes. Swedish TV [35] stands out among these by utilizing the isochrones functionality of OpenRouteService [36] (see Figure 13.4, thus extending beyond the "OSM as basemap" type of data usage. This is related to the unique restrictions imposed in Sweden which were defined by driving time instead of Euclidean distance, hence requiring more complex spatial querying capabilities.

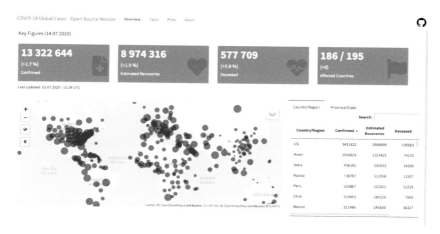

FIGURE 13.2
A dashboard focused on global COVID-19 cases. Source: [37].

FIGURE 13.3
World Bank map showing the measures of each country to support small and medium-sized enterprises (SMEs) in response to COVID-19. Source: [38].

Typology of websites and services using OSM data, with examples

- **Website type: COVID-19 data visualizations**

  - *Dashboards:*
    Examples: Global [33, 37, 39–41]; continental/regional [42]; national/local [40, 43–48];

  - *Dynamic visualizations:*
    Examples: the spread of virus infections over time [49]; the phylogeny of SARS-CoV-2 viruses from the ongoing novel coronavirus COVID-19 [50].

- **Website type: COVID-19 related geospatial services**

  - *Geospatial information services:*
    Examples: measures supporting small to medium-sized enterprises [38]; social media posts [51]; change in mobility patterns [52]; 3-d printing of masks for medical staff [53]; locations of clinical trials [54]; locations of food resources [55]; resilience measures for businesses [56] and population [57]; locations for testing for COVID-19 [58]; stocks of masks in pharmacies [59]; queuing time in border crossings [60]; change in air quality during lockdowns [61]; state of public transport [62];

  - *Services facilitating (non-OSM) data contribution:*
    Examples: 3-d printing of masks for medical staff [53]; initiating joint delivery of goods [63]; queuing times in supermarkets [64];

  - *Services performing geospatial queries:*
    Examples: assessment of exposure to COVID-19 using location history [65–67]; identification of areas allowed for travel from a location, given travel restrictions [35, 68].

The dashboards and web maps above make use of a wide range of different OSM basemaps. Many of these are provided by commercial mapping companies such as CARTO [69] and Mapbox [70]. Other websites and services, especially community-developed projects without financial means to afford using commercial providers, rely on the freely available tiles provided by OSM. To assess whether OSM tiles were used in connection with COVID-19 response, we compared tile usage statistics between two greatly affected regions (Lombardy in Italy and Wuhan in China) with their relatively unaffected counterparts within the same countries (Sicily and Beijing). The left panel of Figure 13.5. a-b plots the number of times tiles were loaded for study sites between January 1 and June 30, 2020. The baseline for the comparison was set to a 3-week-long period between January 1 and January 21 (purple, shaded vertical area), which were compared to 3-week-long affected periods (orange, shaded vertical area, February 5 - 25 in China and March 11 - 31 in Italy). Control and

FIGURE 13.4
Swedish Television's interface using OSM road network data and the isochrones function of OpenRouteService for computing areas within 2 hours driving distance from a location in Sweden (example shows the isochrones from Stockholm's center). Source: [35].

affected periods start with a Wednesday and end with a Tuesday 3 weeks later to eliminate the daily temporal trend that is visible in the left side of Figure 13.5. We assume that the seasonal trend is constant across affected areas and their unaffected counterparts within the same country, therefore seasonal patterns were left untreated. Plots in the right panel of Figure 13.5 show the difference between normalized tile usage patterns for a region. A value of 1 means that tiles were only loaded during the period affected with COVID-19, and -1 means the opposite. The red horizontal shows that equal numbers of tiles were loaded during the control and affected periods on a given day. The normalized difference is higher in Lombardy and in Wuhan than in Sicily and Beijing respectively, which suggests that areas greatly affected by COVID-19 were viewed more frequently than would be expected under normal conditions as seen in the tile logs. Two paired t-tests were conducted, which confirmed that the increased attention affected areas were experiencing was statistically significant, $t(20) = 5.00$, $p < 0.001$ for Italy and $t(20) = 8.63$, $p < 0.001$ for China.

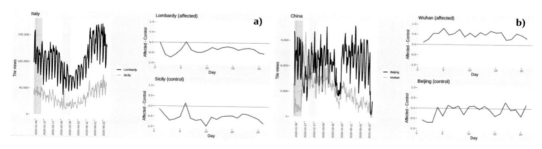

FIGURE 13.5
Tile usage statistics for selected areas in Italy (a) and China (b). The left side of figures shows the number of times tiles were loaded. Purple vertical area is the control period where orange vertical area shows a 3-week-period affected by COVID-19. The right side of sub-plots show the difference of normalized tile usage patterns for an area.

13.5   Collection of OSM Data for COVID-19

The ongoing COVID-19 pandemic has also seen an unprecedented amount and type of activities to collect new OSM data. Not surprisingly, May 2020 has set the all-time records for the numbers of daily OSM contributors $(7, 209)$, newly registered OSM users $(6, 259)$ and newly registered users who contributed data $(1, 019)$ - all of them on May 14 [71]. This section summarizes the main nature of such activities and provides, whenever possible, details on the reasons for collecting OSM data and/or the communities or organizations which actually requested those data. However, a key strength of any VGI project is the chance that data can be used by anyone, at any time, and for purposes that might be different and even unknown to the users who originally collected those data [72]. Proliferation of Artificial Intelligence (AI), which has reached a massive uptake during the COVID-19 crisis [73], does nothing but reinforce this statement. OSM data collection to address the COVID-19 pandemic has happened in all the ways described in Section 13.1. Remote mapping is by far the method by which most data was contributed and it is not surprising that such efforts were led by HOT. At the time of writing (mid-July 2020), the HOT TM lists 183 projects targeted at COVID-19 emergencies worldwide with aims for the collection of baseline OSM data such as buildings, road networks, land use areas and placenames [74]. These projects mainly address regions in African and South American countries where baseline maps are still not available, with Peru being the most popular one with a total of 84 projects. The OSM contribution records mentioned above were directly attributed to increased activity in HOT's projects in Peru, Botswana and Central African Republic, with a mapping peak in the Cusco region in Peru [71]. A recent tweet from HOT [75] reported about more than 10,000 volunteers who have mapped over 1.7 million buildings and over 41,000 km of roads in COVID-19 projects so far. The organizations requesting the activation of these HOT projects, which will use the collected OSM data afterwards, are national or regional governments, health authorities, humanitarian organizations and NGOs. As usual, also during COVID-19 times mapathons (mostly virtual, given the mobility restrictions) have been extensively organized by several organizations worldwide to perform coordinated remote mapping in specific areas, with HOT itself providing tips and suggestions on how to map COVID-specific OSM objects [76].

In addition to the HOT TM, another tool that has been widely used during the COVID-19 crisis is `healthsites.io` [77], which aims to build an open geospatial dataset of every health care facility in the world, allowing to map e.g. hospitals (`amenity=hospital`), pharmacies (`amenity=pharmacy`) and doctors (`amenity=doctors`) and to add tags to the already available ones. This type of mapping clearly requires a personal knowledge of the health facilities to add and therefore it is not a task for remote users like those involved in HOT projects. Similarly in the MapRoulette application for fixing OSM data bugs [78], projects were created for improving health-related OSM data, e.g. by adding information about the number of beds in hospitals. Other different types of OSM mapping activities require field surveys to record the locations of specific objects. As an example, in Cape Town (South Africa) communal pit latrines pose a COVID-19 transmission risk, similar to other places frequented by many people, such as public transport, shopping centres or communal water taps. In the Cape Town area (Dunoon), the Western Cape Government used OSM to map at least 900 communal toilets in informal areas, and these were included in their risk analysis and risk management approach [79–81].

The ways to contribute OSM data during the COVID-19 pandemic have been very different in other countries where the baseline cartography was already available and the focus was placed on adding detailed COVID-19 information. For example, the popular application *Ca reste ouvert* [83], created by the OSM French community and then extended to other countries (including Italy, Germany, Austria and Switzerland), offers a thematic visualization of commercial activities based on whether they are open during the COVID-19 crisis; information on the COVID-19 specific opening hours, takeaway and delivery service are also shown and can be added/edited by users. This explains how dynamically the OSM communities reacted to the emergency by creating new OSM tags such as `opening_hours:covid19=*`, `takeaway:covid19=*`, `delivery:covid19=*`. Given that such information was either not available elsewhere or made available only in a very fragmented way (e.g. lists of activities that were open or offered takeaway/delivery services were published as plain

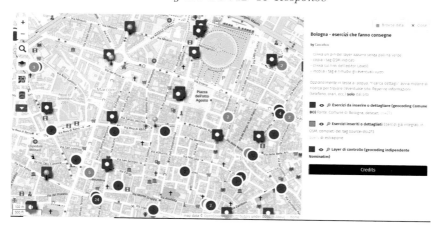

FIGURE 13.6
uMap project to facilitate the OSM import of commercial activities offering delivery service in the Municipality of Bologna, Italy. The colors of the OSM markers distinguish the activities already imported from those still to be imported. Source: [82].

text on websites of local governments or newspapers), OSM has acted as the only platform to store and offer such data in a structured way. As an exception to the general situation described above, some Italian municipalities provided the datasets of commercial activities offering delivery services on their open data portals under OSM-compatible licenses to allow their import. An example is a dataset from the Municipality of Bologna[84], that was imported in OSM by the Italian community through a documented procedure [85] based on a collaborative uMap project [82] (see Figure 13.6).

Another key dataset in Italy that was made available for integration in OSM was the dataset of all Italian pharmacies provided by the Italian Ministry of Health. In this case, given that most pharmacies were already available in OSM, the work performed by the community was not a bulk import but a manual integration of the missing information. Finally, given the high use of OSM data in Italy from emergency agencies such as Red Cross, Civil Protection and fire fighters, the Italian community also decided to focus the mapping efforts during COVID-19 times on substantial imports that were prepared or started in the past but not yet completed, e.g. the one for all addresses in the Municipality of Milan [86].

13.6 Academic Research with OSM During the COVID-19 Response

Although the literature covering COVID-19 is fast changing, there is evidence that OSM is a valuable resource for the scientific community. Published research in the early months of the pandemic mainly appeared in medical and health related outlets, however, at the time of writing, there are several examples of utilizing OSM data and related infrastructures spanning across different scientific disciplines. French-Pardo et al. [87] reviewed 63 articles on the spatial dimensions of COVID-19 and found that most national and regional web viewers use the ArcGIS Online platform [88], however, they also noted that some works utilized OSM because it was free. Some studies used a passive approach and utilized OSM data only for display, such as showing aggregate survey results based on neighborhoods extracted from OSM in Israel [89], or displaying detected hotspots on an OSM basemap [90]. Another study went beyond the basic use of OSM data and extracted social concentration places (e.g. ATMs, bus stops) from OSM to predict mortality trends as part of the first comprehensive study of COVID-19 in Iran [91]. Qazi et al. [92] compiled more than 524 million COVID-19 tweets and used OSM's Nominatim service to geocode and reverse geocode toponyms found in tweets [92]. This highlights that the ecosystem built around OSM data provides researchers with free to use tools for a number of use cases. Apart from these few examples, a quick literature search on Google Scholar for "OpenStreetMap" and "Covid-19" keywords yields several early stage research hosted on arxiv, medrxiv, ResearchGate and other preprint publishing services.

If one had to share data representing the home locations of COVID-19 infected people, their location privacy would be infringed. Geographic masks make it possible to share data in a representative way, without risking the individual's location privacy. Swanlund et al. [93] propose a new method for masking locations of individuals. Instead of displacing locations randomly to other houses (which is done in traditional methods), they move them along a street in the OSM road network. One of the advantages of this method is that OSM data is readily available. For other methods address data and/or population data are required, both of which are more difficult to get hold of.

13.7 Conclusions and Future Work

OSM is mostly used as a basemap, whether for dashboards or for other services. This is not unique to OSM, as there are many dashboards and services using Google Maps and the like. The only cases we have found (so far) that actually used OSM data was when the restrictions called for complex spatial queries that could be completed by OSM-based tools. Yet, this is still not something that is inherently unique to OSM and could be developed also with other frameworks. Given the unique nature of OSM we had expected a more widespread utilisation in the situation of a global pandemic. However, OSM usage is still impressively high and global. Humanitarian efforts in OSM are well suited for disasters and hazards, but not to rolling events like epidemics. While OSM has a very flexible data model and many easy-to-use data contribution methods there is a tendency to map permanent entities (at least for the short term) while much of the mapping during COVID-19 is all about temporary response (e.g. stocks of masks, exposure, supermarket queuing, changes in opening times). There is probably a need to produce a practice of COVID-19 tagging in OSM which requires discussion and coordination in order to make tagging practices fit for pandemic response purposes. Given the global nature of the pandemic, such non-trivial efforts should in principle involve all OSM communities worldwide and would benefit from the coordination of the OpenStreetMap Foundation, which supports the OSM project but does not take decisions about tags [94]. However, the establishment of global COVID-19 tagging practices appears to be hard, not only because of the traditional differences in OSM tagging practices across the world [95], but also due to the legal and ethical aspects that COVID-19 information might bring, at least in some countries or areas of the world.

OSM provides citizens and agencies an easy way to contribute or help in a pandemic response as opposed to not being able to contribute to authoritative datasets. Even if OSM data does not exist before the event it can be created almost in real-time by citizens locally or around the world. The data is accurate and high quality. The increased tile usage in badly affected COVID-19 areas also suggests that there is a need for freely accessible map services. OSM has been utilised in a wide variety of ways during the early phase of the pandemic. However, because OSM is truly open data we may never know of all the uses of OSM data during this period and estimation of usage could be difficult.

There are a number of very interesting questions for future work. Further investigation is required to understand if, and why, governments predominantly used proprietary tools and basemaps during the COVID-19 pandemic whilst research institutions, universities, community organisations used OSM. Analysis of the OSM contribution history will help to understand COVID-19 related OSM data contributions and/or data contributions during the pandemic. This could provide insights into possible correlations between the volume/activity/nature of contributions and the spread/evolution of the pandemic in a given country. The contribution of new data in OSM to address pandemics such as COVID-19 followed different contribution patterns than those observed before and these will offer fruitful grounds for future research work [96]. In Mooney and Juhász [97] the authors comment that many web-based maps produced during the early stages of the COVID-19 pandemic appear different or even contradictory. Urgent attention is required in order to consider how to deliver this information effectively within the constraints of the web-based map. Finally, it would be very interesting to consider a deeper exploration of the causes for differences between OSM communities during the pandemic given that COVID-19 has affected both developed and developing regions in the world.

References

[1] OpenStreetMap community. Openstreetmap wiki, 2020. URL https://wiki.openstreetmap.org/wiki/Main_Page.

[2] Peter Mooney and Marco Minghini. A Review of OpenStreetMap Data. In *Mapping and the Citizen Sensor*, pages 37–59. Ubiquity Press, London, 2017.

[3] OpenStreetMap community. Map Features, 2020. URL https://wiki.openstreetmap.org/wiki/Map_Features.

[4] Toshikazu Seto, Hiroshi Kanasugi, and Yuichiro Nishimura. Quality Verification of Volunteered Geographic Information Using OSM Notes Data in a Global Context. *ISPRS International Journal of Geo-Information*, 9(6):372, Jun 2020. ISSN 2220-9964. doi: 10.3390/ijgi9060372. URL http://dx.doi.org/10.3390/ijgi9060372.

[5] Peter Mooney, Marco Minghini, and Frances Stanley-Jones. Observations on an OpenStreetMap mapping party organised as a social event during an open source GIS conference. *International Journal of Spatial Data Infrastructures Research*, 10:138–150, 2015. URL https://ijsdir.sadl.kuleuven.be/index.php/ijsdir/article/view/395/382.

[6] Maria Antonia Brovelli, Peter Mooney, Ludovico Biagi, Marco Brambilla, Irene Celino, Eleonora Ciceri, Nicola Dorigatti, Haosheng Huang, Marco Minghini, and Vijaycharan Venkatachalam. *Mapping Parties at FOSS4G Europe: Fun, Outcomes and Lessons Learned*, pages 3–34. Springer International Publishing, Cham, 2018. ISBN 978-3-319-70878-2. doi: 10.1007/978-3-319-70878-2_1. URL https://doi.org/10.1007/978-3-319-70878-2_1.

[7] Matthew Zook, Mark Graham, Taylor Shelton, and Sean Gorman. Volunteered Geographic Information and Crowdsourcing Disaster Relief: A Case Study of the Haitian Earthquake. *World Medical & Health Policy*, 2(2):6–32, January 2010. ISSN 1948-4682. doi: 10.2202/1948-4682.1069. URL http://doi.wiley.com/10.2202/1948-4682.1069.

[8] Humanitarian OpenStreetMap Team. Humanitarian OpenStreetMap Team, 2020. URL https://www.hotosm.org/.

[9] Thiago Henrique Poiani, Roberto dos Santos Rocha, Livia Castro Degrossi, and Joao Porto de Albuquerque. Potential of Collaborative Mapping for Disaster Relief: A Case Study of OpenStreetMap in the Nepal Earthquake 2015. In *2016 49th Hawaii International Conference on System Sciences (HICSS)*, pages 188–197, Koloa, HI, January 2016. IEEE. ISBN 9780769556703. doi: 10.1109/HICSS.2016.31. URL http://ieeexplore.ieee.org/document/7427206/.

[10] Leysia Palen, Robert Soden, T. Jennings Anderson, and Mario Barrenechea. Success & Scale in a Data-Producing Organization: The Socio-Technical Evolution of OpenStreetMap in Response to Humanitarian Events. In *Proceedings of the 33rd Annual ACM Conference on Human Factors in Computing Systems*, CHI '15, pages 4113–4122, Seoul, Republic of Korea, April 2015. Association for Computing Machinery. ISBN 9781450331456. doi: 10.1145/2702123.2702294. URL https://doi.org/10.1145/2702123.2702294.

[11] Humanitarian OpenStreetMap Team. Tasking Manager, 2020. URL https://github.com/hotosm/tasking-manager.

[12] Marco Minghini, Alessandro Sarretta, Fulvio Lupia, Maurizio Napolitano, Alessandro Palmas, and Luca Delucchi. Collaborative mapping response to disasters through OpenStreetMap: the case of the 2016 Italian earthquake. *GEAM - Geoingegneria Ambientale e Mineraria*, 54(2):21–26, 2017.

[13] Stefan Scholz, Paul Knight, Melanie Eckle, Sabrina Marx, and Alexander Zipf. Volunteered Geographic Information for Disaster Risk Reduction—The Missing Maps Approach and Its Potential within the Red Cross and Red Crescent Movement. *Remote Sensing*, 10(8):1239, August 2018. ISSN 2072-4292. doi: 10.3390/rs10081239. URL http://www.mdpi.com/2072-4292/10/8/1239.

[14] Crowd2Map Tanzania. Crowd2Map Tanzania, 2020. URL https://crowd2map.org/.

[15] Missing Maps. Putting the World's Vulnerable People on the Map, 2020. URL https://www.missingmaps.org/.

[16] Pascal Neis, Peter Singler, and Alexander Zipf. Collaborative mapping and emergency routing for disaster logistics - case studies from the Haiti earthquake and the UN portal for Afrika. In *Proceedings of the Geoinformatics Forum*, pages 1–6, Salzburg, Austria, 2010.

[17] Naik Nitin. Flooded streets — A crowdsourced sensing system for disaster response: A case study. In *2016 IEEE International Symposium on Systems Engineering (ISSE)*, pages 1–3, Edinburgh, United Kingdom, October 2016. IEEE. ISBN 978-1-5090-0793-6. doi: 10.1109/SysEng.2016.7753186. URL http://ieeexplore.ieee.org/document/7753186/.

[18] Peter Mooney, Padraig Corcoran, and Blazej Ciepluch. The potential for using volunteered geographic information in pervasive health computing applications. *Journal of Ambient Intelligence and Humanized Computing*, 4(6):731–745, December 2013. ISSN 1868-5137, 1868-5145. doi: 10.1007/s12652-012-0149-4. URL http://link.springer.com/10.1007/s12652-012-0149-4.

[19] Patricia Solís, Brent McCusker, Nwasinachi Menkiti, Nuala Cowan, and Chad Blevins. Engaging global youth in participatory spatial data creation for the UN sustainable development goals: The case of open mapping for malaria prevention. *Applied Geography*, 98:143–155, September 2018. ISSN 01436228. doi: 10.1016/j.apgeog.2018.07.013. URL https://linkinghub.elsevier.com/retrieve/pii/S0143622818300456.

[20] Jennifer L Chan, Robert Colombo, and Altaf Musani. Mapping Libyan Health Facilities -A Collaboration Between Crisis Mappers and the World Health Organization. In *Proceedings of the 9th international ISCRAM Conference*, Vancouver, Canada, 2012.

[21] Benjamin Herfort, Eckle Eckle, Melanie, Joao Porto de Albuquerque, and Alexander Zipf. Towards assessing the quality of volunteered geographic information from OpenStreetMap for identifying critical infrastructures. In *Proceedings of the ISCRAM 2015 Conference*, Kristiansand, Norway, 2015.

[22] Rajib Chandra Das and Tauhidul Alam. Location based emergency medical assistance system using OpenstreetMap. In *2014 International Conference on Informatics, Electronics & Vision (ICIEV)*, pages 1–5, Dhaka, Bangladesh, May 2014. IEEE. ISBN 978-1-4799-5180-2 978-1-4799-5179-6 978-1-4799-5178-9. doi: 10.1109/ICIEV.2014.6850695. URL http://ieeexplore.ieee.org/document/6850695/.

[23] William J. Ferguson, Karen Kemp, and Gerald Kost. Using a geographic information system to enhance patient access to point-of-care diagnostics in a limited-resource setting. *International Journal of Health Geographics*, 15(1):10, December 2016. ISSN 1476-072X. doi: 10.1186/s12942-016-0037-9. URL http://www.ij-healthgeographics.com/content/15/1/10.

[24] Daniel Lindholm, Stefan James, Bo Lagerqvist, Mark A. Hlatky, and Christoph Varenhorst. New Method for Assessing the Effect of Driving Distance to Hospital Care: Using OpenStreetMap Routing in Cardiovascular Research. *Circulation: Cardiovascular Quality and Outcomes*, 10(9), September 2017. ISSN 1941-7713, 1941-7705. doi: 10.1161/CIRCOUTCOMES.117.003850. URL https://www.ahajournals.org/doi/10.1161/CIRCOUTCOMES.117.003850.

[25] Godwin Yeboah, João Porto Albuquerque, and Olalekan John Taiwo. Examining spatial proximity to health care facilities in an informal urban setting. *Proceedings of the Academic Track at the State of the Map 2020 Online Conference*, July 2020. doi: 10.5281/ZENODO.3923053. URL https://zenodo.org/record/3923053. Publisher: Zenodo.

[26] Martin Dittus, Giovanni Quattrone, and Licia Capra. Mass Participation During Emergency Response: Event-centric Crowdsourcing in Humanitarian Mapping. In *Proceedings of the 2017 ACM Conference on Computer Supported Cooperative Work and Social Computing*, pages 1290–1303, Portland Oregon USA, February 2017. ACM. ISBN 978-1-4503-4335-0. doi: 10.1145/2998181.2998216. URL https://dl.acm.org/doi/10.1145/2998181.2998216.

[27] Audrey Lessard-Fontaine, Mathieu Soupart, and Sylvie de Laborderie. Supporting Ebola Combat with Satellite Images: The MSF Perspective. *GI_Forum*, 1:445–448, 2015. ISSN 2308-1708, 2308-1708. doi: 10.1553/giscience2015s445. URL http://hw.oeaw.ac.at?arp=0x00324a9d.

[28] Robert Peckham and Ria Sinha. Satellites and the New War on Infection: Tracking Ebola in West Africa. *Geoforum*, 80:24–38, March 2017. ISSN 00167185. doi: 10.1016/j.geoforum.2017.01.001. URL https://linkinghub.elsevier.com/retrieve/pii/S0016718517300015.

[29] Laura M. Nic Lochlainn, Ivan Gayton, Georgios Theocharopoulos, Robin Edwards, Kostas Danis, Ronald Kremer, Karline Kleijer, Sumaila M. Tejan, Mohamed Sankoh, Augustin Jimissa, Jane Greig, and Grazia Caleo. Improving mapping for Ebola response through mobilising a local community with self-owned smartphones: Tonkolili District, Sierra Leone, January 2015. *PLOS ONE*, 13(1):e0189959, January 2018. ISSN 1932-6203. doi: 10.1371/journal.pone.0189959. URL https://dx.plos.org/10.1371/journal.pone.0189959.

[30] Levente Juhász and Hartwig H. Hochmair. User Contribution Patterns and Completeness Evaluation of Mapillary, a Crowdsourced Street Level Photo Service. *Transactions in GIS*, 20(6):925–947, 2016. ISSN 1467-9671. doi: 10.1111/tgis.12190. URL https://onlinelibrary.wiley.com/doi/abs/10.1111/tgis.12190.

[31] OpenStreetMap Foundation Operations Working Group. Tile Usage Policy, 2020. URL https://operations.osmfoundation.org/policies/tiles/.

[32] OpenStreetMap Foundation. Planet OSM, 2020. URL `https://planet.openstreetmap.org/`.

[33] Johns Hopkins University Center for Systems Science and Engineering (JHU CSSE). COVID-19 Data Repository by the Center for Systems Science and Engineering (CSSE) at Johns Hopkins University. URL `https://github.com/CSSEGISandData/COVID-19`.

[34] David Coleman, Yola Georgiadou, and Jeff Labonte. Volunteered geographic information: The nature and motivation of produsers. *International Journal of Spatial Data Infrastructures Research*, 4(4):332–358, 2009.

[35] Sveriges Television AB. Så långt kommer du på två timmar (this is how far you get in two hours), 2020. URL `https://www.svt.se/datajournalistik/sa-langt-kommer-du-pa-tva-timmar/`.

[36] Heidelberg Institute for Geoinformation Technology. OpenRouteService Services, 2020. URL `https://openrouteservice.org/services/`.

[37] Christoph Schoenenberger. COVID-19 Global Cases - Open Source Version, 2020. URL `https://chschoenenberger.shinyapps.io/covid19_dashboard/`.

[38] The World Bank. Map of SME-Support Measures in Response to COVID-19, 2020. URL `https://www.worldbank.org/en/data/interactive/2020/04/14/map-of-sme-support-measures-in-response-to-covid-19`.

[39] Scriby, Inc. The Coronavirus App, 2020. URL `https://coronavirus.app`.

[40] Berliner Morgenpost. Corona: Echtzeit-Karte zeigt Fallzahlen und Neuinfektionen in Deutschland und weltweit, 2020. URL `https://interaktiv.morgenpost.de/corona-virus-karte-infektionen-deutschland-weltweit/`.

[41] University of Pretoria and University of Neyshabur. COVID-19 Dashboard, 2020. URL `https://mahdisalehi.shinyapps.io/Covid19Dashboard/`.

[42] European Commission Joint Research Centre. ECML COVID, 2020. URL `https://covid-statistics.jrc.ec.europa.eu/`.

[43] Francesco Paolicelli. Online coronavirus for italy - Daily cases and mortality rates, 2020. URL `https://www.piersoft.it/covid19/`.

[44] The Detroit News. Map: Tracking Michigan's coronavirus cases. 2020. URL `https://www.detroitnews.com/story/news/nation/coronavirus/2020/03/17/map-tracking-michigan-coronavirus-cases-covid-19/5070633002/`.

[45] geo-spatial.org. Coronavirus COVID-19 România, 2020. URL `https://covid19.geo-spatial.org/`.

[46] Government of Alberta. COVID-19 relaunch status map, 2020. URL `https://www.alberta.ca/coronavirus-info-for-albertans.aspx`.

[47] Mark Nichols, Mitchell Thorson, and Carlie Procell. Maps of COVID-19 in rich and poor neighborhoods show big disparities. *USA Today*, July 2020. URL `https://www.usatoday.com/in-depth/graphics/2020/06/30/maps-covid-19-rich-and-poor-neighborhoods-show-big-disparities/3257615001/`.

[48] Observatory Earth Analytics. Nigeria's COVID-19 scenario board with live predictions, 2020. URL `http://response.oeaconsults.com/`.

[49] HealthMap. COVID-19, 2020. URL `https://www.healthmap.org/covid-19/`.

[50] Nextstrain team. Nextstrain COVID-19 Simulation, 2020. URL `https://nextstrain.org/ncov/global`.

[51] Cedric Moro. Kenya COVID-19 Tracker, 2020. URL `http://covid-19-africa.sen.ovh/`.

[52] C-19 Global Data Science Project. Quantifying Physical Distancing, 2020. URL `https://www.covid19analytics.org/project-details/social-distancing`.

[53] Kaplan Open Source. 3D printing for hospitals, 2020. URL `https://corona.kaplanopensource.co.il/3d-printing/`.

[54] Heidelberg Institute for Geoinforamtion Technology. Mapping COVID-19 Research, 2020. URL `https://covid-19.heigit.org/clinical_trials.html`.

[55] City of Boston. Map of food resources in Boston, March 2020. URL `https://www.boston.gov/departments/food-access/food-resources-map`. Library Catalog: www.boston.gov.

[56] Grey County Economic Development, Tourism & Culture. Community and Business Resiliency Map, 2020. URL `https://grey.maps.arcgis.com/apps/webappviewer/index.html?id=e9e96e39335d48e69b08c9473498293f`.

[57] Colombia National Administrative Department of Statistics. Vulnerabilidad: Map of groups by vulnerability levels, 2020. URL `http://visor01.dane.gov.co/visor-vulnerabilidad/`.

[58] Victoria State Government. Getting tested for coronavirus (COVID-19), 2020. URL `https://www.dhhs.vic.gov.au/where-get-tested-covid-19`.

[59] Finjon Kiang. Stocks of masks in pharmacies in Taiwan, 2020. URL `https://kiang.github.io/pharmacies/`.

[60] Sixfold GmbH. Truck Border Crossing Times, 2020. URL `https://covid-19.sixfold.com/`. Library Catalog: covid-19.sixfold.com.

[61] European Environment Agency (EEA). Air quality and COVID-19, 2020. URL `https://www.eea.europa.eu/themes/air/air-quality-and-covid19`.

[62] Kaplan Open Source. Changes in the public transport map during the times of the Coronavirus, 2020. URL `https://corona.kaplanopensource.co.il/bus/`.

[63] Kaplan Open Source. Want to join a shipment?, 2020. URL `https://corona.kaplanopensource.co.il/shipments/`.

[64] Filaindiana. Filaindiana, 2020. URL `https://filaindiana.it/#no-user-position`.

[65] IsraelCoronaMap. IsraelCoronaMap, 2020. URL `https://israelcoronamap.co.il/`.

[66] Kaplan Open Source. Don't wait for Shin Bet - come and check by yourself your proximity to people infected with Coronavirus, 2020. URL `https://corona.kaplanopensource.co.il/`.

[67] Pietro Rampazzo. 200 metri da casa, 2020. URL `https://200-metri-da-casa.netlify.com/map.html`.

[68] Kaplan Open Source. How far are you allowed to go out?, 2020. URL `https://corona.kaplanopensource.co.il/stayhome/`.

[69] CARTO. CARTO: Unlock the power of spatial analysis, 2020. URL `https://carto.com`.

[70] Mapbox. MapBox: Maps and location for developers, 2020. URL `https://www.mapbox.com/`.

[71] OpenStreetMap. A new record for daily mappers and new users!, June 2020. URL `https://blog.openstreetmap.org/2020/06/30/a-new-record-for-daily-mappers-and-new-users/`.

[72] Peter Mooney, Marco Minghini, Mari Laakso, Vyron Antoniou, Ana-Maria Olteanu-Raimond, and Andriani Skopeliti. Towards a protocol for the collection of vgi vector data. *ISPRS International Journal of Geo-Information*, 5(11):217, Nov 2016. ISSN 2220-9964. doi: 10.3390/ijgi5110217. URL `http://dx.doi.org/10.3390/ijgi5110217`.

[73] Massimo Craglia, Sarah de Nigris, Emilio Gomez-Gonzalez, Emilia Gomez, Bertin Martens, Maria Iglesias Portela, Michele Vespe, Sven Schade, Marina Micheli, Alexander Kotzev, Irena Mitton, Lucia Vesnic Alujevic, Francesco Pignatelli, Jiri Hradec, Stefano Nativi, Jose Ignacio Sanchez Martin, Ronan Hamon, and Henrik Junklewitz. Artificial Intelligence and Digital Transformation: early lessons from the COVID-19 crisis. JRC Science for Policy Report, Joint Research Centre, 2020.

[74] Humanitarian OpenStreetMap Team. Tasking Manager projects on COVID-19, 2020. URL `https://tasks.hotosm.org`.

[75] Humanitarian OpenStreetMap Team. HOTOSM on Twitter: HOT's COVID-10 response, July 2020. URL `https://twitter.com/hotosm/status/1282744216850964484`.

[76] Humanitarian OpenStreetMap Team. Volunteer mappers, 2020. URL `https://www.hotosm.org/volunteer-opportunities/volunteer-mappers/`.

[77] healthsites.io. Building an open data commons with health facility data with OpenStreetMap, 2020. URL `https://healthsites.io/`.

[78] Edoardo Neerhut. Improving Maps for Better Capacity Planning in the Fight Against Covid-19, April 2020. URL `https://blog.mapillary.com/update/2020/04/08/better-capacity-planning.html`.

[79] Jacques Du Preez. OpenStreetMap - mapping informal settlements to assist with COVID-19 preventions and interventions, June 2020.

[80] Jason Corburn, David Vlahov, Blessing Mberu, Lee Riley, Waleska Teixeira Caiaffa, Sabina Faiz Rashid, Albert Ko, Sheela Patel, Smurti Jukur, Eliana Martínez-Herrera, et al. Slum health: arresting covid-19 and improving well-being in urban informal settlements. *Journal of Urban Health*, 97(3), pages 1–10, 2020.

[81] Lesley Gibson and David Rush. Novel coronavirus in Cape Town informal settlements: feasibility of using informal dwelling outlines to identify high risk areas for COVID-19 transmission from a social distancing perspective. *JMIR Public Health and Surveillance*, 6(2):e18844, 2020.

[82] Italian OpenStreetMap community. uMap project Bologna - esercizi che fanno consegne, 2020. URL `http://umap.openstreetmap.fr/en/map/bologna-esercizi-che-fanno-consegne_448911#9`.

[83] Ca reste ouvert. Ça reste ouvert: It remains open, 2020. URL `https://www.caresteouvert.fr/`.

[84] Comune di Bologna. CORONAVIRUS - Spesa a domicilio, 2020. URL http://dati.comune.bologna.it/node/4273.

[85] Italian OpenStreetMap community. Import/Catalogue/BO - EserciziCommerciali - OpenStreetMap Wiki, 2020. URL https://wiki.openstreetmap.org/wiki/Import/Catalogue/BO-EserciziCommerciali.

[86] Italian OpenStreetMap community. Import/Catalogue/Milan addresses import - OpenStreetMap Wiki, 2020. URL https://wiki.openstreetmap.org/wiki/Import/Catalogue/Address_import_for_Milan.

[87] Ivan Franch-Pardo, Brian M. Napoletano, Fernando Rosete-Verges, and Lawal Billa. Spatial analysis and GIS in the study of COVID-19. A review. *Science of The Total Environment*, 739:140033, October 2020. ISSN 0048-9697. doi: 10.1016/j.scitotenv.2020.140033. URL http://www.sciencedirect.com/science/article/pii/S0048969720335531.

[88] ESRI. ArcGIS Online, 2020. URL https://www.arcgis.com/index.html.

[89] Hagai Rossman, Ayya Keshet, Smadar Shilo, Amir Gavrieli, Tal Bauman, Ori Cohen, Esti Shelly, Ran Balicer, Benjamin Geiger, Yuval Dor, and Eran Segal. A framework for identifying regional outbreak and spread of COVID-19 from one-minute population-wide surveys. *Nature Medicine*, 26(5):634–638, May 2020. ISSN 1546-170X. doi: 10.1038/s41591-020-0857-9. URL https://www.nature.com/articles/s41591-020-0857-9. Number: 5 Publisher: Nature Publishing Group.

[90] Alexander Hohl, Eric M. Delmelle, Michael R. Desjardins, and Yu Lan. Daily surveillance of COVID-19 using the prospective space-time scan statistic in the United States. *Spatial and Spatio-temporal Epidemiology*, 34:100354, August 2020. ISSN 1877-5845. doi: 10.1016/j.sste.2020.100354. URL http://www.sciencedirect.com/science/article/pii/S1877584520300320.

[91] Hamid Reza Pourghasemi, Soheila Pouyan, Bahram Heidari, Zakariya Farajzadeh, Seyed Rashid Fallah Shamsi, Sedigheh Babaei, Rasoul Khosravi, Mohammad Etemadi, Gholamabbas Ghanbarian, Ahmad Farhadi, Roja Safaeian, Zahra Heidari, Mohammad Hassan Tarazkar, John P. Tiefenbacher, Amir Azmi, and Faezeh Sadeghian. Spatial modeling, risk mapping, change detection, and outbreak trend analysis of coronavirus (COVID-19) in Iran (days between February 19 and June 14, 2020). *International Journal of Infectious Diseases*, 98:90–108, September 2020. ISSN 1201-9712. doi: 10.1016/j.ijid.2020.06.058. URL http://www.sciencedirect.com/science/article/pii/S1201971220304938.

[92] Umair Qazi, Muhammad Imran, and Ferda Ofli. GeoCoV19: a dataset of hundreds of millions of multilingual COVID-19 tweets with location information. *SIGSPATIAL Special*, 12(1):6–15, June 2020. ISSN 1946-7729, 1946-7729. doi: 10.1145/3404111.3404114. URL https://dl.acm.org/doi/10.1145/3404111.3404114.

[93] David Swanlund, Nadine Schuurman, Paul Zandbergen, and Mariana Brussoni. Street masking: a network-based geographic mask for easily protecting geoprivacy. *International Journal of Health Geographics*, 19(1):26, December 2020. ISSN 1476-072X. doi: 10.1186/s12942-020-00219-z. URL https://ij-healthgeographics.biomedcentral.com/articles/10.1186/s12942-020-00219-z.

[94] OpenStreetMap Foundation. OpenStreetMap Foundation, 2020. URL https://wiki.osmfoundation.org/wiki/Main_Page.

[95] Nikola Davidovic, Peter Mooney, Leonid Stoimenov, and Marco Minghini. Tagging in Volunteered Geographic Information: An Analysis of Tagging Practices for Cities and Urban Regions in OpenStreetMap. *ISPRS International Journal of Geo-Information*, 5(12):232, 2016.

[96] Marco Minghini, Serena Coetzee, A. Yair Grinberger, Godwin Yeboah, Levente Juhász, and Peter Mooney. Editorial: OpenStreetMap research in the COVID-19 era. In Marco Minghini, Serena Coetzee, Levente Juhász, Godwin Yeboah, Peter Mooney, and A. Yair Grinberger, editors, *Proceedings of the Academic Track at State of the Map 2020*, pages 1–4. Zenodo Online: https://doi.org/10.5281/zenodo.3922054, July 2020. doi: 10.5281/zenodo.3922054. URL https://doi.org/10.5281/zenodo.3922054.

[97] Peter Mooney and Levente Juhász. Mapping COVID-19: How web-based maps contribute to the infodemic. *Dialogues in Human Geography*, 10(2):265–270, 2020. doi: 10.1177/2043820620934926.

14

Utilization of Geospatial Network Analysis Technique for Optimal Route Planning During COVID-19 Pandemic

Pravin Kokane, Mohd. Ammar Ashraf and Vinita Shinkar

The local government bodies (LGBs) in India have taken several steps to reduce the spread of the virus. Disinfection of common public spaces such as roads and streets are one such step adopted by municipal council of Basmat city after lock down from March 2020. Basmat city is a 'B' class municipal council with 80,000 population located in Hingoli district of Maharashtra, India. The spraying of Sodium Hypochlorite (NaClO) solution on roads and government establishments with the help of firefighting services is a novel as well as cost effective responsive measure as per guidelines of the central government of India. This chapter aims to analyze the efficiency of disinfection with the help of Network Analysis tools in Arc GIS. Various components such as shortest route analysis for refilling the tanks and analysis of various impedance factors such as time-cost analysis and route tracking form an integral part of the study. In addition to this, the availability of stock and consumption pattern of disinfectant are also analyzed. This research focuses on the attributes of distance traversed, cost of fuel and labor and time taken for sanitization vehicles at service stops. The results are evident that with the use of geospatial technology, all the attributes have reduced values as compared to the previous situation.

14.1 Introduction

Since the outbreak of the novel coronavirus in 2019, a substantial amount of research has been carried out to address the inter-relationship between technological advancements and the pandemic. The research particularly deals with the spatial aspect of the COVID-19 outbreak and analyzing the use of Geographical Information Systems (GIS) as a tool for providing effective measures in containment of the outbreak. Geographic tracking of spatial features enables us to keep a record of the entities and GIS offers multiple tools for spatial accounting. Recent advancements in Geographic Information Systems, has provided with improved decision making about a location. Spatial analytics and location intelligence are the key aspects which make GIS beneficial for improved geographic recording of assets. GIS enables for effective communication in the form of visualizations and maps by better understanding of geographical attributes.

The multidisciplinary nature of GIS technology means that the diffusion, appropriation and use of GIS technologies are distributed in a variety of subject domains and its application in day to day problems of human beings [1]. GIS applications has covered a varied range of sectors including health geography, cultural and anthropological geography, transportation, and land dynamics.

Many researches have studied the spatial aspect of diseases in purview of its nature and behavior with respect to a geographical area. The most famous paradigm of early medical geography was Dr. John Snow, considered to be the father of modern epidemiology, who demonstrated the water-borne origin of cholera by plotting cholera-related deaths in London during the most severe 1854 epidemic on maps [2]. Disease maps have been used since historic times and with GIS it is now possible to keep a track of diseases in a digital format.

Considering the wide range of analysis tools offered by GIS, the spatial aspect of COVID-19 can be analyzed comprehensively with them. Recent technical features of GIS such as location intelligence and live tracking have made it possible for COVID-19 to be potentially mapped and understand the spread of the outbreak. Features such as temporal analysis have aided in understanding the timely spread of the disease. This research particularly focuses on the utilization of network analysis feature of Arc GIS in decision making for the Municipal authorities. The network analysis toolset has been linked with the spraying of disinfectants in municipal areas. To contain the spread of the outbreak, disinfecting public places such as public buildings, major and minor roadways with Sodium Hypochlorite (NaClO) solution is undertaken by the municipal authorities of multiple Indian cities. As per the Central Government of India, spraying of disinfectants has been mandated in Indian cities to avoid the virus from sustaining at public places.

Spraying of disinfectants over large urban areas involve attributes such as cost and time on account of Government officials. This makes it important to utilize modern technologies that can aid the decision-making abilities of the officials. The purpose of this research is to utilize the potential of geospatial technology in order to aid the Municipal authority officials of Basmat City to reduce the cost and time required to spray the disinfectant using the Vehicle Routing Problem (VRP) for devising the optimal paths for fire-fighting vehicles.

14.2 Literature Review

In this section, the literature reviewed in accordance with the network analysis tools in GIS is presented. Utilization of GIS for effective healthcare planning is presented in many studies across the world. A study by [3] presents the use of network analysis in developing a GIS based emergency response system for Delhi, India. The study focuses on integrating real time traffic data with the existing transportation network. Optimal route planning was used to analyze the best route for reaching the emergency site by avoiding congested routes. Network analysis attributes such as shortest path analysis, Origin destination survey and proximity analysis were deployed for building the emergency response system. In another study by [4] the practicality of the shortest path analysis tool in GIS is improved. The Dijkstra's Algorithm which is the principle that works at the backend of the shortest path analysis is optimized by changing the starting node with the search process. This enables to maintain the nodes using a stack structure to avoid revisiting the nodes. In this case, the real time traffic information is not considered.

Another relevant study carried out for Ghana region by [5] is also based on emergency response service by the firefighting services. This service was developed for the Ghana National Fire Services (GNFS) in the metropolis of Kumasi where the GNFS can take better decisions. The optimal route planning in case of a fire incident in the metropolis was devised by considering model attributes such as slope of the roads, travel distance and time and the delays in travel time. Optimal route planning for determining effective evacuation methods in San Diego is performed by [6]. In this study, GIS network analysis is used for public issuing of evacuation orders in case of emergency situations by using 2007 Wildfire datasets. An Origin-Destination (OD) ranking model was deployed to determine evacuation routes between affected areas and nearest shelters. Multiple road features and land-based attributes were considered while building the OD model.

Advancement in the geospatial technologies have upgraded the GIS tools and services. GIS packages are now being introduced in the market with better spatial analysis capabilities. Services and complex businesses involving fleet of vehicles with multiple orders, stops, restrictions, using roadside utilities need a solution to avoid scaled cost in the process of transportation. These issues are now the things of the past since the introduction of network analyst toolset in the ArcGIS platform. Vehicle Routing Problem (VRP) is one such tool in the package, which can find the best route for a single vehicle to visit many stops (for delivering order or for servicing at the stop). The primary goal of these kinds of analysis is to reduce the transportation time and reduce the overall operating cost. VRP can used to solve much complex problems, involving multiple vehicles with multiple capacities and matching vehicles capacity with order quantities, multiple vehicles with special tools and matching their service capabilities, giving breaks to drivers, pairing multiple orders so the same route delivers them.

14.3   Methodology and Materials

The following section presents the detailed methodology that was followed to conduct this research. The methodology flowchart depicts the steps that are performed using Arc GIS 10.2 software. The data preparation includes digitizing road vector layer using Open Street Map (OSM) and satellite imagery from Google Earth. The administrative boundary of ward map has been obtained from the municipal council of Basmat city. The major public government buildings and landmarks have been located from ground verification and satellite imagery. Following this, the georeferencing process of municipal boundary map has been performed, and the geodatabase has been created.

After the data preparation, the network layers have been created. The network layers include the service stops of spraying the disinfectant. The attributes such as road name, design speed of the road, road type, length of the road and time taken for the fire-fighting vehicle to traverse the road have all been updated in the network layers. Further, the network topology and network dataset have been created. Finally, the vehicle routing problem for the firefighting services to spray the disinfectant has been solved.

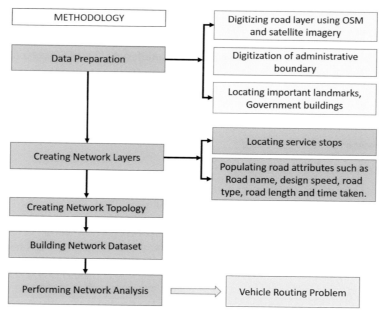

FIGURE 14.1
Methodological Framework of Study

14.3.1   Data Preparation

The data preparation includes downloading the OSM network data and satellite imagery of Basmat city, preparing the network layout, and linking the attribute data. The study area is the Basmat city located in Hingoli district of the state of Maharashtra. This city is a 'B' class municipal council.

The study area is extended from 19° 33' 02" N to 77° 15' 89" E. The Basmat city area is of 12.06 sq.km with 14 ward divisions. The base map and road network data of Basmat city was downloaded from Open street map. OSM has been accessed through Arc GIS online web mapping service. The road network data has an attribute named Road name for names of the roads that have been matched with Google earth imagery. The Design speed attribute includes design speed of the roads which were assigned by taking IRC 86 – 1983 as reference. The Road type attribute consists of classification of the roads according to the hierarchy which includes Arterial Roads, Sub-Arterial Roads, Collector and Local roads. The Road length attribute includes length of the roads that are calculated using calculate geometry tool.

14.3.2   The Network Dataset

The next step is preparing the network dataset to carry out network analysis for fire-fighting vehicles. The topology tool is deployed to remove unnecessary pseudo nodes and dangles in the network that occur during the digitization process. The road network is integrated using the Integrate tool in Data Management and other layers such as road and stops are included in the feature dataset. Further, the road name and landmarks are assigned for directional flow of vehicles.

14.3.3   Building the VRP Route

After building the network dataset, the Vehicle routing problem layer is created and all the VRP layers are activated from the toolbar. The stops which are assigned for spraying of NaClO solution are imported for a shift of the day. The service time which is the spraying time for the fire-fighting vehicle is assigned to the stops. The spraying time data is provided by the Basmat Municipal Council. The filling stations which are the depots are the locations where the Sodium Hypochlorite (NaClO) solution is filled in the tanks of fire-fighting vehicles. After this the routes through which the fire-fighting vehicles traverse are assigned to the route layer. The initial stop of filling station and terminating stop of filling station are assigned. The Start time of the vehicle is taken as 7 a.m. and end time is taken as 8 a.m.

14.4   Results and Discussion

This study presented the analysis of Vehicle Routing problem of fire fighting vehicles that are used for sanitisation to spray Sodium Hypochlorite solution. With the surge of Covid-19 cases, the sanitisation process of public buildings and was taken up by the Basmat Municipal Council. Municipality assigned this task to the sanitation department, which must be carried out in a stipulated time. Major landmarks, government buildings, major religious places, markets, colonies with symptomatic patients were identified for disinfection. Fire-fighting vehicles were assigned for transportation of sanitation workers to the service locations where disinfection was supposed to be carried out. From the ground-based questionnaire survey conducted on 28, 29 and 30 March 2020 and the recorded odometer readings, the time taken by the fire-fighting vehicles was higher as the routes taken to reach the sanitisation destinations were random. This incurred higher time and cost for the government officials being spent on the sanitisation process. The government officials expected a sound way for reducing the cost and time. To address this issue, study tried to address this issue using geospatial technology to analyse whether the cost and time spent on sanitisation process can be reduced. For the same, this study applied the Vehicle Routing Problem to the fire-fighting sanitisation vehicles. For this the optimal route analysis was carried out for all the routes. The optimal route analysis generates the most optimal route between two locations.

With the network analysis extension in Arc GIS, it becomes very easy to set the network parameters for optimal route analysis such as the travel time that is the impedance factor, the start time of the travel and restrictions such as road directions whether unidirectional or bidirectional. The starting point and terminating point of travel is the Sodium Hypochlorite (NaClO) filling station.

The route for sanitization is developed such that all the locations where the service is to be provided (service locations) are visited once during the total travel. From the table 1 given below, comparison between the previous route and the optimal route is analysed based on pre-determined attributes. The three major routes are divided over the period of three days from 28th March to 30th March.

The VRP for the three major routes is given i n the following maps for the three consecutive days (Figure 14.2) respectively. The odometer reading, time taken for travel by the fire-fighting vehicle, the fuel cost spent by the government officials and the labor cost are compared for the previous route taken and the optimal route taken later. It can be inferred from the readings that all the factors considered perform better in case of optimal routes. Time taken for the fire fighting vehicles, fuel cost and labor cost are all comparatively lesser in case of optimal routes when compared with the routes originally followed. The comparison is also presented in graphical format.

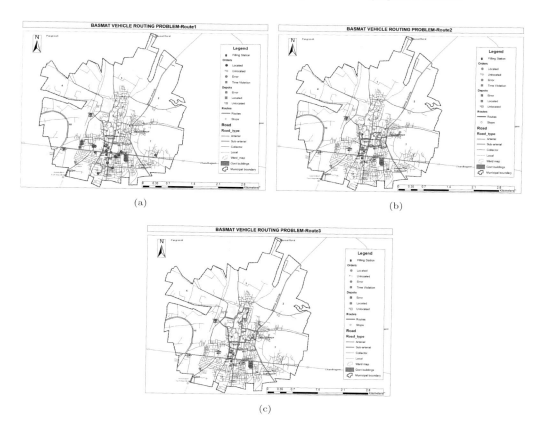

FIGURE 14.2

Basmat Vehicle Routing Problem: a) Route 1; b) Route 2; c) Route 3

TABLE 14.1

Comparative Analysis of Attributes between Previous and Optimal Route

Shift	Previous Route	Optimal Route
Route-1	Odometer reading: 11000 m	Analyzed distance: 9377.8m
	Time Taken: 12 hours	Time Taken: 9 hours 52 min
	Fuel cost: Rs.389	Fuel cost: Rs.329
	Labor cost= Rs.1320	Labor cost= Rs.1070
Route-2	Odometer reading: 6250 (approx.)	Analyzed distance: 5224m
	Time Taken: 8hrs. (approx.)	Time Taken: 7hrs. 38 min
	Fuel cost: Rs.221	Fuel cost: Rs.184
	Labor cost= Rs.840	Labor cost= Rs. 795
Route-3	Odometer reading: 7500 (approx.)	Analyzed distance: 6874 m
	Time Taken: 7hrs. 30 min (approx.)	Time Taken: 6 hrs. 10 min
	Fuel cost: Rs.265	Fuel cost: Rs.240
	Labor cost= Rs.780	Labor cost= Rs. 619

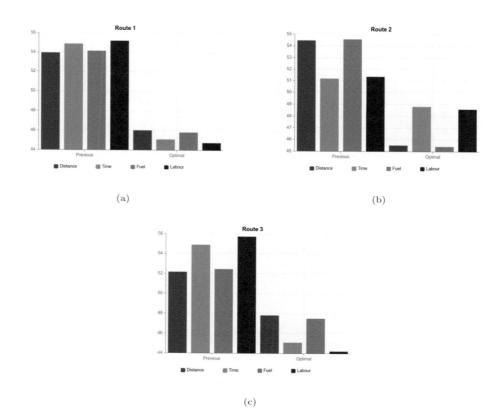

(a)

(b)

(c)

FIGURE 14.3

Comparative Analysis between attributes of: a) Route 1 in percentage; b) Route 2 in percentage; c) Route 3 in percentage

14.5   Conclusion

In this research, an augmented approach of Arc GIS based network analysis using Vehicle Routing problem is applied to the Basmat city area. With the outbreak of Covid-19, sanitisation of public spaces has been made mandatory and this involves spending of huge monetary cost and time on account of government authorities. The Djikstra optimal routing algorithm in Arc GIS offers best results for network analysis. The vehicle routing problem applied in this research to find the optimal route which saves time and cost. The VRP for route 1 has reduced the travel distance and fuel cost by 8% and the travel time taken by 12%. The labor cost is reduced by 10%. Similarly, for route 2, the travel distance is reduced by 8% and the travel time by 4%. The labor cost is reduced by 2% and the fuel cost by 10%. For VRP route 3, the travel distance is reduced by 4% and travel time by 8%. The labor cost is reduced by 4% and fuel cost by 12%. After obtaining positive results with the use of network analysis, in future research this study propose to utilize geospatial technology for analyzing the attributes of cost, time and quantity of disinfectant spraying for building level data by incorporating building level information data such as height of building, size and total floor area , material, building use etc. to predict the attributes for sanitisation automatically. Result out of such studies will help in better emergency preparedness and quick response of Urban Local Bodies (ULB's) as like Basmat.

Acknowledgements

We deeply acknowledge Mr. Ashok Sabale, Chief Officer, Basmat Muncipal Council for extending kind support and help during this project. We also thank all fire brigade personnel for their support during interview and data collection.

References

[1] Hao Ye, Michael Brown, and Jenny Harding. Gis for all: exploring the barriers and opportunities for underexploited gis applications. *OSGeo Journal*, 13(1):19–28, 2014.

[2] George J Musa, Po-Huang Chiang, Tyler Sylk, Rachel Bavley, William Keating, Bereketab Lakew, Hui-Chen Tsou, and Christina W Hoven. Use of gis mapping as a public health tool—from cholera to cancer. *Health services insights*, 6:HSI–S10471, 2013.

[3] Anshul Bhagat and Nikhil Sharma. Gis-based application for emergency preparedness and management accelerating response system through gis. In *14th Esri India User Conference*, pages 1–7, 2013.

[4] Dechuan Kong, Yunjuan Liang, Xiaoqin Ma, and Lijun Zhang. Improvement and realization of dijkstra algorithm in gis of depot. In *2011 International Conference on Control, Automation and Systems Engineering (CASE)*, pages 1–4. IEEE, 2011.

[5] Eric K Forkuo and Jonathan A Quaye-Ballard. Gis based fire emergency response system. 2013.

[6] J Yi Carine, Roy S Park, Osamu Murao, and Eiji Okamoto. Emergency management: Building an od ranking model using gis network analysis. *Journal of Disaster Research*, 7(6):1, 2012.

15

Formalizing Informal Settlements to Empower Residents Against COVID-19 and Other Disasters

Chryssy Potsiou

With the COVID-19 it became obvious that the significant social and economic benefits of the urbanization and globalization era may be accompanied by a globalized threat and risk. This deadly virus struck fast and hard and with little warning and all countries, even the most developed, have proved to be unprepared. Governments have urgently explored short- and long-term actions on how to sustain a resilient economic and social activity while keeping their people safe, but also on defining policies that would help them to deal with the post-COVID-19 challenges. In this respect, the 2019 UNECE publication on Guidelines for Formalization of Informal Constructions may be useful to facilitate a global planning process to support a large number of states that face the challenge of construction informality in developing fit-for-purpose policies while preparing for a post-COVID era. According to UNECE, benefits from formalizing informal constructions could contribute to economic recovery by integration into land markets with clear ownership titles and registration. Security of tenure and rights to ownership of land and property provide access to credit; environmental planning, construction, and utility-provision improvements can be initiated to a standard by which people can live in adequate and healthy homes to the benefit of all. This chapter provides an insight of the above issues and draws the attention to the benefits of a clear and inclusive strategy and of a fit-for-purpose formalization framework.

15.1 Introduction

The COVID-19 pandemic is threatening cities and settlements all over the world, endangering not only public health but also the economy and the structure of society, forcing us apart as we try to slow the spread of the virus. However, we - as individuals - are still finding ways to help each other, inspiring and showing appreciation for those helping our communities, keeping in touch with family members wherever they may be, and most importantly, helping the poorest and most vulnerable, those least able to respond.

But how can we, as experts, do more? How can we support governments to do the same at a larger scale successfully? More specifically, how can surveyors, as geospatial and land professionals, provide appropriate tools that will support governments in their efforts to be more efficient in empowering those most vulnerable, increasing recognition of disease and pandemics? "Who" and more importantly "where" are the most vulnerable, those exposed most to the pandemic?

This discussion will address the following questions:

1. how can geospatial experts and land surveyors provide the technically driven policy tools to

support governments to identify and empower those most vulnerable and those exposed most to the pandemic?

2. why the measures taken by governments to empower people against the pandemic are also related to the good management of land and therefore need to be more "localized", evidence-based, and fit-for-purpose? and

3. how governments may develop "fit-for-purpose" formalization projects to empower residents in informal settlements for the benefit of all?

15.2   The Need for Geospatial Data and Tools to Improve Decision-making

It is said that flooding and other natural disasters are more or less "localized" and authorities, with the support of geospatial experts, know that they may turn "there" to help, while the current COVID-19 disaster is or may exist "everywhere", which complicates recovery actions, and that affects everyone with a priority for the elderly, those with chronic health problems, and those who have difficulty protecting themselves.

As with any natural disaster, the way countries and communities prepare for a damaging event makes the difference for a successful, long-term resilience and recovery. Decision-making for such preparation must be evidence-based; therefore, availability of reliable and affordable geospatial data in a timely manner is crucial. This is at the center of surveyors' professional skills, interests and activities. There are already several modern, low-cost but still reliable tools and methods that may be used for acquiring the needed geo-referenced information including information derived from social media and crowdsourcing [1] and several applications for contact tracing, that may help in providing sound decision-making for applying more "localized" rather than "general" measures, and for providing humanitarian support when dealing with such disasters [2].

Unfortunately, this virus struck fast and hard and without warning and all countries, even the most developed, were unprepared. It has been a common and long-established public confidence that medicine has improved significantly and that humanity has managed to overcome problems caused by pandemics that once killed large numbers of people, and which have thus influenced the history and the future of many cities [3]. Since that development in the history of medicine, and for several years since, research in infectious diseases has lost its institutional urgency.

As a result, rapid and dense urbanization became more and more a global trend for several decades and has been considered as the tool to deal with poverty which would lead us to economic growth for all. A globalized economy has developed and the world has been on a constant move to urbanization. Surveyors have always been in the front line aiming to provide the most appropriate policies, methods and tools to provide the required geo-referenced data to support the management of the emerging mega cities [4]. A global action plan on how to deal with deadly pandemics is still missing; there is a significant lack of awareness among populations and unfortunately a dangerous lack of coordination among governments in terms of disaster-response measures. The result is a dangerous confusion. Coronavirus was a test, and the world's supposedly most advanced nations have all too visibly failed [5].

Governments are now urgently exploring short- and long-term actions on how to sustain a resilient economic and social activity while keeping their people safe, but also on how to deal with post-COVID-19 challenges; it is anticipated that the pandemic will have a continuing multidimensional impact. Such actions and policies should be based on reliable geospatial data.

The situation becomes worse in unplanned and/or dense informal settlements and slums that often exist on the outskirts of many large urban areas, but which also provide unskilled service support to the nearby urban economies. Residents in informal settlements usually are not registered, they may even lack citizenship, identity cards and addresses but also health care, basic services like clean water and sewage disposal, etc. It has become obvious that unfortunately COVID-19 has a higher, "localized" concentration among informal settlement residents where people are not prepared, basic infrastructures are poor, and where there is a significant lack of reliable geo-referenced data. (A strategy for containment of the virus is "contact tracing" in which an attempt is made to track the progress of the disease from population center to population center, requiring an efficient geo-referenced measuring and monitoring system.)

The World Bank reports that the COVID-19 pandemic has plunged the global economy into its deepest recession since World War II. It estimates that this particular disaster will create the worst economic contraction in decades, with numerous job losses and the creation of 60-100 million of "new poor", mainly those self-employed, many informally, which will soon join those most vulnerable - those poor living in the informal settlements; and foresees that the COVID-19 pandemic is a once-in-a-century crisis that presents extraordinary challenges to policymakers around the world [6].

According to the IMF the economic impact of this crisis will be like no other; GDP is expected to fall by some 6-7% this year in the advanced economies, and it will not return to its pre-virus peak until at least 2022. Given the uncertainty around how long the pandemic will last, it may be far worse. Entire sectors of the economy are at risk. Millions of people have already lost their source of income. The International Labor Organization (ILO), at its press release of 29 April 2020, estimated that 1.6 billion workers in the formal or informal economy, amounting to nearly half the global workforce, are at risk of losing their livelihoods. This is due to the lockdown measures and/or because these people are occupied in the hardest-hit sectors, such as wholesale and retail, manufacturing, accommodation and food services, or the real estate sector [7]. What is even worse is the fact that usually these people have no access to credit.

It is "there", at such settlements, that governments should turn their attention to help and provide the means for improvements and resilience.

These people are least able to protect themselves. *"As the pandemic and the jobs crisis evolve, the need to protect the most vulnerable becomes even more urgent"* said ILO Director-General Guy Ryder. *"For millions of workers, no income means no food, no security and no future. Millions of businesses around the world are barely breathing. They have no savings or access to credit. These are the real faces of the world of work. If we don't help them now, these enterprises will simply perish"* [8].

The informal economy includes informal construction - self-made, usually substandard, houses - along with the informal labor force and illegal businesses. Informally, self-made cities/settlements in general [9], with informal, unregistered property rights, lacking property titles and/or planning, construction and operational permits, have no access to credit. Informal rights and informal construction constitute a wide-spread challenge threatening sustainability and although *"... access to basic services, ownership and control over land and other forms of property, inheritance, natural resources,..."* is included at SDG1 (target 1.4) of the UN Sustainable development Agenda 2030 [10], so far few countries have reported on real progress in this field in the five years of implementation period, as emphasized at the recent webinar "Five years into the SDGs - Are we on track to deliver the land targets?" [11], with the World Bank predicting that *"the global community's significant progress on poverty reduction in recent decades will likely be partly reversed and that it will also be more difficult to achieve broader development goals by the end of this decade"* [6].

UNECE and FIG have long worked in this field and land surveyors have built experience in developing fit-for-purpose technical, administrative, legal and policy tools both for the registration of informal tenure rights as well as for the formalization of informal constructions. There is an urgent need that governments will now integrate such tools to improve the preparedness measures for the pandemic.

15.3   Measures Taken by Governments to Manage the Pandemic

A common, immediate response of many governments during the disease outbreak was to request their citizens to "stay at home", "work from home", "keep social distance", "follow basic hygienic measures" and "wash hands with soap and clean water frequently".

These measures have been successfully adopted by many citizens, but unfortunately they seem unrealistic for some people as well as for most residents of informal settlements; residents of informal settlements simply cannot cope with such requirements. A number of issues need to be taken into consideration:

1. Housing conditions in informal settlements are usually substandard, lacking access to basic hygienic services such as drinking water and/or sanitation, waste collection and access to basic health care, while density in such areas does not allow residents to maintain the necessary social distancing.

2. These people cannot earn their daily income while social distancing; they can rarely work from home. Occupants of such informal constructions are usually unregistered workers, or are occupied on a temporary basis, in a myriad of businesses, small or medium enterprises, usually informal; these people, every morning, afternoon or night must leave their homes to go out, to ensure that they will bring back enough food for family members while keeping the economy running for the rest of the urban citizenry, experiencing emotional, physical and mental stress every day.

3. A large percentage of such informal labor force is occupied in transportation, construction, and agriculture/food production, supplying farmers and handling food from "farm to fork;" in many cases this is crucial for maintaining sustainability in the supply chain.

4. A significant number of residents of informal settlements, either rural or urban, are women who are harshly impacted by land tenure insecurity due to discriminatory laws and a lingering social bias. The COVID-19 virus threatens to exacerbate a situation of social gender inequality.

As COVID-19 continues to spread through society common measures are not being adopted by all governments and it becomes clear that strict measures that radically change everyday activities cannot easily be enforced and cannot easily control the disease. While restoring global health remains the uppermost priority, as mentioned above, it is apparent that the strict measures required have caused massive economic and social shock. The prolongation of a lockdown, physical distancing and other isolation measures used to eliminate transmission of the virus will lead the global economy into a recession. Unemployment, loss of income and the risk of more homelessness are the result.

Many countries are using additional "social safety net programs" to respond and protect families from the impact of economic shock. They provide, among other devices, loans with low interest, cash, in-kind transfers, social pensions, public works, and school feeding programs targeted to poor and vulnerable households. Some have enacted measures to secure housing tenure for tenants and occupants of camps and informal settlements in response to this crisis. Among those jurisdictions who have put in such measures, many have moved to enact moratoriums on evictions and utilities shut-offs, and some have put in measures to reduce rents or offer moratoriums to non-performing housing loans and foreclosures, or rental subsidies to the most vulnerable households.

However, the cost of such measures is significantly preventing their broad application. Most frequently beneficiaries of such measures are those registered, meaning those working and living in the formal sector; residents in informal settlements are once again likely to be left behind. But, we should acknowledge that allowing substandard conditions in some areas is not only a threat to those residents, but to the general population as well. Infected residents through their activity very soon will transfer the virus to the people they have job contacts within the city or other regions.

Moreover, the COVID-19 crisis is also anticipated to accelerate a disruption in the housing sector that started well before this crisis. The construction and real estate sector is an industry that tends to be vulnerable to economic cycles. External market factors, combined with fragmented and complex industry dynamics and an overall aversion to risk, already had made the provision of formal affordable housing adequate for all, a problematic process. This is expected to worsen due to the virus thus anticipating larger numbers of people seeking an alternative and affordable but informal housing solution.

Governments need to seriously consider new fit-for-purpose ways and tools to manage and administer land [12] as well as to formalize existing informal constructions in order to enable access to credit for those residents, to improve their living conditions and to enhance the needed hygienic and safety improvements in such constructions. It is more important than ever for all actors to see what the "next normal" will look like and make the bold, strategic decisions to create a better future for all by solving the persistent shortage of formal housing.

15.4 How to Formalize Informal Construction in Order to Empower Residents against COVID-19

Informal development is a social phenomenon in which people settle on land that may be owned by others or by the state, where they build dwellings usually sub-standard and temporary in nature. These settlements may have limited or no infrastructure. Informal development may even appear on legally owned land while its illegality is related to zoning, planning, or building regulations. An illegal building is one built without a construction permit, or in violation of a legally issued permit or against the verified basic legal land plan. In many cases illegal construction in the European transition countries is of a good, permanent type, and can be characterized as self-made "affordable housing" rather than as "slums", although they may not meet all construction stability, safety and environmental standards. Illegal buildings are usually out of the economic circle, not registered, not taxed and unable to be transferred or mortgaged. These constructions represent "dead capital" of a country's economy; the problem is well known in the UNECE region. Unregistered, informal constructions cannot be used as collateral to provide access to vital credit for their occupants (and do not appear on the public record for land taxation purposes). A great support that governments may provide to residents in informal settlements may be to enable formalization of informal constructions, where possible, thereby integrating them into the land administration systems and into property markets. As a result access to credit will be enabled and people may use this funding to improve their living situations with improved protection against the disease. But which is the most appropriate method of formalization?

The UNECE and the Working Party on Land Administration (WPLA) initiated joint research together with the International Federation of Surveyors (FIG) in 2007 on the topic of informal development in the region. The main objective of this research was to identify the size of the problem in the UNECE region, the causes, the types of informal constructions and to assess the formalization methods used by governments in eight countries [13–20], and to identify good practices.

The research identified that more than 50 million people in 15 member States of the United Nation Economic Commission for Europe (UNECE) live in informal settlements. The causes of current informal settlements include major political changes in law and regulation coupled with rapid urbanization, and often uncontrolled, massive internal migration. Conflict, marginalization, cumbersome authorization processes for home improvements and modernization, and corruption resulted. But the list of causes is more complex, including the absence of policies by the states and their failure to adopt pro-growth planning as well as affordable housing policies; weaknesses of the private sector; the lack of knowledge and political will to develop land policies to facilitate recognition of existing tenure and private property rights to aid the transition from centrally planned to market economies; and the failure or reluctance of state agencies to implement measures to support economic reforms to facilitate the digital economy and the UN Sustainable Development Agenda 2030.

The types of informal constructions in the region include a large range of buildings from small single family houses to multi-story apartment buildings, shops, hotels and public buildings. They may lack ownership titles and/or building and planning permits, or they may have been built in excess of legally issued permits. Formalization policies adopted from the various governments to address the problem often lack a clear fit-for-purpose strategy and in many countries formalization is a long bureaucratic and expensive procedure; or may start with the best of intentions but become bogged down due to administrative bottlenecks or change of government. Governments often understand the problem but do not fully recognize the extent of its impacts. Therefore, it was necessary to develop guidelines which would explain why a country would choose to go beyond the established scientific/engineering/planning practice in order to successfully deal with property market challenges, funding challenges, structural stability challenges, environmental challenges and difficult ethical challenges as well as the many hostile reactions to a formalization project by otherwise law-abiding citizens [21].

This long research resulted in the compilation of guidelines for a fit-for-purpose formalization framework in support of those countries seeking a quick and sustainable formalization solution in an affordable, reliable, inclusive and timely manner to improve residents' health, living and working conditions and to meet the SDGs by 2030. The guidelines focus mainly on providing instructions on how to organize the formalization project, but it also provides information about the necessary preparatory work (e.g., how to identify the problem's magnitude and how to develop a strategy to achieve a general political acceptance), as well as information about important post-formalization factors.

It is important that the formalization process, as well as its strategy, will clarify and quantify the anticipated economic, environmental and social benefits and ensure that everyone, not just the residents of informal settlements, sees benefits from formalization. The process should be based on three main pillars: (a) to facilitate increased tenure security, (b) to recognize the right to adequate housing for all, and (c) to provide access to credit for the residents in informal settlements. Guidelines are aligned with the UN SDGs, especially SDG 1, target 1.4, SDG 11, SDG 5, the FAO Voluntary Guidelines on the Responsible Governance of Tenure of Land, Fisheries and Forests (VGGT) and the New Urban Agenda.

These guidelines, published in 2019 by the United Nations, are written mainly for countries within the UNECE region where informal constructions are of fairly good quality (not slums) and therefore could be considered as a commodity, which may provide access to credit and funds to be used by the residents either for construction improvements or for other general improvements of the neighborhoods e.g., to enable disaster recovery, education and health services, or to develop businesses. The guidelines are meant to be used by all sectors and stakeholders involved, such as politicians, government members, state agencies, all involved professionals, as well as academics, NGOs and banks.

It is anticipated that the guidelines will be applicable in other regions, too. In the "new normal" era titling provision and registration should be quick and of low cost and should be independent from other types of informalities (lack of planning and/or construction permits). Post-formalization or parallel planning, environmental considerations, construction improvements as well as service-provision should be enabled not only for social and environmental reasons, but also to make these properties more economically viable and attractive in order to become part of the broader legal real estate market and to enable access to credit. Otherwise, it is hard to realize equity in a house that cannot be sold or is without interest in the real estate market.

However, there is no "one size fits all" general rule for improvement provision; such improvements can be initiated and funded by the residents in partnership with national and local authorities, as well as the private sector. Tools to be used for urban regeneration may include consolidation of parcels and land readjustment. Such land reforms require a broad public awareness and acceptance, as well as trust and willingness of residents to participate voluntarily to secure ownership rights to their homes. In general, the success of such a project is based on the voluntary participation of residents. Eliminating the informality phenomenon in future requires, apart from title provision and property registration, comprehensive land policies and reforms that may include pro-growth planning, flexible permitting/inspection processes for development, property valuation, policies for creating job opportunities, fair taxation and affordability. Other issues relevant to the establishment of real estate markets should be also addressed, which include the existence of funding mechanisms, professional education, professional ethics and an effective role for the private sector [22].

When dealing with formalization one should remember that demand in real estate markets is defined not only by consumer need, but also by consumer desire and when neither the state nor the private sector provide, legally, the supply of appropriate real estate types and quantities to satisfy the current demand, people may build informally with a result that is inherently risky.

Also, one should remember that security of tenure is a social issue and a human right; security of ownership rights and of titles may also be a social issue as it is fundamental to the well-being of residents. But security of tenure alone cannot facilitate access to credit, while security of ownership rights may. A country without an inclusive formal system for registering property rights limits its own economic development and prevents its citizens from realizing their full potential.

The formalization of informal constructions, among several other improvements, will enable:

1. reduction of evictions by the establishment of updated cadastral systems and increased security of rights;

2. risk reduction thus enabling occupants' access to credit at affordable interest rates, as well as a significant tool for funding their housing and resistance to any natural and/or manmade disasters;

3. occupants to improve their housing and business conditions; improvement of planning of neighborhoods and construction stability; improvement to family health issues; children's education; security;

4. authorities to use this updated spatial data infrastructure for evidence-based decision-making for a series of issues, e.g., to enable digital transformation of society; to build reliable basic registers; to add other necessary information or improve various statistical records; to apply good and fair land and property policies; to monitor and improve important health and other SDG indicators, such as for environmental issues; to support agriculture and food production, education and employment, gender equality and transportation and to provide humanitarian support;

5. the transformation of dead capital locked up in informal constructions to become productive capital thus increasing a nation's GDP with faster economic recovery and poverty alleviation. Such assets as formalized constructions may provide collateral and increased revenue from land taxation to improve basic infrastructure and provide electricity and digital access to all people, which is basic for a restart of national economies especially in the poorest countries.

The UNECE Guidelines for formalization of informal constructions may be of particular interest to governments preparing for the post-COVID era. Benefits from a fit-for-purpose formalization of informal settlements could contribute to economic recovery by providing property titles, registering them in the cadastral systems and integrating them into the local economies.

Experts involved in the compilation of these Guidelines are currently working under the guidance of UNECE for identifying ways to monitor the implementation of the Guidelines in the region. More specifically, a follow up project is carried on with a purpose to review how well countries that face the challenge of informal development have progressed with their formalization projects and if there is a need for some revision of the process, what is actually the impact of Covid-19 in these regions, and what are the actions taken by governments during the Covid-19 period. Some seminars and lectures will be organized soon aiming to raise awareness about the importance of the Guidelines and their fast and inclusive implementation. It is highly recommended though that the experience gained from UNECE region will be shared in other regions, too, that are facing similar challenges.

References

[1] V. Cetl, C. Ioannidis, S. Dalyot, Y. Doytsher, Y. Felus, M. Haklay, H. Mueller, C. Potsiou, E. Rispoli, and D. Siriba. New Trends in Geospatial Information: The Land Surveyors Role in the Era of Crowdsourcing and VGI. *International Federation of Surveyors (FIG): FIG Publication No. 73*, 2019.

[2] United Nations UN. *Sendai Framework for Disaster Risk Reduction 2015–2030*. URL https://www.preventionweb.net/files/43291_sendaiframeworkfordrren.pdf.

[3] C. Potsiou. Spatial Data Infrastructures in Support of Land Governance and Natural Disaster Prevention and Management - The FIG Com3 activity. In *2nd GIS National Congress in Turkey on "NSDI and working cooperatively for a liveable future"*. FIG, 2009.

[4] Y. Doytsher, P. Kelly, R. Khouri, R. McLaren, H. Mueller, and C. Potsiou. Rapid urbanization and mega cities: the need for spatial information management. Denmark. *International Federation of Surveyors (FIG): FIG Publication No. 73*, 2010.

[5] J. Crabtree. How to manage a pandemic, 2020. URL https://www.technologyreview.com/magazines/the-coronavirus-issue/. MIT technology review Magazine.

[6] The World Bank Group WB. Global Productivity: Trends, Drivers, and Policies, 2020. URL https://www.worldbank.org/en/research/publication/global-productivity.

[7] ILO. A policy framework for tackling the economic and social impact of the COVID-19 crisis, 2020. URL https://www.ilo.org/wcmsp5/groups/public/@dgreports/@dcomm/documents/briefingnote/wcms_745337.pdf. Press release.

[8] ILO. As job losses escalate, nearly half of global workforce at risk of losing livelihoods, 2020. URL https://www.ilo.org/global/about-the-ilo/newsroom/news/WCMS_743036/lang--en/index.htm.

[9] S. Tsenkova, C. Potsiou, and A. Badyina. Self-made Cities. *Search for Sustainable Solutions for the Informal Settlements in the United Nations Economic Commission for Europe Region*, 2009.

[10] United Nations UN. UN transforming the world: the 2030 Agenda for Sustainable Development, . URL https://sustainabledevelopment.un.org/post2015/transformingourworld.

[11] Land Portal. Five years into the SDGs: are we on track to deliver the land targets? URL https://www.youtube.com/watch?v=uxYjO9BVbjQ.

[12] S. Enemark, K. C. Bell, C. Lemmen, and R. McLaren. Fit-For-Purpose Land Administration. *International Federation of Surveyors (FIG): FIG Publication No. 60*, 2015.

[13] C. Potsiou. *Informal Urban Development in Europe - Experiences from Albania and Greece*. UN Habitat, 2010.

[14] C. Potsiou and S. Basiouka. Security of ownership versus public benefit: A case study for land taking for infrastructure in Greece as an EU member state. *Survey Review*, 44(325):111–123, 2012.

[15] C. Potsiou and S. Basiouka. Policies for formalization of informal development: recent experience from southeastern Europe. *Land Use Policy*, 36(325):33–46, 2014.

[16] C. Potsiou and K. Dimitriadi. Tools for Legal Integration and Regeneration of Informal Development in Greece: A Research Study in the Municipality of Keratea. *Surveying and Land Information Sciences (SaLIS)*, 68(2):103–118, 2008.

[17] C. Potsiou, M. Theodorou, and E. Elikkos. Informal Development Due to Market Pressure-A Case Study on Cyprus and the Role of Land Administration. *Nordic Journal of Surveying and Real Estate Research*, 2009.

[18] C. Potsiou and K. Dimitriadi. Illegal Development in a State Controlled Economy in transition: the case of Montenegro. *South-Eastern European Journal of Earth Observation and Geomatics*, 3(1a):71–85, 2014.

[19] C. Potsiou. *Formalizing the Informal: Challenges and Opportunities of Informal Settlements in South-East Europe*. United Nations, 2015.

[20] C. Potsiou and C. Ioannidis. Informal settlements in Greece: The mystery of missing information and the difficulty of their integration into a legal framework. In *Proceedings of 5th FIG Regional Conference for Africa, Accra, Ghana*. FIG, 2006.

[21] C. Potsiou, S. Nystrom, R. Wouters, and A. Figueiredo. *Guidelines for the formalization of informal constructions*. UNECE, 2019.

[22] Estate Market Advisory Group UNECE. *Policy Framework for Sustainable Real Estate Markets*. United Nations, 2010.

16

Spatially Enabled COVID-19: A Review of Applications and Systems

Abbas Rajabifard, Yiqun Chen, Yibo Zhang and Katie Potts

The ongoing COVID-19 pandemic has profoundly reshaped the world and impacted the lives of billions globally across many facets, including health, economy, culture, education, environment and politics. Since declared as a public health emergency of international concern (PHEIC) in January 2020, the outbreak has attracted significant research attention globally. Governments, industries and academics altogether are investigating various means for monitoring the spread of the virus, assessing the impacts, and planning strategies and policies for reopening. Many tools and applications have been developed to support government and emergency agencies for critical decision-making and situation monitoring at various stage of the outbreak. This paper reviews existing COVID-19 emergency management tools and applications currently being adopted by different countries and jurisdictions, and identifies and compares their key capabilities and functionalities.

16.1 Introduction

The outbreak of the COVID-19 virus has fundamentally changed the way our world operates. The impact of this virus has been felt in almost every country around the globe, disrupting and putting extreme pressure on various industry sectors – such as building and construction, retail, transport, hospitality, education, financial services, agriculture, aviation and tourism, and healthcare. In response to the pandemic, the governments of many countries have adopted strategies to minimise the spread and impact of the virus, which involves quarantining communities through lockdown mandates which have had enormous economic and social impacts. As the spread of infectious disease is inherently a spatial process, the geospatial industry which specialises in geospatial data, technologies, and analytical methods play a critical role in understanding and responding to the coronavirus disease 2019 (COVID-19) pandemic [1]. To contribute and assist with the escalating problem, the geospatial industry, like many other industries, have focused their attention to this global challenge and have founded solutions and developed tools which aid and assist officials in their role of managing this unprecedented event.

Areas of focus which fit within the scope of the geospatial industry's expertise include: developing spatial data infrastructures (SDI) for surveillance and data sharing; incorporating mobility data into infectious disease forecasting; using geospatial technologies for digital contact tracing; integrating geographic data in COVID-19 modelling; investigating social vulnerabilities and health disparities; communicating the status of the disease or status of facilities for return-to-normal operations; and tracking, monitoring and optimisation of the location of necessary health and safety resources such as personal protective equipment (PPE), ventilators, and available hospital beds [1].

One early contribution from the geospatial industry has been the development of smartphone apps to assist contact tracing. Contact tracing involves identifying persons who may have come into contact with an infected person, and the management these people who have been exposed to COVID-19 to prevent onward transmission [2]. It is an essential activity conducted by public health organisations for controlling the virus. Through tracing of the contacts of infected individuals, testing them for infections, and then isolating the infected, public health aims to reduce the infections in the population. In order to effectively perform contact tracing, specific location and time details are required. To assist with this task, the geospatial industry has responded with a range of applications which can facilitate the tracing, some assisting from the public health side, and others from the citizen side. The apps take advantage of the inbuilt location and timestamp records of smart phones, GPS data from cars, credit card transactions, travel histories and CCTV footage to determine where and at what time a person has been in a specific location, and through analysis can use this information to determine intersections of individuals to determine who has been potentially exposed. Identifying the exact location of sick people, tracing their movements, and isolating them minimises the need to impose mobility restrictions or business closures [3].

Another application which has seen geospatial technology play a critical role has been in the identification and proximities of individuals to essential services. The geospatial industry has developed smartphone applications for use by citizens and also complex platforms to perform detailed analysis for government health departments. Government, industry and academia have put significant efforts and resources to build these applications, which fall into two categories of tracing apps and map-enabled dashboards. These applications are all built upon the same COVID-19 test data, and utilise various technologies and aggregate additional data sources to serve their purposes.

16.2 Tracing Apps

Tracing apps are critical means for the pandemic control, particularly when widely deployed, as they help to detect and notify people who contact with a carrier and can also monitor who breach the isolation rules. In March 2020, Ferretti et al. [4] suggested using digital contact tracing to quantify the virus transmission and proposed a schematic of a tracing app (Figure 16.1 (a)). Contacts of carrier A are traced by the app, and when carrier A is confirmed by a positive test result, the app triggers an instant notification to all the contacts with risk-stratified quarantine (i.e., close contacts B, C, D, E, F, G and low-risk contacts H, I) and physical distancing advice. CDC also released a COVID-19 contact tracing workflow (Figure 16.1 (b)) which can help scientists follow the chain of infection to understand how the virus transmits among crowd [5].

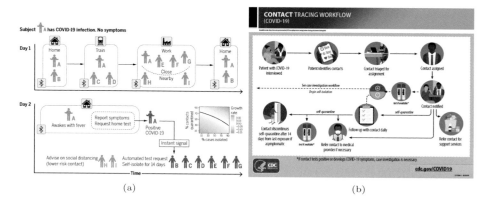

(a)   (b)

FIGURE 16.1
a) A schematic of a tracing app, b) COVID-19 contact tracing workflow

Most of the apps adopt Bluetooth technology to detect the proximity to other mobile devices. Unlike GPS or Wi-Fi data, the Bluetooth technology only tracks which device has been near one another, rather than reporting users' actual locations. They are usually classified as "Decentralised Contact Tracing" and considered to be better privacy-preserving and less intrusive, comparing with "Centralised Contact Tracing" methods which utilise cellular network and GPS to determine the location of users. In March 2020, in collaboration with CoEPi [6], Covid Watch [7] was the first team in the world to develop an open-source, anonymous, decentralised Bluetooth digital contact tracing protocol, the CEN (Contact Event Numbers) Protocol. It now has been renamed as TCN (Temporary Contact Numbers) Protocol[8]. In April 2020, similar decentralised protocols like DP-3T (Decentralized Privacy-Preserving Proximity Tracing) [8], PACT(Private Automated Contact Tracing) [9] and Google/Apple Exposure Notification framework [10] were also prevailing. By adopting such a decentralised protocol, contact tracing apps will create and broadcast short-lived pseudorandom values over Bluetooth. These values are recorded by nearby devices and reveal no information about users' identity or location history as they are pseudorandom. When a user is developing symptoms or tested positive, the app will send a report to any potential contacts by uploading a packet of data to a server. Other users can monitor data published by the server to learn whether they have received any reports [11, 12].

Several issues impact the effectiveness of tracking apps in the real world. First, inferring physical distance based these technologies can be unreliable. The range (3-10 m) of Bluetooth-enabled device varies dramatically due to the environment or the way the device is held [13, 14]. GPS-based proximity detection can also be unreliable, smartphones are typically accurate to within a 4.9-meter radius in open space, with accuracy decreasing further in the presence of signal blockage [15, 16]. The cellular network-based proximity reasoning also depends on the density of antenna towers (base stations) and the precision of positioning can achieve down to 50 meters in urban areas [17]. While, in most countries, the social distancing guidelines recommend 1.5 to 2 meters, which could not be reliably and accurately detected by any of these means. False positives might lead to unnecessary self-quarantine and could cause the public to ignore warnings when they find these warnings are untrustworthy. Another problem is the update ratio of tracing apps. The effectiveness of a tracing app depends on how many people use it regularly. If only a small proportion of people participate in, the app is worthless and could be harmful as its indications will be highly inaccurate and could even instill a false sense of security [18]. In Singapore, by the end of September 2020, 2.4 million people (41% population) downloaded the TraceTogether App. The uptake was lower than the optimal number of users required for the contact tracing system to work well, which was 75% of the population [19].

Australia launched its contact tracking app CovidSafe in April, which is completely voluntary. By the end of September, it has accumulated over 7 million downloads (28% population), while how and whether the app is being used has yet been revealed [20, 21]. In the UK, the second version of the NHS Covid-19 app has over 10 million downloads (around 15% population) since it launched in September 2020 [13, 22–24]. As the tracing apps are characterised by strong network effect [18], its efficacy is the square of the proportion of the population using the app, multiplied by the probability of the app detecting infectious contacts, multiplied by the fractional reduction in infectiousness resulting from being notified as a contact [4]. Simulation model shows that approximately 60% of the whole population are required to use the app and adhere to the app's recommendations to stop virus contagion [25].

16.3   Map-Based Dashboard

The history of using maps to understand the spread of disease can go back to 1850's when Dr. John Snow connected location and illness to trace the source of a cholera outbreak in London, as shown in Figure 16.2 (a) [26]. From disease atlases in early 20th century to more recent web mapping of Ebola (Figure 16.2 (b) [27]) and Zika, maps have been considered as a critical tool in coping with contagious viruses [28]. The reason behind is that global mobility is faster and easier than ever before, and a carrier can become a super spreader, infecting a large number of people across a large geographic area [28].

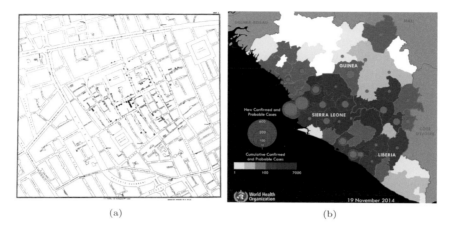

(a)   (b)

FIGURE 16.2

a) Cluster map of cholera cases in London, 1854, b) Web mapping of Ebola virus in Africa, 2014

The most famous COVID-19 dashboard (see Figure 16.3) has been created and maintained by Johns Hopkins University since late January 2020. It is a map-based web application, aggregating real-time information about the pandemic at the global level (190 countries and regions included), and has been cited as official COVID-19 data and statistics by many media channels. The dashboard sources and aggregates data globally and reports cases at the province level in China; at the city level in the USA, Australia, and Canada; and at the country level otherwise [29, 30]. The interactive maps of the dashboard include accumulated cases, active cases, incidence rate, case-fatality rate and testing rate. Besides, it also offers critical trends analysis and interactive visualisation, which help user unfold details about the outbreak spread patterns at various geographical levels [31–33].

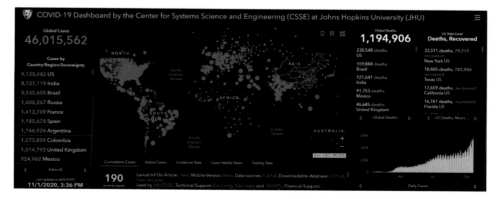

FIGURE 16.3

COVID-19 Dashboard developed by Johns Hopkins University

The Johns Hopkins COVID-19 dashboard has a significant impact on the coming COVID-19 dashboard design and functionalities. Within a short period, many countries and organisations have adopted similar web mapping technology (mostly powered by ESRI Live Atlas) to build their dashboard and customise with additional information [28]. Figure 16.4 shows four dashboards for Italy (top-left), China (top-right), Japan (bottom-left) and Germany (bottom-right) respectively [34–37]. They are all built upon ESRI ArcGIS online map applications and share the same style with

Johns Hopkins University's COVID-19 dashboard. Figure 16.5 illustrates the COVID-19 dashboards created by India (top-left), Brazil (top-right), Australia (bottom-left) and WHO (bottom-right) using different web tools. Though the appearances are different from each other, the maps and statistics charts all remain as the key components [38–41].

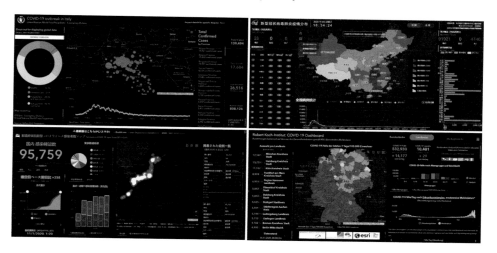

FIGURE 16.4
A series of similar COVID-19 dashboards created with ESRI ArcGIS Online

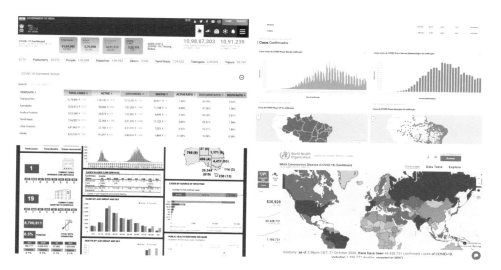

FIGURE 16.5
COVID-19 Dashboards created using different web tools

Besides diseases statistics, dispersion maps and propagation animations, there is another category of dashboards particularly focus on the pandemic impact analyses including mobility, health, economy and society. For example, the COVID-19 Impact Analysis Platform [42, 43] developed by the University of Maryland placed emphases on the mobility and social impact of the virus by incorporating over 30 variables, including social distancing index (top-left), percentage of hospital bed utilisation (top-right), unemployment rate (bottom-left) and COVID death rate (bottom-right), as shown in Figure 16.6.

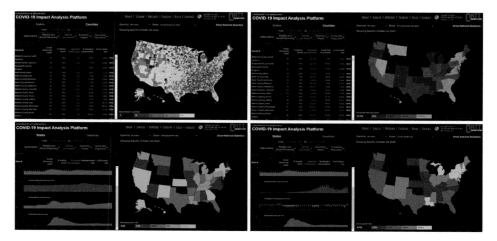

FIGURE 16.6

COVID-19 Impact Analysis Platform developed by University of Maryland

The Australia COVID-19 Location Tracker developed by the Centre for Disaster Management and Public Safety (CDMPS) jointly with the Centre for SDIs and Land Administration (CSDILA), both at the University of Melbourne also comes with a set of ready-for-use analytics tools by utilising live data through multiple sources for Australia.

The system can perform capacity and service area (e.g., 3, 5, 10 km) analysis for COVID-19 related hospitals and clinics and provide insights medical resource supply chain management at various scenarios. It plots the distribution of the vulnerable population (e.g., 65+ years old) at a fine geospatial unit level based on the latest Census data and identifies regions required particular attention by cross-referencing health condition datasets. The system compiles and visualises the number of closed non-essential businesses during various stage of lockdown, and estimates the impacts on the local economy such as unemployment rate and scale of subsidies etc.

FIGURE 16.7

Australia COVID-19 Location Tracker developed by the University of Melbourne

In general, the map-based dashboards prevail in the COVID-19 pandemic and have been adopted worldwide at various administrative scales. By aggregating, analysing and conveying data in a timely manner, it serves as a critical and effective tool for government and public to communicate and understand the spread of disease and hence helps to increase the pandemic situational awareness and preparedness.

16.4   Conclusion

The geospatial community has a fundamental and critical role to play in supporting government management of COVID-19 through contact tracing and map development applications. In this paper tracing apps that have been developed have been presented and discussed revealing their strengths and weaknesses as well as challenges faced when trying to successfully implement these apps at a large scale to produce valuable data for management of the virus. Successful map dashboards that are serving both government and the community were also presented and discussed. Consensus on these applications are that map dashboards have been the most useful and more widely accepted and adopted, proving an effective tool for presenting and relaying information for government and public understanding and situational awareness on COVID-19.

References

[1] Charlotte D. Smith and J. M. Incorporating Geographic Information Science and Technology in Response to the COVID-19 Pandemic. 2020. URL https://www.cdc.gov/pcd/issues/2020/20_0246.htm. Accessed on 10 October 2020.

[2] WHO. Rolling updates on coronavirus disease (COVID-19). 2020. URL https://bit.ly/39fHuz8. Accessed on 10 October 2020.

[3] Mika-Petteri Torhonen, S.E., Dongkyu Kwak Antos, and Alvaro Federico Barra. The role of geospatial information in confronting COVID-19 – Learning from Korea. 2020. URL https://bit.ly/33iQGPo. Accessed on 1 August 2020.

[4] L. Ferretti and et al. Quantifying SARS-CoV-2 transmission suggests epidemic control with digital contact tracing. *Science,* 368(6491): eabb6936, 2020.

[5] CDC. Monitoring and tracking the disease. 2020. URL https://bit.ly/3fwD6g4. Accessed on 21 October 2020.

[6] CoEpi. Monitoring and tracking the diseaseCoEpi: Community Epidemiology in Action. 2020. URL https://www.coepi.org/. Accessed on 10 October 2020.

[7] Covid Watch. 2020. URL https://www.covidwatch.org/. Accessed on 10 October 2020.

[8] DP-3T. Decentralised Privacy-Preserving Proximity Tracing. 2020. URL https://github.com/DP-3T/documents. Accessed on 10 October 2020.

[9] MIT. PACT: Private Automated Contact Tracing. 2020. Accessed on 10 October 2020.

[10] Google. Exposure Notifications: Using technology to help public health authorities fight COVID-19. 2020. URL https://www.google.com/covid19/exposurenotifications/. Accessed on 29 August 2020.

[11] T. Coalition. TCN Protocol. 2020. URL https://github.com/TCNCoalition/TCN. Accessed on 10 October 2020.

[12] HD VALENCE. Private Contact Tracing Protocols Compared: DP-3T and CEN. 2020. URL https://bit.ly/2KvLmRY. Accessed on 15 Septermber 2020.

[13] D Leprince-Ringuet. Contact-tracing apps: Why the NHS said no to Apple and Google's plan. 2020. URL https://zd.net/39cjblk. Accessed on 29 August 2020.

[14] J. Larsson. Distance estimation and positioning based on Bluetooth low energy technology. *KTH Royal Institute of Technology,* 2015.

[15] Frank van Diggelen and P.E. The World's first GPS MOOC and Worldwide Laboratory using Smartphones. in Proceedings of the 28th International Technical Meeting of the Satellite Division of The Institute of Navigation (ION GNSS+ 2015). *Tampa, Florida,* 2015.

[16] GPS.GOV. How accurate is GPS? 2020. URL https://www.gps.gov/systems/gps/performance/accuracy/. Accessed on 29 August 2020.

[17] H. Laitinen, J. Lahteenmaki, and T. Nordstrom. Database correlation method for GSM location. *IEEE*.

[18] Chiara Farronato, M.I., Marcin Bartosiak, Stefano Denicolai, Luca Ferretti, and Roberto Fontana. How to Get People to Actually Use Contact-Tracing Apps. 2020. URL https://hbr.org/2020/07/how-to-get-people-to-actually-use-contact-tracing-apps. Accessed on 1 September 2020.

[19] H. Baharudin. Contact-tracing device will not track location; people can use TraceTogether if they prefer, says Vivian Balakrishnan. 2020. URL https://bit.ly/33esKfX. Accessed on 29 August 2020.

[20] A. COVIDSafe app Department of Health. he COVIDSafe app is a tool that helps identify people exposed to coronavirus (COVID-19). 2020. URL https://www.health.gov.au/resources/apps-and-tools/covidsafe-app. Accessed on 10 September 2020.

[21] T. Guardian. Releasing Covidsafe app usage numbers could risk public safety, government claims. 2020. URL https://bit.ly/33fqxka. Accessed on 1 October 2020.

[22] Matt Burgess. Everything you need to know about the new NHS contact tracing app. 2020. URL https://bit.ly/3nUG01g. Accessed on 25 October 2020.

[23] Department of Health and Social Care. NHS COVID-19 app has been downloaded over 10 million times. 2020. URL https://bit.ly/2UZj707. Accessed on 22 October 2020.

[24] Joe O'Halloran. NHS Covid-19 app exceeds 10 million downloads, but has teething troubles. 2020. URL https://bit.ly/313L69x. Accessed on 25 October 2020.

[25] Oxford University. Digital contact tracing can slow or even stop coronavirus transmission and ease us out of lockdown. 2020. URL https://bit.ly/378Gz0u. Accessed on 21 October 2020.

[26] Wikipedia. John Snow. 2020. URL https://en.wikipedia.org/wiki/John_Snow. Accessed on 28 August 2020.

[27] WHO. Ebola maps. 2016. URL https://www.who.int/csr/disease/ebola/maps/en/. Accessed on 20 October 2020.

[28] E. Geraghty. Coronavirus: World Connectivity Can Save Lives. 2020. URL https://bit.ly/3l52bQv. Accessed on 29 August 2020.

[29] E. Dong, H. Du, and L. Gardner. An interactive web-based dashboard to track COVID-19 in real time. *The Lancet Infectious Diseases*. 20(5) 533-534, 2020.

[30] Johns Hopkins University. COVID-19 Data Repository by the Center for Systems Science and Engineering (CSSE) at Johns Hopkins University. 2020. URL https://github.com/CSSEGISandData/COVID-19. Accessed on 29 October 2020.

[31] Johns Hopkins University. Animated Maps. 2020. URL https://coronavirus.jhu.edu/data/animated-world-map. Accessed on 1 November 2020.

[32] Johns Hopkins University. Daily Confirmed New Cases (7-Day Moving Average). 2020. URL https://coronavirus.jhu.edu/data/new-cases. Accessed on 1 November 2020.

[33] Johns Hopkins University. Cases and mortality by country. 2020. URL https://coronavirus.jhu.edu/data/mortality. Accessed on 1 November 2020.

[34] UNWFP. COVID-19 outbreak in Italy. 2020. URL https://bit.ly/2KDLG1g. Accessed on 1 November 2020.

[35] C. CHINA. 2020. URL http://2019ncov.chinacdc.cn/2019-nCoV/. Accessed on 1 November 2020.

[36] J.A.G JAPAN Corp. Coronavirus COVID-19 Japan Case by Each Prefecture. 2020. URL https://bit.ly/3nZguId. Accessed on 1 November 2020.

[37] R. Koch-Institut. COVID-19 Dashboard. 2020. URL https://experience.arcgis.com/experience/478220a4c454480e823b17327b2bf1d4. Accessed on 1 November 2020.

[38] Government of India. COVID-19 Dashboard. 2020. URL https://www.mygov.in/covid-19/. Accessed on 1 November 2020.

[39] M.d.S. Brazil. COVID19 Painel Coronavírus. 2020. URL https://covid.saude.gov.br/. Accessed on 1 November 2020.

[40] Australian Government Department of Health. Coronavirus (COVID-19) at a glance. 2020. URL https://bit.ly/3kZRnTL. Accessed on 1 November 2020.

[41] WHO. WHO Coronavirus Disease (COVID-19) Dashboard. 2020. URL https://covid19.who.int. Accessed on 1 November 2020.

[42] University of Maryland. COVID-19 Impact Analysis Platform. 2020. URL https://data.covid.umd.edu/about/index.html.

[43] Lei Zhang, Sepehr Ghader, Michael L Pack, Chenfeng Xiong, Aref Darzi, Mofeng Yang, Qianqian Sun, AliAkbar Kabiri, and Songhua Hu. An Interactive COVID-19 Mobility Impact and Social Distancing Analysis Platform. *medRxiv*, 2020. doi: 10.1101/2020.04.29.20085472.

17

COVID-19 Spatiotemporal Hotspots and Prediction Based on Wavelet and Neural Network

Neda Kaffash Charandabi and Amir Gholami

In this chapter, a global model of the COVID-19 is proposed to determine the important periods of each country, prediction of confirmed cases, and discover spatiotemporal hot/cold spots. The importance of the COVID-19 periods is assessed for each country and the most important periods are selected as time series prediction delays and temporal neighborhood steps of spatiotemporal analysis. The COVID-19 cases are predicted based on wavelet and neural network with an average RMSEIQR of 0.974 for all countries. Finally, the hot/cold spot maps are prepared by the specified temporal neighborhood steps and the patterns are identified. More than 61% of the earth's surface is surrounded by COVID-19 hot spots.

17.1   Introduction

The novel Coronavirus Disease 2019 (COVID-19) has spread all over the world since it first appeared in Wuhan, the capital city of Hubei province, on 31 December 2019. The number of cases is well above 35 million and the number of deaths is more than 1 million till 5 October 2020, according to the World Health Organization (WHO) situation reports [1]. The WHO announced COVID-19 as the sixth the world's public health concern on January 30, 2020. It is transmitted via human-to-human droplets or direct contact, and the mean incubation period for infection has been estimated to be 6.4 days [2]. However, there is little information about this new virus, researchers in different fields are working towards discovering an appropriate solution to this global issue [2]. One of the new approaches to better management of epidemics is the use of spatiotemporal analyses. These analyses are important tools for preventing and reducing the spread of disease, with the potential to detect trends and critical points of the disease outbreaks.

The Geographic Information System (GIS) is an analytical tool for collecting, editing, managing, and processing of spatial data. GIS is also used as a platform for spatiotemporal analyses by integrating temporal data with location and attribute data. Conventional GIS analyses are very useful in the identification of spatiotemporal patterns and clusters. However, it needs to be combined with robust algorithms to predict time series. Neural network algorithms are among the most common families of non-parametric methods that can be used for predicting epidemic peaks. But they alone are not enough to predict variable, nonlinear, and uncertain issues. Wavelet is used as one of the most powerful methods in signal processing and time series analysis. It is possible to predict complex time series with high accuracy by combining the wavelet with neural networks [3].

In recent years, more researchers have concentrated on predicting epidemic outbreaks. Al-Ahmadi et al. investigated MERS-COV data in Saudi Arabia from 2012 to 2019. The disease was analyzed by extracting spatial, temporal, seasonal, and spatial-temporal clusters [4]. Mongkolsawat and Kamchai identified the critical areas of Avian influenza in Thailand. This study highlighted the use of GIS to investigate the prevalence and identification of critical areas in different epidemics [5]. Li et al. described the spatial and temporal characteristics of human H7N9 virus infections in China using data from 2013 to 2017 and ArcMap^{TM}10.2 along with SaTScan [6]. Zhu et al. used the multi-channel Long Short-Term Memory (LSTM) to predict influenza in China. The neural network training process was performed with number of legal influenza cases and outbreaks, affected cases with different ages, Chinese patent cold medicines, other cold medicines, temperature, rainfall, air pressure, and relative humidity for nine years in nine regions of China [7]. Venna et al. applied data-driven machine learning to predict flu based on environmental factors. Meteorological, proximity, and influenza data from 1997 to 2016 were analyzed using the LSTM deep learning model [8]. Spataru utilized the ArcMap^{TM}10.2 "space-time pattern mining" tool to analyze polio disease. He had extracted space-time clusters and critical locations of the disease based on Mann-Kendall and Getis-Ord Gi* statistic [9]. According to the previous studies, the use of spatiotemporal analysis has been very useful in studying epidemics. However, spatiotemporal clustering and time series analysis had been carried out separately in previous researches.

Numerous studies have started in the field of treatment and management of the COVID-19. Guan et al. studied data from 1099 patients of 552 hospitals in 30 different provinces. Based on their findings over the first 2 months, the COVID-19 has spread around the world with different conditions and symptoms [10]. Lai et al. studied COVID-19 patient data in countries around the world until February 11 and used graphs and maps to examine their patient numbers and specific symptoms [2]. Kuniya predicted the epidemic peak of Coronavirus using the SEIR model in Japan. In his study, early middle summer was known as the peak of the COVID-19 in Japan, so forecasting for all countries based on suitable methods seems to be necessary [11]. Al-qaness et al. proposed a method for forecasting confirmed cases of the COVID-19 in China based on an Adaptive Neuro-Fuzzy Inference System (ANFIS) using an enhanced Flower Pollination Algorithm (FPA) along with the Salp Swarm Algorithm (SSA) [12]. Chakraborty and Ghosh forecasted Coronavirus cases base on wavelet and AutoRegressive Integrated Moving Average model (ARIMA) for Canada, France, India, South Korea, and the UK [13]. Tamang et al. predicted Covid-19 cases based on an Artificial Neural Network (ANN) curve fitting technique [14]. These predictions have been made in line with the current trend of rising cases in different countries and the patterns of change in China and South Korea for one week. The reviewed articles provided an example of researches in the field of space and statistics. In these studies, less attentions have been paid to both the SpatioTemporal Hot/Cold Spot Analysis (STHCSA) and the Coronavirus pandemic time series prediction. Previous research has only been performed in one or some countries and has not been a global model. Periods are not predicted for each country, and the accuracy of the training data is assessed, while the accuracy of the test and train data indicates the actual accuracy of the prediction.

17.2   Materials and Methods

In this chapter, a combined model of wavelet and neural network was used to predict COVID-19 cases based on data reported by WHO, due to its ability to complex time series prediction [3]. Also, its hot/cold spots were identified by specified important periods and features. The theoretical foundations of the methods used in this research were described in this section.

17.2.1   Wavelet transforms

Wavelet transform is a mathematical approach to the decomposition of data into a variety of frequency components. It can extract special patterns hidden in a huge amount of data. The wavelet transform can be used to analyze non-stationary time series data at several different frequencies. Wavelet transforms are generally divided into the Continuous Wavelet Transformation (CWT) and Discrete Wavelets Transformation (DWT) [15]. The DWT and CWT are the wavelet transform implementation using discrete and arbitrary sets of the wavelet scales, respectively. They can be used to decompose wavelets, process signals, extract features, and denoise noisy signals. There are many types of mother wavelets that can be used for wavelet transforms. The different mother wavelets that are used to examine the same signal will yield varying results. Therefore, different mother wavelet types of CWT and DWT were examined to select best of them for capturing the multiscale features of signals [16, 17].

17.2.1.1 CWT

The CWT is an important method for assessing non-stationary signals and providing a number of signal information, such as time, frequency, scale, and local signal correlation. The CWT is used to decompose a signal into small wavelets that are highly localized in time [18]. It generally used short-time Fourier transform for decomposes a signal into unlimited length sines and cosines, basically eliminating all time-localization information and replacing it with time-frequency signal representation that provides very strong time and frequency localization. The wavelet function is defined as Eq. (17.1) The basic functions of the CWT are scaled and shifted versions of a function called the time-localized mother wavelet $\Psi(t)$. Eq. (17.2) express wavelet transform that is the convolution of time series data and wavelets [18, 19].

$$\int_{-\infty}^{\infty} \Psi(t)\mathrm{dt} = 0. \tag{17.1}$$

$$F(a, b) = \frac{1}{\sqrt{a}} \int_{-\infty}^{\infty} f(t)\Psi\left(\frac{t - b}{a}\right)\mathrm{dt}. \tag{17.2}$$

Where a and b are the scale and shift parameters, t is the time, $f(t)$ is the data, $\Psi(t)$ is the mother wavelet, and $F(a, b)$ is the time-scale representation of the signal. Several mother wavelets are available for the CWT, including Mexican hat wavelet, analytic Morlet wavelet, generalized Morse wavelet, Bump wavelet, and so on. The Morlet is a wavelet composed mainly of an exponential function multiplied by a Gaussian window. This wavelet is closely related to human perception and demonstrates good performance in analyzing the periodicity of local signals. Generalized Morse wavelets are a family of analytical wavelets with two parameters, symmetry and time-bandwidth of the product. Bump wavelet has a larger variance in time and smaller variance in frequency. Each of these wavelets has different parameters for studying different behaviors and properties [18, 20].

17.2.1.2 DWT

The DWT is a powerful time series analysis tool used to break down the original time series into different components, each of which can produce meaningful information from the original data. The DWT can be decomposed the signal into low and high frequencies. The low and high frequencies are also called as approximation and detail coefficients. Commonly the approximation is decomposed to a higher level after the first level. The DWT is used to reduce time series data in order to save storage space while losing a small amount of detailed information. The last coefficient of approximation and a few of the high-level detail coefficients are typically chosen for preservation that are the only coefficients needed for perfect reconstruction. Hence, The DWT is known as a lossless transformation, whereby transformed domain data can collectively rebuild the original data [16, 21].

The DWT has several mother wavelet families, such as Daubechies, Coiflets, Symlets, Fejér-Korovkin, discrete Meyer, Biorthogonal, and reverse Biorthogonal, which each of them has different orders. The Daubechies family is an orthonormal wavelet, which makes the analysis of wavelets possible in discrete time. The first order Daubechies (db1) wavelet resembles a simple step function and the higher-order Daubechies functions (db2, db3, db4, etc.) are not easy to define with an analytical expression. The order of this function shows the number of vanishing moments or the number of zero wavelet moments. The Coiflet (coif) wavelet family is more symmetrical and has more vanishing moments than the Daubechies wavelets. Symlets' (sym) properties are similar to Daubechies, that are near-symmetric and have the least asymmetry. Fejér-Korovkin (fk) wavelet family minimizes the gap between the ideal since lowpass filter and the valid scaling filter. The discrete Meyer (dmey) wavelet family is defined in the frequency domain. The Biorthogonal (bio) and reverse Biorthogonal (rbio) families use separate wavelet and scaling functions for the analysis, synthesis, and vice versa [22].

17.2.2   Neural networks

ANNs are human brain-inspired methods that consist of a large number of simple and highly interconnected computing elements and use them as a huge data processing system. ANN-based methods are very useful for prediction problems. Three main parts of the ANN are the input, hidden, and output layers [23]. Different models of the ANNs were introduced to solve specific problems. In this research Multi Layer Perceptron (MLP) was used as a class of feedforward neural networks which is an efficient and popular algorithm. The MLP is a type of supervised learning algorithms that uses backpropagation to train. The MLP contains a number of layers, neurons, weights, and transfer functions. Transfer functions are used to aggregate the input neurons with different weights to the output where the neuron is a link between the layers. First, the input neurons are multiplied by their respective weights, then the output neuron is summed up and determined via the transfer function. Tansig is one of the widely used transfer functions that has been selected for this research. This function makes MLP networks so powerful, because of the ability to represent nonlinear functions [23, 24].

Finally, normalized Root Means Square Error by the Inter-Quartile Ranges (RMSEIQR) was used to evaluate the accuracy of the prediction results of the proposed model because it is suitable for comparing the different values obtained for various countries with a different population and confirmed cases. The RMSEIQR is an interquartile range of the RMSE that normalizes values and is less sensitive to extreme values (outliers) than the RMSE. The RMSEIQR is defined as Eq. (17.3) where $\hat{y}_t$ and y_t are predicted and observed values over T time and IQR is the difference of quartile functions. In other words, the RMSEIQR calculates by dividing the RMSE into the IQR [25].

$$RMSEIQR = \frac{\sqrt{\sum_{t=1}^{T}(\hat{y}_t - y_t)^2}}{IQR\sqrt{T}}. \tag{17.3}$$

17.2.3   Hot/Cold spot analysis

Spatiotemporal analysis was used to identified hot/cold spots by specified important periods and features in previous steps. STHCSA is an important component of spatiotemporal analysis since location and time are two critical aspects of important events such as the Coronavirus epidemic. The outputs of such analyses can provide useful information to guide the activities aimed at preventing, detecting, and responding to pandemic problems [26]. There are various methods for spatiotemporal analysis. In this study, Mann-Kendall test was used to detect trends of data and Getis-Ord Gi^* statistic was used to identify hot/cold spots.

Network Common Data Form (NetCDF) is a file format to store multi-dimensional scientific data such as temperature, humidity, disease, and crime. The NetCDF cube is generated using the COVID-19 x, y, and time data as x, y, and z axes. It summarizes a collection of points into a NetCDF by aggregating them into space-time bins. The Mann-Kendall p-values and z-scores show the statistical significance of the trend in a hot spot (spatial clusters of high values) or cold spot (spatial clusters of low values) at a location. A positive or negative z-score indicates an upward or downward trend respectively [9, 27]. Then, the pattern in the spatiotemporal data was identified with Getis-Ord Gi^* statistic based on neighborhood distance and neighborhood time step. The Getis-Ord Gi^* statistic is calculated for each bin as follows [28, 29]:

$$\bar{x} = \frac{\sum_{j=1}^{n} x_j}{n}. \tag{17.4}$$

$$s = \sqrt{\frac{\sum_{j=1}^{n} x_j^2}{n} - \bar{x}^2}. \tag{17.5}$$

$$G_i^* = \frac{\sum_{j=1}^{n} w_{ij} x_j - \bar{x} \sum_{j=1}^{n} w_{ij}}{s \sqrt{\frac{n \sum_{j=1}^{n} w_{ij}^2 - (\sum_{j=1}^{n} w_{ij})^2}{n-1}}}. \tag{17.6}$$

Where x_j is the value of feature x at location j, n is the number of data and w_{ij} is the element of the weight matrix. The G_i^* is recorded as a z-score for each variable in the dataset. The more intense the clustering of high values or hot spots are, the larger positive z-scores become and the more intense the clustering of low values or cold spots are, the smaller negative z-scores get. Based on p-values and z-scores of this statistic, 17 pattern types include: no pattern detected, new hot spot, consecutive hot spot, intensifying hot spot, persistent hot spot, diminishing hot spot, sporadic hot spot, oscillating hot spot, historical hot spot, new cold spot, consecutive cold spot, intensifying cold spot, persistent cold spot, diminishing Cold Spot, sporadic cold spot, oscillating cold spot and historical cold spot are extracted [9].

17.3   Results of Proposed Model

In this chapter, the confirmed cases of the COVID-19 in all countries around the world based on WHO reports until June 24 were used as input signals. The proposed model of this research was implemented in four steps: 1) identification of significant periods using CWT, 2) extraction of effective features using DWT, 3) prediction of cases with neural network based on the outputs of steps 1 and 2, and 4) extraction of hot/cold spot patterns. The procedure and the results of each step are discussed below.

17.3.1   Identification of significant periods using CWT

The COVID-19 epidemic is a highly contagious disease and may have a long incubation period, which means that patients understand it late and therefore quickly infects others without regarding social distance. Therefore, many people get the disease in a short period of time, and after an incubation period, the number of patients suddenly increases significantly. This trend is easily understood from the COVID-19 confirmed cases data and important periods can be deduced from them.

The confirmed cases of the COVID-19 were divided into train and test data as input signals. The data for the last 7 days (17 to June 24, 2020) of each country was selected as the test data. Due to the high outbreak of COVID-19 and its long and short incubation periods, signal behavior can be analyzed, its relative and absolute maxima can be identified, and significant periods can be recognized for each country. The CWT was used to extract significant periods and these periods were used as delays in the prediction step. The significant frequency (reverse of the period), the date of its occurrence, and the magnitude were calculated for each country and shown on 3D plot (Figure 17.1). Based on the 3D surfaces, relative or local maxima were identified to determine the peak of important periods. For each country, periods, magnitudes, and dates of its occurrence have been identified by the CWT. The aim of this chapter is to investigate the longer and shorter serial intervals of COVID-19 that are associated with the incubation periods. The period of incubation for COVID-19 is the time between virus exposure and the onset of symptoms, which can be contagious to some people during this period. Understanding the incubation period enables health authorities to establish more effective quarantine systems for people suspected of carrying the virus as a means of monitoring and preventing the spread of the virus [1].Based on WHO reports, the incubation period for seasonal influenza, SARS, and MERS was typically around 2-14 days. Various studies have been conducted to determine the period of COVID-19. Qun Li et al. has found the incubation period to be 5.2 days on average [30] but in another research these periods were between 3 and 7 days, up to 14 days [31]. In addition, other cases with 19 and 27 incubation periods were reported by Hubei province. These periods were between 2-14 and 2-10 days based on the United States' CDC and WHO reports, respectively [1].

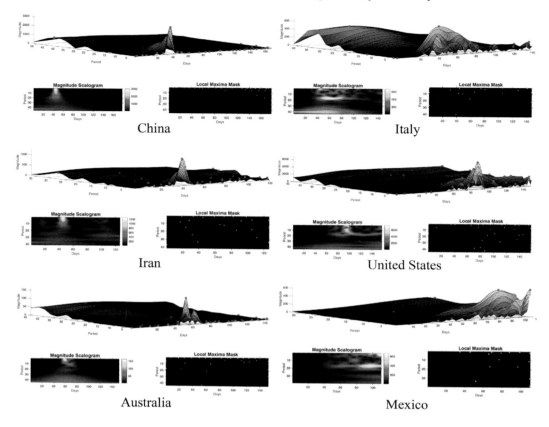

FIGURE 17.1
The CWT results for COVID-19 confirmed cases of six countries.

Previous research, based on clinical trials, identified incubation periods for some countries using restricted cases. While in this chapter, significant periods (the longer and shorter serial intervals of COVID-19) for all countries have been identified based on CWT and the input signal that their accuracy depends on the accuracy of WHO reports. They can considerably represent incubation periods. For example, according to the results of this research, significant periods for China were 2.72, 4.41, 5.43, 16.46, 17.64, 40.53, and 65.85 days which 2.71 and 40.53 days were more important than others. Also, COVID-19 important periods for Italy were about 3, 4, 7, 9, 38, 47, and 53 days while these periods for Iran were about 3, 4, 6, 12, 14, 22, and 47 days. It was done for each country and the important periods of each country were identified. For example, periods in China, Italy, Iran, the United States, Australia, and Mexico are shown in Figure 17.1. The results indicate that the three days period was important in most countries. Periods of 2-14 days and periods greater than 25, 40, and 65 days were also very notable. In particular, the (2-7)-day period was very important as one of the results of this research that was emphasized in previous clinical studies. The range and frequency of important periods that were extracted for all countries are shown in Figure 17.2. Comparison of CWT results and clinical studies reveals that the research outcome is highly accurate, which can be easily derived from the reported COVID-19 cases for all countries.

Also, due to the different results of the use of different mother wavelet functions, each CWT function was examined for each country and the function that had better RMSE was selected for each country. For instance, the best CWT function for the United States, China, Italy, Australia, and Mexico was bump and morlet (amor) for Iran.

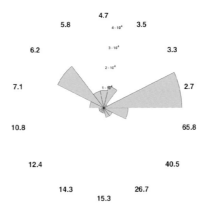

FIGURE 17.2
The range and frequency of important periods of all countries around the world based on CWT results.

17.3.2   Extraction of effective features using DWT

After identifying the significant periods of each country in the previous step, they can be used as a time series prediction delay. In other words, previous days which had an impact on the number of cases each day were determined by these periods for the neural network. The input signal (or the probability density function of patients) alone is not sufficient to predict accurately and it is better to extract the features from the original signal. Because the confirmed number of patients with COVID-19 is affected by many different factors that are not easily identifiable. For example, cultural factors in the timely referral of patients, a number of tests in each country, the integrity of governments in reporting cases, and so on, have a direct impact on the number of reported cases, although they are almost impossible to characterize due to lack of data. Therefore, it is better to extract the features of the daily COVID-19 reports from the input data signals. Artificial intelligence can consider features without identifying the name and type of features.

The DWT is one of the most popular tools for feature extraction. In this study, the five signal levels for each country were calculated by DWT. In the first step, the DWT was applied to the input signal and the approximation and detail were extracted. In the next step, this transformation was applied to the approximation extracted from the previous level. This process continued for five levels and finally, five approximations and details were obtained. All details of the levels and the approximation of the last level were used as ANN features. For example, the result of applying DWT to Iran confirmed cases is shown in Figure 17.3 with D1, D2, D3, D4, D5, and A5. The DWT has been done for all countries, and the features of each country have been identified for entry into the ANN.

Also in DWT, different mother wavelet functions with different orders were evaluated and the function that led to the lowest RMSE for each country was selected. For example, the best DWT functions for the United States, China, Italy, Iran, Australia, and Mexico were fk22, coif1, d6, sym9, db1, and coif5, respectively. Figure 17.4 shows the results of CWT and DWT implementation of different mother wavelet functions for each country. For 213 countries and territories around the world, 3 mother wavelet families of CWT and 6 mother wavelet families with 40 types of DWT functions were implemented. For example, in the 152nd country, Russia, bump and rbio were chosen as the appropriate mother wavelet functions. The numerical proportions of the use of CWT and DWT mother wavelet functions are also shown in the left and right pie charts of Figure 17.4. The results show that morse and bior1.1 were the most desirable functions among the CWT and DWT functions which were used 41.95% and 16.0976%, respectively.

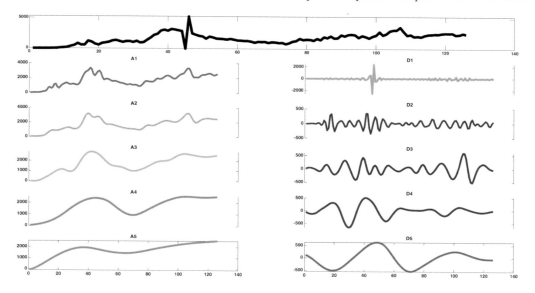

FIGURE 17.3
The DWT results for COVID-19 confirmed cases of Iran.

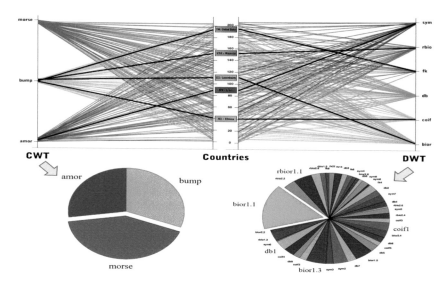

FIGURE 17.4
Comparison of CWT and DWT mother wavelet functions.

17.3.3 Prediction model based on a neural network

The extracted features must be delayed according to the detected periods before entering the ANN. Thus, the number of input features was $(ns+k)^*np$, where k is the number of input signals (k=1), ns is the number of sub-series, and np is the number of important periods for each country. In this study, ns was six because there were five levels of detail (D1, D2, D3, D4, and D5) and one level of approximation (A5). For example, the most important periods for Australia were about 3, 4, 9, and 41 days. They applied to the main signal and all subseries (k, D1, D2, D3, D4, D5, and A1) and

$4^*(6+1)$ features (28 features) were prepared as the network inputs. A single-layer perceptron neural network with a sigmoid transfer function has been implemented for each country. The advantages of the MLP network and the reason for choosing the sigmoid function were described in the materials and methods section. As a generalization error is so important in predicting time series, an attempt has been made to select a network size as small as possible to prevent overfitting.

After selecting the features and creating an optimal network, based on the confirmed cases of the COVID-19 up to June 17, the networks were trained and, for the last seven days, the forecast was carried out as test data. The prediction models have been developed for all countries and the results for the six countries: the United States, China, Italy, Iran, Australia, and Mexico are presented in Figure 17.5. In these plots, the horizontal axis is the number of the days, the vertical axis is the number of patients, the red dashed line is the observed cases, the continuous blue line is the predicted cases, and the white and gray parts are the train and test sections of data, respectively. These plots show the spread of the disease, its peaks, sudden increases, and the results of predictions in each country. The RMSE of train and test data has been calculated to evaluate the results of the prediction. The best and worst RMSE of predictions among these six countries were for Australia and the United States with 4.23 and 2264.92 for test data as well as 61.6852 and 3631.14 for train data. For a more detailed review, the test and train RMSE values, CWT and DWT mother wavelet functions, and the significant periods in 14 countries that are more affected by the COVID-19 are shown in Table 17.1.

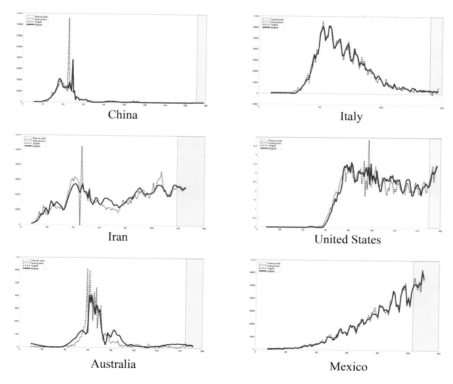

FIGURE 17.5
Prediction results of the COVID-19 confirmed cases for six countries.

TABLE 17.1
List of detailed information about inputs and results of prediction in 14 counties.

Country	Train RMSE	Test RMSE	CWT	DWT	Periods
Australia	61.6852	4.23448	bump	db1	2.72- 4.41 9.46- 40.54
Brazil	2094.0814	6800.2734	amor	rbio1.1	2.72- 3.34 3.58- 5.43 6.69- 7.68 21.72- 43.45
Canada	154.2365	30.5101	morse	bior1.5	2.72- 4.12 8.23- 13.37 26.74- 53.49
China	1101.6565	8.70	bump	coif1	2.72- 4.41 5.43- 16.46 17.64- 40.53 65.85
Germany	356.2333	81.2454	amor	coif3	2.72- 6.69- 10.86 13.37- 15.36 53.49
India	208.8657	1329.085	morse	bior1.5	2.72- 2.91 3.58- 5.07 6.24-7.17 8.82-20.27
Iran	456.87	82.5656	amor	sym9	2.72-3.84 6.24-11.64 14.33-21.72 46.56
Italy	219.5788	329.0488	bump	db6	2.72- 3.58 6.69- 9.46 37.82-46.56 53.49
Mexico	135.006	329.0488	bump	coif5	2.72- 2.91 3.84-4.12 6.69- 13.37 17.64-30.72
Russia	162.9836	145.0177	bump	rbio2.4	2.72-3.84 6.69-18.91 20.27- 30.72 53.49
South Korea	625.2626	12.3547	morse	sym9	2.72-3.58 4.12- 4.73 5.07-7.17 28.66- 43.45
Spain	411.7153	83.6592	amor	db2	2.72- 3.34 5.82-6.24 7.17- 8.23 13.37- 49.91
Turkey	77.9651	297.4952	morse	db5	2.72- 3.84 4.41-5.82 7.68- 9.46 18.91-37.82
United States	3631.1439	2264.9258	bump	fk22	2.72- 3.12 4.12-6.69 768- 28.66 43.45- 57.33

17.3.4 Extraction of hot/cold spot patterns

Finally, the COVID-19 pattern maps were prepared with the STHCSA at different periods. The neighborhood time step must be specified in the preparation of this map. The neighborhood time step is the number of time-step intervals to be used in the neighborhood of analysis. This value specifies which features are evaluated together to determine local clustering in space-time cube [28]. Hot/Cold spots of the COVID-19 confirmed cases in the world countries with one-day neighbors until March 21, 2020 are presented in Figure 17.6.

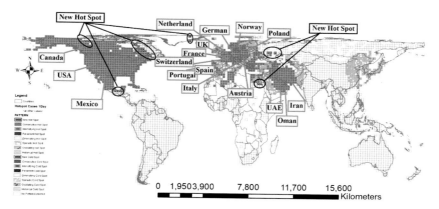

FIGURE 17.6
The STHCSA results for confirmed cases with a day temporal neighborhood steps.

The spatiotemporal patterns were identified with respect to the number of confirmed cases, the area, the spatial and temporal neighbors of each country. Countries such as the USA, Italy, Germany, France, Portugal, Mexico, Iran, Poland, Austria, Switzerland, Netherlands, and UAE have consecutive hot spots according to the results in Figure 17.6. The consecutive hot spot is a location with a single continuous run of statistically notable hot spot bins in the final time-step intervals. New hot spots in countries like Canada, Mexico, Cuba, Egypt, and Russia were also identified. Other countries were recognized as the oscillating hot spot or without a pattern. The new hot spot area is a location that is statistically significant for the final time step and has never been a statistically significant hot spot before. The oscillating hot spot is a region with high temporal oscillation patterns. With the temporal neighborhood increasing to three days, parts of Australia and Venezuela had been identified as historic cold spots and western China as oscillating cold spots. New hot spots had been detected in Brazil, Mexico, Russia, and Australia based on data until March 21, and after this date, there was a huge increase especially in Brazil and Russia.

Then, the spatiotemporal patterns were re-examined and shown in Figure 17.7 by entering all the data until June 24. The temporal neighborhood steps were entered as 3, 6, and 66 days according to the important periods extracted for the whole world and results are shown in Figure 17.7.a, 17.7.b, and 17.7.c, respectively. With increasing temporal neighborhood steps from 3 to 66 days, oscillation and consecutive hot spots have increased by 14% for Asian and European regions and about 10% for the United States. Countries like India, Brazil, Mexico, and Russia have become oscillation and consecutive hot spots. According to the results, many parts of the southern hemisphere have been identified as persistent and intensifying cold spots due to their low confirmed cases and cold spots have also increased by 20%.

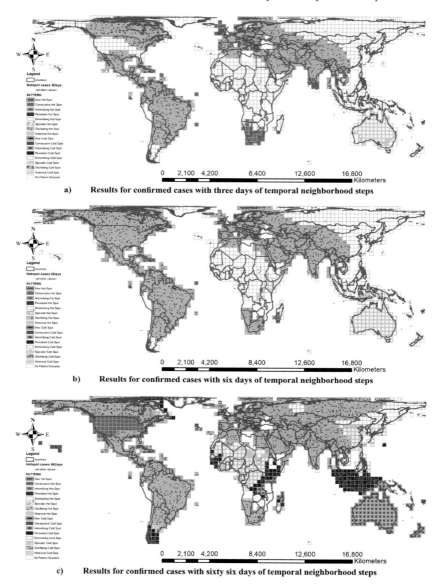

a)   **Results for confirmed cases with three days of temporal neighborhood steps**

b)   **Results for confirmed cases with six days of temporal neighborhood steps**

c)   **Results for confirmed cases with sixty six days of temporal neighborhood steps**

FIGURE 17.7
The STHCSA maps.

17.4   Discussion

The (2-7)-day period had a large magnitude in the results of this research, which had also been highlighted in clinical research. Results also highlighted periods greater than 25, 40, and 65 days which should be considered, whereas clinical trials had recorded only periods about 25 days. It seems that if the time series data are recorded correctly in terms of number and time, the higher the rate of infection and the incubation period of the diseases, the more possible it will be to extract important periods from them. The 3, 6, and 66-day periods with a large magnitude are shown in Figure 17.8. The size of the symbols indicates the normalized magnitude of the periods and their colors show the importance of the classes that are classified by the k-means.

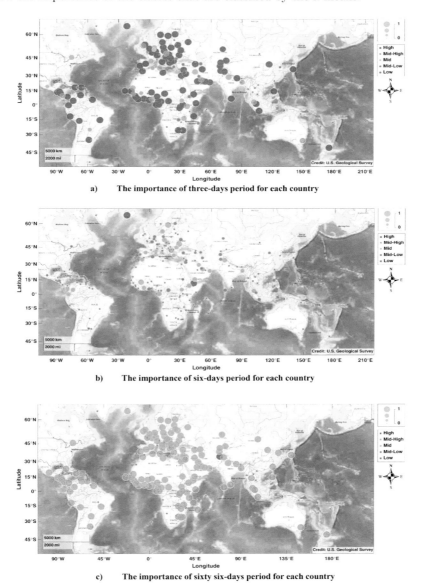

a) The importance of three-days period for each country

b) The importance of six-days period for each country

c) The importance of sixty six-days period for each country

FIGURE 17.8
The important periods of the COVID-19 with their magnitude.

There have been periods of 3 and 66 days in many countries, but the magnitude of three days periods was much greater than 66 days. Periods of six days have been observed in many parts of Europe, some parts of Africa, and South America. Neighboring countries may have an impact on the similarity of the importance of periods.

In the COVID-19 prediction for each country, the performance of the proposed model was investigated in different situations based on the test and train RMSE, and the DWT and CWT mother wavelet functions were determined as well as an optimal network was built. Since train data was larger than test data and there had been significant changes and sudden increases in the train data, test accuracy was higher than train accuracy in many countries. Therefore, the train data was much more irregular than the test data.

Due to the different populations, confirmed cases and periods of infection in different countries, the RMSE is not sufficient to compare the accuracy of prediction for various countries. RMSEIQR can be more compatible to compare different data sets through IQR normalization. It has been determined for train and test data in all countries and the best and worst values are shown in Figure 17.9. According to the proposed model and the train data, Russia with RMSEIQR of 0.018 was the best, and Mauritania with 54.2689 was the worst prediction of this study.

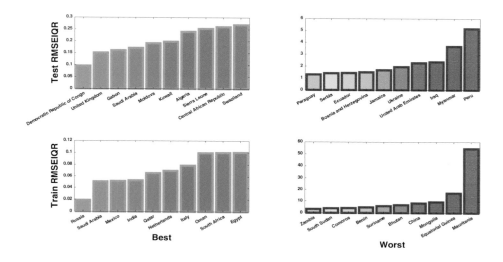

FIGURE 17.9
Comparison of test and train RMSEIQR.

Based on the test data, the Democratic Republic of Congo with RMSEIQR of 0.095 was the best, and Peru with 5.14 was the worst. The results indicate that the performance of the prediction was sufficient for almost all countries. In particular, the networks of countries such as Russia, Mexico, Italy, the United Kingdom, India, Saudi Arabia, and the Congo were the most efficient.

17.5   Conclusion

In this chapter, daily reports of the COVID-19 cases through different countries of the world were used to discover important periods of the disease. The results indicate that the COVID-19 has different short-term and long-term periods in different countries of the world, but in general, the main important periods were between 2 and 7 days, which had been demonstrated by clinical study for limited countries. Significant long periods, such as 66 days and 41 days, have also been detected by CWT. Then, by DWT, the features were extracted and important periods were used as a delay on the main signal and the extracted features. The neural network was then built based on the results of the previous steps and the COVID-19 cases were predicted. Results were acceptable with an average train and test RMSEIQR equivalent to 1.2785 and 0.6695, respectively.

Finally, hot/cold spots were identified by analyzing spatiotemporal patterns. The existence of 48.78% and 13.20% of oscillation and consecutive hot spot patterns around the world indicate the widespread spatiotemporal distribution of this epidemic. Prediction and analysis of hot/cold spots are useful for finding high-risk areas. Accurate predictions of cases and deaths can help politicians and decision-makers to legislate until the COVID-19 vaccine is discovered. A comparison of various neural networks and their tunes with optimization methods may be discussed in future research. Also, effective environmental and social factors in the COVID-19 and the impact of neighboring countries will be extracted which are recommended for further study in this field.

References

[1] Novel Coronavirus (2019-nCoV) situation reports - World Health Organization (WHO), https://covid19.who.int [accessed on 5 October 2020].

[2] Lai, Ch. Ch., Shih, T. P., Ko, W. Ch., Tang, H. J., Hsueh, P. R., 2020. Severe acute respiratory syndrome coronavirus 2 (SARS-CoV-2) and coronavirus disease-2019 (COVID-19): The epidemic and the challenges. International Journal of Antimicrobial Agents, 55, 105924. doi: 10.1016/j.ijantimicag.2020.105924.

[3] Celso A. G. Santos, C. A. G., Freire, P. K. M. M., Akrami, S. A., Silva, R. M. D., 2019. Hybrid Wavelet Neural Network Approach for Daily Inflow Forecasting Using Tropical Rainfall Measuring Mission Data. Journal of Hydrologic Engineering 24(2). doi: 10.1061/(ASCE)HE.1943-5584.0001725.

[4] Al-Ahmadi, Kh., Alahmadi, S., Al-Zahrani, A., 2019. Spatiotemporal Clustering of Middle East Respiratory Syndrome Coronavirus (MERS-CoV) Incidence in Saudi Arabia, 2012–2019. International Journal of Environmental Research and Public Health, 16(14), 1-14. doi:10.3390/ijerph16142520.

[5] Mongkolsawat, Ch., Kamchai, T., 2008. GIS Modeling for Avian Influenza Risk Areas, 2nd international conference on HealthGIS, Bangkok, 14-16 January.

[6] Li, Z., Fu, J., Lin, G., Jiang, D., 2019. Spatiotemporal Variation and Hotspot Detection of the Avian Influenza A(H7N9) Virus in China, 2013–2017. International Journal of Environmental Research and Public Health, 16, 648; doi:10.3390/ijerph16040648.

[7] Zhu, X., Fu, B., Yang, Y., Ma, Y., Hao, J., Chen, S., Liu, Sh., Li, T., Liu, S., Guo, W., Liao, Zh., 2019. Attention-based recurrent neural network for influenza epidemic prediction. BMC Bioinformatics, 20(18), 575. doi: 10.1186/s12859-019-3131-8.

[8] Venna, S.R., Tavanaei, A., Gottumukkala, R. N., Raghavan, V. V., Maida, A. S., Nichols, S., 2019. A novel data-driven model for real-time influenza forecasting. IEEE Access, 7, 7691–7701. doi: 10.1109/ACCESS.2018.2888585.

[9] Spataru, R., 2018. Spatial-temporal GIS analysis in public health: a case study of polio disease, Master Thesis, Department of Physical Geography and Ecosystem Science, Centre for Geographical Information Systems, Lund University, Sweden.

[10] Guan, W., Ni, Z., Hu, Y., Liang, W., Ou, C., He, J., Liu, L., Shan, H., Lei, C., Hui, D. S. C., Du, B., Li, L., Zeng, G., Yuen, K. Y., Chen, R., Tang, C., Wang, T., Chen, P., Xiang, J., Li, S., Wang, J. L., Liang, Z., Peng, Y., Wei, L., Liu, Y., Hu, Y. H., Peng, P., Wang, J. M., Liu, J., Chen, Z., Li, G., Zheng, Z., Qiu, S., Luo, J., Ye, C., Zhu, S., Zhong, N., 2020. Clinical Characteristics of Coronavirus Disease 2019 in China. The New England Journal of Medicine. doi: 10.1056/NEJMoa2002032.

[11] Kuniya, T., 2020. Prediction of the Epidemic Peak of Coronavirus Disease in Japan, Journal of Clinical Medicine, 9, 789; doi:10.3390/jcm9030789.

[12] Al-qaness, M. A. A., Ewees, A. A., Fan,H ., Aziz, M. A. E., 2020. Optimization method for forecasting confirmed cases of COVID-19 in China. Journal of Clinical Medicine, 9, 674. doi:10.3390/jcm9030674.

[13] Chakraborty, T., Ghosh, I., 2020. Real-time forecasts and risk assessment of novel coronavirus (COVID-19) cases: A data-driven analysis. medRxiv. doi:10.1101/2020.04.09.20059311.

[14] Tamang, S. K., Singh, P. D., Datta, B., 2020. Forecasting of Covid-19 cases based on prediction using artificial neural network curve fitting technique. Global J. Environ. Sci. Manage, 6 (SI): 53-64. doi:10.22034/GJESM.2019.06.SI.06.

[15] Dyllon, Sh., Xiao, P., 2018. Wavelet Transform for Educational Network Data Traffic Analysis. Wavelet Theory and Its Applications, IntechOpen,eBook (PDF) ISBN: 978-1-83881-536-3. doi: 10.5772/intechopen.76455.

[16] Nourani Esfetanaj, N., Nojavan, S., 2018. The Use of Hybrid Neural Networks, Wavelet Transform and Heuristic Algorithm of WIPSO in Smart Grids to Improve Short-Term Prediction of Load, Solar Power, and Wind Energy. Chapter 4, Operation of Distributed Energy Resources in Smart Distribution Networks. doi: 10.1016/B978-0-12-814891-4.00004-7.

[17] Conejo, A.J., Plazas, M., Espinola, R., Molina, A.B., 2005. Day-ahead electricity price forecasting using the wavelet transform and ARIMA models, Power Systems, IEEE Trans, 20, 1035-1042. doi: 10.1109/TPWRS.2005.846054.

[18] Ahmed. O., Ovinis, M., Hashim, F., 2017. Osei, H. Time Delay Estimation Using Continuous Wavelet Transform Coefficients. Journal of Computational and Theoretical Nanoscience 23(2):1299-1303. doi: 10.1166/asl.2017.8377.

[19] Farge, M., 1992. Wavelet Transforms and Their Application to Turbulence. Ann. Rev. Fluid. Mech., 24, 395–457. doi: 10.1146/annurev.fl.24.010192.002143.

[20] Lilly, J. M., 2016. jLab: A data analysis package for Matlab, version 1.6.2., http://www.jmlilly.net/jmlsoft.html [accessed on 8 July 2020].

[21] Chaovalit, P., Gangopadhyay, A., Karabatis, G., Chen, Zh., 2011. Discrete wavelet transform-based time series analysis and mining. ACM Computing Surveys, 43(2), 1-37. doi: 10.1145/1883612.1883613.

[22] Merry, R. J. E., 2005. Wavelet theory and applications: a literature study. (DCT rapporten; Vol. 2005.053).

[23] Rosenblatt, F., 1961. Principles of Neurodynamics: Perceptrons and the Theory of Brain Mechanisms. Spartan Books, Washington DC.

[24] Klimasauskas, C. C., 1991. Applying neural networks, part III: Training a neural network. PC-AI, 20-24.

[25] Li, L., Girguis, M., Lurmann, F., Wu, J., Urman, R., Rappaport, E., Ritz, B., Franklin, M., Breton, C., Gilliland, F., Habre, R., 2019. Cluster-based bagging of constrained mixed-effects models for high spatiotemporal resolution nitrogen oxides prediction over large regions. Environment International, 128, 310–323.doi: 10.1016/j.envint.2019.04.057.

[26] Zeng D, Chang W, Chen H., 2004. A comparative study of Spatio-temporal hotspot analysis techniques in security informatics. The 7th International IEEE Conference on Intelligent Transportation Systems, doi: 10.1109/ITSC.2004.1398880.

[27] NetCDF Home Page,https://www.unidata.ucar.edu/software/netcdf/ [accessed on 8 July 2020].

[28] ESRI, 2016, ArcGIS Resources Center. https://pro.arcgis.com/en/pro-app/latest/tool-reference/spatial-statistics/h-how-hot-spot-analysis-getis-ord-gi-spatial-stati.htm [accessed on 26 March 2020].

[29] Abdulhafedh A., 2017. A Novel Hybrid Method for Measuring the Spatial Autocorrelation of Vehicular Crashes: Combining Moran's Index and Getis-Ord Gi* Statistic. Open Journal of Civil Engineering, 7, 208-221. doi:10.4236/ojce.2017.72013.

[30] Qun Li et al., 2020. Early Transmission Dynamics in Wuhan, China, of Novel Coronavirus–Infected Pneumonia - New England Journal of Medicine, 382(13), 1-9. doi: 10.1056/NEJMoa2001316.

[31] Bai, Y., Yao, L., , Wei, T., Tian, F., Jin, D. Y., Chen, L., Wang, M., 2020. Presumed Asymptomatic Carrier Transmission of COVID-19. JAMA, 323(14), 1406-1407. doi: 10.1056/NEJMoa2001316.

Part III

Regional, Country and Local Applications

18

London in Lockdown: Mobility in the Pandemic City

Michael Batty, Roberto Murcio, Iacopo Iacopini, Maarten Vanhoof and Richard Milton

This chapter looks at the spatial distribution and mobility patterns of essential and non-essential workers before and during the COVID-19 pandemic in London, and compares them to the rest of the UK. In the 3-month lockdown that started on 23 March 2020, 20% of the workforce was deemed to be pursuing essential jobs. The other 80% were either furloughed which meant being supported by the government to not work, or working from home. Based on travel journey data between zones (983 zones in London; 8,436 zones in England, Wales and Scotland), trips were decomposed into essential and non-essential trips. Despite some big regional differences within the UK, we find that essential workers have much the same spatial patterning as non-essential for all occupational groups containing essential and non-essential workers. Also, the amount of travel time saved by working from home during the Pandemic is roughly the same proportion – 80% – as the separation between essential and non-essential workers. Further, the loss of travel, reduction in workers, reductions in retail spending as well as increases in use of parks are examined in different London boroughs using Google Mobility Reports which give us a clear picture of what has happened over the last 6 months since the first Lockdown. These reports also now imply that a second wave of infection is beginning.

18.1   The 2020 Pandemic in Britain

On 23 March 2020, Britain locked down to protect its population against what by then was widely recognised as a global Pandemic. Its population watched in horror the reports from Northern Italy of rising deaths and a health system that was simply overwhelmed with serious cases requiring intensive care. Spain was not far behind while the rest of Europe was catching up fast. COVID-19 had overwhelmed the city of Wuhan where the virus was first detected in a wildlife market in early November 2019 but the serious nature of the disease was not appreciated until it was literally on our doorstep. By March, it was clear that the disease was particularly serious for older age groups whose mortality rates for those above 80 who were admitted to hospital were close to 50%. The Lockdown introduced in late March was designed to stop the spread of the disease, using the time honoured method of keeping people apart until the disease could be contained which was generally assumed to have occurred when the so-called R number – its rate of change – dropped below 1. Although the Lockdown was reviewed every three weeks, in fact it lasted some three months to mid-June when it became apparent that the virus had been contained. It was then deemed 'safe' to open up parts of the economy again to social interactions, notwithstanding fairly strict measures of social distancing that mandated people to keep 2 metres apart from one another, wear masks to avoid spreading the virus through respiratory means, and to wash hands frequently to remove any traces of the virus that might have been picked up from surfaces.

The restrictions imposed by the Lockdown were designed to protect the UK National Health Service which to some extent, is the most revered public service in Britain, the only function of government to have survived the dismantling of the Welfare State that proceeded apace as Britain emerged from its industrial past. The key elements of the Lockdown involved staying at home to stop the disease spreading between households. To this end, the only exceptions were shopping for basic necessities, one form of exercise a day, medical needs, care for the vulnerable, and travelling to or from work to carry out essential services. These mandates meant no household mixing, no meeting friends or family members living in separate homes, no gatherings of more than two people in public, and no social or sporting events. Schools and churches were closed. These were Draconian measures by peacetime standards and essentially put the economy and social life into cold storage. The summer months saw a gradual opening up of the economy but in a dramatically constrained way. However by the late summer in September, it was clear that a second wave could be detected through a rapid increase in testing for the virus [1]. Hospital admissions began to rise and at the time of writing (end October 2020) half the country is now back in some form of Lockdown, a little less severe perhaps than the original with some hospitality, schools, shops and work still open, but with strong advice to continue working from home wherever possible and with no household mixing in the most infectious hotspots. With winter approaching, the predictions are that although the shows no signs of loosening its grip and becoming less virulent, there are vaccines on the horizon whilst our medical knowledge of how to combat the disease with pharmaceutical inventions has increased. The hope is that although the number of cases may well outstrip the peak earlier in the year, the overall impact will be less severe. However assuming a vaccine becomes available by early 2021, it will take a Herculean effort to mass vaccinate an entire population.

If you lockdown an economy in the way many governments have to combat the spread of this disease, the impact on where people work, live, and entertain is dramatic. The effect of the Pandemic has and continues to have largely destroyed our quest to travel using public or group transport. Although our focus here is not on the economic impact, there are obvious changes to the locations which we traditionally visit or frequent where we engage in the routine activities of working, shopping, educating ourselves, socialising and so on, all activities that usually require us to gather together in groups of all sizes and at all scales. The mandates of social distancing operate at the most local level but these translate themselves into how we might travel more globally throughout the metropolitan area, regionally, nationally and internationally for we need to observe the mandates for keeping apart when we use public transport of any kind [2].

In this chapter, we will illustrate the impact of COVID-19 on changes in mobility in both the UK and in a world city where changes in where and how we travel have been dramatic. London has one of the biggest central areas of any city worldwide, diversified into financial, retail, and government functions in several distinct cores all of which have been emptied of workers since the hit. In the financial quarter – the 'square mile' or the City – which is the traditional heart of the metropolis, half a million people usually work largely in financial and legal services and cognate activities but most have been absent, working from home, for the last 6 months since the Pandemic began. In the inner part of the metropolis, the Greater London Authority (GLA) area, home to a population of some 8 million, about 40% of all those travelling use public transport and these services have been operating at little more than 30% capacity. It is estimated that 16% of the 5 million workers in this GLA area were classed as 'key' or 'essential, with permission to work during the first Lockdown. There has been an exodus of population to the outer suburbs and to the countryside, just as happened in the last great plague that hit London in 1665 when Parliament moved to Oxford. Retail activity within the City has all but ceased and many outlets have closed, reportedly more than 1,000 in the GLA area with little sign that these closures are anywhere near complete.

In some respects, a full analysis of a city under a Pandemic is an impossible task until the Pandemic ends because the restrictions on normal life are continually changing. Here, however, we will focus on mobility examining the extent to which the patterns of movement we have already noted have been disrupted by the need to social distance on all spatial scales. We will begin by examining the location patterns of essential and non-essential workers in London which are defined in terms of occupations and which are assumed to separate workers who have remained at their place of work during the Pandemic from those who are either furloughed and supported by the government (to not work) or are working from home. We will extend this analysis to how different types of workers travel between home and work under the Pandemic.

Although our analysis is largely inconclusive with respect to defining distinct differences between essential and non-essential workers in terms of their geospatial attributes, we then follow up this analysis by examining a more detailed picture of changes in travel patterns using Google's Mobility Reports. These reveal significant differences between movements associated with several physical activities ranging from transit to the use of parks and using this type of data, we can easily demonstrate how mobility varies systematically across the metropolis illustrating quite profound differences between the city core, the inner area and the outer suburbs. In fact a full analysis of all this data for cities and regions in the UK is still to be attempted but the particular case of London does provide a focus for informed speculation about how the Pandemic might end with respect to possible changes in mobility. From this data too, because it relates to how visits to different activities vary throughout the Pandemic starting in mid-February 2020 providing data each day until 18 October (the time of writing), we can see detailed change in the time series and in this way, detect the rise of the second wave and the difficulties of bringing the economy back until a vaccine is in sight. Last but not least, we will use this particular analysis to hint at ways in which London might transition to a new normal different but similar to the old normal once the Pandemic ends.

18.2   Defining Essential Workers

When the government locked the country down, it first defined a group of 'key' or 'essential' workers whose endeavours were required to keep the country running. It produced a list of such workers defined in terms of the proportion of the numbers of persons in the 9 occupational classes defined by the Office of National Statistics and used in the Population Census. By applying the proportions to the numbers in each of the occupational classes, it is possible to derive the numbers of essential workers in each class and it is possible to do this at the level of the standard regions in the UK of which there are 12. This is the finest level of granularity we have for occupational classes at the level of the resident population which we need to work with because we need to disaggregate our trip patterns for the journey to work by occupational class so that we can generate the distribution of such classes at the workplace end of the trip. In short, our basic data involves the flows of workers from their place of residence to their place of work, data collected by the UK Population at the census year, the latest of which is 2011, updated to 2019 by proportional factoring. As all this data is grounded at the place of residence, we need to work backward by disaggregating trips by occupation at the residence and then computing occupational classes at the workplace end of the trip. This then enables us to calculate the number of essential workers at both ends of the trip.

To indicate how we generate this data, trips between a workplace i and a residential location j are first defined by mode of travel k as T_{ij}^k from the updated Census data. This is consistent with employment E_i in workplace i and working population P_j at residential location j defined from $E_i = \sum_j \sum_k T_{ij}^k$ and $P_j = \sum_i \sum_k T_{ij}^k$. As we know the proportions of occupations o at the residential end of the trip ρ_j^o, we can apply these first to generate a disaggregate pattern of trips $T_{ij}^{ko} = \rho_j^o T_{ij}^k$ from which we can compute both the working population and the employment by occupational group at the residential and workplace ends of the trip $P_j^o = \rho_j^o P_j = \rho_j^o \sum_i \sum_k T_{ij}^k$ and $E_i^o = \sum_j \sum_k \rho_j^o T_{ij}^k$. We also need to divide employment, working population and trips into essential (es) and non-essential (ne) workers. We have this for the residential end of the trip from more aggregate data where we define $\rho_j^o = \rho_j^o(es) + \rho_j^o(ne)$ and we then use these proportions to generate the essential and non-essential workers and working populations as

$$\left.\begin{array}{l} E_i^o(es) = \sum_j \sum_k \rho_j^o(es) T_{ij}^k \quad , \quad E_i^o(ne) = \sum_j \sum_k \rho_j^o(ne) T_{ij}^k \\ P_j^o(es) = \rho_j^o(es) \sum_i \sum_k T_{ij}^k \quad , \quad P_j^o(ne) = \rho_j^o(ne) \sum_i \sum_k T_{ij}^k \\ E_i = E_i^o(es) + E_i^o(ne) \quad , \quad P_j = P_j^o(es) + P_j^o(ne) \end{array}\right\} \tag{18.1}$$

We now need to consider the volumes of essential workers from the data before we embark on our first foray into examining the distribution of those who are still working during the first

Lockdown. To get some sense of the variation in the distribution of essential and non-essential workers, we can aggregate the employment and working populations given in equation 18.1 to the UK and then to Greater London. In Table we show $E^o = \sum_i E_i^o$ and $E^o(es) = \sum_i E_i^o(es)$ and $E_{GLA}^o = \sum_{i \in GLA} E_i^o$ and $E_{GLA}^o(es) = \sum_{i \in GLA} E_i^o(es)$ and it is clear that there are substantial differences between different locations as well as between the volume of different occupations for different levels of spatial aggregation.

The way the government defined essential workers was based on particular subcategories of occupation whose families required support such as child care [3], and these subcategories varied in size for each occupational class in different areas and were defined from the Standard Occupational Classification (SOC) which has a very detailed breakdown of the 9 basic occupations. The percentages of workers in each basic occupation determined to be essential are illustrated in Table 18.1 for the UK and for London. It is immediately clear that the proportion of essential workers in London is much smaller than in the whole UK, 16% compared to 24% and although we do not have space here to examine these variations over the whole country, they are significant and thus make a big difference to the sheer volume of mobile workers during the Lockdown for the entire country. In fact in this project we have extended our analysis to England, Scotland and Wales using the Census geography of the middle-layer super output areas (MSOAs) of which there are 8,436 in Great Britain (where we use the term Britain as a short hand for the three countries involved) but here we will focus only on London. Our figure of 24% working in essential services in the UKL compares well with the figure of 22% from the Institute of Fiscal Studies which is also based on the list of key occupations provided by government [4] but applied slightly differently.

In Table 18.1, where we show total and essential workers by occupational categories for the UK and London, we first note that the relative importance of managerial and professional groups (the first three categories) which are much greater for essential workers in the UK than in London. The table also shows that the proportions of carers acting as essential workers in the UK is twice that of London. If we look at the last two columns in Table 18.1 where we have computed the proportions of non-essential and essential occupational groups for the UK and London in terms of the total employment of each area, we see that proportions of non-essential and essential managerial-professional groups is a little higher in London with skilled trades a little lower and caring and leisure services somewhat higher. A closer analysis of Table 18.1 suggests that London is weighted more to managerial occupations and service occupations than the UK in general but that in these occupations there are less proportions in the essential workers category than the UK in general. This bears out in very broad terms the fact that there are less non-essential workers in London with the implication that is non-essential are likely to be working from home, mobility levels will be a lot less than other parts of the country.

Our preliminary analysis of this data involves examining the relative distributions of essential and non-essential workers at their place of work and at their place of residence. In the analysis, we aggregated the occupational data, thus, working with essential and non-essential workers at their workplace and residence. These are defined from the above employments as

$$\left. \begin{array}{l} E_i(es) = \sum_o E_i^o(es) \\ E_i(ne) = \sum_o E_i^o(ne) \\ P_j(es) = \sum_o P_j^o(es) \\ P_j(ne) = \sum_o P_j^o(ne) \end{array} \right\} \tag{18.2}$$

We initially speculated that essential workers would travel less distances to work than non-essential, especially in London and this would be reflected in their work and home locations. We would expect non-essential to be more clustered towards the centre of the city although the complications of the London housing market could well obscure such a clear pattern because central and inner London are now so highly priced. Therefor we might also be able to detect some evidence that essential workers might actually travel further to work so that they can access lower priced housing. The trade-off in London between house price and travel cost however is complicated and the data to measure this is problematic. If we first look at the correlations between essential and non-essential workers at their place of work for the UK aggregated now over occupations, this is 0.981 in comparison with their place of residence where it is 0.882. However the correlations between essential and non-essential between workplace and home are very low. In short, there is a very dramatic difference in the UK between where workers live and work which is perhaps somewhat greater than what one might have expected. Correlation is one of many measures we can use to look at this covariance and it does not tend to pick up the autocorrelation in these data but it does bear out the fact that there are big differences particularly in London where people live and work for both essential and non-essential workers. These bear out similar correlations to the UK.

TABLE 18.1
Total and Essential Workers by Occupational Categories for the UK and London (Source: [3])

UK	Employment	Essential	Ess/ Emp	NEss/ Total	Ess/ Total
1 Managers, directors & senior officials;	3,149,600	168,800	0.054	0.127	0.007
2 Professional	5,532,200	1,170,300	0.212	0.186	0.050
3 Associate professional, technical occupations;	3,854,300	919,600	0.239	0.125	0.039
4 Administrative and secretarial occupations;	2,050,900	312,100	0.152	0.074	0.013
5 Skilled trades	2,932,400	570,800	0.195	0.101	0.024
6 Caring, leisure & other service occupations;	1,700,900	973,200	0.572	0.031	0.042
7 Sales & customer service occupations;	719,700	71,800	0.100	0.028	0.003
8 Process, plant & machine operatives;	1,754,200	796,200	0.454	0.041	0.034
9 Elementary	1,752,400	542,500	0.310	0.052	0.023
Total	23,446,600	5,525,300	0.236	0.764	0.236

LONDON	Employment	Essential	Ess/ Emp	NEss/ Total	Ess/ Total
1 Managers, directors & senior officials;	617,300	14,800	0.024	0.130	0.003
2 Professional	1,230,000	242,900	0.197	0.213	0.052
3 Associate professional, technical occupations;	870,100	120,000	0.138	0.162	0.026
4 Administrative and secretarial occupations;	412,100	52,100	0.126	0.078	0.011
5 Skilled trades	317,800	46,000	0.145	0.059	0.010
6 Caring, leisure & other service occupations;	328,200	80,200	0.244	0.054	0.017
7 Sales & customer service occupations;	265,300	10,900	0.041	0.055	0.002
8 Process, plant & machine operatives;	210,700	98,000	0.465	0.024	0.021
9 Elementary	377,500	76,700	0.203	0.065	0.017
Total	4,629,000	741,600	0.160	0.840	0.160

Our data represent counts of workers in the small zones called MSOAs which on average have some 2,378 employees at their workplace and the same working populations at their residences. In fact the standard deviation for workplaces is much bigger than for residences (5,360 compared to 760) and this shows the very skewed distribution of the workplace data compared to the residential areas. To generate normalised distribution which are somewhat more comparable, we have defined densities as follows $E_i(es)/L_i$, $E_i(ne)/L_i$, $P_j(es)/L_j$, and $P_j(ne)/L_j$ where L_i, L_j are the land areas of the zones in question. We have also correlated these variables for the UK and London and this shows a slightly different pattern; all these are shown in the heat maps in Figure 18.1 which, for counts and densities of the data in MSOAs, show almost exact correlations between essential and nonessential workers at their workplace and very strong correlations at their residence (home). Only for essential and non-essential workers at their residence is there any clear and obvious difference, and this is with respect to counts data where the absolute non-normalised size effect is more dominant.

To complete this preliminary picture of how locations of essential and non-essential workers at their workplaces and residences are spatially distributed, we begin with the counts data that we show in Figure 18.2 for the UK and Figure 18.3 for London. Because these distributions are so skewed with very few large values and many small, we plot the logarithms of these data. The distinction between correlations associated with workplaces and residential areas in terms of essential and non-essential workers is reflected in these maps, first for the UK in Figure 18.2.

It is clear that at the workplaces the UK distributions of essential and non-essential are very close as reflected in the correlations in the Heatmaps in Figure 18.1(a) and Figure 18.1(c). When we examine the home-based data in Figures 18.2(b) and 18.2(d), the biggest differences between essential and non-essential areas are in rural locations where travel times are much longer to reach workplaces and homes. Essential workers tend to be a little less concentrated near the bigger cities. We map the same distributions for London (the GLA area) in Figure 18.3 and the same sorts of conclusion emerge.

From Figure 18.3, the workplace distribution of essential workers is quite close to the non-essential for London and there is little to suggest any real spatial differences. In terms of the distribution of these same employments at the home-residence locations, the non-essential appear to be more clustered than the essential with the essential living a little closer to the centre. To explore these differences further, we can generate the same maps for the density distributions. As before, we first map the national density distributions of essential and non-essential workers at their workplace and home in Figure 18.4. From this first analysis, we can conclude that the spatial distributions of essential employment differs very little from non-essential at their place of work, as much because these distributions are very highly skewed and follow power laws. This is the reason we have been plotting them as logarithmic transforms to get rid of extreme variations and make them as comparable as possible, visually. At the home location, there is more variation but in terms of the UK and then London, it is more difficult to generalise other than saying that non-essential appear to be more randomly distributed than essential which are lower in rural and remote areas.

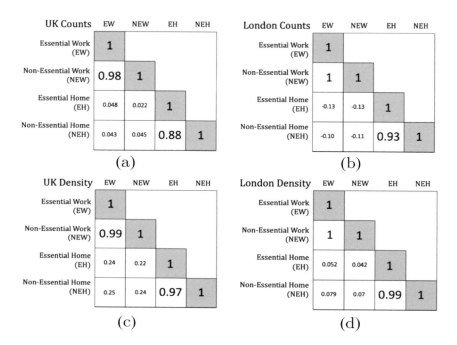

FIGURE 18.1

Heat Maps Showing the Correlations for the UK and London For Count and Density Data a) UK Count Data, b) London Count Data, c) UK Density Data, and d) London Density Data

FIGURE 18.2

UK: Essential and Non-Essential Employment at Workplace (a and b) and at Home (Residence c and d)

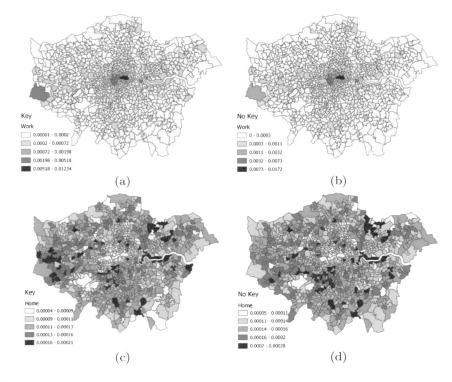

FIGURE 18.3
London: Essential and Non-Essential Employment at Workplace (a and b) and at Home (Residence c and d)

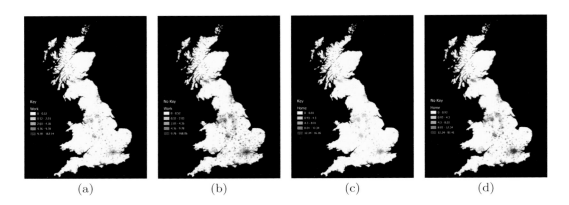

FIGURE 18.4
UK: Essential and Non-Essential Employment Densities at Workplace (a and b) and at Home (Residence c and d)

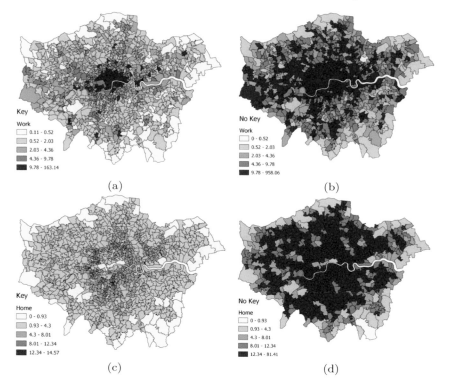

FIGURE 18.5
London: Essential and Non-Essential Employment Densities at Workplace (a and b) and at Home (Residence c and d)

18.3 The Movement Patterns of Essential and Non-Essential Workers

Rather than simply focussing on how different are the location patterns for essential and non-essential workers, a more important aspect of the analysis is to examine the different trip lengths for the basic variable T_{ij}^{ko}. We do this for the overall distribution and then for the aggregations that we have introduced above. The mean trip length C over the entire system measured in minutes is

$$C = \sum_i \sum_j \sum_k \sum_o T_{ij}^{ko} d_{ij}^k \ / \ \sum_i \sum_j \sum_k \sum_o T_{ij}^{ko} \tag{18.3}$$

and then for the overall aggregations for occupations, modes and occupations by mode, these means are

$$\left.\begin{array}{l} C^o = \sum_i \sum_j \sum_k T_{ij}^{ko} d_{ij}^k \ / \ \sum_i \sum_j \sum_k T_{ij}^{ko} \\ C^k = \sum_i \sum_j \sum_o T_{ij}^{ko} d_{ij}^k \ / \ \sum_i \sum_j \sum_o T_{ij}^{ko} \\ C^{ko} = \sum_i \sum_j T_{ij}^{ko} d_{ij}^k \ / \ \sum_i \sum_j T_{ij}^{ko} \end{array}\right\} \tag{18.4}$$

We can also aggregate these to workplace zones and all sub-aggregations to occupations, modes and occupations by mode

$$\left.\begin{array}{l} C_i = \sum_j \sum_k \sum_o T_{ij}^{ko} d_{ij}^k \ / \ \sum_j \sum_k \sum_o T_{ij}^{ko} \\ C_i^o = \sum_j \sum_k T_{ij}^{ko} d_{ij}^k \ / \ \sum_j \sum_k T_{ij}^{ko} \\ C_i^k = \sum_j \sum_o T_{ij}^{ko} d_{ij}^k \ / \ \sum_j \sum_o T_{ij}^{ko} \\ C_i^{ko} = \sum_j T_{ij}^{ko} d_{ij}^k \ / \ \sum_j T_{ij}^{ko} \end{array}\right\} \tag{18.5}$$

and then to residential destinations

$$\left.\begin{array}{l} C_j = \sum_i \sum_k \sum_o T_{ij}^{ko} d_{ij}^k \ / \ \sum_i \sum_k \sum_o T_{ij}^{ko} \\ C_j^o = \sum_i \sum_k T_{ij}^{ko} d_{ij}^k \ / \ \sum_i \sum_k T_{ij}^{ko} \\ C_j^k = \sum_i \sum_o T_{ij}^{ko} d_{ij}^k \ / \ \sum_i \sum_o T_{ij}^{ko} \\ C_j^{ko} = \sum_i T_{ij}^{ko} d_{ij}^k \ / \ \sum_i T_{ij}^{ko} \end{array}\right\} \tag{18.6}$$

We need to note that the variable d_{ij}^k is the travel time between origin i and destination j on the modal network k of which there are three – bus, rail and road – but this does not include travel time at the trip ends. It is solely the travel time on the mode of transport – the time spent on the bus, in the train, or in the car. It is very likely that these times would double if the trip end times were added to them.

The breakdown of total modal trips into essential $T^k(es) = \sum_i \sum_j \sum_o T_{ij}^{ko}(es)$ non-essential $T^k(ne) = \sum_i \sum_j \sum_o T_{ij}^{ko}(ne)$, and total $T^k = \sum_i \sum_j \sum_o T_{ij}^{ko}$ is shown in Table 18.2 where it is clear that the percentage divisions for each mode do not differ very much from the 20-80 split which is roughly the overall split advised by government. In terms of the trip lengths, these are shown in Table 18.3 for each mode and overall and they differ very little between essential and non-essential. The minor differences in terms of proportions are such that what this probably means is that essential and non-essential trips patterns are very close to each other across all modes and this is echoed throughout this analysis. The aggregate mean trip length for the whole UK system C is 15.89 minutes. When we disaggregate these into modes C^k, the longest is the rail at 30.63 minutes ($C^{(k=2)}$), followed by bus at 26.64 ($C^{(k=1)}$), and then there is a large drop to road (largely meaning car) with 12.46 minutes travelled on average ($C^{(k=3)}$). In terms of the modal split, the proportions in each mode are

$$\rho^k = E^k \ / \ \sum_k E^k = \sum_i \sum_j \sum_o T_{ij}^{ko} \ / \ \sum_i \sum_j \sum_o \sum_k T_{ij}^{ko} \tag{18.7}$$

and these are calculated approximately as 10% for bus, 11% for rail and 79% for road.

TABLE 18.2
UK Total, Essential and Non Essential Workers $T^k(es)$, $T^k(ne)$, T^k

	Total Workers Essential Workers $T^k(es)$	Non-Essential Workers $T^k(ne)$	Total T^k	% Essential	% Non-Essential
Road	3105661	12717370	15823031	0.2	0.8
Rail	353080	1833292	2186372	0.16	0.84
Bus	383304	1667827	2051131	0.19	0.81
Total	**3842045**	**16218489**	**20060534**	**0.19**	**0.81**

Although we examine the trip lengths by mode in Table 18.2, we should also note the division of the country into its standard regions – namely Wales (W), Scotland(S) and 9 English regions – East Midlands (EM), East of England (EE), London (L), North east (NE), North West (NW), South East (SE), South West (SW), West Midlands (WM) and Yorkshire/Humberside (YH). The variations in trip lengths across modes still dominate the regional variations although there are some large deviations from the overall means. For example, in terms of road travel, the shortest travel times are in London (9.25) and the largest are in Wales (14.43) while rail travel is also smallest in London (22.98) and largest in Wales (45.82), the East Midlands (50.09) and the South West (64.88). The bus times are pretty even across all the regions with the largest being London but this is only 29.62 minutes compared to the average of 26.62, 11% more. Note that it is easy to

London in Lockdown: Mobility in the Pandemic City

confirm these statistics in that we can show if we add the mean trip lengths together for the three modes and weight them in the way we have shown in equation (18.7) above, then it is clear that

$$\sum_k \rho^k C^k = \left\{ \rho^1 \frac{\sum_i \sum_j \sum_o T_{ij}^{10} d_{ij}^1}{\sum_i \sum_j \sum_o T_{ij}^{10}} + \rho^2 \frac{\sum_i \sum_j \sum_o T_{ij}^{20} d_{ij}^2}{\sum_i \sum_j \sum_o T_{ij}^{20}} + \rho^3 \frac{\sum_i \sum_j \sum_o T_{ij}^{30} d_{ij}^3}{\sum_i \sum_j \sum_o T_{ij}^{30}} \right\} = C \quad (18.8)$$

A brief examination of the variances between these three modes between the 11 regions suggests that for bus, the standard deviation is about 6.68 minutes, followed by rail where it is 5.42, and then road which is 4.80. We can casually interpret these deviations as being due to the fact that most travellers have less control of the timing of their use of bus compared to rail and that the greatest control, hence the lowest variance, is for car use where the user has most control. However as all these effects are compounded across many zones and many travel times in different regions, it is not clear whether we can attribute such variation simply to the spatial differences across the nation or to the modes themselves.

When we examine the overall trip lengths by occupation and by region C^o, we find that managers and professionals travel some 33% more in time than the average while less professionally qualified occupations such as sales, technicians and some caring services travel some 25% less. London is a massive outlier where the managerial and professional occupations tend to have much less variation than in the regions but the less professional travel more than 40% of the national average. The North West and West Midlands tend to have lower travel times over most occupations than other regions. The singly-biggest difference with respect to occupations and regions is between an average travel time of some 20 minutes for professionals in all regions with the exceptions of the North West, West Midlands and Yorkshire-Humberside. The caring occupations only commute some 10-11 minutes while London is again the outlier and more peripheral regions such as Wales and Scotland do not appear to be dramatically different from the average. It is hard not to conclude from this brief analysis that London is dramatically different from the national average largely because of its size and the fact that its housing market and its transport systems are so different from the rest of the country.

We have one further disaggregation that we need to focus on and that is our basic distinction between essential and nonessential workers. In fact we can explore these through the occupations but as this would involve us in too much detailed analysis here, we will aggregate these essential and nonessential occupations into a total of essential and nonessential at the zonal, then the regional and the national levels. We will thus produce the same analysis that we have already developed for the essential and non-essential aggregates. Noting that we define the essential trips and non-essential as $T_{ij}^{ko}(es)$ and $T_{ij}^{ko}(ne)$, the mean trip lengths by mode as $C^k(es)$ and $C^k(ne)$, and by occupation as $C^o(es)$ and $C^o(ne)$, it is immediately apparent that the orders of magnitude of all these variables are very similar in values to C^k and C^o. In fact, the essential and non-essential mean trip lengths for occupations and regions hardly reveal any differences from the combined distributions of all populations: the main difference is in the overall mean trip lengths $C(es)$ and $C(ne)$, which are 15.63 and 15.95, respectively, which is a difference of only about 2%. These are shown in Table 18.3 for the modes as well.

TABLE 18.3
UK Mean Trip Lengths $C^k(es)$, $C^k(ne)$, C^k

Mean Costs	Essential Workers $C^k(es)$	Non-Essential Workers $C^k(ne)$	Total C^k
Road	12.52	12.44	12.46
Rail	31.23	30.52	30.63
Bus	26.48	26.68	26.64
Total	**15.63**	**15.96**	**15.89**

In short, this means that on average, essential workers only travel about 2% less than nonessential workers over all modes. The occupation data suggests all changes are less than 2% and these do not vary much within regions. In fact each of the 9 categories of worker by occupation has essential and non-essential workers and in general over all occupations, the essential travel is only very slightly less than the nonessential. In terms of modes, there is no more difference than between regions and occupations and it would appear that the essential workers are distributed in a very similar way to the nonessential across the country, probably due to the fact that to keep the system running, one has to have roughly the same pattern of workers everywhere. This is particularly pronounced for London as Table 18.4 reveals. In short the differences are hardly worthy of comment and our anticipation that essential workers differ in their journey patterns radically from non-essential is not borne out. In fact it is more likely that essential and non-essential differ in their spatial locations than in the amount of time spent in travelling but what we require is a new framework to handle all these variations so that we can apportion the relative importance of minor differences between category types.

TABLE 18.4
London Mean Trip Lengths $C_{GLA}^k(es)$, $C_{GLA}^k(ne)$, C_{GLA}^k

Mean Costs	Essential Workers $C^k(es)$	Non-Essential Workers $C^k(ne)$	Total C^k
Road	9.12	9.28	9.25
Rail	22.98	22.98	22.98
Bus	29.76	29.95	29.62
Total	**18.86**	**19.16**	**19.12**

If we now look at the total amount of travel, rather than the trip lengths, we can begin noting that we can multiply the mean trip lengths by the total trips for whatever aggregation of the trips we are dealing with from $T_{ij}^{ko}(es)$ and $T_{ij}^{ko}(ne)$. First, we will look at total travel in the essential and non-essential sectors and these are defined as $T(es) = \sum_i \sum_j \sum_k \sum_o T_{ij}^{ko}(es)d_{ij}^k$ and $T(ne) = \sum_i \sum_j \sum_k \sum_o T_{ij}^{ko}(ne)d_{ij}^k$ which add to the total travel in the system as

$$T = \sum_i \sum_j \sum_k \sum_o T_{ij}^{ko}d_{ij}^k = \sum_i \sum_j \sum_k \sum_o \left[T_{ij}^{ko}(es) + T_{ij}^{ko}(ne) \right] d_{ij}^k = T(es) + T(ne) \quad (18.9)$$

These statistics suggest that before the Pandemic, the total amount of travel for work during the day was about 5.31 million hours per day in the UK as shown in Table 18.5. If we look at essential workers, the number of hours travelled after the lock down was about 1 million hours which means that some 4.31 million hours has been saved by persons working from home. This is a fall of some 81% in travel time which reflects the number of essential workers in the whole economy. It is worth saying that this is not the total reduction in travel because people working from home still go shopping and take exercise. Note that if we divide these total travel times by the respective total trips, then this gives the mean travel times, in this case of $C(es) = 15.63$, $C(ne) = 15.95$, and $C = 15.89$.

TABLE 18.5
UK Total Hours Spent in Essential Travel and Saved in Home Working $C^k T^k/60$

Hours	Essential Workers	Non-Essential Workers	Total
Road	648,048	2,636,735	3,285,916
Rail	183,778	932,535	1,116,143
Bus	169,165	741,627	910,702
Total	**1,000,853**	**4,314,118**	**5,312,698**

18.4 Drilling Down Into Individual Locations in London

So far, we have only examined the aggregate pattern of essential and non-essential workers at their workplace and home where the distribution of workers has been mapped prior to the Pandemic. Then those who are furloughed and work from home who are deemed non-essential are subtracted from the total leaving those who are essential workers dominating the journey to work during the 3 months period from 23 March 2020 when the country was first locked down. However, we are able to approach the problem of the fall in travel in a more oblique manner using Google Mobility Reports [5] which collate data from anyone who users Google services on mobile devices such as Google Maps and who has switched on their Location History (which is off by default). This is available for many places around the world and in the UK is available for all local authorities. In London, this means that we have good data on the changes in trips day by day from 10 February 2020 to 18 October 2020 for six categories of activities: residential occupancy, workplace volumes, visits to parks, volumes of workers using transit which in the case of London is overground and underground rail and buses, retail sales, and then grocery store volumes of visits. What these data show is the decrease or increase in volume from the baseline. In this case for the UK, it is some 37 days before Lockdown and covers the period from then to our cut-off date when we retrieved the data giving us a series of 247 days. The horizontal axes of the trajectories that we show below in Figures 6 to 9 span these 247 days on a scale from 0 to 250. In fact, the baseline is the median value of activity volumes in the 5-week period from 3 January to 6 February 2020. The data continues to be collected.

For each place and aggregation thereof, the data provides a detailed time series of the level of activity before the Lockdown with the baseline data as 10 February. Then the subsequent change in activity which at the beginning of the period is a massive drop in visits due to the fact that people were mandated not to travel (as we noted in the introduction) suggest a slow recovery towards the baseline. In the case of the UK, and London in particular, there is no return to the baseline and there has in fact been a levelling off and even a slight drop in some activities in the last 40 or so days as a second wave of infection appears to be beginning. There is a wealth of data here but with all the caveats of course pertaining to its representativeness for only if you have Location History on and access to Google services can any such data be collected. The representativeness of the data is thus unknown and only if the data were integrated with other sources would we be able to say very much about its overall quality. What we can say, however, is that the data is accurate in terms of its geo-positioning.

Our analysis in this paper merely touches the surface of what we can do with data such as this and as yet we have not embarked on a full scale analysis of all areas of the UK and any aggregation thereof. What we do here is begin with the data for the UK and use this as our spatial baseline, thence comparing three different parts of the Greater London Authority with this baseline and with each other. These locations are the City of London – the so-called dead heart of the metropolis [6], the more prosperous borough of Richmond-on-Thames in west London and the less prosperous borough of Newham in east London. The average income/wage of those in the City is about £27 per hour (ph), in Richmond it is £20 ph and in Newham £13 ph, all compared with a London average of £15 ph and a UK average of £13 ph. This gives a very crude idea of the relative prosperity of these places and we might expect this to have some effect on the degree to which mobility patterns might have altered during the Pandemic. There are many other estimates of income but these appear to be the least controversial (see [7] and [8]).

We show the profiles of the change in the six activities for the UK in Figure 18.6 and the same for the three London boroughs – the City in Figure 18.7, Richmond on Thames in Figure 18.8, and Newham in Figure 18.9. For the UK, the growth in those working at home peaked early in the Pandemic at about an additional 30% staying home to work or furlough, then gradually falling back to about 10% more than the baseline. There is no data for the City of London as only 8,000 people live there and many only do so during the working week but the richer borough of Richmond had up to 50% and this has fallen back to some 25% now. Newham is similar to the UK baseline. The only other activity which has seen any real increases in activity are in parks, which fell nationally in the early and then quickly increase to a peak of 150% about average through the summer months

well above the baseline. This has fallen back to some 25% above the baseline. Richmond is similar to this profile but in Newham there has been massive increase up to 500% of above the baseline of people visiting parts where in the City of London where half a million workers use pocket parks during the day, volumes have fallen by over 90% rising back to some 60% below the baseline but now back down to 70% as winter approaches.

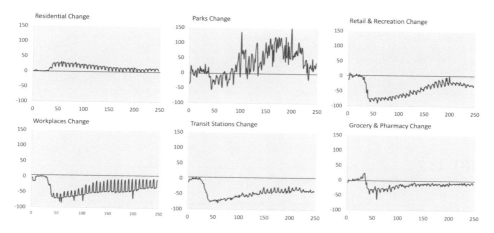

FIGURE 18.6

National UK Percentage Changes in Use of Activities from the February Baseline

The horizontal axes relate to the number of days from the 10th Feb and the vertical axes are the negative or positive percentage shifts in activity volumes from the baseline. This applies to all subsequent figures.

The other four activities – retail, workplaces, use of transit and grocery shopping – all show a big drop when Lockdown took place and then a gradual recovery but only in the case of grocery shopping has this recovered almost to the baseline – the old normal. This is apart from the City where grocery shopping is mainly based on office workers who are no longer at work. Retail change is startling with a national fall by about 90% at the beginning of the and then a steady rise back to about 20% below the baseline by the late summer but with a distinct fall back to about 35 percent below the line during the last 50 days. There is evidence here of a second peak but this is compounded by a drop in income and as yet the picture is unclear. Richmond and Newham are fairly similar to the national UK profile apart from two massive spikes in Richmond on 23rd February and 7th March which relate to key Rugby matches at Twickenham where England played Ireland and Wales in the 6 Nations Cup in the days before the Lockdown occurred. The same picture occurs in transit usage with spikes in Richmond but quite dramatic falls in usage in all four examples. In the UK, volumes using transit fell to about 70% below the baseline but then have recovered to about 50%, while in the City these have fallen even more by about 95% but have only recovered to within some 70 percent of their normal baseline. Richmond and Newham have a similar profile to the UK but have only recovered to about 60% of their previous normal volumes. This is a major problem in that public transport is being completely subsidised by government and local authorities throughout England and is effectively bankrupt. National Rail have more or less been re-nationalised and Transport for London is in negotiation with the UK government. Congestion charging has been increased already in London and fare rises much greater than inflation have been suggested but not yet agreed. The public transport picture is much confused and at the time of writing, where a new national Lockdown is under discussion, the picture for transit looks bleak.

The key changes of course with respect to the focus here on essential and non-essential workers pertain to change in workplace volumes which imply changes to those working in their traditional workplace and those who have elected to work from home. When we look at the national picture in Figure 18.6 for workplace change, the profile is fairly typical of other declines: the national fall is

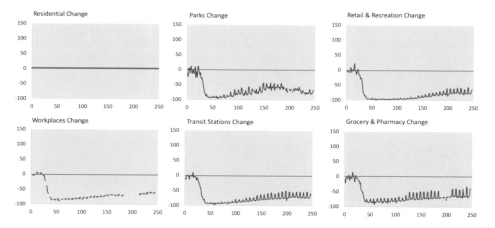

FIGURE 18.7

The City of London Percentage Changes in Use of Activities from the February Baseline

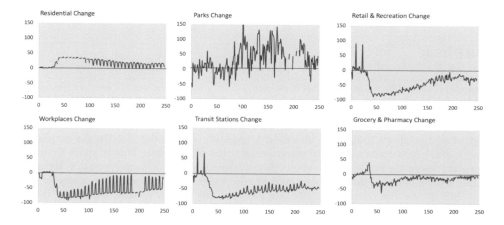

FIGURE 18.8

The Borough of Richmond on Thames Percentage Changes in Use of Activities from the February Baseline

about 70 precent which then recovers to some 30% less than the baseline. In Richmond, the decline is similar to the UK and to Newham but the decline in the City of London is much more fractured due to gaps in data collection during the weekends while in the three other cases the impact of the weekend versus the weekday is very pronounced. In short, the succession of spikes along the trend from a big fall and then recovery back towards the baseline marks the way the weekend and weekdays impact on work journeys to places of work. Without more information, it is difficult to precisely gauge these movements but these are quite pronounced in Richmond where the impact of the weekday seems to generate many less workers than the weekends.

The last activity we need to examine is very local – grocery shopping which drops the least of any activity after Lockdown – to no more than 50% of normal activity. In all but the City, this recovers to near normality by the end of the period. In fact, there is spike at the onset of the Pandemic with grocery shopping increasingly above the baseline, largely we suspect when people were stocking up on products ready to shop far less in the early months of the Pandemic. This is the case for three of our cases but not the City of London where there is a pronounced drop to about 90% of normal activity which slowly climbs back but to no more than 50% less than the

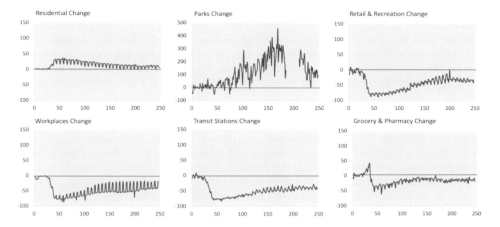

FIGURE 18.9
The Borough of Newham Percentage Changes in Use of Activities from the February Baseline

baseline. This is largely due to the fact that most grocery shopping in the City is by workers from their place of work, not their home and it is interesting that these features are reflected in the data. This is also true of the spikiness of the trajectories which reflect differences between home and work with the distortions posed by working from home, affecting this drop in activity much more on weekdays than is represented on weekend days.

Overall, these trajectories confirm what we know from our casual experience of the Pandemic, but what is interesting is that they do give us some insight into changes in activities even though they only come from one source, Google. We cannot prove that this data is representative but little differences such as the impact of sporting events which show up in the data are likely to show up in similar activity patterns from other mobile operators. Moreover, what is of current interest is in how these patterns will be reflected in another Lockdown. As we have had a series of partial Lockdowns of varying severity in the UK during the last 3 months, it may be possible to trace the impact of these once the full Lockdown becomes active on 05 November. Although this data is useful, it is hard to tie it to independent data sets, and during the Pandemic it is difficult to mount special surveys to examine more conventional flow data, notwithstanding the work that the Office of National Statistics are undertaking.

18.5 Conclusions and Next Steps: A More Integrated Analysis

The most surprising conclusion from the analysis involves the dramatic differences between the regions of the UK with respect to average travel times on different modes of transport, and the minimal differences between average travel times between essential and non-essential workers in each region. To an extent, this may be due to the fact that the way the government has defined essential workers is close to the distribution of non-essential workers and if this is the case, the transport networks and modal split will not make any real difference to the patterns of distribution which essentially are the same for these two groups.

A key issue which is raised by this paper is data. From data prior to the Pandemic, which is the only detailed data we have on flow patterns and locational volumes, it is of little surprise that we cannot generate many new insights into spatial differences that might be exploited in handling the Pandemic. To this end we need much better data on the spatial progression of the Pandemic, and we need to tie the sort of data produced by Google (with equivalent mobility data from IT platforms such as Apple [9] from their map products, and Amazon Web Services, etc.) to more conventional transport data such as traffic counts from sensors, data from smart card ticking systems and so on.

What we need to do now is to regionalise the country into localities and regions that might be highly clustered with respect to similarities (and differences in an alternative analysis) so that we can examine where there are significant differences that might be exploited in countering the Pandemic. In part of the country where people travel more or travel less than the average, this has implications for how we might lockdown certain areas. Currently, many governments in Western Europe are moving towards a total Lockdown to combat the second wave but these kinds of blunt instrument approaches are too crude to effectively exploit the differences in the way the wave of infections is diffusing. In this work, what we urgently need, as in all work on the spatial, is some way of linking the location of the incidence and intensity of the disease to human behaviours pertaining to location and mobility. This is essential and probably requires moving to a much more individual scale where we can tie health data to the location of workers and the population. This will require us to disaggregate our data down to the individual and household level so that we can then associate this with the diseases and susceptibility to disease, before we then aggregate this back up so we can link these attributes to those we have explored in this paper, which focus on how people move and how movement is connected to location.

Acknowledgements

The Future Cities Catapult funded the early stage of this research (2016-2018) and the **QUANT** model is now supported by The Alan Turing Institute under **QUANT2**–Contract–CID–3815811. Partial support has also come from the UK Regions Digital Research Facility (UK RDRF) EP/M023583/1.

References

[1] R Murcio. Local Lockdown Stories: Leicester Commuting Patterns, 2020. URL https://citiescience.org.

[2] Michael Batty. Social distancing at scale. *Environment and Planning B: Urban Analytics and City Science*, 47(9):1533–1536, 2020. doi: 10.1177/2399808320972506.

[3] Cabinet Office. Guidance On Critical Workers Who Can Access Schools Or Educational Settings. *Department of Education and Science*, 2020. URL https://www.gov.uk/government/publications/coronavirus-covid-19-maintaining-educational-provision/guidance-for-schools-colleges-and-local-authorities-on-maintaining-educational-provision#vulnerable-children-and-young-people. Accessed 31/10/20.

[4] C. Farquharson, I. Rasul, and L. Sibieta. Key Workers: Key Facts and Questions. *Institute of Fiscal Studies, London*, 2020. URL https://www.ifs.org.uk/publications/14763. Accessed 31/10/20.

[5] Google. COVID-19 Community Mobility Reports, 2020. URL https://www.google.com/covid19/mobility/. Accessed 31/10/20.

[6] V. Gruen. *The Heart of Our Cities : The Urban Crisis, Diagnosis and Cure*. Simon and Schuster, New York, 1964.

[7] London Data Store. Earnings by Place of Residence, Borough. *London Data Store*, 2020. URL https://data.london.gov.uk/dataset/earnings-place-residence-borough. Accessed 31/10/20.

[8] ONS. Employee Earnings in the UK: 2019, 2020. URL https://www.ons.gov.uk/employmentandlabourmarket/peopleinwork/earningsandworkinghours/bulletins/annualsurveyofhoursandearnings/2019. Accessed 31/10/20.

[9] Apple. Mobility Trends Reports, 2020. URL https://covid19.apple.com/mobility.

19

Americas' Geospatial Response to COVID-19

Rosario Casanova, Paloma Merodio Gómez, Álvaro Monett Hernández and
Andrea Ramírez Santiago

*In the Americas region, the Regional Committee of the United Nations for Global
Geospatial Information Management (UN-GGIM: Americas) in a joint work with the
Economic Commission for Latin America and the Caribbean, have been facilitating
exchange of good practices and monitoring geospatial tools to respond to the pandemic.
This exchange has conveyed an analysis of the different institutional arrangements, data
management and technological approaches taken by countries in the region to control the
outspread of COVID-19. This chapter provides an overview of the regional geospatial
response to COVID-19. We analyze the implementation and use of UNGGIM global
frameworks in the geospatial response to COVID-19. Through the regional meetings and
consultations carried out in the context of the pandemic, we have been able to verify
that countries, to a greater or lesser extent, have knowledge on methods and geospatial
tools to face critical situations such as the COVID-19 pandemic. However, some gaps and
challenges have also been identified that must be addressed. From a regional perspective, we
encourage countries to take full advantage of these guiding frameworks, through a collective
and collaborative approach.*

19.1   Introduction

In December 2019, a new virus called SARSCoV-2 causing severe acute respiratory syndrome
coronavirus disease (COVID-19) emerged in Wuhan, China, and rapidly spread to other parts
of the world [1]. March 11, 2020, the World Health Organization (WHO) officially declared the
COVID-19 outbreak a pandemic [2]. The disease is characterized by a long incubation period, high
infectivity, and difficulty in detection, which has contributed to the rapid outbreak and development
of the epidemic [3].

This situation has required that experts in different areas like doctors, disease trackers, modelers,
logisticians, and supply chain experts are designing and implementing measures to stop the
transmission and spread of the virus. In this way, it is essential for the exchange of information and
the development of tools, to deliver data in real time on websites and via messaging networks,
identification of locations to establish additional hospitals, quarantine bases and virus testing
locations, and effective communication on the situation.

The COVID-19 pandemic is full of unknowns, and many of them have a spatial dimension [3],
in this way, GIS has become a vital tool in analyzing and visualizing the spread of COVID-19
[4]. Modern GIS technologies center around web-based tools, improved data sharing and real time
information to support critical decision-making, an example of these are online dashboards have
been extremely popular to sharing and understanding the spread of COVID-19, since they offer
accessible information to people around the world, improves data transparency and helps authorities

disseminate information [1]. The most notable example is the online dashboard developed by John Hopkins University Centre for Systems Science and Engineering [5].

In this way, this chapter provides an overview of the regional use of geospatial data and GIS tools to support the response measures and manage the containment of COVID-19, based on the outputs of the Virtual Geospatial Summit, the webinar "COVID-19: Strategies for a Geospatial Response in the Americas" and the regional questionnaire on geospatial support to COVID-19 in the Americas. Furthermore, we analyze the role and implementation of UNGGIM global frameworks in the geospatial response to COVID-19.

Available Global Frameworks to Support the Geospatial Response to COVID-19

The geospatial response to COVID-19 at country level can be supported by sound global guidelines provided by the United Nations Committee of Experts on Global Geospatial Information Management (UNGGIM [6]). This committee has the objective to make joint decisions and establish directions on the use of geospatial information within national and global policy frameworks.

In this chapter, we will show how the geospatial response to COVID-19 -being conducted by member states is transiting to the alignment with these frameworks and how these frameworks can help so that .an improved geospatial response to this emergency and others that may occur in the future is sustainable.

The first one is the Integrated Geospatial Information Framework (IGIF [7]) that provides a guide for developing, integrating, strengthening, and maximizing geospatial information management and related resources in all countries [8]. The IGIF has been proven to be integrative and of practical implementation. Any of the nine IGIF strategic pathways have been implemented by member countries in the Americas, by establishing institutional arrangements and governance agreements, referencing policies to protect privacy and confidentiality of data, promoting partnerships between stakeholders from different sectors (public, private, and academy), leveraging innovation to deliver better technological platforms, and creating communication tools to reach the wide spectrum of users that need this geospatial resources for different purposes.

The second framework endorsed by UNGGIM and the Statistical commission of the United Nations Statistics Division that has proven to be usefully implemented to monitor COVID-19 is the Global Statistical and Geospatial Framework (GSGF [9]) which enables a range of data to be integrated from both statistical and geospatial communities and, through the application of its five Principles and supporting key elements, permits the production of harmonized and standardized geospatially enabled statistical data. The resulting data can then be integrated with statistical, geospatial, and other information to inform and facilitate data-driven and evidence-based decision making. The integration of statistics and geospatial has been vital in this pandemic. Sociodemographic variables such as age, health status, have been analyzed even at block level to detect vulnerable populations.

And the third one is the Strategic Framework on Geospatial Information and Services for Disasters [10], elaborated by the UN-GGIM Working Group on this topic, which aims to bring all stakeholders and partners involved in Disaster Risk Reduction and/or Emergency Management together to ensure that quality geospatial information and services are available and accessible in a timely and coordinated way to support decision-making and operations within and across all sectors and phases of disaster risk management. The strategic framework draws from the principles included in the Sendai Framework for Disaster Risk Reduction [11]; the UN General Assembly resolution on international cooperation on humanitarian assistance in the field of natural disasters, from relief to development; the 2030 Agenda for Sustainable Development; and the UN-GGIM Global Statistical Geospatial Framework [9].

19.2 Overview On the Regional Geospatial Response to COVID-19

As reported in the abstract of this article in a joint effort between the United Nations Regional Committee for Global Geospatial Information Management (UN-GGIM: Americas) and the Economic Commission for Latin America and the Caribbean (ECLAC [12] with the support of the Secretariat of UN-GGIM at a global level, two regional webinars and a regional consultation on regarding geospatial response to COVID-19 were conducted, in order to collect information and share experiences and knowledge from different approaches ranging from institutional to technological.

In order for geospatial data users and providers across governments, the private sector, academia, students and the general public could know and shared how the global community of geospatial scientists have been leveraging geospatial, Earth Observation and statistical data, creating innovative tools to support response measures and manage the containment of COVID-19, was made the Virtual Geospatial Summit 2020 under the theme "GIS Response to COVID-19", in which they showed some of the geospatial tools that have been developed in different countries including the Americas region, as well as the good practices that have been implemented, including the challenges in collecting geospatial health data.

The seminar COVID-19: Strategies for a Geospatial Response in the Americas was held on May 15, 2020, facilitated by UN-ECLAC and UN-GGIM: Americas. Through this activity an enriched exchange of experiences in Member States on how they have met the challenge of COVID-19 was conducted, reviewing progresses, and identifying the challenges being faced. Demonstrations on developing national dashboards and tools were also shared, highlighting data needs and available resources. The seminar helped the discussion on how to optimize resources to respond in the short and medium-term impact of COVID-19, while preparing for the long-term implications of public health and safety crises or emergencies.

The regional consultation was carried out by UN-GGIM: Americas and ECLAC to promote dissemination actions and exchange of practices and experiences around the use of geospatial information, to support the management of the COVID-19 pandemic.

In this consultation, information was collected from national geospatial data infrastructures or from national cartographic agencies in collaboration with other public bodies. Information regarding data integration, development of indicators and implementation of platforms, among others was reported. The identified use cases and good practices were disseminated on the UN-GGIM: Americas website [13], and on the COVID-19 Observatory [14] in Latin America and the Caribbean.

Overview On the Regional Geospatial Support

The following section presents the response approach, from different countries in the region, regarding institutional aspects and the use of geospatial data.

Governance and Institutions

A central component of geospatial support for disaster management is governance. This is established by the UN-GGIM Strategic Framework on Geospatial Information and Services for Disasters, assigning institutional agreements, collaboration, and coordination a fundamental role. In this context, through this consultation it was possible to identify various forms of governance and participation in the countries that responded to the regional consultation, basically through the formation of multisectoral work teams to support decision-makers and the entities in charge of disaster management.

In order to articulate national organizations and to make geospatial information available for decision-making, several countries have activated protocols to support to the entities in charge of disaster management, like the National Emergency Response System in Jamaica, the Emergency Operations Center in Sint Maarten or the National Risk Management System in Honduras. These protocols organize the collection of spatial information, the integration of statistical and geospatial data and the way in which this information is processed to help the decision making.

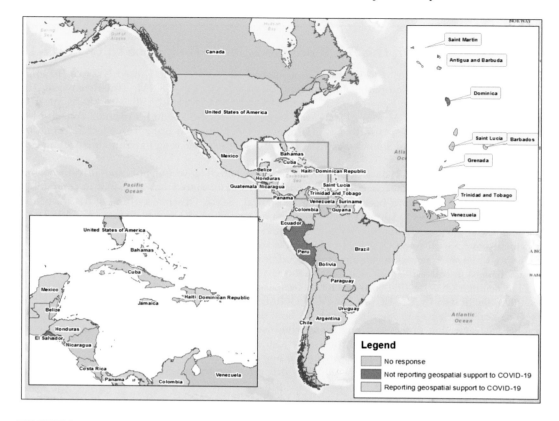

FIGURE 19.1
Map representing the geospatial response to COVID-19 of Americas countries. Source: Regional consultation carried out by UN-GGIM: Americas-ECLAC Regional consultation, 2020.

Other frequent institutional arrangement observed in the region is the creation of special working committees and/or groups to assist the national geospatial response to the pandemic. This allows to collect information from various sources, keep the inter-institutional communication permanently opened and generate added value products helping to implement logistical actions and carry out territorial analysis regarding the advance of the pandemic. These working groups in some cases also examine political issues affecting employee activities, travel, and public events, among others.

In this regional overview, the institutions that most frequently participate in geospatial support are the ministries and institutes of statistics and geography of each country. An example of the above is Mexico, where statistical data on COVID-19 is provided by the Ministry of Health, and then these are processed by the National Institute of Statistics and Geography (INEGI), to be displayed on platforms for presentation to the public; Chile follows a similar process, but in this case it is through the country's Spatial Data Infrastructure (IDE-Chile) that collects and disseminates the information provided by the different associated Ministries or Institutions.

Following the foregoing, in many countries emergency systems or institutions are the first access route in geospatial support, an example of this is Uruguay, where the National Emergency System (SINAE) is the body in charge of being in contact with all institutions from which you can receive information; In Antigua and Barbuda, the National Disaster Office (NODS) performs a similar function, coordinating the collaboration of geospatial information from different Ministries or offices such as the statistical office. Also, national / civil defense institutions are organizations that have been mentioned as organizations that deliver information to the coordinating entity, as is the case of Guyana, Barbados, the Dominican Republic and Jamaica. Finally, to a lesser extent, agencies, private entities, or foundations are independent organizations that have valuable information useful for the country, for which they work collaboratively. This is the case of Brazil, where data provided by the Oswaldo Cruz Foundation is disseminated; or in the Dominican Republic, where support is obtained from private geomatic companies.

The integration of statistical and geospatial information has been made explicit through the examples mentioned above, where countries are using geocoded health and population data referenced to a specific location and the information is being displayed in geospatial dashboards. This use of fundamental geospatial infrastructure and geocoding in a data management environment, using common geographies for the dissemination of statistics in an accessible and usable platform is the core of the five principals of the GSGF [15].

Data and Technology

From the collected information through the different activities and consultations carried out in the region, it was possible to realize that the most frequent technological resources being utilized to disseminate COVID-19 statistics, are geospatial dashboards. Secondly, interactive websites with maps, charts and dynamic statistics. Most countries are using GIS to disseminate statistics related to confirmed cases, active cases, recovered cases, and deaths, at different levels of disaggregation, such as political-administrative divisions, gender, or age groups. A first group of countries report that they are using GIS to prepare distribution maps, networks and flows of people to access health services, or other services that offer basic goods. Others have informed to be carrying out spatial analysis of vulnerable groups, such as the elderly, the chronically ill or areas of high population density. There are also cases of mapping households with confirmed cases, quarantined areas and isolation centers, as well as constant monitoring of confirmed and suspected cases.

In the case of the regional consultation, it was informed that, from a total of 20 countries that answered the questionnaire, fifty percent declared that they had public access platforms for the dissemination of data regarding COVID-19. In general terms, the information is disaggregated to the second or third hierarchical level of the political-administrative division and the topics represented are diverse: confirmed cases, examinations, intensive care patients and deceased patients, vulnerable population disaggregated by age ranges, information on employability, poverty and population at risk, tests carried out and results, among others.

Regarding some specific country examples in the use of national platforms and dashboards, the National Institute of Statistics and Geography of Mexico developed a geoportal called "Analytical Visualizer for COVID-19", which allows information on COVID-19 how number of confirmed, negative, suspected cases and deaths to be seen at the municipal and state levels. Information that is aligned to the information issued by the Ministry of Health.

In addition to this information, the displayed integrates information of others 8 themes: population, ethnicity educational characteristics, economic characteristics, health services, households, hospital infrastructure and deaths due to various registered conditions 2018. Each one of the topics has its corresponding indicators for a total of 28, some of the indicators that can be viewed are density (inhabitants per square kilometer), total population, population over 60 years of age, population affiliated with health services, average number of occupants per dwelling, dwellings that do not have piped water and risk diseases.

Other interesting experience is that conducted collaboratively between the National Planning Department, the Institute of Technological Evaluation in Health and the National Administrative Department of Statistics (DANE) of Colombia, which collaborated with the Ministry of Health and Social Protection and the National Institute of Health to provide statistical information and build tools[1] that facilitate senior government to make decisions with greater certainty for emergency response caused by COVID-19.

In this case, the demographic characteristics of the population and their conditions of health helped to determine who may have more complications in case of getting COVID-19. This, by taking into account, among others considerations, the identified epidemiological criteria, based on information from the 2018 National Census of Population and Housing, administrative records of the National Identification File, the Civil Birth Registry, the National Registry of Marital Status, the Unique Database of Health Affiliation and the individual records of provision of Health services.

---

[1] Reference: http://visor01.dane.gov.co/visor-vulnerabilidad/

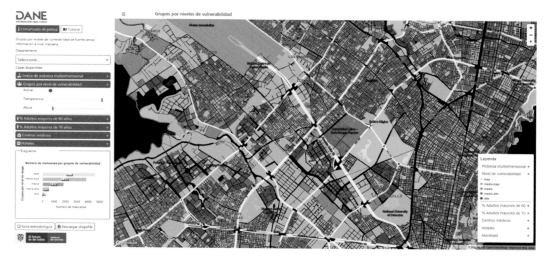

FIGURE 19.2
Viewer of vulnerability levels in Colombia Source: National Administrative Department of Statistics of the Republic of Colombia, 2020.

In the Caribbean subregion, it can be mentioned the work carried out by the GIS unit of the Survey and Mapping Division, which has been providing geospatial support to the National Emergency Operation Center, mainly through the development of GIS solutions and data gathering. This work has been conducted in coordination and collaboration with the National Office of Disaster Services, the Ministry of Health, Wellness and the Environment, the Central Board of Health and the Statistics Division. As a result, a geospatial hub is in the public domain to disseminate data on the timeline of cases and basic associated information, primarily focused on the local level, but complemented by a section regarding regional response efforts. Internally, a monitoring dashboard is still being setup to effectively manage the operations and coordination between all stakeholders.

In Central America, the National Geographic Institute Tommy Guardia (IGNTG) of Panamá formed a work team to support with cartographic information and mapping, two relevant government initiatives to confront COVID-19. The first on is the plan "Protégete Panamá" led by the Ministry of Health in collaboration with the Social Security Fund, WHO experts, and national and international Health experts. The second one is the "Solidarity Plan", in charge of the Economic Advisory Council led by the Ministry of the Presidency and integrated by several institutions. Both programs seek to mitigate the impact of the pandemic and guarantee that Panamanians affected by the health crisis can obtain essential products.

The IGNTG, leading the Panamanian Spatial Data Infrastructure, has facilitated data cooperation to integrate information from different sources, for example, on educational centers location (provided by the Ministry of Education) and a wide range of statistical data made available by the Institute of Statistics and Censuses, which has been combined with other geospatial information.

The committee prepared a special map of the republic with presidential indications for the Solidarity Plan for food delivery logistics and solidarity bonds to affected families: Route maps for garbage collection; Maps to assist aid distribution and logistics for municipalities; Statistical information to generate information layers of housing areas for people over 60 years, beds by province, chronic diseases, location of health centers and hospitals; Maps for aircraft landing areas and secondary collection centers.

19.3 Gaps and Challenges

The outcomes from the regional consultation show that countries have been able to capitalize the power of geospatial tool to respond to COVID-19. Nevertheless, challenges persist in the region and further work needs to be done in order to have an integrated geospatial response and to be prepared for future disasters.

- The most urgent gap detected by the regional encounters and consultations is related to data accessibility. To respond geospatially to the pandemic countries have faced challenges in: accessing updated real time data; lack of access to quality data and satellite images; unavailability of disaggregated fundamental data at different levels (political-administrative divisions, sex, age, etc.). Moreover the low interoperability between statistical and geospatial data, the absence of regulation regarding the use of information, and the need to create a national address systems are the most frequent challenges among the countries that responded the questionnaire conducted by ECLAC/UN: GGIM-Americas.

- Farther, there is an urgent need to improve the GIS technical capacities of current personnel. Some of the weaknesses, that have been exposed in this pandemic, refer to the lack of technical and professional resources available to make appropriate use of geospatial data, as well as lack of knowledge about the accessibility to free geographic data and applications.

- Raising awareness of authorities regarding the importance of GIS can promote its effectiveness in capturing, analyzing and disseminating spatial information. Countries recognize the challenge to support software financing and human resources. Finally, it is important to have an appropriate Spatial Data Infrastructure (SDI) that allows them to collect data from the different institutions, to have a cadaster and organize national information.

On the other hand, two major advancements identified in the regional consultation are related to dissemination geospatial tools and partnerships.

- The urgent need to access high quality data has been enabled through geospatial dissemination tools. The public visibility of geographic data, gained during this pandemic, has made geographic information take on unexpected relevance. Fact that opens some opportunities and challenges for the geomatic community. Moments in which the relevance of geographic data, as a tool for processing and making analysis, is an unquestionable fact open opportunity to promote and raise awareness of the importance of having upgraded and good data quality of the information. Data that should be accessible at the national level and acquired with the specific needs of each country. An aspect that should be included, in the current agenda, refers to the use of geospatial information in support of the new "normality", in which sustained physical distance is the only way to minimize the effects of the pandemic. Now it is time to move from response to recovery and reopening. Once, commercial life, educational centers, recreational spaces, etc. have been reestablished, the relative distance between the inhabitants begins to take on a leading role in the new way of life. And it that place is where geomatic tools have a lot to contribute.

- The wealth of professional exchanges carried out in these times has been one of the most outstanding aspects of this pandemic. As stated in the ninth pathway of the IGIF, cross-sector and interdisciplinary cooperation, coordination and collaboration with all levels of government, the geospatial industry, private sector, academia, and the international community is a premise to developing and sustaining an enduring response to disasters [8]. The collaboration and partnership generated by various professionals, from different countries, has resulted in the use of good practices that have no frontiers and are being applied in different parts of the continent. As geospatial professionals, practitioners and stakeholders strategic actions reinforcing the power of collaboration and true humanity.

19.4   Conclusions

In the previous sections, valuable experiences in the use of geospatial information to support the response to COVID-19 in countries of the region have been described,. Various institutional arrangements to coordinate the actions of the different national actors, to establish the links between geospatial agencies, ministries of health, and other relevant actors, with the offices in charge of emergency management. We also provided an overview of methodologies for the integration and analysis of geospatial data and its dissemination through accessible platforms for decision-makers and citizens.

Through the regional meetings and consultations carried out in the context of the pandemic, we have been able to verify that the countries, to a greater or lesser extent, have knowledge on methods and geospatial tools to face critical situations such as the COVID-19 pandemic. However, some gaps and challenges have also been identified that must be addressed, regarding to interoperability, data access policies, higher levels of disaggregation, capacity building, increased awareness at the level of authorities and availability of greater financing, among other.

Considering the above, in the region of the Americas there are strengths which support future crises of this or another nature. We also have weaknesses and challenges that open the way to strengthen our geospatial response. The crucial question then is, what should we do to capitalize our strengths, address gaps and achieve a comprehensive and sustainable geospatial response over time?

From UN-GGIM: Americas and ECLAC, we recognize a great opportunity in the new guidelines delivered by the working agenda of the UN-GGIM Initiative, and the need to bring down global frameworks in the countries of the region. These frameworks would make it possible to take advantage of and strengthen the response that we have today, provide cross-cutting work elements to the countries' management in geospatial matters, and prepare roadmaps with concrete actions to cover the existing gaps.

The Integrated Geospatial Information Framework (IGIF) and the Implementation Guide for its nine strategic pathways -governance and institutions, legal and policy issues, financing, geospatial data, innovation, standards, partnerships, education/capacity building, and communication- exhaustively and didactically provides a vision of what actions can be carried out to strengthen geospatial information management.

In particular, the Implementation Guide provides valuable guidance to address the five priorities of action of the Strategic Framework on Geospatial Information and Services for Disasters, which are connected and aligned with the IGIF's strategic pathways. For example, for the Disaster Framework Governance action priority, the IGIF explains how to establish working groups, define strategies, develop action plans, and monitor their progress, among other.

The same applies to other priorities of action such as data management, where the IGIF implementation guide suggests on the application of inventories (in this case to support disasters management), the development of geospatial data profiles, the analysis of gaps, the formulation of roadmaps for thematic data, and the generation of guidelines for the maintenance and custody of data, among others.

On the other hand, the Global Statistical Geospatial Framework (GSGF) provides tools for the territorial disaggregation of data, a fundamental requirement to have accurate diagnoses and to effectively guide the activation of alerts and decision-making for the management and recovery of this health, social and economic crisis. The GSGF highlights the importance of geocoding processes and the fundamental geospatial dataset that support it, for example, geo-referenced postal addresses, buildings, cadastral parcels, and other highly granular data.

From the regional level, we encourage countries to take full advantage of these guiding frameworks, through a collective and collaborative review among all public, private and academic actors, and then put them into operation on the basis of institutional agreements, intersectoral alliances, capacity building plans, and sustainable communication mechanisms over time.

References

[1] Maged N Kamel Boulos and Estella M Geraghty. Geographical tracking and mapping of coronavirus disease covid-19/severe acute respiratory syndrome coronavirus 2 (sars-cov-2) epidemic and associated events around the world: how 21st century gis technologies are supporting the global fight against outbreaks and epidemics, 2020.

[2] World Health Organization. World health organization website, 2020.

[3] Ivan Franch-Pardo, Brian M Napoletano, Fernando Rosete-Verges, and Lawal Billa. Spatial analysis and gis in the study of covid-19. a review. *Science of The Total Environment*, page 140033, 2020.

[4] Abolfazl Mollalo, Behzad Vahedi, and Kiara M Rivera. Gis-based spatial modeling of covid-19 incidence rate in the continental united states. *Science of The Total Environment*, page 138884, 2020.

[5] Johns Hopkins University and Medicine. Johns hopkins coronavirus resource center website, 2020.

[6] UN-GGIM: Américas. Un-ggim: Américas website, 2020.

[7] United Nations. Integrated geospatial information framework (igif), 2020.

[8] United Nations-Statistics Division and World Bank. Integrated geospatial information framework: A strategic guide to develop and strengthen national geospatial information management part 1: Overarching strategic framework, 2018.

[9] United Nations-Statistics Division. Global statistical geospatial framework, 2019.

[10] United Nations-Committee of Experts on Global Geospatial Information Management Working Group on Geospatial Information and Services for Disasters. Strategic framework on geospatial information and services for disasters, 2017.

[11] United Nations Office for Disaster Risk Reduction. Sendai framework for disaster risk reduction, 2015.

[12] ECLAC United Nations. Economic commission for latin america and the caribbean website, 2020.

[13] UN-GGIM: Americas. Un-ggim: Americas website, 2020.

[14] ECLAC United Nations. Observatorio covid-19 en américa latina y el caribe: Impacto económico y social, 2020.

[15] United Nations Expert Group on the Integration of Statistical and Geospatial Information. The gsgf implementation guide, 2019.

20

Spatio-Temporal Information Management to Control the COVID-19 Epidemic: Country Perspectives in Europe

Marije Louwsma and Hartmut Müller

The COVID-19 pandemic puts a heavy burden on populations, health care systems and governments alike. Europe has been one of the first epicenters of the pandemic, with a huge number of reported cases and fatalities. National governments in Europe applied a range of measures to mitigate the impact of the outbreak. Infectious diseases such as COVID-19 spread from person to person and thus in space and time. Local outbreaks occur frequently and different spatial distribution patterns can be observed. Therefore, policy makers and health care services have to respond to regional dynamics of new infections on a local basis. Theis chapter illustrates the state-of-the-art of providing COVID-19 information using selected EU countries as examples. From a supranational perspective, it can be stated that the most up-to-date data at national and sub-national level can be found in national dashboards, at the most detailed NUTS 3 level or even more detailed. The integrated view and analysis of COVID-19 data from different sources reveals a wide variety of difficulties, such as timeliness of reporting, ambiguous definitions of cases and fatalities, to name a few. In Europe, the potential of an integrated system is not yet fully exploited due to the obstacles identified. It remains to be seen to what extent and when this situation will improve in the future.

20.1 Introduction

After having recently published a Global Influenza Strategy 2019-2020 [1], on 11 March 2020, the World Health Organization WHO 'made the assessment that COVID-19 can be characterized as a pandemic' [2]. On 13 March 2020 WHO stated that 'Europe has now become the epicenter of the pandemic, with more reported cases and deaths than the rest of the world combined, apart from China'. On 19 March 2020 UN Secretary-General stated that 'the coronavirus pandemic is a crisis unlike any in the UN's 75-years history'. Apart from the people that contracted the disease, the epidemic put a heavy burden on health care and governments the like. Early detection, laboratory testing, isolation, contact tracing and referral of patients had to be managed. Furthermore, the demands of responding directly to COVID-19 while maintaining essential health service delivery had to be balanced.

20.2 Spatiotemporal Spread of Infectious Diseases

Infectious diseases spread from person to person and thus by their very nature in space and time. Depending on the characteristics of the disease, different spatial distribution patterns can be observed [3]. Since COVID-19 was not known before the start of the outbreak, little information was available about the circumstances that influence contamination and consequently the spatial distribution by infected people. The limited amount of information available from the first epicentres in China had to be used as the best assumption. From a global perspective, the influence of long-range airline traffic which shapes the spatiotemporal pattern of a global epidemic by forcing infections due to multiscale processes in the disease dynamics [4] is also of particular interest [5]. Experience with COVID-19 in China [6] suggests that in many cases the disease spreads under particular circumstances related to specific local environments. This results in spatially very heterogeneous distribution patterns in larger geographical areas.

To assess the impact of COVID-19 the British Health Foundation has compared the nationwide excess mortality rates in several European countries to the excess mortality rates in the COVID-19 hotspots of these countries [7, 8]. The parameter excess mortality was chosen because the number of registered deaths in all countries can be considered as one of the most reliable statistics, which is for various reasons regarded more reliable than the figures related to the dissemination of the disease itself. Many countries do have a longstanding registration system for census data, contrary to the registration of COVID-19 patients and related casualties. There is no risk of misrepresentation due to different definitions used, as is the case with the number of deaths registered with COVID-19 as the cause of death (see discussion below).

Spatiotemporal heterogeneous distributions of disease cases demand for analyses with special consideration of the spatiality of the underlying phenomena. The national figures might not be representative for the local and regional situation, due to uneven spreading of the disease. A first step to analyze the geographical distribution of the disease is to visualize diagnosed cases on maps. Meanwhile, distribution maps as a medium of COVID-19 representation can be found all over the world in a mass of official publications, newspapers, on social media platforms, in dashboards etc. A list of resources can be found at the website of the Open Geospatial Consortium [9].

Data visualization of territories, mostly at country level, through mapping, dashboards and other techniques, is a valuable tool to present the characteristics of spatiotemporal phenomena. Geospatial analysis of the underlying geospatial data can do much more. Trends in outbreaks over time and space, hotspots of infection, applicable rules and regulations, and available resources for medical treatment can be identified and disseminated to a wider public. In times of a pandemic such as COVID-19 a global view is needed to take appropriate action at all governance levels; global, supranational, national, and local.

In health context, individual humans represent the basic unit of spatial analysis. However, publicly available data are regularly being aggregated to a sufficient extent to adhere to privacy standards and regulations to protect individuals in their right for privacy [10].

An integrated statistical and geospatial framework [11] can be used as an excellent basis for managing such aggregated health data. Once a harmonized framework of spatially referenced territorial units is given, health data can be aggregated to the predefined territorial units and be used for presentation and further spatiotemporal analysis. In fact, many national health authorities already take advantage from these possibilities by providing national COVID-19 data within their national framework used for managing statistical national data. The following section will start by describing the reference system NUTS (Nomenclature des Unités Territoriales Statistiques) used for managing statistical information in Europe. After that, a number of use cases presenting COVID-19 related epidemic data by using the NUTS system will be briefly discussed.

20.3 NUTS (Nomenclature Des Unités Territoriales Statistiques), the European Union's Spatial Reference for Statistical Data

The Nomenclature of Territorial Units for Statistics (NUTS) provides a breakdown of the economic territory of the European Union into territorial units. It has been used in EU legislation since 1988, and it was converted to a formal Regulation of the European Parliament and the Council in 2003 [12]. While the national level of Member States is above NUTS, the NUTS classification consists of three hierarchical levels: each Member State is divided into NUTS 1 regions, then divided further into NUTS 2 regions, which in turn are subdivided into NUTS 3 regions. The NUTS regions regularly coincide with existing administrative units within the Member States, because the statistical data of the Member States are available for these units. A legislative procedure is in force to renew the classification, following changes in the Member States' administrative units. At EU level, the NUTS serves as a reference for the collection, development and harmonization of the European Union's regional statistics, for socio-economic analyses of the regions, and for the framing of EU regional policies.

The current NUTS nomenclature subdivides the territory of the European Union into 104 regions at NUTS 1 level, 281 regions at NUTS 2 level and 1,348 regions at NUTS 3 level. The NUTS Regulation defines the population size as a key indicator for comparability, laying down minimum and maximum thresholds for the population (Table 20.1).

TABLE 20.1
Population Size of the European Union's Administrative Units
(Source: [12])

Level	Min. number of inhabitants	Max. number of inhabitants
NUTS 1	3 million	7 million
NUTS 2	800.000	3 million
NUTS 3	150.000	800.000

Following the heterogeneous population density across the EU territory this definition results in a wide span of both area size and population number: the largest NUTS 1 region is Manner-Suomi (Finland), covering 336,859 km^2, the smallest region, Région de Bruxelles-Capitale (Belgium) covers 161 km^2. At NUTS 2 level, Pohjois-ja ltä-Suomi (Finland) covers 227,150 km^2, Ciudad Autónoma de Melilla (Spain) 13 km^2, at NUTS 3 level the figures are Norrbottens län (Sweden), 105,205 km^2 and again Ciudad Autónoma de Melilla (Spain), 13 km^2.

20.4 COVID-19 Pandemic Data Using the NUTS System

20.4.1 EU Level

Eurostat, the statistical office of the European Union situated in Luxembourg, concentrates on providing relevant statistics to tackle the implications of the Covid-19 outbreak. Eurostat maintains an interactive dashboard regarding Covid-19 developments within Europe, based on the data provided by its member states (Figure 20.1).

Note: The map in Figure 20.1 is based on information provided to ECDC by the EU/EEA Member States and UK on their subnational levels of COVID-19 transmission (NUTS 2 regions) according to the categories defined by the World Health Organization. When no information has been provided by the countries on the level of COVID-19 transmission, the region is marked as 'not reported'.

The European Union is a union of sovereign states. The EU design gives the maximum respect for the sovereignty of its member states. At the same time, it ensures that the system is operational

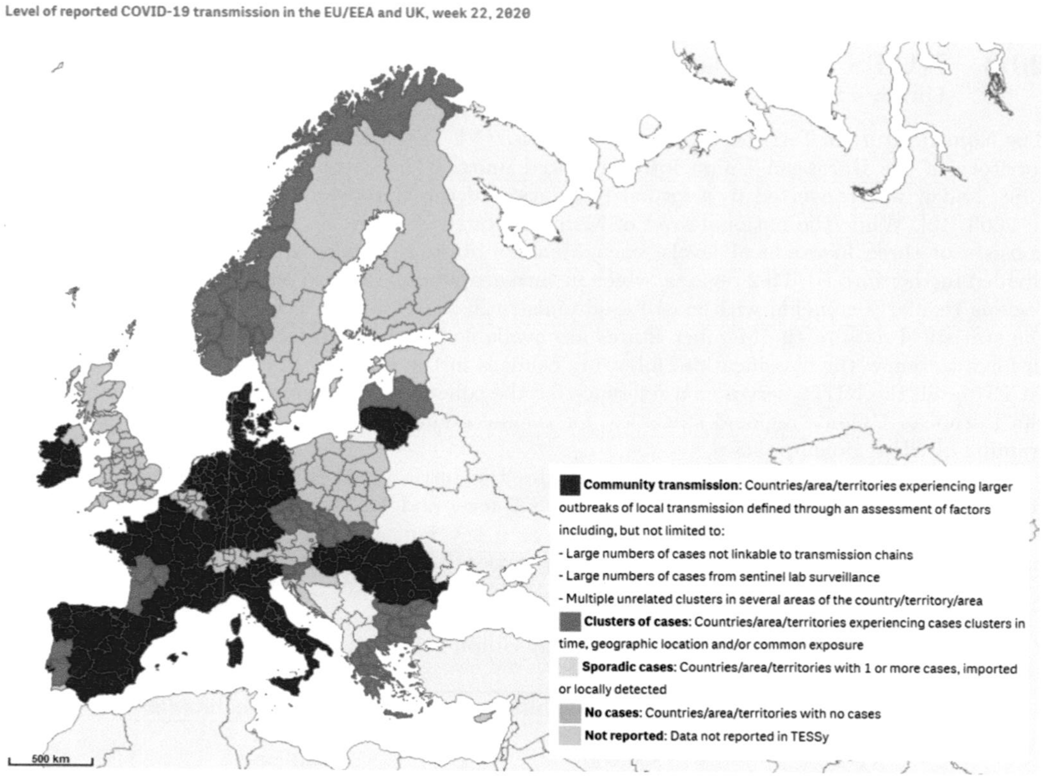

Level of reported COVID-19 transmission in the EU/EEA and UK, week 22, 2020

Community transmission: Countries/area/territories experiencing larger outbreaks of local transmission defined through an assessment of factors including, but not limited to:
- Large numbers of cases not linkable to transmission chains
- Large numbers of cases from sentinel lab surveillance
- Multiple unrelated clusters in several areas of the country/territory/area

Clusters of cases: Countries/area/territories experiencing cases clusters in time, geographic location and/or common exposure

Sporadic cases: Countries/area/territories with 1 or more cases, imported or locally detected

No cases: Countries/area/territories with no cases

Not reported: Data not reported in TESSy

FIGURE 20.1
Country Level Information on COVID-19 in Europe (Source: [13])

and decisions can be taken. The role of EU institutions has evolved over time, but national institutions also continue to play key roles by performing their traditional functions at the national level. This fact became very evident again in the initial phase of the COVID-19 outbreak, when political decisions were predominantly taken by the national member governments. From a certain level, this also applies to the provision of information, including geospatial health information. In the following sections, this will be illustrated using selected EU countries as examples.

20.4.2 National and Sub-National Level

Providing up to date information about the distribution of the virus and prevailing measures is key to make informed decisions on the one hand and on the other hand to inform citizens and organisations to comply with the policy within a country (awareness raising or sensitization). Most up-to-date data at sub-national level, either at NUTS 3 level or even more detailed, can be found in national dashboards. Some use cases will be presented here.

20.4.2.1 France

The French government has published a dashboard on the internet that presents COVID-19 related information geographically. It is possible to retrieve the information on a particular date. Hence it is possible to consult the course of the disease geographically. Various information is included: the current level of precautionary measures based on the number of detected cases (Figure 20.2), the transfer of patients within France and Europe, test sampling locations and their status and the test results per administrative unit.

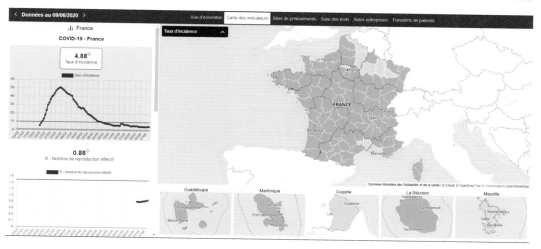

FIGURE 20.2
Vigilance Map for France on 9 June 2020 (Source: [14])

20.4.2.2 The Netherlands

After the crisis team became operable, the national insitute for public health and the environment (RIVM), operating under the Ministry of Health, Welfare and Sport, became responsible for dissemination of Covid-19 related data and figures. The government in the Netherlands chose to publish most Covid-19 related information in traditional graphs instead of mapping it. Only the relative number of Covid-19 cases and hospitalized people per 100,000 inhabitants per municipality were visualized geographically. Compared to absolute numbers, this relative number allows to compare between municipalities with varying population densities. The media mapped the confirmed hospitalized patients over time at municipality level to show the spreading of the disease of the country over time [15]. Here, one can see that the disease was spread across the country from the south to the west and north due to various events, e.g. spring holiday and carnival, and movements of people between the regions. The three most norther provinces were hardly affected, most likely due to their remote character relative to the location of the big cities in the west and south.

20.4.2.3 Germany

At March 2020, Germany had introduced consistent measures to combat COVID-19 that were implemented nationwide. Over time, it became clear that the spread of infection is mainly concentrated in local hotspots, without it being possible to predict such locations precisely. Therefore, on 6 May 2020 policy makers agreed to respond to regional dynamics of new infections on a local basis, using the NUTS 3 level administrative units as the spatial reference. It was decided that in districts or urban municipalities, the German NUTS 3 level units, with a cumulative rate of more than 50 new cases of infection per 100,000 inhabitants within the previous seven days, restrictions adapted to the local situation will immediately be implemented. A cumulative rate of more than 35 new cases of infection per 100,000 inhabitants within the previous seven days was set as threshold for early warning [16].

Figure 20.3 shows the temporal dynamics of infections over time including the numbers as of 12 June 2020, with one NUTS 3 unit surpassing the intervention threshold of 50 infections per 100,000 inhabitants within the previous seven days (LK Aichach-Friedberg, 59 cases), and five units reaching the early warning limit of 35 infections per 100,000 inhabitants within the previous seven days (LK Cuxhaven 44 cases, SK Bremerhaven 41 cases, LK Sonneburg 41 cases, LK Göttingen 37 cases, LK Coburg 35 cases).

The Robert-Koch-Institute, Germany's public health institute, collects data on, among others,

12 Dynamics of infections.png

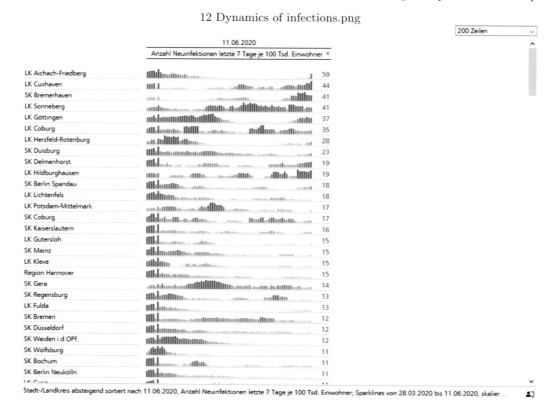

FIGURE 20.3
Dynamics of Infections per 100,000 Inhabitants in Germany at the Nuts 3 Level (Source: [17])

infectious diseases; it communicates information by a COVID-19 specific dashboard and offers the underlying data to the general public on a daily updated basis. The data can be downloaded in different formats. Retrieving the data via an ESRI ArcGIS Feature Service is a very versatile way to get direct access to the attributes and geometries of the layers. Geospatial data retrieved via a Web Feature Server make it possible to use the complete set of GIS tools for comprehensive spatiotemporal analyses. For example, the period of time and further spread of local outbreaks can be tracked. At the same time, using such spatially aggregated data preserves data protection and data privacy.

A major event illustrating the benefits of locally adapted measures occurred in June 2020, when a COVID-19 outbreak was detected at a German meat processing plant in the week ending 21 June 2020 [18]. The outbreak near Gütersloh (see Figure 20.4, prism in red) was first reported on Wednesday 17 June, when 400 workers tested positive. By Friday 19 June, that number had doubled to 803 and it climbed further to 1,331 by Sunday 21 June. The number of confirmed infections for the corresponding NUTS 3 unit LK Gütersloh rose to 264 per 100,000 inhabitants within one week, thus far exceeding the intervention threshold of 50 infections. Seven days high incidences in neighbouring districts are linked to the outbreak in Gütersloh [19]. The now localised lockdown strategy permitted the local authorities to limit the quarantine order to the 5,500 employees of the plant and their families, rather than imposing a broad lockdown affecting the social and economic lives of many millions of people in the whole country.

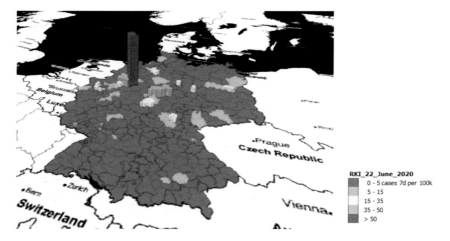

RKI_22_June_2020
0 - 5 cases 7d per 100k
5 - 15
15 - 35
35 - 50
> 50

FIGURE 20.4
Visualization at Nuts 3 Level of a Major Local COVID-19 Outbreak in Germany, June 2020. Source: Own Representation, Data Based on Robert Koch-Institut (Rki), DL-de/by-2-0, Map Tiles by Stamen Design, Under CC by 3.0. Data by Openstreetmap, Under CC by SA

20.5   Shortcuts and Challenges of COVID-19 Data Provision

Data problems in providing COVID-19 data are manifold. The Washington Post expresses the facts in this perfect, concise statement: 'Case counts are consistently inconsistent. Reporting practices differ from country to country, state to state, even county to county' [20].

The Johns Hopkins University, Baltimore, Maryland, USA, maintains a coronavirus resource center [21], a globally intensively used resource for better understanding of and information about the virus. The researchers of Johns Hopkins University are doing very valuable work by collecting data and, at the same time, by managing a list of open issues [22]. At the time of writing this article, the list consists of 1,344 open issues, with 899 issues already closed. A comprehensive review of the existing data problems is beyond the scope of this article. For illustration purposes, however, some relevant exemplary problems shall be addressed briefly.

1. The Quest for Reliable Data
   The number of confirmed cases depends largely on the number of conducted diagnostic tests: the more laboratory tests are conducted, the more positive cases are discovered. A lack of test material or testing capacity hampered some countries to produce reliable data regarding the number of positive tested persons. As an alternative other data were used to monitor the progress of the disease, such as the number of hospitalized people.

2. The Timeliness of Reporting
   There is no obvious reason why both the number of confirmed cases of disease and the number of disease-induced deaths should be lower on weekends than on working days. However, this is exactly what most country statistics display. It seems to be much more likely that a smaller number of cases are registered at weekends because fewer diagnostic tests are conducted at weekends, or because there are delays in reporting due to staff at health offices not being on the job, or for other reasons. The timeliness of the data therefore fluctuates without this being precisely documented in many cases.

3. The Need for Unambiguous Definitions
   Differences in the definition of diagnosed and reported cases, even changes in the definition occur. For illustration purposes, some application cases shall be mentioned.

China reported 15,132 new cases for a single day, February 12 2020. The reason for this spike was a change in how cases are diagnosed and reported in Hubei province starting on the same day. In the Hubei province only, medical professionals can classify a suspected case of COVID-19 as a clinically confirmed case, without having to have a laboratory confirmation. Of the 15,132 new cases reported, only 1,820 were new laboratory confirmed cases, all others were due to the changed counting method of the cases [23].

In a similar way the U.S. moved from counting only laboratory confirmed cases to counting 'confirmed and probable cases and deaths' [24].

In early April, France reported 17,827 additional cases and 532 plus 884 additional deaths from nursing homes, that had not previously been included in the official counts. Similarly, the daily figures for COVID-19 deaths in one country might, for example, only include those dying in hospitals, while other countries include deaths in nursing homes in their figures [23].

20.6 Discussion

Due to the epidemic character and unfamiliarity with the disease, no standardized methodology to collect data was available. This makes it difficult to compare between countries and to provide decision-makers and the public with reliable information. For logic reasons, each country drafted their own procedures and policy regarding the testing strategy, and these might have been altered over the course of the epidemic. Many variables influenced the strategy, for example the availability of testing material, the capacity of health care to treat patients, and political viewpoints. Some countries (initially) ignored or underestimated the impact of the infectious disease, which led to a more severe outbreak. The country examples show nicely which data was collected and were regarded 'reliable' enough to be published.

Apart from variations in the type of data collected, also the purpose of geospatial data – i.e. the use case – differed. On the one hand, geospatial information played an important role to inform the public about the severity of the outbreak, the spatial distribution and possible measures that applied in particular local regions or municipalities. Graphics and maps in a complementary dashboard are an important means for communication.

The other role of geospatial information relates to analytical purposes. Governments need reliable information to decide how to respond to the crises. Of course, with a new disease, much is unknown, and politicians have few resources to rely on, except for knowledge and expectations from the experts. However, over the course of the epidemic, it is essential to collect data to monitor progress and effectiveness of imposed measures, such as the closure of facilities and restrictions to travel.

The purpose for which geospatial information is used, should relate to how the geospatial information is presented and which means are used. Can it best be presented in a simple graph or is a map better? And how to include specific spatial developments related to spread of the disease across the country, or across the region? The level of detail provided should be considered and related to the purpose as well. A comparison between countries or between continents requires a different presentation of data, e.g. more accumulation is needed, then a detailed location-specific analysis for decision-makers.

20.6.1 The Data Problem

Every presentation and analysis of geospatial information is a result of the underlying data. Responding to a global epidemic requires coordinated action at all levels, both global and supranational, as well as national and local. As discussed in section 'Shortcuts and challenges of COVID-19 data provision', there is a lack of internationally harmonized standards for data collection and data provision of COVID-19 data. This limitation makes it difficult, if not impossible, to compare data collected in different countries and thus hinders information and possibly informed joint political action at the international level.

Other global issues, such as achieving the Sustainable Development Goals (SDG) 2030, face similar data problems. In July 2017, the United Nations General Assembly adopted a Global Indicator Framework consisting of 232 statistical indicators designed to measure the SDG goals and targets [25]. Populating those indicators poses enormous challenges, which is even described as an 'unprecedented statistical' challenge [26]. MacFeely [27] distinguishes two different groups of SDG indicators: Indicators that are conceptually clear, have an internationally established methodology, and for which standards are available, and indicators, for which internationally established or standards are not yet available, but are being (or will be) developed or tested.

20.6.2 Public Health Data and Statistical Information

As discussed above, health data are regularly provided by national health authorities in an aggregated form within the same national framework that is used to manage statistical national data. For this reason, a globally well-defined integrated statistical and geospatial framework could serve as an excellent basis for managing not only relatively low-dynamic statistical data, but also highly-dynamic health data, such as those generated in the event of a global epidemic. In this way spatiality of statistical information [28] and dynamic health data could go hand in hand. INEGI, the National Institute of Statistics, Geography and Informatics of Mexico [29] implemented one of the first geostatistical dashboards presenting COVID-19 data and statistical indicators in an integrated form [30]. The analysis of confirmed, suspected, negative COVID-19 cases and COVID-19 deaths in the context of statistical indicators at both state and municipality level (population density, population aged 60 and over, educational and economic characteristics, health services, hospital infrastructure, etc.) makes it possible to assess the level of vulnerability of the population (see [31]).

20.6.3 Public Health Data and Spatial Data Infrastructures

By definition, a pandemic is 'the worldwide spread of a new disease' [2]. Consequently, a pandemic requires a worldwide coordinated response. Due to global dependencies and exchange of goods and people, there is a need to coordinate actions to limit further spreading of the disease. However, each country has its own authority and powers to take decisions. In Europe, countries developed their own strategy to counteract the disease despite a shared understanding of the potential impact of the outbreak on society. A parallel can be drawn with the management of geospatial COVID-19 data. Each country made their own decisions regarding which data to collect, how to measure and monitor progress of the outbreak, and how to display and disseminate the information to the public.

At the beginning of this century, a similar situation existed with regard to the Spatial Data Infrastructures (SDI) of the EU Member States. To overcome the unsatisfactory situation of lack of interoperability between the different National Data Infrastructures (NSDI), it was decided to create a European Spatial Data Infrastructure to enable the sharing of environmental geospatial information among public sector organisations, to facilitate public access to geospatial information across Europe and to support policy-making across national borders. In 2007 the INSPIRE (INfrastructure for SPatial InfoRmation in Europe) Directive came into force, with full implementation required by 2021 [32]. INSPIRE is based on the National Data Infrastructures established and operated by the Member States of the European Union.

Although long-established standards for a European Spatial Data Infrastructure are available, it does not currently seem possible to provide a high-quality European dashboard capable of disseminating COVID-19 data from individual Member States in a standardized form. Part of the reason lies in the novice nature of the disease in combination with the diverse institutional settings in each country. Most of these institutions are not oriented towards geospatial information, but deal with healthcare, public health and public order and safety.

Murgante et al. [33] publish the results of a comprehensive research on the COVID-19 outbreak in Italy, in which health, geographical and planning aspects were equally considered and integrated. The aim of the study was to conduct a fine and disaggregate analysis at the local level. The analysis demonstrated the spatial diffusion and the distribution of the COVID-19 outbreak in Italy by referencing some major groups of variables: land use, air quality, climate and weather, population, health and life expectancy. Many high-resolution data on land use, air quality, climate and weather, population, health and wellness were needed as input data for such detailed analyses. The authors report that they had to collect data from many different sources, COVID-19 data from the Italian Ministry of Health, from regional administrations, from local health agencies, even from newspapers. Socio-economic and demographic data came from the Italian Statistical Institute, environmental data and indicators had to be collected from different sources, such as the Higher Institute for Environmental Protection and Research, the World Health Organization, the European Environmental Agency, the Italian Automobile Club. Weather and wind data had to be retrieved from other websites, data on air quality and weather conditions from special dashboards.

Considerable preparatory work was needed to integrate those data so that could be used as input for analyses. Most of this data could be provided within a well-defined spatial data infrastructure, directly and instantly accessible, clearly linked to georeferenced statistical, health and other relevant information.

20.6.4 Integration of Public Health Data, Statistical Data and Basic Geospatial Data

To take full advantage of the wealth of information available in the various institutions it is necessary to develop and implement solutions for the integrated management of public health data, general statistical data and basic geospatial data.

Since 2016, the global 'integration of spatial, statistical and other related information' has been explicitly on the agenda of the UN Committee of Experts on Global Spatial Data Management [34, 35]. The COVID-19 epidemic demonstrates in a perhaps unparalleled way the need to provide globally integrated spatial, statistical and health-related information, adapted to the needs of very diverse users.

20.7 Conclusions

A pandemic, a worldwide-spread of a new disease, requires a worldwide coordinated response. An infectious disease spreads over space and time at different speeds and can cause local outbreaks. A new disease calls for new insights, which must be gained through synoptic observations from different perspectives, medical, social and economic. Spatio-temporal analysis can help to gain such new insights by relating disease-related data, such as case numbers, hospital occupations, fatality rates, etc. which evolve over time, to statistical indicators and to the locations to which they refer.

In order for spatio-temporal information systems to develop their full potential, the characteristics of the data they contain must be clearly defined and the underlying spatial reference units must be consistently defined. Such high-quality and trusted information can help decision-makers to intervene at the right time and at the right place, rather than relying on general figures. More than that, a quality controlled spatiotemporal database can support post-pandemic analysis in many different areas of interest.

Much groundwork has already been done in the domain of spatial data infrastructures, both at national and supranational level. At this stage, committees and working groups are concentrating on the development of solutions for the integration of statistical information into such infrastructures, which will then be implemented by the individual countries.

The epidemic demonstrates the urgent need for an integrated spatial and statistical information system at the global level, but also at the country level and beyond. This chapter showed how various countries implemented a system at the national level, which led to a range of diverse solutions, interfaces, and management information. This pluralism in national solutions was integrated at the European level into a data platform based on the input from individual member states and their systems. After some initial hick-ups, the information was used to discuss interventions at the European level and feed these back into national actions, e.g. regarding cross-border travel regulations between countries. However, the potential of an integrated system at the country level and the European level is not fully taken advantage of yet due to mentioned barriers. Once the systems at the country level have matured and aligned, it will leverage the benefits for both government and societal resilience at the country level and at European level.

An integrated system providing basic geospatial data, statistical data, and public health data in one and the same framework would make it possible to retrieve georeferenced information in near real time at all levels – global, supranational, national and local – in a timely and user-oriented manner.

It remains to be investigated to what extent and how the organizational, technical, and legal challenges of such an initiative can be mastered.

References

[1] WHO World Health Organization. Global influenza strategy 2019-2030. *License: CC BY-NC-SA 3.0 IGO, 31 p., ISBN 978-924-151532-0. World Health Organization*, 2019. URL https://apps.who.int/iris/handle/10665/311184.

[2] WHO World Health Organization. Coronavirus Disease (COVID-2019) Situation Reports. *World Health Organization*, 2020. URL https://www.who.int. Accessed on June 2020.

[3] Mark D Verhagen, David M Brazel, Jennifer Beam Dowd, Ilya Kashnitsky, and Melinda C Mills. Forecasting spatial, socioeconomic and demographic variation in COVID-19 health care demand in England and Wales. *BMC Med 18*, 203, 2020. URL https://doi.org/10.1186/s12916-020-01646-2.

[4] Duygu Balcan, Vittoria Colizza, Bruno Gonçalves, Hao Hu, José J. Ramasco, and Alessandro Vespignani. Multiscale mobility networks and the spatial spreading of infectious diseases. *Proceedings of the National Academy of Sciences of the United States of America*, 106(51), 2009. URL https://www.pnas.org/content/106/51/21484.

[5] J.A Backer, Don Klinkenberg, and Jacco Wallinga. Incubation period of 2019 novel coronavirus (2019-nCoV) infections among travellers from Wuhan, China, 20-28 January 2020. *Euro Surveill*. URL https://www.eurosurveillance.org/content/10.2807/1560-7917.ES.2020.25.5.2000062#html_fulltext.

[6] Wentao Yang, Min Deng, Chaokui Li, and Jincai Huang. Spatio-Temporal Patterns of the 2019-nCoV Epidemic at the County Level in Hubei Province, China. *International Journal of Environmental Research and Public Health*, 17:2563, 2020. doi: 10.3390/ijerph17072563. URL www.mdpi.com/journal/ijerph.

[7] The Health Foundation. Excess mortality rates for the period from 28 February 2020 March to 22 May 2020, nationwide figures. 2020. URL https://www.health.org.uk/news-and-comment/charts-and-infographics/understanding-excess-deaths-countries-regions-localities. Accessed on June 2020.

[8] The Health Foundation. Excess mortality rates for the period from 28 February 2020 March to 22 May 2020 in hotspots. 2020. URL https://www.health.org.uk/news-and-comment/charts-and-infographics/understanding-excess-deaths-countries-regions-localities. Accessed on June 2020.

[9] OGC. 2020. URL https://www.ogc.org/resources-for-COVID-19-from-ogc. Accessed on October 2020.

[10] Pierre Goovaerts. Geostatistical analysis of health data: State-of-the-art and perspectives. In *A. Soares et al. (eds.), geoENV VI – Geostatistics for Environmental Applications*, pages 3–22. C Springer Science+Business Media B.V., 2008. doi: 10.1007/978-1-4020-6448-7_1.

[11] UN-GGIM. 2020. URL https://ggim.un.org/IGIF/. Accessed on October 2020.

[12] EUROSTAT. Regions in the European Union, edition 2018, Nomenclature of territorial units for statistics -NUTS 2016/EU-28. *Publications Office of the European Union, Luxembourg*, 2018. doi: 10.2785/475524.

[13] European Centre for Disease Prevention and Control. Country level information on COVID-19 in Europe. 2020. URL https://qap.ecdc.europa.eu/public/extensions/COVID-19/COVID-19.html. Accessed on 4 June 2020.

[14] French government. Vigilance map for France at 9 June 2020. 2020. URL https://www.gouvernement.fr/info-coronavirus/carte-et-donnees#activite-epidemique. Accessed on 8 September 2020.

[15] RTL nieuws. 2020. URL https://www.rtlnieuws.nl/nieuws/nederland/artikel/5128431/corona-gemeente-nederland-verspreiding-wanneer-haard-besmettingen. Accessed on June 2020.

[16] German Federal Government. Press release number151/20 of 6May2020. 2020. URL https://www.bundesregierung.de/resource/blob/973812/1751456/c197062365f7e60780e9039dc4e336ee/2020-05-06-beschluss-bund-laender-eng-data.pdf?download=1. Accessed on June 2020.

[17] Bissantz Business Intelligence. Dynamics of infections per 100,000 inhabitants in Germany at the NUTS 3 level. 2020. URL https://data.bissantz.de/Session.aspx?application=2000#s-237. Accessed on 13 June 2020.

[18] World News. German coronavirus outbreak at abattoir infects more than 1,000. 2020. URL https://www.reuters.com/article/us-health-coronavirus-meat-toennies/german-coronavirus-outbreak-at-abattoir-infects-more-than-1000-idUSKBN23R0Q5.

[19] Robert Koch Institute. Coronavirus Disease 2019 (COVID-19) Daily Situation Report of the Robert Koch Institute22/06/2020 - UPDATED STATUS FOR GERMANY. 2020. URL https://www.rki.de/DE/Content/InfAZ/N/Neuartiges_Coronavirus/Situationsberichte/2020-06-22-en.pdf. Accessed on June 2020.

[20] The Washington Post. Millions track the pandemic on Johns Hopkins's dashboard. Those who built it say some miss the real story, by Kyle Swenson, June 29, 2020 at 9:50 p.m. GMT+2. 2020. URL https://www.washingtonpost.com/local/johns-hopkins-tracker/2020/06/29/daea7eea-a03f-11ea-9590-1858a893bd59_story.html. Accessed on June 2020.

[21] Johns Hopkins University. 2020. URL https://coronavirus.jhu.edu/. Accessed on October 2020.

[22] GitHub. 2020. URL https://github.com/CSSEGISandData/COVID-19/issues. Accessed on June 2020.

[23] Worldometer. COVID-19 coronavirus pandemic. 2020. URL https://www.worldometers.info/coronavirus/.

[24] CDC. Centers for Disease Control and Prevention. 2020. URL https://www.cdc.gov/coronavirus/2019-ncov/cases-updates/cases-in-us.html. Accessed on June 2020.

[25] UN (United Nations) General Assembly. Resolution adopted by the General Assembly on 6 July 2017 – Work of the Statistical Commission pertaining to the 2030 Agenda for Sustainable Development. Seventy-first session. A/RES/71/313. 2017. URL https://undocs.org/A/RES/71/313. Accessed on June 2020.

[26] Lebada A.M. Member states, statisticians address SDG monitoring requirements. 2016. URL http://sdg.iisd.org/news/member-states-statisticians-address-sdg-monitoring-requirements/. Accessed on June 2020.

[27] Steve MacFeely. Measuring the Sustainable Development Goal Indicators: An Unprecedented Statistical Challenge. *Journal of Official Statistics*, 36(2):361–378, 2020. doi: 10.2478/jos-2020-0019.

[28] UN (United Nations). Economic Commission for Europe, Conference of European Statisticans, In-depth review of developing geospatial information services based on official statistics. *Meeting of the 2015/2016 Bureau, Luxembourg*. 2016. URL https://www.unece.org/fileadmin/DAM/stats/documents/ece/ces/bur/2016/February/02-In-depth_review_on_developing_geospatial_information_final.pdf. Accessed on June 2020.

[29] INEGI. 2020. URL https://en.www.inegi.org.mx. Accessed on October 2020.

[30] INEGI. 2020. URL https://gaia.inegi.org.mx/covid19/. Accessed on October 2020.

[31] INEGI. Covid-19: Context indicators GeoStatistical-dashboard. 2020. URL https://www.cepal.org/sites/default/files/presentations/covid-19-strategies-geospatial-response-lac-mexico_0.pdf. Accessed on October 2020.

[32] European Union (EU). Directive 2007/2/EC of the European Parliament and of the Council of 14 March 2007 establishing an Infrastructure for Spatial Information in the European Community (INSPIRE). OJ L 108, 25.4.2007, p. 1–14 (BG, ES, CS, DA, DE, ET, EL, EN, FR, IT, LV, LT, HU, MT, NL, PL, PT, RO, SK, SL, FI, SV) Special edition in Croatian: Chapter 13 Volume 030 P. 270 – 283. 2007. URL https://inspire.ec.europa.eu/documents/directive-20072ec-european-parliament-and-council-14-march-2007-establishing.

[33] B Murgante, G Borruso, G Balletto, P Castiglia, and M Dettori. Why Italy First? Health, Geographical and Planning Aspects of the COVID-19 Outbreak. *Sustainability*, 12, 2020, 5064.

[34] UN-GGIM. UN Committee of Experts on Global Spatial Data Management, Sixth session New York. 2016. URL http://ggim.un.org/knowledgebase/Attachment1651.aspx?AttachmentType=1. Accessed on June 2020.

[35] European Union/United Nations. The integration of statistical and geospatial information — a call for political action in Europe, UN-GGIM: Europe, Work Group on Data Integration, subgroup 1. Luxembourg: Publications Office of the European Union, Luxembourg, 2019, ISBN 978-92-76-05474-0. 2019. URL https://ec.europa.eu/eurostat/documents/4031688/10158240/KS-03-19-423-EN-N.pdf/c8f75ee1-2181-288c-1efa-1622c5abb980. Accessed on June 2020.

21

Practicing Online Higher Education Facilitated by ICT in China: In the Context of COVID-19 Pandemic

Zhixuan Yang

The impact of COVID-19 pandemic on higher education pushes forward the transformation of traditional in-class education to fully online education. The chapter analyzes the experience of online education firstly in literature, particularly, the external and internal elements that influence learning outcomes in flipped classrooms and Massive Open Online Courses (MOOC). Besides, the chapter also touches base on the learning behavior change in online higher education to reveal the internal driving force of self-regulation in the distancing learning environment. The results of a survey in the course of GIS for Real Estate to analyze the importance of the crucial elements in the learning practice suggest that COVID-19 pandemic has a crucial influence on the teaching-learning process. It has been also noticed that the resilience of the community to the shock of health disaster and the speed of reaction to the preparedness for the change in the broader sense is meaningful to the success of the practice of higher online education.

21.1   Introduction

COVID-19 pandemic is a devastating global crisis which has caused millions of confirmed cases and hundreds of thousands of death. It is the most serious global epidemic since the Spanish pandemic 100 years before. In China, the pandemic is a nationwide epidemic, reshaping social activities as well as causing changes in higher education. The online higher education has become a teaching-learning routine since the spring semester in 2020, influencing approximately 32 million students studying in colleges and universities. The fully online higher education causes the transformation of such a vast amount of students studying remotely from home.

There is limited information on online higher education in practice. Different from theoretical research, practical research requires a solid investigation of operations in online education, particularly, the ICT preparedness, the monitoring process, and the evaluation of performance. In general, the prerequisites of the practice influence the most in terms of successful implementation. That means the following three points are important. First, ICTs should be ready and accessible. Teachers and students have access to the internet as well as mobile devices. Second, mobile devices and online applications can be applied to the learning management system. Users' devices can access learning management systems and online applications. Third, sufficient and informative online courses should be available. Teachers have recorded teaching videos and calibrate digital materials for teaching purposes.

The practice of online higher education officially started on 1st March 2020 when the spring semester began. Up till the end of the semester in July, it has shown that the practice was generally successful. It is necessary to introduce the experience in practice and analyze the pros and cons. Therefore, the chapter focuses on the current practice of online higher education facilitated by ICT to illustrate the crucial elements of maintaining the performance in the context of the COVID-19 pandemic in China.

21.2   Literature Review

21.2.1   ICTs and Online Accessibility

It has been a long history of discussion of online higher education in theory. By definition, online education refers to educational activities in cyberspace which are facilitated by the internet, information communication technology (ICT), and geospatial information system. Due to the innovative way of remote teaching and distancing learning, online education creates the virtual reality of study anytime, anyplace for anyone. To be exact, the virtual environment bases on the internet and ICT, leveraging the advantages of flexibility, accessibility, content diversity, scalability, and cost-effectiveness in modern education. In that sense, ICTs are the fundamental instruments in the knowledge delivery, engaging teachers together with learners in problem-solving and critical thinking [1].

As remote teaching and learning require the accessibility of online courses, the ICT facilitation is critical regarding the successful performance of distancing education. It also matters the engagement of students in the technology-enriched learning environment which is important to identify and evaluate the students' needs and help teachers to calibrate the teaching content to the knowledge in their need.

Apart from the facilitation of ICT, online higher education also requires students to have strong self-directed and self-regulated inner drives. In that sense, the design of an online learning environment is crucial. The supportive online learning environment includes three layers, i.e. participants, micro-level and macro-level environments [2]. The layers overlap and cooperate in the creation of a satisfactory and accessible virtual learning environment. In the three layers, the participants are the central roles as instructors, responders, and actors; the micro-level environment refers to the learning management system (LMS) that forms the digital interactive platform; the macro-level environment consists of the cyber and digital environment and ICTs' facilitation.

As the online learning environment is important regarding course performance, the previous researches reveal the elements that foster a good environment. For example, researchers find that the appropriate instructional design of prediction, observation, explanation, and evaluation (POEE) is necessary for the inquiry learning process. Besides, the course design in the scaffolding modular structure is meaningful to a better understanding environment and it can also provide support for self-learning [3, 4]. In addition, the online self-assessment toolbox in the learning management systems (LMS) and the virtual learning environment (VLE) interface facilitates leaning performance as well [5]. Furthermore, the design of sociable environments can enhance learners' social presence and interaction, which enables confidence in the learning process [6].

21.2.2   Experience Learned from Flipped Classroom and MOOC

As discussed, the readiness of digital infrastructure is crucial regarding the preparation of online education. The ICT infrastructure requires high-speed digital signals, mobile smart devices as well as environment friendly leaning management systems (LMS). Before the pandemic, the online higher education facilitated by ICT has been prevalently used in blended learning (BL), such as flipped classroom and Massive Open Online Courses (MOOC), which is known as one of the major trends in higher education [7]. In the face of the epidemic, the former experience of flipped classroom and MOOC is beneficial to teachers as it is helpful in terms of appropriate online resources and adjustable video courses to different levels of learners.

21.2.2.1 Flipped Classroom

The flipped classroom is a model that the in-class teaching course is deliverable outside the classroom via virtual online LMS, leaving the time in the classroom effective for questions and discussions [8]. The flipped classroom is regarded as an advanced teaching method due to the power of online teaching technology, driving the significant contribution to efficient learning outside the classroom, and leaving the time in class open for the innovative collision of deep thoughts.

There are arguments about the pros and cons of flipped classroom and experiences can be referential to online education. As the teaching content is taught in the video course, the well-designed video course is crucial to efficient learning outside the classroom. Besides, knowledge, skills, engagement with students' satisfaction, and advanced organization via e-learning management system (LMS) are the fundamental dimensions of the flipped classroom [9].

The flipped classroom emphasizes the teacher's ability of course control regarding the course design in terms of the percentage of the video course and in-class interaction, the skill of instilling various knowledge in class monitoring, the organization's ability as well as the engagement of students in the teaching-learning process. However, the flipped classroom is not the fully-online education as the part of education is still conducted in the classroom. The teachers and students still have the chance of face-to-face interaction, so traditional ways of the class organization such as group discussion can be fulfilled. The outside and inside classrooms are complementary to the goal of good performance of the learning process. Even if the failure of teaching outside the classroom fails, there are still chances of monitoring teaching outcomes. In contrast, MOOC has more common features with fully-online higher education.

21.2.2.2 MOOC

The MOOC stands for Massive Open Online Course and represents an instructional approach that provides students access to online courses from places anywhere around the world [10]. Alhazzani [11] reveals that MOOCs have a significant direct impact on higher education as it improves education outcomes [11]. Besides, studies of MOOC are contributable to online higher education as the MOOC can be the fully-online and outside the classroom. Generally, the researches touch base on the advantages of MOOC in practice regarding the sharing of high-quality education resources as well as flexible self-study via portable ICTs. In a sense, MOOC has become global evaluation criteria regarding the level of the university.

However, the difficulties of monitoring the performance of MOOC is also of great concern as it requires high self-regulation and remains uncertain of students involvement via distancing education. Researchers find that good performance of MOOC requires concerns on students' engagement in the learning process as the vast majority of students may drop out before completing courses when the loose engagement undermining learning performance [10].

Teachers' facilitation can foster a positive environment by offering informative course materials, which enables the students' engagement. Besides, the teachers' facilitation improves the efficiency of knowledge transmission and quality of interaction, which enhances the engagement, motivation, and satisfaction of students. But importantly, the students' confirmation, satisfaction, and attitude have directly or indirectly influenced the intention to continue using MOOCs [12].

It is suggested that the intention of use, interaction, engagement, motivation, and satisfaction, are the five pillars of MOOC [13]. Among those, the quality of interaction is regarded as the paramount element in solving the problem of learning retention. For example, Dai et al found that there was no direct relation of interaction quality and satisfaction with the learning experience, but the learning habit of MOOCs as a learning model could significantly increase continuance intention [14]. In addition, the interaction can promote students' attitudes and enhance their persistence. Besides, the interaction enables motivation and self-regulation, which is a positive impact on the MOOC performance as well [15].

In contrast to the flipped classroom, MOOC emphasizes the promotion of students' inner drive on learning performance through teachers' facilitation as well as mediation. The practice of two innovative educations, reshaping students' learning behavior, bring forward the valuable experience of online higher education.

21.2.3   Learning Behavior Change

The learning behavior change is an unavoidable challenge of fully online higher education. The open and distance online learning environment changes the traditional face-to-face mode. And the most apparent change from the students' side is the learning behavior change. Such change also causes a change in teacher's instruction and mediation in learning activities [16].

In the time when the teaching is in class, the students' learning behavior is easy to predict, observe, explain, and evaluate (POEE), while online education is on the contrary. Students' learning behavior relies on the instructions given by teachers through virtual interaction, but importantly, the inner drive of self-learning behavior plays vital roles in the learning process, which directly affects education outcomes.

Typically, the importance of learning behavior regarding the performance of online education has been illustrated by the technology acceptance model (TAM). According to the original TAM [17], the external variables function the perceived usefulness and perceived ease of use, which impact on the attitude towards behavior, and influence the behavior intention to use, and lastly the actual system use.

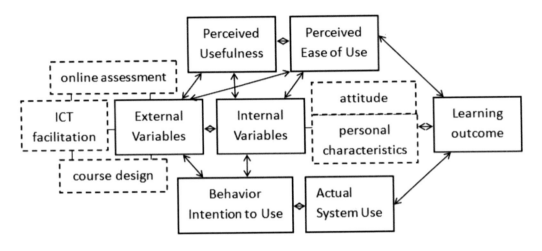

FIGURE 21.1
Modified TAM (Based on original TAM [17])

The external variables consist of ICT facilitation, course design, online formative assessment as well as course monitoring. Taking the online course design affecting learning behavior, for example, [18] finds that a course design enticing students' behavior, emotional and cognitive engagements can promote achievement [18]. Among the different types of engagements, behavior engagement is relatively easier to measure and collect, especially with the help of learning management systems (LMS). [3] highlights that the learner-centered course design helps the collaborative learning and social inclusion, widening participation in education. It is also suggested that the scaffolding modular structure of the learning environment is convenient for observation and evaluation [3, 19]. Also, as regards the performance of online higher education, the online formative assessment is in need. As effective online formative assessment can foster a learner's assessment centered focus through "formative feedback and enhanced engagement with valuable learning experiences" [20].

The internal variables, such as personal characteristics, are also focused on relevant research. For example, the learners' characteristics have a strong influence on learning behavior, such as note-taking behavior, and the impact on learning performance during a fully online course [16]. The strong self-determination and persistence in the learning process can assist the learning behavior and so forth [21].

21.3 Practice of Online Higher Education in China

21.3.1 Background

China started early as a certified distancing higher education. Back in 1998, the Ministry of Education officially approved Tsinghua University, Beijing University of Posts and Telecommunications, Zhejiang University, and Hunan University as the first batch of National Modern Distancing Education Pilot Universities (NMDEPU). And 68 universities have been officially approved by the Ministry of Education regarding the certified online higher education by 2019.

Meanwhile, China has a good foundation of cyber technology. The internet and mobile technology are prevalently used by Chinese entities, universities as well as individuals. And the level of digital infrastructure and the popularity of broadband has been continuously improved. The users of bandwidth 100M have surpassed 60% in 2018. Also, the 4G network coverage is remarkable. In 2019, the total number of 4G users reached 1.23 billion, covering nearly 98% of users, ranking first in the world. At the same time, the construction of new infrastructure, 5G, and gigabit optical fiber networks is in acceleration.

As the key support for the development of digital society, the leading role of broadband network and 4G fiber network becomes increasingly prominent. It provides strong support for the smooth development of online education.

21.3.2 Online Learning Environment in Practice

The learning management system (LMS) supports the online learning environment. There are three modules in the system, they are, administration module, teaching module, and learning module. And LMSs are embedded in the intranet of certain universities. The design of the learning environment is versatile due to the verified needs of users. Recently, commercial online education platforms are gradually established, which is encouraged by the Ministry of Education in the 13th five-year plan. But the commercial platforms are open to the education market and independent from universities' LMSs. Those functions of modules are slightly different as the commercial platforms emphasize more on technical services as well as flexible unified learning modules.

During the period of the pandemic, the commercial online educational platforms are in great popularity as the learning materials and video courses are enriched and well-established before the incident. Thus, the market shows a strong demand for merging the internal LMS in universities with commercial online open courses. Therefore, that type of cooperative online higher education is in rapid development.

Accordingly, the commercial platform adopts an updated marketing strategy during the epidemic, including free use and open learning resources, which attracts massive users to register in the open platforms, providing chances for the teachers to integrate video courses into their curriculum construction.

The commercial platforms support either recorded course or live broadcasting course. Table 21.1 showed the features of popular platforms ICourse, Chaoxing, Yuketang, Zhihuishu, Wechat, and Tencent Meeting. They have different publishers, but all have open access to end-users. Most of them have enriched course resources, such as pre-recorded courses and sufficient learning materials. Besides, they all support desk-top and cell phone apps. But the technical maturity is slightly different. For example, not all of the platforms support live broadcasting.

21.3.3   Case Study

For the analysis of users' experience as well as the online education performance in the incorporated LMS, the chapter elaborates on a survey in this section. The course GIS for Real Estate is the investigated case.

TABLE 21.1
Commercial learning platform (Based on this research)

Name	Publisher	User access	Curriculum resources	Convenience of use	Live broadcasting	Curriculum construction	Desktop app	Mobile phone app
ICourse (https://www.icourse163.org/)	Higher Education Society & Netease	Open access (limited time)	☆☆☆☆☆	☆☆☆☆☆	Yes	☆☆☆☆☆	Yes	Yes
Chaoxing (http://erya.mooc.chaoxing.com/)	Beijing superstar company	Open access (limited time)	☆☆☆☆	☆☆☆☆☆	Yes	☆☆☆☆☆	Yes	Yes
Yuketang (https://www.yuketang.cn/)	Tsinghua Uni	Open access (limited time)	☆☆☆☆	☆☆☆☆☆	Yes	☆☆☆☆☆	Yes	Yes
Zhihuishu (https://www.zhihuishu.com/)	Shanghai Zhuoyue Ruixin Digital Technology Co., Ltd	Open access (limited time)	☆☆☆	☆☆☆☆☆	Yes	☆☆☆☆☆	Yes	Yes
Wechat (https://weixin.qq.com/)	Tencent group	Open access	☆	☆☆☆☆☆	Yes	☆☆☆	Yes	Yes
Tencent Meeting (https://meeting.tencent.com/)	Tencent group	Open access	☆	☆☆☆☆☆	Yes	☆☆☆	Yes	Yes

Notes: ☆ represents for the level of readiness of the curriculum on different online platforms, The marks base on the observation of users in general in this research.

The course was a selective course open to the sophomore in the major of Real Estate Development and Management. The teaching weeks were 18 weeks for 2 credits. Students needed to finish the entire online course, weekly assignment, and participate in the final exam to get the full credit. Due to the situation of the pandemic, the course had been pre-recorded in videos and uploaded to the Chaoxing Platform according to the weekly teaching schedule. The learning system recorded students' learning behavior and marked individual scores accordingly. The weekly course opened from Monday to Friday to students. The flexible learning arrangement was encouraged as a test of self-management. The teacher used an online discussion whiteboard for questions and answers of weekly learning content. Besides, the teacher also interacted face-to-face with students in the Tencent Meeting and Wechat. The final exam was conducted in the universites' LMS.

The course focused on the application of GIS analysis in real estate industry in terms of market analysis, real estate development, and property analysis. The pre-recorded videos were the main learning resources for students, which was convenient to use as a digital interpretation of the textbook. But it was not easy to trace the GIS operation online. In that case, the course gave weekly instructions in the text before the assignment, so the students could follow the instructions step by step in the GIS tool operation. The evaluation of the assignment based on the analysis outcome of the work. Also, the course used ad-hoc online meetings and group chat devices to solve students' problems.

For evaluating the performance of students, the chapter delivered a survey at the end of the semester. The class was divided into two groups. Each of them consisted of 29 students, with 58 students in total. A survey was delivered to students online at the end of the semester. The purpose of the survey was to test significant elements that influence students' performance in their learning experience.

The survey included 13 question items, those were, Satisfaction of online learning platform, Satisfaction of fully online course, Habit's influence, ICT facilitation, Personality influence, Attitude and persistence influence, Behavior influence (taking notes), Modular design, Course management, Weekly assignment, Time flexibility, Final exam, and Barriers of the online course. Among those, the first twelve questions were in a Likert 5 scale (full score 100) for the evaluation, and the last question was a structural deigned semi-open question. The survey was distributed to students via the back-to-back method to ensure respondents to have no communication. The valid responses were 58. The survey result is shown as follows (Table 21.2).

TABLE 21.2

Factor loading matrix for self-evaluated online education performance (Based on the survey in this research)

No.	Question Item	Satisfaction/Importance (Score)	
		Group 1 (mean)	Group 2 (mean)
1	Satisfaction of online learning platform	82.11	88.42
2	Satisfaction of fully online course	62.91	65.91
3	Habit's influence	83.65	86.33
4	ICT facilitation	81.54	91.58
5	**Personality influence**	**45.76**	**59.48**
6	Attitude and persistence influence	81.6	86.8
7	Behavior influence (taking notes)	81.58	83.68
8	**Modular design**	**89.49**	**94.74**
9	Course management	82.14	89.99
10	Weekly assignment	85.27	91.03
11	Time flexibility	70.53	81.03
12	Final exam	84.22	81.58
13	Barriers of online course	-	-

The mean score in both groups was homogenous, without apparent variance. The top five question items (basing on the mean score) were No. 8, 10, 4, 9, and 1. The observation showed that the top items were external variables that influenced students' learning performance. In contrast, the lowest two items were No. 5 and 3, which were internal variables influencing students' performance.

Besides, the students highlighted barriers of the online course in the regard of self-regulation, eye-contact and interaction, focus and concentration of video course, in-class monitoring, learning atmosphere and efficiency, internet congestion, time management, pop-up advertisement disturbance, and reading inconvenience of the digital document.

21.4 Conclusion

COVID-19 pandemic is an overwhelming health disaster. The shock of the epidemic causes the reconsideration of building community resilience in the field of online higher education. Due to the closure of the campus, millions of university students receive online courses remotely. The fully online transformation changes the face-to-face learning process to distancing online self-study mode. The transformation is not merely a temporary change in educational evolution. It is influencing the revolution of higher education deeply.

Practicing online higher education is a predominant issue facing the epidemic. The experience shows the readiness of online education, such as ICT facilitation, video courses, online learning materials, LMS and commercial platforms, etc, is the prerequisite. Meanwhile, the external drives for interaction and engagement of students in the teaching-learning process are vital.

The lessons learned from flipped classrooms and MOOCs are that crucial elements for the improvement of learning performance are both external and internal. A good combination of external and internal drives can enhance students' learning behavior.

The case study in the chapter shows that external elements, such as modular design, weekly assignment, ICT facilitation, course management, and convenient online LMS, are the most significant elements influencing respondents' performance. Whereas, the internal drives, such as personality and learning habits, have insignificant influence. Besides, the step-by-step technical instructions to GIS operation and sufficient online interaction are crucial in the online learning environment.

The continuation of on-going research of online higher education in the reaction of health disaster will be in need, particularly, regarding building community resilience. The experience that the research learned from the practice in China shows the preparedness of ICT facilitation, flexible structure of the organization, the readiness of online course resources, effective communication of participants as well as the clear instructions to students in the GIS-related course are crucial to the successful implementation of the online higher education.

References

[1] Serhat Kurt. Technology use in elementary education in turkey: A case study. *New Horizons in Education*, 58(1):65–76, 2010.

[2] Young Hoan Cho, Hyoseon Choi, Jiwon Shin, Him Chan Yu, Yoon Kang Kim, and Jung Yeon Kim. Review of research on online learning environments in higher education. *Social Behavioral Sciences*, 191:2012–2017, 2015.

[3] Sarah R Lambert. Do moocs contribute to student equity and social inclusion? a systematic review 2014–18. *Computers & Education*, 145:103693, 2020.

[4] Md Abdullah Al Mamun, Gwendolyn Lawrie, and Tony Wright. Instructional design of scaffolded online learning modules for self-directed and inquiry-based learning environments. *Computers Education*, 144: 103695, 2020.

[5] Maja Ćukušić, Željko Garača, and Mario Jadrić. Online self-assessment and students' success in higher education institutions. *Computers & Education*, 72:100–109, 2014.

[6] Joshua Weidlich and Theo J Bastiaens. Designing sociable online learning environments and enhancing social presence: An affordance enrichment approach. *Computers & Education*, 142:103622, 2019.

[7] Yeonjeong Park, Ji Hyun Yu, and Il-Hyun Jo. Clustering blended learning courses by online behavior data: A case study in a korean higher education institute. *The Internet and Higher Education*, 29:1–11, 2016.

[8] Sathyendra Bhat, Ragesh Raju, Shreeranga Bhat, and Rio D'Souza. Redefining quality in engineering education through the flipped classroom model. *Computer Science*, 172:906–914, 2020.

[9] Abdellah Ibrahim Mohammed Elfeky, Thouqan Saleem Yakoub Masadeh, and Marwa Yasien Helmy Elbyaly. Advance organizers in flipped classroom via e-learning management system and the promotion of integrated science process skills. *Thinking Skills and Creativity*, 35:100622, 2020.

[10] Justin M Weinhardt and Traci Sitzmann. Revolutionizing training and education? three questions regarding massive open online courses (moocs). *Human Resource Management Review*, 29(2):218–225, 2019.

[11] Noura Alhazzani. Mooc's impact on higher education. *Social Sciences & Humanities Open*, page 100030, 2020.

[12] Young Ju Joo, Hyo-Jeong So, and Nam Hee Kim. Examination of relationships among students' self-determination, technology acceptance, satisfaction, and continuance intention to use k-moocs. *Computers & Education*, 122:260–272, 2018.

[13] Waleed Al-Rahmi, Ahmed Aldraiweesh, Noraffandy Yahaya, Yusri Bin Kamin, and Akram M Zeki. Massive open online courses (moocs): Data on higher education. *Data in Brief*, 22:118–125, 2019.

[14] Hai Min Dai, Timothy Teo, and Natasha Anne Rappa. Understanding continuance intention among mooc participants: The role of habit and mooc performance. *Computers in Human Behavior*, 112, page 106455, 2020.

[15] Reparaz Charo, Aznárez-Sanado Maite, and Mendoza Guillermo. Self-regulation of learning and mooc retention. *Computers in Human Behavior*, 111, page 106423, 2020.

[16] Minoru Nakayama, Kouichi Mutsuura, and Hiroh Yamamoto. Impact of learner's characteristics and learning behaviour on learning performance during a fully online course. *The Electronic Journal of e-Learning*, 12:394–408, 2014.

[17] Fred D Davis. Perceived usefulness, perceived ease of use, and user acceptance of information technology. *MIS Quarterly*, 13(3), pages 319–340, 1989.

[18] Feng Hsu Wang. An exploration of online behaviour engagement and achievement in flipped classroom supported by learning management system. *Computers & Education*, 114:79–91, 2017.

[19] Ilya V Osipov, Anna Y Prasikova, and Alex A Volinsky. Participant behavior and content of the online foreign languages learning and teaching platform. *Computers in Human Behavior*, 50:476–488, 2015.

[20] Joyce Wangui Gikandi, Donna Morrow, and Niki E Davis. Online formative assessment in higher education: A review of the literature. *Computers & Education*, 57:2333–2351, 2011.

[21] Arnon Hershkovitz and Rafi Nachmias. Online persistence in higher education web-supported courses. *Internet and Higher Education*, 14:98–106, 2011.

22

Time-Series Analysis of COVID-19 in Iran: A Remote Sensing Perspective

Nadia Abbaszadeh Tehrani, Abolfazl Mollalo, Farinaz Farhanj, Nooshin Pahlevanzadeh and Milad Janalipour

This chapter reports on a national study of COVID-19 using remote sensing (RS) indicators in Iran. Time-series analysis is performed on RS indicators (n=12) including wind speed, temperature, evaporation, carbon monoxide (CO), nitrogen dioxide (NO₂), Sulphur dioxide (SO₂), ozone (O₃), formaldehyde (HCHO), cloud cover, precipitation, air pressure and soil moisture (SM) to identify remotely sensed products that may contribute to COVID-19 transmission. Mann-Kendall test is employed to summarize time-series observations. Further, a correlation analysis is performed between Z-scores obtained from the Mann-Kendall test and the number of COVID-19 cases. Findings indicated that the precipitation, NO₂, and SO₂ have high correlations with number of COVID-19 cases with Spearman correlation coefficient of -0.39, -0.33, and -0.31, respectively. Findings may provide useful insights for public health decision makers by improving the accuracy of predicative models.

22.1 Introduction

As of 1 July 2020, Iran has been identified as one of the top ten countries with the highest number of reported COVID-19 cases. Several neighboring countries such as Bahrain, Iraq, Georgia, Kuwait, Oman, Afghanistan, Lebanon, and Pakistan reported that their first cases of COVID-19 was imported from passengers traveling from Iran [1]. As of 3 September 2020, over 381,000 confirmed cases and almost 22,000 deaths had been reported from Iran. However, the real figure is largely underestimated [2]. It is predicted that the country will face several waves of the pandemic due to ineffective controlling strategies such as early reopening and ease of restrictions.

Several studies have identified associations between environmental indicators and COVID-19 transmission. For instance, in China, Yongji et al. (2020) examined the relationship between ambient air pollution and daily (confirmed) COVID-19 cases using generalized additive models. They found a positive association between COVID-19 and particulate matter 2.5, carbon monoxide, nitrogen dioxide, and ozone, while Sulphur dioxide was negatively associated with the disease [3]. Ma et al. (2020) modeled the relationship between daily COVID-19 mortalities and temperature and relative humidity variations using time-series analysis. They found a positive association with temperature and negative association with relative humidity [4].

Epidemiological investigations of infectious diseases mostly concentrate on medical aspects and infection control and disregard the geographic components of the diseases [5–7]. Geospatial technologies such as Remote Sensing (RS) and geographic information system (GIS) have been identified useful in monitoring a variety of infectious diseases when they are coupled with data-driven techniques [8, 9]. GIS and RS have been utilized in the study of COVID-19 across the world. For instance, Liu et al. (2020) used RS data such as nighttime light and air quality index to assess the impact of COVID-19 lockdown on human lives in Mainland, China. Their results suggested that with the implementation of lockdown policies, the nighttime light radiances generally decreased in the entire Mainland, and a significant decline was observed in commercial center regions. Meanwhile, air quality significantly improved [10]. In a GIS-based study in the United States, Mollalo et al., (2020) utilized multi-scale geographically weighted regression to explain the variations of COVID-19 incidence at the county level across the country. They compiled a geodatabase of 35 explanatory variables, including environmental, behavioral, and socio-economic factors. Their results indicated that socio-economic variables, particularly income inequality, could explain more than 68% of variations of disease incidence compared to environmental factors [11, 12].

To our knowledge, there are limited studies that have utilized remotely sensed data to monitor COVID-19 in any region of Iran, especially at the national level. To bridge the gap, we examined the applicability of RS coupled with time-series analysis in Iran as our study area.

22.2 Materials and Methods

In this section, we describe the study area, data used and methodology for identifying time-series relation among COVID-19 and environmental indicators obtained from satellite observations.

22.2.1 Study Area

The study area covers Iran. This country with the area of 648,195 km^2 is considered as the 17th largest country in the world. Iran is divided into 31 provinces (Figure 22.1). Two types of datasets including the number of COVID-19 cases and remotely sensed data were compiled. Figure 22.1 shows the geographic location of study area together with the normalized number of COVID-19 cases by the population.

22.2.2 Disease Dataset

The number of COVID-19 cases in each province was obtained from the Ministry of Health and Medical Education. The data were only available for 22 provinces, excluding Alborz, Isfahan, Qom, Razavi Khorasan, Semnan, and Tehran provinces, which are shown in Figure 22.1. The actual number of cases is presented in NCD column of Table 22.2. The number of COVID-19 cases is registered from 20 February 2020 to 19 April 2020, which is about 53000 cases.

22.2.3 Remotely Sensed Data

In this study, various satellite data sources and products were obtained from Google Earth Engine (GEE) platform (https://earthengine.google.com/). GEE is an efficient cloud computing tool that provides georeferenced and calibrated RS data of a variety of satellite imagery [13]. It allows researchers and users to simultaneously process, visualize, and analyze time-series geospatial data in a simple and quick way [14]. GEE was utilized to provide 12 spatial indicators including wind speed, temperature, evaporation, carbon monoxide (CO), nitrogen dioxide (NO$_2$), Sulphur dioxide (SO$_2$), ozone (O$_3$), formaldehyde (HCHO), cloud cover, precipitation, surface pressure, and soil moisture (SM) (Table 22.1). The selection of parameters is based on literature review and available RS indicators [3, 4, 10–12].

In order to extract time-series RS indicators (n=12) from GEE, Terra Moderate Resolution Imaging Spectroradiometer (MODIS), Sentinel-5 Precursor (Sentinel-5P), Global Precipitation Measurement (GPM), Soil Moisture Active Passive (SMAP), National Centers for Environmental Prediction (NCEP) Climate Forecast System Reanalysis (CFSR), and Global Land Data

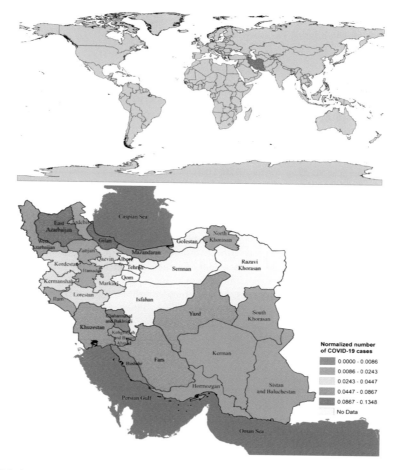

FIGURE 22.1
The geographic location of Iran in world map, and the normalized number of COVID-19 cases obtained until 19 April 2020 for each province

Assimilation System (GLDAS) were used. These data were acquired from February 20, 2020 (starting date of COVID-19 outbreak in Iran) to 19 April 2020.

22.2.3.1 MODIS Data

According to previous studies, the number of COVID-19 cases may be influenced by the changes of temperature and evaporation [15, 16]. Terra MODIS MOD11A1 Collection 6 (C6) product provides daily daytime, and nighttime land surface temperature (LST) at a spatial resolution of 1 km [17]. We selected Terra MODIS data, because the atmosphere is more stable at the early hours of the day. Atmospheric instability can influence dispersion of aerosols, pollutants, and smoke plumes in some areas [18, 19]. This product is vastly used and evaluated by many researchers across the world [20, 21]. The MOD11A1 with scientific datasets (SDS) name of "LST-Day-1km" ($^{\circ}K$) was obtained from GEE data catalog during the study period.

Terra MODIS level 4 MOD16A2 C6 product, which provides land surface total evapotranspiration (ET) (kg/m^2) datasets in 8-day at 500 m resolution, have also been used [22]. ET product can be used to calculate regional water and energy balance. Provinces with high ET values may have high COVID-19 cases, therefore researchers believe that ET may be an effective indicator. Hence, change of ET and its effect on COVID-19 are investigated. The MOD16A2 product with SDS name of "ET-500m" was also downloaded from GEE data catalog. This product has been applied, evaluated, and validated by many researchers [23, 24].

22.2.3.2   GPM Data

Previous studies indicate that precipitation is an important indicator that may lead to an influence on microbial pollution which may effect on the number of COVID-19 cases [25]. For this reason, this indicator is incorporated in the dataset. GPM is an international earth's precipitation observation science mission that measures amounts of rainfall and snowfall (mm/hr) for every three hours at a spatial resolution of 0.1 arc degrees ($\approx$ 11.1 km). GPM data products can improve analyzing climate data all over the world [26, 27]. The data were previously validated by some researchers [28–31]. GPM version 6 with SDS name of IR (Infrared) precipitation was utilized.

22.2.3.3   NCEP CFSR Data

Surface pressure (SP) is an indicator that effects some respiratory diseases such as chronic obstructive pulmonary disease, therefore it is employed in this study [32]. NCEP CFSR, one of the global reanalysis datasets, designed to compute an estimation of the global interaction between atmosphere, ocean, sea ice, and land surface [33]. Surface pressure (Pa), albedo (%), sea surface temperature (^oK), soil temperature (^oK), snow depth (m), vegetation cover (%), relative humidity (%), planetary boundary layer height (m), and surface roughness (m) were available variables in the datasets at 0.2 arc degrees ($\approx$ 22.2 km) resolution. These reanalysis datasets were widely used and evaluated in many studies [34, 35]. Among these, surface pressure with SDS name of "Pressure-surface" was the only variable used in this study.

22.2.3.4   SMAP Data

Soil Moisture (SM) is an environmental indicator that can be provided by RS data. Change of SM may influence COVID-19 cases. Hence, this indicator is included in this study. SMAP measures surface values and subsurface SM (mm) every 3 days at 0.25 arc degrees ($\approx$ 27.75 km) resolution with the combination of passive (radiometer) and active (radar) instruments [36]. Scientists can use SMAP data products to better investigate different environmental applications, such as drought monitoring, climate change analyzing, flood prediction, and monitoring of agricultural crop growth [37–39]. These data were evaluated and validated in some research projects [40, 41]. In this study, level 3 surface soil moisture (SSM) with SDS name of SSM was acquired.

22.2.3.5   GLDAS Data

Similar to surface pressure, wind speed can be an influential factor that may be associated with the transmission of respiratory diseases [42]. GLDAS utilizes different earth observation satellites and ground-based data. It is mainly used to generate wind speed (m/s), albedo (%), and soil temperature (^oK). These data are provided at 0.25 arc degrees ($\approx$ 27.75 km) resolution every 3 hours, which are used and evaluated in many research projects, such as water resource management, drought monitoring, weather forecasting, and flux cycle studies [42, 43]. In this study, wind speed (WS) was extracted from GLDAS data products using GEE platform.

22.2.3.6   Sentinel-5P Data

Copernicus program provides some environmental parameters that can present appropriate information about diseases [44]. They can show crowded and industrial areas that people have a high interaction. Hence, it is employed to extract some environmental indicators and the their effects on COVID-19. Sentinel-5P sensor called TROPOspheric Monitoring Instrument (Tropomi) is designed to monitor the atmosphere, climate, air quality, and solar radiation, at a spatial resolution of 0.01 arc degrees ($\approx$ 1.11 km), and a spectral range of (270-495), (675-775), and (2305-2385) nm [45]. In this study, Near Real-Time (NRTI) air pollutant concentrations, including CO, NO2, SO2, O3, and HCHO were obtained. Also, cloud cover fraction data among NRTI level 3 cloud products of Sentinel-5P was extracted from GEE data catalog and utilized as explanatory variable.

TABLE 22.1

Remotely sensed data used in this study together with spatial resolution and sources.

Source	Indicator	Spatial resolution	Citation
MODIS	LST	1 km	[15–17, 46]
	Evaporation	500 m	
GPM	Precipitation	11 km	[47]
NCEP CFSR	Surface Pressure	22 km	[32]
SMAP	Soil Moisture	27 km	[40, 41, 48]
GLDAS	Wind Speed	27 km	[32, 49]
Sentinel-5P	CO, NO$_2$, SO$_2$, O$_3$, HCHO, Cloud Cover	1 km	[44]

22.2.4 Methodology

In the proposed method, time-series analysis of 12 spatial indicators including wind speed, temperature, evaporation, NO$_2$, SO$_2$, CO, O$_3$, cloud cover, HCHO, precipitation, surface pressure and SM obtained from GLDAS, MODIS, Sentinel-5P, GPM, NCEP CFSR, and SMAP satellites/datasets. Pre-processing tasks including some scale factors were performed. Further, the average of each indicator was estimated. Mann-Kendall test was employed to produce Z score maps of time-series observations for each indicator. Mann-Kendall test was used to indicate the general trend of a variable resulted from the processing of time series data. Finally, correlation between Z values and the number of COVID-19 cases was calculated to identify the most effective indicators. Figure 22.2 depicts the workflow of the research.

22.2.4.1 Mann-Kendall Test for time-series Analysis

Mann-Kendall test was utilized to study time-series changes of the selected environmental RS indicators. The main advantage of this test is that it is not influenced by observations with the drastic changes [50, 51]. Mann-Kendall test was also employed for two main reasons: 1- To study severe time-series and changes of spatial indicators in the study area, 2- since the number of registered COVID-19 cases have been registered in period of two months, we need to make a parameter from daily and weekly satellite observations to compare it with the number of COVID-19 cases. Z score of Mann-Kendall test provides a change of an indicator in period of two months, therefore it is possible to perform a correlation analysis among them.

Suppose n observations in accordance with $x_1, x_2, \ldots, x_n$ in the Mann-Kendall test, S variable is calculated based on Equation (22.1):

$$S = \sum_{k=1}^{n-1} \sum_{j=k+1}^{n} \operatorname{sgn}(x_j - x_k) \tag{22.1}$$

where, sgn (x) is calculated as:

$$sgn(x) = \begin{cases} 1 & if\, x > 0 \\ 0 & if\, x = 0 \\ -1 & if\, x < 0 \end{cases} \tag{22.2}$$

The variance of S is calculated as:

$$\operatorname{var}(S) = \frac{[n(n-1)(2n+5) - \sum_{i=0}^{m}(t_i(t_i-1)(2t_i+5)))]}{18} \tag{22.3}$$

where m is the number of groups with similar values and t_i is the number of points in group i. After calculating the variance, the Z score is calculated using the Equation (22.4). Positive Z scores indicate positive changes in the variable trend, while negative Z scores indicate decreasing trend of the studied variable. Values greater than 1.96 and smaller than -1.96 indicate significant changes

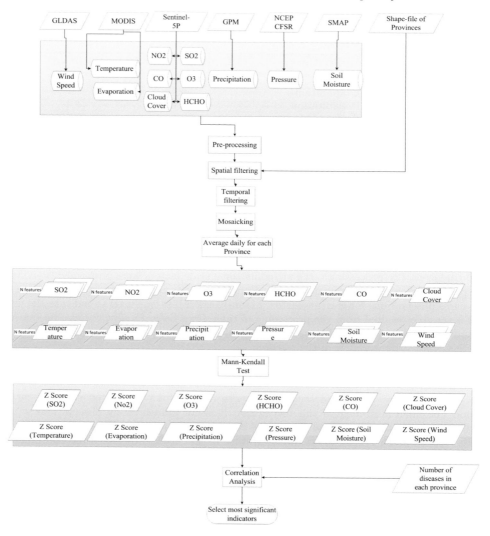

FIGURE 22.2
Workflow of the proposed method to identify effective time-series RS indicators on COVID-19

at 95% confidence level.

$$ZScore = \begin{cases} \dfrac{(S-1)}{\sqrt{Var(S)}} & if S > 0 \\ 0 & if S = 0 \\ \dfrac{(S+1)}{\sqrt{Var(S)}} & if S < 0 \end{cases} \tag{22.4}$$

22.2.4.2 Correlation Analysis for Validation

The relation between COVID-19 and spatial indicators was investigated using correlation analysis. Correlation analysis was examined between Z score of each indicator and the number of COVID-19 cases. Three correlation coefficients including Pearson, Spearman, and Kendall were utilized, which were frequently used in previous studies [52]. If at least two correlation methods confirm high correlation values, it can be concluded the spatial indicator may be related to the COVID-19.

Pearson is a linear approach to measure correlation among two variables, which was frequently used in previous researches. The range of values in Pearson is changing between -1 and 1. Values approaching -1 and 1 show high correlation between variables [53]. Spearman is another correlation estimation method which assesses monotonic relationships between variables [54]. The Kendall rank correlation coefficient is another way to measure correlation of two variables [55]. To assess the significance level of the three correlation approaches, P-values were also computed.

22.3   Results and Discussion

Figure 22.3 shows the map of average time-series of each indicator across Iran. According to cloud cover map, maximum cloud was observed in North and West regions of Iran. Maximum values of CO were seen in regions near Caspian Sea, Persian Gulf and Oman Sea. While, minimum values were observed in central areas. Precipitation of the wettest regions in Iran was higher than other regions. While, precipitation of central and east regions were lower than other regions. Maximum precipitation was occurred in south regions of Iran, where some flood events were also reported during 2020. HCHO over Tehran, Gilan, Mazandaran, Khuzestan, and Bushehr provinces was more than others during the study period. Temperature of north and west regions of Iran was lower than south and east, which is true based on climate of those areas. Wind speed of east regions was more than north and west ones during the study period.

Maximum value of NO_2 was observed in Gilan, Mazandaran, Albourz, Tehran, Qom, Markazi, Isfahan, and Khuzestan. High density population in the mentioned areas may be a possible explanation for this finding. Moreover, a high number of COVID-19 cases were registered in the mentioned provinces. Time-series analysis of O_3 showed a higher density in higher longitude compared to lower altitudes.

According to time-series analysis, the larger amount of SO_2 values were observed in Gilan, Mazandaran, Tehran, Khuzestan, Bushehr, East Azarbaijan, and Kerman provinces. Surface pressure of south, west and central regions of Iran was more than other areas. In addition, SM of north and west regions of Iran was more than other areas, while central regions had the lowest values compare with the other regions.

The Z scores of each indicator obtained from Mann-Kendall test were presented in Table 22.3. Cloud cover time-series analysis shows that the percentage of cloud cover in south and north regions including Alborz, Isfahan, Fars, Hormozgan, Semnan, Sistan and Baluchestan, and Yazd have been significantly increased during study period (Z score < 1.96). While, a significant decrease with Z Score lower than -1.96 in cloud cover was observed over Kordestan and West Azarbaijan (Wazar). Among the mentioned provinces, Alborz, Isfahan, Semnan and Yazd have a high number of COVID-19 cases. In general, according to Z score results, it seems that the cloud cover is not an effective indicator to find provinces with low and high numbers of COVID-19 cases were not detected.

Although the amount of evaporations over all provinces has been increased during the study period, it is not significant (0 < Z score < 1.96). Therefore, it seems that ET is not a related indicator to COVID-19.

According to satellite observations and Mann-Kendall test, precipitation was significantly increased over Bushehr, Isfahan, Fars, Hormozgan, Kerman, Kohgiluyeh and Buyer Ahmad, North Khorasan (Nkhorsan), Razavi Khorasan (Rkhorasan), Semnan, Sistan and Bluchestan, and South Khorasan (Skhorasan). During the study period, the number of COVID-19 diseases in the mentioned provinces was lower than others. It seems that Z score of precipitation is negatively correlated with the number of COVID-19 cases.

Z score of temperature over all provinces was positive and greater than 1.96, which shows an increase in temperature in all provinces. Since the research period was between winter and spring, the results seem to be correct. There was no significant association between the number of COVID-19 cases and surface pressure and the association has not changed over majority of provinces. Based on SMAP observations, SM of central and east regions of Iran i.e., Fras, Kerman, Razavi Khorasan, South Khorasan, and Yazd were increased. Moreover, the Z scores of west regions

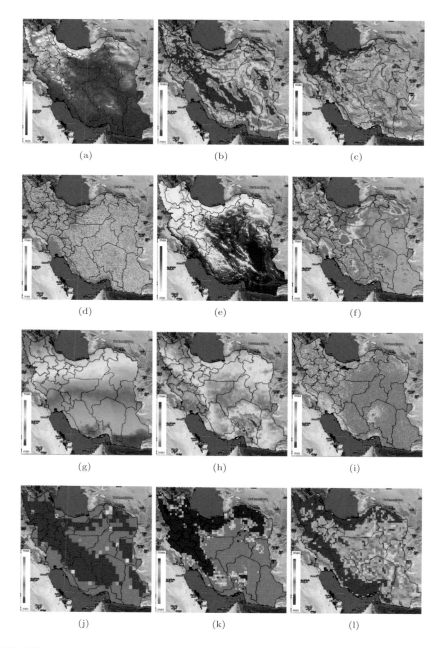

FIGURE 22.3

Average maps of indicators obtained from Iran in time of study(a) Cloud cover (b) CO (c) ET (d) HCHO (e) LST (f) NO2 (g) O3 (h) Precipitation (i) SO2 (j) Surface pressure (k) SM (l) Wind speed

of Iran i.e., Ilam, Kermanshah, Khuzestan, Kordestan, Lorestan, Mazandaran, and Zanjan were decreased. According to the results, a strong relation among SM and the number of COVID-19 cases is not observed.

The values of CO, O3 and HCHO indicators in all provinces were increasing, decreasing and increasing, respectively. NO2 was decreased in some provinces, especially in regions that the number of patients was higher than others. Moreover, based on the Z score, SO2 was decreased over all provinces. Due to several limitations of government on industries, universities, schools, and transportation, it appears that the results of NO2 and SO2 were reasonable. Since results of these indicators are complex, we use correlation analysis to find relation among these two indicators and COVID-19.

All the correlation coefficients (i.e., Pearson, Kendall, and Spearman) between spatial parameters and the number of COVID-19 cases, were calculated and presented in Table 22.3. A significant correlation is not observed between number of COVID-19 diseases and spatial indicators including evaporation, cloud cover, SP, SM, temperature, wind, CO, formaldehyde, and O3 (P value > 0.05). Their correlation values were closer to zero with large P values.

Unlike the study of Yongjian [3] that showed a positive correlation among CO, O3, and the number of COVID-19 cases, the correlation values of Pearson, Kendall, and Spearman for CO and O3 were (0.04, 0.06, 0.09) and (0.24, 0.02, 0.04), respectively. This suggests that there is no correlation among the mentioned indicators and the number of COVID-19 cases in Iran.

Based on outcomes of [4], a high correlation among humidity, temperature, and number of death due to COVID-19 is observed. In this study, Kendall and Spearman correlation values for ET are 0.19 and 0.24, respectively, which shows a correlation among them, but it is not significant enough. Also, a low correlation value (<0.1) is obtained between temperature and number of COVID-19 cases in this study.

According to our findings, precipitation, NO2, and SO2 are the most effective indicators that were highly correlated with the number of COVID-19 cases. Correlation values of Pearson, Kendall, and Spearman for precipitation were -0.35, -0.28, -0.39, respectively. Based on low P-values of each correlation value (P-P value=0.08, K-P value=0.05, S-P value=0.05), it can be deduced that these associations are not due to the chance alone. Moreover, the P values of two correlation analysis methods confirmed that the correlation between precipitation and COVID-19 cases with confidence level of 95% is meaningful. Moreover, NO2 with the correlation values of -0.25, -0.24, -0.33 for Pearson, Kendall, and Spearman is another important indicator. Likewise, SO2 seems to be associated with the number of COVID-19 cases. P-values of NO2 and SO2 are higher than precipitation. Based on P-values of Kendall and Spearman, results with a confidence level of 85% are acceptable. This suggests that Kendall and Spearman correlation analysis methods confirm a significant correlation among NO2, SO2, and number of COVID-19 cases. Results of [3] are in agreement with our findings about NO2 and SO2.

Although this is a new study about the effect of RS indicators on COVID-19 in Iran, there are some limitations that should be considered. As the spatial and temporal resolutions of the used indicators are inconsistent, the integration of those indicators in data level would be a great limitation. Moreover, there are some no-data pixels in products of some days that should be corrected by interpolation methods. Another limitation is that the used products such as SO2 and NO2 should be calibrated based on ground observations for Iran to achieve more reliable outcomes. Finally, we employed the number of registered COVID-19 cases for two months. Since satellite observations can be provided on a daily basis, the use of daily statistics regarding COVID-19 cases can help us to perform a more robust validation on environmental indicators. The most important limitation is related to lack of detailed understanding of the nature of COVID individual cases & deaths, or correcting for epidemiological & personal health issues.

TABLE 22.2

The Z scores of spatial indicators over all provinces

Province / Indicators	Cloud cover	Evaporation	Precipitation	Surface pressure	Soil moisture	Temperature	Wind speed	CO	HCHO	NO2	O₃	SO2	NCD
Alborz	2.00	1.22	0.36	-0.37	0.53	4.53	-1.22	0.01	-2.35	-4.37	4.37	-1.83	N/A
Ardebil	0.84	0.73	0.19	0.09	0	1.82	1.08	2.60	-1.67	2.48	5.31	-3.61	0.018
Bushehr	0.97	-0.24	3.01	-4.42	0.07	4.24	0.37	0.92	0.01	-2.25	4.60	-1.31	0.006
Ch-Mahal & Bakh[*]	1.48	1.22	0.76	-0.25	-1.28	2.81	0.47	4.30	-1.88	1.95	5.12	-0.31	0.008
East Azarbaijan	-0.53	1.22	-0.38	-0.79	1.51	5.16	2.07	3.52	-2.21	0.01	4.53	-3.56	0.111
Fars	3.61	1.22	2.74	-0.96	2.34	2.16	0.27	2.22	-1.78	-1.36	4.52	-1.56	0.077
Gilan	-0.11	1.22	-0.56	0.12	-0.30	2.18	1.35	2.88	-0.56	-1.24	5.42	-0.95	0.134
Golsetan	1.71	1.71	0.22	0.08	-1.11	1.62	0.03	2.31	-1.16	-0.20	4.40	-2.80	N/A
Hamedan	-1.17	1.22	-0.14	-0.83	-0.68	3.79	1.05	4.85	-1.19	-0.95	4.70	-2.10	0.023
Hormozgan	2.06	0.73	4.12	-3.03	0.75	2.87	0.67	0.77	-0.67	-1.20	2.44	-1.25	0.024
Ilam	0.24	1.22	0.02	-1.99	-3.78	5.71	-0.17	3.38	-0.38	0.56	4.68	-0.60	0.011
Isfahan	2.60	1.22	2.21	-0.77	0.62	2.72	0.06	3.71	-2.86	-2.81	5.232	-2.55	N/A
Kerman	3.97	1.22	5.39	-1.35	2.27	2.30	0	2.78	-1.23	0.50	3.12	-0.80	0.017
Kermanshah	-0.55	1.22	0.33	-1.04	-2.12	3.61	0.04	3.92	-0.62	-0.81	4.99	-1.37	0.035
Khuzestan	-0.44	0.24	0.95	-4.09	-2.49	4.32	0.61	3.24	0.51	-0.88	4.91	-0.81	0.086
Kohg & B-Ahmad[**]	0.80	0.73	1.99	-1.47	0.90	3.94	0.54	2.01	-1.26	0.10	4.96	-1.02	0.010
Kordestan	-1.93	1.71	-0.68	-0.85	-2.58	4.49	2.78	4.88	-3.0	0.22	4.60	-1.81	0.034
Lorestan	0.01	1.71	0.12	-0.75	-2.27	3.58	0.24	5.04	-1.35	0.40	4.62	-0.51	0.044
Markazi	0.72	0.73	1.11	-0.68	-0.07	2.95	0.44	4.37	-1.71	-1.28	4.74	-1.21	0.033
Mazandaran	0.91	1.71	-0.68	0.17	-2.04	3.27	-1.80	2.63	-0.46	-1.55	4.34	-3.75	0.072
North Khorasan	1.46	1.71	2.54	0	1.25	2.87	0.01	3.28	-0.93	0.57	4.27	-3.56	0.023
Qazvin	0.28	0.73	0.29	-0.25	-0.30	2.12	1.01	2.11	-1.59	-2.74	4.97	-2.91	0.038
Qom	0.58	0.73	1.64	-0.75	0.15	3.05	-0.03	4.45	-3.10	-3.09	4.82	-3.07	N/A
Razavi Khorasan	1.70	1.22	3.86	0.02	2.80	1.76	-0.03	3.44	-1.81	1.17	3.81	-2.18	N/A
Semnan	2.07	0.73	2.77	-0.28	1.21	3.70	-0.40	3.62	-3.45	-3.15	4.64	-2.89	N/A
Sistan & Baluch[***]	2.27	0.73	4.07	-2.02	1.13	3.94	0.84	1.87	-0.68	1.89	2.05	0.94	0.015
South Khorasan	2.30	0.73	4.85	-0.25	2.87	0.98	0.03	4.05	-0.61	5.39	2.79	0.50	0.011
Tehran	1.49	0.73	0.85	-0.16	-0.22	4.85	-1.29	0.08	-3.22	-3.82	4.36	-2.94	N/A
West Khorasan	-1.81	1.71	0.16	-1.04	0.07	6.27	2.41	3.68	-0.99	1.26	3.98	-2.47	0.061
Yazd	2.59	0.24	3.16	-1.08	3.21	3.83	-0.23	3.24	-1.86	2.58	3.87	-0.92	0.077
Zanjan	-1.43	1.22	-0.23	-0.69	-2.04	3.79	1.39	3.67	-0.89	0.089	4.86	-2.71	0.020

[*] Chaharmahal and Bakhtiari
[**] Kohgiluyeh and Boyer-Ahmad
[***] Sistan and Baluchestan

TABLE 22.3

Correlation and P value obtained from Pearson, Kendall, and Spearman, Pearson P-Value: P-P value; Kendall P-value: K-P value; Spearman P-value: S-P value.

Indicators	Pearson	P-P value	Kendall	K-P value	Spearman	S-P value
Cloud Cover	-0.16	0.43	-0.18	0.20	-0.29	0.15
ET	0.13	0.53	0.19	0.24	0.24	0.25
P	-0.35	0.08	-0.28	0.05	-0.39	0.05
SP	0.14	0.49	0.11	0.44	0.19	0.36
SM	0.06	0.74	-0.05	0.70	-0.06	0.77
T	0.10	0.62	0.03	0.80	0.06	0.77
Wind	0.15	0.47	0.12	0.41	0.16	0.43
CO	0.04	0.82	0.06	0.69	0.09	0.65
HCHO	-0.03	0.88	-0.10	0.50	-0.12	0.54
NO2	-0.25	0.22	-0.24	0.09	-0.33	0.10
O3	0.24	0.24	0.02	0.86	0.04	0.84
SO2	-0.22	0.27	-0.19	0.19	-0.31	0.13

22.4 Conclusion

In this study, we examined the association between 12 spatial indicators obtained from satellite observations and COVID-19 cases in Iran using time-series analysis. Our findings indicated that changes of SO2, NO2, and precipitation were highly correlated with the number of COVID-19 cases. At least two correlation analysis methods including Pearson, Kendall, and Spearman and their P-values confirm that there was a relation between the three mentioned indicators and the number of COVID-19 cases. Changes of the effective indicators can be measured in other periods, so results may be useful for public health decision makers to mitigate the disease effects. As a future work, it is recommended to apply the methodology based on the number of COVID-19 deaths. Moreover, spatial modeling disease using these indicators is recommended as another topic for future studies.

Acknowledgement

The authors would like to thank the National Aeronautics and Space Administration (NASA) Land Processes Distributed Active Archive Center (DAAC, NASA's Goddard Earth Sciences Data and Information Services Center (GES DISC, National Oceanic and Atmospheric Administration (NOAA) National Weather Service (NWS) National Centers for Environmental Prediction (NCEP), NASA's Goddard Space Flight Center (GSFC), and European Space Agency (ESA) Copernicus, for providing temperature, evaporation, precipitation, surface pressure, soil moisture, wind speed, carbon monoxide (CO), nitrogen dioxide (NO2), sulphur dioxide (SO2), ozone (O3), formaldehyde (HCHO), and cloud cover datasets.

References

[1] Najmul Haider, Alexei Yavlinsky, David Simons, Abdinasir Yusuf Osman, Francine Ntoumi, Alimuddin Zumla, and Richard Kock. Passengers' destinations from china: low risk of novel coronavirus (2019-ncov) transmission into africa and south america. *Epidemiology & Infection*, 148, 2020.

[2] Adrianna Murphy, Zhaleh Abdi, Iraj Harirchi, Martin McKee, and Elham Ahmadnezhad. Economic sanctions and iran's capacity to respond to covid-19. *The Lancet Public Health*, 5(5):e254, 2020.

[3] Zhu Yongjian, Xie Jingu, Huang Fengming, and Cao Liqing. Association between short-term exposure to air pollution and covid-19 infection: Evidence from china. *Science of the Total Environment*, page 138704, 2020.

[4] Yueling Ma, Yadong Zhao, Jiangtao Liu, Xiaotao He, Bo Wang, Shihua Fu, Jun Yan, Jingping Niu, Ji Zhou, and Bin Luo. Effects of temperature variation and humidity on the death of covid-19 in wuhan, china. *Science of the Total Environment*, page 138226, 2020.

[5] Abolfazl Mollalo, Abbas Alimohammadi, Mohammad Reza Shirzadi, and Mohammad Reza Malek. Geographic information system-based analysis of the spatial and spatio-temporal distribution of zoonotic cutaneous leishmaniasis in golestan province, north-east of iran. *Zoonoses and Public Health*, 62(1):18–28, 2014. doi: 10.1111/zph.12109.

[6] Abolfazl Mollalo, Abbas Alimohammadi, and Mostafa Khoshabi. Spatial and spatio-temporal analysis of human brucellosis in iran. *Transactions of The Royal Society of Tropical Medicine and Hygiene*, 108(11): 721–728, 2014.

[7] Abolfazl Mollalo, Jason Blackburn, Lillian Morris, and Gregory Glass. A 24-Year Exploratory Spatial Data Analysis of Lyme Disease Incidence Rate in Connecticut. *Geospatial Health*, 12(2), 2017. doi: 10.4081/gh. 2017.588.

[8] Abolfazl Mollalo, Liang Mao, Parisa Rashidi, and Gregory E Glass. A gis-based artificial neural network model for spatial distribution of tuberculosis across the continental united states. *International Journal of Environmental Research and Public Health*, 16(1):157, 2019.

[9] Abolfazl Mollalo, Ali Sadeghian, Glenn D Israel, Parisa Rashidi, Aioub Sofizadeh, and Gregory E Glass. Machine learning approaches in gis-based ecological modeling of the sand fly phlebotomus papatasi, a vector of zoonotic cutaneous leishmaniasis in golestan province, iran. *Acta Tropica*, 188:187–194, 2018.

[10] Qian Liu, Dexuan Sha, Wei Liu, Paul Houser, Luyao Zhang, Ruizhi Hou, Hai Lan, Colin Flynn, Mingyue Lu, Tao Hu, et al. Spatiotemporal patterns of covid-19 impact on human activities and environment in mainland china using nighttime light and air quality data. *Remote Sensing*, 12(10):1576, 2020.

[11] Abolfazl Mollalo, Kiara M Rivera, and Behzad Vahedi. Artificial neural network modeling of novel coronavirus (covid-19) incidence rates across the continental united states. *International Journal of Environmental Research and Public Health*, 17(12):4204, 2020.

[12] Abolfazl Mollalo, Behzad Vahedi, and Kiara M Rivera. Gis-based spatial modeling of covid-19 incidence rate in the continental united states. *Science of the Total Environment*, page 138884, 2020.

[13] Noel Gorelick, Matt Hancher, Mike Dixon, Simon Ilyushchenko, David Thau, and Rebecca Moore. Google earth engine: Planetary-scale geospatial analysis for everyone. *Remote Sensing of Environment*, 2017. doi: 10.1016/j.rse.2017.06.031. URL https://doi.org/10.1016/j.rse.2017.06.031.

[14] Andrii Shelestov, Mykola Lavreniuk, Nataliia Kussul, Alexei Novikov, and Sergii Skakun. Exploring google earth engine platform for big data processing: Classification of multi-temporal satellite imagery for crop mapping. *Frontiers in Earth Science*, 5:17, 2017.

[15] Jalonne L White-Newsome, Shannon J Brines, Daniel G Brown, J Timothy Dvonch, Carina J Gronlund, Kai Zhang, Evan M Oswald, and Marie S O'Neill. Validating satellite-derived land surface temperature with in situ measurements: A public health perspective. *Environmental Health Perspectives*, 121(8):925–931, 2013.

[16] Fikre Enquselassie, ANNETTE J DOBSON, HILARY M ALEXANDER, and PAULA L STEELE. Seasons, temperature and coronary disease. *International Journal of Epidemiology*, 22(4):632–636, 1993.

[17] Z Wan, S Hook, and G Hulley. Mod11a1 modis/terra land surface temperature/emissivity daily l3 global 1km sin grid v006. *NASA EOSDIS Land Processes DAAC*, 6, 2015.

[18] C Donald Ahrens. *Essentials of meteorology: an invitation to the atmosphere*. Cengage Learning, 2011.

[19] Ling-jun Li, WANG Ying, Qiang Zhang, YU Tong, ZHAO Yue, and JIN Jun. Spatial distribution of aerosol pollution based on modis data over beijing, china. *Journal of Environmental Sciences*, 19(8):955–960, 2007.

[20] Lei Lu, Tingjun Zhang, Tiejun Wang, and Xiaoming Zhou. Evaluation of collection-6 modis land surface temperature product using multi-year ground measurements in an arid area of northwest china. *Remote Sensing*, 10(11):1852, 2018.

[21] Thanh Noi Phan and Martin Kappas. Application of modis land surface temperature data: a systematic literature review and analysis. *Journal of Applied Remote Sensing*, 12(4):041501, 2018.

[22] Steven W Running, Qiaozhen Mu, Maosheng Zhao, and Alvaro Moreno. Modis global terrestrial evapotranspiration (et) product (nasa mod16a2/a3) nasa earth observing system modis land algorithm. *NASA: Washington, DC, USA*, 2017.

[23] Dario Autovino, Mario Minacapilli, and Giuseppe Provenzano. Modelling bulk surface resistance by modis data and assessment of mod16a2 evapotranspiration product in an irrigation district of southern italy. *Agricultural Water Management*, 167:86–94, 2016.

[24] Marjolein FA Vogels, Steven M de Jong, Geert Sterk, Niko Wanders, Marc FP Bierkens, and Elisabeth A Addink. An object-based image analysis approach to assess irrigation-water consumption from modis products in ethiopia. *International Journal of Applied Earth Observation and Geoinformation*, 88:102067, 2020.

[25] Andreas Tornevi, Olof Bergstedt, and Bertil Forsberg. Precipitation effects on microbial pollution in a river: lag structures and seasonal effect modification. *PloS One*, 9(5):e98546, 2014.

[26] Arthur Y Hou, Ramesh K Kakar, Steven Neeck, Ardeshir A Azarbarzin, Christian D Kummerow, Masahiro Kojima, Riko Oki, Kenji Nakamura, and Toshio Iguchi. The global precipitation measurement mission. *Bulletin of the American Meteorological Society*, 95(5):701–722, 2014.

[27] George J Huffman, David T Bolvin, Dan Braithwaite, Kuolin Hsu, Robert Joyce, Pingping Xie, and Soo-Hyun Yoo. Nasa global precipitation measurement (gpm) integrated multi-satellite retrievals for gpm (imerg). *Algorithm Theoretical Basis Document (ATBD) Version*, 4:26, 2015.

[28] Ji-Hye Kim, Mi-Lim Ou, Jun-Dong Park, Kenneth R Morris, Mathew R Schwaller, and David B Wolff. Global precipitation measurement (gpm) ground validation (gv) prototype in the korean peninsula. *Journal of Atmospheric and Oceanic Technology*, 31(9):1902–1921, 2014.

[29] Kiyoung Kim, Jongmin Park, Jongjin Baik, and Minha Choi. Evaluation of topographical and seasonal feature using gpm imerg and trmm 3b42 over far-east asia. *Atmospheric Research*, 187:95–105, 2017.

[30] Luiz Octavio Fabricio dos Santos, Carlos Alexandre Santos Querino, Juliane Kayse Albuquerque da Silva Querino, Altemar Lopes Pedreira Junior, Aryanne Resende de Melo Moura, Nadja Gomes Machado, and Marcelo Sacardi Biudes. Validation of rainfall data estimated by gpm satellite on southern amazon region. *Revista Ambiente & Água*, 14(1), 2019.

[31] Wei Sun, Yonghua Sun, Xiaojuan Li, Tao Wang, Yanbing Wang, Qi Qiu, and Zhitian Deng. Evaluation and correction of gpm imerg precipitation products over the capital circle in northeast china at multiple spatiotemporal scales. *Advances in Meteorology*, 2018, 2018.

[32] Uta Ferrari, Teresa Exner, Eva R Wanka, Christoph Bergemann, Julian Meyer-Arnek, Beate Hildenbrand, Amanda Tufman, Christian Heumann, Rudolf M Huber, Michael Bittner, et al. Influence of air pressure, humidity, solar radiation, temperature, and wind speed on ambulatory visits due to chronic obstructive pulmonary disease in bavaria, germany. *International Journal of Biometeorology*, 56(1):137–143, 2012.

[33] Suranjana Saha, Shrinivas Moorthi, Hua-Lu Pan, Xingren Wu, Jiande Wang, Sudhir Nadiga, Patrick Tripp, Robert Kistler, John Woollen, David Behringer, et al. The ncep climate forecast system reanalysis. *Bulletin of the American Meteorological Society*, 91(8):1015–1058, 2010.

[34] Dong-Ik Kim and Dawei Han. Comparative study on long term climate data sources over south korea. *Journal of Water and Climate Change*, 10(3):504–523, 2019.

[35] Tiina Nygård, Timo Vihma, Gerit Birnbaum, Jörg Hartmann, John King, Tom Lachlan-Cope, Russell Ladkin, Christof Lüpkes, and Alexandra Weiss. Validation of eight atmospheric reanalyses in the antarctic peninsula region. *Quarterly Journal of the Royal Meteorological Society*, 142(695):684–692, 2016.

[36] Dara Entekhabi, Simon Yueh, Peggy E O'Neill, Kent H Kellogg, Angela Allen, Rajat Bindlish, Molly Brown, Steven Chan, Andreas Colliander, Wade T Crow, et al. Smap handbook–soil moisture active passive: Mapping soil moisture and freeze/thaw from space. 2014.

[37] Nereida Rodriguez-Alvarez, Sidharth Misra, and Mary Morris. The polarimetric sensitivity of smap-reflectometry signals to crop growth in the us corn belt. *Remote Sensing*, 12(6):1007, 2020.

[38] Nazmus Sazib, Iliana Mladenova, and John Bolten. Leveraging the google earth engine for drought assessment using global soil moisture data. *Remote Sensing*, 10(8):1265, 2018.

[39] Huan Wu, John S Kimball, Naijun Zhou, Lorenzo Alfieri, Lifeng Luo, Jinyang Du, and Zhijun Huang. Evaluation of real-time global flood modeling with satellite surface inundation observations from smap. *Remote Sensing of Environment*, 233:111360, 2019.

[40] Chengwei Li, Hui Lu, Kun Yang, Menglei Han, Jonathon S Wright, Yingying Chen, Le Yu, Shiming Xu, Xiaomeng Huang, and Wei Gong. The evaluation of smap enhanced soil moisture products using high-resolution model simulations and in-situ observations on the tibetan plateau. *Remote Sensing*, 10 (4):535, 2018.

[41] BG Mousa and Hong Shu. Spatial evaluation and assimilation of smap, smos, and ascat satellite soil moisture products over africa using statistical techniques. *Earth and Space Science*, 7(1):e2019EA000841, 2020.

[42] Josh M Colston, Tahmeed Ahmed, Cloupas Mahopo, Gagandeep Kang, Margaret Kosek, Francisco de Sousa Junior, Prakash Sunder Shrestha, Erling Svensen, Ali Turab, Benjamin Zaitchik, et al. Evaluating meteorological data from weather stations, and from satellites and global models for a multi-site epidemiological study. *Environmental Research*, 165:91–109, 2018.

[43] Wen Wang, Wei Cui, Xiaoju Wang, and Xi Chen. Evaluation of gldas-1 and gldas-2 forcing data and noah model simulations over china at the monthly scale. *Journal of Hydrometeorology*, 17(11):2815–2833, 2016.

[44] Elie El Khoury, Elsy Ibrahim, and Sophia Ghanimeh. A look at the relationship between tropospheric nitrogen dioxide and aerosol optical thickness over lebanon using spaceborne data of the copernicus programme. In *2019 Fourth International Conference on Advances in Computational Tools for Engineering Applications (ACTEA)*, pages 1–6. IEEE, 2019.

[45] Hichem Omrani, Bilel Omrani, Benoit Parmentier, and Marco Helbich. Spatio-temporal data on the air pollutant nitrogen dioxide derived from sentinel satellite for france. *Data in Brief*, 28:105089, 2020.

[46] S Running, Q Mu, and M Zhao. Mod16a2 modis/terra net evapotranspiration 8-day l4 global 500m sin grid v006. *NASA EOSDIS Land Processes DAAC*, 6, 2017.

[47] GJ Huffman, EF Stocker, DT Bolvin, EJ Nelkin, and T Jackson. Gpm imerg final precipitation l3 half hourly 0.1 degree x 0.1 degree v06, greenbelt, md, goddard earth sciences data and information services center (ges disc), 2019.

[48] PE O'Neill, S Chan, EG Njoku, T Jackson, and R Bindlish. Smap l3 radiometer global daily 36 km ease-grid soil moisture, version 4, boulder, colorado usa, nasa national snow and ice data center distributed active archive center, 2016.

[49] Matthew Rodell, PR Houser, UEA Jambor, J Gottschalck, K Mitchell, C-J Meng, K Arsenault, B Cosgrove, J Radakovich, M Bosilovich, et al. The global land data assimilation system. *Bulletin of the American Meteorological Society*, 85(3):381–394, 2004.

[50] Hossein Ahani, Mehrzad Kherad, Mohammad Reza Kousari, Mehdi Rezaeian-Zadeh, Mohammad Amin Karampour, Faezeh Ejraee, and Saeedeh Kamali. An investigation of trends in precipitation volume for the last three decades in different regions of fars province, iran. *Theoretical and Applied Climatology*, 109 (3-4):361–382, 2012.

[51] Mohammad Reza Kousari, Mohammad Amin Asadi Zarch, Hossein Ahani, and Hemila Hakimelahi. A survey of temporal and spatial reference crop evapotranspiration trends in iran from 1960 to 2005. *Climatic Change*, 120(1-2):277–298, 2013.

[52] Jean Dickinson Gibbons and Subhabrata Chakraborti. *Nonparametric Statistical Inference: Revised and Expanded*. CRC press, 2014.

[53] Jacob Benesty, Jingdong Chen, Yiteng Huang, and Israel Cohen. Pearson correlation coefficient. In *Noise reduction in speech processing*, pages 1–4. Springer, 2009.

[54] Douglas G Bonett and Thomas A Wright. Sample size requirements for estimating pearson, kendall and spearman correlations. *Psychometrika*, 65(1):23–28, 2000.

[55] H Abdi. The kendall rank correlation coefficient. encyclopaedia of measurement and statistics (pp. 508-510), 2007.

23

Creating a Set of High-Resolution Vulnerability Indicators to Support the Disaster Management Response to the COVID-19 Pandemic in South Africa

Alize Le Roux, Antony K. Cooper, Chantel Ludick, Kathryn A. Arnold and Gerbrand Mans

This chapter presents the "COVID-19 Vulnerability Dashboard" for South Africa, developed by the CSIR for the National Disaster Management Centre (NDMC). It maps vulnerability to COVID-19 for the whole of South Africa, down to the level of the 103 576 enumerator areas (EAs). The COVID-19 Vulnerability Dashboard aims at helping the NDMC, local authorities and other stakeholders with disaster risk reduction (DRR) and evidence based decision making. Several national government departments have used the Dashboard for planning support. South Africa has large populations around the country vulnerable to COVID-19 because of the triple challenges of poverty, inequality and employment, and the high levels of HIV/AIDS and tuberculosis; high potential for rapid spread because of many dense informal settlements; and limited health resources. The COVID-19 Vulnerability Dashboard draws on our expertise in spatial analysis and disaster risk reduction of human settlements, and our tools, data and expertise — including the Green Book, *also developed in partnership with the NDMC, to deal with the likely impacts of climate change. Using a multi-criteria analysis approach, we created a set of vulnerability indicators based on domain knowledge, which was peer-reviewed by expert groups. These are disseminated by dynamic spatial mapping through an interactive, online dashboard.*

23.1 Background

Released in 2019, the *Green Book* is an online planning support tool providing quantitative scientific evidence on the likely impacts climate change will have on South Africa at the local authority level. It was co-funded by the CSIR and the Canadian International Development Research Centre (IDRC), and developed by the CSIR in partnership with the National Disaster Management Centre (NDMC) and others [1, 2]. For more, see Section 23.3.

The CSIR has been helping the NDMC deal with the COVID-19 pandemic in several ways, including disseminating the *COVID-19 Vulnerability Dashboard*, built rapidly using the technologies and expertise (strong spatial analysis and deep understanding of risk and vulnerability analysis of human settlements) used for the Green Book. This dashboard provides indicators at a high resolution for all of South Africa, to help role players understand better the risks COVID-19 poses to communities and the health system, and the associated vulnerabilities. The focus is on the location and vulnerabilities of communities, and the required response mechanisms (coping capacities) [3].

Note that these COVID-19 vulnerability indicators are not based on epidemiological modelling, but were intended to support the early prevention, mitigation and preparedness phase of the disaster management cycle. As more data become available, updated versions of the COVID-19 vulnerability indicators will be released and shared to improve their usability and accuracy. Unsurprisingly, several organisations have been conducting research on SARS-CoV-2 and COVID-19 in South Africa and these initiatives collaborate with one another, such as through the *COVID-19 Modelling Webinar Series* [4].

This chapter then reports on this COVID-19 Vulnerability Dashboard developed following disaster management principals for the NDMC and used by several national government departments (particularly the Department of Health) for planning support. It has three main components: the *COVID-19 Vulnerability Index*, the *COVID-19 Transmission Potential Indicator* and the *COVID-19 Health Susceptibility Indicator*. See Section 23.5 for details.

Significantly, this link between the Green Book and addressing the COVID-19 pandemic demonstrates that modelling climate change risk (a potential disaster) and pandemics (as a disaster emanating from a biological hazard), and their impacts, are closely related. Hence, adaption and mitigation for both could be intertwined [5, 6].

This section has provided the background to the COVID-19 Vulnerability Dashboard. The next section provides some background on South Africa and the context for developing the COVID-19 Vulnerability Dashboard. This is followed by sections on the situation regarding SARS-CoV-2 and COVID-19 in South Africa, the Dashboard itself and the challenges encountered. This chapter ends with some conclusions and a look at the way forward.

23.2   Government Structures in South Africa

Since 1994, South Africa has had a constitutional, multiparty democracy with three spheres of government: national, provincial and local. South Africa has nine provinces and 8 metropolitan (metro), 44 district and 205 local municipalities. Within these, there are 4392 wards and 103 576 census enumerator areas (EAs) [7, 8]. The metros and districts are contiguous, each consisting of a mix of urban, peri-urban and hinterland or rural areas (even in the metros). Within each district, the local municipalities are contiguous. Unfortunately, too many municipalities are dysfunctional, due to corruption, incompetence, limited resources and limited capacity [9].

This obviously complicates dealing with the COVID-19 pandemic effectively, efficiently and fairly, such as accessing data and resources. Our COVID-19 Vulnerability Dashboard helps by providing a mechanism to obtain data and map the very vulnerable spaces, etc. The Auditor-General of South Africa (AGSA) has found *"clear signs of overpricing, unfair processes, potential fraud … delays in the delivery of personal protective equipment and quality concerns"* and many problems with relief payments [9]. Subsequently, the AGSA has been conducting *real-time auditing*[1] of the key COVID-19 [10].

To deal with the pervasive poor municipal management, the South African Government initiated the *Khawuleza*[2] *District Coordination Service Delivery Model* on 18 October 2019. It aims to break the pattern of municipalities operating in silos and the *"lack of coherence in planning and implementation* [that] has made monitoring and oversight of government's programme difficult", to improve service delivery and beat the triple challenges of poverty, inequality and employment [11]. There will then be a single, integrated plan for each district and the national and provincial budgets and programmes will be referenced spatially to districts. Implementation began with the 2020/21 Budget cycle (from 1 April 2020), though this has probably been disrupted by the COVID-19 pandemic.

The mid-year estimate for 2020 for the population of was 59.62 million, with about 51,1% being female, about 28,6% being aged younger than 15 years and about 9,1% being 60 years or older. Life

---

[1] As opposed to conventional annual audits in the months after a financial year-end.
[2] *Khawuleza* means "hurry up" in Zulu.

expectancy at birth was estimated at 62,5 years for males and 68,5 years for females, with infant mortality at about 23,6 per 1000 live births. Internal migration is high, estimated to average over 550 000 per year between provinces during 2016-2021 [7, 12]. Many South Africans, even amongst the poorest, have two family homes, one in a traditional rural area and one close to the job market, so there is also much travel between the provinces — adding to the COVID-19 risks.

23.3   The Green Book

In 2008, the South African Department of Science and Technology (DST)[3] published a ten-year Innovation Plan to meet five grand challenges, including "global-change science with a focus on climate change" [13]. DST then published its draft *Global Change Grand Challenge National Research Plan, South Africa* [14] and its ten-year *Global Change Research Plan* [15].

A *flagship science-into-policy initiative* of this Challenge is the *South African Risk and Vulnerability Atlas* (SARVA). The first edition of SARVA was published in 2010 [16]. SARVA targets local government specifically, but is also aimed at academia and was in South Africa's submissions to the COP17 meetings on climate change [17]. The second edition of SARVA was peer-reviewed and published in 2017 [18].

Building on our experience with SARVA, the concept of the *Green Book* was initiated by the CSIR and released in 2019. It is an online planning support tool providing quantitative scientific evidence on the likely impacts climate change will have on South Africa at the local authority level. The Green Book also presents various adaptation actions that can be implemented by local government to support climate resilient development. The Green Book was co-funded by the CSIR and the IDRC and developed by the CSIR in partnership with the NDMC and others [1, 2].

The key problem is the rapid urbanisation in South Africa (largely into informal settlements), but with poor economic performance and growth (now exacerbated by the COVID-19 lockdown) and the constrained capacity of many municipalities to cope. Further, many people are very vulnerable to any shocks, be they social, economic or environmental — or a pandemic. The Green Book has been developed to help municipalities across the country understand their threats and plan suitable adaptation and mitigation [2].

The Green Book integrates the *grounding in science* of climate change adaption (CCA) with the *practical planning and operations* of disaster risk reduction (DRR). This *interplay* or *overlapping-world* for understanding risk better, particularly disaster risk, makes the work multidimensional and opens-up future possibilities — as has now happened with dealing with the COVID-19 pandemic.

The Green Book has been flexible enough to be adapted for other types of disasters, such as the COVID-19 pandemic.

23.4   SARS-CoV-2 and COVID-19 in South Africa

On 15 March 2020, a national state of disaster was declared [19]. A severe lockdown for 21 days was then declared and subsequently extended [20]. The lockdown caused a short-term decline in the rate of new COVID-19 cases [21] ("flattening the curve") and initially, the South African Government received praise for the rapid and drastic response, still before the first death from COVID-19. However, by 22 May 2020, arrests for allegedly contravening the lockdown regulations were made in almost 230 000 cases [22] and as at 29 June 2020, the Independent Police Investigative Directorate (IPID) was examining 588 complaints, including 11 deaths allegedly due to police action [23].

A risk-adjusted strategy of five Alert Levels was created on 23 April 2020 [24], ranging from

---

[3]Now the Department of Science and Innovation (DSI).

level 1, being almost normal (but with a curfew), to level 5, with drastic measures such as confining everyone to their home (except for essential services and goods), closing most businesses and complete bans on the sales of alcohol and tobacco products [25–27]. The then existing *hard lockdown* effectively morphed immediately into Alert Level 5 on 23 April 2020. Some of the Regulations were found to be distressing, arbitrary and irrational [28]. South Africa moved to Alert Level 1 on 21 September 2020 [29].

Unfortunately, COVID-19 cases increased rapidly in South Africa with 364 328 confirmed cases by 19 July 2020, behind only the USA, Brazil, India and Russia in total cases. From 28 August 2020, the rate of new infections in South Africa slowed to the extent that Peru (621 997 cases) overtook South Africa (620 132 cases), followed by other countries. However, the death rate in South Africa has been relatively lower. As at 30 September 2020, South Africa had the tenth highest number of cases, at 674 339, but the thirteenth highest number of deaths, at 16 734 [30–33]. A sentinel surveillance study in July/August 2020 in Cape Town of women attending public-sector antenatal clinics and public-sector patients living with HIV, found that 40% had SARS-CoV-2 antibodies, but only 4% of those with the antibodies had COVID-19. Such herd immunity "is likely the main contributor to the observed decline in the epidemic curve in the Cape Town Metro" [34].

There has been some contention over the modelling of infections and their consequences, with forecasts of deaths from COVID-19 in South Africa ranging from as high as 351 000 (made in March 2020) [35] to as low as less than 10 000 [36]. Excessively high forecasts of deaths have been made in other countries, as well [37] and there are several reasons for why such forecasting has failed [38]. On the other hand, some consider the actual deaths from COVID-19 to be much higher. The South African Medical Research Council (SAMRC), for example, estimate that the excess deaths (including from COVID-19) between 6 May 2020 and 15 September 2020 were 44 481 [39].

23.5   The COVID-19 Vulnerability Dashboard

23.5.1   Background

With the looming threat of the SARS-CoV-2 and COVID-19 pandemic, the NDMC approached the CSIR in March 2020 to assist with supporting under-capacitated municipalities in responding to the COVID-19 disaster and mitigating all possible risks. The focus was to provide conceptual and guiding input to the NDMC's approach to the national crisis. A key part of this response is the *COVID-19 Vulnerability Dashboard*, developed using the CSIR's tools, data and expertise, including the Green Book [3].

For modelling the COVID-19 risks, we provided conceptual input and supported the NMDC's spatial mapping of the vulnerabilities of communities to COVID-19, packaged into a spatial dashboard with vulnerability indices (using a web-based geographical information system(GIS)) to show how and where the NDMC should focus its efforts. We report here only on this *COVID-19 Vulnerability Dashboard*, which is underpinned by strong spatial analysis and deep understanding of risk vulnerability analysis of human settlements,as gained through the Green Book project [40].

The COVID-19 vulnerability indicators for all of South Africa are calculated at the level of the 103 576 EAs, but are displayed and reported in the Dashboard at the level of the 4 392 wards, as that is the relevant granularity for making interventions (each ward is represented by a municipal councillor). These indicators were developed with conceptual input from the Albert Luthuli Centre for Responsible Leadership (University of Pretoria), and help role players understand better the risks COVID-19 poses to communities and the health system, and the associated vulnerabilities. The questions most often asked by these role players are:

- Where are the communities that will struggle to apply the principles of social distancing?

- Are there areas that will struggle to maintain the principles of good basic hygiene due to a lack of basic water and sanitation services?

- Where are the elderly and other vulnerable communities located?

- Can the potential hospitalization demand be met with an adequate supply of beds, equipment, health workers and emergency personnel [3]?

These questions fall into two groups: the location and vulnerabilities of communities, and the required response mechanisms (coping capacities). One needs to understand these vulnerabilities to anticipate the risks and identify the high-risk intervention areas. The following are the main indicators that have been developed:

- Risk = Exposure to hazard × (Vulnerability / Coping capacity)

- COVID-19 vulnerability index = Transmission potential + Health susceptibility

- Transmission potential = Informality + Lack of access to basic services + High population density

- Health susceptibility = Weighted age factor + (Amplification correction factor × Weighted age factor)

- Amplification correction factor = Disease burden + Poverty rate

The COVID-19 Vulnerability Dashboard was created on 3 April 2020, made fully public on 6 May 2020 and as of 22 July 2020 had received 2601 views. It has been used by the NDMC, the National Department of Health, other departments, municipalities and others for planning support.

23.5.2 The Dashboard Platform

Esri's ArcGIS Dashboard [41] was used as the technology platform for rapidly disseminating the analytical results and for them to be openly accessible by national, provincial and local government officials and decision-makers in South Africa. The ArcGIS Dashboarding environment was chosen because of the wide user reach, reliability and immediate availability of the data assured by an openly accessible web-based platform. The use of dashboarding technology also allowed users of the COVID-19 Vulnerability Dashboard to explore interactively the COVID-19 vulnerability analysis data by dynamically filtering data for the spatial extent of their choice (national, provincial, district municipal level, local municipality or ward level), making the COVID-19 Vulnerability Dashboard an invaluable decision support tool at all levels of South African government. Lastly, the COVID-19 Vulnerability Dashboard, as the single source for accessing the COVID-19 Vulnerability Index data, ensured decision makers the trusted reliability of accessing the data and metadata for decision making directly from the CSIR as the COVID-19 Vulnerability Index data custodian.

A valuable outcome has been the development and provision of data-sharing facilities, such as the COVID-19 Vulnerability Dashboard, to help with the effective planning and management of the response to the pandemic. Using dashboards for health evolved as web-based GIS platforms became more capable at providing ready access and real-time sharing of spatially-referenced operational data, a vital component for evidence-based decision-making in disaster situations. Dashboarding technology has played an important role in the spatial analysis and rapid data-sharing related to the COVID-19 pandemic around the world (such as [31, 32, 42, 43]), where accurate and timely information is required to support decision-makers so that epidemic prevention, control and management can be efficiently carried out.

23.5.3 Overview of the COVID-19 Vulnerability Dashboard

The following are some details of how the *COVID-19 Vulnerability Dashboard* has been assembled and how it functions.

- **Version control and updates**: The COVID-19 vulnerability indicators were designed and developed based on currently available data and knowledge. Given the unfolding and evolving nature of the COVID-19 pandemic, both locally and internationally, the assumptions that informed the creation of these indicators, the input data and critical weights used in calculating the indicators should be updated, corrected and refined as new information and understandings emerge. As more data becomes available, the aim is to release updated versions of the COVID-19 vulnerability indicators and to share these to improve their usability and accuracy.

- **Limitations and considerations in use**: The COVID-19 vulnerability indicators are not based on epidemiological modelling. The development of the indicators was intended to support the early prevention, mitigation and preparedness phase of the disaster management cycle, and their use should, therefore, be restricted to supporting and informing disaster management decision making. Care has been applied in testing the assumptions on which the indicators are based with a small expert user group, but we recommend that those who use these indicators should familiarise themselves with the input data and assumptions made, acknowledging that the resultant indicators might not reflect the reality on the ground.

- **Background of the disaster management cycle**: Four important phases (mitigation/prevention, preparedness, response, and recovery) are applicable in any disaster management cycle. Disaster management is the process of focusing on reducing and/or avoiding the potential or expected losses from any hazard (e.g. loss of life or livelihoods, economic loss); ensuring that timely assistance is provided to affected, or potentially affected, communities; and facilitating the rapid and effective recovery from a disaster event through "building-back" better. When a disaster strikes (e.g. the spread of an infectious disease such as COVID-19), government departments and sectors, businesses, NGOs, industries and civil society will engage and respond differently with the disaster management cycle according to their mandates, responsibilities and contingency plans. Although the phases can overlap, differ concerning their purpose and objective and last varying lengths of time it is assumed that the phases would strive to:

  1. **Mitigation/prevention phase**: Minimising the devastating impacts of the disaster. The focus here is on preventing or reducing the exposure to the disaster and mitigating vulnerability;

  2. **Preparedness phase**: Planning the response strategy and capacitating emergency managers to provide the best response possible. The focus here is on strengthening various coping capacities;

  3. **Response phase**: Implementing efforts to minimise the consequences of the disaster and reduce associated mortality and morbidity. In this phase, humanitarian action and aid are often applicable. The focus here is on coordinating of various efforts to preserve life and livelihoods, and to provide essential services and/or subsistence to those affected by the disaster; and

  4. **Recovery phase**: Returning the community and affected groups to a new state of normal. The focus here is on striving to "building-back" better.

- **Purpose of the indicators**: In the early phase of the disaster management cycle (mitigation/prevention and preparedness), data and information are vital to the success of the subsequent phases (response and recovery). With the COVID-19 pandemic in South Africa, many sector departments faced similar questions at the start of the outbreak. Departments were concerned with understanding better the risks posed by COVID-19 to communities and the health system, and the associated vulnerabilities.

- **Role of the indicators**: The questions outlined above can be divided into two groups, those relating to the vulnerabilities of communities and their location, and those relating to the response mechanisms (coping capacities) to be put in place to offset these vulnerabilities. To anticipate the risks and identify high-risk intervention areas, it is vital to understand the vulnerabilities of communities. The subset of indicators presented in the following sections is thus concerned with looking at the vulnerabilities present in communities and identifying areas in need of targeted coordinated interventions and early response.

23.5.4   COVID-19 Vulnerability Index

The *COVID-19 Vulnerability Index* attempts to indicate the vulnerability of communities to the potential impact of COVID-19, based firstly on how effectively the spread of COVID-19 can be contained (the transmission potential), and secondly on the population's susceptibility to severe disease associated with contracting COVID-19 (the health susceptibility). For this, the following formula is used:

$$Vulnerability\ index = Transmission\ potential + Health\ susceptibility \qquad (23.1)$$

We used an indicator-based assessment method to construct the composite COVID-19 vulnerability indicator. This indicator was computed using multi-criteria analysis (MCA), a spatial analysis technique that combines similar descriptive variables into indicators, and indicators into a final descriptive composite index. The different variables contributing to the indicators were standardized using the min-max normalisation process, which allowed the different variables to be added together to form the indicators. Min-max normalisation linearly scales data to fall within a specified range and we used 1–100 for this standardization process. In this method, each Enumeration Area (EA) in South Africa was compared and related to all the other EAs in the country, thus ensuring the COVID-19 Vulnerability Index could facilitate a coordinated national response. The following formula is used to normalise the data:

$$MinMax = \frac{X_i - X_{min}}{X_{max} - X_{min}} \times (End\ of\ range - Start\ of\ range) + Start\ of\ range \qquad (23.2)$$

After the standardization process, an equal-weighted multi-criteria analysis was performed in order to add the different indicators (*transmission potential* and *health susceptibility*) together to form the vulnerability indicator. A weighted average was calculated to provide the final score for each feature (variable/indicator), thus producing a score between 1 and 100 for each EA, where 1 is least vulnerable and 100 is most vulnerable.

Figure 23.1 is a screen shot of the COVID-19 Vulnerability Dashboard, showing high vulnerabilities in the rural areas in the eastern areas. However, the extremely vulnerable areas (red dots) are actually scattered across the country, particularly in high density but small EAs in urban areas, though they are unsurprisingly not so obvious in such a small-scale map.

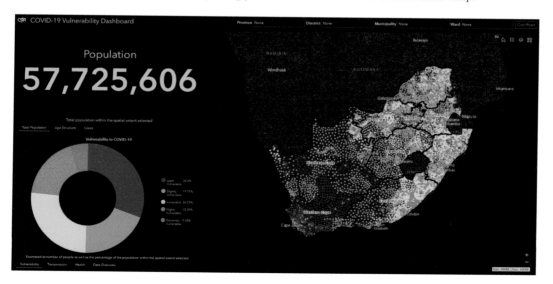

FIGURE 23.1
COVID-19 Vulnerability Dashboard, showing vulnerability [44].

23.5.5 COVID-19 Transmission Potential Indicator

The *COVID-19 Transmission Potential Indicator* identifies areas where existing living conditions could make it difficult to maintain social distancing and practice good basic hygiene in order to contain the spread of COVID-19. The following formula is used:

$$Transmission\ potential = Informality + Basic\ services + Population\ density \qquad (23.3)$$

This indicator classifies EAs throughout South Africa according to transmission risk, producing a score between 1 and 100 (where 1 refers to least risk and 100 to extreme risk), indicating areas where the virus might spread more rapidly than other areas in the country. Three main variables were used as inputs into this indicator (the higher the value for each, the worse the risk):

- **Informality**: Number of informal dwellings per EA (informal dwellings and informal backyard structures).

- **Basic services**: The *lack of access* to basic services, being the number of households without basic access to running water and sanitation.

- **Population density**: Number of people per hectare.

Transmission potential has a similar pattern to that of vulnerability, see Figure 23.1.

23.5.6 COVID-19 Health Susceptibility Indicator

The *COVID-19 Health Susceptibility Indicator* provides an indication of areas where larger numbers of people are potentially more susceptible to being adversely affected by COVID-19 (suffering more severe disease). Given that current observations indicate that mortality rates associated with COVID-19 tend to be higher in elderly populations and those individuals with underlying health conditions (one or more co-morbidities), these two factors were included in the health susceptibility (sometimes referred to as epidemiological vulnerability) indicator. Since information on the epidemiological vulnerability of population groups is limited, it is suggested that this indicator be complemented and refined based on local assessments and observations. The health susceptibility indicator was derived by assigning specific weights to various age categories and assigning a higher susceptibility to groups of people with known co-morbidities. The following formula is used:

$$\begin{aligned} Health\ susceptibility &= Weighted\ age\ factor+ \\ &(Amplification\ correction\ factor \times Weighted\ age\ factor) \end{aligned} \qquad (23.4)$$

Weighted age factor: Weights were assigned according to observed death rates. The known death rates reported for Asian and European countries were used to weight the various age groups in each EA to estimate how many people might be more susceptible to severe disease (the 0–4 age category was elevated in certain provinces/local municipalities based on high infant/child mortality rates in South Africa). The following formula is used:

$$\begin{aligned} Weighted\ age\ factor = Total[total0\_4(age0\_4 \times CMRF) \\ + total5\_39(age5\_9 + \cdots + age35\_39) \times 0.002) \\ + (total40\_49(age40\_44 + age45\_49) \times 0.004) \\ + (total50\_59(total50\_54 + total55\_59) \times 0.013) \\ + (total60\_69(total60\_64 + total65\_69) \times 0.036) \\ + total70\_79(total70\_74 + total75\_79) \times 0.008) \\ + total80over(age80over \times 0.21)] \end{aligned} \qquad (23.5)$$

Where,

- **Child mortality rate factor (CMRF)** = Value between 0.002 (low infant/child mortality rates) to 0.004 (high infant/child mortality rates), based on observed child mortality rates in local municipalities.

- **Amplification correction factor**: This factor was derived from taking both disease burden and known poverty rate into account. Current observations show that people with a history of one or more co-morbidities (disease burden) are at higher risk of more severe disease from COVID-19. There has been much speculation as to the severity of the impact of the COVID-19 virus and whether it will affect low and middle-to-low income countries more severely due to factors such as access to medical facilities, malnutrition, poverty and/or lifestyle. The following formula is used:

$$Amplification\ correction\ factor = Disease\ burden + Poverty\ rate \qquad (23.6)$$

- **Disease burden**: Prevalence of HIV infections as well as life expectancy (as a proxy for underlying health conditions).

- **Poverty rate**: Household income below R76 400 *per annum* (as a proxy for malnutrition, healthy food choices, lifestyle choices and access to medicine and health support).

Figure 23.2 is a screen shot of the COVID-19 Health Susceptibility Dashboard. This shows a different pattern from those for vulnerability (Figure 23.1) and transmission potential, with lower risks in the Transkei (eastern part of the Eastern Cape) but higher risks in KwaZulu Natal and the south-western parts of the Western Cape, for example.

FIGURE 23.2
COVID-19 Vulnerability Dashboard, showing health susceptibility [44].

23.6   Challenges

23.6.1   Data Sources

Concerns have been raised at the general lack of access to data about SARS-CoV2 and COVID-19, which could be constraining unified action against the pandemic [45]. In particular, case data at a high (fine) spatial resolution are critical for complete and full risk assessments for successful disaster response and planning. Many feel that open data should be the default [46], with even the Organisation for Economic Cooperation and Development (OECD) declaring that open science is critical to combatting COVID-19 [47].

Fortunately, we were able to draw on our extensive data holdings, for which we have done quality assurance, cleaning and integration over the years for various products and services. For the COVID-19 Vulnerability Dashboard, the key data sources used to compile the indicators at the EA level are:

- Population demographics 2018, from GeoTerra Image.

- Building Based Land Use 2018, from GeoTerra Image.

- Mid-year population estimates at the district council level for 2002-2018, from Statistics South Africa (StatsSA).

- 2011 Population census and its EA demarcation, from StatsSA.

- Health Data for 2016, from Quantec.

23.6.2   Quality

There are several problems with the quality of the data on COVID-19 cases, recoveries and deaths. The first is identifying the relevant cases and documenting and reporting them correctly. This has been an issue in South Africa, as some clinicians and pathology laboratories did not complete the documentation properly for all the patients who presented for tests, even though it is a notifiable disease. This increased the administrative burden on the NICD, as its staff had to search for the missing patient information of the confirmed cases, so that the patients could be contacted to see if they actually needed treatment and to trace everyone with whom they had been in direct contact, so that they could be warned, etc [48].

This obstacle is systematic, unfortunately: Table 23.1 shows *Number and percentage distribution of deaths by method used to ascertain the cause of death, 2017,* from the report, *Mortality and causes of death in South Africa: Findings from death notification, 2017* [49]. The data for this report are "completed by medical practitioners and other certifying officials", yet in one third of the cases (33.3%), these professionals did not know how they ascertained the cause of death!

TABLE 23.1
Method of ascertaining the cause of death [49]

Method of ascertaining the cause of death	Number	Percent
Autopsy	44 848	10,0
Post mortem examination	116 246	26,0
Opinion of attending medical practitioner	64 663	14,5
Opinion of attending medical practitioner on duty	7 777	1,7
Opinion of registered professional nurse	52 810	11,8
Interview of family member	5 238	1,2
Other	6 033	1,4
Unknown	344	0,1
Unspecified	148 585	33,3
Total	**446 544**	**100,00**

Then comes tracking each case to its conclusion: recovery (which requires the case file to be closed and reported properly) or death. A key issue with the latter is the structuring of the death certificate and whether COVID-19 gets recorded as the immediate cause, an underlying cause, a significant condition contributing to death, or not at all [50].

It is also necessary to get accurate data on the locations of cases, for tracing potential contacts and other interventions. While South Africa has a suite of standards for addresses [51], it is not yet widely used and the forms for COVID-19 do not cater for it. The result is that municipalities, provinces and national departments are having to manually and laboriously geocode the addresses [52]. A consequence is over-counting, such as when an infected person is tested several times but each test gets recorded as a separate case of COVID-19: this could result in the total number of cases fluctuating as the duplicates get identified and removed later.

Finally, of course, there needs to be metadata, that is, documentation of the data.

23.7 Conclusions and the Way Forward

This chapter has presented the *COVID-19 Vulnerability Dashboard* for South Africa, developed by the CSIR originally for the NDMC. The Dashboard provides the *COVID-19 Vulnerability Index*, *COVID-19 Transmission Potential Indicator* and *COVID-19 Health Susceptibility Indicator* at ward level. It provided critical information for sector departments and under-capacitated municipalities early in the disaster management cycle. The purpose was to highlight the high-risk intervention areas so that decision makers could intervene with the appropriate adaptation measures where needed. The COVID-19 Vulnerability Index, COVID-19 Transmission Potential Indicator and COVID-19 Health Susceptibility Indicator were made available for free and were peer-reviewed by various stakeholders.

The ESRI dashboard environment was used as this supported an interactive, dynamic and accessible approach in which to convey these critical datasets in an open-access manner. Open access to data is critical in the disaster management cycle if anyone is to respond effectively and timeously. The open access nature of the dashboard proved highly affective as more than 2600 entries to the dashboard where recorded between May 2020 and July 2020. Since the dashboard was created, published and hosted by the CSIR infrastructure, it provided the opportunity to correct, alter or add any information deemed necessary with little additional effort.

When the open dashboard was released, many of the users of the dashboard requested additional supportive information to be added and loaded. The most requested included the location and capacity of hospitals, hospital admission rates and the location of quarantine facilities. Including these datasets into the COVID-19 Vulnerability Dashboard proved a much harder task as the team ran into data custodian restrictions, data censorship, fragmented data capturing techniques and a general lack of critical information being made open and accessible to decision makers. The lack of cooperation and sharing of critical datasets resulted in these datasets being excluded in the dashboard.

An additional request made by users was to gain access to the spatial information in the back-end. Many of the decision makers and researchers with in-house GIS and analytical capability requested copies of the information for their own decision-making purposes. Since the dashboard did not support the functionality to download the spatial information, a file hosting service was set-up in the cloud to share the information with these decision makers. This resulted in many copies of the various vulnerability indicators being used even more effectively and widely for various processes.

Acknowledgement

We would like to thank the CSIR for funding the development of the COVID-19 Vulnerability Dashboard. We would also like to thank GeoTerraImage (GTI) for providing the raw data that was utilised in the indicator development process. Finally, we would like to thank the referees for their useful comments.

References

[1] CSIR. Green Book: Adapting settlements for the future, 2019. URL http://www.greenbook.co.za/. Accessed on 2020-06-04.

[2] Willemien Van Niekerk, Alize Le Roux, and Amy Pieterse. CSIR launches novel online climate risk profiling and adaptation tool: The Green Book. *South African Journal of Science*, 115(5/6):3, 29 May 2019. ISSN 0038-2353. doi: 10.17159/sajs.2019/6238.

[3] CSIR. Creating a set of COVID-19 vulnerability indicators for South Africa. Project Overview, CSIR, Pretoria, South Africa, 14 April 2020.

[4] CSIR. Modelling a changed world: Providing expert insight for modelling of COVID-19, 30 June 2020.

[5] Jonathan A. Patz, Valerie J. Stull, and Vijay S. Limaye. A Low-Carbon Future Could Improve Global Health and Achieve Economic Benefits. *JAMA*, 323(13):1247–1248, 7 April 2020. ISSN 0098-7484. doi: 10.1001/jama.2020.1313.

[6] Gustav Engström, Johan Gars, Niko Jaakkola, Therese Lindahl, Daniel Spiro, and Arthur van Benthem. What policies address both the coronavirus crisis and the climate crisis? SSRN Scholarly Paper ID 3633650, Social Science Research Network, Rochester, NY, USA, 23 June 2020.

[7] South African Government. Government systems. In *South Africa Yearbook 2018/19*, page 20. Government Communications (GCIS), Pretoria, South Africa, twenty-sixth edition, July 2019. ISBN 978-0-620-83194-9.

[8] MDB. Frequently Asked Questions About MDB and Services. FAQ, Municipal Demarcation Board, Centurion, South Africa, 2020.

[9] Kimi Makwetu. Consolidated General Report on the Local Government Audit Outcomes: MFMA 2018-19. Audit RP208/2020, Auditor-General of South Africa (AGSA), Pretoria, South Africa, 1 July 2020.

[10] Kimi Makwetu. First special report on the financial management of government's COVID-19 initiatives. Special Report 1, Auditor-General of South Africa (AGSA), Pretoria, South Africa, 2 September 2020.

[11] DPME. Khawuleza District Development Model, 2019. URL https://www.dpme.gov.za/news/Pages/KhawulezaDistrictModel.aspx. (Accessed on 2020-06-26).

[12] StatsSA. Mid-year population estimates, 2020. Statistical Release P0302, Statistics South Africa, Pretoria, South Africa, 9 July 2020.

[13] DST. The ten-year plan for science and technology: innovation towards a knowledge-based economy 2008-2018. White Paper, Department of Science and Technology, Pretoria, South Africa, 2008.

[14] DST. Global Change Grand Challenge National Research Plan, South Africa. Plan, Department of Science and Technology, Pretoria, South Africa, June 2009.

[15] DST. 10-Year Global Change Research Plan for South Africa. Plan, Department of Science and Technology, Pretoria, South Africa, 2010.

[16] Emma RM Archer, Francois Engelbrecht, Willem Landman, Alize Le Roux, Elsona Van Huyssteen, Christina Fatti, Coleen Vogel, Is'Haaq Akoon, Rebecca Maserumule, Christine Colvin, David C. Le Maitre, Daleen Lötter, Jane Olwoch, Caradee Wright, Alan Aldrin Meyer, Andre K Theron, Gerhardus P. J. Diedericks, Ashton Maherry, Marius Rossouw, Guy Midgley, Claire L. Davis, Nikki Stevens, Lee-Ann Sinden, Michele Warburton, and Caesar Nkambule. *South African Risk and Vulnerability Atlas: Mapping the way to a resilient future.* Department of Science and Technology, Pretoria, South Africa, first edition, April 2010. ISBN 978-0-620-45659-3.

[17] DEA. South Africa's Second National Communication under the United Nations Framework Convention on Climate Change. Report, Department of Environmental Affairs, Pretoria, South Africa, November 2011.

[18] Julia Mambo and Kristy Faccer. *South African Risk and Vulnerability Atlas: Understanding the social & environmental implications of global change.* African Sun Media, Stellenbosch, South Africa, second edition, 2017. ISBN 978-0-9922360-6-9.

[19] Cyril Ramaphosa. President Cyril Ramaphosa: Measures to combat coronavirus COVID-19 epidemic. Technical report, South African Government, 15 March 2020.

[20] Cyril Ramaphosa. President Cyril Ramaphosa: Escalation of measures to combat coronavirus COVID-19 pandemic. Technical report, South African Government, 23 March 2020.

[21] Cyril Ramaphosa. President Cyril Ramaphosa: Extension of coronavirus COVID-19 lockdown to the end of April. Technical report, South African Government, 9 April 2020.

[22] Bheki Cele. Minister Bheki Cele: Coronavirus Covid-19 regulations levels of compliance and adherence. Technical report, South African Government, 22 May 2020.

[23] IPID. IPID investigates 588 complaints for the Covid-19 period. Technical report, Independent Police Investigative Directorate (IPID), Pretoria, South Africa, 29 June 2020.

[24] Cyril Ramaphosa. President Cyril Ramaphosa: South Africa's response to coronavirus COVID-19 pandemic. Technical report, South African Government, 23 April 2020.

[25] South Africa. Disaster Management Act: Amendment of regulations: Coronavirus COVID-19 lockdown, 16 April 2020. URL `https://bit.ly/3nuiIQc`. (Accessed on 2020-06-23).

[26] South Africa. Disaster Management Act, 2002: Regulations issued in terms of Section 27(2) of the Act, 18 March 2020. URL `https://bit.ly/30Ldxln`. (Accessed on 2020-06-26).

[27] South African Government. Disaster Management Act: Regulations to address, prevent and combat the spread of Coronavirus COVID-19: Amendment, 20 April 2020. URL `https://bit.ly/3iDcZnt`. (Accessed on 2020-06-26).

[28] N Davis. De Beer and Others v Minister of Cooperative Governance and Traditional Affairs (21542/2020) [2020] ZAGPPHC 184, 2 June 2020.

[29] South Africa. Disaster Management Act, 2002: Amendment of Regulations Issued in Terms of Section 27(2), 18 September 2020. URL `https://www.gov.za/sites/default/files/gcis_document/202009/43725gon999.pdf`. (Accessed on 2020-10-01).

[30] CSSEGISandData. COVID-19 Data Repository by the Center for Systems Science and Engineering (CSSE) at Johns Hopkins University. Johns Hopkins University, 29 September 2020.

[31] Ensheng Dong, Hongru Du, and Lauren Gardner. An interactive web-based dashboard to track COVID-19 in real time. *The Lancet Infectious Diseases*, 20(5):533–534, 1 May 2020. ISSN 1473-3099, 1474-4457. doi: 10.1016/S1473-3099(20)30120-1.

[32] Johns Hopkins University of Medicine. Johns Hopkins Coronavirus Resource Center, 2020. URL `https://coronavirus.jhu.edu/`. (Accessed on 2020-09-28).

[33] NICD. COVID-19 Alerts, 2020. URL `https://www.nicd.ac.za/media/alerts/`. Accessed on 2020-10-02.

[34] Martin Hsiao, Mary-Ann Davies, Emma Kalk, Diana Hardie, Michelle Naidoo, Chad Centner, Gert van Zyl, Zivanai Chapanduka, Jessica Opie, Hassan Mahomed, Annibale Cois, Mariette Smith, David Pienaar, Heleen Vrede, Elizabeth Mayne, Kamy Chetty, and Andrew Boulle. SARS-COV-2 seroprevalence in the Cape Town Metropolitan sub-districts after the peak of infections. Report Vol 18, Supp Issue 5, National Institute for Communicable Diseases (NICD), Johannesburg, South Africa, 28 September 2020.

[35] Kyle Cowan. EXCLUSIVE — The terrifying coronavirus projections that pushed govt into lockdown. *News24*, 19 March 2020.

[36] Nick Hudson, Shayne Krige, and Ian McGorian. Covid-19 epidemiologists: Fortune-tellers or witches? PANDA reviews the evidence, 10 July 2020.

[37] David Richards and Konstantin Boudnik. UK's COVID-19 modelling derided as 'totally unreliable' and a 'programming mess', 20 May 2020.

[38] John P A Ioannidis, Sally Cripps, and Martin A Tanner. Forecasting for COVID-19 has failed. Technical report, International Institute of Forecasters, Medford, MA, USA, 14 June 2020.

[39] SAMRC. Report on weekly deaths in South Africa, 22 September 2020. URL `https://www.samrc.ac.za/reports/report-weekly-deaths-south-africa`. (Accessed on 2020-09-28).

[40] CSIR. CSIR helps NDMC determine communities most vulnerable to COVID-19 pandemic, 30 June 2020.

[41] Esri. ArcGIS Dashboards. Esri, Inc, 2020.

[42] SARVA. COVID-19 preparedness indicators, 2020.

[43] Julia de Kadt, Christian Hamann, Gillian Maree, Alexandra Parker, Graeme Götz, Melinda Swift, Rob Moore, Samkelisiwe Khanyile, Christina Culwick, Samy Katumba, Yashena Naidoo, Sandiswa Mapukata, and Darlington Mushongera. Responding to the COVID-19 pandemic in Gauteng. Technical report, Gauteng City-Region Observatory (GCRO), Johannesburg, South Africa, 2 June 2020.

[44] CSIR. COVID-19 Vulnerability Dashboard, 2020. URL https://bit.ly/3iFU4Zo. (Accessed on 2020-07-09).

[45] Craig Schwabe and Michael O'Donovan. A lack of access to information is constraining a unified fight against Covid-19. *Daily Maverick*, 14 June 2020.

[46] Vukosi Marivate. The COVID-19 data conundrum - why open should be default. In *COVID-19 Modelling Webinar Series: Webinar 02*, Online, 20 May 2020. CSIR.

[47] OECD. Why open science is critical to combatting COVID-19. Technical report, Organisation for Economic Co-operation and Development (OECD), Paris, France, 12 May 2020.

[48] Zweli Mkhize. Minister Zweli Mkhize confirms total of 554 cases of Coronavirus COVID-19. Alert, National Department of Health, Pretoria, South Africa, 24 March 2020.

[49] StatsSA. Mortality and causes of death in South Africa: Findings from death notification, 2017. Statistical Release P0309.3, Statistics South Africa, Pretoria, South Africa, 26 March 2020.

[50] James R. Gill and Maura E. DeJoseph. The importance of proper death certification during the COVID-19 pandemic. *JAMA*, 10 June 2020. doi: 10.1001/jama.2020.9536.

[51] SABS. SANS 1883-1:2009, Geographic information - Addresses Part 1: Data format of addresses. Standard 1883-1, South African Bureau of Standards, Pretoria, South Africa, 2009.

[52] Serena Coetzee, Antony K. Cooper, and Samy Katumba. Strengthening governance in the Gauteng City-Region through a spatial data infrastructure: The case of address data. GCRO Provocation 05, Gauteng City-Region Observatory (GCRO), Johannesburg, South Africa, May 2020.

24

Rapid Development of Location-based Apps: Saving Lives during a Pandemic – the South Korean Experience

Bola Michelle Ju, Lesley Arnold and Kathrine Kelm

The first confirmed case of COVID-19 in South Korea was recorded in January 2020. The government took swift wide-ranging measures to protect the health and wellbeing of citizens using geospatial data and information communications technology, which included immediate upgrades to the Emergency Broadcast System. Several location-based applications were developed during the height of the evolving pandemic. The speed with which these applications were developed and subsequently used by the community was a remarkable feat, and one that has set a benchmark for other countries aiming to flatten the curve of infections. These Apps have delivered benefits contributing to the prevention of community transmissions, particularly from the influx of overseas travellers. The Smart City Data Hub system enhanced resiliency during the second wave in Daegu where mass infections eventuated at a large religious gathering. The system enabled the analysis of pathway tracings of people who attended the event using big data analytics and data provided by credit card, transport and mobile companies. This chapter describes seven major location-based applications. It discusses the mechanisms behind each system, the technological and data foundations that enabled their development and operation, and how they are contributing to strengthening resiliency efforts during the COVID-19 crisis. The chapter also describes how the South Korea Government has previously made use of geospatial information and data processing systems to respond to past pandemics, and how the lessons learned from these earlier developments has contributed to the success of COVID-19 response efforts today. The major technology, data, policy and institutional arrangements that enabled the COVID-19 applications to be developed in such a short space of time are discussed, including broad direction for future research and development opportunities to manage future pandemics.

24.1   Introduction

Global pandemics have occurred with devastating impact over the past centuries. The well-known Black Death outbreak in the 14th century killed around 50 million lives [1], and the Spanish flu is typically estimated to have caused between 17 and 50 million deaths worldwide from 1918 to 1920 [2] [3]. In the 21st century, major pandemics include SARS (Severe Acute Respiratory Syndrome) in 2002, Swine flu in 2009, MERS (Middle East Respiratory Syndrome) in 2015, and the most recent COVID-19 from late 2019.

The first confirmed COVID-19 case in South Korea was recorded on 19 January 2020 – a Wuhan resident visiting South Korea [4]. The number of cases increased rapidly over the following months with over 13,550 confirmed cases, recorded as of 15 July 2020 [5]. The spread of the disease was exponential. In January, there were only 11 confirmed cases. By February, the number grew to 3150 and in March 9786. With government interventions and the deployment of location-based applications to enable social distancing, the curve began to flatten, with the number of cases increasing to 10,765 in April and then 11,468 in May[1] [6].

The COVID-19 outbreak globally, is proving inherently difficult to manage because transmission can occur when people are pre-symptomatic or asymptomatic and not just when they have symptoms. This has meant that people may be unaware that they have the virus and are inadvertently spreading the disease [7]. The range of channels through which people can become infected has also made the spread of COVID-19 difficult to manage, with 'contact-based' transmissions caused by respiratory droplets, direct contact with contaminated objects and surfaces, and so forth [7].

To limit the spread of the disease and prevent community infections, the South Korean government launched a location-based service that uses mobile phone GPS technology to send notifications, via the Emergency Broadcasting Service, to people living in the vicinity of reported COVID-19 case/s. This service communicates the routes taken by COVID-19 patients and the places they visited. This official information is being released so that people will be able to go for COVID-19 screening in case they find overlapping pathways [8], and to permit people to avoid visiting affected areas if they are still being disinfected [6].

Private companies have also leveraged location-based health-related data to create more sophisticated visualisation applications using geospatial data so that people can see the contaminated areas and pathways of confirmed cases throughout the country. By taking prompt action with location-based applications and services, the government and private sector have jointly enabled South Korea to successfully flatten the curve - saving many lives and increasing community resiliency against COVID-19 in the longer term.

Between 30 January to 18 March 2020, several location-based applications were developed; each application playing a vital (but different) role in managing COVID-19 transmissions and needs – from tracking and tracing COVID-19 cases to locating pharmacies with available mask stocks, and so on. This chapter describes seven applications that have played a substantial role in communicating essential services to citizens during the pandemic, and controlling and preventing community-spread infections. The applications are:

- **Emergency Broadcasting Service** (CBS, cellular broadcasting service): Emergency text messaging transmission service that alerts people in the near vicinity of pathways taken by the COVID-19 infected people.

- **Coronavirus Map**: A website showing the location of all confirmed cases.

- **Corona Now**: A map-based information service providing information on national and international confirmed cases and mortalities, as well as real-time news broadcasts and the location of nearby COVID-19 screening centres, quarantined areas, and testing locations.

- **Now and Here**: Developed by ITL (Innovative Technology Lab), the 'Here and Now' App calculates a mix of risk factors and the percentage of risk associated with commuting routes based on identified COVID-19 cases.

- **CoBaek Plus**: Launched by a private developer Tina3D, CoBaek Plus App sends an alarm to a user when they are within 100 meters of a place that has had a confirmed case.

- **Masks Stock App**: An information system developed to resolve 'mask stock' shortages by showing the availability of face masks at various locations and recording purchases - where, when and by whom - to manage supply equitably.

---

[1]KCDC Statistics are accessible at https://github.com/jooeungen/coronaboard_kr/blob/master/kr_daily.csv

- **Self-Quarantine App**: A self-monitoring and self-diagnosis service for citizens that is also used by government to monitor self-quarantined individuals when they are outside of designated quarantine areas.

There are numerous factors that contributed to the rapid development of COVID-19-related Apps, but the overreaching factors can be categorized into two major components:

1. Systems

2. Policy/legal and institutional arrangements

In terms of systems, the South Korean Government has a robust National Spatial Data Infrastructure (NSDI) in place. The NSDI provided the underpinning development environment for COVID-19 location-based applications. The NSDI consists of modern technologies, governance and policy frameworks, and wide-ranging fundamental and specialist data themes. The success of the NSDI is a result of a comprehensive and continuously updated NSDI Development Strategy that had guided enhancements to the NSDI over the past 20 years. The NSDI elements and policy/legal and institutional factors that have contributed to the success of the COVID-19-related applications and systems are described further in Section 24.4.

24.2 Location-based Apps

Location-based services are defined as 'services that integrate a mobile device's location (or position) with other information to provide added value to a user' [9]. Location-based applications (Apps) or websites, such as the Self-quarantine App, are created using these location-based services (Figure 24.1). Location data is used to pinpoint, visualise and integrate data, making it easier for people to understand the complex relationships between people, the economy and the environment.

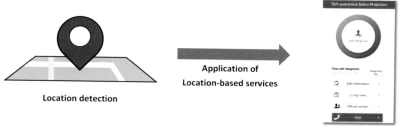

Location detection → Application of Location-based services → E.g. Self-quarantine App

FIGURE 24.1
Location-based services (LBS) and example of LBS App: Self-quarantine App

According to Seoul economy statistics, between February and April 2020, South Korea was ranked as having the highest growth rate (135%) in monthly downloads of medical Apps during the COVID-19 pandemic. This contrasts with 65% growth rates, globally [10].

As COVID-19 spreads by personal contact, private companies and individuals quickly faced the challenge of developing location-based applications to show the locations of people with infections, enable social distancing, self-monitoring and self-diagnosis, and provide updates about new local cases, and the mitigation of face mask stockpiling. These applications, developed between January and March 2020, have played a significant role in saving lives and flattening the rate of infections.

The rapid development of COVID-19 applications was facilitated by several overarching factors including a high-level of science and technology education in both the developer- and user-community; a robust NSDI built on modern technologies, a solid data foundation and an open data policy; ubiquitous internet access and a high-number of mobile users able to access free smartphone Apps; and public trust in authorities and a 'collective' community culture.

The seven major Apps and websites' services, represented in Figure 24.2, are described below including their features, data sources and the location-based services used to control and prevent the spread of COVID-19 during the height of the pandemic.

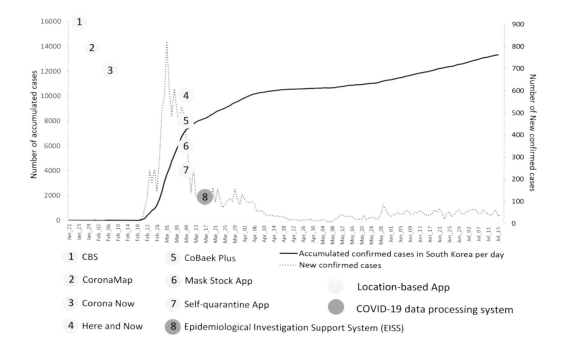

FIGURE 24.2
COVID-19-related location-based Apps in different timelines, and number of COVID-19 cases in South Korea; Statistics source: [5]

24.2.1   Emergency Broadcasting Service

The Emergency Broadcasting Service or CBS (Cellular Broadcasting Service) was first implemented for 2G cellular phones in 2005 by the Ministry of Interior & Safety (MOIS). The service was developed to alert citizens to impending natural and manmade disasters in their local area so they could prepare early for potential eventualities [11], and to enable authorities to quickly respond to those natural disasters and avoid missing the 'golden time' [12], which occurs within the first hour following the onset of an emergency or disaster.

While the Ministry of Interior and Safety (MOIS) oversees the central CBS system and its operation, metropolitan and local governments can also send CBS messages to local residents and visitors in the vicinity of an emergency. The CBS service is an 'opt-in' subscriber service. Subscribers consent to having their mobile phone GPS location identified so that they can receive alerts. There is also an option to receive translated messages in English and Chinese.

In an endeavour to curb the contagion, municipalities throughout South Korea have been using Code 3 alerts to notify subscribers in the vicinity of COVID-19 infectious people.

The CBS uses COVID-19 confirmed patient 'pathway' data made available by the Korea Centers for Disease Control & Prevention (KCDC). More specific information on COVID-19 patients' pathways is provided by local government. In South Korea, the data about COVID-19 patients is considered public data (i.e. the data collected from confirmed patients).

In addition to sending CBS alert messages to people living in the nearby vicinity of a patient, pathway tracing data is also uploaded to the MOIS CBS official website. In this way, all citizens can access the pathway data and, in turn, make informed decisions about social distancing and personal safety while commuting.

South Korean Laws on managing and openly sharing information on patients with infectious disease were enforced after the MERS outbreak in 2015 [8]. At the time of the MERS outbreak, South Korea ranked second for MERS confirmed cases, and the country was criticized for not having released patient location data publicly. This led the government to bring in new laws to enforce the sharing of information on the location of patients with infectious diseases.

However, while CBS has brought about far-reaching beneficial outcomes in the prevention of secondary infections, there have been criticism over privacy issues. Even though patients are not identified outright (i.e. by their name and address, which is protected data), citizens still dread stigma, fear losing their jobs or experiencing other potential hardship [13].

24.2.2 CoronaMap

The CoronaMap website enables people to make a visual inspection of where confirmed COVID-19 cases are using a map interface. This was an important design feature; while health officials release locations of COVID-19 patients, the official information is not very visual. CoronaMap not only pinpoints patient locations, it also connects the places they have visited with lines to show their pathways.

The data for CoronaMap is derived from the KCDC official website and managed by the CoronaMap database management team. An open API map from the Naver[2] cloud platform provides the base map detail. CoronaMap includes a function that can determine a user's location using their mobile phone GPS. This enables them to compare their location with COVID-19 cases on the map and make an informed decision to go for COVID-19 screening because they have overlapping pathways (Figure 24.3).

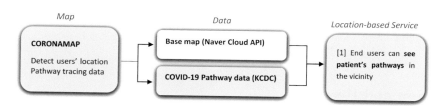

FIGURE 24.3
CoronaMap data components and service provided to end users

A link to CoronaMap was communicated through social media channels, such as Kakaotalk (a free mobile instant messaging application for smartphones) and Facebook. News of the application spread quickly, and the website had over 2.4 million viewers on the day it was launched [14]. According to in an article published by Hankyoreh Press,[3] Dong-Hoon Lee expressed on his Facebook page 'The coding and the UI (User Interface) is still messed up. But I hope the website provides a useful service to the local community'. The public responded with messages of thanks and comments of gratitude for freely providing the CoronaMap website.

---

[2]NAVER Co., Ltd. is South Korea's largest web search engine, as well as a global ICT brand that provides services including LINE messenger, currently with over 200 million users from around the world, the SNOW video app, and the digital comics platform NAVER WEBTOON. Retrieved from: https://www.navercorp.com/en/naver/company

[3]Hankyoreh Press is accessible at https://www.w3newspapers.com/south-korea/

24.2.3   Corona Now

Corona Now was initially developed to provide COVID-19 national and international statistics dashboard and to fill an information delivery gap [15]. At the time, KCDC statistics on confirmed patients' pathways were only available via CBS messaging and there was a lack of information delivery on national and international dashboard in which people could see confirmed cases, number of discharged patients, or number of deaths at a glance. National statistics were only available at the country-level, and people wanted to have more accurate data at the district, province and neighbourhood levels, and be able to compare statistics at a global level. In addition to the statistics dashboard, Corona Now has added a location-based information service including the 'find the closest screening centre' feature.

Since its development, the community have used Corona Now extensively. Like CoronaMap, the Corona Now website link was communicated via social media. The Website was visited over 30,000 times in the first few days it was released. By 25 February, the total number of web visitors reached 2 million and was ranked first in the 'Naver Search' [16].

A key success of Corona Now stems from the fact that it draws information from reliable sources. Having access to authoritative data from the Korea Centres for Disease Control & Prevention (KCDC), Johns Hopkins University Centre for Systems Science and Engineering (CSSE), and the China Medical information website[4] [17] has meant that developers could analyse and process the data with confidence (Figure 24.4). This, in turn, has led to a high-level of community trust in location-based services.

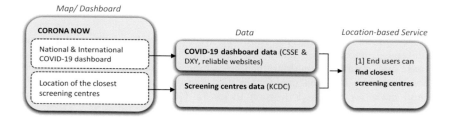

FIGURE 24.4
Corona Now data source, features and location-based service

24.2.4   Now and Here

The 'Now and Here' App is a community-based information sharing platform developed by private company Innovative Technology Lab (ITL). On 3 March 2020, ITL launched a new COVID-19 preventive service on the 'Here and Now' platform. The new feature calculates a mix of risk factors by detecting users' location and nearby infected areas. It also shows the percentage of 'risk' associated with commuting routes based on identified COVID-19 cases [18].

The Now and Here App not only shows the relative locations of the users to recent patient pathways in the vicinity, but also shows the closet COVID-19 screening centres, nearby ShinCheonJi churches, and recent news posts on COVID-19 (Figure 24.5). In March 2020, the mass outbreak of COVID-19 confirmed cases surged from a large gathering at the ShinCheonJi church in Daegu and spread the virus throughout the country. ShinCheonJi believers returned to their local ShinCheonJi churches and continued to spread the virus to the local community. Each local government hence decided to collect all ShinCheonJi Church locations, which were officially disclosed via the local government's official website (i.e. Seoul Metropolitan website, or Incheon city website), from which people could locate the church locations in their vicinity and avoid those areas [19]. The confirmed patients' data is sourced from KCDC, while news information is collected from reliable websites.

---

[4]China Medical information website is accessible at www.dxy.cn

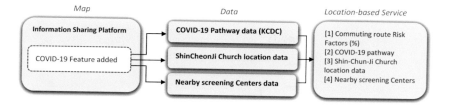

FIGURE 24.5
Here and Now data source and website services

The value of the new feature in the Now and Here App is that information is updated and refined as more information becomes available. For example, if a user posts a question in the App (e.g. where can I purchase face masks?); other users respond by uploading answers, relating to the user's region of interest within a radius of 0.5 km, 1 km, 2 km, 5 km, 10 km from the user's current location [20].

The Now and Here App has become one of the most essential Apps to have during the COVID-19 pandemic, particularly for commuters. In March 2020, the Now and Here App was ranked as one of the most downloaded Apps in Korea [21], because it provides diverse 'community-driven' location-based services that support both social-distancing measures and community well-being though knowing where essential services can be located [18].

24.2.5   CoBaek Plus

The 'Corona 100m' App was launched February 2020 and rereleased as 'CoBaek Plus' App on 18 March 2020 by private company Tina3D.[5] Corona 100m was first created to provide a visualisation of COVID-19 patient pathways, including the ability to send alarm messages to users, when they approach within a 100m radius of a confirmed patients' recent pathways. In March 2020, the company updated 'Corona 100m' as 'CoBaek Plus' by adding new features such as Mask stock availability, and COVID-19 pathway tracing and withdrew the Corona 100m App.

'CoBaek Plus' has proven to be an ideal App for commuters and travellers who do not receive CBS messages nor regularly check COVID-19 pathway information. It is one of the most downloaded Apps in Korea. CoBaek Plus has achieved over 112,515 downloads and the earlier version Corona 100m over 3,400,000 downloads as of February 26 [22]. One of the key success factors, is that the App is intuitive and easily downloaded by users. The developer, Tina3D, has not only received attention from the South Korean community but also from international communities and organizations. Mr. Bae, a board member of the company, said in an interview: 'We are currently in discussions with the Inter-American Development Bank (IDB) and the World Bank, Mexico and Spain' [22].

CoBaek Plus uses COVID-19 Pathway data released publicly by KCDC, and Mask Stock data is sourced from the government's open data platform.[6] A map API (Naver) is used as the base map for the App and other location-based data, such as mask stock and pathway tracing data, are sourced from the Mask API (Figure 24.6) and pathway tracing API (from reliable sources such as Kaggle), respectively. National and International COVID-19 statistics data are sourced from KCDC for the national data, from WHO for international statistics and from BIDU for COVID-19 Statistics in China [22].

---

[5]TINA3D is accessible at http://www.tina3d.com/
[6]South Korea Open Data Platform is accessible at www.data.go.kr

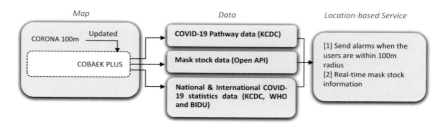

FIGURE 24.6
CoBaek Plus App data source and location-based services

24.2.6   Masks Stock App

Due to the scarcity of masks, the government launched the 'Five-day Rotation Face Masks' policy
and distribution system on 9 March 2020. Under this policy, the general public can only purchase
2-3 face masks per week, and only on designated days. For instance, people with an ID number
ending with 1 or 6 can only buy public masks on Monday, ID number ending with 2 or 7 on Tuesday,
ID numbers ending with 3 or 8 on Thursday, and so on. Since people have only one day to buy
public masks, checking on the mask stocks before heading to the nearby pharmacy was essential.

Masks are distributed to government-designated pharmacies, post offices and Nonghyup Hanaro
Mart[7] stores. The sales of face masks are recorded by the government designated retailers, and then
uploaded to the Health Insurance Review and Assessment Service (HIRA).

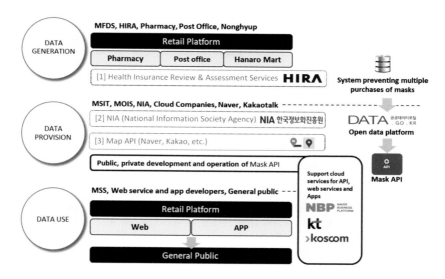

FIGURE 24.7
Publicly Distributed Face Mask Information Service

However, in order to manage the 'mask stock' shortage and direct the public to available stock,
the government had to rapidly develop an information system showing the status of face mask stocks
across the nation. To achieve this objective, the government took a Public-Private Partnership
approach to development. In this partnership, the government released the data on face masks sold

---

[7]Name of a supermarket.

at public designated-retailers through the public data centre of the National Information Society Agency (NIA). The NIA processed and published the HIRA data so it was accessible to the general public (as Open Data). Private companies could then develop cloud and other mapping services and Apps, through an Open API cloud service, provided free by the private sector (Figure 24.7).

The Public-Private Partnership approach was hugely successful. The face mask data was released by the government on 10 March 2020, and an App service was launched the very next day. The availability of Open Data through a sophisticated data infrastructure meant that it only took 13 hours to develop and deploy the first App service. Since then, more than 150 Apps have been developed to assist the public to purchase face masks.[8] The number of data calls, related to mask distribution, through the API cloud reached 570 million (around 9.64 million per hour) from 11-31 March 2020 [12].

24.2.7 Self-Quarantine

The South Korean government developed the 'Self-quarantine Safety Application' to effectively support the monitoring of those under self-quarantine. The Android version was launched on 7 March and the iOS version on 14 March 2020. The Self-quarantine Safety Application supports three languages Korean, English and Chinese [12]. It comprises 3 main functions:

1. Self-diagnosis instructions for the users to conduct and submit results to an assigned government officer;

2. GPS-based location tracking to identify those outside their designated area; and

3. the provision of necessary health information including self-quarantine guidelines.

The App allows users to self-monitor their condition by uploading body temperature and answer survey questions relating to four symptoms: fever, cough, sore throat and respiratory difficulties (Figure 24.8). These survey results are automatically shared with their assigned officer. An alarm is triggered when a self-quarantine user does not submit their result. In addition, a monitoring officer gets an alarm when a person under self-quarantine violates self-quarantine restrictions (e.g. moving outside of the quarantine area). This information is retrieved from a person's mobile phone and submitted to designated officials.

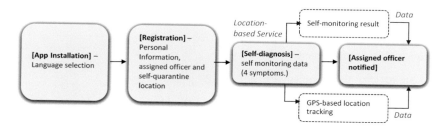

FIGURE 24.8
Process of Self-quarantine App use, and data generated

24.3 Real-time Data Processing Systems

Since 1954, the South Korean Government has been obligated to report all kinds of diseases, but omissions and delays were still apt to occur. As a consequence, the government decided to

---

[8]Apps for mark stock locations are accessible at http://mask.paas-ta.org

take measures by introducing the 'Integrated Information Support System for Infectious Disease Control' in 2013 [23] to aggregate different disease-related reporting and management systems [24]. In 2015, the system was integrated with the 'Automatic Infectious Disease Report Support System', in which diagnosis results could be directly reported in real-time [24]. The integrated system has played a substantial role in controlling previous pandemics, MERS and SARS.

In 2015, the *Infectious Disease Prevention and Control Act*, originally enacted in 2009, was revised to enforce the disclosure of infectious disease patients and the collection and use of the data. This Act established a legal basis for the reporting, handling, securement, and disclosure of information required for epidemic investigations. Based on the Act, the Epidemic Investigation Support System (EISS) was developed as an application platform on the Smart City data platform [22].

24.3.1 Integrated Information Support System for Infectious Disease Control

The project to develop the 'Integrated Information Support System for Infectious Disease Control' was developed over a number of years and consisted of several development phases:

The Government was able to control the growth of infections for previous pandemics, MERS and SARS, solely by making use of these systems, mainly because the total confirmed cases and the rate of infections were fewer and with slower transmission rates than the recent COVID-19 pandemic. However, the Integrated Information Support System for Infectious Disease Control alone was not enough to manage and contain the spread of the virus, as COVID-19 is infected by contact, requiring more accurate location data.

24.3.2 Smart City Data Hub

The 'Smart City Data Hub' is a real-time platform that automatically collects city data using IoT devices (sensors and automatic reporting systems), which permit the analysis and visualisation of Big data without manual input, using technologies such as AI and machine learning. Data is collected across a wide range of sectors such as energy, transportation and city administration. The South Korean government launched the 'Smart City Innovation and Growth Project' at the national level in 2018. The project consists of three different focus areas:

1. Smart City Modelling;

2. Daegu Smart City Development Project; and

3. Si-Heung Smart City Development Project [25].

When the ShinCheonJi church-related COVID-19 outbreak occurred in March with hundreds of confirmed cases per day, the Ministry of Science and ICT, the Ministry of Land Infrastructure and Transport (MOLIT), KCDC, Police Department, Financial Service Committee, the Board of Audit and Inspection decided to launch the Epidemic Investigation Support System (EISS) into the 'City Data Hub' [26]. The EISS was therefore developed as an application built on the Smart City Data Hub [27] (Figure 24.9), that has been legally supported by the 'Infectious Disease Prevention and Control Act'. EISS contributed greatly to reducing time spent on analysing real-time analysis of large scale outbreak areas, including the visualisation of patients' pathways and hot spot locations. EISS also enabled App developers to use real-time data for other services.

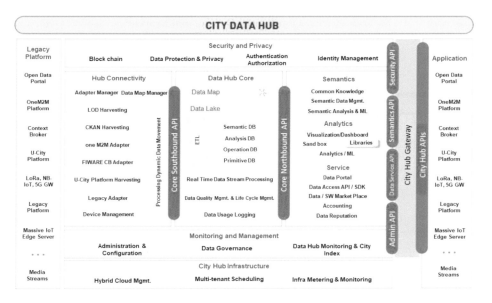

FIGURE 24.9
Structure of City Data Hub [27]

24.3.3 Epidemiological Investigation Support System (EISS)

According to the *Infectious Disease Prevention and Control Act*[9] and its enforcement Decree,[10] COVID-19-patient data are collected by the KCDC, under the Ministry of Health and Welfare (MOHW). The Act grants authority to the Police Department to ask for location information on infectious disease patient data that are normally retained by private mobile network companies. The Act also allows other responsible (designated) departments to collect additional data such as details of credit card usage (that has to be approved by the credit card association), visits to medical institutions, transport card use, entry and departure from the country, and closed-circuit television video footage.

In addition, the *Infectious Disease Prevention Act* has a provision to rapidly disclose the tracking information of infectious disease patients, depending on the outbreak situation [27]. The provision for the use of personal information amended in the *Infectious Disease Prevention Act*, including the disclosure of information for tracking purposes, was enforced during the MERS outbreak on 8 July 2015. To prevent the introduction and spread of dangerous infectious diseases, the Act was amended to enable the use of specific measures to rapidly control infectious diseases in the early stage of inflow [27].

According to the Infectious Disease Prevention Act, EISS has two different approval processes:

1. Location data: the Police Department has the authority to directly ask telecommunication companies (3 main national telecoms companies) to provide the requested data; and

2. Credit card-related data: the approval must be granted by the credit card association (22 credit card companies).

Following the EISS pilot operations conducted 16 March 2020, the system was officially launched on 26 March 2020 by the Ministry of Land, Infrastructure, and Transport (MOLIT), together with

---

[9]Infectious Disease Prevention and Control Act is accessible at http://elaw.klri.re.kr/eng_mobile/viewer.do?hseq=53530&type=part&key=36
[10]The Decree is accessible at http://elaw.klri.re.kr/eng_mobile/viewer.do?hseq=43547&type=part&key=36

the Ministry of ICT and Korea Centres for Disease Control and Prevention (KCDC) [26]. The EISS is operated in collaboration with private companies that provide location and card use data.

24.4 COVID-19 Response Success Factors

There are a number of factors that have contributed to South Korea's success in managing the COVID-19 pandemic. These factors include having a robust National Spatial Data Infrastructure (NSDI) that has provided the foundation for:

1. integrated geospatial data management and technological innovation;

2. an Open Data Policy that has stimulated the development of COVID-19-related systems and applications by government, private sector and individuals in the community;

3. institutional arrangements that have fostered a strong culture of data sharing;

4. high-quality fundamental and specific datasets; and

5. application development.

24.4.1 National Spatial Data Infrastructure

South Korea is recognized as one of the most influential digital economies powered by a well-coordinated NSDI [28], supportive policies and leadership. The NSDI success is founded on well-established and integrated geospatial datasets, interlinked Ministry and regional systems, a central database system, accessible information portals and cloud-based services that support application development.

It is the development of geospatial information-related technologies that has played a key role in enabling COVID-19 location-based products and services to be developed rapidly. In line with Industry 4.0, the geospatial information sector has experienced rapid innovation in parallel with major national agendas, such as Smart Cities and Ubiquitous Cities [29].

South Korea has continually developed and revised its overarching NSDI Basic Plan since 1995, and several major NSDI projects have been completed. The current 6th NSDI Basic Plan (2018-2022) aims to:

1. encourage the use of geospatial information in a way that creates social and economic value;

2. implement geospatial platforms to share information innovatively;

3. advance the geospatial information industry to stimulate job creation, and

4. augment geospatial information management through a public-participatory environment to enhance data quality and usability.

The presence of a well-established NSDI framework, including the legal system, and standards has provided the groundwork for base maps as an Open API format, which is essential for the development of COVID-19 location-based applications.

24.4.2 Open Data Policy

The rapid development of fit-for-purpose COVID-19 location-based Apps has provided far-reaching benefits for local communities faced with social distancing and precautionary travel. However, debate has sparked on the disclosure of private data: The Open Data Policy and other Acts, such as the Infectious Disease Prevention Act, have made it possible to legally disclose COVID-19 confirmed patient data. While the Government took precautionary measures when sending CBS messages during the onset of the pandemic, the number of confirmed cases was so low to start with, that people could identify patients from news and media reporting.

As a consequence, people were more concerned about being stigmatized through news reports than benefitting from the released data [13]. As the severity of COVID-19 grew and there was increased fear in the virus, people came to trust the government in the management of their personal data.

24.4.3 Institutional Arrangements

A robust NSDI governance model, underpinned by a central coordinating body (NSDI Committee) and supportive institutional networks, has been an influencing factor in the development of COVID-19 applications and services, which rely on effective collaboration and data sharing. In addition, South Korea has embraced public-private partnerships (PPP). In 2011-12, an NSDI project introduced a new collaboration and data sharing model between local governments, central government and the private sector. This collaboration has since become entrenched in the fabric of government.

In order to better promote geospatial information-related industries, the government established the Spatial Information Industry Promotion Institute (SPACE N), to support geospatial information-related industries, support the operation of 3D geospatial maps (vWorld), promote research and development, and provide consultation for start-ups and other private sector businesses [30]. SPACE N has encouraged the development of new and innovative technologies, datasets and platforms, which have since become vitalizing components of the geospatial data market in South Korea and enablers for COVID-19 applications.

24.4.4 Fundamental and Specific Dataset

Fundamental datasets are provided through the 'NSDI Portal' and 'V-World Portal'[11] (comprising 3D geospatial data), launched and operated by MOLIT. The list of fundamental datasets is based on the South Korean 'National Framework Data', which is progressively being translated to the set of Fundamental Data Themes endorsed by Member States at the Seventh Session of United Nations Committee of Experts on Global Geospatial Information Management (UN-GGIM).

Fundamental datasets are distributed via data portals and made available in various formats so that companies and individuals have greater options when developing new application and services. Formats include shapefiles, GPS (Global Positioning Systems) data and LBS (Location Based Services), Real-time data and open APIs. It is this breadth and variety of available high-quality integrated data that has made it possible to develop COVID-19 applications and services so quickly.

24.5 Conclusion

Several factors have contributed to the rapid development of these COVID-19 applications and services. The Spatial Information Industry Promotion Institute (SPACE N), established under MOLIT in 2012, has been promoting business start-ups and capacity building through education programs since 2012. The Open data policy adopted in 2013 played a substantial role in releasing base map data needed for the development of location-based Apps, supported by the robust NSDI that contributed in integrating geospatial data into one coordinate system (including for Smart City Data Hub) and aggregate the data into real-time geospatial platform.

These factors are categorized as:

1. **Factor 1: Systems**, which consist of technical components such as automation supported

---

[11] http://map.vworld.kr/map/maps.do

by real-time systems that have contributed to processing COVID-19 mass data efficiently (discussed in Section 24.3); while

2. **Factor 2: Policy/legal and institutional arrangements**, including capacity development from national institutions such as SPACE N, which contributed to building highly skilled professionals in geospatial information and supported businesses and start-ups with enabling technologies and policy, which in turn had far- reaching impacts in procuring, releasing and sharing the base maps, which were essential to creating the location-based applications.

South Korea has been lauded for rapidly controlling and flattening the COVID-19 curve, but the location-based services and release of personal data has raised concerns with the public as they are used to trace and track people's movements, and are thus an invasion of privacy. These concerns remain unanswered, and the balance between public good and privacy is still debated.

In summary, hundreds of COVID-19 Apps were developed between the first outbreak up until to today (September 2020). However, privacy issues remain a key concern. Some Apps demand access to users' location and to other mobile device features, such as camera, to enable the collection of individuals private data. Legal enforcement, bridging the gap between public good and privacy, needs to be thoroughly addressed. In addition, with so many Apps available, there is need for a platform with a regularly updated list of COVID-19 Apps to enable the avoidance of similar services. This platform is expected to increase the efficiency and effectiveness of App development, enabling private developers to rapidly bridge communities' need in times of a pandemic.

What is clear from the Korean experience is that location-based Apps, in the hand of citizens, have delivered huge benefits in reducing the spread of COVID-19 because people have been able to make informed decisions about social distancing, their welfare and the welfare of others.

References

[1] J. Ole. The black death: The greatest catastrophe ever. *History Today*, 55(3), 2005.

[2] A. Trilla, G. Trilla, and C. Daer. The 1918 'spanish flu' in spain. *Clinical Infectious Diseases*, 47(5):668–673, 2008.

[3] CDC. 1918 pandemic (h1n1 virus), centre for disease control and prevention, 2019. URL https://www.cdc.gov/flu/pandemic-resources/1918-pandemic-h1n1.html.

[4] S. Koh. The first covid-19 confirmed case in south korea, 2020. URL https://www.doctorsnews.co.kr/news/articleView.html?idxno=133009.

[5] Korea Centres for Disease Control and Prevention (KCDC). Statistics of covid-19 confirmed cases, 2020. URL http://ncov.mohw.go.kr/bdBoardList_Real.do.

[6] Korea Centres for Disease Control and Prevention (KCDC). Covid-19 statistics – regular briefing as of 21 may 2020, 2020. URL http://ncov.mohw.go.kr/tcmBoardView.do?contSeq=354638.

[7] World Health Organisation. Coronavirus disease 2019 (covid-19): situation report, 2020.

[8] BBC. Why is it the pathway tracing of the new covid-19 confirmed so detailed?, 2020. URL https://www.bbc.com/korean/news-51352575.

[9] J. Schiller and A. Voisard. *Location-based services*. Elsevier, 2004.

[10] J. Oh. Which country experienced rapid growth of medical applications during the height of covid-19 pandemic?, 2020. URL https://www.sedaily.com/NewsVIew/1Z44JU847J.

[11] MOIS. Sending sms (information service) for emergency disasters from the ministry of interior and safety (mois, 2017. URL https://www.gov.kr/portal/ntnadmNews/1219011.

[12] Republic of Korea. Flattening the curve on covid-19: How korea responded to a pandemic using ict, 2020.

[13] BBC. Coronavirus privacy: Are south korea's alerts too revealing?, 2020. URL https://www.bbc.com/news/world-asia-51733145.

[14] J. Gang. Distribution of covid-19 confirmed cases at a glance, 2020. URL http://www.hani.co.kr/arti/society/society_general/926540.html.

[15] J. Moon. 'coronanow' developed by two middle school students in daegu... profits used for masks donation, 2020. URL https://www.ytn.co.kr/_ln/0103_202002241510065315.

[16] M. Kim. 'coronanow' app made naver company to reach out to the two middle school developers, 2020. URL http://news.imaeil.com/Society/2020022615263206129.

[17] BBC. Coronanow, coronamap...when pandemics meet technology, 2020. URL https://www.bbc.com/korean/news-51541390.

[18] H. Lee. Covid-19 feature added in 'now and here' app, a community-based information sharing platform, 2020. URL https://m.etnews.com/20200303000313.

[19] P. Rosle. South korean church linked to many covid-19 cases is being sued for r1 billion in damages, 2020. URL https://www.businessinsider.co.za/south-korea-doomsday-church-shincheonji-sued-daegu-coronavirus-damages-2020-6.

[20] Maekyung. Now and here app, real-time information to market sales information, 2020. URL https://www.mk.co.kr/news/it/view/2018/08/532441/.

[21] B. Hwang. Masks and covid-19 pathway tracing... life with covid-19 became a routine, 2020. URL http://www.dt.co.kr/contents.html?article_no=2020031802101958054004.

[22] J. Park. Tina3d receives love calls after developing coback plus app, 2020. URL http://www.newspim.com/news/view/20200327000767.

[23] Korea Centres for Disease Control and Prevention (KCDC). Automatic infectious disease report support system, 2020. URL http://www.cdc.go.kr/npt/biz/npp/portal/nppAtRptMain.do.

[24] Korea Centres for Disease Control and Prevention (KCDC). Integrated information support system for infectious disease control, 2020. URL http://www.cdc.go.kr/contents.es?mid=a20301140000.

[25] Smart City Korea. Smart city innovation and growth r&d, 2020. URL https://smartcity.go.kr/rd/.

[26] MOLIT. Covid-19 pathway tracing becomes faster and easier, 2020. URL http://m.molit.go.kr/viewer/skin/doc.html?sfn=374f741a7cee499222a2ac204d1c2f2d&rs=/viewer/result/20200325.

[27] Y.J. Park, S.Y. Cho, J. Lee, O. Lee, W. Park, S. Jeong, S. Kim, S. Lee, J. Kim, and O. Parka. Development and utilization of a rapid and accurate epidemic investigation support system for covid-19. *Osong Public Health and Research Perspectives*, 11(3):118, 2020.

[28] E.H. Kim. A study on the strategic nsdi model for developing countries based on korean experiences. *Spatial Information Research*, 21(6):11–21, 2013.

[29] D.H. Shin. Ubiquitous city: Urban technologies, urban infrastructure and urban informatics. *Journal of Information Science*, 35(5):515–526, 2009.

[30] SPACE N. Introduction of space n, 2020. URL http://www.spacen.or.kr/spacen_intro/history.do.

25

Spatial Analysis of Urban Parks and COVID-19: City of Whittlesea, Victoria, Australia

Sultana Nasrin Baby, Adrian Murone, Shuddhasattwa Rafiq, and Khlood Ghalib Alrasheedi

Parks are an important part of the urban fabric of cities. The Victorian Government has made it clear that everyone with a pre-existing medical condition, needs to play a part in controlling the spread of the novel COVID-19 virus. Self-isolation and social distancing from other people will reduce the spread of the virus but may also be impacting negatively on people's physical and mental health. The Government allows people to leave their homes to exercise. For this reason, parks remain open, providing that visitors observe the protocols of not being in groups larger than two (apart from households) and keeping a safe distance of two metres between each other. The purpose of this paper is to explore the mental health conditions across age groups within spatial relationships between park availability and age care facilities in the City of Whittlesea. The association between having a park within 800 m from an aged care facility and the likelihood of having zero, one, two or more aged care facilities nearby was examined.

25.1   Introduction

Urban parks have received attention in recent years as a possible natural factor that could encourage physical activity, prevent obesity, and reduce the incidence of chronic conditions [12]. Despite long hypothesized benefits of parks for mental health, few park studies incorporate mental health measures. COVID-19 related restrictions have accentuated the community's reliance on open space to maintain its physical fitness and stabilise its mental health. It has also been demonstrated that older people are among the most vulnerable to both the effects of policy-induced isolation and disease itself. The benefits gleaned from being able to access open spaces and associated walking trails were demonstrated in Australia [29] and proximity to a park was inextricably linked to an increased frequency of park use, regular exercise and improved mental health [28]. However, the government has encouraged older people to stay at home for their own protection during the pandemic and implemented physical distancing measures to slow the spread of the disease. Unfortunately, older people, especially those in aged care facilities, may not have access to open spaces large enough to enable them to adhere to physical distancing measures within their facilities whilst spending time outdoors. This results in a reduction in social interaction even with the people that they live with and effects their mental health. Those living in aged care homes face additional mobility and psychological challenges that they (and their carers) must overcome before they are able to obtain the benefits associated with spending time in nature. One barrier faced by people in aged care facilities is access to public open space. Population forecasting indicates that, by 2036, there will be an 87% increase in people aged 50+ years in the City of Whittlesea

[17]. The city has committed to investing in, maximising and delivering recreation infrastructure that improves connectivity between places and removes the barriers experienced by older people to promote physical activity, active travel and incidental exercise (profile.id, 2019). To future-proof its investments and deliver equitable wellbeing outcomes there is a need to identify where existing and potential open spaces are situated, and their proximity to aged care facilities.

Aims of the Study

To identify the proximity between urban parks and aged care facilities and whether there is a link between proximity and clusters of older adults (60 years and over) who consider themselves impacted by mobility, or from mental health or physical health issues. The suburbs and towers associated with the inception of a second wave of COVID-19 in Melbourne have demonstrated that the most vulnerable members of our communities are those living close to limited open space.

This paper aims to contribute to two different strands of relevant literature. The first relates to the effect of park and open space proximity to aged care facilities on health. A relatively common finding in this literature is that people living near park areas report being in better physical and mental health and experience lower levels of stress, this is largely attributed to the size of the open space available, cleaner natural environments and better-quality air found in parks [2]. Through facilities, outdoor settings, and services provided, smaller public parks enable people of all ages, socio-economic backgrounds, and ethnicities to obtain these same benefits. Several studies show that that council parks provide opportunities for people to increase their rigorous physical activity, thereby reducing obesity. The literature consistently reveals that those living in close proximity to parks and other recreation facilities have superior physical activity levels, physical and mental health [7, 10, 11, 13, 15, 21, 27].

A second strand of the literature to which the paper contributes investigates the drivers of the COVID-19 pandemic, including the role of crucial factors such as lockdowns, human and economic activity, climate and pollution. On the role of social distance, Greenstone and Nigam [8] find that the mortality benefits of social distancing are about $8 trillion for the US $60,000 per US household. Fang et al. [6] analysed the impact of restrictions on human mobility and calculated that without the Wuhan lockdown, contagion cases would have been 64.81% greater in the 347 Chinese cities outside Hubei province, and 52.64% higher in the 16 non- Wuhan cities inside Hubei. Several authors have examined the drivers of Italy's severe COVID-19 outbreak [9, 20, 22, 24] with Ciminelli and Garcia-Mandicó [4] demonstrating that the congestion of the health care system exacerbated the number of deaths in Italy.

These research findings contribute to both research strands by showing that park areas play an important positive role in health outcomes specifically under the context of a pandemic, and that environmental factors impact geographical spread of the disease. In the final part of the paper, we discuss methodological issues, directions for future research and policy implications of our results.

25.2 Urban Parks

Public and private urban parks are critical to the long-term health, liveability and resilience of communities. Access to nature helps individuals to stay physically healthy [16]. Physical activity in nature (e.g. walking, cycling, gardening and other outdoor activities) can lower anxiety [14] and reduce post-traumatic symptoms [19], which might prove to be important after the COVID-19 world-wide social distancing orders are liberalized [1]. Using data from Kansas City, Kaczynski et al. [12] documents having a park within 800 metres from home and the likelihood of having 0, 1, or 2 or more chronic health conditions (CHCs). Rosenfeld et al. [25] reveal that urban parks induce increased physical activities of nearby communities in Dublin, Ireland. Dharmarajan et al. [5] provides evidence of positive mental health outcome due to residing close to parks in Los Angeles. In a recent study, Rice and Pan [23] argue that during these extraordinary circumstances, urban nature offers resilience for maintaining well-being in urban populations, while enabling social distancing.

In the Australian context, the benefits gleaned from being able to access open spaces and associated walking trails have been demonstrated in Temple Lang [29]. The results of this study strengthen the growing body of evidence that mental health is significantly related to residential distance from parks, with the aged care facility, residents within short walking distance from the park (400 m) and decreasing significantly as the distance increases. The number of visits and physical activity minutes are significantly and independently related to distance.

25.3   Study Area

The study area was the entire CoW municipality, which is one of Melbourne's largest urban municipalities, located about 20 kilometres north of the city and the fastest growing area in the north of Melbourne. The CoW has established urban areas in the south and urban growth areas (new communities) and rural areas in the north. It has been designated as one of six 'growth areas' along the fringes of Melbourne. Between 2016 and 2041, it is projected to grow by 175,000 people in 62,400 additional households. While the population is ageing, it will continue to mainly attract a diverse group of younger families moving to outer areas to establish a home. Some residents are less advantaged than those in other parts of Melbourne and the new suburbs, migration from a wide range of areas across Melbourne means some residents will have fewer community connections. This growth is said to provide significant benefits derived from the critical mass required to make businesses, services, clubs and infrastructure viable. Diversity may provide an interesting culture and the type of vibrancy in which tourism, education, and other activities thrive. However, growth and diversity also make Whittlesea vulnerable to some of the negative effects of emerging challenges such as:

- Increasing demand for infrastructure.

- Changing work patterns.

- Increasing transport issues.

- Climate change.

- Social disconnection.

Suburban development in Whittlesea began after World War 2 and has progressed north since (Figure 25.3). In 2002, an Urban Growth Boundary for Melbourne was put in place that divides Whittlesea's urban and rural areas. There was a lull in new housing development in the late 2000s, but in the last few years, several large subdivisions in previously rural areas, and infill development in the established suburbs, have rapidly increased the number of households.

Despite ageing, the population will continue to be dominated by family households. Whittlesea currently has a markedly younger population than the rest of Melbourne. By 2041, all population groups will grow, but the population will age, with an increased proportion of older people (aged over 55). There will also be an increase in the proportion of the population aged 5 to 19, while those aged 20-54 will decrease. The median age is projected to increase only slightly, from 34 in 2016 to 35 in 2041 (Figure 25.4).

25.4   Methodology

To identify the proximity between urban parks and aged care facilities in CoW and its impact on older adults (60 years and over) who consider themselves impacted by mobility, or from mental

FIGURE 25.1

CoW and Surrounding Area (Northern Melbourne comprises LGAs of Banyule, Darebin, Hume, Moreland, Nillumbik and Whittlesea). Source: SGS Economics and Planning 2018 Data: Victoria State Government 2017, Plan Melbourne

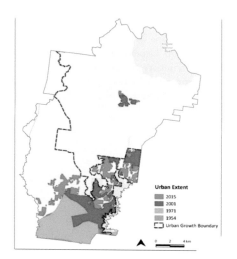

FIGURE 25.2

Figure 2. Extent of Urban Development 1954–2015. Source: SGS Economics and Planning 2018 Data: Victoria State Government 2017, Plan Melbourne

health or physical health issues in this study we conduct an individual survey and a GIS based proximity analysis. The results from both methods are presented in order.

25.4.1   Survey

Analyses of the City of Whittlesea 2019 Household Survey (1,083 respondent households and 3,083 individual respondents) were conducted looking specifically at the results for people who reported being 60 years of age or older [18]. 676 (62%) respondents identified as being over the age of 60 years, 674 respondents indicated their residential location, 2 did not. The distribution of these respondents is presented in Figure 25.4.

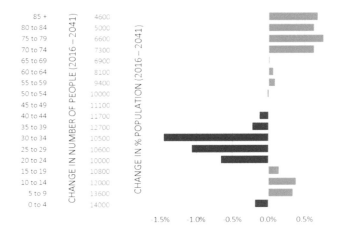

FIGURE 25.3
Whittlesea Population Change by Age Group. Source: SGS Economics and Planning 2018 Data: Victoria State Government 2017, Plan Melbourne

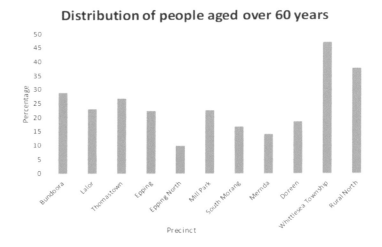

FIGURE 25.4
The top five concentrations of respondents aged older than 60 by precinct (in order of highest to lowest) were in the Whittlesea Township (47%), Rural North (37.3), Bundoora (29%), Thomastown (26.9) and Mill Park (22.6)

According to the survey undertaken in CoW, older adults and senior citizens (aged 60 years and over) – respondents were measurably more likely than average to have done less than five hours moderate to vigorous physical activity.

There was measurable and significant variation in the amount of moderate to vigorous physical activity undertaken 'in the last week' observed by respondent profile (age structure, gender, and language spoken at home). The following graph provides a summary of the results for respondents doing less than 5 hours last week and those doing five hours or more, as follows:

Of all respondents, 62% answered the questions pertaining to disabilities, within the 60 plus age group, 33.4% of respondents indicated that they had permanent or long-term disability. Ranked in order of highest to lowest, the top three precincts with the highest percentage of people reporting a disability linked with mobility and/or mental health and/or a medical condition were Epping North, Bundoora and Lalor. On average, in this demographic;

- 2% of total respondents identified mobility as their disability.

- 1% identified mental health as their disability.

- 5% of respondents identified as having a permanent or long-term medical condition.

By precinct, the top three precincts where respondents identified 'Mobility' as their disability resided in Lalor (30%), Epping (24%), Mill Park (22%). The top three precincts where respondents identified 'Mental Health' as their disability were Mernda (31%), Thomastown (26%), South Morang (21%), followed by Bundoora and Lalor (both 19%). The top three precincts where respondents identified as having a 'Permanent or long-term medical condition' were Epping North (86%), Bundoora (69%) and Mill Park (65%).

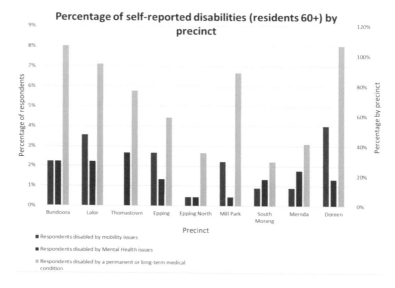

FIGURE 25.5
Percentage of Self-Reported Disabilities (residents 60+) by Prescient

Figure 25.5 offers distribution of residents self-reporting disabilities and the types of disabilities reported among precincts. For each disability reported, the following rates were the highest among respondents. Four percent (4%) of residents aged over 60 residing in Lalor reported being disabled by 'Mobility' issues, 3% of residents aged over 60 residing in Thomastown reported being disabled by 'Mental Health' issues and 8% of residents aged over 60 residing in Bundoora reported being disabled by a permanent or long-term medical condition.

Respondents aged over 60 were also asked to self-report whether they undertook vigorous physical activity in the week prior to the survey. The results indicated that those who resided in Mernda and Doreen performed vigorous activity for longer periods than respondents in any other precinct. Interestingly, most residents in Bundoora, Lalor, Thomastown, Epping, Epping North and Mill Park who performed vigorous activity, only did so for less than 2.5hrs over the week.

Figure 25.6 indicates that a high percentage (29%) of residents aged over 60 years reported a need for support (data not shown), and that those in Lalor were in highest need of support for daily tasks, to overcome the limitations of their mobility and to be able to participate in social events.

By precinct, in order of highest to lowest, the top 3 precincts with the highest levels of access

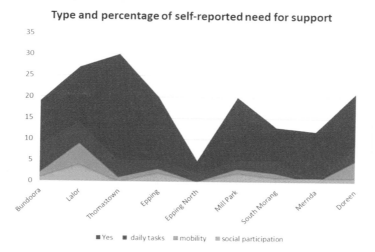

FIGURE 25.6
Type and Percentage of Self-Reported Need for Supports

to or used Aged care services were Lalor (12.6%), Doreen (6.7%) and Bundoora (5.7%). The top 3 precincts with the highest levels of access to or used Mental health services were Epping (9%), and Lalor (8.8%) and Doreen (8.6%). The top 3 precincts with the highest levels of access to, or used Other social services were Bundoora (4.6%), Thomastown (3.9%), and Lalor (3.0%). The data also indicates that between 87.4 and 99 percent of respondents indicated they did not have access to aged care, mental health or other social services, though only two individual respondents specifically identified that distance was a barrier to access.

25.4.2 GIS Based Proximity Analyses

GIS users bring a wealth of knowledge about physical space, particularly geographic space, into the process of interpreting GIS data. The proximity toolset in the analysis ESRI ARCGIS software toolbox can be used to discover proximity relationships. These tools output information with buffer features or tables. Buffers are usually used to delineate protected zones around features or to show areas of influence. For example, one can buffer an aged care facility by one mile and use the buffer to select all the parks that are more than one mile from the park in order to plan for the transportation of aged-care residents to and from their facility to that park. One could also use the multi-ring buffer tool to classify the areas around a feature into near, moderate distance, and long-distance classes for analysis. Buffers are sometimes used to clip data to a given study area, or to exclude features within a critical distance of something from further consideration in an analysis. Buffer and Multiple Ring Buffer create area features at a specified distance (or several specified distances) around the input features. In this research we conducted proximity analysis on multiple ring buffers to identify suitable parks for aged-care residents to visit and completed a gap analysis of aged care facilities and reserves, local parks and smaller urban spaces for the CoW.

Data were collected for parks and Aged care facilities and the distance from each point was calculated. This table can be used for statistical analyses, or it can be joined to one of the feature classes to show the distance to points in the other feature class. Use the Point Distance tool to look at proximity relationships between two sets of things. For example, you might compare the distances between one set of points representing several types of businesses (such as theatres, fast food restaurants, engineering firms, and hardware stores) and another set of points representing the locations of community problems (litter, broken windows, spray-paint graffiti), limiting the search to one mile to look for local relationships. You could join the resulting table to the business and problem attribute tables and calculate summary statistics for the distances between types of business and problems. You might find a stronger correlation for some pairs than for others and use your results to target the placement of public trash cans, or police patrols [26]. Use Point Distance to find the distance and direction to all the water wells within a given distance of a test well where you identified a contaminant. Below is an example of point distance analysis. Each point in one feature class is given the ID, distance, and direction to the nearest point in another feature class. proximity findings are incorporated to make the framework more relevant to the users of Geographic Information Systems (GIS) concerning their spatial circumstances.

Urban parks, along with other natural elements like conservation reserves and waterways are a key mechanism that will enable the CoW to cope with future urban challenges linked to densification. They will also make the community more resilient to human health, wellbeing and environmental challenges such as heatwaves, flooding and soil contamination. A park hierarchy groups parks into distinct types and defines how each type of park is used, what it contains, and what service levels are associated with them. The hierarchy and naming conventions adopted by CoW, park types include:

Figure 25.7 present number of parks near aged care facilities identified at 100 metres apart. While only nine (9) aged care facilities were located within 100 metres of a nearby park, 125 aged care facilities were within 800 metres. For a person living in an aged-care facility, walking a distance of 800 meters could prove to be a demotivating factor; whether many of them would have enough energy to cover those distances unsupported is also unknown.

TABLE 25.1

Distance between Parks and Aged Care Facilities in CoW

Distance from aged care 100 m interval	100 metres	200 metres	300 metres	400 metres	500 metres	600 metres	800 metres	Grand Total
Civic & Commercial Facilities			5	4	3	3	4	19
Conservation Area	1	1		2	4	3	10	21
Landscape Site	2	8	14	17	19	33	43	136
Major Community Parks				1	1	1	1	4
Municipal Open Space		5	7	9	8	11	12	52
Neighbourhood & Local Open Space	6	18	29	30	40	40	55	218
Special Purpose Site					1			1
Grand Total	9	32	55	63	76	91	125	**451**

From Figure 25.8a we can easily understand that most of the aged care facilities (marked as a solid black circle) are located in the lower section of the map, while most of the larger conservation areas, open space and landscape sites are located in the top right section of the lower half, too far away to access. Even some of the neighbourhood and municipal open spaces, and major community parks are quite distant from aged care facilities.

In Figure 25.8b while the aged care facilities in this map are comparatively small, a lot of them are quite distant from conservation areas, landscape sites, and major community parks which are often the most equipped to service the needs of senior citizens and those who live in aged-care facilities.

Park and recreation professionals are seeking answers to key questions as they move into a response and prevention mode in the coming days and weeks, especially in communities that are starting to document confirmed cases of COVID-19 (Figure 25.9). As part of hazard identification and mitigation process, it is important to identify any parks near aged care facilities, to provide adequate communication to affected residents when closing or cleaning these facilities or providing advice on the nearest open space at which residents may find natural respite.

The numbers of confirmed coronavirus cases on 12 July are:

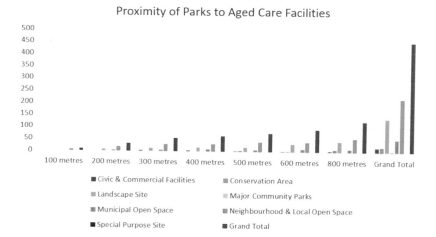

FIGURE 25.7
Proximity of Parks to Aged Care Facilities

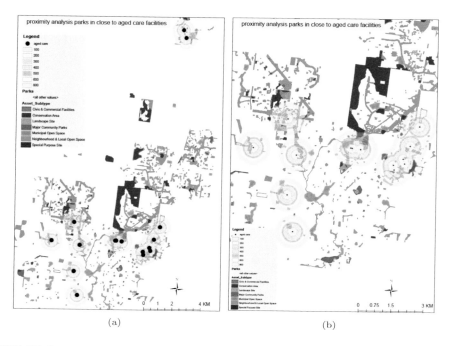

(a)   (b)

FIGURE 25.8
(a) Proximity of Parks to Aged Care Facilities (b) Proximity analysis parks in close to aged care facilities

- **In Australia:** 9797 cases – 7728 recovered (108 deaths)

- **In Victoria:** 3967 cases – 2329 recovered (24 death)

- **In Whittlesea:** 33 cases (including 2 active cases)

Community transmissions of second wave started to spread across Victorian aged care families.

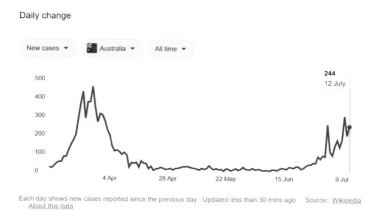

FIGURE 25.9
Daily change coronavirus cases from April to July

As of July 14, 2020, a total of 14 residents and 17 staff at the Menarock Life Essendon aged care facility in Essendon have tested positive to coronavirus, the largest cluster in the state. In this backdrop while planning for location choice for aged care facilities or parks two major criteria should be proximity of recreational facilities to aged care facilities as well as the design of these facilities to ensure social distancing while people are using these facilities.

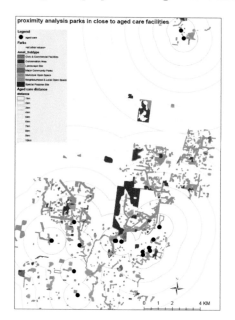

FIGURE 25.10
Age care distance from 1 km to 10 km

25.5 Results Discussion and Limitations

The proximity analysis indicates that aged care facilities are clustered in the south west and west of the municipality and that these centres are in closer proximity to parks. It also reveals that in the northeast (newly developed areas) aged care facilities have not been collocated with parks. The model also reveals that the distribution of Aged care facilities is less dense in the newly developed areas in comparison to older suburbs like Epping, South Morang. Whittlesea, and Lalor. The demographic analysis shows that in order of highest to lowest, the top three precincts consisting of residents who reported they were living with a disability were Epping North, Bundoora and Lalor.

By analysing the impact of multiple demographic factors such as the methodology used herein, information can be gleaned to determine the spatial location of those in most need. Our data analysis shows that residents over the age of 60 who resided in Lalor needed the most support. Lalor had the highest number of people reporting they experienced limitations due to mobility and needed the most support with daily tasks and to overcome limitations they faced when trying to socially participate. Interestingly, the precinct of Lalor also recorded the most respondents to use and have access to aged care facilities and the lowest rate (87.4%) of respondents who indicated they needed the services but could not access them. These results do not directly correlate with the proximity analysis because there were no aged care facilities located in Lalor.

A nearby urban park has been associated with the same mental health benefits as decreasing local unemployment rates by 2 percentage points, suggesting at least the potential for environmental interventions to improve mental health [28]. There are limitations to the application of the proximity analysis we have conducted. It is cross-sectional, making it impossible to control for important confounders, including residential selection, and assumes that the park needs to be in proximity of an Aged-care facility to be utilised by its occupants. The analysis does not provide an evaluation of the impact of the quality, location or suitability of park infrastructure such as seats, barbeques, walking or cycling paths for older people. Another limitation of the study is that it has not evaluated the impact of the modes of transport that would be utilised by residents of Aged-care centres or their carers to facilitate park visitation. Similarly, other than to locate them within a spatial precinct, the survey data does not identify the spatial location of the resident who filled in the survey. This is critical because the likelihood of a person in an aged care facility completing the household survey would be very low; it is complex and requires a certain level of cognitive ability to complete. It could be argued that the survey results reflect more about the composition of households and that specific surveys of residents living in aged care facilities focusing on their interaction with nearby open space within these precincts is required to understand the effect of the proximity to open space on the mental health of residents therein.

Implications for planning and open space policy makers

Mental health policy has traditionally focused on interventions required to cure an illness at an individual scale, such as providing clinical support or improving access to services for sufferers in need of support. It is our contention that mental health policy should shift its focus from curing the individual to prevention by maximising the benefits of environmental determinants such that both the most vulnerable and the broader population may benefit substantially from such measures.

25.6 Conclusions

The paper set out to explore the importance of several parks and the spatial relationship between park availability and COVID-19 across age groups in the CoW. Park-based physical activity is a promising means to satisfy current physical activity requirements for COVID-19 time. However, there is little research concerning what park environmental and policy characteristics might enhance physical activity levels. This paper analysis and proposes a spatial model to guide thinking and suggest hypotheses. This paper also describes the relationships between park benefits, park use, and physical activity, and the antecedents/correlates of park use.

This paper suggests that in councils policies regarding spatial design, the provision of park space close to residential areas aged care facility and should be considered so that individuals can engage in activities such as walking and exercise [3]. As indicated through our analyses as well as some earlier studies, having a well-designed landscape planning with proximity between aged care and recreational facilities help develop an agile and resilient community ready to physically and mentally cope up with unprecedented events like COVID-19 pandemic. In future research will discuss classification scheme, the discussion focuses on park environmental characteristics that could be related to physical activity, including park features, condition, access, aesthetics, safety, and least cost path analysis and policies. Data for these categories should be collected within specific geographic areas in or around the park, including activity areas, supporting areas, the overall park, and the surrounding neighbourhood. Future research also focuses on how to operationalize specific measures and methodologies for collecting data, as well as measuring associations between individual physical activity levels and specific park characteristics. Collaboration among many disciplines is needed.

Acknowledgments

We would like to acknowledge the support of City of Whittlesea Council.

References

[1] Samantha K Brooks, Rebecca K Webster, Louise E Smith, Lisa Woodland, Simon Wessely, Neil Greenberg, and Gideon James Rubin. The psychological impact of quarantine and how to reduce it: rapid review of the evidence. *The Lancet*, 2020.

[2] Matthew HEM Browning, Katherine J Mimnaugh, Carena J van Riper, Heidemarie K Laurent, and Steven M LaValle. Can simulated nature support mental health? comparing short, single-doses of 360-degree nature videos in virtual reality with the outdoors. *Frontiers in Psychology*, 10, 2019.

[3] Jacquelin Burgess, Carolyn M Harrison, and Melanie Limb. People, parks and the urban green: a study of popular meanings and values for open spaces in the city. *Urban Studies*, (6):455–473, 1988.

[4] Gabriele Ciminelli and Sílvia Garcia-Mandicó. Covid-19 in italy: an analysis of death registry data. *VOXEU, Centre for Economic Policy Research, London*, 22, 2020.

[5] Sai Dharmarajan, John P Bentley, Benjamin F Banahan III, and Donna S West-Strum. Measuring pharmacy performance in the area of medication adherence: addressing the issue of risk adjustment. *Journal of Managed Care Pharmacy*, 20:1057–1068, 2014.

[6] Lei Fang, George Karakiulakis, and Michael Roth. Are patients with hypertension and diabetes mellitus at increased risk for covid-19 infection? *The Lancet. Respiratory Medicine*, 8:e21, 2020.

[7] Penny Gordon-Larsen, Melissa C Nelson, Phil Page, and Barry M Popkin. Inequality in the built environment underlies key health disparities in physical activity and obesity. *Pediatrics*, 117:417–424, 2006.

[8] M Greenstone and V Nigam. Does social distancing matter? university of chicago, becker friedman institute for economics working paper., 2020.

[9] Jill Hallin, Lars D Engstrom, Lauren Hargis, Andrew Calinisan, Ruth Aranda, David M Briere, Niranjan Sudhakar, Vickie Bowcut, Brian R Baer, Joshua A Ballard, et al. The krasg12c inhibitor mrtx849 provides insight toward therapeutic susceptibility of kras-mutant cancers in mouse models and patients. *Cancer Discovery*, 10:54–71, 2020.

[10] Don R Hansen, Maryanne M Mowen, and Tom Madison. Cornerstones of cost accounting. *Issues in Accounting Education*, 25:790–791, 2010.

[11] Nancy Humpel, Neville Owen, and Eva Leslie. Environmental factors associated with adults' participation in physical activity: a review. *American Journal of Preventive Medicine*, 22:188–199, 2002.

[12] Andrew T Kaczynski, Gina M Besenyi, Sonja A Wilhelm Stanis, Mohammad Javad Koohsari, Katherine B Oestman, Ryan Bergstrom, Luke R Potwarka, and Rodrigo S Reis. Are park proximity and park features related to park use and park-based physical activity among adults? variations by multiple socio-demographic characteristics. *International Journal of Behavioral Nutrition and Physical Activity*, 11:146, 2014.

[13] Sahib S Khalsa, Ralph Adolphs, Oliver G Cameron, Hugo D Critchley, Paul W Davenport, Justin S Feinstein, Jamie D Feusner, Sarah N Garfinkel, Richard D Lane, Wolf E Mehling, et al. Interoception and mental health: a roadmap. *Biological Psychiatry: Cognitive Neuroscience and Neuroimaging*, 3:501–513, 2018.

[14] Emma Lawton, Eric Brymer, Peter Clough, and Andrew Denovan. The relationship between the physical activity environment, nature relatedness, anxiety, and the psychological well-being benefits of regular exercisers. *Frontiers in Psychology*, 8:1058, 2017.

[15] Merry-Jo Levers, Carole A Estabrooks, and Janet C Ross Kerr. Factors contributing to frailty: literature review. *Journal of Advanced Nursing*, 56:282–291, 2006.

[16] Iana Markevych, Julia Schoierer, Terry Hartig, Alexandra Chudnovsky, Perry Hystad, Angel M Dzhambov, Sjerp De Vries, Margarita Triguero-Mas, Michael Brauer, Mark J Nieuwenhuijsen, et al. Exploring pathways linking greenspace to health: theoretical and methodological guidance. *Environmental Research*, 158:301–317, 2017.

[17] City of Whittlesea. City of Whittlesea Population Forecasts. 2016. Accessed on 8 May 2018.

[18] City of Whittlesea. A Positive Ageing Strategy for the Whittlesea Municipality 2016 – 2025. 2019. Accessed on 8 March 2019.

[19] Lauren M Oppizzi and Reba Umberger. The effect of physical activity on ptsd. *Issues in Mental Health Nursing*, 39:179–187, 2018.

[20] Matteo Paradisi and Gianluca Rinaldi. An empirical estimate of the infection fatality rate of covid-19 from the first italian outbreak. *Available at SSRN 3582811*, 2020.

[21] Nirav P Patel, Michael A Grandner, Dawei Xie, Charles C Branas, and Nalaka Gooneratne. 'sleep disparity' in the population: poor sleep quality is strongly associated with poverty and ethnicity. *BMC Public Health*, 10:475, 2010.

[22] A Pluchino, G Inturri, A Rapisarda, AE Biondo, R Le Moli, C Zappala, N Giuffrida, G Russo, and V Latora. A novel methodology for epidemic risk assessment: the case of covid-19 outbreak in italy. *arXiv preprint arXiv:2004.02739*, 2020.

[23] William L Rice and Bing Pan. Understanding drivers of change in park visitation during the covid-19 pandemic: A spatial application of big data. 2020.

[24] Gianluca Rinaldi and Matteo Paradisi. An empirical estimate of the infection fatality rate of covid-19 from the first italian outbreak. *medRxiv*, 2020.

[25] Daniel L Rosenfeld, Emily Balcetis, Brock Bastian, Elliot Berkman, Jennifer Bosson, Tiffany Brannon, Anthony L Burrow, Daryl Cameron, CHEN Serena, Jonathan E Cook, et al. Conducting social psychological research in the wake of covid-19. 2020.

[26] Lauren M. Scott and Mark V. Janikas. *Spatial Statistics in ArcGIS*, pages 27–41. Springer Berlin Heidelberg, Berlin, Heidelberg, 2010.

[27] Lilly Shoup and Reid Ewing. The economic benefits of open space, recreation facilities and walkable community design. *A Research Synthesis. Princeton, NJ, Active Living Research, a National Program of the Robert Wood Johnson Foundation*, 2010.

[28] Roland Sturm and Deborah Cohen. Proximity to urban parks and mental health. *The Journal of Mental Health Policy and Economics*, 17:19, 2014.

[29] John Temple Lang. Three possibilities for reform of the procedure of the european commission in competition cases under regulation 1/2003. *Centre for European Policy Studies (CEPS) Special Report*, 2011.

26

The Economic Impact of COVID-19 in Pacific Island Countries and Territories

Phil Bright and David Abbott

This chapter describes the impact of COVID-19 on the socio-economic situation of the Pacific Island Countries and Territories (PICTs) during the first nine-months of 2020. Fortunately, only six of the PICTs have had cases of COVID-19 to date, but the far-reaching social and economic effects on such a vulnerable region are significant. This chapter highlights the economic impacts currently being felt, and those which are being forecast for the near future. The chapter is primarily focused on the tourism sector, which is one of the principal industries for the region providing livelihoods for people in both the formal and informal sectors. Spatial analysis of the Pacific situation is limited, but a few examples are presented.

26.1 Introduction

When people think of the Pacific Islands, they often imagine the postcard photo of coconut trees, white sand and turquoise water. This is certainly the case for parts of the Pacific, but in reality the region is very varied with low-lying atoll countries interspersed with high, mountainous and sometimes volcanic islands. The region is made up of thousands of islands spread out across a vast ocean ranging in size from the atoll country of Tokelau with a population of a little over 1,500, to the rugged, and mountainous country of Papua New Guinea with a population of almost 9 million.

The region is also very cultural and ethnically diverse. This is manifest in the more than 800 individual languages in Papua New Guinea (PNG) and the regionally recognised Melanesian, Micronesian and Polynesian sub-regions. Each with its own distinct, yet varied cultures and customs.

In total the Pacific region currently comprises a little over 12.3 million inhabitants and is characterized by relative fast population growth in many countries, notably in Melanesia, and rapid urbanisation (as nationally defined) in countries across the region. The population is expected to increase by more than fifty percent and to pass 20 million in the next 30 years[1].

The region is also among the most vulnerable to natural disasters and climate change. Excluding PNG, 90% of Pacific Islanders live within 5km of the coast [1] making them highly susceptible to sea level rise and extreme weather events, including storm surges, cyclonic damage and coastal flooding. There have also been incidents of earthquake-related tsunamis causing serious loss of life and infrastructure damage in Samoa, Solomon Islands and PNG; and volcanoes have caused similar damage in Vanuatu. Having geospatial data that accurately maps these areas of vulnerability will be essential as the consequences of climate change affect the fragile island environments.

---

[1] Pacific Data Hub.stat. Population Projections. https://stats.pacificdata.org/

26.2   Socio-economic Context

Although PICTs being small islands in a vast ocean, are often regarded as isolated from the rest of the world and the vagaries of the global economy, in reality they are as fully integrated as any other nation. The economies of the Pacific are very open with merchandise trade, the aggregate value of both imports and exports often exceeding the value of their national Gross Domestic Product (GDP). And most of the smaller, resource-poor, small island states experience persistent balance of trade deficits that amount in some cases to over 70 percent of GDP. In recent years increases in fishing licence fees, revenues from sovereign wealth and trust funds have helped to cover these deficits.

PICTs are also highly dependent on foreign development assistance (increasingly so in the current pandemic environment), worker and family remittances, and receipts from tourism, all of which are directly and closely linked to the state of the global economy. This means they are highly susceptible to the impact of external events or shocks, including the consequential effects of the pandemic even when the health aspects have been largely avoided.

The region is therefore very dependent on the "outside" with remittances being equivalent to around 40% of Tonga's GDP[2], and tourism is estimated to account for between 20-30% of economic activity in many countries including Samoa, Tonga and Vanuatu [2]. There is also a significant dependency on Overseas Development Assistance (ODA) with half of the PICTs falling in the top 15 countries in the world in terms of net ODA received per capita (US$)[3].

Lack of economic opportunities in the small island economies of the Pacific have led to high rates of youth unemployment and significant rural-to-urban-to-overseas migration. This has led to rural depopulation in a number of countries, increasing rural dependency ratios and a reduction in the contribution of rural agriculture to national GDPs. Gender inequality, increasing levels of hardship and basic-needs poverty and the incidence of domestic violence also present significant challenges in the region. Poor health outcomes, largely the result of the prevalence of non-communicable diseases (NCDs) which represent a very high, 75%, of mortality, putting the region above the global average, are also a major challenge [3]. The high prevalence of NCDs also makes Pacific people potentially highly susceptible to the COVID-19 virus and its complications; a major reason for the strict border controls and international movement instituted by most of the island governments.

26.3   Coming of COVID-19 and How It Is Reported in the Pacific Region

26.3.1   The Spread of Covid-19 in the Region

The first case of COVID-19 appeared in French Polynesia on 10 March 2020. Over the next 3 weeks, Guam, New Caledonia, Fiji, PNG and the Commonwealth of the Northern Marianas detected their first cases.

As has been the case globally, PICTs adopted strict measures to close their borders and restrict domestic movement. The timeliness of these measures have resulted in many PICTs recording no cases of COVID-19, and others being able to effectively limit, at least initially, the numbers of cases entering the country. New Caledonia for example, significantly reduced international travel starting on the 18th of March when the first case of COVID was diagnosed. The authorities then enforced a nation-wide four weeks of confinement from the 24th of March, closing schools and non-essential services, and prohibiting leisure activities apart from limited exercise within 1 km of place of

---

[2]World Bank Data. Personal Remittances, received (% of GDP) https://data.worldbank.org/indicator/BX.TRF. PWKR.DT.GD.ZS?most_recent_value_desc=true

[3]World Bank Data. Net ODA received per capita (current US$) https://data.worldbank.org/indicator/DT.ODA. ODAT.PC.ZS?most_recent_value_desc=true

residence. Shopping was allowed, though any movement outside the place of residence required an *"attestation de déplacement dérogatoire"* which meant everyone moving outside of their immediate residential area needed to carry a statement indicating why the person had left the house. Such an attestation needed to be carried by every household member[4].

As of 15 September there were 3,656 COVID-19 cases (Figure 26.1) and 38 reported deaths in the Pacific, with significant increases reported in the previous four weeks, notably in Guam, French Polynesia and PNG (Figure 26.2)[5]. In New Caledonia where border restrictions were still some of the tightest globally, there were only 26 cases, with none of them being from community transmission.

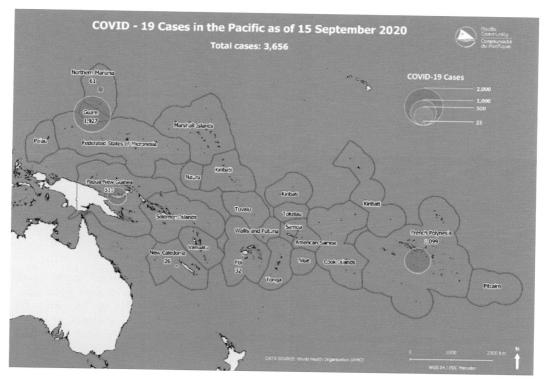

FIGURE 26.1
COVID-19 Cases in the Pacific as of 15 September 2020 (Source: See footnote 5)

26.4   Mapping COVID-19 in the Pacific

Robust spatial data infrastructures in the Pacific's twenty-two countries and territories would be ideal to prepare for and manage a pandemic like COVID-19; "A virus-resilient economy requires knowing exactly where infected people are, living conditions, and access to medical services – all of which hinges on geospatial information" [4].

Although there has been increased adoption of GPS-locational data, satellite and drone imagery, and improvements in the mapping of services and infrastructure, what is generally lacking across

---

[4]Gouvernement de la Nouvelle Calédonie. Info coronavirus Covid-19. https://gouv.nc/coronavirus
[5]Pacific Community. COVID-19: Pacific Community Updates. https://www.spc.int/updates/blog/2020/09/covid-19-pacific-community-updates

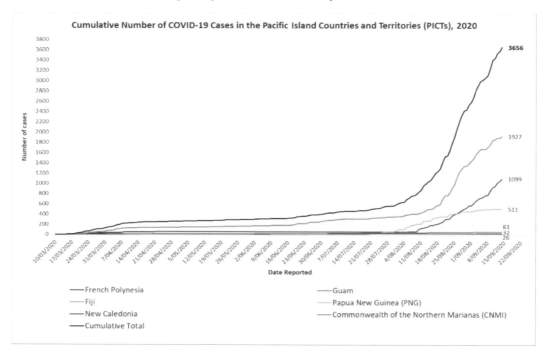

FIGURE 26.2
Cumulative COVID-19 Cases in the Pacific as of 15 September 2020 (Source: See footnote 5)

the region is a way to easily access, utilise and link these disparate data sources. Mobile phone data is also being more frequently utilised and some crowdsourcing of data in disaster situations.

Population grids such as the one shown in Figure 26.3, developed by the Statistics for Development Division (SDD) at the Pacific Community (SPC)[6], are an example of where value-added spatial analysis has been undertaken and can be used in applications such as disaster preparedness and also disaster relief.

To date the use of geospatial tools to analyse the COVID-19 situation at a sub-national level in the region has not been widespread. This is to a large degree because of the limited availability of detailed COVID incidence data, the required local-level socio-economic data, and the resources to perform the analysis. The most detailed mapping the authors are aware of, is that which has been done by the World Health Organisation (WHO) which shows data at a provincial level for most of the PICTs affected by COVID-19.

There is also the Pacific COVID-19 Response Map created by the Australian National University (ANU) CartoGIS, the Australia Pacific Security College (PSC), and the ANU Department of Pacific Affairs to monitor the ongoing responses of Pacific Island Countries and Territories[7]. The map is updated weekly.

26.4.1   Communicating the Pandemic

Communicating nationally important health messages across the countries of the region is frequently very difficult. Internet, TV and mobile phone penetration is very low in many of the poorer and widely dispersed mountainous countries of Melanesia, and amongst the small atoll and island states with widely scattered, small and often isolated communities. Not only is communication difficult but also the collection of the "real-time" data required to monitor and

---

[6]Pacific Community, Statistics for Development Division. Covid-19. https://sdd.spc.int/disasters-data/covid-19

[7]Policy Forum. Pacific COVID-19 Map. https://www.policyforum.net/pacific-covid-19-map/

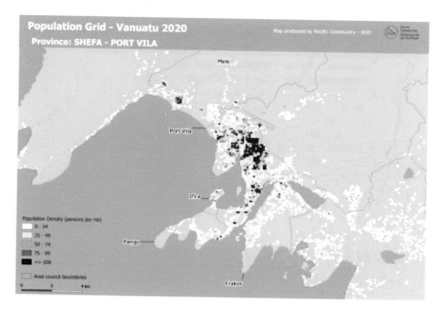

FIGURE 26.3
Population Grid of Port Vila, Efate, Vanuatu with each cell representing 100m² (Source: See footnote 6)

address disaster-related events, such as the COVID-19 pandemic and the tropical cyclones that are a regular occurrence for many.

26.4.2 Awareness and Coping Strategies

In an attempt to overcome this information and communication constraint, the World Bank conducted the first round of High Frequency Phone Monitoring (HFPM) Surveys at the end of June 2020, interviewing more than 3,000 respondents in PNG [5] and over 2,600 in Solomon Islands [6]. The surveys showed that fortunately there was a high degree of COVID awareness, with over 95% of PNG respondents and 91.8% of respondents in Solomon Islands reporting that they were aware of the pandemic; awareness in the Solomon Islands urban centres at 97.4% was however a little higher than in the rural areas (90.9%).

The most important sources of information were reported as the radio 53.2% and 28.4% in Solomon Islands and PNG respectively, followed by family & friends (7.1% & 14.7%), community leaders (9.0% & 13.0%) and newspapers (2.1% & 15.2%). In Solomon Islands the internet and social media (7.4%) and health clinics (6.2%) were also important. These results were reflected across all levels of respondent suggesting that radio is a cost effective and equitable means of providing information to the public at large [6]. See Figures 26.4 and 26.5 below for the PNG results.

The PNG HFPM survey also looked at the coping strategies of those who had lost their jobs or seen their income reduced as a result of the pandemic. Coping strategies for these families included both selling some of their own local produce or livestock to raise needed cash (over one-third of respondents in PNG and just over seventeen percent in Solomon Islands), and/or reducing food or non-food consumption expenditure, an average of 28% in PNG and just over 52% in Solomon Islands. Around one quarter of households in PNG and almost half of households in Solomon Islands reported receiving cash or borrowing from family or friends and in PNG a quarter also reported receiving other forms of assistance from this source. In Solomon Islands almost 45% found ways to earn extra money, 27% used credit or delayed payments and 18.8% received assistance from their church, in PNG only 10.9% reported receiving assistance from this last source.

Of particular concern however was the report from PNG that just over 50% of households had

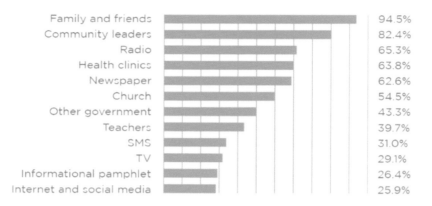

FIGURE 26.4

Sources of Information on COVID-19. World Bank High Frequency Phone Survey, PNG Round 1 June 2020 [6]

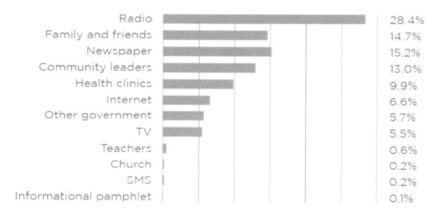

FIGURE 26.5

Main Source of Information on COVID-19. World Bank High Frequency Phone Survey, PNG Round 1 June 2020 [6]

removed children from school. The HFPM did not provide sufficient information to definitively identify the underlying reason for this and it could have been a combination of many factors including financial cost, concern at school-level COVID-19 transmission and the need for additional help in domestic food cultivation. Subsequent rounds of the surveys are expected to delve more deeply into the effects on inequality, gender and children.

26.5   What Is Being done to Monitor the Impact of COVID-19 via Economic Statistics?

The pandemic is adversely affecting almost all activities in the economic and social spheres of the Pacific region. Economic activity in the Pacific Islands has slowed at an unprecedented rate and scale, triggering major crises in the tourism, trade, financial, construction, personal services and government sectors.

It is also having a serious impact on the informal parts of Pacific economies. For example, many women are involved in selling food and other items in local markets or handicrafts in hotels and tourism sites. With many of these now closed or devoid of tourists the livelihoods of a large number of these informal vendors will have been destroyed. Job losses, restrictions on small businesses and declining remittance flows are therefore likely to be having a major impact on the levels of hardship and poverty being experienced by households and families across the region.

More than three-quarters of the respondents in both HFPM Surveys said they were worried about their household finances in the next month. In PNG there was a bias towards those in the bottom 40% (poorer population) where more than 85% of households were worried (Figure 26.6).

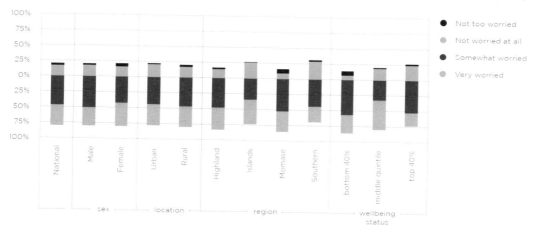

FIGURE 26.6

Financial Anxiety (by sex, location, and well-being status). World Bank High Frequency Phone Survey, PNG Round 1 June 2020 [6]

26.5.1 Economic Impacts and Fiscal Responses

All Pacific countries announced immediate fiscal responses to COVID in March or April [7]. Many have expanded on these as the pandemic has continued to disrupt economic activity, for example the US$37.5 million the Solomon Islands Government is injecting into key sectors. These measures include tax breaks for tourism operators; subsidies for copra and cocoa exporters; concessional loans for large private companies and equity injections for public/private companies. There is also a ramping up of donor-funded infrastructure projects with a focus on local employment [8].

Notwithstanding these early fiscal responses, the extent of the initial and underlying economic impacts are now being seen in available quarterly GDP data and budget forecasts from countries across the region. For example, in the first half of 2020 GDP in Samoa was an estimated 7.7% (in constant 2013 prices) below the level of the first half of 2019. The tourism-related sectors in the Samoa economy were the worst affected with the value-added contribution to GDP of the accommodation and restaurant industries falling by 53.3% and manufacturing, including of food and beverages, falling by a quarter over the same period[8].

The state of the tourism sector in Fiji and elsewhere tells a similar story. In the second quarter of 2020 there were effectively zero tourist arrivals to Fiji, Samoa and Solomon Islands. Employment in the accommodation industry in Samoa was down by 26.6% in the second quarter of 2020 compared to the same period of 2019; decreases in employment in construction (-6.0%), restaurants (-3.0%) and personal services (-4.3%) were also recorded.

---

[8]Samoa Bureau of Statistics; Gross Domestic product June 2020, September 2020

With tourism being so important to the Pacific, the impact will be felt in areas including government finances, supply chains and transport. The tourism industry in Fiji accounts for roughly 35% of GDP which is why the impact of COVID-19 is estimated to be creating such a large contraction in the Fijian economy.

The impact on the Fiji economy was clearly outlined by the Fiji Finance Minister in his 2020-21 budget address. The Minister reported that by July 115,000 workers, approximately one-third of Fiji's total workforce, had either had their hours reduced or had lost their jobs entirely as a result of the collapse in tourism [9]. As a consequence, the 2020-21 budget projected a 21.7% contraction in GDP in 2020 leading to a forecast budget deficit of 20.2% of GDP in the 2020-21 fiscal year[9].

Somewhat unusually it is those in formal employment that are experiencing the worst of the economic impacts. Most natural disasters deprive rural populations of their livelihoods through destroyed crops and damaged rural infrastructure. This time the pandemic is causing job and income losses principally amongst those previously in formal employment, especially in the tourism and services sector. The border closures and lockdowns have left rural populations relatively unscathed and with continued access to their crops, livestock and fishing grounds. There is, however, anecdotal evidence to suggest that many urban families are returning to their traditional villages and that such return migration, is having adverse impacts through the over-exploitation of coastal fisheries and traditional plantations.

A reduction in sources of income and disturbed supply chains are also impacting Pacific food systems. Governments across the region are implementing various initiatives to enhance the production of healthy local produce. These include distribution of fruit and vegetable seedlings to farmers and families; fast-tracking of existing agriculture initiatives; and distribution of Tilapia fingerlings and feed to stock backyard ponds. Government authorities in some countries have also been buying produce from farmers and delivering to vendors during lockdown periods, where trade in local produce declined due to domestic travel restrictions [10].

The coming fiscal year is likely to be very tough for all Pacific countries. Reduced public revenues coupled with increasing demands for higher public expenditure to support struggling businesses, to provide social protection for the most vulnerable and those being made unemployed by the closed borders, are undermining fiscal stability for many Pacific countries. Demands for external budget support from bilateral donors, international finance institutions and borrowing are increasing [11].

26.5.2   Social Protection

Prior to the arrival of the pandemic and its serious consequences for employment and incomes, it was estimated that across the region as a whole, around one-in-four families were living at or below their respective national basic-needs poverty lines [12]. This suggests that over 3 million Pacific Islanders were struggling to meet a minimum standard of living in their own countries. Estimates by the Australian National University (ANU) Development Policy Centre [13] and the Statistics for Development Division of the Pacific Community (SPC). indicate that if household consumption expenditure declines by an average of between 30%-50% an additional one million people will likely fall below the basic-needs poverty lines during the pandemic[10].

Throughout the Pacific region national governments play a significant role in almost all Pacific economies. However social protection has not generally been a high priority in public expenditure. Traditional Pacific systems of caring and sharing amongst families, kinship groups, communities and church congregations have been left to carry much of the burden. However, these traditional systems have come under pressure as Pacific economies have monetized, migration has increased and the structural nature of societies has changed. Only in a few Pacific countries have social protection systems kept pace with the changing social environment.

Although spending on social protection has increased in recent years (from the equivalent of 4.1% of GDP in 2009 to 6.0% in 2015) [14, p 74] the distribution of benefits tends to favour those in the formal sectors of the economy, primarily through the social insurance provided by national

---

[9]Pacific Community, Statistics for Development Division. Covid-19. `https://sdd.spc.int/disasters-data/covid-19`

[10]Pacific Community, Statistics for Development Division. Covid-19. `https://sdd.spc.int/disasters-data/covid-19`

provident funds and social security administrations. Frequently those engaged in the informal or semi-subsistence sectors have been excluded.

Social assistance is usually universally available to those who meet the criteria for each particular benefit but is nevertheless estimated to only reach around 20% of intended beneficiaries across the region. Social assistance benefits generally provide limited payments for vulnerable people, including the elderly, people living with a disability and for child welfare. Although benefits are comparable, on average, to those seen in Asia, social protection spending in the Pacific reportedly favours the nonpoor over the poor, and men over women [14, p 63]. In 2015 the ADB estimated that, in total, social protection covered only 31.2% of intended beneficiaries in the region [14, p 21]. The extent of the social and economic damage caused by the pandemic has caught most countries off-guard, and social protection responses to COVID are therefore building on a limited base.

With fiscal constraints and limited institutional structures to establish and manage large scale social protection schemes, to date only a few countries have introduced new or increased levels of social protection benefits; these include Cook Islands, Fiji, Samoa and Tuvalu. Only Fiji has a broad poverty-targeted social welfare programme, and thus has institutional arrangements in place to introduce new social protection measures.

But like most other Pacific countries the social protection system in Fiji does not provide comprehensive support for those experiencing such sudden and widespread loss of employment and income. In its 2020-21 budget Fiji allocated around US$50 million (approximately 1% of GDP) in funding for unemployment assistance in 2020-21. If the pandemic-induced economic recession lasts well into 2021 that allocation will not go very far to alleviate the increasing hardship being experienced. The newly unemployed in Fiji and elsewhere across the region will need to find coping strategies to meet their final commitments and basic needs. The newly unemployed in Fiji and elsewhere are largely on their own.

Many governments including Fiji, have allowed those being made unemployed to access a proportion of their own savings in national provident funds. This is generally a nil-cost measure for governments, and one that favours the minority who have provident fund savings. It certainly assists in alleviating the most urgent needs but comes at the expense of depleting savings for retirement. Moreover, it does little for those in the informal sectors. Indeed, some countries, including Fiji, have a condition that access to central government assistance is only available to those who have completely exhausted their own provident fund and other savings, and even then, will receive only FJD220 per fortnight.

26.6   What We Can Learn from COVID-19 for Future Pandemics or Other Disasters?

The social and economic impact of COVID-19 in the Pacific, as with the rest of the world, will likely long outlast the discovery and application of the first vaccines and the reopening of economies. Many small businesses have already closed with their cash flows having already dried up and with no access to additional capital or lines of credit. The confidence of these small entrepreneurs and family businesses, and that of other investors will likely take years to fully recover, indeed if ever [15].

The Pacific is a vulnerable region, whether it be from impacts related to cyclones, earthquakes or other natural disasters, or from pandemics such as COVID-19. Indeed, it might be argued by many in the health sectors of the PICTs that there is an ever-present epidemic situation involving NCDs. These might not have the same macroeconomic consequences as the current COVID pandemic, but at the household and family levels the impact can be just as devastating as the complications often associated with NCDs that remove individuals from the labour force, either as sufferers or as carers.

Travel restrictions and lockdowns have created a perfect storm of social and economic disruption to the small, fragile economies which are highly dependent on external drivers and resources. With small domestic economies and few economies of scale it is hard to offset the magnitude of the economic losses caused by the closing of borders and disruptions to trade.

"Fiscal space" to enable more resources to be channelled towards public health, providing economic stimulus and improving social "safety nets" [16] can be created through avoiding wasteful spending and improving cost-effectiveness in situations where raising additional revenues might be difficult. Likewise, encouraging household production of fresh produce for home consumption or sale in local markets can reduce dependency on purchased goods, particularly imports of food.

Although the pandemic has raised the profile of social protection as a major policy concern, much remains to be done. For example, would it be desirable or affordable to introduce a national minimum income or social protection floor and better targeting of those in need, especially people with disabilities, the poorest and most vulnerable. The social impact of COVID-19 further highlights the need for improved public sector performance in the delivery of essential public sector service provision including health, education and welfare. The inter-related issues of affordability, social preferences and performance might be better served by engaging more cooperatively and effectively with civil society and the private sector.

26.7   Building Preparedness Through Better Data

Administrative systems and data collection processes lack the efficiencies which generally exist in more developed countries. This can result in data being hard to access and collate, and in some countries with limited statistical capacity the data might not be collected at all. This makes it difficult to effectively prepare for a pandemic or such a similar event, or to monitor the impacts should such an event occur. In addition, sub-national disaggregation is either non-existent or data is only disseminated in a highly aggregated form, making detailed spatial analysis difficult. This is an area which needs to be improved, not only to assist with the management of pandemics, but to assist in infrastructure planning and building climate change resilience.

The collection of locational data has improved with the utilisation of Global Positioning Systems (GPS) and Computer Aided Personal Interviews (CAPI) during census and survey fieldwork which has facilitated the development of population grids for many PICTs. If pandemic case data were also recorded and disseminated at a highly disaggregated level then more complex analysis would be possible.

More could be done to prepare for future events including natural disasters and pandemics through better data compilation and monitoring of emerging trends and issues. In particular, sharing of administrative data between government ministries, agencies and state-owned enterprises and the national statistics offices could enable data to become available more quickly and more comprehensively.

As connectivity across the Pacific region also improves, the use of "big data" and the wider use of geo-spatial and satellite data from global platforms will allow much greater understanding of how and where Pacific people are living, and how their local environments and livelihoods are being affected by climate change, migration and other shocks and disasters.

The long-term sustainability of the Pacific islands, especially the low-lying atolls and islands depends on the regular monitoring and assessment of these factors and events on the people and their social-economic environments.

References

[1] Neil L. Andrew, Phil Bright, Luis de la Rua, Shwu Jiau Teoh, and Mathew Vickers. Coastal proximity of populations in 22 Pacific Island Countries and Territories. *PLOS ONE*, 14(9):1–15, 09 2019. doi: 10.1371/ journal.pone.0223249.

[2] International Monetary Fund. Pacific Islands Threatened by COVID-19. URL https://www.imf.org/en/News/Articles/2020/05/27/na-05272020-pacific-islands-threatened.

[3] Pacific Community. COVID-19 is compounding the Pacific's non- communicable disease crisis. URL https://www.spc.int/updates/blog/2020/06/covid-19-is-compounding-the-pacifics-non-communicable-disease-crisis.

[4] World Bank. The role of geospatial information in confronting COVID-19 – Learning from Korea. URL https://blogs.worldbank.org/eastasiapacific/role-geospatial-information-confronting-covid-19-learning-korea.

[5] Kristen Himelein, James Carroll Waldersee, and Bagus Arya Wirapati. Papua New Guinea High Frequency Phone Survey on COVID-19 – Results from Round 1. *World Bank*, September 2020.

[6] Kristen Himelein, James Carroll Waldersee, Bagus Arya Wirapati, and Stephanie Eckman. Solomon Islands High Frequency Phone Survey on COVID-19 – Results from Round 1. *World Bank*, November 2020.

[7] Devpolicy. Constraints on the Pacific response to COVID-19. URL https://devpolicy.org/constraints-on-the-pacific-response-to-covid-19/.

[8] RNZ. Details of Solomon Islands Economic Package Revealed by PM. URL https://www.rnz.co.nz/international/pacific-news/415823/details-of-solomon-islands-economic-package-revealed-by-pm.

[9] Hon. Aiyaz Sayed-Khaiyum. 2020-2021 National Budget Address. *Fiji Parliament*. 17 July 2020.

[10] Food and Agriculture Organisation of the United Nations. Impacts of COVID-19 on the Food Systems in the Pacific Small Island Developing States (PSIDS) and A Look into the PSIDS Responses. URL http://www.fao.org/uploads/pics/COVID-19_impacts_on_food_systems_in_PICs_CRFS_.pdf.

[11] Stephen Howes and Sherman Surandiran. COVID-19 spending across the Pacific: the self-funded, the aid-financed, and the constrained. *Australian National University DevPolicy Blog*, 20 August 2020. URL https://devpolicy.org/covid-19-spending-across-the-pacific-20200820/.

[12] United Nations Development Programme. The State of Human Development in the Pacific: A Report on Vulnerability and Exclusion in A Time of Rapid Change. *UNDP Pacific Centre*, 2014. URL https://www.undp.org/content/dam/rbap/docs/Research%20&%20Publications/poverty/State_Human_Development_Pacific_report.pdf.

[13] Chris Hoy. Poverty and the pandemic in the Pacific. *Australian National University DevPolicy Blog*, 15 June 2020. URL https://devpolicy.org/poverty-and-teh-pandemic-in-the-pacific-20200615-2/.

[14] Asian Development Bank. The Social Protection Indicator for the Pacific Assessing Progress. *Asian Development Bank*, 2019. URL https://www.adb.org/sites/default/files/publication/513481/spi-pacific-2019.pdf.

[15] Abbott and Pollard. From Response to recovery. *Australian National University DevPolicy Blog*, 28 August 2020. URL https://devpolicy.org/how-to-get-from-response-to-recovery-in-the-pacific-20200828/.

[16] United Nations Development Programme. The Social and Economic Impact of COVID-19 in the Asia-Pacific Region. *UNDP Regional Bureau for Asia and the Pacific*, April 2020. URL https://www.undp.org/content/dam/undp/library/km-qap/UNDP-RBAP-Position-Note-Social-Economic-Impact-of-COVID-19-in-Asia-Pacific-2020.pdf.

27

Promoting Resilience While Mitigating Disease Transmission: An Australian COVID-19 Study

Freya M. Shearer, Niamh Meagher, Katitza Marinkovic Chavez, Lauren Carpenter, Alana Pirrone, Phoebe Quinn, Eva Alisic, James M. McCaw, Colin MacDougall, David J. Price and Lisa Gibbs

In this Chapter, we present evidence to inform evolving COVID-19 response planning by analysing how Australians were thinking, feeling and behaving in response to the so-called "first wave" of the COVID-19 epidemic and the associated public health measures. These topics were explored through an online survey of Australian adults (n=999) between 3–6 April 2020, less than one week after "stay-at-home" restrictions were enacted nationally to mitigate the spread of COVID-19. To explore if and how people's thoughts, feelings, and behaviours may have changed over time, we fielded the same survey between 28 April and 6 May 2020 (n=1020), with 732 respondents completing both surveys. Overall, our study found high levels of community acceptance and adherence to physical distancing measures. While physical distancing measures have proven highly effective at mitigating disease transmission worldwide, they have substantial social and economic costs. Our results highlight the negative social and emotional impacts of physical distancing and the importance of complementary policies that enable social connection and self- and collective efficacy to minimise these impacts and promote community resilience.

27.1   Introduction

Australians watched with concern when the novel coronavirus SARS-CoV-2 was first reported in Wuhan, China in December 2019 [1]. Concern turned to alarm as, by March 2020, the virus had spread to all global regions, and COVID-19 (the disease caused by SARS-CoV-2) was threatening to overwhelm some of the world's economies and strongest health systems [2, 3]. In the absence of an effective treatment or vaccine for COVID-19, physical distancing measures soon formed the cornerstone of the global response — at a scale that was not typically contemplated by existing pandemic plans [4–8].

There is so much that is new about this pandemic that "unprecedented" soon became the most used word in formal and informal discussions about how to deliver a proportionate public health response. Indeed, in free text responses to our first survey (described later), respondents referred to it by emotive names such as "rotten", "disgusting", and "invisible". Some worried that scientists did not understand its basic biological processes.

This chapter presents evidence to inform continued, evolving response planning in Australia, and where relevant, in other countries around the world. It includes findings from two nationwide surveys [9, 10] asking the overall question: How were Australians thinking, feeling and behaving in response to the "first wave" of the COVID-19 epidemic and the associated public health measures?

By doing so, we aim to guide decision-making on how best to manage disease transmission and promote community resilience.

Specifically, we provide insight into levels of transmission-reducing behaviours, how these changed over time, and how these behaviours related to people's concerns and perceptions. We explore how these trends differed between lower- and higher-impacted Australian states and territories.

Next, the chapter reports on the social and emotional impact of COVID-19 on Australians. Internationally, it is agreed that five elements are essential to support people and communities confronted with large scale-disaster and loss in the immediate and mid-term [11]. These elements, which also underpin Psychological First Aid [12, 13], are the promotion of: a sense of safety; calm; a sense of self- and community efficacy; connectedness; and hope. We conclude with insights into how these elements interacted with people's mental health and wellbeing during pandemic restrictions.

27.2   Early Phase of the Australian Epidemic and the Public Health Response

Australia has a federated political system featuring overlapping responsibilities between a federal government, eight state and territory governments and local governments. The political geography of Australia, as an island continent, has informed the shape of the responses. Over two decades, one of the most strident political positions for successive federal governments has been to use its authority to control the national borders to reduce the number of refugees arriving by boat to seek asylum in Australia. By contrast, the eight states and territories, with different climates, industry, population structures and geography, have their own powers to close borders to other jurisdictions. In response to COVID-19, a National Cabinet was quickly formed to improve communication, co-ordination across states and territories, and joint decision making.

The first case of COVID-19 was detected in Australia on 22 January 2020 [14]. On 1 February, when China was the only country reporting uncontained transmission, Australia closed its borders to mainland China [15]. Australia only reported 12 cases of COVID-19 through February. By contrast, globally the number of confirmed cases and geographic extent of transmission continued to increase drastically [16]. By early March, Australia faced the threat of importation from all global regions, and governments and health authorities were concerned when daily case counts rose sharply through the first half of March. Although more than two thirds of cases were connected to returned travellers who acquired their infections overseas, pockets of local transmission were reported in the cities of Sydney and Melbourne [17].

As a result, from 16 March 2020 the eight state and territory governments of Australia used their own authority to progressively implement physical distancing measures to prevent and reduce community transmission of SARS-CoV-2 [18]. By 29 March 2020, all Australians were strongly advised to leave their homes only for limited essential activities and public gatherings were limited to two people (known as "stay-at-home" restrictions). These measures were in addition to self-isolation advice for (mild) confirmed cases and their contacts, as well as for returned overseas travellers.

By late March, daily counts of new cases were declining, and the effective reproduction number was estimated to be below 1 [19], indicating that the collective actions of the Australian public and government authorities had successfully mitigated a first epidemic wave. Of the 7,075 confirmed cases of COVID-19 in Australia up to 17 May 2020, 70% were acquired overseas [20].

27.3 Understanding the Response of Australians to COVID-19

To develop a timely understanding of how people in Australia were thinking, feeling, and behaving in relation to the COVID-19 pandemic and the associated response measures, we conducted two nationwide surveys.

The first survey was conducted online from 3 to 6 April, shortly after the activation of "stay-at-home" restrictions in response to the initial wave of imported infections, and the other three weeks later (29 April to 6 May) when restrictions remained in most state and territories (Figure 27.1). Western Australia commenced easing of restrictions on 27 April [21], followed by the Northern Territory and New South Wales on 1 May [22, 23]. Note that all data were collected during the first epidemic wave, prior to the establishment of a second wave in the state of Victoria in late June 2020 [24].

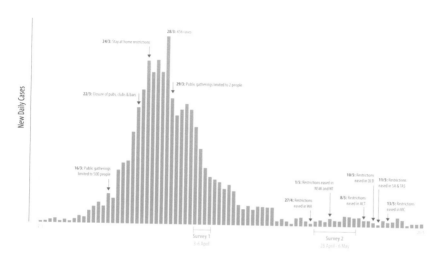

FIGURE 27.1

Plot of national daily new case notifications in Australia [25], timings of key national response policies and Surveys 1 (teal) and 2 (blue). Note: we include both overseas and locally acquired cases in the daily case counts. Of all cases in Australia notified up to 17 May 2020 with a known place of acquisition (95%), 70% were acquired overseas [20]

27.4 Overview of Data Collection and Analysis

The sample size of Survey 1 was 999 Australian residents aged 18 years and over. The sample size of Survey 2 was 1020 individuals, of which 732 (71.8%) had previously completed Survey 1. Results were weighted and are representative of the adult population in Australia (as described below).

The two surveys were based on research developed and conducted by Imperial College in the UK in mid-March 2020 [26]. Some questions in the Australian survey were modified slightly to reflect local response measures and terminology. Additional questions were added to the Australian survey to measure social and emotional impacts. Data collection in both the UK and Australia was conducted by the online market research agency YouGov.

We used a structured questionnaire addressing the following three domains:

- perceptions of risk and consequences of COVID-19 infection;

- measures taken by individuals to protect themselves and others from COVID-19 infection; and

- social and emotional impact.

Finally, we included an open-ended question to allow people to express their main concern regarding the COVID-19 pandemic. The question requiring a free text response was: "What is your biggest concern at the moment?" All respondents answered the question as it was mandatory. We conducted thematic coding, informed by Framework analysis [27] which was designed to code qualitative data in order to inform policy and practice. The data reported here are primarily a sub-section of the total coding frame, designed to illustrate key points in the quantitative analysis.

The questionnaire was administered online to members of the YouGov Australia panel of individuals who have agreed to take part in surveys of public opinion (over 120,000 Australian adults). Panellists, selected at random from the base sample, received an email inviting them to take part in a survey, which included a survey link. Once a panel member clicked on the link and logged in, they were directed to the survey most relevant to them available on the platform at the time, according to the sample definition and quotas based on census data. A plain language statement appeared on screen and respondents were required to electronically consent prior to the survey questions appearing. Proportional quota sampling was used to ensure that respondents were demographically representative of the Australian adult population, with quotas based on age, gender, income and location (state and metropolitan or regional).

The study was by approved by the University of Melbourne Human Research Ethics Committee (2056694).

27.5 Geographic Variation in COVID-19 Epidemiology and Public Health Response in Australia

Our analyses differentiated between lower-impacted and higher-impacted jurisdictions because of the geographical variation in COVID-19 epidemiology and the associated physical distancing policies. Australia's two most populous states, New South Wales (more than 8.1 million people) and Victoria (more than 6.1 million people), also the most exposed to international travellers, experienced considerably higher total numbers of confirmed cases and peak daily incidence than other jurisdictions [14]. Consequently, people living in New South Wales and Victoria also experienced longer periods of restriction on their movement and social gatherings. New South Wales and Victoria are therefore defined as higher-impacted jurisdictions and all other jurisdictions as lower-impacted jurisdictions (Figure 27.2).

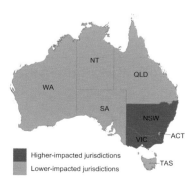

FIGURE 27.2
Map of the higher and lower impacted jurisdictions in Australia.

27.6 Findings

27.6.1 How did people perceive the risk and consequences of SARS-CoV-2 infection?

Respondents perceived that their risk of SARS-CoV-2 infection decreased between the two survey periods, which coincided with a reduction in disease prevalence across Australia. Fewer respondents believed that it was likely they would be infected with SARS-CoV-2 at some point in the future at Survey 2 (29.6%) compared to Survey 1 (38.2%). This change was similar across lower- and higher-impacted jurisdictions.

There was little difference in perceived severity of SARS-CoV-2 infection between surveys. In both surveys, older adults were more likely than younger adults to believe that, if infected themselves, SARS-CoV-2 would be life-threatening or very severe (requiring hospitalisation). Respondents with a self-reported health status of "poor" or "fair" were also more likely to believe that, if infected, their infection would be very severe or life-threatening compared to those who reported being in "good", "very good", or "excellent" health. These self-assessments are consistent with risk profiles for COVID-19 where increasing age and comorbidities are associated with more severe outcomes [28]. Despite having different risk profiles, responses between males and females were very similar.

27.6.2 How did people change their behaviours to prevent the spread of COVID-19?

Overall, very high levels of physical distancing behaviour were reported at both Surveys 1 and 2 (Figure 27.3).

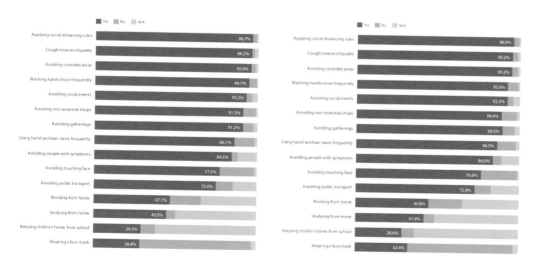

FIGURE 27.3

Percentage of respondents taking measures to protect themselves and others from SARS-CoV-2 infection at Surveys 1 (left) and 2 (right). Applying social distancing rules = "staying 1.5m apart, not shaking hands etc". Keeping children home from school = "keeping children home from school when schools are open". N/A = not applicable to me.

SARS-CoV-2 spreads via close contact between infectious and susceptible individuals. The rate of spread depends on a number of factors, including 1) the number of social contacts made by an infectious individual and 2) the nature of those encounters (how long they were, whether there was physical contact, whether they occurred indoors/outdoors). Both of these factors are impacted by changes in physical distancing behaviour. Accordingly, we used two types of physical distancing behaviour in our analyses. Firstly, behaviour that reduces the number of daily contacts made by an individual (excluding members of their household), such as working from home or avoiding social gatherings ("macro-distancing" behaviour). Secondly, behaviour that reduces the per contact probability of transmission such as handwashing, avoiding physical contact, and staying 1.5m apart from others ("micro-distancing" behaviour). Distinguishing between these two types of behaviour and directly measuring them through population surveys has been critical to monitoring the transmission potential of SARS-CoV-2 [29].

In the longitudinal subsample, there was no meaningful difference in the percentage of respondents applying micro-distancing measures (keeping 1.5 metres away from others, not shaking hands, etc.) between Survey 1 (97.0% [96% CI: 95.9, 98.2]) and Survey 2 (96.5% [95% CI: 95.4, 97.9]). There was no meaningful change in the overall percentage of respondents washing their hands more frequently at Survey 2 (92.1% [95% CI: 90.3, 94.0]) compared to Survey 1 (94.6% [95% CI: 93.1, 96.2]).

Our results indicate that Australians reached high levels of self-reported adherence to micro-distancing measures recommended in March 2020 and maintained these behaviours into early May.

On the other hand, our results provide evidence of a reduction in macro-distancing behaviour between early April and May. In the longitudinal subsample, there was an increase in the number of people reporting 2–3 non-household contacts and a decrease in the number of people reporting 0 daily non-household contacts between Survey 1 and 2 (Figure 27.4). The easing of restrictions in both lower- and higher-impacted jurisdictions overlapped with the timing of Survey 2.

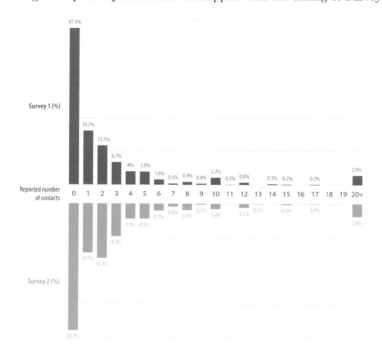

FIGURE 27.4

Reported number of non-household contacts at each Survey. A contact was "considered either a face to face conversation of a least three words or any form of physical contact, such as a handshake". Note that the bar charts are truncated at a maximum of 20 contacts, to better visualise spread values > 20, which comprised only 3% of respondents.

In both surveys, younger adults were more likely than older adults to report having a high number of contacts. However, the number of contacts was also linked to profession, with respondents working in health and medical services, air travel, restaurant services and retail more likely to report a high number of contacts outside of their household unit.

27.6.3 How were people's concerns and perceptions related to their adherence to prevention measures?

We examined how the change in reported perception of infection risk was associated with changes in the number of daily non-household contacts made and adherence to certain preventative measures. We report only associations between variables and make no attempt to infer causative relationships. For repeat respondents, the mean change in reported non-household contacts in the previous 24 hours showed an increase of 0.7 (95% CI: -1.6, 3.0) additional contacts at Survey 2 compared to Survey 1. This varied by change in perceived risk of infection. At Survey 2, those who believed they were less likely to be infected had a mean reduction in non-household contacts (1.83 fewer contacts on average than Survey 1). This varied between lower-impacted (0.75 fewer contacts) and higher-impacted (2.54 fewer contacts) jurisdictions. Those who showed no change or an increase in perceived risk of infection at Survey 2, showed a slight increase in non-household contacts (0.15 additional contacts on average).

A univariate multinomial regression showed that those who said they were at lower risk of SARS-CoV-2 infection at Survey 2 had a 1.1-fold [95% CI: 0.65, 1.86] increase in odds of reporting fewer non-household contacts at Survey 2 than those who reported no change in perceived risk of infection. Note that the wide confidence interval spanning 1 does not preclude the possibility of no effect or an effect in the opposite direction.

Analysis of the free text responses from Survey 2 showed a new (relative to Survey 1) and dominant theme linking community complacency, distancing, and a second wave of infections. Respondents were not so much blaming people, but suggesting that as time goes by there is a natural tendency to become complacent, contributing to a second wave, for example:

"Australians will become complacent, and the second wave of outbreaks will not be able to be controlled effectively."

Together with the quantitative findings of high levels of physical distancing behaviour, this suggests that some respondents were indeed maintaining distancing measures irrespective of the risk of personal infection: perhaps explained by their concern about the population (rather than personal) level implications of a second wave.

27.6.4 What was the social and emotional impact of COVID-19?

At both Surveys 1 and 2, a significant minority of respondents reported symptoms indicating high levels of anxiety (24.2% and 19.9%, respectively) and high levels of depressive symptoms (17.5%, and 17%, respectively).

Conversely, 60.8% (Survey 1) and 65.1% (Survey 2) of respondents were either somewhat or very optimistic about their future. People experiencing higher feelings of hope for their future were more likely to report lower levels of depression and anxiety.

In our longitudinal subsample, there was a statistically significant decrease in mean anxiety scores [1] between Survey 1 (6.9) and Survey 2 (6.4). This result suggested that most survey respondents experienced a slight decrease in anxiety symptoms but remained in the normal range. However, the percentage of respondents who reported high levels of anxiety and may require professional mental health support increased between Survey 1 (15.4%) and Survey 2 (19.4%).

Free text responses revealed fewer expressions of worry about the pandemic between Surveys 1 and 2. At Survey 1, the dominant themes in concerns named by respondents were people, virus and

---

[1] As measured with the Hospital Anxiety and Depression Scale, out of a maximum of 21 points, scores between 0 and 7 are considered in the normal range, while cases with scores of 11 or above may require professional mental health support.

health. "People" referred both to fears for the health of family and close friends, and concerns that not everyone was adopting distancing measures. Respondents used many different words expressing concern about economy, income and family and social factors. At Survey 2, people remained the dominant concern while the statements raising concerns about virus and health decreased in number. There was a large increase in the word "restriction", and more mentions of economy. At Survey 2, the words used to describe the virus were very different. There were fewer emotive statements about the scary or unknown characteristics of the virus. Although there were similar comments about spread in the virus compared with Survey 1, new concerns emerged about lack of herd immunity, winter coming in Australia, and a fear of a new spike or second wave. Some thought the health system would not be able to cope. Others had very serious personal concerns such as being about to give birth to their first child or the health of vulnerable family members.

27.6.5   How did COVID-19 affect people's connection to others and people's connection to others influence their experience of COVID-19?

At both surveys, higher levels of community connectedness were significantly associated with lower levels of depression and anxiety (see Table 27.3). Regarding social support, 68.7% (Survey 1) and 67.2% (Survey 2) of respondents said that they could rely on two people or more for assistance or support during the pandemic if they needed it. Meanwhile, 9.9% (Survey 1) and 10.0% (Survey 2) reported that they had no one to rely on. These individuals may be at increased risk of negative mental health effects as higher levels of anxiety and depression were significantly associated with having fewer people to rely upon for assistance or support during the pandemic.

Additionally, 68.4% (Survey 1) and 68.0% (Survey 2) of respondents said that two or more people relied on them for assistance or support during they pandemic. Those with more people who relied on them for assistance or support showed lower levels of anxiety and depression.

Free text responses in both surveys revealed evidence of altruism expressed in concerns for other groups of people, society in general and social justice. Respondents were concerned about "the loss of jobs of many vulnerable groups in the society, leading to unemployment and homelessness:" "temporary residents" and "survival of the less privileged in the society." Some said that while they were "financially OK," they were "concerned for the world in general and the impact on those who have lost more" leading to "an even larger gap between the rich and the poor." A small number of respondents were concerned for their employers:

> "If I had to self-isolate, would have a dramatic impact on my employer; I would find that hard to deal with."

There were more responses about altruism and social justice in Survey 2 than in Survey 1, for example:

> "I am fine. My biggest concern is for those who are not or will not be. That I will catch it without knowing and pass it on to the more vulnerable."

Some also spoke of concerns about domestic violence, aggressive behaviour and crime.

27.6.6   Level of worry about the COVID-19 outbreak in Australia

Respondents were asked to report their level of worry about the COVID-19 situation in Australia. Considering only those who responded to both surveys, the percentage of respondents who reported being worried about the COVID-19 outbreak in Australia decreased from 84.0% at Survey 1 to 69.2% at Survey 2. This trend was consistent across lower- and higher-impacted jurisdictions.

Respondents who were less worried about the COVID-19 outbreak in Australia at Survey 2 (compared to Survey 1) had a mean increase in non-household contacts (1.37 more contacts), however respondents residing in higher-impacted jurisdictions had a smaller mean increase (0.56) compared to lower-impacted jurisdictions (2.35).

Respondents who were more worried about the COVID-19 outbreak in Australia had an overall mean decrease in contacts at Survey 2 (1.11 fewer contacts), however respondents residing in higher-impacted jurisdictions had a mean 2.44 fewer contacts and those in lower-impacted jurisdictions had a mean 1.75 more contacts.

We propose that individuals who were less worried once relative control of the epidemic was achieved (by the time of Survey 2), may have had lower levels of adherence to macro-distancing measures. Individuals who were more worried at Survey 2, appeared to be more cautious about making contacts. In both groups, individuals residing in higher-impacted jurisdictions made less contacts than those in lower-impacted jurisdictions, potentially reflecting different levels of restrictions. However, the easing of restrictions in both lower- and higher-impacted jurisdictions overlapped with the timing of Survey 2. It should be noted that our study does not distinguish between types of contacts (e.g., social versus workplace) and how "essential" these contacts might be deemed under different levels of restrictions: for example, the limited choices available to front line workers to reduce their contacts.

TABLE 27.1
Daily number of non-household contacts.

	More worried at Survey 2	Less worried at Survey 2
Higher-impacted jurisdictions	2.44 fewer	0.35 more
Lower-impacted jurisdictions	1.75 more	2.35 more
Overall	1.11 fewer	1.37 more

27.6.7 Perceptions of the future for Australia and the world

At the time of data collection for Survey 2, the majority (95.4%) of respondents were confident they could manage until the restrictions due to COVID-19 were over, however only 52.8% were confident that Australia could manage until the restrictions were over.

Feelings of confidence were also reflected in some of the answers to the survey's open question, for example: "I am feeling very confident that Australia has beaten this virus so am just looking forward to going out again."

High numbers of respondents in both Surveys provided free text responses criticising the behaviour of other people, suggesting some sort of moral, character or behavioural flaw. In Survey 1 there were more concerns about such behaviour: very many spoke of *"Not adhering to rules"* and a number about *"Hoarding and panic buying"*. Concerns about behaviour were linked to the invisibility of the virus and young people's actions.

At Survey 2, 60.4% of respondents were either somewhat or very optimistic about the future of Australia, and 47% felt the same way about the future of the world.

The answers to the survey's open question on people's biggest concern were not, however, all bleak. Some spoke of qualified hope or optimism, for example:

"I don't want to imagine anything negative right now, hope for the best."

"That we all stay positive"

Higher feelings of hope for the future of Australia and the world were significantly associated with lower levels of depression and anxiety. These results were consistent with Survey 1.

27.6.8 Five elements to support people and communities confronted with disaster

In this section, we summarise patterns of responses to the five elements to support people and communities confronted with large scale-disaster and loss in the immediate and mid-term [6]. We also explored how these five elements interact with people's mental health and wellbeing during pandemic restrictions.

Overall, we found that higher feelings of hope, connectedness, self and community efficacy, calm and safety were significantly associated with lower levels of anxiety and depression (Table 27.3).

TABLE 27.2
Summarises patterns of responses to the five elements to support people and communities confronted with large scale-disaster and loss in the immediate and mid-term.

Element	Findings
Calm	During both surveys, most poll respondents said that they could sit at ease and feel relaxed (66.1% at Survey 1 and 70.6% at Survey 2).
Sense of safety	The proportion of respondents who believed it was very likely or somewhat likely that they would become infected with COVID-19 was 38.2% at Survey 1 and 29.7% at Survey 2. In our longitudinal subsample, respondents' perceived likelihood of becoming infected decreased between Surveys 1 and 2.
Efficacy	**Self-efficacy**: during both surveys, most respondents felt they could manage until restrictions due to COVID-19 were over (89.9% at Survey 1 and 68.1% at Survey 2). Although the percentage of people who felt confident decreased between Survey 1 and 2, respondents' mean scores in self-efficacy tended to increase. **Collective efficacy**: the percentage of respondents who felt Australia could manage until restrictions due to COVID-19 were over was lower at Survey 2 (77.4% at Survey 1 and 52.8% at Survey 2).
Community connectedness	In Survey 1, out of a total score of 30 points, the mean score for community connectedness * was 22.36 (standard deviation = 4.59). Meanwhile, in Survey 2, the mean score was 22.68 (standard deviation = 4.54).
Hope	**About one's future**: in Survey 1, 60.8% of respondents were either somewhat or very optimistic about their future, and 65.1% felt this way at Survey 2. **About the future of Australia**: in Survey 1, 56.5% of respondents were either somewhat or very optimistic about the future of Australia, and 60.4% felt this way at Survey 2. **About the future of the world**: in Survey 1, 46% of respondents were either somewhat or very optimistic about the future of the world, and 47% felt this way at Survey 2.

* Measured with the Social Solidarity Index [30]

TABLE 27.3
Bivariate correlations (2-tailed) between the five elements of mid to long-term recovery[11] and levels of depression and anxiety measured with the Hospital Anxiety and Depression Scale (HADS)

	Correlation [95% CI]			
	Anxiety		Depression	
	Survey 1	Survey 2	Survey 1	Survey 2
Calm	-0.208	-0.202	-0.099	-0.126
	[-0.269, -0.147]	[-0.264, -0.140]	[-0.162, -0.037]	[-0.189, -0.063]
Sense of safety	-0.248	-0.225	-0.041	-0.132
	[-0.318, -0.179]	[-0.292, -0.158]	[-0.114, -0.032]	[-0.201, -0.063]
Self-efficacy	-0.204	0.046	-0.261	0.060
	[-0.265, -0.143]	[-0.015, 0.108]	[-0.321, -0.201]	[-0.002, 0.121]
Collective efficacy	-0.032	-0.039	-0.099	-0.002
	[-0.094, -0.030]	[-0.101, 0.022]	[-0.161, -0.037]	[-0.064, 0.059]
Community connectedness	-0.163	-0.168	-0.196	-0.254
	[-0.232, -0.095]	[-0.239, -0.098]	[-0.264, -0.129]	[-0.322, -0.187]
Hope for one's future	-0.251	-0.292	-0.348	-0.381
	[-0.313, -0.190]	[-0.352, 0.232]	[-0.407, -0.288]	[-0.439, -0.323]
Hope for the future of Australia	-0.123	-0.170	-0.224	-0.249
	[-0.186, -0.060]	[-0.232, -0.108]	[-0.286, -0.162]	[-0.310, -0.189]
Hope for the future of the world	-0.059	-0.127	-0.158	-0.183
	[-0.123, 0.005]	[-0.189, -0.064]	[-0.221, -0.095]	[-0.244, -0.121]

27.7   Discussion and conclusions

In this chapter we have presented evidence to inform evolving COVID-19 response planning by analysing how Australians were thinking, feeling and behaving in response to the first wave of the COVID-19 epidemic and the associated public health measures. We explored these topics through an online survey of Australian adults (N=999) between 3–6 April, less than one week after "stay-at-home" restrictions were enacted nationally. To explore if and how people's thoughts, feelings, and behaviours may have changed over time, we fielded the same survey between 28 April and 6 May (N=1020), with 732 respondents completing both surveys.

High levels of adherence to physical distancing measures were reported in early April and high levels of micro-distancing behaviour (e.g., hand washing, staying 1.5m from others) were maintained into May. There was some evidence of a decrease in macro-distancing behaviour (i.e., number of non-household contacts), which differed by jurisdiction and level of worry (see Table 27.1 for detail). Free text responses revealed fears that lockdown would be eased too early leading to a second wave. Added to concerns that people would become complacent, this suggests strong support for distancing measures.

While the level of worry about the pandemic in Australia decreased between early April and May 2020 overall, the group of individuals who reported increased levels of worry, reported lower rates of non-household contacts. This suggests that people's level of concern about the outbreak may impact their adoption of physical distancing behaviours. The trend was most marked for individuals residing in higher-impacted jurisdictions (New South Wales and Victoria). It should be noted that our study does not distinguish between types of contacts (e.g., social versus workplace) and how "essential" these contacts might be deemed under different levels of restrictions: for example, the limited choices available to front line workers.

Our findings are consistent with a number of other studies assessing people's response to COVID-19 public health measures. Recent studies conducted in China [31], Hong Kong [32], Japan [33], Korea [34], the Philippines [35], the United Kingdom [26], the United States [36], Germany, Italy and the Netherlands [37] report high levels of adoption of and broad support for physical distancing measures, during the period under study. Other studies conducted during/after the epidemics of severe acute respiratory syndrome (SARS) in 2003 [38], influenza A(H1N1)pdm09 in 2009 [39], and more recently, during the COVID-19 pandemic [40], have reported that higher levels of worry and/or perceived risk of infection were associated with the adoption of infection-prevention behaviours. However, it is important to also consider the influence of sense of self-efficacy on behaviours because previous evidence [41] shows that "when the threat was high as compared to low, people changed their behaviour in the advised direction only when efficacy was high, and not when efficacy was low". In fact, when efficacy was low, the behaviour change showed, if anything, an effect in the unhealthy direction" [42]. Further analyses are required to examine the relationship between the perception of risk, self- and community efficacy, and behaviour change [43]. At the time of writing, we did not identify any published longitudinal studies assessing how perceptions and behaviours may have changed during the course of the COVID-19 pandemic and response.

Since the success of physical distancing measures relies on people changing their behaviour, a challenge that lies ahead for policymakers is the potential for community fatigue. Individuals may not respond as quickly or assiduously if/when physical distancing measures are re-established in response to future outbreaks. Overall, our study found high levels of community acceptance of physical distancing measures. There was also evidence that distancing behaviours decreased between April and May; however, it is unclear whether this was due to reduced compliance or the easing of restrictions.

While physical distancing measures have proven highly effective at suppressing transmission of COVID-19 [44], they place a significant emotional and psychological burden on individuals, as highlighted by our study and others [45–47] — not to mention the economic consequences and potential longer-term health impacts. Governments around the world are currently grappling to balance the risks associated with an uncontrolled outbreak of COVID-19 against those associated with intensive and/or prolonged physical distancing measures. Studies such as ours can help to understand and guide the management of mental health risks associated with physical distancing measures.

Our findings about the association between mental health and sense of safety, calm, self and community efficacy, social connectedness and hope suggest ways forward in informing the public about support as communities emerge from pandemic restrictions. Previous evidence about use of fear to promote health behaviours [42] shows there is a risk in conveying the seriousness of the health risk unless it is accompanied by messages that promote sense of self- and community efficacy. Our qualitative data also suggested levels of hope, altruism, and trust in science counterbalance difficult decisions and bad news. At the same time, previous studies have shown that individual and community empowerment must go beyond promoting feelings of competence — they require having access to and control over the resources in one's environment [48, 49]. In line with this, we argue that policies and services that support people experiencing economic adversity (such as Australia's income support payments "JobSeeker" and "JobKeeper" [50]), and those associated with childcare, mental health and family violence can be a crucial source of individual and community resilience during the response and recovery phases of the pandemic.

Other studies conducted during COVID-19 have found that access to reliable health information and precautionary measures like hand hygiene and wearing a mask was associated with lower levels of emotional distress [45, 51]. In our study, having a larger number of people to rely on for assistance or support or being the source of assistance or support for other people was associated with lower levels of anxiety and depression, highlighting the importance of social connections for supporting mental health and wellbeing. Our findings are consistent with previous evidence about the human impacts of disasters, including the COVID-19 pandemic, and show how important it is to find ways to maintain social connections while following the physical distancing guidelines. Since pandemics have the potential to perpetuate and exacerbate existing social disparities [52], the social structures of populations most at risk of negative outcomes from the disease and/or transmission-mitigating policies, should be closely considered if the goal is an equitable response strategy.

Our study was necessarily rapidly conceived and implemented in response to the evolving epidemiological and policy situation in Australia. While useful for gaining rapid insights into people's feelings and behaviours, our results need to be interpreted in the context of the limitations of the research design. The sampling strategy did not allow for surveying individuals without internet access, low literacy or limited English language skills, or communication or cognitive difficulties. Additionally, people who register to complete YouGov surveys may also be different from the general population in ways that we cannot identify. Subgroup analyses may be limited by smaller participant numbers; and qualitative data was from one free text response, limiting potential analyses.

In conclusion, studies such as this are necessarily conducted with short lead times and rely on the skills and capacity of public health researchers to work quickly within resource constraints. We therefore offer reflections and recommendations for research design in this and other pandemics. A formal and collegial review of studies to date would also be prudent, so we can learn and make methodological suggestions for future rapid onset research.

Studies such as ours provide broad, population-level insights, and near-real-time data for estimating transmission potential and forecasting epidemic activity [29]. COVID-19 epidemiology and response policy will continue to change rapidly over the coming months and years. In order to capture/monitor associated shifts in people's feelings and behaviours, public health researchers should plan flexible studies where data collection (repeated cross-sectional or longitudinal) is timed to occur in response to key changes in epidemiology and public health policy. Data collection and participant recruitment methods should ensure the representation of higher-transmission groups, in terms of their demography and geography.

Ultimately, more in-depth studies of the social, emotional and behavioural dimensions of physical distancing should be conducted to supplement findings from structured online surveys. These studies may include less structured interviews and/or surveys with more opportunities for individuals to respond in their own words. Follow-up studies should also target population groups most impacted by COVID-19 — in terms of disease outcomes and restrictions — in order to understand what different groups may need to help them to follow public health guidelines and to support the development of tailored and targeted public health policy. For example, this may include exploring the potential barriers to cooperating with physical distancing, isolation, and quarantine regulations experienced by individuals with insecure employment or higher-density housing conditions.

27.8   COVID-19 Developments and Further Research

In late June 2020, the state of Victoria experienced a significant resurgence of COVID-19 epidemic activity. By late July, daily case counts reached nearly 20 times those seen in March and stay-at-home restrictions had been reinstated across Victoria [53].

The epidemiology of Victoria's second COVID-19 incursion has been distinct from the first. While caseloads in March and April were dominated by overseas acquired infections, the June outbreak has seen the establishment of community transmission, and heightened transmission within groups that are less able to practice physical distancing (e.g., healthcare workers, public housing residents including communities from migrant and refugee backgrounds and residents of aged care facilities). At the time of writing, a third survey of Victorian residents, including interviewer-assisted surveys of individuals from migrant and refugee backgrounds, was in progress to help inform the State's response.

Insights from this study have been considered by various policy and strategy structures and this chapter, along with further analyses, can help to inform public health planning for the management of COVID-19 and other diseases of epidemic potential.

Acknowledgements

The authors acknowledge funding support from the Melbourne School of Population and Global Health, The University of Melbourne. We also thank Professors Nancy Baxter and Jodie McVernon for their support of this project.

References

[1] World Health Organization. Novel Coronavirus (2019-nCoV) Situation Report – 1. 2020. URL https://www.who.int/docs/default-source/coronaviruse/situation-reports/20200121-sitrep-1-2019-ncov.pdf?sfvrsn=20a99c10_4. Accessed on September 24, 2020.

[2] Andrea Remuzzi and Giuseppe Remuzzi. COVID-19 and Italy: what next? *The Lancet,* 395(10231):1225-1228, 2020. doi: 10.1016/S0140-6736(20)30627-9.

[3] The Lancet. COVID-19 in the USA: a question of time. *Lancet,* 395(10232):1229, 2020. doi: 10.1016/S0140-6736(20)30863-1.

[4] Australian Government Department of Health. Australian Health Management Plan for Pandemic Influenza.

[5] Qualls N, Levitt A, Kanade N, Wright-Jegede N, Dopson S, Biggerstaff M, and Reed C UA. Community Mitigation Guidelines to Prevent Pandemic Influenza-United States. *MMWR Recomm Rep. 2017;66(No. RR-1):1-34.* URL http://www.cdc.gov/mmwr/cme/conted.html.

[6] Public Health England. Pandemic Influenza Response Plan.

[7] Ministry of Health Labour and Welfare of Japan. National Action Plan for Pandemic Influenza and New Infectious Diseases.

[8] Ministry of Health Singapore. MOH Pandemic Readiness and Response Plan For Influenza and Other Acute Respiratory Diseases. URL https://www.moh.gov.sg/docs/librariesprovider5/diseases-updates/interim-pandemic-plan-public-ver-_april-2014.pdf. Accessed on October 18, 2020.

[9] Shearer FM, Gibbs L, Alisic E, and et al. Distancing Measures in the Face of COVID-19 in Australia. Summary of National Survey Findings. *Survey 2 Report*, 2020. URL https://www.doherty.edu.au/uploads/content_doc/social_distancing_survey_wave1_report_May142.pdf. Accessed on September 24, 2020.

[10] Meagher N, Carpenter L, Chavez KM, and et al. Distancing Measures in the Face of COVID-19 in Australia. *Summary of National Survey Findings: Survey Wave 1.*, 2020. URL https://www.doherty.edu.au/uploads/content_doc/Covid_report_2.pdf. Accessed on September 24, 2020.

[11] S Hobfoll, P Watson, C Bell, R Bryant, M Brymer, M Friedman, et al. Five essential elements of immediate and mid-term mass trauma intervention: empirical evidence. *Psychiatry*, 70(4):283–315. doi: 10.1521/psyc.2007.70.4.283.

[12] Australian Red Cross. Psychological First Aid: An Australian guide to supporting people affected by disaster. *Published 2013*. URL https://www.psychology.org.au/getmedia/c1846704-2fa3-41ae-bf53-7a7451af6246/Red-crosspsychological-first-aid-disasters.pdf. Accessed on September 24, 2020.

[13] World Health Organization. War Trauma Foundation and World Vision International. Psychological first aid: Guide for field workers. URL https://apps.who.int/iris/bitstream/handle/10665/44615/9789241548205_eng.pdf;jsessionid=8B079EB2CED837997893970749D3ED67?sequence=1. Accessed on September 24, 2020.

[14] COVID-19 National Incident Room Surveillance Team. 2019-nCoV acute respiratory disease, Australia: Epidemiology Report 1 (Reporting week 26 January - 1 February 2020). *Communicable Diseases Intelligence*, 44, 2020. doi: 10.33321/cdi.2019.44.13.

[15] COVID-19 National Incident Room Surveillance Team. COVID-19, Australia: Epidemiology Report 2 (Reporting week ending 19:00 AEDT 8 February 2020). *Commun Dis Intell*, 44, 2020. doi: 10.33321/cdi.2020.44.14.

[16] World Health Organization. Coronavirus disease 2019 (COVID-19). *Situation Report – 41*, 2020. URL https://www.who.int/docs/default-source/coronaviruse/situation-reports/20200301-sitrep-41-covid-19.pdf?sfvrsn=6768306d_2. Accessed on September 24, 2020.

[17] COVID-19 National Incident Room Surveillance Team. COVID-19 , Australia: Epidemiology Report 12 (Reporting week ending 23:59 AEST 19 April 2020). *Commun Dis Intell – 44*, 2020.

[18] COVID-19 National Incident Room Surveillance Team. COVID-19, Australia: Epidemiology Report 9 (Reporting week to 23:59 AEDT 29 March 2020). *Commun Dis Intell*, 44, 2020. doi: 10.33321/cdi.2020.44.29.

[19] Raj Dandekar, Shane G Henderson, Hermanus M Jansen, Joshua McDonald, Sarat Moka, Yoni Nazarathy, Christopher Rackauckas, Thomas M Stace, Peter G Taylor, and Aapeli Vuorinen. Early analysis of the australian covid-19 epidemic. *Elife*, 9:1-14, 2020. doi: 10.7554/ELIFE.58785.

[20] COVID-19 National Incident Room Surveillance Team. COVID-19, Australia: Epidemiology Report 16: Reporting week ending 17 May 2020. *Commun Dis Intell*, 44, 2020.

[21] Government of Western Australia. Media statement: Cautious easing of restrictions thanks to WA's COVID-19 progress. 2020. URL https://www.mediastatements.wa.gov.au/Pages/McGowan/2020/04/Cautious-easing-of-restrictions-thanks-to-WAs-COVID-19-progress.aspx. Accessed on September 24, 2020.

[22] Northern Territory Government. Media statement: The Territory's Roadmap to the New Normal. 2020. URL https://coronavirus.nt.gov.au/updates/items/2020-04-30-the-territorys-roadmap-to-the-new-normal. Accessed on September 24, 2020.

[23] New South Wales Government. Media statement: Update on COVID-19 restrictions. 2020. URL https://www.nsw.gov.au/media-releases/update-on-covid-19-restrictions. Accessed on September 24, 2020.

[24] COVID-19 National Incident Room Surveillance Team. COVID-19, Australia: Epidemiology Report 19 (Fortnightly reporting period ending 21 June 2020). *Commun Dis Intell*, 44, 2020. doi: 10.33321/cdi.2020.44.54.

[25] O'Brien T. Coronavirus (COVID-19) in Australia. 2020. URL https://www.covid19data.com.au/. Accessed on September 24, 2020.

[26] Christina J Atchison, Leigh Bowman, Charlotte Vrinten, Rozlyn Redd, Philippa Pristera, Jeffrey W Eaton, and Helen Ward. Perceptions and behavioural responses of the general public during the COVID-19 pandemic: A cross-sectional survey of UK Adults. *medRxiv*, 1-21, 2020. doi: 10.1101/2020.04.01.20050039.

[27] Ritchie J and Spencer L. Qualitative data analysis for applied policy research. In: Bryman A, Burgess RG, eds). *Analysing Qualitative Data. London: Routledge; 1994:173-194*, 2020.

[28] Annemarie B Docherty, Ewen M Harrison, Christopher A Green, Hayley E Hardwick, Riinu Pius, Lisa Norman, Karl A Holden, Jonathan M Read, Frank Dondelinger, Gail Carson, et al. Features of 20 133 uk patients in hospital with covid-19 using the isaric who clinical characterisation protocol: prospective observational cohort study. *bmj*, 369:m1985, 2020. doi: 10.1136/bmj.m1985.

[29] Golding N, Shearer FM, Moss R, and et al. Estimating Temporal Variation in Transmission of SARS-CoV-2 and Physical Distancing Behaviour in Australia). 2020.

[30] Pekka Räsänen, James Hawdon, Matti Näsi, and Atte Oksanen. Social solidarity and the fear of risk: Examining worries about the recurrence of a mass tragedy in a small community. *Sociological Spectrum*, 34, 06 2014. doi: 10.1080/02732173.2014.917248.

[31] Jing Huang, Fangkun Liu, Ziwei Teng, Jindong Chen, Jingping Zhao, Xiaoping Wang, Ying Wu, Jingmei Xiao, Ying Wang, and Renrong Wu. Public behavior change, perceptions, depression, and anxiety in relation to the covid-19 outbreak. *Open forum infectious diseases*, 7(8):ofaa273–ofaa273, 2020. ISSN 2328-8957. doi: 10.1093/ofid/ofaa273.

[32] Emily Ying Yang Chan, Zhe Huang, Eugene Siu Kai Lo, Kevin Kei Ching Hung, Eliza Lai Yi Wong, and Samuel Yeung Shan Wong. Sociodemographic predictors of health risk perception, attitude and behavior practices associated with health-emergency disaster risk management for biological hazards: The case of COVID-19 pandemic in Hong Kong, SAR China. *Int J Env Res Public Heal*, 17(11):1–18, 2020. doi: 10.3390/ijerph17113869.

[33] Kaori Muto, Isamu Yamamoto, Miwako Nagasu, Mikihito Tanaka, and Koji Wada. Japanese citizens' behavioral changes and preparedness against COVID-19: An online survey during the early phase of the pandemic. *Plos one*, 15(6):e0234292, 2020. URL https://doi.org/10.1371/journal.pone.0234292.

[34] Jang WM, Jang DH, and Lee JY. Social distancing and transmission-reducing practices during the 2019 coronavirus disease and 2015 middle east respiratory syndrome coronavirus outbreaks in Korea. *J Korean Med Sci*, 35(23):e220, 2020. doi: 10.3346/JKMS.2020.35.E220.

[35] Lincoln Leehang Lau, Natalee Hung, Daryn Joy Go, Jansel Ferma, Mia Choi, Warren Dodd, and Xiaolin Wei. Knowledge, attitudes and practices of COVID-19 among income-poor households in the Philippines: A cross-sectional study. *Journal of global health*, 10(1), 2020. doi: 10.7189/JOGH.10.011007.

[36] Mark É Czeisler, Michael A Tynan, Mark E Howard, Sally Honeycutt, Erika B Fulmer, Daniel P Kidder, Rebecca Robbins, Laura K Barger, Elise R Facer-Childs, Grant Baldwin, et al. Public Attitudes, Behaviors, and Beliefs Related to COVID-19, Stay-at-Home Orders, Nonessential Business Closures, and Public Health Guidance — United States, New York City, and Los Angeles, May 5–12, 2020. *MMWR Morbidity and Mortality Weekly Report*, 69(24):751–758, 2020. doi: 10.15585/mmwr.mm6924e1.

[37] Karien Meier, Toivo Glatz, Mathijs C Guijt, Marco Piccininni, Merel van der Meulen, Khaled Atmar, Anne-Tess C Jolink, Tobias Kurth, Jessica L Rohmann, Amir H Zamanipoor Najafabadi, et al. Public perspectives on protective measures during the COVID-19 pandemic in the Netherlands, Germany and Italy: A survey study. *PloS one*, 15(8):e0236917, 2020. doi: 10.1371/journal.pone.0236917.

[38] JTF Lau, X Yang, H Tsui, and JH Kim. Monitoring community responses to the SARS epidemic in Hong Kong: From day 10 to day 62. *J Epidemiol Community Heal*, 57(11):864–870, 2003. doi: 10.1136/jech.57.11.864.

[39] James Holland Jones and Marcel Salathe. Early assessment of anxiety and behavioral response to novel swine-origin influenza A (H1N1). *PLoS one*, 4(12):2–9, 2009. doi: 10.1371/journal.pone.0008032.

[40] Holly Seale, Anita E Heywood, Julie Leask, Meru Steel, Susan Thomas, David N Durrheim, Katarzyna Bolsewicz, and Rajneesh Kaur. COVID-19 is rapidly changing: Examining public perceptions and behaviors in response to this evolving pandemic. *PLoS One*, 6(15):e0235112, 2020. doi: 10.1371/journal.pone.0235112.

[41] Gjalt-Jorn Y Peters, Robert Ruiter, and Gerjo Kok. Threatening communication: a critical re-analysis and a revised meta-analytic test of fear appeal theory. *Health Psychol Rev. 7(Suppl 1):S8-S31*, 2013. doi: 10.1080/17437199.2012.703527.

[42] Gerjo Kok, Gjalt-Jorn Y Peters, Loes TE Kessels, Gill A Ten Hoor, and Robert AC Ruiter. Ignoring theory and misinterpreting evidence: the false belief in fear appeals. *Health Psychology Review*, 12(2):111–125, 2018. doi: 10.1080/17437199.2017.1415767.

[43] Bavel JJ Van, Baicker K, Boggio PS, and et al. Using social and behavioural science to support COVID-19 pandemic response. *Nat Hum Behav. 4(5):460-471.*, 2020. doi: 10.1038/s41562-020-0884-z.

[44] Flaxman S, Mishra S, Gandy A, and et al. Estimating the effects of non-pharmaceutical interventions on COVID-19 in Europe. *Nature, 584(7820):257-261*, 2020. doi: 10.1038/s41586-020-2405-7.

[45] Nadia Yanet Cortés-Álvarez, Regino Piñeiro-Lamas, and César Rubén Vuelvas-Olmos. Psychological effects and associated factors of covid-19 in a mexican sample. *Disaster Med Public Health Prep*, pages 1–12, 2020. doi: 10.1017/dmp.2020.215.

[46] Brett Marroquín, Vera Vine, and Reed Morgan. Mental health during the COVID-19 pandemic: Effects of stay-at-home policies, social distancing behavior, and social resources. *Psychiatry Res*, 293, 2020. doi: 10.1016/j.psychres.2020.113419.

[47] Matthew T Tull, Keith A Edmonds, Kayla Scamaldo, Julia R Richmond, Jason P Rose, and Kim L Gratz. Psychological outcomes associated with stay-at-home orders and the perceived impact of covid-19 on daily life. *Psychiatry Res, 289*, page 113098, 2020. doi: 10.1016/j.psychres.2020.113098.

[48] Danielle Kohfeldt, Lina Chhun, Sarah Grace, and Regina Day Langhout. Youth empowerment in context: Exploring tensions in school-based yPAR. *Am J Community Psychol*, 47(1-2):28–45, 2011. doi: 10.1007/s10464-010-9376-z.

[49] Julian Rappaport. In praise of paradox: A social policy of empowerment over prevention. *Am J Community Psychol, 9(1):1*, 1981. doi: 10.1007/bf00896357.

[50] Australian Government. Payments and services during coronavirus (COVID-19).

[51] C Wang, R Pan, X Wan, et al. Immediate Psychological Responses and Associated Factors during the Initial Stage of the 2019 Coronavirus Disease (COVID-19) Epidemic among the General Population in China. *Int J Env Res Public Heal*, 17(5), 2020. doi: 10.3390/ijerph17051729.

[52] Debruin D, Liaschenko J, and Marshall MF. Social Justice in Pandemic Preparedness Social Justice in Pandemic Preparedness. *Am J Public Heal*, 102(4):586–591, 2012. doi: 10.2105/AJPH.

[53] COVID-19 National Incident Room Surveillance Team. COVID-19, Australia: Epidemiology Report 21: Fortnightly reporting period ending 19 July 2020. *Commun Dis Intell*, 44, 2020.

28

Impacts of COVID-19 Lockdown Restrictions on Housing and Public Space Use and Adaptation: Urban Proximity, Public Health, and Vulnerability in Three Latin American Cities

Raul Marino, Elkin Vargas and Mariana Flores

This chapter presents the results of an investigation about the lack of access to public space and social interactions in three Latin-American cities by using literature review, location data and online survey (quantitative and qualitative information) from household members on how these restrictions affected their daily life and their relationship with community and public space use. Focused on Bogota, Quito, and Mexico DF (n = 650), geospatial tools are used to correlate the survey's respondents' answers with official COVID-19 reports from government. The results show the correlation between the number of contagions by zones and users' behavioral shifts in terms of housing and public space use and adaptation. This could support the efforts of communities and decision makers to improve public health standards, reduce vulnerability to COVID-19, improve their resilience and enhance urban proximity to essential services and public spaces.

28.1 Introduction

In order to mitigate and manage the incidences of the pandemic, the World Health Organization [1] suggests the management of reliable information, as well as the isolation associated with social distancing, hand washing and treatment in case of contagion. The risks of a pandemic increase when community health and wellbeing weakens, however, there is a high incidence of contagions in land use, life expectancy, displacement, climatic disability and poor air quality. Confinement has undoubtedly transformed everyday life [2].

For the present study, a descriptive and causality analysis was carried out to explore the impacts of the COVID-19 pandemic on housing and public space use and adaptation, based on a survey that was applied online in different countries, but focusing in three cities of interest: Bogota (Colombia), Quito (Ecuador) and Mexico City (Mexico). An innovative methodology was proposed using official data, our survey results and geospatial analysis. Geospatial analysis allows integrating themes in disease mapping such as spatio-temporal analysis, health and geography, environmental variables, data mining and web mapping, and understanding the spatial conditions of propagation for the design of mitigation strategies, in decision-making, planning and community action. The importance of geospatial analysis methodologies lies in the possibility of strategically identifying vulnerable sectors, either due to their location, services or nearby infrastructure, geographical conditions, or particularities in the case of informal settlements [3].

28.1.1 Proximity and density

The urban factors identified in the spread of the pandemic in Wuhan were the intensive urban growth, hospitals, shopping centres, mixed uses, the population ageing index and roads, among others, which evidenced the need for planning strategies focused on understanding the transmission of infectious diseases in urban settings [4, 5]. Physical distancing as a health measure does not imply social distancing, which is why it suggests the proximity argument based on the dichotomy of "being in the place" and "being connected" [6]. The urban density allows numerous complex social and economic interactions, which are associated with prosperity by being close to work centres and services. Communities exhibit demographic and socioeconomic differences associated with vulnerability [7]. Urban density as a key metric of sustainability, can be defined as the proportion of the total number of inhabitants living within a delimited urban footprint of a city. Research indicates that inhabitants of a compact city with a higher urban density will be closer to others, which will make moving from one place to another more efficient and sustainable. Some indicators to measure urban density are the urban footprint, the total population, residential occupancy, parcel coverage, the height of the buildings, the efficiency of the plants, the occupancy level, and people per dwelling unit. Studies have revealed a number of benefits of compactness: more productivity; lower cost public services; greater social and economic mobility, as well as diversity; increased use of public transport; lower energy use and emissions; and improved health and wellbeing [8, 9].

The current pandemic suggests investigating how connectivity influences spread more than density, since large metropolitan areas are closely linked through economic, social and transport relationships, so dense areas may have better access to care facilities and further implementation of distancing policies and practices [10]. The most marginalized populations are seen to be more likely to get sick and die from being exposed to unequal conditions [11]. In terms of community, density is not related to infection rates and is inversely related to mortality rates [12].

28.1.2 Vulnerability and public health

COVID-19 has exposed urban structural weaknesses and inequalities, where health is the best element of cohesion to insert proposals for development and progress in contaminated communities. Due to their inability to access adequate medical care, transportation, and nutrition, socially vulnerable populations are at increased risk of health problems during disasters [13]. The greater degree of vulnerability is accompanied by demographic change, infrastructure, and governance, which is why the virus occurs mostly in more developed areas. In this case, migration, urban population growth, and high population density are important factors influencing the spread of disease. Associated with science and technological responses to COVID-19, it is necessary to integrate more critical and reflective analysis in addition to theoretical knowledge. According to Polko et al. [14], public space is an open and impartially accessible geographic dimension for all, which includes social interactions, subject to restrictions such as physical distancing, and is a key characteristic of a resilient city due to its ability to transform itself for health purposes of emergency, and the flexibility to adapt to new needs [14]. Urban designers seek to create places where people feel welcome, comfortable, and safe. In this way, urban residents experience nature most of the time at "the cognitive level of urban space", that is, at the level where "the people on the street" live in the city. The questions from architecture and urban planning in the face of the crisis are focused on how it will affect our relationship with public space [15–19].

28.1.3 Accessibility, adaptation and resilience

The adaptation processes include aspects of housing and the city such as morphology, spatial distribution, connectivity and resilience, where green areas represent important cores that are added to concepts such as proximity, access and quality [20]. Resilience provides an adaptive approach to environmental problems, natural hazards, and public health emergencies. At the urban context, resilience is understood as the ability of cities to absorb and respond to disasters through five dimensions: scale, structure, form, function and urban spatial network [21]. According to Urban Resilience Hub of United Nations, it is the "measurable ability of any urban system, with its inhabitants, to maintain continuity through all shocks and stresses, while positively adapting and transforming towards sustainability" [22]. Resilience allows a system to adapt to changes, regarding environment/ecology, infrastructure and governance/institutions. Meanwhile, accessibility considers access to urban and public services, health, food, financial resources, places, etc., for the entire population and vulnerable sectors [23].

28.2 Case Studies Context Summary

28.2.1 México city, Bogota, and Quito: common urban realities

For our study, we focused on three of the main Latin American capitals that have special conditions of interest for our research: Mexico City in Mexico, Bogotá in Colombia, Quito in Ecuador (see Figure 28.1). These cities share among each other similar economic, social, and cultural characteristics; moreover, some other particularities in common such as geographical and climatic condition as well as similar environmental challenges. We consider that a comparative approach between these cities would allow us to evaluate more in detail certain hypotheses related to relationship between the spreading and impact of the COVID-19 pandemic with geographic, environmental, social, and climatic variables. The data collected, apart from those by official sources, were obtained through an online global survey with emphasis on Latin American region, where the three study cities represent almost the 50% of the total surveys gathered (n = 1538). Another reason for doing a comparative analysis is the possibility to identify the successes or failures of policies and regulations implemented by local governments in relation to pandemic and its behaviour, by setting up possible linkages between these data and the results with variables such as urban density, centrality and proximity.

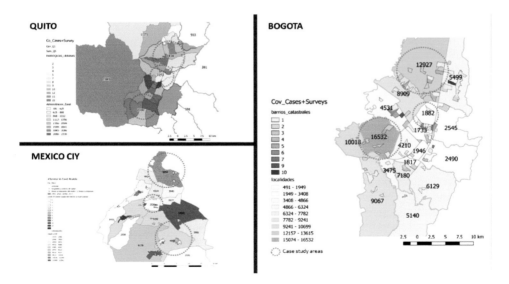

FIGURE 28.1
Case study cities: Quito, Mexico DF (left), and Bogota (right) – COVID-19 cases, survey participants and study area locations

Other common characteristics among the three study cases are related to high altitude (Mexico City: 2200 mamsl while Bogotá and Quito are located at 2800 mamsl) and geographical and climatic conditions. These cities have been built up on wetlands surrounded by mountains, and in the case of Mexico City and Quito nearby to volcanos. Their urban humidity levels are quite similar as well as the climate, especially in Quito and Bogotá along the year because there are no seasons as in Mexico City. In terms of population and density (as indicated in Table 28.1), Mexico City is the largest with 8,928,653 inhabitants and a density indicator of 5,966 p / km^2; Bogotá is the second in population with 7,181,469 inhabitants and the third in density with 4,907.45 p / km^2; Quito has 2,011,678 inhabitants and the second highest density rate among the three cities with 5,401.29 p / km^2 after Mexico City (see Table 28.1).

TABLE 28.1
Comparative city data [24–26]

City	Population	Population density (pop/Km2)	Covid-19 cases (31/07/20)	Covid-19 mortality rate (31/07/20)	Covid-19 contagions/ million	People per household	Public space per inhabitant (M2)	Gini coefficient	Territorial Administrative Division	number of surveys
Ciudad de México	8,928,653	5,966	76,169	8,731	8,530	3,4	5,4	0,532	16 (Delegaciones)	158
Quito	2,011,678	5,401	13,438	640	6,679	3,5	21,6	0,492	8 (Administraciones Zonales)	325
Bogotá	7,181,469	4,907	101,955	4,900	14,196	2,8	4,5	0,504	19 (Localidades)	184

For the spatial analysis, two scales of analysis were selected: a Metropolitan scale and a municipality scale as it allows us to have a similar observation patterns in each of the three cities (see Figure 28.1). In this sense, Mexico City is divided into 17 sectors or "Delegaciones". In the case of Quito, the homologous territorial administrative division is called "Administración Zonal" with eight such subdivisions. Finally, in the case of Bogotá, the political-administrative unit is called "Localidad", with a total of 19 localities.

28.2.2 Informality and public health

One of the main common patterns in our three case study cities is urban informality. This concept is understood not exclusively from the economic perspective; informality is also related to spatial features. It is considered as a pattern of land occupancy that characterizes the Latin American city and the global south in general and shapes most of the marginal peripheries where a large percentage of low-income population lives [27]. From public space view, the street vendors add an activity buzz become a vital part of the urban, cultural and social landscape of many cities and towns in the Global South [28, 29]. Millions of households depend on informal economy, which mostly take place on public space [30]. Only in Mexico City, the informality rate is 49.7%, that is, almost 5 out of 10 workers in the capital have an informal job [31]; a very similar indicator is shared by Bogotá [32] and Quito [26].

The impact of informality in public space becomes more complex during the current quarantine restrictions, as many street vendors are forced to keep crowding the streets as these are their only source of income. This risk increases in the case of Bogotá and Quito where large numbers (450,000 in Bogota alone) of migrant refugee population from Venezuela, is engaged in informal economic activities, as public vendors, increasing their vulnerability and contagions rates [33]. The policies of physical distancing and staying at home are not only difficult, they are often impossible to meet for large percentage of the population in developing countries [34].

Related to the current public health crisis, according to information available by 31 July 2020 (our baseline date), the impact of COVID-19 in terms of number of infections responds as follows: in Mexico City[1], 76,169 cases and 8,731 deaths (mortality rate: 11.5%); in Quito[2], 13,438 cases and

---

[1] https://datos.cdmx.gob.mx/pages/covid19/

[2] https://coe-pichincha.senescyt.gob.ec/wp-content/uploads/2020/08/Infografi%CC%81a-Cantonal-01_08_2020.pdf

640 deaths (mortality rate = 4.8%); in Bogotá[3], 101,955 cases and 4,900 deaths (mortality rate = 4.8%). Additionally, on the basis of COVID-19 test taken per 100,000 inhabitants in each city, the city with the highest impact of virus spreading is Bogotá with 14,196 infections per million inhabitants, as indicated in Table 28.1.

In this sense, it is likely that the pandemic will push street vendors and other informal workers to a long-term economic recession without precedent in modern times. In fact, the recession will not be exclusively in terms of informal activities, the most of formal economic sectors are currently affected. However, informality, increases the state of emergency in Latin American countries where this sector represents around 40% of the labour force [35]. This condition in the global south and our case study cities makes even more important the capacity of reorganization and resilience of governments and communities in the face of current regulatory absence and political legitimacy crisis of governments, especially in Latin America.

28.3   Research Methodology

The analysis of the impacts of the COVID-19 pandemic were undertaken using a mixed methods approach, based on firsthand data collected by the authors through an online survey covering the three selected case study cities: Bogota, Quito and Mexico, and the results of a proximity analysis on Points of Interest (POI): public space, health facilities and public transport access (see Figure 28.2). So far, the analysis of the discussion of the impacts of the COVID-19 pandemic has been mostly focussed on secondary data or observations of public space use by researchers [36], with few published papers showing firsthand results. Also, most research on COVID-19 and the built environment has focused on either housing [10] or public space [37]. Only a small percentage of previous research addressed the integrated study of housing and public space.

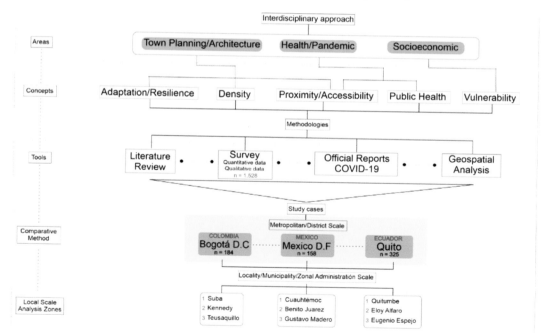

FIGURE 28.2
Research Methodology Scheme 1

[3]http://saludata.saludcapital.gov.co/osb/index.php/datos-de-salud/enfermedades-trasmisibles/covid19/

Geospatial analysis has been used widely to understand the factors driving the contagion of cases in urban areas, from the first cholera cluster maps in the London Epidemic in 1854 done by Snow, to the use of advanced tools using artificial intelligence and advance algorithms calculations [38]. The challenges of public health management in the last decades had led medicine research to support itself with geographical analysis, especially GIS systems, to understand the development and trends of infectious diseases in urban and rural contexts [39]. Important discoveries related to patterns of incidence and spread of the some of the main diseases affecting human population such as cancer, diabetes and lung and heart problems, and their correlation with the urban form and structures of cities, their density and their access to public transport [40, 41].

Surveys have been used as a method to collect information on sociodemographic characteristics of urban population and their housing and mobility behaviour [42, 43]. Its focus change according to the information needs, from surveys covering all the population in a given city or urban area (census), to surveys focused on specific segments of the population (by age, income, housing type, etc) and also focused on specific areas of the city where a certain phenomenon or trends needs to be investigated [44]. Based on these experiences, this paper follows a mixed method of collection of the required data for our analysis (see Figure 28.2), integrating two analytic tools: the analysis of the results of the survey conducted by our team on impacts of quarantine in housing and public space use; and the geospatial analysis of the case study cities selected in this paper: Bogota, Quito and Mexico DF.

28.3.1   Data collection

The collection of data was performed using two approaches, an Online Survey and collection of COVID-19 contagions reports from our case study cities.

- **Online survey**: The online survey collected information about the impact of quarantine's restrictions on housing and public space and adaptation. The survey was open for any person or household currently (from 25 April to 31 July 2020) experiencing restrictions on their daily activities due to governments emergency regulations to COVID-19, such as curfews, lockdowns, mobility restrictions, and other. The survey was divided into 7 categories (socioeconomic profile, housing, community, public space, mobility, working/education, and public health), with a total of 42 questions and a running time of 14 mins. The questions were divided into multiple selection and questions with open-ended responses, to collect a wider variety of observations from the participants. The delivery system used was through academic and professional online networks from the main authors in several countries in Latin America, Europe, and Oceania, focusing on Colombia, Ecuador, and Mexico as main case study areas for this research. To access the online survey site please see: https://www.surveymonkey.com/r/urbanmappingagency-English

- **Collection of COVID-19 data and geospatial data from the case study countries:** The data and figures related to the number of COVID-19 cases per city and analysis zones were collected from the government's official portals (see Bibliography for references on COVID-19 Portals) and reports to the closing date of the study: 31 July 2020. It is important to mention that being this pandemic such a dynamic and changing phenomenon, from which we are still trying to learn its nature and behaviour, the reported COVID-19 cases reports from each country and city can differ from the real number on COVID-19 contagions [1].

28.3.2   Data analysis

The collected data was analysed following a mixed methods approach:

- **Online survey:** (a) Qualitative information: The collected answers were analysed using content analysis and sentiment analysis tools [45], looking to understand the opinions and experiences of the participants in front of the quarantine's restrictions. (b) Quantitative information: The quantitative data were tabulated and analysed using statistical analysis tools (SPSS and Minitab), however the results of this analysis will be presented in a separate follow-up report.

- **Geospatial analysis**: This paper focused on the relationship of spatial variables such as density, accessibility and proximity to the points of interest: public space, health facilities and public transport hubs, and their relationship with the location of COVID-19 contagions clusters in our case study cities. The geospatial analysis tools used were selected to map and measure accessibility and proximity levels in a combined mapping of the local zones selected in each city. To achieve this, the Cost Distance tool [46] was selected to evaluate the accessibility and proximity to parks, health facilities and public transport hubs. To create the Cost Distance Maps, we converted the street network to raster format used Euclidean Distance tools to get the cost raster as an input parameter in cost distance tools.

- **Limitations and assumptions**: The study's limitations relate to availability of data for the case study cities, and possible small errors in the spatial files used to run the geospatial analysis. Also, the reports of the COVID-19 might have also misreporting information on the number and location of cases. The authors gave their best effort to minimize these errors.

28.4 Results

28.4.1 Survey results (housing, public space, mobility, community)

This section presents the results of the online survey and geospatial analyses described in Section 28.3, Methodology. The information is presented in the form of comparative figures, matrix of proximity mappings per case study city (see Figures 28.4, 28.5 and 28.6) and comparative table integrating all results (Table 28.2).

The online survey had a final number of 1,568 of complete answers by the cut-off date of 31 July 2020. The survey was opened to all persons or households experiencing quarantine restrictions in any city in the world, and the survey collected information from 38 countries and 121 cities (see COVID-19 preliminary Survey Report, 2020). From this complete sample (n=1,568), the 45.6% corresponded to our three case study cities, with a sample of 189 complete answers in Bogota, 320 in Quito and 155 in Mexico DF. The survey collected information on the impact of the restrictions of the COVID-19 pandemic in housing and public space use and adaptation, including information about impacts on mobility, community, working and education. In this chapter, we focus on the results related to public space use, mobility, and community responses to the crisis. More information about the survey's results on housing use and adaptation can be found in the preliminary report cited above.

Changes in house use and restrictions to access public space have an impact as well in the change of use of public space, driving shifts in behaviour and mobility [47]. Most of the participants in the three case study cities (65.18%) expressed that they make some changes in the use of the houses, in response to the restrictions imposed by the quarantine. Studies in Mexico and Bogota also arrived at similar conclusions [48, 49]. This number indicates that the restrictions are having a profound impact on the life of people and families, which should be further investigated to provide a better quality of life in the face of new conditions arising from COVID-19 pandemic.

Housing flexibility is one of the main factors that enable rapid adaptation to new living and working conditions. When asked about their houses' flexibility to adapt to new uses such as working and education, 46.3% of the participants indicated that their houses did not have flexibility to cope with the change of lifestyles and permanent cohabitation with the other members of their family groups or households. Therefore, it is essential that governments and institutions provide guidelines for housing adaptation to new uses such as working, education, gym and others, and also promote the development of new housing typologies that could adapt faster to the needs of their inhabitants and be more resilient to the impacts of the pandemic.

One of the main impacts of the COVID-19 pandemic has been the lack of face-to-face interaction with other community members. This increased the cases of psychological stress and depression on populations under severe quarantine restrictions. Question 32 of the survey asked participants which activity in public space they missed the most, and 35.7% of the participants expressed that it was the lack of social interaction with other people in public space, followed by walking (19.9%) and working out in public space/parks (14.3%). The survey also asked about the impact of the lack of social interaction on the participants' mental health and 81% indicated have some alteration to their mental health, mainly anxiety, irritability, and depression. These findings are similar to the ones presented by some surveys and studies on the same topic, which described the lack of social interaction as one of the main impacts on people's health during the COVID-19 pandemic [37, 50].

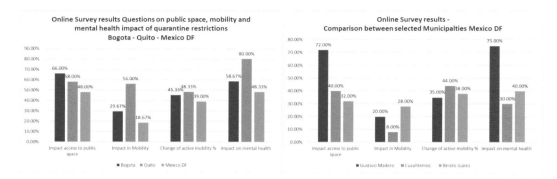

FIGURE 28.3

Online survey results comparison – Case Study cities analysis areas average (left) and results for Mexico City (right)

Access to public space and green areas is vital for the social and community life of cities [51]. According to survey results, 74.5% of the participants have a park or green area close to their homes (500 m), and the 52.4% expressed being affected by the restrictions in access and use of public spaces such as parks, recreation areas, public gyms and playgrounds (see Figure 28.3). This indicates that the strategies to manage the impacts of the COVID-19 pandemic in cities should consider more actively how to keep open these vital infrastructure, instead of just closing all parks and green areas as many cities in the world did (including our case study cities). The lack of access to public sport facilities and gyms had also created rising problems in public health, accelerated by the sedentarism of homeworking and home-schooling [36].

28.4.2   Geospatial analysis results (proximity, accessibility, density, etc.)

This section presents the results of the geospatial analysis of the selected variables (proximity, accessibility, density) in our three case study areas. The results are presented in a matrix of maps per case study to facilitate the comparison amongst the three selected local areas. As described above, our three-case study Metropolitan Areas (Bogota, Quito, Mexico), were analysed at municipality level, to enable a finer grain analysis of the urban conditions of each zone. These three subdivisions for each Metropolitan area are: Bogota (Kennedy, Suba, Teusaquillo), Quito (Espejo Alfaro, Eugenio Espejo and Quitumbe) and Mexico DF (Gustavo Madero, Cuauhtemoc and Benito Juarez). The results are described briefly in this section and will be analysed in more detail and compared with the survey information in the next section, Discussion.

In general, the three areas selected show a degree of lack of proximity to public space (parks), health facilities, and public transport. Proximity to Public Transport was more evenly distributed in Quito and Mexico, with large areas of Bogota's analysis zones showing a lack of accessibility to the BRT Transmilenio system (specially in Kennedy and Suba localities). The following part presents the results of these analyses per city in a comparison matrix. To see more details in each of the maps, please see: https://burodap.co/project-details/habitar-bajo-condiciones-de-cuarentena

In the case of the three analysis zones in Bogota, the analysis show that there are large contrasts amongst them, with localities such as Suba containing large areas that are not covered by public transport system, health facilities and have no parks (see Figure 28.4). One of the reasons for these

TEUSAQUILLO   **KENNEDY**   **SUBA**

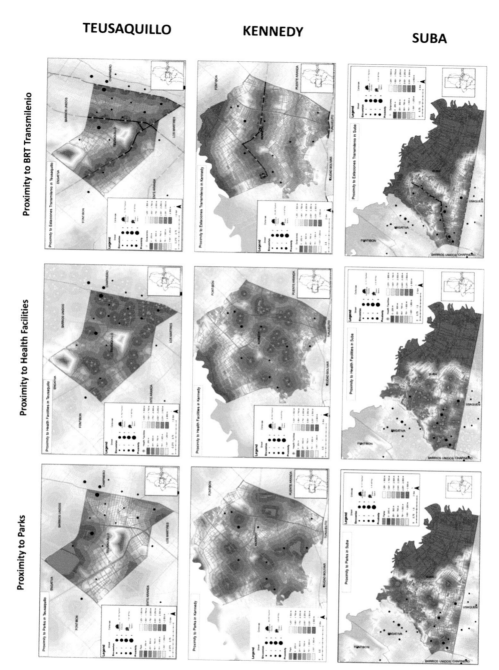

FIGURE 28.4

Geospatial proximity analysis Bogota (Kennedy, Suba, Teusaquillo)

results can be that a large part of the north part of Suba locality is a protected reservation zone which contains some small industries, and very low population density.

The selected zones In Quito also showed differences in proximity to parks, health facilities and public transport (see Figure 28.5). However, these differences were smaller than our other

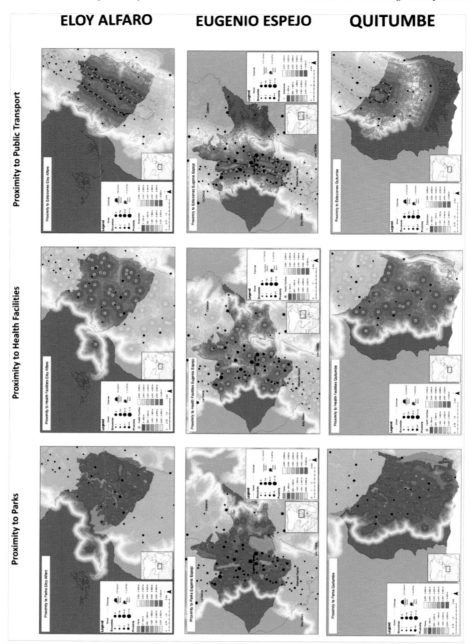

FIGURE 28.5

Geospatial proximity analysis Quito (Eloy Alfaro, Eugenio Espejo, Quitumbe)

case study cities, which can be related to the smaller population size in Quito, together with a denser distribution of population driven by the geographical features of the mountains conforming the metropolitan area of Quito. In some of the selected administrative zones, the analysis show a higher lack of accessibility to these infrastructure, which can also be related to the land use classification in these areas, which are more of an urban-rural character located at the periphery of the city.

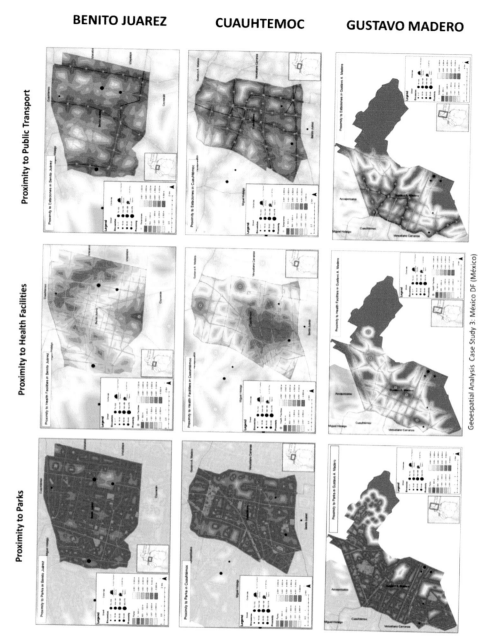

FIGURE 28.6

Geospatial proximity analysis Mexico City (Benito Juarez, Cuauhtemoc, Gustavo Madero)

For Mexico, the three municipalities selected showed a larger lack of accessibility to health facilities, but also have a better distribution of green areas and parks than our other case study cities (see Figure 28.6). One of the municipalities analysed, Gustavo Madero, displayed a lower coverage of public transport network, especially in the north part, which is located at a peripheral area of the city and mostly consisting of low-income households.

28.4.3 Integration of survey and geospatial results

The areas of analysis in each city were selected considering their number of COVID-19 cases, and also the urban characteristics of the areas, with areas located close the city centre and other located at the peripheries, with the aim to cover a larger variety of urban configurations. Also, the selected areas were considered related to the number of survey participants located in these areas, to be able to compare our survey results about the experience of users in public space and mobility during the restrictions of the COVID-19 quarantine. The maps of the geospatial analysis shown in Figures 28.4, 28.5, 28.6 above display the survey's participant number in a black circle magnitude scale (the larger the circle more surveys according to scale in the legend) (see Figures 28.4, 28.5, 28.6 from one result to nine or more results. These results were geolocated using the survey's information on location of the participant (neighbourhood), collected in Question 13. The following section will discuss first the results of this survey in each city related to the use and changes in public space and mobility, and secondly, it will discuss the results compared with the result of the geospatial analysis of proximity to parks, health facilities and public transport for each selected zone in the case study cities.

TABLE 28.2
Integration of Survey and proximity analysis results per case study cities and localities

Area of analysis per city	Density/Public space		Geospatial Analysis results			Online Survey Results				Covid19 Reports
	Pop. Density (pop/km2)	M² parks per person	% Proximity Parks (1500 m)	% Proximity Health (1500 mt)	% Proximity Public Transport (1500 m)	Impact access to public space	Impact in Mobility	Change of active mobility	Impact on mental health	Covid Cases 31 july/2019
Bogota			71.74%	76.92%	62.59%	66.00%	29.67%	45.33%	58.67%	107826*
Kennedy	28206	0.69	93.34%	83.35%	58.16%	70.00%	39.00%	52.00%	62.00%	16532
Suba	12117	0.35	41.30%	50.29%	34.08%	65.00%	35.00%	43.00%	67.00%	12927
Teusaquillo	10782	7.67	80.57%	97.11%	95.52%	63.00%	15.00%	41.00%	47.00%	1733
Quito			39.71%	21.99%	25.60%	58.00%	56.00%	48.33%	80.00%	9450
Eloy Alfaro	13100	11.02	7.60%	6.90%	5.03%	60.00%	42.00%	50.00%	90.00%	1945
Eugenio Espejo	3571	21.32	70.29%	57.47%	34.89%	63.00%	46.00%	40.00%	70.00%	1434
Quitumbe	3614	17.09	41.23%	1.60%	36.89%	60.00%	80.00%	55.00%	80.00%	2330
Mexico DF			93.59%	19.67%	69.03%	48.00%	18.67%	39.00%	48.33%	76169
Gustavo Madero	11779	7.58	81.03%	9.07%	28.09%	72.00%	20.00%	35.00%	75.00%	9254
Cuauhtemoc	14572	4.07	99.88%	42.24%	89.36%	40.00%	8.00%	44.00%	30.00%	4314
Benito Juarez	13992	2.38	99.87%	7.71%	89.64%	32.00%	28.00%	38.00%	40.00%	2536

Table 28.2 shows the integration of the results of the proximity analysis to our POI (parks, public transport, and health facilities). The values represented in each cell in the geospatial analysis section represent the percentage of the municipality area that have access to the interest point within 1,500 m. This range was selected as a class measure based on different urban planning studies supporting the development of 15-minute city in Paris [52] the 20-minute city in Melbourne [53], and the 20-minute neighbourhood in UK [54]. These plans promote the idea of a closer integration of activity hubs in the city subcentres, advocating for a better land use and reducing sprawl, increasing active transport (walking, bicycle) and reducing the need for long commuting to work, education, shops and recreational activities. The second part of the table shows the results of the survey's questions related to: impact of lack of access to public space, impact of mobility restrictions, shift towards active transport and impact on mental health. The values presented in these cells represent the percentage of the respondents in each city that indicate being affected by the restrictions of the quarantine in these activities. The last column presents the COVID-19 confirmed cases per city, as presented by official reports (see references in Section 28.2).

28.4.4 Statistical analysis: Multiple Linear Regression analysis results

The results of the proximity analysis were analysed using multiple linear regression analysis approach, with a backward stepwise tool to run several iterations of the data to find the best fit. The regression had our variables of interest (proximity, density, accessibility) as predictors (expressed as Proximity to Parks, Proximity to Health Facilities, Proximity to Public Transport and population density), and the amount of COVID-19 cases reported in our baseline data (31 July 2020), as dependent variable. The first round of the stepwise analysis showed that the variables Proximity to Health Facilities and population density did not have a significant impact on the dependent variable, so they were removed from the regression. The results of the final regression are shown in Table 28.3:

TABLE 28.3
Multiple Linear Regression analysis results

Coefficient Table Iteration 3 (adjusted R-squared = 0.737)								
	Coeff	SE	t-stat	lower (0.045(5))	upper (0.955(5))	Stand Coeff	p-value	VIF
b	3.819534	0.120283	31.754476	3.567200	4.071869	0.00000	5.81668e-7	
Log(X2) M2 Public Space	-0.562034	0.123662	-4.544935	-0.821455	-0.302612	-0.857770	0.00614089	1.081498
Log(X3) Prox.Parks	1.216468	0.509843	2.385967	0.146901	2.286035	1.061661	0.0326999	3.011498
Log(X5) Prox. Public Transport	-1.112501	0.456156	-2.438859	-2.069442	-0.155560	-1.098922	0.0487361	2.164527

As the results in Table 28.3 show, the selected research variables have a reasonably good fit for the model with an adjusted R^2 of 0.737. Public space per person (p=0.006), Proximity to Public Transport (p=0.058) and Proximity to Parks (p=0.0062) are significant predictor variables.

28.5 Discussion

28.5.1 Main findings of analysis

The three case study cities showed some similarities related to the patterns of contagions concentration, with peripheral areas of Bogota, Quito and Mexico DF registering the largest number of COVID-19 contagions. Also, when viewed separately, the patterns of proximity to the POIs (parks, health facilities and public transport) showed that these peripheral areas also have the lowest levels of proximity to the POI, especially in public transport accessibility and health facilities, indicating that there is a correlation between the access to these POI and the clustering of contagions in the local level areas analysed in each city.

Working and study activities have been also affected by the restrictions of the quarantine, shifting towards an online working, and learning model. 78% of the surveyed households have one member working remotely, 38% two members and 11.97% three members. This indicates the large amount of people that needed to adapt their houses to be able to work from home, with households having more than one member working at the same space, which creates problems related to privacy, concentration, noise and others. Regarding online education, the 63% of participants have one or more people learning online, and the 38.7% expressed having similar problems to be able to perform these activities in their homes.

The unit of spatial analysis in the three case study cities was based on certain criteria such as socio-economic and infrastructure characteristics of neighbourhoods and its densities. In this way, we classified the study sectors according to their urban proximity to our POI in low, medium, or high level. In the case of Bogotá, the sector or locality with the best indicators of proximity is Teusaquillo, based on proximity to health service infrastructure, public spaces, and connectivity with the rest of the city (see Table 28.2). It is followed by the Suba sector and in third place we see the Kennedy sector, which coincides with the highest contagion rate and population density despite of having a good proximity average to public spaces, health facilities and transport services. In this regard, it seems that high population density plus a weak socioeconomic condition are the aspects that might be more directly correlated with the high number of infections in these sectors.

It is worth noting that when comparing the three areas across the case study cities, with the highest urban deficits in the three cities, we find out that it coincides with the highest COVID-19 contagion rates, but also in terms of proximity as they are the most disconnected and distant from the public transportation system; especially in Quitumbe (Quito) and Gustavo Madero (Mexico). Although this last sector is not the most public transport deficient in Mexico City, it matches with Quitumbe in Quito regarding the impact of mobility and proximity to health infrastructures. On the other hand, the sectors of Teusaquillo (Bogotá), Eugenio Espejo (Quito) and Benito Juarez (CDMX), register the least contagion rate and the best indicators of proximity to POI and socioeconomic conditions. They are also the ones with the lowest population density. However, when comparing these proximity results with the results of the survey, these same three sectors, being the most favoured in this research, reflect the greatest impacts and limitations on access to public space and mobility. Several reasons could be offered for this contrast, mainly related to the strict quarantine restrictions enforced in the case study cities which restricted access to most public parks, playgrounds, and other communal facilities.

In the case of middle-income sectors, such as Suba (Bogotá), Eloy Alfaro (Quito) and Cuauhtemoc (Mexico), the greatest impact due to restrictions is connected with the lack of access to public space, according to qualitative data from online survey, despite the fact that the indicator of proximity to parks remains high in the study sectors of Quito and Mexico. On the other hand, one of the most revealing indicators among these sectors is observed in the percentage of people who answered affirmatively to the question about the impact of quarantine on their mental health. In this field, it is evident that the most affected population corresponds to residents of the sectors with higher population densities and those who have less access to parks or green infrastructure. Taking this into consideration, the sectors with closer proximity relationships to public space, transportation and health facilities show a lower impact on the mental health of their residents.

Density of population is another factor that has been investigated in relation with COVID-19 contagions rates [10]. Some research show that there is no or little correlation between density and the number of cases [55]. However, some factors associated to urban density, such as pedestrian congestion and crowding in public space and public transport could increase the contagion cases. In our survey, 52.35% of participants think that density is an important risk factor, while 32.34% expressed that density was an important factor, but there were other more important such as urban hygiene, crowding avoidance, access to health facilities and social behaviour to follow the norms stablished in each city to manage the pandemic. In comparison Table 28.2, the municipalities with largest density had higher register of COVID-19 cases in each city. Also, when comparing the results of the proximity to parks and public transport we noticed that with less proximity to these areas, the rate of COVID-19 contagions tends to increase. However, this was not true for all cases in our case study cities, as some municipalities such as Gustavo Madero in Mexico City had a high proximity value but also higher COVID-19 cases in the city.

Regarding the concept of urban proximity investigated in this research, one of the important findings has to do with the relationship among community, neighbourhood or districts with public space access, and the amount of public space area per person (parks and squares). These kinds of urban infrastructures have an influence in quality of life and public health when there is a close proximity relation between them and residential areas in the case study cities. In this sense, we notice a close correlation of a high contagious rate with the lack of proximity between urban health facilities to housing or residential zones. Additionally, there is also a difference between the case study cities of this type of health infrastructure in terms of service coverage and concentration with the health system in each of the three countries. For instance, the health system in Colombian cities is financed by public resources but outsourced by private operators. On the other side, in Mexico and Ecuador the public sector is still the main operator of health services, therefore most of the health facilities are centralized and managed by the public sector, consequently the coverage of health infrastructure is less dispersed along the city and more concentrated in large hospital complexes and multipurpose medical buildings.

Urban mobility has been also greatly disturbed by the restrictions of quarantine. 36% of the survey's participants in the case study cities expressed being affected in their mobility, and 74% report changing their transport modes towards more active transport such as walking and bicycling. On the other hand, 23% of the participants said that they would prefer to use private car to avoid any risk of contagion in public space. This shift towards active transport is an important trend that could support a change in urban transport planning, favouring bicycle networks and walkable pathways into the city's mobility infrastructure. Regarding these networks, 54% of the participants said that their cities did not have a bicycle network system, and 11% reported that such systems were currently under constructions in their cities.

Cities have adopted different strategies to manage the spread of the COVID-19 pandemic, mainly based on restrictions of mobility and agglomerations in public transport and public space. In this sense, our survey asked the participants about what strategy could be more effective to manage the reduction of contagions, and 25% expressed that the option: "Establish body temperature check point, hand washing stations and disinfectant gel in public space" was the best option, followed by the option: "Promote active transport and the expansion of bicycle networks and walkable paths", with 19%, and finally the option: "Redesign public space, urban furniture and green areas to reduce human contact" (16%). These results indicate that most in the urban communities wish to participate in the decision making process regarding the management of this pandemic, and is keen to support the development of active transport options and the redesign of public spaces to offer a safer environment for themselves, their families and the community. Participatory GIS options to collect community feedback on public space use and behaviour could be a valuable tool to support achieving this goal and offer better guidance to city planners in their quest to reduce the spread of the COVID-19 virus while reducing vulnerability in urban communities [56].

28.5.2   Main findings and links to similar COVID-19 studies or reports

Similar studies using online surveys to collect information about the impact of the COVID-19 pandemic restrictions on the life and behaviour of people and household have been published recently [37, 49]. The report presented by Gehl et al analysed the changes in the patterns of use and behaviour in public spaces in four Danish cities (Copenhagen, Helsingør, Horsends and Svenborg) and found that these cities are being used more for recreation, play and exercise, and the use of public space has remained constant, while A to B movements have decreased significantly. Similar results were found in our study regarding reduction of daily travels, however, the use of public space diminished during the pandemic in our case study cities, especially in Bogota. Another interesting observation of this study is that more children and older people are using the city's space than before. However, it is important to point out that the patterns of use and restrictions on the access and use of public space between Europe and Latin America are different, as most Latin-American cities have enforced strict restrictions to access parks, playgrounds, public gyms and other community areas. This is also supported by the results of the Google Community Reports on public space use [57] where it shows an increase of use in European cities (+85%) and a large decrease of public space use in our case study countries (-45%). This change can be driven by different factors, from the restrictions itself to access these spaces, to the change of attitude of people and community towards public space, considering it is now a risk area where there may be a higher probability of COVID-19 contagion [36].

28.5.3   Impact of findings on COVID-19 strategies and planning

As the results of the survey showed, and supported by similar reports [37, 58] in other cities, there is a significant shift towards active mobility (walking, bicycle) in cities in many countries, which could in turn increase the need for new strategies directed to increase and/or extend existing infrastructure to support this change of mobility patterns. On the other hand, there is also the risk that the low demand for public transport (already reported by several cities such as NY, Bogota and Quito), could create economic challenges in the provision and operation of public transport networks, increasing as well the use of private cars as main transportation mode in cities [47]. Urban pollution had decreased as well as collateral effect of the restrictions in mobility, and large percentage of the population currently working and learning from home in the case study areas (65%), according to the data collected in our survey. The tendency towards these kinds of remote working and education has already being growing before the COVID-19 pandemic, and now has accelerated. This trend will likely continue, changing the way our cities and houses function.

Another possible scenario on the future growth of cities could be the increase of urban sprawl driven by the desire of larger housing spaces in low density neighbourhoods. In our survey, 24% of the participants expressed their preference for larger houses located far from the city centre. It is important that this tendency does not become a new wave of unsustainable expansion of cities towards their fringe areas, reversing the efforts of many cities towards better land use, with medium density mix-use areas located in strategic areas or activity clusters in cities, which had proven to be beneficial to reduce impacts of sprawl, pollution, energy use and promote an active community life [59, 60].

Communities have shown a great capacity to support groups vulnerable to the pandemic (migrants, street dwellers, the elderly, children), and a variety of responses have been received that show the potential that communities have to be an important part of management of the pandemic. However, citizen participation in decision-making about the management of this pandemic has been very low or non-existent in the study cities, as well as in many cities in the world.

28.5.4   Recommendations for decision-makers and community-based initiatives

Community participation in the decision making process about strategies to manage COVID-19 and other pandemics could be a vital factor to enhance urban resilience [61]. Most cities, including our case study cities, have not fully included communities in the decision making process in the current crisis. Communities and the civil sector felt ignored and forced to surrender temporarily their liberty to move-around and access public spaces in cities [62]. The social capital and community wisdom how their local neighbourhoods function and adapt are an important source of information that could enrich the decision making process together with local government authorities to better cope with the quarantine restrictions and reduce the adverse effects of forced lockdown measures during COVID-19.

In the proximity analysis, there are large areas in the case study cities with very low proximity and accessibility to green areas and public spaces. The analysis also shows that in the densest areas and with fewer area of public space per inhabitant, the level of contagion to COVID-19 is higher. Therefore, public policies oriented towards the provision of more and better public space should be on the agenda for cities in developing countries, with special emphasis on the informal areas most vulnerable to COVID-19.

The vulnerability to develop serious heath complications from COVID-19 is correlated with diseases such as diabetes, heart problems and high blood pressure and lung problems [1]. The rate of occurrence of these diseases is related to urban areas with low accessibility to green areas and active transport (walking, cycling), which promotes car dependency and sedentary lifestyle. Our research showed that large areas of the case study cities, affected by the highest levels of contagions, have public transport disadvantage and low proximity to parks. It is important to understand this relationship between the characteristics of the virus and urban planning, which should more efficiently promote active transportation and exercise in parks and recreational public spaces.

Another important recommendation to local administrations is to collect higher resolution data and made publicly available, to facilitate the efforts of academy and other institutions to provide better insights on the dynamics of pandemic spread or control. Finally, it is also important for cities to provide small scale disaggregated data on COVID-19, in order to understand the possible impacts of urban form and urban features such as the ones explored in this chapter (public space, mobility, density) on the spread and behaviour of the COVID-19 pandemic at neighbourhood or precinct levels.

28.6 Conclusions and Future Work

28.6.1 Summary of main findings

The impact of quarantine on the use of homes has been high, although its adaptation has been restricted due to lack of flexibility of housing. The development of new housing that can more easily adapt to new conditions and mix or types of uses to respond to the needs of its inhabitants is needed.

The use of public space has decreased considerably in the three study cities, mostly motivated by access restrictions and lack of confidence in the hygienic safety of public space and facilities. This could have a significant impact on public health, and potentially lead to an increase in the rate of diseases related to sedentary lifestyle and social isolation is expected [1]. Therefore, it is essential to avoid total restrictions (all or nothing approaches) in accessing public space and green areas, and instead promote strategies of capacity control, use of real-time data of public space agglomerations, continuous disinfection of urban and sports furniture and signage for social distancing.

The change of paradigm from face-to-face work and education to virtual work/education will be one of the main factors that will guide urban development in the coming years. This trend was already starting to occur in some cities that have decentralized their areas of employment from the city centre to nodes and secondary activity centres in the city. Steps in this direction have been already taken by some cities such as Melbourne and Paris, aiming to apply the 20-minutes city concept to their current and future urban development plans. But this trend has accelerated during COVID-19.

Proximity to public spaces and green areas has a correlation with the level of contagion in the case study cities, however it is important to take into account the impact of the socioeconomic profile and population density, since these could have more influence on the level of contagions by location according to the results of this research. There are several trade-offs between the advantages of density and the risk of contagion in areas with high traffic and urban density, which should be explored in more detail in order to improve resilience to COVID-19 and future pandemics.

Access to green areas and public recreational spaces is vital to better cope with the restrictions and lifestyle changes caused by the pandemic. The shift towards teleworking and online education has led to an increase in lack of physical activity and face-to-face interaction. Therefore, it does not make sense that in times of pandemic, decisions are made to close urban parks, playgrounds and public spaces, which further confines the population and leaves them without options for socialization, exercising and enjoyment of nature. These are considered essential for good mental and community health. Access to parks and public recreational space must be merely regulated, not prohibited. Authorities need to take advantage of the potential of new technology (such as crowd monitoring and public transport real-time data on commuters) to prevent crowding and increase the continuous disinfection of urban/public spaces and furniture.

28.6.2 Contributions to research and practice

Geospatial analysis can contribute to a better management of the COVID-19 pandemic by identifying the most important urban spaces for the community and understanding how the characteristics of each context influence public health and quality of life. After the first wave of the pandemic, COVID-19 control strategies in many cities have been aimed at identifying contagion clusters and selective quarantine of specific areas of the city, which is why it is essential to understand the relationships between the prevalence of contagion of COVID-19 and the urban characteristics at multiple scales of analysis (i.e., zonal, neighbourhood, municipality).

The development of urban centralities or activity hubs that reduce the need for the population for long commute to their jobs, studies, health and recreation areas is one of the strategies that can help reduce the spread of COVID-19, especially in cities with high urban density. The urban sub-centres (centralities) where there is a combination of activities (housing, employment, recreation, health), have the possibility of being more resilient to the impacts of strict quarantine, by being able to organize the development of these activities more efficiently and adapted to their special needs. Generic quarantine and general curfew measures applied to cities may result in a worsening of the population's quality of life and economy, while more targeted and customized solutions and measures for neighbourhoods and communities may have a better chance of success.

28.6.3 Future steps

The relationship between density and COVID-19 involve several variables that should be further investigated to understand the possible trade-offs between the advantages of density and the management of public transport systems and crowded public spaces, especially in cities with a large percent of its population depending on informal trading in public spaces to secure a living, such as the three cities in our case studies. Also, with better data, we can undertake finer grain analysis and explore urban form variables at block or neighbourhood level. Many cities have been publishing their COVID-19 pandemic data through several portals and dashboards, which help to track the spread of the virus and prepare for second wave and other future pandemics.

   The COVID-19 pandemic has highlighted the high vulnerability of cities and communities to manage new forms of risks to public health. Therefore, it is vital to learn from the lessons from the best (and also worst) management strategies that different countries and cities have applied to cope with the pandemic, and be able to adapt quickly to new conditions and be more resilient to future pandemic and other threats. The development of healthier cities, with more robust health infrastructure and multi-mode active transport networks and generous green zones should be included in the planning agenda of cities to reduce the social and economic impacts of current and future quarantine restrictions in cities.

Acknowledgements

The authors wish to acknowledge the sponsorship and research grant funded by Urban Mapping Agency (UMA) and BuroDAP in Colombia. Also, we thank the collaboration of associated researchers to this research project: Arch. Manuel Bobadilla, GIS Analyst Angga Syfarianto, Roxane Dufresne and Arch. Diego Torres for their valuable contributions to data analysis.

References

[1] WHO. Strengthening Preparedness for COVID-19 in Cities and Urban Settings Interim Guidance for Local Authorities. *W. H. Organization, Ed.*, 2020.

[2] Pablo Cabrera-Barona and Andrea Carrión. Voiding Public Spaces, Enclosing Domestic Places: Place Attachment at the Onset of the Pandemic in Quito, Ecuador. *Journal of Latin American Geography, Ahead of Print: JLAG Perspectives*, 2020. doi: 10.1353/lag.0.0145.

[3] Isabel Duque Franco, Catalina Ortiz, Jota Samper, and Gynna Millan. Mapping repertoires of collective action facing the COVID-19 pandemic in informal settlements in Latin American cities. *Environment and Urbanization*, 2020. URL https://doi.org/10.1177/0956247820944823.

[4] R. A Matthew and B Mcdonald. Cities under Siege: Urban Planning and the Threat of Infectious. *Journal of the American Planning Association, 72(1), 109-117*, 2006.

[5] Xin Li, Lin Zhou, Tao Jia, Ran Peng, Xiongwu Fu, and Yuliang Zou. Associating COVID-19 Severity with Urban Factors: A Case Study of Wuhan. *Research Square*, 2020. URL https://doi.org/10.21203/rs.3.rs-34863/v1.

[6] José Antonio Belso-Martínez, Alicia Mas-Tur, Mariola Sánchez, and María José López-Sánchez. The COVID 19 response system and collective social service provision. Strategic network dimensions and proximity considerations. *Service Business*, 2020. URL https://doi.org/10.1007/s11628-020-00421-w.

[7] Ashley Wendell Kranjac and Dinko Kranjac. County-level factors influence the trajectory of covid-19 incidence. *medRxiv and bioRxiv*, 2020. doi: 10.1101/2020.05.05.20092254.

[8] C. Boyko and C. Boyko. Progress in Planning. *Annu Rev Ecol Evol Syst*, 1(76):1–61, 2011.

[9] Shlomo, P. Lamson-Hall, S. Shingad, S. Kumar, and Z. Gonzalez Blanco. Anatomy of Density I: Measurable Factors that Together Constitute Urban Density. *NYU Marron Institute of Urban Management*, 2020. URL https://marroninstitute.nyu.edu/papers/anatomy-of-density-i-measurable-factors-that-together-constitute-urban-density.

[10] Shima Hamidi, Sadegh Sabouri, and Reid Ewing. Does Density Aggravate the COVID-19 Pandemic? Journal of the American Planning Association. *Journal of the American Planning Association*, 2020. doi: 10.1080/01944363.2020.1777891.

[11] Helen VS Cole, Isabelle Anguelovski, Francesc Baró, Melissa García-Lamarca, Panagiota Kotsila, Carmen Pérez del Pulgar, Galia Shokry, and Margarita Triguero-Mas. The COVID-19 pandemic: power and privilege, gentrification, and urban environmental justice in the global north. *Cities & Health*, 2020. doi: 10.1080/23748834.2020.1785176.

[12] Matheus T Baumgartner, Fernando M Lansac-Toha, Marco Tulio P Coelho, Ricardo Dobrovolski, and Jose Alexandre F Diniz-Filho. Social distancing and movement constraint as the most likely factors for COVID-19 outbreak control in Brazil. *meRxiv Health Cities*, 2020. doi: 10.1101/2020.05.02.20088013.

[13] Ibraheem M Karaye and Jennifer A Horney. The impact of social vulnerability on covid-19 in the us: an analysis of spatially varying relationships. *American Journal of Preventive Medicine*, 59(3):317–325, 2020. doi: 10.1016/j.amepre.2020.06.006.

[14] A Polko. Public space development in the context of urban and regional resilience. *Cambridge Journal of Regions, Economy and Society, 3(1)*, 2010.

[15] L. Alter. Urban design after the coronavirus. *Treehugger*, 2020. URL https://www.treehugger.com/urban-design/urban-design-after-coronavirus.html. accessed 4.9.20.

[16] R. Florida. We'll Need To Reopen Our Cities. But Not Without Making Changes First. *CityLab*, 2020.

[17] H. Null, S. anad Smith. COVID-19 Could Affect Cities for Years. Here Are 4 Ways They're Coping Now. *TheCityFix: World Resource Institute (WRI)*, 2020.

[18] D. Roberts. How to make a city livable during lockdown. *Vox*, 2020.

[19] R. van der Berg. How Will COVID-19 Affect Urban Planning? *TheCityFix*, 2020.

[20] Mick Lennon. Green space and the compact city: planning issues for a 'new normal'. *Cities & Health*, 2020. doi: 10.1080/23748834.2020.1778843.

[21] Yuwen Lu, Guofang Zhai, Shutian Zhou, and Yijun Shi. Risk reduction through urban spatial resilience: A theoretical framework. *Human and Ecological Risk Assessment: An International*, 2020. doi: 10.1080/10807039.2020.1788918.

[22] UNHABITAT. What is urban resilience. *Urban Resilience Hub*, 2019. URL https://urbanresiliencehub.org/what-is-urban-resilience/.

[23] CEPAL and S. Huenchuan. COVID-19 Recomendaciones generales para la atención a personas mayores desde una perspectiva de derechos humanos. 2020. URL http://repositorio.uasb.edu.bo/handle/54000/1122.

[24] Dadep. Primer Reporte de Indicadores. 2018.

[25] WRI MÉXICO. Manual "Espacio Público y Vida Pública. 2016. URL https://wriciudades.org/research/publication/manual-espacio-p%C3%BAblico-y-vida-p%C3%BAblica.

[26] INEC. Actualización metodológica:Empleo en el sector informal yla clasificación de los ocupadossegún sectores. 2015. URL https://www.ecuadorencifras.gob.ec/documentos/web-inec/EMPLEO/2015/Junio-2015/Metogologia_Informalidad/notatecnica.pdf.

[27] N. Clichevsky. Informalidad y segregaciónurbana en América Latina. Unaaproximación. medio ambiente y desarrollo. 2000. URL https://repositorio.cepal.org/bitstream/handle/11362/5712/S00100859.pdf?sequence=1.

[28] R. Rocha, F. Sánchez, and L. García. Ventas callejeras y espacio público: efectos sobre el comercio de Bogotá. *Desarrollo y Sociedad*, 2009. URL http://www.scielo.org.co/scielo.php?script=sci_arttext&pid=S0120-35842009000100007&lng=en&tlng=es.

[29] Michael Janoschka and Jorge Sequera. Gentrification in Latin America: addressing the politics and geographies of displacement. *Urban Geography, 1(20)*, 37(8):1–20, 2016. doi: 10.1080/02723638.2015.1103995.

[30] ILO. Woman and Men the informal Economy: a statistical picture. International Labour Organization. 2018. URL https://www.ilo.org/wcmsp5/groups/public/---dgreports/---dcomm/documents/publication/wcms_626831.pdf.

[31] NEGI. Estadísticas de Informalidad. México, Nuevas Estadísticas de Informalidad laboral. 2020.

[32] DANE. Empleo Informal y Seguridad Social. 2019. URL https://www.dane.gov.co/index.php/estadisticas-por-tema/salud/informalidad-y-seguridad-social/empleo-informal-y-seguridad-social-historicos.

[33] ACNUR. Datos Básicos Refugiados. 2020. URL https://www.acnur.org/datos-basicos.html.

[34] Kishinchand Poornima Wasdani and Ajnesh Prasad. The impossibility of social distancing among the urban poor: the case of an indian slum in the times of covid-19. *Local Environment. The International Journal of Justice and Sustainability*, 2020. doi: 10.1080/13549839.2020.1754375.

[35] CEPAL. Estudio Económico de América Latina y el Caribe 2015: desafíos para impulsar el ciclo de inversión con miras a reactivar el crecimiento. *CEPAL*, 2015. URL https://www.cepal.org/es/publicaciones/38713-estudio-economico-america-latina-caribe-2015-desafios-impulsar-ciclo-inversion.

[36] Jordi Honey-Roses, Isabelle Anguelovski, Vincent Chireh, Carolyn Daher, Cecil Konijnendijk, Jill Litt, M. Nieuwenhuijsen, et al. The impact of COVID-19 on public space: an early review of the emerging questions – design, perceptions and inequities. *Cities & Health*, 2020.

[37] Gehl. Public Space & Public Life during COVID-19 Survey Report. *Supported by Realdania and the City of Copenhagen*, 2020. URL https://covid19.gehlpeople.com/.

[38] George J Musa, Po-Huang Chiang, Tyler Sylk, Rachel Bavley, William Keating, Bereketab Lakew, Hui-Chen Tsou, and Christina W Hoven. Use of GIS mapping as a public health tool—from cholera to cancer. *Health services insights*, 2013. doi: 10.4137/HSI.S10471.

[39] I. Franch-Pardo, B. M.Napoletano, and F. Rosete-Verges. Spatial analysis and GIS in the study of COVID-19. *A review. Science of The Total Environment*, 2013. URL https://doi.org/10.1016/j.scitotenv.2020.140033.

[40] D. Kasraian, K. Maat, and B. Van Wee. The impact of urban proximity, transport accessibility and policy on urban growth: A longitudinal analysis over five decades. *Environment and Plannig B: Urban Analytics and City Science*, 2017.

[41] Yuliang Zhang, Wenxiang Li, Haopeng Deng, and Ye Li. Evaluation of Public Transport-Based Accessibility to Health Facilities considering Spatial Heterogeneity. *Methods and Technologies for Next-Generation Public Transport Planning and Operations*, 2020. doi: 10.1155/2020/7645153.

[42] Hugh Barton. Land use planning and health and well-being. *Land Use Policy*, 2009. doi: https://doi.org/10.1016/j.landusepol.2009.09.008.

[43] Joseph Sakshaug. Important considerations when analyzing health survey data collected using a complex sample design. *American Journal of Public Health*, pages 15–16, 2014. doi: 10.2105/AJPH.2013.301515.

[44] Chen Zhong, Xianfeng Huang, Stefan Müller Arisona, and Gerhard Schmitt. Identifying Spatial Structure of Urban Functional Centers Using Travel Survey Data: A Case Study of Singapore. *Conference: Proceedings of The First ACM SIGSPATIAL International Workshop on Computational Models of Place (COMP'13)*, 2013. doi: 10.1145/2534848.2534855.

[45] J. F. Sánchez-Rada and C. A. Iglesias. Social context in sentiment analysis: Formal definition, overview of current trends and framework for comparison. *Information Fusion*, 2019. doi: https://doi.org/10.1016/j.inffus.2019.05.003.

[46] GIS Documentation. Coste de distancia (Spatial Analyst). *ArcGis Pro*, 2016. URL https://pro.arcgis.com/es/pro-app/tool-reference/spatial-analyst/cost-distance.htm.

[47] Mark Stevenson, Jason Thompson, Thiago Hérick de Sá, Reid Ewing, Dinesh Mohan, McClure, et al. Land use, transport, and population health: estimating the health benefits of compact cities. *Urban Design, Transport, and Health*, pages 2925–2935, 2016. doi: 10.1016/S0140-6736(16)30067-8.

[48] E. Rodríguez-Izquierdo, S. Pérez-Jiménez, L. Merino-Pérez, and M. (s.f.) Mazari-Hiriart. Spatial analysis of COVID-19 and inequalities in Mexico City. URL https://www.un.org/development/desa/dpad/wp-content/uploads/sites/45/COVID-19-Mexico-City.pdf.

[49] PROFAMILIA. Health services inequalities affecting the Venezuelan migrant and refugee population in Colombia. *Profamila*, 2020. URL https://profamilia.org.co/wp-content/uploads/2020/06/Health-services-inequalities-affecting-the-Venezuelan-migrant-and-refugee-population-in-Colombia-how-to-improve-the-local-response-to-the-humanitarian-emergency.pdf.

[50] PROFAMILIA. Health services inequalities affecting the Venezuelan migrant and refugee population in Colombia. *Profamila*, 2020. URL https://profamilia.org.co/wp-content/uploads/2020/06/Health-services-inequalities-affecting-the-Venezuelan-migrant-and-refugee-population-in-Colombia-how-to-improve-the-local-response-to-the-humanitarian-emergency.pdf.

[51] A. Bedimo-Rung, A. Mowen, and D.l Cohen. The significance of parks to physical activity and public health: a conceptual model. *Am J Prev Med*, 2005. doi: 10.1016/j.amepre.2004.10.024.

[52] C. Moreno. Prossimità a parigi / proximity in paris. *DOMUS*, 2020. URL http://www.moreno-web.net/domus-prossimita-a-parigi-proximity-in-paris-edition-juin-2020/.

[53] Victoria State Government. Plan Melbourne 2017-2020. *Social Science & Medicine*, 2017. URL https://vpa.vic.gov.au/strategy-guidelines/plan-melbourne/.

[54] N. Corbett. Small is beautiful: Planning for a post-Covid world. *Transforming Cities*, 2020. URL https://www.transformingcities.co.uk/small-is-beautiful-planning-for-a-post-coved-world/.

[55] Villerías Salinas, G. S., Nochebuena, and A. Uriostegui Flores. Análisis espacial de vulnerabilidad y riesgo en salud por COVID-19 en el estado de Guerrero, México. Posición. Análisis geográfico del COVID-19. 2020.

[56] S Michelle Driedger, Anita Kothari, Jason Morrison, Michael Sawada, Eric J Crighton, and Ian D Graham. Correction: Using participatory design to develop (public) health decision support systems through gis. *International Journal of Health Geographics*, page 53, 2007. URL https://ij-healthgeographics.biomedcentral.com/articles/10.1186/1476-072X-6-53.

[57] Google. Google Community Reports. 2020. URL https://www.google.com/covid19/mobility/.

[58] Mario Coccia. Factors determining the diffusion of covid-19 and suggested strategy to prevent future accelerated viral infectivity similar to covid. *Science of the Total Environment*, 2020. doi: 10.1016/j.scitotenv.2020.138474.

[59] Kim Dovey and Elek Pafka. What is walkability? The urban dma. *Urban studies*, 2020. doi: 10.1177/0042098018819727.

[60] R. Marino Zamudio. Assessing the impact of urban form on the energy consumption and Green House Gas (GHG) emissions in Metropolitan Melbourne. *PhD Thesis, Universidad de Melbourne, Melbourne*, 2020. URL https://minerva-access.unimelb.edu.au/handle/11343/241479.

[61] Ayyoob Sharifi. A critical review of selected tools for assessing community resilience. *Ecological Indicators*, pages 629–647, 2016. doi: 10.1016/j.ecolind.2016.05.023.

[62] Harvard Gazzete. Strong signals: Study findings support use of county-level cell phone location data as tool to estimate future trends of the COVID-19 pandemic. 2020. URL https://news.harvard.edu/gazette/story/2020/08/cell-phone-location-data-can-help-monitor-covid-19-rates/.

29

Use of Geospatial Information and Technologies in Understanding the COVID-19 Pandemic in Canada: Examples and Critical Discussion

David J. Coleman and Prashant Shukle

Despite the very uneven distribution and intensity of the spread of COVID-19 in different regions – and considering highly decentralised responsibilities for health care, and shared federal and provincial leadership for national emergency response coordination – Canada has been able to ensure a reasonably effective and well-coordinated response. All Canadian provinces and territories now have data driven dashboards or geospatial tools that highlight the incidence of COVID-19 in their respective jurisdictions. After a number of early independent development initiatives sponsored by different provinces, a nationally-endorsed, geospatially-enabled exposure notification app for cellphones was publicly released at the end of July. While supportive of the overall efforts under difficult circumstances, the authors suggest that specific responses could be improved if proactive work is done to share technology and data within the framework of national pandemic or disaster plans. As well, it would be valuable to ensure that the geospatial tools employed and data collected continue to be used as the public-sector focus shifts from pandemic response to economic recovery. Strong leadership and high levels of both national and international cooperation will be required to address these improvements.

29.1 Introduction

As of early September 2020, the spread of COVID-19 still varies significantly across Canada. Some provinces such as British Columbia, Alberta, Ontario and especially Quebec experienced significantly higher impacts whereas other provinces and territories such as Manitoba, New Brunswick and Newfoundland & Labrador experienced much lower levels of social and economic disruption. Despite this highly asymmetrical national spread of a global pandemic, highly decentralised responsibilities for health care, and shared federal and provincial leadership for national emergency response coordination – Canada has been able to ensure a reasonably effective and well-coordinated response. Governance and a long history of cross-jurisdictional collaboration have been critical success factors for Canada and reliance on data and technology were key enablers.

This chapter provides a very brief introduction to how they were deployed in Canada's COVID-19 pandemic. After providing selected examples of technology-level responses that were employed, the authors highlight early "hits and misses" which can be observed at this stage of the pandemic in Canada. The authors conclude with a look to the future in terms of opportunities for further development and cooperation.

29.2 Context

29.2.1 History and extent of the COVID-19 Outbreak in Canada

Figure 29.1 is a political map showing Canada's provinces and territories. Detailed timelines of events surrounding the COVID-19 outbreak in Canada may be found at Public Health Canada [1] and the Canadian Press [2]. Very early in 2020, as information became available, Canadian efforts moved from a pragmatic "wait and see" approach to one of increased proactivity. By January 25, Canada's first case of COVID-19 was declared. Canada's Public Health Agency activated its Health Operations Centre and triggered Canada's Federal/ Provincial/ Territorial Public Health Response Plan for Biological Events [3]. Thousands of families were affected in the months to come: Prime Minister Trudeau announced on March 12 that he himself was self-isolating as his wife had tested positive for COVID 19. By September 6, 2020, almost 133,000 cases of the virus and 9145 deaths had been confirmed nationally (Public Health Canada, 2020b). Relative numbers of cases varied widely across the country, with three provinces in particular (Québec, Alberta and Ontario) accounting for a disproportionately high rate of those cases (Figure 29.2).

FIGURE 29.1
Map of Canada's Provinces and Territories [4]

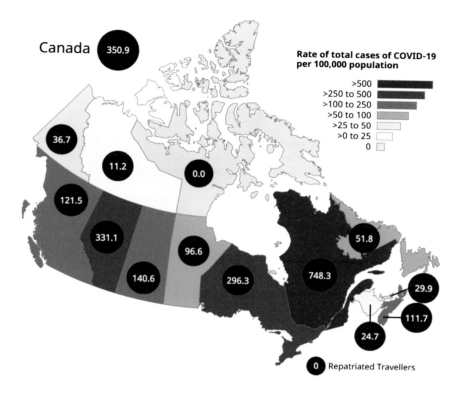

FIGURE 29.2

Rate of Confirmed Cases of COVID-19 per 100,000 population by Province as of September 6, 2020 [5]

No single factor accounts for the differences in the relative rate of cases in different provinces. Clearly the effects were greatest in large metropolitan centres, but that is only part of the picture. The high number of outbreaks in (especially) Nursing Homes and Seniors Care residences accounted for many of the cases found even in more sparsely populated provinces like Nova Scotia. Similarly, cities with busy international airports typically had higher incidence rates than those found elsewhere.

29.2.2 Federal/Provincial Issues and Reactions

Constitutionally, while Canada's federal government provides nation-wide leadership and coordination across all 14 jurisdictions in a national emergency (such as a global pandemic), each provincial government is responsible for adapting and implementing its own regional or local specific emergency management plan. Federal authorities are also required to provide 2-way communication with all provinces and territories when coordinating the influx of returning citizens and international travellers who are exiting or entering the country at the more than 140 land border crossings, 14 international airports, and over 550 port facilities that play a strategic role in Canada's goods and services supply chain.

Approximately 80% of Canadians live within 160 kilometres miles of the Canada – United States border. The other 20% of the population resides in the remaining land mass that stretches a further 5300 kilometres north. If there was ever a crisis requiring an understanding of location and its relation to human health – this was it.

29.3   Institutional and Technical Responses

Interestingly, the first capabilities to which Canadians turned were not geospatial in nature. Rather, governments at all levels relied upon institutional responsiveness and the reach of television, radio, social media, and newspapers. Depending on real-time events coupled with legacy economic and social influences in each province, each provincial government responded to their specific regional and local realities.

Communication strategies leveraged the power of a captive audience and the fact that 93% of Canadian adults are reached by television each week. To an impressive and unusual extent, federal, provincial and even (in major cities) municipal governments aligned to provide messaging that was overwhelmingly consistent, uniform, and readily available. Data initially focussed on the numbers of cases, the spread of the disease and the ongoing provision of expert advice and opinion. From March through May 2020, each provincial premier hosted daily news conferences that were televised on national and local media, usually following the Prime Minister of Canada who conducted his daily briefing for all Canadians. In the same sessions, expert senior public health authorities provided extensive information concerning the impacts, spread, and efforts at addressing COVID-19 in every federal, provincial and territorial jurisdiction.

Through different media channels, Canadians were urged strongly and consistently to: follow specific distancing and masking protocols, adopt telework arrangements, stay quarantined, and minimise exposure to each other by staying at home unless required. Given a tendency towards deference to authority and trust in governments, Canadians overwhelmingly adopted stringent health protocols.

29.3.1   "Dashboard" Services

To minimise speculation and conspiracy theorizing, all major political leaders in Canada threw their support behind expert management of the crisis. All governments established COVID-19 specific websites with extensive information and data about the impacts and preventative measures. For example, the Government of Canada released "Get Updates on COVID-19" a web-based email service that provides subscribers with critical information related to the pandemic. Developed by Health Canada, the Canadian Digital Service and Service Canada, the service ensured that those Canadians who subscribed would get authoritative and institutionally valid content through the Government of Canada website. Another application "ArriveCan", developed by the Canadian Border Services Agency and the Public Health Agency of Canada, allowed digitization of returning traveller information to help manage 14-day isolation information periods, including identification of whether the travellers have quarantine accommodations.

Baranovskiy et al. [6] offer an excellent early discussion of the difficulties in accessing, and organizing Canadian public datasets in order to create easy to understand thematic maps and charts that track the spread of COVID across the country. With "Made-in-Canada" geospatial solutions being initially slow off the mark, global substitutes were employed by national and local media outlets. For example, the John Hopkins Coronavirus Resource Center[1] provided a very effective dashboard highlighting global cases, detailed U.S. caseloads, and other visualisations such as timelines and critical trends such as mortality rates. Another exceptional visualisation tool used by Canadian sources came from the Financial Times[2], whose coronavirus data was used to illustrate not just the vectors and incidence of COVID-19 but also the economic impacts and shocks of the pandemic on global and national economies. Finally, the "COVID-19 Case Data Explorer" developed and maintained by Esri Canada [7] offers a very detailed up-to-date statistics at national, provincial and, in some cases, local health district levels.

It was not until May 2020 when the Government of Canada unveiled its first geospatially enabled dashboard which resulted from a shared collaboration between the Public Health Agency of Canada,

---

[1] See https://coronavirus.jhu.edu/map.html
[2] See https://on.ft.com/3d32Y1Z

Statistics Canada, and Natural Resources Canada[3]. The dashboard, like that provided by Johns Hopkins, was powered by ESRI GIS capabilities and drew upon Government of Canada data and technology. Added visualisations included COVID in the world, a situational awareness dashboard visualising provincial and territorial data and other economic and demographic indicators[4]. All Canadian provinces and territories now have data driven dashboards or geospatial tools that highlight the incidence of COVID-19 in their respective jurisdictions.

29.3.2   Geospatial Monitoring and Analysis – Contact Tracing

Contact tracing is "...the process of identifying, assessing, and managing people who have been exposed to a disease to prevent onward transmission" [8]. Public health agencies have long employed the tracing the contacts of infected individuals (and then their contacts in turn) in order to inform policies and practices which reduce infections in the population. Digital contact tracing today relies on positioning and tracking capabilities of (primarily) mobile personal devices in order to determine contact between a given infected patient and the device user.

Different countries have adopted different technical approaches and sometimes conflicting guiding philosophies to digital contact tracing. There is considerable debate on the user population-base requirements necessary to ensure effective contact tracing as well as the attendant privacy and security implications to individual citizens using contact tracing apps [9, 10].

Exposure notification applications rely on the same basic technology but purports to offer greater privacy protection to individual users [11]. Exposure notification apps notify you if you have been near someone who later tested positive for COVID-19. By comparison, contact tracing apps let people log their location and then share it (voluntarily or involuntarily) with public health authorities.

Through April-May 2020, Canada saw multiple efforts carried out by independent provincial governments in Alberta, Newfoundland & Labrador, Ontario, Manitoba, Saskatchewan and New Brunswick to either procure or develop in-house their own apps to support "exposure notification" [12].

Most of these initiatives intended to incorporate Bluetooth technology provided by Apple and Google. However, to avoid duplication and confusion, those companies made it clear they preferred supporting one nationally-endorsed app rather than many different regional ones [13]. The federally-funded COVID Alert app development project was led by the Canadian Digital Service and being undertaken in cooperation with partners from the Ontario Provincial Government and with help from volunteers from the commercial technology firm Shopify [14]. While originally expected to be rolled out by July 1, 2020, unexpected issues in refinement and testing delayed the national app's introduction until July 31, 2020 – and even then its reception was mixed [15].

From an institutional perspective, widespread public and commercial interest in COVID-19 related contact tracing apps quickly sparked concerns from government Privacy Commissioners and citizen interest groups alike across Canada. Two institutional responses provided early and very useful contributions to this debate. In April 2020, the Office of the Privacy Commissioner of Canada issued an assessment framework [16] intended to "...assist government institutions faced with responding to the COVID-19 crisis, and help organizations subject to federal privacy laws understand their privacy-related obligations during the pandemic". This framework was followed the next month with a more extensive Joint Statement by Federal, Provincial and Territorial Privacy Commissioners articulating their shared position on privacy principles for contact tracing and exposure notification [17].

Given the engagement of the Privacy Commissioner of Canada and other key geospatial departments such as Natural Resources Canada – concerns for individual privacy and protection directed the final application design to utilise Bluetooth to exchange random codes with nearby phones that also have the app involved. If someone within the proximate areas scanned by the phones later tests positive for COVID-19 they are to entire a key or code into the app. If any individual has spent more than 15 minutes and less than the mandated 2 metres apart from the

---

[3]See https://health-infobase.canada.ca/covid-19/
[4]https://health-infobase.canada.ca/covid-19/visual-data-gallery/

infected individual they will be notified. It should be noted that this app will not provide location, names, addresses, places, the time of contact or any health information to anonymise and protect the health information of Canadians.

29.4   Discussion

The "purpose-built" development of the new Canadian Government geospatial dashboard devoted specifically to COVID-19 tracking is notable for two reasons. First, it took well over 3 months for the relevant data and tools on the new dashboard to be configured and launched publicly. At the same time, the Government of Canada already had its own Federal Geospatial Platform [18] as an enterprise wide geospatial capability – one that had been highly touted as one of the Government of Canada's most successful data and technology initiatives. In the authors' opinion, this lack of responsiveness and subsequent duplication requires further study. Second, the time lag in preparing Canadian data dashboards suggests a gap in the institutionally driven pandemic Response Plan. Although this Plan had clearly undergone significant consultations and trial runs beforehand, it suggests the need for greater advance planning to reduce this time lag for data loading in the future.

As well, the authors look forward to seeing reports on the use of geospatially-enabled dashboards and exposure notification *for operational modelling purposes in Canada* through different stages of the pandemic. A significant amount of relevant health data on the spread and incidence of the disease may already be available to public authorities in geospatial and analysis-ready formats, but its veracity is still unclear. While we appreciate there are real and significant difficulties in planning and conducting such analyses effectively [19, 20], critical assessments of examples and lessons learned in this regard will be extremely valuable to the international community. Similarly, there has been no documentation yet on the impact and use of that geospatial data for economic and health recovery in Canada. Geospatially-enabled analysis of supply chains, detailed economic analyses at local levels, and sentiment analyses of citizens in hardest hit areas are all within the grasp of the technology of today. The authors look forward to seeing – hopefully soon – work undertaken in this regard as well.

29.5   Towards the Future

Geography – in particular, the very small number of densely-populated large metropolitan areas in relation to its vast area – has played a key role in Canada's relative success in containing the COVD-19 pandemic. Still, if the number of confirmed cases and mortality statistics are any indication, Canadian responses to the COVID-19 pandemic have been relatively well managed and of the "middle of the pack" variety. While new apps have been developed, websites built, and a variety of data disseminated to citizens, the first priority was clearly to use mass media to communicate information and expert advice in order to ensure that citizens were protected from the effects of COVID-19 and that the general population benefitted from the mitigation of any spread.

That said, the issues highlighted earlier do present significant institutional and technology-development opportunities in Canada.

First, most jurisdictions could respond more quickly if proactive work is done to share technology and data within the framework of national pandemic or disaster plans. Critical questions highlighting which data are essential to report and how should form a critical element of a clear data strategy in each plan.

Second, these pandemic plans should also focus on the recovery – it will be essential to understand how the health recovery is progressing alongside an economic recovery, and key social, environmental and health indicators from national to local perspective would be critical to a well managed and staged set of economic and social policy interventions.

Finally, as we move further away from any pandemic or crisis, there is a clear need to ensure that tools and data enabling pandemic response are transformed and sustainably utilised for the next set of crises that depend on geospatial data.

Global readiness depends on long term vigilance. Leadership and international cooperation will be required in the GGIM academic community and well beyond in order to ensure all nations are able to attain the necessary levels of technical and data readiness.

References

[1] Public Health Canada. History section, Coronavirus disease (COVID-19): Outbreak update. 2020. https://www.canada.ca/en/public-health/services/diseases/2019-novel-coronavirus-infection.html Last accessed 30 June 2020.

[2] Canadian Press. A timeline of events in Canada's fight against COVID-19. 2020. https://www.thestar.com/news/canada/2020/06/18/a-timeline-of-events-in-canadas-fight-against-covid-19.html Last accessed 22 July 2020.

[3] Public Health Canada. Federal/Provincial/Territorial Public Health Response Plan for Biological Events. 2018. https://www.canada.ca/en/public-health/services/emergency-preparedness/public-health-response-plan-biological-events.html Last accessed 22 July 2020.

[4] E.P. Anthony. Map of Canada – by E Pluribus Anthony, transferred to Wikimedia Commons by Kaveh (log), optimised by Andrew pmk. - Own work, Public Domain. 2006. URL https://commons.wikimedia.org/w/index.php?curid=844714. Last accessed 7 September 2020.

[5] Public Health Canada. Current Situation section, Coronavirus disease (COVID-19): Outbreak update. 2020. Map Generated Courtesy of Public Health Canada Web Mapping Site https://health-infobase.canada.ca/covid-19/dashboard/.

[6] Peter Baranovskiy, Ken Coates, and Carin Holroyd. "Designing COVID-19 Data Tools". Part of the JSGS Policy Briefs COVID-19 Series: From Crisis to Recovery, Johnson Shoyama Graduate School of Public Policy, University of Saskatchewan, Saskatoon, SK, Canada. 2020. https://www.schoolofpublicpolicy.sk.ca/research/publications/policy-brief/designing-covid-19-data-tools.php Last accessed 7 September 2020.

[7] Esri Canada. COVID-19 Case Data Explorer. 2020. https://bit.ly/34zmuPN Last accessed 7 September 2020.

[8] World Health Organization. Contact tracing on the context of COVID-19. Interim Guidance Document, Reference No. WHO/2019-nCoV/Contact_Tracing/2020.1. 2020. https://www.who.int/publications/i/item/contact-tracing-in-the-context-of-covid-19 Last accessed 30 June 2020.

[9] Robert A. Kleinman and Colin Merkel. Digital contact tracing for COVID-19. *CMAJ*, 192(24):E653–E656, 2020. doi: https://doi.org/10.1503/cmaj.200922.

[10] Jeffrey Kahn and Johns Hopkins Project on Ethics and Governance of Digital Contact Tracing Technologies. *Digital Contact Tracing for Pandemic Response: Ethics and Governance Guidance*. Johns Hopkins University Press, 2020. https://muse.jhu.edu/book/75831 Last accessed 30 June 2020.

[11] Caroline Haskins. Apple and Google's Coronavirus Tech Won't Actually Do Contact Tracing. Here's Why Exposure Notification Is Different. *Buzzfeed News*, 20 May 2020. https://www.buzzfeednews.com/article/carolinehaskins1/what-are-exposure-notifications-contact-tracing-how-are Last accessed 30 July 2020.

[12] Ruth Promislow, Michael Whitt, and Stephen Burns. COVID-19 and Contact-Tracing Apps in Canada. *Blog entry. Bennett Jones LLP*, 2020. https://www.bennettjones.com/Blogs-Section/COVID-19-and-Contact-Tracing-Apps-in-Canada Last accessed 22 June 2020.

[13] Catharine Tunney. Ottawa looking to endorse 1 coronavirus contact tracing app for the whole nation. *Online news article, Canadian Broadcasting Corporation, Ottawa, Canada*, 2020. https://www.cbc.ca/news/politics/trudeau-app-contact-tracing-1.5580184 Last accessed 22 May 2020.

[14] Government of Canada. Download COVID Alert Today. 2020. https://www.canada.ca/en/public-health/services/diseases/coronavirus-disease-covid-19/covid-alert.html Last accessed 7 September 2020.

[15] Thomas Daigle. Misconceptions persist about effectiveness and privacy of Canada's COVID Alert app. *CBC News, Toronto, Canada*, 2020. https://www.cbc.ca/news/technology/covid-19-alert-app-myths-privacy-1.5684089 Last accessed 7 September 2020.

392   *Understanding the COVID-19 Pandemic in Canada*

[16] Privacy Commissioner. A Framework for the Government of Canada to Assess Privacy-Impactful Initiatives in Response to COVID-19. *Office of the Privacy Commissioner of Canada*, 2020. https://www.priv.gc.ca/en/privacy-topics/health-genetic-and-other-body-information/health-emergencies/fw_covid/ Last accessed 30 June 2020.

[17] Privacy Commissioner. "Supporting public health, building public trust: Privacy principles for contact tracing and similar apps". A Joint Statement by Federal, Provincial and Territorial Privacy Commissioners. *Office of the Privacy Commissioner of Canada*, 2020. https://www.priv.gc.ca/en/opc-news/speeches/2020/s-d_20200507/ Last accessed 30 June 2020.

[18] Government of Canada. Federal Geospatial Platform. 2020. https://www.nrcan.gc.ca/science-data/science-research/earth-sciences/geomatics/canadas-spatial-data-infrastruct/geospatial-communities-canada-ce/federal-geospatial-platform/11031 Last accessed 22 July 2020.

[19] Chenghu Zhou, Fenzhen Su, Tao Pei, An Zhang, Yunyan Du, Bin Luo, Zhidong Cao, Juanle Wang, Wen Yuan, Yunqiang Zhu, Ci Song, Jie Chen, Jun Xu, Fujia Li, Ting Ma, Lili Jiang, Fengqin Yan, Jiawei Yi, Yunfeng Hu, Yilan Liao, and Han Xiao. COVID-19: Challenges to GIS with Big Data. *Geography and Sustainability*, 1(1):77 – 87, 2020. ISSN 2666-6839. doi: https://doi.org/10.1016/j.geosus.2020.03.005. URL http://www.sciencedirect.com/science/article/pii/S2666683920300092.

[20] Kenneth Field. Mapping coronavirus, responsibly. *ArcGIS Blog*, 2020. https://www.esri.com/arcgis-blog/products/product/mapping/mapping-coronavirus-responsibly/ Last accessed 30 June 2020.

30

Geospatial Intelligence in Dealing with COVID-19 Challenges in Czechia

Milan Konecny, Jiri Hladik, Jiri Bouchal, Lukas Herman and Tomas Reznik

This chapter deals with aspects of geospatial support to manage COVID-19 in Czechia. The first three cases of the disease were confirmed on March 1, 2020. Geospatial intelligence has played an important role in analysing and predicting the spread of the disease, in designing and optimizing measures against it, and in reducing harm. Three categories of applications were identified and described when following the conducted analysis of the content and purpose of COVID-19-related geospatial applications and solutions. The first, the visual analytics of COVID-19-related health statistics follows the concept of multiple coordinated views and dynamic queries. This category of applications uses various official or semi-official sources of geospatial data and their presentation in interactive web maps. The second, different tracking applications or tools for analysis of people's movement and identification of risky contacts was implemented. In the Czechia, these are for example eRouska mobile application and movement tracking in the Mapy.cz application. The third category represents decision support systems for public administration, emergency services and volunteers. Example of this category is the interactive map of registered volunteers used by coordination centre established by Masaryk University (MUNI) in Brno, Czechia. The advantages, limitations, and possible future directions of the mentioned applications of geospatial intelligence are discussed in the conclusions.

30.1   Introduction

The United Nations Global Geospatial Information Management (U.N. GGIM), which includes the core idea of creating a global geospatial integrative data ecosystem with potential applications in various situations (incl. pandemic) and on all geographical levels (incl. local and regional), is fundamentally based on the Spatial Data Infrastructure (SDI) concept. The COVID-19 pandemic has again highlighted the need of societies to deal with various kinds of data and to enrich and integrate them "on-line" or "near-online". One of the necessary preconditions is to analyse data fast and provide visual representations such as digital maps and other types of models. Geospatial intelligence proved itself to be an useful bridge combining the already existing authoritative spatial data (as in the Infrastructure for Spatial Information in the European Community - INSPIRE and national SDIs) with referenced health information regularly collected by special governmental institutions (in Czechia, this is e.g. the Institute for Health Information and Statistics - IHIS) or obtained by everyday measurements based on COVID-19 testing among various population groups and regions of Czechia. This paper describes theoretical and practical approaches based on state-of-the-art geospatial intelligence.

Based on the analysis of the content and purpose of existing and newly emerging geospatial applications and solutions [1–3], the authors of this paper have integrated three approaches to improve dealing with COVID-19-related problems:

- Visual analytics of COVID-19-related health statistics,

- Tracking and analysis of people's movement and identification of risky contacts, and

- Decision support systems for public administration, emergency services and volunteers.

30.2   Visual Analytics of COVID-19-related Health Statistics in Czechia

The main goal of visual analytics is to provide interactivity through utilizing the concept of multiple coordinated views and dynamic queries to emphasize the impact of changes in analysed phenomena. A number of applications have been developed around the world for the visual analysis of geospatial data on the spread of COVID-19 [1–3]. Many of these applications are global and use data from the World Health Organization (WHO). Several applications use data from Johns Hopkins University in Maryland; this data source is created by combining several primary data sets (such as WHO) by supplementing them with additional information. In Czechia, applications that visualise global data have also been developed alongside visualisations built to analyse domestic data. Those focused on Czechia primarily use the data provided by the Ministry of Health of the Czech Republic, as well as the IHIS data, which are included. Data collection process includes an aggregation of data from individual Regional Public Health Stations. These data are freely available [3].

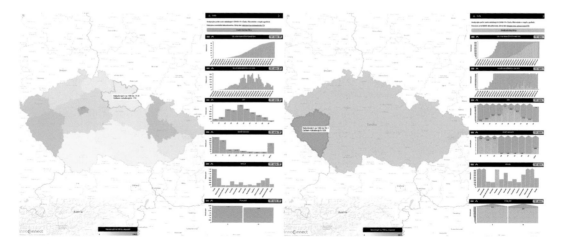

FIGURE 30.1

An interactive map of COVID-19 in Czechia[*]. Note: choropleth maps show the number of infected per 100 thousand inhabitants. Graphs in columns are used to select according to the infected persons' age, region and gender, or according to the date and source country (if infected abroad) of the infection. The map on the left shows the overall situation in Czechia; the situation in the Pilsen Region is displayed on the right.

[*] *http://mapa-koronavirus.innoconnect.net*

A map of COVID-19 spread in Czechia[1] is an example of this kind of visual analytics application.

---

[1] https://mapa-koronavirus.innoconnect.net/

The map allows to analyse the number of people infected by COVID-19 through implementing multiple linked views to present the data. Each of the views (map and charts) enables different interactions, such as brushing, relationship analysis, and filtering that trigger an instant update of the other views. Different combinations of filters can be applied for deeper insights, for instance by selecting a single source country of infection: the distribution of cases originating in that country is then visualised according to time, region, gender and age (Figure 30.1). It is also possible to select people over 70 years of age as a group and highlight the regions with the highest number of infected senior citizens. These functionalities are implemented on top of the WebGLayer open source library[2].

30.3   Tracking and Analysis of People's Movement and Determination of Risky Contacts

The application and procedures described in this section form the technological basis for the deployment of the "smart quarantine system". The main part of this system in Czechia consists in creating "memory maps" based on processing of an individual's movement data obtained from the relevant mobile operator. There are two facts that need to be emphasized. The individual must agree to data processing and no data belonging to any other persons are used in the process. The aim is, therefore, to help the person remember all the places he or she visited and then identify all people (s)he came into contact with. The use of memory maps is supplemented by other voluntary technologies such as the eRouska (eMask in English) mobile application[3] and movement tracking in the Mapy.cz application[4].

eRouska is a mobile application for smartphones that helps authorized officers from Regional Public Health Stations to easily and quickly identify people with whom an infected person came into contact with and who are therefore also potentially at risk of infection. The application uses Bluetooth and records close contact with other users of the application. Tracking within Mapy.cz uses location history data collected by mobile devices. Thanks to location sharing, an increased probability of infection can be calculated; this probability is determined on the basis of whether the observed person stayed in the same place for a significant period of time as a person who has tested positive for COVID-19. By July 2020, 1.4 million users have volunteered to share their location data using the Mapy.cz application (out of the total of 10.7 million inhabitants of Czechia).

The aforementioned tracking data from mobile phones can also be used to improve the population estimates in certain areas, e.g. due to the increased incidence of COVID-19 in these areas. Kubicek et al. [4] describe a proof-of-concept application of tracking data from mobile phones in a crisis management context. A similar approach can also be used in the future to improve the estimates of current population in smaller areas affected by COVID-19 in order to facilitate closure planning or to plan services.

30.4   Decision Support Systems for Public Administration, Emergency Services and Volunteers

Geospatial applications can also serve as a platform for volunteers, community groups and those who need help in connecting with each other, as well as for local authorities and individuals or groups of volunteers matching specific locations and other criteria. Maps can display information and help in navigation to hospitals, clinics, grocery stores or pharmacies, places where personal protective

---

[2]http://webglayer.org/
[3]https://erouska.cz/en
[4]https://napoveda.seznam.cz/en/mapy/covid-19/

equipment can be purchased and similar. In affected areas, this information and connections could improve the organization of assistive services and thus potentially save lives.

Masaryk University (MUNI) in Brno, Czechia, has established a coordination center for volunteers right at the beginning of the COVID-19 crisis[5]. The help offered consisted mostly in the manufacture of face masks, food or medicine delivery to vulnerable people, babysitting, teaching assistance and similar. Both volunteers and requests for help and assistance were collected through online forms, e-mails and phone calls. All data thus obtained included geospatial information; Geographic Information System (GIS) support has been introduced across all these activities to increase the coordination center's efficiency.

An interactive web map based on the Leaflet library[6] has been established to display the location of all registered volunteers. The map also features browsing by attributes and filtering and address search to help operators locate people who are asking for help and to assign a suitable volunteer nearby (Figure 30.2). Input data from Excel sheets were processed using a Python script. To obtain geographic information from the addresses provided, two geocoding services are used: the national Registry of Territorial Identification, Addresses and Real Estate – RUIAN geocoding service[7] operated by the Czech Office for Surveying, Mapping and Cadastre on the one hand, and the geocoding service provided by the Czech online and mobile map application Mapy.cz[8] developed by the private company Seznam.cz on the other hand. The output point dataset was visualized using Leaflet.markercluster plugin[9]. The data processing script was executed automatically every 10 minutes to keep the data in the application up-to-date.

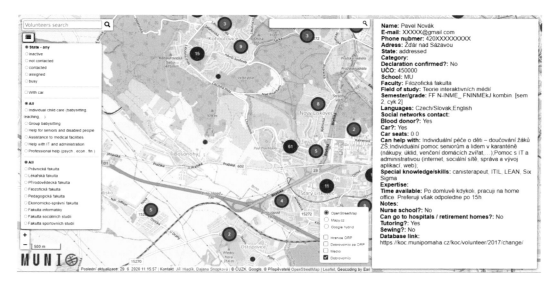

FIGURE 30.2

An interactive map of registered volunteers. Note: elements on the left contain a search bar and data filtering; the right panel contains information on the selected volunteer.

A similar application was established for public use in order to promote the activities of the coordination center and, simultaneously, to invite more help-seekers by providing information on available volunteers nearby. To ensure protection of the volunteers' privacy, the amount of sensitive information was reduced, location data were anonymized and aggregated. The internal version of the map of volunteers was used by 30 people, usually 7 workers per day. Overall, more than 4,000 volunteers have registered, and the center has successfully resolved 2,405 requests for help. The

---

[5]https://munipomaha.cz/en/i-need-help

[6]https://leafletjs.com/

[7]http://ags.cuzk.cz/arcgis/rest/services/RUIAN/Vyhledavaci_sluzba_nad_daty_RUIAN/MapServer

[8]https://api.mapy.cz/geocode

[9]https://github.com/Leaflet/Leaflet.markercluster

map has also helped coordinate efforts with other volunteer groups where they had a shortage of people.

30.5   Conclusions and Discussion

Geospatial information has been an irreplaceable tool across the activities to combat the COVID-19 pandemic in Czechia, regardless of whether the particular application has been provided centrally by the government/public administration, the private sector and/or volunteer activities. Location information, mapping and GIS tools have been used at all stages, from preparedness in areas without infected persons, through response at hotspot areas, to mitigation across the whole country. Open source as well as customized national commercial products have been used with similar frequency. For such purposes, both, national map data sources/registries and open data like OpenStreetMap are combined.

Several applications have been created quickly and spontaneously, many of them initially containing several cartographic mistakes or shortcomings that were later gradually corrected. A typical shortcoming was, for example, the use of a choropleth map to display the absolute number of infected people instead of showing a share of the infected in the population, or using proportional map symbols. Geospatial applications visualizing COVID-19-related health statistics have also suffered from data quality issues such as different data reporting practices in different regions. Potentially, data errors can also occur in processing or in combining input data from different sources.

This use of Geospatial Intelligence based on a combination of the three approaches in dealing with the COVID-19 pandemic represents one of many possibilities. It can also be applied in other crisis situations, other cities, countries and continents if high-quality geospatial data are available.

The tasks related to the COVID-19 pandemic were in public administration and public health bodies firstly addressed via spreadsheets, notes etc. Geospatial intelligence was employed in early stages of the pandemic as it resulted in such bodies in (1) significantly faster processing, (2) more complex tasks, (3) sophisticated predictions and (4) shortening the supply chain. All these benefits are demonstrated during the second wave of the COVID-19 pandemic[10] that is even stronger than the first wave in spring 2020.

Acknowledgement

This research was supported from the European Union's Horizon 2020 research and innovation programme under grant agreement No 769608 titled Policy Development based on Advanced Geospatial Data Analytics and Visualisation (PoliVisu).

References

[1] Maged N. Kamel Boulos and Estella M. Geraghty. Geographical tracking and mapping of coronavirus disease covid-19/severe acute respiratory syndrome coronavirus 2 (sars-cov-2) epidemic and associated events around the world: how 21st century gis technologies are supporting the global fight against outbreaks and epidemics. *International Journal of Health Geographics*, 19(1):8, Mar 2020. ISSN 1476-072X. doi: 10.1186/s12942-020-00202-8.

---

[10]As witnessed in the Czechia from the end of August 2020.

[2] Amy L. Griffin. Trustworthy maps. *Journal of Spatial Information Science*, 2020(20):5–19, 2020. ISSN 1948-660X. doi: 10.5311/JOSIS.2020.20.654.

[3] Vit Pászto, Jaroslav Burian, and Karel Macku. Covid-19 data sources: Evaluation of map applications and analysis of behaviour changes in europe's population. *Geografie (Utrecht)*, 125(2):171–209, 2020. doi: https://doi.org/10.37040/geografie2020125020171.

[4] Petr Kubíček, Milan Konečný, Zdeněk Stachoň, Jie Shen, Lukáš Herman, Tomáš Řezník, Karel Staněk, Radim Štampach, and Šimon Leitgeb. Population distribution modelling at fine spatio-temporal scale based on mobile phone data. *International Journal of Digital Earth*, 12(11):1319–1340, 2019. doi: 10.1080/17538947.2018.1548654.

31

COVID-19 in France: A Multiphase and Multidimensional Approach to a Complex Societal Imbalance

Carmen Martin and François Pérès

This chapter focuses on the effects of the pandemic in France. The first part describes the phased evolution of the perception and treatment of the virus in the first half of 2020. In the second part, a multidimensional analysis describes the societal impact of the health crisis and its negative and positive effects on France in general and, by analogy, in Europe and the world. The study first presents the temporal characteristics of the pandemic associated with the mix of scales, phase shifts, delays, inertia and the random and unpredictable dynamic nature of the crisis evolution. Secondly, a view qualified as functional, depicts the virus in relation to the different roles it played in terms of its capacity to reveal phenomena, accelerate dynamics, divide or reconcile communities together, bring about new behaviours, eliminate or restore weakened entities and generate a questioning of the very meaning of the existence of our societies' lifestyles.

31.1   Introduction

This chapter looks back on four months of exploration of this new world and the experimentation of life in the presence of a deadly virus. A first part deals with the factual nature of the events observed during the first six months of the crisis. An analytical and instantaneous vision of the situation in France is proposed in a second part. Two angles are considered, respectively approaching the temporal and functional views to describe the dynamic parameters characterising the evolution of the crisis and the role played by the virus in the envisaged societal upheavals[1].

31.2   Observation

31.2.1   Evolution of the Crisis, Health Measures, and Risk Perception

The Covid19 pandemic in France followed a phased process. Each of the process stages is to be brought closer to the level of risk perceived or proven by the population and its governing bodies (Figure 31.1)[2].

---

[1]Due to the uncertainties about the evolution of the crisis and the countermeasures imagined to contain its consequences, the sustainability of the ideas developed and the forecast data is not consolidated. Perhaps the future will deny or correct some of the forward-looking ideas or solutions reported here.

[2]This graph is only a snapshot of the evolution recorded during the first half of the crisis. At the time this chapter was written, the evolution of the pandemic was on a downward slope. However, many experts believe that a second wave should hit France at the end of the summer.

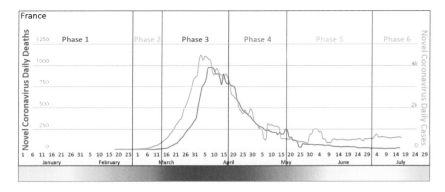

FIGURE 31.1
Graph of the Evolution of the Number of Cases and Deaths in France in the First Half of 2020

31.2.1.1   Phase 1: Observation and Denial - November 2019-February 2020

Even with the announcement by China of the discovery of a new Coronavirus by the Chinese authorities on January 1, 2020, France observes but is not worried [1]. Reinforced by the finally not very alarmist announcements of the World Health Organization, a feeling of indifference reigns, associated with a (false obviously) perception of invulnerability and a denial of the risks of contamination.

31.2.1.2   Phase 2: Awareness and Projection - Early March 2020

Even though the French generally trust their local health services, there is growing concern among the population. Debates are flourishing at all levels of decision-making, on masks usefulness as a protective barrier, on hydroxy-chloroquine effectiveness as a curative treatment, on the choice between distancing strategy and herd immunity [2]. On March 16 2020, the President announces "France is at war". The general confinement of the population is introduced.

31.2.1.3   Phase 3: Adaptation and Resignation. Mid-March to Mid-April

Except for a few derogatory measures, 67 million French people have to limit their movements to what is strictly necessary. The French are taking the full measure of the seriousness of the epidemic situation: 70% of those questioned consider that COVID-19 is particularly contagious [3]. In a volatile public opinion, the Covid-19 epidemic sharpens fear, rehabilitates the performative function of the presidential speech and unites the French around the measures taken by the executive branch.

31.2.1.4   Phase 4: Fatigue and Hope. Mid-April to Mid-May

The first month of confinement is well accepted, and the French (no doubt for fear of sanctions) adhere to the measures taken by the government. But, in France more than elsewhere, the credit given to leaders never lasts very long and, one month later, mistrust takes over with a 58% rate of dissatisfaction. Faced with this prolonged crisis and the executive's procrastination on several subjects (tests, masks, etc.), the confidence of the French people has not collapsed, but it has significantly eroded. Besides, in one month, the number of deaths rose from 150 to nearly 18,000 (Figure 31.2), which understandably cannot drive euphoria. The peak of contamination is reached between 6 and 10 April, and the epidemic begins to recede. The anticipated announcements of deconfinement and a date for its entry into force give new hope. The measures taken by the

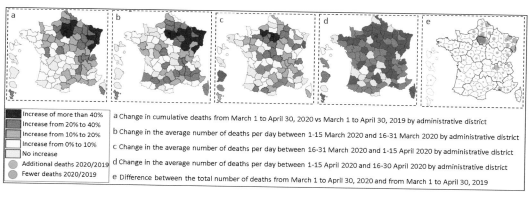

FIGURE 31.2

Spatial and Temporal Evolution of Mortality Linked to COVID 19 in France

executive to support short-time working and the social protection nets set up to help individuals and legal entities cushion (temporarily?) the effects of the health crisis, doubled in an economic depression.

31.2.1.5 Phase 5: Liberation and Concern Mid-May End June 2020

On May 7 2020, the end containment measures are officially announced for gradual implementation from May 11. The government policy is based on a three-pronged strategy: (i) living with the virus, (ii) acting progressively, (iii) adjusting locally. Indicators are established for the implementation of the various measures (reopening of schools, shops, public transport, residences for the elderly, places of worship, parks and gardens, beaches, cultural sites, etc.).

FIGURE 31.3

Spatial visualisation of the virus incidence rate indicator on May 7, 2020

These indicators indicate whether a department is classified as green, orange or red zone (Figure 31.3). They are based on the incidence rate of new cases accumulated daily over seven days, the virus reproduction factor, the occupancy rate of resuscitation beds by patients with COVID-19, the positivity rate of tests collected three days previously, and the number of tests performed. The deconfinement phase is a relief for a majority of French people. It is also a source of concern. Health authorities are worried, however, about the slackening observed at the end of the containment period and the feeling of a few that the war is won. Warnings are constantly being repeated to remind people that the virus is still circulating and that barrier gestures remain essential.

31.2.1.6   Phase 6: Learning and Release July 2020

Even if this number remains relatively constant, one still observes, in a somewhat irrational way, a downward trend in the systematic adoption of preventive measures. This decline in vigilance is undoubtedly linked to deconfinement which favours social interactions and makes it more challenging to adopt physical distancing measures. It is also related to the decrease in the number of hospitalisations and deaths, which may question the usefulness or relevance of maintaining the systematic adoption of these behaviours. (Figure 31.4). It should also be noted that among preventive measures, the wearing of masks is gradually becoming part of everyday life.

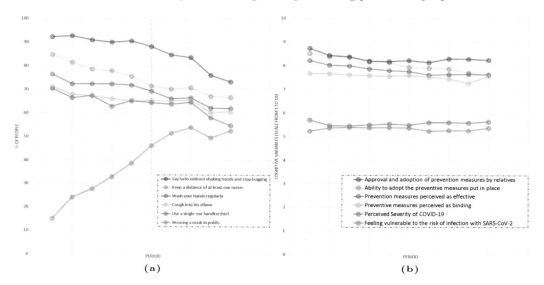

FIGURE 31.4
(a) Social Distancing and Barrier Gestures Application (b) Perception of Risk and Preventive Measures

31.2.2   Synthesis

The study of this phased process and the observed behaviour of the French population highlights the definition of risk, based on the exposure between a potentially vulnerable entity and a potentially dangerous event. The perception of risk requires being able to evaluate these different components (levels of vulnerability, danger and exposure), to aggregate them into a single measure and then to compare its value to a reference system capable of providing information on its level of criticality. The exercise is not simple, and very often, the perceived risk is not related to the real threat [4, 5].

Unable to refer to scientifically validated figures or statistics representative of their specific environment or lifestyle, the French have constructed their own indicators based on their interpretation of the signals received, mainly relayed by the media. Still, the distinction in risk assessment according to age groups combined with morbidity factors shows that the severity index is really taken into account in the perception of danger. On another level, the possible distortion between perceived risk and real threat can also be induced by a multiple relaxation risk. The probability of catching the virus is not equal to the likelihood of dying from it. Many people are asymptomatic and do not suffer the pangs of the disease they carry within them. If it does occur, it is usually mild and flu-like. If, however, a worsening is observed and hospitalisation is necessary, only a small proportion of patients will be transferred to intensive care. Here again, the chance of survival is high. In the end, the risk of death can be minimised by the various emergency exits along the path of the infected person.

31.3 Multidimensional Analysis

The analysis proposed in this paragraph, which is inevitably incomplete, focuses on a few particularities related to different dimensions, in particular those connected with the temporal, functional and sectoral views of the health crisis induced by the appearance of the virus.

31.3.1 Temporal View

Beyond the different chronological phases discussed in the observation paragraph, one of the major difficulties in the management of this health crisis can be explained by temporal factors [6]. Several phenomena appear to coexist in this respect. We detail them below.

31.3.1.1 Time Scale Mixtures

Two crises overlap: a health crisis with immediate effects and lethal consequences and an economic crisis with delayed impact and societal repercussions. The short-term solution aimed at annihilating the virus by confining the people, vectors of its spread, has proved its effectiveness in health terms but leads to economic and social disaster on a more distant horizon. Conversely, refusing to give in to the pandemic comes down to sacrificing thousands of people on the altar of growth and prosperity without any real control of the human cost generated. Both paths seem to be dead ends, and only a subtle compromise should make it possible to limit the damage. At the political level, there is also confusion. The short-term view aimed at keeping endangered businesses alive by rapidly releasing financial aid leads to indebtedness with perhaps postponed devastating consequences in economic terms. The political and the economic horizons differ, as do the time frames at the individual or collective scales.

31.3.1.2 Dephasing

Delayed effects are also very significant in the Coronavirus crisis. First of all, there is a natural delay between infection and symptom appearance or between the different stages of the pathology's evolution. Acting on this dephasing seems to be futile. However, some delays can be reduced due to the slow or delayed effects of political or medical strategies. These delays are due to a lack of knowledge of the pathogenic agents or the evolution of the disease. This is the case, for example, in the search for curative treatments (anti-viral drugs, steroid anti-inflammatory medications, triple therapy, etc.), the results of which are still pending because of incompressible development times but also because of regulatory complications associated with normative issues. Sources of delay may also be linked to a lack of logistical support.

In France, several controversies emerged concerning this issue. First of all, the obligation to wear a mask was declared ineffective by hazardous state communication. The delay in the application of this barrier gesture was, in fact, linked to a lack of masks and an inability to produce them on French soil at the required rate. The same observation could be made about the diagnosis procedure. Implementing virological or serological tests was delayed by the lack of available structures and material shortages. Another controversy was widely talked about, related to the delay (or even absence) of attention by care structures for older adults affected by the coronavirus in retirement homes due to a lack of hospital beds.

31.3.1.3   Space-Time Shift

The erratic spread of the virus highlights a two-speed process.

The circulation of the virus between continents or between countries was not immediate; at the level of the large blocks of contamination, South East Asia was first impacted. Europe was then affected with a delay of about two months. One month later, the United States was hit hard. A few weeks after, South America, Russia and India were in turn, overwhelmed.

When a region is affected, however, the spread can be very rapid, with cases of contamination that can increase at a rate corresponding to an $R_0=4$ (one person contaminates four others on average) and a number of daily cases increasing exponentially. In France, this discrepancy has been observed between regions. The Great East was first affected, then the Ile de France, the Hauts de France and Burgundy. The rest of the regions were spared overall. However, the paralysing effects of the pandemic affected all of France. The same measures were applied throughout the country. This spatial and temporal gap amplified the immediate effects of the crisis and contributed to the blocking of economies by desynchronisation of supply and demand in the framework of interregional or international industrial relations.

31.3.1.4   Inertia

The temporal view also concerns the economy [7]. While the cessation of a commercial or industrial activity may be rapid, recovery can sometimes be more complicated as it cannot be achieved alone and relies on the one hand on synchronisation with the upstream and downstream logistics chain and, of course, on the return of consumption and customers. The recovery, just like the start-up of a business, is likely to come up against the so-called "Bullwhip" phenomenon. This phenomenon, which is well known in production management, is generally initiated by the uncertainties inherent in the demand of each stakeholder in an unstable market. It leads to distortions between current needs and effectively committed production. In addition to the unnecessary increase (or reduction) in production and the associated additional logistics costs, it results in undesirable inertia related to the number of links in the supply chain and their reactivity in processing information (order taking) and in the production (delivery of goods or provision of services).

This inertia is all the more critical in a health crisis that the state of the partners involved in a supply chain is subject to a high uncertainty level (on the partner responsiveness but also the expected product quantity, itself depending on the pandemic evolution).

The launch in France of the manufacture of respirators is the most typical example of this. Companies that were not in the business (notably industrial groups in the automotive sector: PSA, Valeo and Schneider Electrique), commissioned to speed up the marketing of this medical equipment have been confronted with this phenomenon. The inertia induced by the start-up of this new activity combined with a lack of awareness of the need for respiratory assistance devices led, on the one hand, to significant delays in delivery and, on the other hand, to overproduction. The newly manufactured respirators were not needed anymore. The essential nature of the demand and the emergency logistics put in place to meet it eventually led to costly and prohibitive expenses without any return on investment or profitability.

31.3.1.5   Chaotic Dynamics

Even if day by day research is making progress and the state of knowledge is improving, the transmission factors and conditions necessary for the transmission of the virus remain poorly understood. Some variables seem to be preponderant (age, morbidity factors, etc.). Others require confirmation (gender, antibody generation, pollution, climate, etc.). It is difficult to explain, for the time being, the low level of contamination in Africa compared to South America, for example. The seasonality of the virus is not certain either. Has a periodic phenomenon been initiated requiring, like the flu, an annual vaccine? Is it, on the contrary, a "one-shot" cellular disorder caused by a natural or human-made accident? Virus mutation, improved detection techniques or advances in treatment are also likely to change the curves. The uncertain nature of all these factors makes it impossible to rationalise the dynamics of evolution and renders challenging to forecast the number of people infected and the projection in terms of expected mortality [8].

In France, the dynamics observed showed a radical effect of containment and barrier gestures in the spread reduction of the virus. Knowledge of the time constants: incubation (1 to 14 days), contagiousness (8 to 37 days) turned out to be accurate and in line with prognosis. What will happen when life returns to normal? What trajectory will the pandemic follow? At the time of writing, all is conjecture.

31.3.2 Functional View

This paragraph discusses the contributory role attributed to the coronavirus. For the most part, the effects of the pandemic are obviously deleterious and have resulted or will result in human and social (excess mortality, depression, domestic violence, school dropout), economic (corporate bankruptcies, debt) tragedies. Nevertheless, as a famous French expression says, "à quelque chose, malheur est bon" which means that however unpleasant an experience can be, you will probably learn from it. The appearance of the coronavirus does not deny the precept. Faced issues, new situations, lived experiences can be sources of inspiration and renewal. In this sense, and without erasing or compensating for the harmful effects of the pandemic, the health crisis can have a role to play and a beneficial character. These aspects are briefly described below. A synthesis in the form of a table is available (`https://tinyurl.com/covidappendix`); this presents a more comprehensive view of the contributory character of COVID 19 on nine major themes: Health Medicine / Economy Business Work / Ecology Sustainable development / Tourism Leisure Sports Culture / Education - Schools - Universities / Society - Lifestyles / Politics State / Justice / Science Technologies.

31.3.2.1 Detector, Scanner and Demonstrator Function

The appearance of the virus has had a significant role in confirming or highlighting the qualities and defects that were until then inconspicuous, or even invisible, of all our systems (immune protection, health management, etc.), organisations (political, industrial, etc.) or strategies (economic, environmental, social) [9]. In France, like a scanner, it has revealed unsuspected weaknesses or, on the contrary, hitherto unknown forms of resilience. It should be noted that the revelation of negative aspects is in itself something positive in that it allows us to ask ourselves questions in order to remedy them and thus offers indirect benefits.

We list below some of the main lessons revealed by the crisis in France:

- **Vital Importance of Public Service and Role of the State.** The vital and unconditional support of the state has marked a disassociation from purely liberal doctrines. Based on market self-regulation and individual self-management, these policies are proving unsuitable for identifying and implementing solutions based on collective and social utilities.

- **Highlighting a Need for National or, at the Very Least, European Sovereignty.** The lack of medicines, health equipment or the shutdown in logistics chains due to the outsourcing of markets has revealed in a patent manner the need to sustain on its soil the means and knowledge necessary to maintain industrial autonomy.

- **Central State Limitations and Administrative Burdens.** The uniformity of containment policies, the slowness observed in the implementation of directives descending from Paris to the regions have shown a need for decentralisation of decision-making, a policy more based on territorialisation and administrative simplification.

- **Impact of Pollution on Health and the Need for a More Environment-Oriented Policy.** While coronavirus has already claimed more than 30,000 victims, fine particles and nitrogen oxides are responsible for approximately 67,000 deaths (lung cancer, stroke, heart attack, ...) every year. The recovery plans devised for a new future must integrate this ecological dimension.

- **Preponderant Role of Feminised Professions in Crisis Management.** Carers, nurses, cashiers,... these often feminised and poorly paid jobs, found themselves in the front line and of vital importance. A pay rise for these professions and a rebalancing of skills within social categories are necessary.

31.3.2.2   Enabler, Trigger, Facilitator, Catalyst, Promoter, Accelerator Function

The pandemic facilitated the outbreak of many phenomena that could not have been observed or would not have developed so rapidly without the presence of the virus, its consequences and the solutions put in place to counter it [10–13]. This role as a catalyst has had consequences, often positive and sometimes negative, by creating the conditions necessary to promote new practices, encouraging the development of new activities and stimulating novel ideas or theories.

A non-exhaustive list of this almost chemical function assigned to the virus in France is provided below.

- **Accelerating the Development of Alternative Energy Vehicles.** The crisis seems to have precipitated environmental awareness and encouraged energy transition. In the automotive sector, manufacturers are favouring the hypothesis that the crisis could accelerate the spread of electric or hybrid models.

- **Enhancement of Scientific Output.** Coronavirus-related research has been boosted: publications, clinical trials, and modelling have increased to unprecedented proportions. However, biases have appeared in the development and results validation, as well as in the monitoring capacity required for the professional to process this surplus of knowledge.

- **Increase in Governance Mistrust and Crisis Communication.** The discredit of the institutional voice (politicians, scientists, media) accelerated during the crisis. Polemics about the effectiveness of treatments and barrier gestures fuelled suspicions of manipulation and lies.

- **Simplification of Labour Law.** MPs adopted the bill on various legislative measures related to the health crisis, which relaxes the rules governing relations between employers and employees. These changes, justified by the need to allow companies to adapt to the consequences of the recession, have however been criticised by the opposition.

- **Amplification of Conspiracy Theories.** "Citizen-investigators", extremist militants or populist leaders refer to scientific studies, often contradictory, in support of their sometimes collusion suspicions. These plot ideologues aim to criticise authority figures and use them to discredit theories hostile to their models which often remain unclear.

31.3.2.3   Unifier or Divider Function

COVID 19 has also contributed to bringing together or federating, previously distinct domains, based on the observation of common interests, behavioural similarities or structural affinities [14]. It has also favoured the reconciliation, sincere or opportunistic, of historically divided entities but reunited again around shared problems. Conversely, the pandemic has led to separations or divisions by highlighting imbalances in treatment, differences of opinion and distinct perceptions of the situations to be managed [15].

This role of matchmaker or splitter is illustrated in the following examples.

- **Convergence Between Pandemic and Climate Change.** The decline in activity induced by the crisis led a Stanford researcher to state that "reducing pollution in China probably saved twenty times more lives than those lost to the virus". Perhaps the demonstration that economic deceleration or decline would be strategies for the future.

- **Divergence Between Health Protection and Individual Freedom.** French experts have diverged on the technical solutions proposed to facilitate the identification of "contact cases" of the virus. The reliability of the technologies and their health effectiveness, but above all, the risk of state surveillance or ethical questions have deeply divided the scientific community.

- **Coordination Between Science and Society.** The crisis showed that involving in the decision-making, those who will experience its application leads to more appropriate and better-lived choices. Crossing social and scientific issues requires a body to coordinate public debate, decompartmentalise disciplines and bring together experts and politicians to guide the governmental action.

- **Ecological and Social Opposition.** COVID 19 has shown the impossibility of achieving carbon neutrality without creating mass unemployment. In order not to dissociate the pillars of sustainable development, the ecological transition must, therefore, reconcile environmental constraints, strategic independence, localism and decarbonised and rural reindustrialisation.

- **Reconciliation of Retired Population and Working People.** The lack of resources dedicated to the elderly must lead to a redefinition of the policy on old age. This sector appears as a source of employment and an opportunity for researchers and companies to create innovative solutions. Retired and working people come together in a win-win logic.

31.3.2.4   Singular Point or Emergence Function

The Coronavirus crisis has imposed or will impose a brutal change on our (old?) world and the observed pandemic will undoubtedly be considered in history as a singular point at which lifestyles, behaviours and political strategies will be at odds with past attitudes. Nevertheless, the "France of the future" will not be achieved in a snap of the fingers. Consciences have evolved, which no doubt was the sine qua non condition for the revolution to get underway. Many obstacles to change remain, mostly related to the financial capacity to make the necessary structural changes but also to the possible release of emotional factors once the crisis is over. The health and economic damage caused by the virus seems to have triggered the emergence of irreversible trends [16].

Some illustrations proposed below come to illustrate this singular character.

- **Digital Revolution.** Digitalisation has shown the extent of its capabilities in the treatment of the coronavirus crisis. E-work, e-education, e-commerce, e-services are all areas of activity whose usefulness has been revealed by confinement. A digital upheaval has begun in France. It goes beyond the framework of the State and will be amplified in the future.

- **Break in Hospital Policy.** The neo-liberal trend observed recently in the hospital has undoubtedly had its days. The ethical rule of appropriate care for the patient at the least cost to the community must prevail over the commercial rule of seeking profitability based on the optimisation of its value chains and billing maximisation.

- **Urban Exodus.** The Covid-19 pandemic has highlighted the fragilities of contemporary urban globalisation. By paralysing global operations and freezing metropolises under confinement, the present epidemic has triggered a movement of depopulation of large cities (Paris, Toulouse Bordeaux, Lille, ...), to the benefit of medium-sized towns and rural areas.

- **Changing Traditions.** Sanitary crisis obliges, the kiss disappeared. This affectionate greeting, very French, had nevertheless crossed the centuries and civilisations until it became a tradition. New signs have begun to replace the kiss: the "elbow to elbow", the hello with the feet, the inclination of the bust, the hand on the heart... Definitive rupture?

- **European Debt.** The virus has enabled a decisive political breakthrough for the affirmation of Europe's sovereignty. On a Franco-German proposal, the historic resolution to issue a mutualised European debt on the financial markets triggered a new political era enabling Europe to catch up with the major economic blocs.

31.3.2.5   Purifier or Sanitiser Function

If preserving the planet means accepting the rules of nature, perhaps human mortality should be considered as an adjustment variable. This hypothesis is obviously not audible to society, but nature, through this health crisis, should perhaps ask us about the intrusive behaviour of our lifestyles and their deleterious role in environmental imbalance. Like cyclones leading to the renewal of wooded areas and the elimination of debilitated species, nature seems to be setting up natural purification processes eliminating the weakest elements to encourage the growth of the strongest. The pandemic engendered by the coronavirus and its induced or forced consequences seem to be part of this logic. It thus takes on, in turn, the function of a cleaner, leading to the elimination of the most feeble entities, or a sanitiser by natural consequences or via the implementation of anthropic actions to restore systems or situations affected by the crisis [17].

Examples of this function are given here below.

- **Deaths of Vulnerable Individuals.** People with physiological co-morbidities or heavy therapeutic treatments (chemotherapy, dialysis, organ transplantation, . . .) are more likely to suffer from and succumb to a severe form of COVID 19. Independently, social precariousness, another form of vulnerability is also a risk factor for death.

- **Cessation of Payment or Bankruptcies.** Business insolvencies in France could increase by 80% in 2020 as a result of the crisis. Businesses already weakened before the pandemic (airlines, car manufacturers, restaurants, leisure activities, . . .) are the first to be affected. Some emerging countries that have defaulted on payments are also close to bankruptcy (Angola, Zambia, etc.).

- **Reduced Noise Pollution and Improved Air Quality.** While containment has significantly reduced pollutant emissions, another more insidious pollution has decreased: noise. Marked by the decline in industrial activities, car or air traffic, a reduction in the average noise level of between 4 and 6 dB has been observed. Unfortunately, the truce is only provisional.

- **Smoking and Drug Use Cessation.** Even though 25% of French smokers have temporarily increased their consumption, the increased risk of infection by the coronavirus and the severe forms of the disease it might cause has prompted many of them to stop smoking. Moreover, difficulties in the supply of drugs have led to a decrease in drug trafficking.

- **Retreat of Extremist Ideas.** In France, extreme parties have not taken advantage of the effects of the crisis to increase their hold. Worse, they have regressed. By deciding to close the borders, the leaders have deprived the extreme right of their flagship argument. The sterile polemics launched by the extreme left on the government's negligence have not received favourable echoes.

31.3.2.6   Questioner and Validator Function

Beyond the simple questioning of the biological and medical aspects related to the appearance of the virus and its curative or preventive treatment, the global and multisectoral crisis engendered by the pandemic has questioned all social and professional categories in every field of activity. The exceptional nature of the scenarios provoked by this type of cataclysm, never experienced or even imagined in the contemporary era, has provided a breeding ground for scientific questions [18]. It also offers a real test basis for the experimentation and validation of the answers that could be given to this type of event or to others with similar consequences.

Without attempting to answer them, we list below a few high-level questions among all the scientific questions raised by the health crisis and its management.

- **Democracy or Totalitarianism.** Which regime is best suited to deal with this type of crisis? How far can freedom go if individual behaviour harms the majority? Is free will compatible with collective security? Are totalitarian regimes better suited to ensure security through coercive or even repressive measures?

- **Globalisation of Health.** Do the economic interests of pharmaceutical companies in the development of a vaccine and the confidentiality that it requires match the need for its rapid availability calling upon nations for transparency of data, sharing of ideas, and results? Is non-profit health globalisation conceivable?

- **Moving From Protectionism to the Precautionary Principle.** Should quality standards and norms replace customs tariffs? Should people first be protected from the risks they face or should companies (and their employees) be protected from competitive threats? Is the resilience of a state a higher value than the efficiency of its economy?

- **Emergency and Caution.** Should administrative or scientific protocols, which are sources of rigour but also of slowness, be relaxed in times of crisis? Therapeutic trials are subject to a methodology and legislation guaranteeing respect for the individual, non-maleficence and justice. What level of urgency can legitimise the lifting of these procedures?

- **Dynamics Between Science and Politics.** The health crisis has raised the question of the contribution of research to government action. Is academic expertise sufficient to legitimise decision-making in times of pandemic? How to reconcile scientific advice and political measures? Are the time horizons of science and politics aligned?

31.4   Conclusion

This chapter aimed to give a panoramic view of the impact of the coronavirus crisis in France. After an observation round describing the phased evolution of the course of events, an analysis was proposed. Considered from a multidimensional angle, dissociating temporal and functional views, the study highlighted the notions linked to the dynamics of the evolution of the phenomena induced by the crisis and the contribution of the virus to proven or potential societal modifications. The analysis shows that all facets of our lifestyles are affected, in one way or another, by this crisis of such an exceptional nature. The impact is, of course, negative in the short term, but looking at the longer term, the fallout from the crisis may have paved the way for beneficial changes in our society. All major social issues are concerned: health, freedom, solidarity, justice, globalisation, sustainable development, national sovereignty, ... The academic world must now take up these subjects. Physical sciences, life sciences, social sciences, applied sciences, engineering sciences, the entire research community must now act in a coordinated manner to find solutions to the harmful effects of this virus but also take advantage of this crisis to build the foundations of a safer, fairer and more respectful world.

References

[1] Jean-Paul Moatti. The french response to covid-19: intrinsic difficulties at the interface of science, public health, and policy. *The Lancet Public Health,*, 5:e255, 2020. doi: 10.1016/S2468-2667(20)30087-6.

[2] H Chen, W Xu, C Paris, A Reeson, X Li, et al. Social distance and sars memory: impact on the public awareness of 2019 novel coronavirus (covid-19) outbreak. medrxiv. 2020. doi: 10.1101/2020.03.11.20033688.

[3] Wändi Bruine de Bruin. Age differences in covid-19 risk perceptions and mental health: Evidence from a national us survey conducted in march 2020. *The Journals of Gerontology: Series B, gbaa074*, 2020. doi: 10.1093/geronb/gbaa074.

[4] Yin-Yin Lek and George D Bishop. Perceived vulnerability to illness threats: The role of disease type, risk factor perception and attributions. *Psychology and Health*, 10(3):205–217, 1995. doi: 10.1080/08870449508401950.

[5] Susan G Millstein and Bonnie L Halpern-Felsher. Perceptions of risk and vulnerability. *Journal of adolescent health*, 31(1):10–27, 2002. doi: 10.1016/S1054-139X(02)00412-3.

[6] Kathakali Biswas and Parongama Sen. Space-time dependence of corona virus (covid-19) outbreak. *arXiv preprint arXiv:2003.03149*, 2020.

[7] Yadollah Dadgar. Coronavirus and emergence of an extraordinary political economy: editorial note. *International Journal of Economics and Politics*, 1(2):1–11, 2020.

[8] Mohsen Maleki, Mohammad Reza Mahmoudi, Mohammad Hossein Heydari, and Kim-Hung Pho. Modeling and forecasting the spread and death rate of coronavirus (covid-19) in the world using time series models. *Chaos, Solitons & Fractals*, 140:110151, 2020.

[9] Hari Bapuji, Charmi Patel, Gokhan Ertug, and David G Allen. Corona crisis and inequality: Why management research needs a societal turn. 2020. doi: 10.1177/0149206320925881.

[10] Gila Kriegel, Sigall Bell, Tom Delbanco, and Jan Walker. Covid-19 as innovation accelerator: cogenerating telemedicine visit notes with patients. *Nejm Catalyst Innovations in Care Delivery*, 2020.

[11] BS Robynn Rixse. Coronavirus: Catalyst for change. *Dental Assistant*, 89(3):8–9, 2020.

[12] Anne-Laure Mention, João José Pinto Ferreira, and Marko Torkkeli. Coronavirus: a catalyst for change and innovation. *Journal of Innovation Management*, 8(1), 2020.

[13] Christine Riefa. Coronavirus as a catalyst to transform consumer policy and enforcement. *Journal of Consumer Policy*, 43(3):451–461, 2020.

[14] Vasee Moorthy, Ana Maria Henao Restrepo, Marie-Pierre Preziosi, and Soumya Swaminathan. Data sharing for novel coronavirus (covid-19). *Bulletin of the World Health Organization*, 98(3):150, 2020.

[15] Matt Apuzzo and David D Kirkpatrick. Covid-19 changed how the world does science, together. *New York Times*, 2020.

[16] Dmitry Ivanov and Ajay Das. Coronavirus (covid-19/sars-cov-2) and supply chain resilience: A research note. *International Journal of Integrated Supply Management*, 13(1):90–102, 2020.

[17] Usman W Chohan. A post-coronavirus world: 7 points of discussion for a new political economy. 2020.

[18] Philip N Britton and Ben J Marais. Questions raised by covid-19 case descriptions. *Journal of Paediatrics and Child Health*, 2020.

Part IV

Stakeholder Perspectives

32

Digital Earth: A World Infrastructure for Sustaining Resilience in Complex Pandemic Scenarios

Richard Simpson

This perspective makes the case for an improved multidisciplinary global collaboration that more effectively leverages our technological prowess to improve how we share and communicate the best science-based information. The concept of Digital Earth - the aspirational digital representation of our physical, social, and natural world - is introduced to serve as a critical digital infrastructure for proactively informing policy, investment, planning, design, and our behavioural responses to managing crisis situations, including pandemics.

32.1   Spatial Information During a Pandemic

We live in an intricately interconnected and increasingly globalised world. Within hours a viral infection can rapidly spread throughout a community. Despite the advances in sciences and technologies, a pandemic such as COVID-19 can cost the global economy many trillions of dollars and have far reaching global social, economic, and political consequences.

Spatial information has long been recognised as a critical enabler in the forensic management of infectious diseases ever since 1854 when Dr. John Snow, one of the founders of modern epidemiology, applied maps to trace the source of cholera outbreaks to a single contaminated pump in Broad St. Soho, London [1].

During the COVID-19 pandemic there has been a plethora of innovative applications using spatial information to resolve issues at specific points in the response, and also recovery phases. These location-enabled apps have in many instances been helpful to specific tasks such as contract tracing, drug delivery and presenting signage via drones and robots, finding ventilators, dashboards, spatial enablement of e-learning and e-health systems, finding availability and location of public services, and informing us on lock-down policies.

However, despite the benefits of impressive technological and scientific advances, we are still effectively applying maps as Snow did over one and half centuries ago, except now the maps are digital. With uncoordinated international cohesion; siloing of information across disciplines, organisations and jurisdictions; and a lack of trusted integrated information resources, we have seen a cargo cult emerge with Government organisations practicing rituals to win public and political favour as hero warriors in this 'war' on the virus. We are not facing up to these challenges and their multi-dimensional dynamics as emergent complex adaptive systems, instead we are too often simplifying problems down into the arbitrary domains convenient to focus mono-disciplinary application of commercial-off-the-shelf point 'solution' technologies. We also lack adequate regulations, policies and data mandates to support the governance and sustained use, provisioning and sharing of spatial information. The accumulative crisis now facing humanity and our inabilities to address it objectively is the result of failing to account for the aggregate impact of decisions initially made for short-term comforts and political gain.

New thinking is sought to revitalize these cultural and societal approaches towards spatial information and its metaphorical expression of objective science and our own identity and associations with places. This renaissance culminating in the realisations of a Digital Earth will expand our horizons for the interpretation of events, and create new ways for expressing our situational awareness through the arts, philosophy and scientific inquiry.

32.2   A New Paradigm of Thinking

To advance beyond this stalemate we need to shift the paradigm and adopt a more holistic and deterministic perspective on the challenge. We need to consider spatial information as an integrating enabler for a common open and innovative digital infrastructure, not just as a location enabler for point applications.

The rapid urbanisation, easy mobility and dense interconnectivity of cities is creating environments where pandemics will thrive. There is irony in the fact that the built and social environments of our city centric civilisation has made us more vulnerable to severe impact from disasters. Unbridled complexity of our built environment exposes our cities to risks of catastrophic failure. We have seen this demonstrated repeatedly in recent history with floods, earthquakes, bushfires, wars, tsunamis, landslides, and cyclones. The intensity of these disasters is increasing in the wake of our changing climate, and accelerating competition for essential resources.

Disasters can happen concurrently, as demonstrated by the spread of cholera following the Haiti Earthquake in 2010 [2]. The Spanish flu of 1918 brought acute illness to over a quarter of the world's population and death to an estimated 40 million people in the aftermath of 10 million killed in World War One.

The likelihood for disasters to happen concurrently is now more probable with the changing climate and city-driven global economy in the wake of rapid urbanisation. The significant human impact on the Earth's ecosystems and climate change increases the risk as this is creating situations more conducive to breeding pandemics [2].

Snow's identification of a contaminated water pump illustrates how even the infrastructure we depend upon and trust or fresh water and sanitation in a city can fail with disastrous consequence.

Despite so many advances in asset information management, for the greater part maintenance practices still remain reactive – just as they would have been in Snow's time. There is a pressing need for our cities' utilities to transform their business processes, policies and mandates to shift their traditional practices to a paradigm where there is massive integration of trusted evidence-based spatial data with real-time cyber-physical systems. Through this more dynamic ability to digitally mirror the objects and processes of the physical world such organisations and their supply chains can improve resilience with the applications of AI and machine learning with more proactive predictive and prescriptive asset management [3].

Similarly, decision making must also be driven by scientific evidence and effective use of spatial information to more effectively meet the challenges of pandemics such as COVID-19. Government and business institutions have traditionally been enabled by technical data and information but the power structures from twentieth century mean decisions are often made for short term vested interests rather than public good. Recent wide access to emerging communication technologies and social media platforms have revealed an emerging public capability for use and sharing of expert data in more productive ways to inform human behaviour for survival.

This pandemic has demonstrated that effective responses demands transparent governance and collaboration between all tiers of Government, related agencies and civilians. Snow's achievement not only illustrates the power of maps in the visualisation of correlated data, but also how spatial indexing helps build evidence with veracity and provides a referencing system for the aggregation of the collated information. Any disaster, especially a pandemic demands a coordinated real-time response from diverse interdisciplinary teams that may include scientists, politicians, health workers, supply chain operators, data scientists, foreign diplomats, and technologists.

It therefore helps if all these stakeholders have access to the same trusted spatially referenced data. For population wide implementation of an emergency response, such data needs to be communicated clearly and accurately to the civilian population in ways that engage their cooperation and inform their personal choices to change habitual behaviours.

32.3 Digital Earth

Digital Earth is a multidisciplinary collaboration to build a comprehensive digital twin of our planet's built, natural and social environments [4]. It is envisioned as a massively integrated multi-disciplined digital representation of our knowledge expressed through spatial metaphor of a globe. For example, a Digital Earth could spatially integrate our planet's thermodynamic performances with associated environmental, epidemiological, economic, and other social phenomena so we can more effectively monitor situations and inform better decisions during all phases of a disaster. Digital Twins are the building blocks of a Digital Earth. They integrate multi-dimensional geometric, topological, behavioural and semantic representations with Internet of Things (IoT), artificial intelligence (AI) and analytics. Graph based digital threads trace all lifecycle transactions and associations to ensure the integrity of this cyber-physical coupling [3]. Through metaphors such as virtual globes [5] we can apply this digital framework to build a deeper and more collaborative understanding of the complex dynamic interactions in our physical world and what bearing these may have on our individual and collective wellbeing.

As a global scientific project, Digital Earth sits on a seamless multi-scaled continuum with other big-science initiatives including the Physiome project [6] to model our physiology for drug discovery and testing, and its predecessor the Human Genome project to functional and physically map our genes. These mathematical models provide insight into the dynamic complex adaptive systems that we have evolved into and become part of.

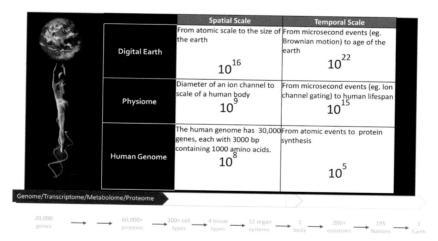

FIGURE 32.1
Big Science continuum - Adapted from Hunter, PJ and Borg, TK. Integration from proteins to organs: The Physiome Project. *Nature Reviews Molec & Cell Biol.* 4:237-243, 2003

For example, the models could reveal the interaction between COVID-19 the environment and physiological functions at different scales from genes to the whole living organism to the environmental factors. At the scale of the Physiome, genome and other initiatives in this continuum such as the metabolome and transcriptome [6] valuable insights are being sought to accelerate the quest for a vaccine and improve patient treatment. Similarly, at the next magnitude in scale there is exciting potential for Digital Earth to provide predictive early warnings and deliver trusted evidence-based prescriptive course of action in real-time at every phase and inter-phase transition of a multi-hazard crisis situation.

A Digital Earth could also serve as an integrating foundation for a next generation of digital passports to enable us to safely travel and serve as an augmented super-sense to protect us from harm. This will only be possible if the Scientific and technical developments underpinning this project are effectively shared with, questioned, and trusted by civilian populations so they become a part of the civil and political process of learning and reconceptualising our impact on our shared global habitat and the laws for our engagement with each other.

32.4   Conclusion

There are remedial lessons to learn from this pandemic about appreciating how we are all connected, and how technologies can shape our daily existences and our survival outcomes. In the past we have embraced a vision of a world of machines for living in and enabling our mobility on demand. Until now we have only superficially applied technologies to conveniently interpret the realities of the world as a simple metaphor. Even with the benefit of computer technologies we model this world rather simplistically with a domain-based point 'solution' approach, avoiding complexity of the multi-disciplinary and massive data integration. This has so often given us a mistaken mental picture of possibilities and led us astray. There is now some urgency to rethink the design of our habitats, make scientifically informed decisions, transparently communicate trusted information and to consider how we can cyber-physically engage in the flux of the emergent complex adaptive systems of the world we live in rather than the one we picture.

A Digital Earth is a critical digital infrastructure to ensure our future survival as it consolidates our collective knowledge and liberates new wisdom. Realising a Digital Earth will demand prioritisation, fresh new 'moon-shot' thinking and international collaboration and determination. There are many intellectual, ethical and philosophical challenges, but a Digital Earth may become the most significant scientific and technological achievement in our civilised history and the definitive achievement of the 21st Century.

References

[1] Tom Koch. Cholera, chloroform, and the science of medicine: A life of john snow. *Cartographic Perspectives*, 60:62–64, 06 2004. doi: 10.14714/CP48.461.

[2] Bapon Fakhruddin, Kevin Blanchard, and Durga Ragupathy. Are we there yet? The transition from response to recovery for the COVID-19 pandemic. *Progress in Disaster Science*, 7:100102, 2020. ISSN 2590-0617. doi: https://doi.org/10.1016/j.pdisas.2020.100102.

[3] D Jackson and R Simpson. *Digital City Manual for Digital Earth part 3 chapter 15*. Springer, New York, 2020. URL https://link.springer.com/content/pdf/10.1007%2F978-981-32-9915-3_16.pdf.

[4] Michael F Goodchild, Huadong Guo, Alessandro Annoni, Ling Bian, Kees De Bie, Frederick Campbell, Max Craglia, Manfred Ehlers, John Van Genderen, Davina Jackson, et al. Next-generation digital earth. *Proceedings of the National Academy of Sciences U S A*, 109(28):11088–11094, 2012. doi: 10.1073/pnas.1202383109.

[5] Albert Gore. *Earth in the balance-ecology and the human spirit*. Houghton Mifflin Harcourt, New York, 1992.

[6] Peter J. Hunter and Thomas K. Borg. Integration from proteins to organs: the physiome project. *Nature Reviews Molecular Cell Biology*, 4(3):237–243, Mar 2003. ISSN 1471-0080. doi: 10.1038/nrm1054.

33

COVID-19: The Open Data Pandemic

Jamie Leach

The COVID-19 pandemic highlighted the need for trustworthy data and science to guide the response of authorities, institutions and the public. Open data, open and collaborative science are needed to hasten the development of solutions to bring this pandemic and any future crisis to an end.

33.1 Unlocking the Value of Data

I wouldn't be the first to compare data to raw material. Data in isolation and without context is as useful as a piece of rock ripped from the Earth. But what if that rock was polished, washed, cleaned, smelted and extruded? Suddenly that piece of innocuous rock may resemble the makings of steel created from Iron Ore.

Data in isolation lacks purpose or value and may pose little danger to its custodian from privacy or from the ability to manipulate it. Before COVID-19, data was coveted by its creators. The owners or custodians of data either protected it for fear of breach or recognizing the economic value in the data locked it up for future benefit and gain.

33.2 From Data Sharing to Open Science

The advent of COVID-19 has shaken the world with anxiety levels of the public and governments rising to a fever pitch. Suddenly, the potential for greater good through collaboration to overcome a united enemy has prompted the barriers to data sharing to be rapidly lowered, and in some cases, removed altogether [1–3].

Through a shared desire to find treatments and cures for the pandemic, and through a need to fact check directives issued by governments and world leaders, data is being shared at unprecedented levels. Frustrated by swathes of policies and political advice, more people are turning to science.

Examples of COVID-19 data sharing is occurring around the globe. In Europe, the launch of several COVID-19 data portals is enabling collaboration between Bioinformatics Institutes and their partners [4]. By creating a shared space, the portals address a need to share data, create an accessible and safe storage facility and analysis tools for future data development and manipulation.

Another partnership between NASA, the European Space Agency and the Japan Aerospace Exploration Agency strives [5] to find a cure to COVID-19 and to utilize the learnings to further progress sustainability. No stranger to the concept of citizen science and crowdsourcing of ideas, the partnership participants have long been affiliated with innovation and mountains of data. Wanting to lend a hand to fight the Global pandemic, scientists and engineers' thought the best way to find solutions, would be to work as collaboratively as possible, and nothing screams collaboration as loudly as the Hackathon they held in May 2020 [6].

Not all governments have been slow to react, however. Renowned for its tech-enabled civic culture with Taiwan's revered Digital Minister Audrey Tang at the helm, a bottom-up information sharing approach, coupled with the public-private partnership model, has resulted in a participatory collective action; central to the country's success in handling pandemics and regional crises [7]. Based on hard-learned lessons from the 2003 SARS epidemic, Taiwan has experienced significantly lower COVID-19 cases than other nations. Minister Tang stated that no one decision alone had yielded their low rate of infection, but rather a unified approach to data and technology has contributed significantly [8].

33.3   The Future

Despite the groundbreaking results of data sharing between the scientific and research communities, factions of the government are resisting the adoption of open and transparent data processes. The urgent and pressing need for a cure is forcing researchers and scientists to put the benefit in front of the legalities: sharing models, research and analytics accelerating science ahead of regulation. I hope that this surge in open data, open research and overall sharing for the greater good will not only aid the quest for a solution for COVID-19, but will forever change large-scale attitudes towards data sharing and open science.

In the number of months since the pandemic recorded its first case, open science has led to the isolation of the virus, a standardized list of symptoms, COVID-19's genome has been sequenced and shared, multiple formats of testing have evolved and the potential of global vaccines have been developed across multiple jurisdictions. Prior to the pandemic, science was largely publicly funded, but not publicly accessible. To progress the current breakthroughs of the scientific and medical fraternities post pandemic, a standardization of data practices, maintaining open access and a willingness to continue mass collaboration is essential. To create and promote resilience across the community will come from their faith in a united scientific community, achieving a solution to bring this pandemic and any future crisis to an end. If open access, open science and open data are maintained, this becomes the new normal. Anything less will be regression without justification.

References

[1] https://bit.ly/39uhXlN

[2] http://www.oecd.org/coronavirus/en/

[3] https://www.nature.com/articles/d41586-020-01246-3

[4] https://techcrunch.com/2020/04/20/eu-data-portal-launches-to-support-covid-19-research/

[5] https://www.nasa.gov/press-release/nasa-partner-space-agencies-amass-global-view-of-covid-19-impacts

[6] https://covid19.spaceappschallenge.org/

[7] https://bloom.bg/3qesORP

[8] https://link.medium.com/niQHMnonRbb

34

The Challenge of Mapping COVID-19 Data

Menno-Jan Kraak

This perspective discusses the design choices to make while dealing with multivariate COVID-19 data; the most common errors made in this process; and how to avoid them and present data in meaningful and effective ways.

34.1   The Mapping Challenge

In reporting about the COVID-19 pandemic, many plots, maps and other diagrams showing the current situation at local and global levels and comparing regional developments have appeared in the media.

The complexity of these graphics varies both in design and technology. You can find ingenious online story maps and simple single variable maps in the print media. The data behind the graphics is most often related to three different variables: the infected, the hospitalized and the dead. It is quite a cartographic challenge to visualize all these numbers properly, especially together. This because there is a wide variety over space and time, and a large range between the lowest and highest values, as well as between and within these variables.

The numbers available can be very revealing but also should be interpreted with caution. It is revealing because when plotted over time they show where the pandemic started and how it spread over the world. Caution is needed because countries do not necessarily have the same definition for each variable nor follow the same data collection approach. Some publish everything while others virtually nothing. Some numbers only include those tested while other also those suspected. Numbers after a weekend tend to be higher because most weekend cases are reported only after the weekend. Reading this you might wonder how do we then create trustworthy maps? My advise is that we look at maps critically and realize that there might be a data problem.

34.2   How-to

Here I would like to address two issues:

1. professional cartographic design challenges and choices; and

2. the mapmakers problem (or the most common cartographic mistakes in the media).

Let us discuss the challenges based on variations of three familiar questions: where? what? and when? At what spatial scale do we map? Like nearly all phenomena, a pandemic is not homogeneously distributed over space. In some places one would prefer a larger scale than in other locations. In addition, the collecting of the numbers does not necessarily happen at the same level of geographical units, and even if so, these might vary in size quite a lot. Inset maps for the more crowded areas could be useful.

How do we symbolize the numbers? The large range between the lowest and highest values is often a delicate design problem. How to select symbol sizes that avoid the big symbols covering the whole map, but still allow us to see the smallest values? This problem gets amplified when all high values are in the same region. One solution is to classify the data, and group individual values together according to a formula. The choice of a classification method is critical because you want to avoid hiding existing patterns or reveal non-existing patterns. It would also be possible to apply logarithmic scales, but one can wonder if users (esp. the public) can easily understand and interpret this. Yet another commonly applied alternative is to normalize the data, for instance display the number of infected per hundred thousand inhabitants.

How do we visualize the trends over time? Similar to the non-homogeneous distribution over space the course of the pandemic over time is also erratic. The depiction of time can be done in a single map, but more often is done in a set of maps or even by animation. Often dashboard like views are used, allowing the display of multiple perspectives with maps and additional time-line diagrams.

34.3   Case in Point

A final design will be based on a combination of the above considerations with the overall purpose of the map in mind. In Figure 34.1, we see a detail of a COVID-19 related map of Europe providing data on country level. The map background supports the theme, and shows roads, airports and harbors, the human infrastructure potentially used by the virus to enter a country. The red half circles represent the number of deaths, and the blue halve circles the number of infected. Both half circles have a different scale because the number of infected is a magnitude bigger than the number of deaths. This stresses the importance of a clear map legend. To avoid that the large circles covers too much map, they have been made transparent above a certain size, as for instance can be seen for France and Germany. More information on this map's design choices, can be found in [1]. Following this lead, you can also download this and other maps.

From a cartographic domain perspective, it is great to see so many maps on COVID-19 in the news media. However, despite the creativity of the mapmakers, bad design choices have been made. The most common error is the choice of the wrong map type, especially when the mapmakers try to visualize absolute numbers. Some just plot the number as text in the geographic unit, but such maps have to be literally read unit by unit and will not provide an overview. The 'worst' mistake is when, instead of a map with proportional point symbols like in the map in Figure 1, a choropleth map is used. This map type is only suitable for relative data. The problem is that two geographical units in the same class could differ substantially in size and this results in an over attention for the large unit. Also, the overall pattern might be misleading. Often these choices are due to the default options in the software used.

When choropleths are correctly used, for instance, to display normalized data, such as the number of infected per hundred thousand inhabitants the choice of a map projections is also critical. Since people use these maps to discover patterns and compare regions, only so-called equal area projections should be used. A common error is the use of the Mercator projection which disproportionally exaggerates the size of land masses towards the north and south pole. Its use is - again - often driven by the default options in the software used.

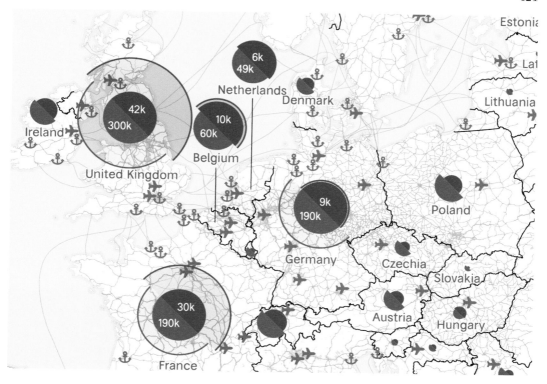

FIGURE 34.1
Detail of a map about the COVID-19 pandemic in Europe

34.4 From Data to Insights... to Actions

The dynamics and variability of the data related to pandemics such as COVID-19 is a real challenge for cartographers and requires creative but critical thinking about solutions which are also influenced by the final environment where the maps are published. Well-designed maps will attract attention and enlighten, providing insights that tell the story at hand and lead to appropriate decisions and actions.

References

[1] Franz-Benjamin Mocnik, Paulo Raposo, Wim Feringa, Menno-Jan Kraak, and Barend Köbben. Epidemics and pandemics in maps – the case of covid-19. *Journal of Maps*, 16(1):144–152, 2020. doi: 10.1080/17445647.2020. 1776646. URL https://doi.org/10.1080/17445647.2020.1776646.

35

Better Engagement to Build Smarter, Resilient Communities

Alice Kesminas

Community resilience can be better achieved with geospatial information and technology, but only if we can determine what needs to be done for them to be accepted by communities. The challenge of trust, and concern about what else might be done with personal data beyond its initial purpose, need to be addressed to enable geospatial information to be used effectively to plan and manage resilient communities. We need to extend data anonymisation techniques to big data and understand what their limitations are when multiple data sources are linked.

35.1 Introduction

Geospatial information can improve our insights, understanding and management of events such as the COVID-19 pandemic, as well as the ongoing administration and planning of resilient communities and cities. Emerging technologies offer the opportunity to monitor our cities in real-time and gain an unprecedented level of location intelligence from a range of inputs – including mobile and wearable devices and other sensors that can identify an individual or household. Community reactions to tracing apps during the current COVID-19 pandemic have demonstrated that the public's concerns and expectations about technology and the privacy and security of their personal location data will determine how information can be used by decision makers. In this instance, technological capabilities have come second to the expectations of our communities. Community resilience can be better achieved with the help of geospatial information and technology, but only if we can determine what needs to be done for them to be accepted by communities.

Even with the potential for life-saving benefits, only around 7 million of Australia's 17 million adult population have downloaded the Australian Government's COVIDSafe app to date. "Like any health-care intervention, coronavirus apps need to conform to the highest standards of safety and efficacy. And yet, and there are no global standards" [1]. Lack of standards coupled with concerns about government use of data are possibly factors behind the current resistance to tracing apps. More than 60% of the population are "very concerned or concerned about their data being used by the Australian Government to make unfair decisions" [2]. Nonetheless there is support for data being made available to researchers (especially those in universities) and being used within government but there is much less support for multiple sources of data to be linked. The challenge of trust, and concern about what else might be done with personal data beyond its initial purpose, need to be addressed to enable geospatial information to be used effectively to plan and manage resilient communities.

35.2   Learning from Experience

Open data is critical to smart growth and urbanisation. Sharing of sensor data, such as traffic flow, can allow multiple parties to develop insights that can improve day-to-day liveability and, via planning, the sustainability of our cites. While the benefits of sensors may be clear to councils, the installation of sensors to capture data has been known to cause issues. The City of Darwin found their "smart city" installation of sensors and cameras created issues within the community. In response to community expectations and privacy concerns, The City of Darwin committed to establishing a Privacy Framework to set the expectations and decision-making criteria for deployment of technology and data collection and management. They found it necessary to go beyond current privacy laws and help the community understand when their personal information is being collected and limit its use [3].

In retrospect, better community consultation could have reduced risks to the Victorian Smart Meter rollout. The technology was backed by a strong business case for better customer service, networks and safety but there was a need to clearly communicate benefits to individuals and address their concerns and lack of understanding about the new technology [4]. The sale of smart meter data to third parties to market alternative electricity plans and products to reduce energy consumption was pitched as a benefit by champions of the technology but is seen as a risk by some consumers. This mandated rollout was met with strong opposition and demonstrated that individual choice needs to be considered.

Engaging with the community from the outset was the key to success in the implementation of the Yackandandah mini grid [5]. By talking about the proposed new technology and listening to communities' concerns and vision, it was possible to co-develop a solution that would provide the network operator valuable insight into how to adapt to accommodate distributed energy resources and help the community to achieve their renewable energy vision. This is an example of what can be achieved when community, industry and government work together. We can learn from projects such as this by laying the foundation of trust and transparency for emerging geospatial technologies.

Community engagement can be costly, but there is also a cost when technology is not widely accepted in the community. The COVIDSafe app offered the promise of benefits to the community via reduced transmission, fewer lockdowns and less economic impact but still the download numbers were relatively small. The Australian Government's COVIDSafe app also suffered from public confusion about whether it even worked on some operating systems. If there was clearer communication, improved implementation and higher downloads, would we have captured critical transmissions earlier and avoided further costly lockdowns? What is the price we are paying, for not knowing where COVID-19 cases are sooner and having more robust contact tracing? What is the cost of not having community trust and acceptance of this technology?

35.3   Extending Anonymisation to "Big" Geospatial Data

With the increase in data being generated by the individual and analysed, maintaining privacy levels will be an increasingly complex issue. Data privacy has been identified as one of the biggest issues of the next decade [6]. There are several existing approaches to providing privacy for location data that includes sensitive or personal information such as address. These methods have been developed so that researchers and decision-makers can perform valuable spatial analysis, without the loss of personal privacy. Methods of anonymisation include, but are not limited to, aggregation and a range of masking, such as isomasks, where spatial analysis is performed in an offset location. As data and systems evolve, there is a need for new ways of ensuring privacy in increasingly complex systems. To achieve this, we need to extend data anonymisation techniques to big data and understand what their limitations are when multiple data sources are linked to support artificial intelligence. Once we understand privacy expectations, we can build the required solutions and legislation to support them. This means undertaking research now to ensure privacy can be guaranteed in increasingly complex systems, understanding de-anonymisation risks and determining who has the responsibility for protecting against them. It also means understanding the limitations of current acts as we transition to big data.

35.4 Building Trust for Future Resilience

Government, industry and communities can work together to: build trust and a mutual understanding of benefits technology offers to building resilient communities; provide expected levels of geospatial data security and privacy and; develop the standards and legislation that underpin these factors. Then we will be able to use smart technologies and geospatial data effectively build resilient communities.

The COVID-19 pandemic has provided valuable insight into the gap between technological possibilities and community acceptance of technology. As we ramp-up development digital twins as virtual replicas of our physical world and roll-out technology for smart cities technology, the reaction to tracing apps provides a timely reminder. Community engagement needs to underpin the process, not come as an afterthought. A range of issues have contributed to people's decision not to download tracing apps including bad press, rushed roll-out, platform incompatibilities and concerns about on selling of data. Similar issues in the future could be addressed with better community engagement as well as better design and implementation. If the community understands and accepts new geospatial technology, we can better use these technologies to build community resilience. We have an opportunity to learn from the reaction to tracing apps and achieve better outcomes in our future cities.

References

[1] Nature Editorial. Show evidence that apps for COVID-19 contact-tracing are secure and effective, 2020. URL https://go.nature.com/36TiT1w.

[2] N Biddle, B Edwards, M Gray, and S McEachern. Public attitudes towards data governance in Australia, 2018.

[3] City of Darwin. Switching On Darwin Privacy Framework, 2019. URL https://bit.ly/2GDoOgE.

[4] R. Bolt. The evolving engineer is the best engineer, ghd thoughtbook, 2020. URL https://bit.ly/2GErJpl.

[5] AusNet Services. Australia's first community mini grid launched in Yackandandah, 2017. URL https://bit.ly/3iMLYOC.

[6] P Thaine. Perfectly Privacy-Preserving AI, Towards Data Science, 2020. URL https://bit.ly/3nwna0Z.

36

How the Coronavirus Could Change Urban Planning

Frank Friesecke

Does urban planning determine humanity's chances of survival in our cities during periods of pandemics? The great importance of sustainable and health-promoting urban development is already evident from history. This chapter clarifies the connection and offers initial considerations as to whether and how the distance between humans, cars and buildings should be reappraised. The city of the future will be more digital, it will have to become more resilient to future pandemics, all of which will lead to a different planning culture. The basic functions of existence for urban society, namely living, working, basic essentials and mobility, are used to examine how the current corona crisis affects architecture and urban planning. The explanations in this chapter show that integrated urban development solutions are possible, without fundamentally calling into question the compact and dense city built on the principle of mixed use.

36.1   Introduction

Closed schools and shops, cordoned off children's playgrounds, deserted squares, buses and trains, orphaned pedestrian zones and virtually car-free streets: The effects of the corona crisis on urban areas are immense and can be observed worldwide. Whether it be Wuhan, New York or in the cities of Europe - the images are similar despite the great differences in architecture and urban planning.

Although the topics of hygiene and health promotion have played a role in the urban development debate since the second half of the 19th century at the latest, due to the current pandemic it can be assumed that the planning culture will once again change fundamentally as a result of the coronavirus.

Currently more than half of humanity lives in cities or urban conurbations. This trend will continue. By 2050, it is estimated that three quarters of the world's population, i.e. around 7 billion people, will live in cities [1]. Does the Smart City, however, including tracking the movement profiles of infected city dwellers, provide the ideal image for the city of the future? Or, as a corollary of pandemics, can we anticipate a return to cities of shorter distances, in which the jobs in the "home office" or in co-working spaces are located, and where online retail has largely replaced brick-and-mortar retail premises?

The chapter deals with these and other questions. After a brief review of the urban development governing principles and concepts of the past, the intention is to present a first vision of the direction in which the city of the future could develop towards in the light of corona and other potential pandemics of the future.

36.2   Present: Urban Development in Corona Times

With the spread of the coronavirus, urban planning and urban development are once again obliged to address hygiene in cities. While until recently the lack of affordable housing and, above all in Europe, the climate debate were the determining factors, the urban development policy debate is now expanding to include epidemiological issues.

Of course, the subject is not completely unknown even today. The current debate on clean air and noise reduction planning in smog-contaminated cities, as well as health promotion measures in socially disadvantaged urban districts, testify to the importance of eliminating social and health inequalities. What is new, however, is the imperative of "social distancing", i.e. measures to control infection with the aim of spatial distancing. Since it is not a matter of social isolation of individuals, the terms "spatial distancing" or "physical distancing" would be more appropriate but have not become established in the English language. In everyday life, spatial distancing means in particular keeping physical distance and avoiding physical contact (1.5 to 2 m distance, no hand shaking, no group formation, mask protection etc.), in the most extreme case up to restrictions on outdoor activities and contact bans.

Not only for the individual, but also from the point of view of urban planners, these restrictions are enormous, for after all the main aim in designing squares and other public and semi-public spaces is to create opportunities for social interaction. The importance of one's own living environment, local amenities, as well as parks and urban squares, is one of the key findings of recent months. Public spaces have made the pandemic more bearable. While jogging, walking or sitting on a bench, city dwellers rediscovered their surroundings, so to speak. It is likely that green spaces have never been appreciated as much as in spring 2020, when people moved outside to escape isolation at home.

In addition, the inner cities and district centres are determined by trade and consumption, by festivals, art and culture - in corona times the urban infrastructure seems strangely skeletal and meaningless. While shopping in stores poses a risk of infection, shopping at home on a smartphone or PC is completely risk-free. It is feared that numerous owner-operated shops, but also theatres, clubs, cinemas and pubs, will have disappeared after the crisis.

The current impact of the corona crisis on mobility structure has been profound, and indeed initially significantly positive. Social distancing and in particular working from home ensure less traffic, less traffic jams and fewer accidents. The proportion of people traveling to work or training places every working day has decreased significantly as a result of mobility restrictions that have been in effect almost worldwide since mid-spring 2020. In many cities, empty lanes are released for healthier forms of mobility, in particular the bicycle or e-bike, preserving individual freedom and thus becoming a solution to the many hindrances produced by the crisis.

However, there is also a major loser in the transport sector: the declining number of passengers in public transport is posing serious concerns for the future of municipal transport companies. How can the risk of infection be reduced in buses, underground and suburban trains, but also in long-distance transport? Will the car become the winner arising from the crisis after all?

36.3   Future: The Smart, Participatory and Resilient City

Cities are social organisms that are constantly changing. It is therefore not surprising that urban planners and architects, but also philosophers and scientists, are constantly thinking about the future of our cities. The desired spatial (and usually also social) future state is usually quickly formulated. However, a look into the past also shows how quickly a designed vision of the future can prove to be a mistake or has already been replaced by the next vision of the future.

Current developments, which in many ways represent an unprecedented watershed, require us to be cautious about coming to premature conclusions about future urban development. To call fundamentally into question the viability of the densely populated city in the wake of corona ignores the fact that at least Asian cities such as Hong Kong, Singapore and Tokyo have so far successfully dealt with the crisis. So density in itself is not the problem. It is about being well organized and well designed.

It cannot be denied that certain developments will accelerate significantly in the course of crisis management. The top priority is the digitalization of administrations and public institutions - digital offerings and work from home have so far not yet been standard in many countries. The digital transformation enables more transparent, more efficient processes; actually having to visit authorities can be circumvented thanks to new online procedures. In the medium term, there is no way around e-Government. It should also be noted that the digital city needs an administrative apparatus that can keep up with the rapid pace of technological progress.

36.3.1   The smart city

Smart City solutions can improve the quality of life in existing and new urban structures, which ultimately also serve to enhance public space. A city is considered "smart" if intelligent solutions for very different areas of urban development such as infrastructure, buildings, mobility, services or security are achieved in it through the use of innovative information and communication technologies [2]. The challenges in setting up these solutions currently lie less in data collection, storage and processing than in the development of inter-faces between the individual "sub-markets" of the smart city (Smart Mobility, Smart People, Smart Economy, Smart Environment, Smart Government and Smart Living). In many European countries, corona warning apps have been developed on behalf of governments, which turn the smartphone into a warning system. Not only in China, the colour of the personalised QR Health Code scanner on the smartphone now determines whether the person should go into quarantine or is allowed to visit a reopened restaurant (red/green).

Beyond the undisputed advantages of digital solutions, the Smart City is also about personal rights issues in the area of conflict between informational self-determination and digital monitoring and control. Which personal data may be used in the event of a pandemic? A "real" Smart City would use digital technologies not only for hazard prevention or public safety, but also for less relevant public issues with urban spatial relevance.

The Smart City has not yet established itself as a model for urban development, at least not in Europe. However, the current crisis shows us more than clearly how important digital technologies are in periods of social distancing.

36.3.2   The participatory city

While the Smart City describes an overarching, strategically designed solution approach, the issue of citizen participation in urban development requires short-term municipal action. Ongoing planning and dialogue processes, which up to now have mainly taken place "offline" in the form of information events, future and idea workshops, but also outreach activities such as site inspections and activating surveys, must be adapted, and in many cases completely rethought.

The "digitalization of participation" [3] through websites, apps, social networks and web-based communication platforms has long been used, but habitually only in addition to analogue formats.

In these times of the corona crisis new ways of participation will have to be followed. These include online dialogues in large groups, online surveys and virtual residents' meetings. With the digital participation system DIPAS, citizens in Germany will in future be able to call up digital maps, aerial photographs, plans, 3D models and geodata and provide precisely localised feedback on planning projects. DIPAS is currently being developed by the Hamburg Ministry of Urban Development and Housing together with the State Office for Geographic Information and Surveying and the City Science Lab of the HafenCity University Hamburg (HCU). The software is open source and is to be made available as "Public Code" to other institutions for subsequent use and further development from the end of 2020.

Some European cities have already opened online participation portals, and the number of users is likely to increase significantly during corona times (see www.stuttgart-meine-stadt.de).

In order to prevent a Hamburg resident from voting on planning processes in Stuttgart, registration is required that is tied to his or her place of residence. Inappropriate comments will be deleted immediately by an online editorial team.

FIGURE 36.1
Participation and social distancing during Corona times, Stuttgart, Germany, Source: die STEG Stadtentwicklung GmbH

In addition to the Internet, video conferences in the exchanges between administrations and planning offices have become an everyday medium within a very short time - inevitably the question arises whether some travel routes could not have been avoided even before the crisis. It is also conceivable that consultations with owners in urban renewal areas via telephone or video could be used, but the physical surveying of the building condition of the property on-site still seems to be a continuing necessity in the future.

Despite the proven advantages of web-based interaction, it is to be hoped that the tried and tested communication channels can be used again as soon as possible after the pandemic has been overcome. Civic participation is more than just a website; good communication still always requires meeting in person.

36.3.3   The resilient city

From the point of view of urban decision-makers, it will be essential to review the resilience of a city or infrastructure in the future with regard to pandemic events. Adaptation concepts have so far mainly referred to natural disasters such as earthquakes, floods and heat waves [4, 5], but not to epidemics and, in the worst case, pandemics.

As many people live together in a relatively small area in cities, many people are affected all at once when a disaster occurs. At the same time, however, spatial concentration also creates opportunities for dealing with risks and giving better control options. The decisive factor in determining whether these advantages can be effectively utilized or whether an event turns into a disaster for many people is how these risks are handled. New York serves as an example of a metropolis that was severely affected by the coronavirus in March 2020, but was also able to contain its spread quickly through a large number of coordinated measures [6].

A good plan for urban resilience is based on a multi-dimensional approach. Holistic strategies for resilience in the event of the current corona crisis lead to a change in the planning culture, which primarily extends to the areas of living, working, shopping and moving around. The following section deals with the initial approaches that will have an impact on future urban planning and architecture.

36.4 Rethinking urban planning

What can we learn from the corona crisis for the future? On the one hand, the current pandemic is challenging the resilience of our society and especially our cities. On the other hand, coping with it will trigger processes of change that offer a wide range of opportunities for sustainable urban development.

Unintentionally, the corona crisis is becoming a kind of real-life laboratory for the city of the future. So what can cities learn from the lockdown? What structures for the resilient city after corona are already emerging?

Based on the essential functions of existence for urban society, namely living, working, basic essentials and mobility, the following outlines the changes resulting from the current crisis and which solutions urban planning and architecture can respond with.

36.4.1 Housing

As an elementary basic need, housing is one of the central urban functions. However, the demands on housing are very heterogeneous and vary greatly according to region, social affiliation and individual preferences. Housing needs depend on demographic, technical, social and economic parameters that are volatile over time and can only be controlled to a limited extent.

Despite these differences, it has become clear, especially in the current crisis, that the single-family home in the suburbs or in the countryside, which has been critically judged for decades, was a relatively pleasant place to spend lockdown: stable neighbourhoods, long-standing and personal shopping relationships, private garden areas and generous floor plans for one's own family and home office are extremely helpful to this end. Owners were also often at an advantage over tenants because they were able to generate added value through repairs and improvements during the period of short-time work.

However, this is not the only reason why the demand for housing will increase even more than expected in the future: thanks to digital technologies, many companies have made it possible to work from home, and many working people may not even return to their open-plan offices. Yet, there is still a lack of flexible floor plans at home that allow living and working in a home office and that provide sufficient privacy and retreat.

For architects, this means building apartments in such a way that different forms of living coexist in one house. So small apartments, large apartments, and that there is perhaps one dedicated apartment for guests set in every apartment building. That there are work or common rooms in the house, which can be shared not only in times of crisis. It is about establishing forms of living that bring living and working closer together again.

For urban planners, this means making public spaces that were often neglected in the past more attractive when planning new quarters, but also in existing areas. If the expensive city apartment is small, the living environment becomes even more important - public green spaces and places within walking distance, short distances to shopping and to medical practices. More open spaces on which urban agriculture is practised can also be a solution along the lines of the urban gardening movement. The demand for allotment gardens, at least in Germany, has more than doubled compared to the previous year. The waiting time for one of the almost 1 million allotments in certain regions has been several years [7].

In principle, the city has everything to survive quarantine periods - if it is planned consistently. What is new is that there should be an overview of the necessary separation distance areas, especially in public facilities, shops and restaurants.

36.4.2 Work

As can be seen from the previous section, the urban functions of living and working are mutually dependent and cannot be substituted for a functioning city. A return to the functionally segregated city is no longer appropriate in times of climate change anyway.

Overall, it can be assumed that corona will have the most lasting impact on the world of work. Working from home will become a permanent and steadily growing part of the working world. As a result, oversized office buildings and even more space will become available in the city. The role of the central office could be taken over by the study in the (larger) apartment, but also by decentralised offices close to the apartment. In their own neighbourhood or district, between grocery stores, hairdressers, snack bars and cafe's, people could work in co-working spaces and thus avoid commuting to work.

Structural changes will not be avoided for the hitherto open plan office space. An obvious concept is the return to the so-called Cubicles. This technique of dividing an open-plan office into smaller personal areas, which had been in use since the 1970s, had actually seemed to have run its course, but is now experiencing something of a renaissance.

On the other hand, in the medium term it is necessary to convert offices in the city centres that are no longer needed. Demand has been great for centrally located apartments not only since corona, yet in many places the (still) very high prices for condominiums and the high rent level prevent affordable living in the city. This could change in the future, since in addition to office properties, retail properties are even more threatened by non-occupancy. Living and possibly also working in a previous office premises converted into an apartment - or a former ground floor shop - this too could represent a future for the city centre.

36.4.3 Retail business

One of the greatest threats to the inner cities has already been identified. The gradual creeping disappearance of the classic activity of going shopping, at least in the city, has been now greatly accelerated by the pandemic.

The competition against brick-and-mortar retail is already clear: Online business is the great beneficiary of the crisis. When non-food stores in the inner cities had to close, many consumers switched to existing online offerings. Although not all industries benefited equally from the boom in online retailing, online giant Amazon alone was able to increase its sales by 26 percent in the first quarter of 2020 compared to the previous year [8].

In order to prevent city and town centres from becoming deserted, one of the aims will be to designate smaller core zones in which trade has priority over other uses. Outside these areas, vacant buildings will be given a new use, either by conversion or by demolition and new construction. In growing cities, it will be primarily residential use that will replace the previous retail use.

In many cases, however, quick, creative solutions are also needed to mitigate the crisis: In Berlin, Boston, Paris and elsewhere, "pop-up street restaurants" have been approved relatively easily – restaurateurs are allowed to use adjacent parking spaces as extended outdoor terraces.

In order to prevent a final decline of the inner city as a location for basic essentials, it will be important to actively shape the structural change. The affected owners must act jointly in the same direction, and this requires above all new forms of cooperation. Municipal authorities will have to play a leading role in the renewal process, but private initiatives can also make their contribution to strengthening the inner cities (e.g. business improvement districts). Much of this will only work in small-scale – property by property, street by street.

For urban planners, the change in consumer behaviour also impacts the outskirts of cities: If the currently forced change in shopping behaviour continues to move in the direction of online trading, this will be accompanied by an increase in logistics centres, warehouses and other large-scale infrastructures. For a long-term and resilient urban development, the high-quality design of these new commercial megastructures is absolutely essential.

In order to avoid these area-intensive developments, considerations regarding more compact spatial production structures should also be realized in urban areas. One approach could be the "urban factory" concept, which integrates industrial production into the urban context by means of a city-factory interface [9].

In the light of current events, the overall question is whether certain services should be decentralised, not only in the health sector but also in the provision of care in general. This in turn has implications for urban planning and architecture.

36.4.4   Transport and mobility

Does the pandemic also serve as an accelerator for new urban transport concepts? The spread of the coronavirus and the resulting initial restrictions led to a forced, unprecedented, breathing space for traffic. People have reduced their everyday mobility to a minimum and shifted it significantly: The proportion of walking and cycling has increased, while that of local public transport has fallen dramatically [10].

During the crisis it has become clear that urban transport areas are not divided up according to demand. In the current situation, at least 1.5 meters distance from other people in public spaces should be kept to minimize the risk of infection. Narrow or non-existent bicycle lanes and sidewalk parking make it difficult to comply with the prescribed distance rules.

Many cities have reacted to the changed mobility behaviour with appropriate measures in the short term. In Brussels, the city centre (Pentagon Zone) is being converted to an extensive pedestrian and cycling zone, Paris is investing 300 million euros in new (pop-up) cycling infrastructure to connect the entire city and prepare it for increased cycling after the lockdown. Oakland in California has developed the concept of slow streets, where 10 percent of all roads are closed to through traffic. Already today, one in two households in the inner city of Berlin no longer owns a car, simply because they no longer need one [11].

Is the car-friendly city a thing of the past? Against this background, the size of a city makes a significant difference. The smaller the city, the higher the proportion of car journeys, the longer the distances travelled and the lower the proportion of public transport. Even if mobility after corona will not be different everywhere, the same is true for small towns: Urbanity is created primarily where people get around on foot or by bicycle, and not by a solid line of cars meandering through the city centres, district centres or town centres.

In addition to the newly forming traffic flows, it is digitalization and smart technologies that are leading to more efficient traffic control. This applies in particular to motorised private transport, which is one of the great benefiters of the crisis. An infrastructure that thinks ahead helps to steer traffic flows in such a way that traffic jams do not occur in the first place. Finding a parking space can soon be a thing of the past if networked vehicles know where the next gap in the parked cars will be.

A great many people are already traveling intermodally, so they use several means of transport on their journeys. IT applications and apps on smartphones can link data on the location of vehicles and people, tariffs and route information and both create new, networked transport offers and facilitate access to them.

Is the corona crisis a catalyst for changing transport behaviour? Will the old mobility patterns return afterwards? The everyday behaviour of each individual will depend on whether transport and urban planners succeed in making public space attractive for health-promoting forms of mobility.

36.5   Conclusion

How pandemic based must future urban planning be? In his major work "The Man Without Qualities", first published in 1930, Robert Musil came to the following observation: "Modern man is born in the clinic and dies in the clinic: therefore he should also be living like he is in a clinic" [12].

Even if the requirements of leading architects at the time of the Neues Bauen are judged differently nowadays, the question of integrating hygiene regulations, larger spacing and changed floor plans for apartments, retail, offices and public facilities into urban development is still being raised. The illustrations in this chapter show that (urban) construction and architectural solutions are possible in this respect, without fundamentally calling into question the compact and dense city built on the principle of mixed use.

With regard to the changed trading and transport behaviour in corona times, only the future will show whether there will be a reversion to old consumption and mobility patterns, or whether there will be a sustainable and lasting change. Conversion strategies for empty properties require ideas to make commercial and district centres more attractive again, but also eco-nomic stimulus programmes are needed in order to be able to finance the necessary measures in the foreseeable slump in municipal finances.

One conclusion is thus obvious: The far-reaching changes in all essential functions of existence for the urban society, i.e. living, working, basic essentials and mobility, do not only mean loss or deprivation, but above all an opportunity for future urban and transport planning. Urban development and spatial planning do not have to be reinvented, but what is required is an urban experimentalism in the cities, combined with municipal decision-making power and civil society commitment [13].

For a successful integration of adaptation measures in urban planning and development, a societal process is required that can only succeed if it is anchored beyond politics and administrative spheres involving private sector stakeholders (including retail, housing industry) and involving residents too. There is no doubt that digitalization and new technologies will play a significant role in this process.

References

[1] United Nations, Population Division of the Department of Economic and Social Affairs. *World Population Prospects 2019*. 2019.

[2] Gassmann, O., Böhm, J., Palmié, M. *Smart Cities: Introducing Digital Innovation to Cities*. Melbourne: Emerald Publishing Limited, 2019.

[3] Selle, K. Partizipation 8.0 – Bürgerinnen und Bürger in Prozessen der Stadtentwicklung. In: Informationen zur Raumentwicklung, Heft 6/2017. page 12ff, 2017.

[4] BBSR Bundesinstitut für Bau-, Stadt und Raumforschung (Hrsg.). Stresstest Stadt – wie resilient sind unsere Städte? Unsicherheiten der Stadtentwicklung identifizieren, analysieren und bewerten. 2018.

[5] Vale, L.W. *The Resilient City: How Modern Cities Recover from Disaster*. Oxford University Press, 2005.

[6] New York State Government. NY Forward - A Guide to Reopening New York & Building Back Better. URL https://www.governor.ny.gov/sites/governor.ny.gov/files/atoms/files/NYForwardReopeningGuide.pdf. (Accessed: 30.06.2020).

[7] Süddeutsche Zeitung vom 1.6.2020. Corona-Beschränkungen sorgen für "Run auf Kleingärten". URL https://www.sueddeutsche.de/leben/freizeit-corona-beschraenkungen-sorgen-fuer-run-auf-kleingaerten-dpa.urn-newsml-dpa-com-20090101-200601-99-260144.

[8] Weise, K. Amazon Sells More, but Warns of Much Higher Costs Ahead, in: The New York Times from April 30, 2020. URL https://www.nytimes.com/2020/04/30/technology/amazon-stock-earnings-report.html. (Accessed: 30.06.2020).

[9] Bucherer, M., Clausen, U., Herrmann, C. et al. Urban Factory – Entwicklung ressourceneffizienter Fabriken in der Stadt. Abschlussbericht. Braunschweig, 2019. URL https://publikationsserver.tu-braunschweig.de/receive/dbbs_mods_00066906.

[10] Meyer, H. Corona und Mobilität: Mehr Homeoffice, weniger Berufsverkehr. Onlineartikel vom 08.04.2020. URL https://www.adac.de/verkehr/standpunkte-studien/mobilitaets-trends/corona-mobilitaet/. (Accessed: 22.04.2020).

[11] Jacobs, S., Keilani, F., Betschka, J., Seeling, B., Van Bebber, W. "Meinen eigenen Wagen habe ich lange verkauft", in: Der Tagesspiegel vom 5.1.2020. URL https://www.tagesspiegel.de/berlin/autofreie-innenstadt-meinen-eigenen-wagen-habe-ich-lange-verkauft/25388382.html. (Accessed: 1.07.2020).

[12] Musil, R. *Der Mann ohne Eigenschaften, Band 1: Erstes und Zweites Buch*. Hamburg: Rowohlt Verlag., 1971.

[13] Roesler, S. Epidemiologie und Stadtplanung haben eine gemeinsame Geschichte und auch Zukunft. In: Neue Zürcher Zeitung vom 03.04.2020. URL https://www.nzz.ch/feuilleton/epidemiologie-und-stadtplanung-haben-eine-gemeinsame-geschichte-und-auch-zukunft-ld.1549809. (Accessed: 30.06.2020).

37

Toward Agile Strategies for Enhancing Community Resilience Following the COVID-19 Pandemic: An Interview Study

Hossein Mokhtarzadeh

The global Pandemic as a result of a recently discovered coronavirus has affected every aspect of our lives. In this observational study, I interviewed a small group of experts in different fields on how they cope with this global crisis. Have they modified their strategies to achieve their goals and whether this has affected them negatively or positively? The interviewees were from academia, and industry. Almost all participants found the lockdowns quite positive, however, a sentiment analysis revealed a negative outcome with moderate confidence (54.3%) with Australian participants; and positive (96.2% confidence) when all participants were included. Some of the positive outcomes included more time with family, more physical activities, and creative ways to perform tasks. Negative outcomes involved some of their team members who could not handle the new norms. Further research is required to be conducted with a wider range of stakeholders to better understand how we can recover more efficiency from this pandemic in Australia and beyond.

37.1 Introduction

Global pandemic was announced on 11 March 2020 by World Health Organization (WHO) as a result of COVID-19 outbreak. Since its first identification in Wuhan, China, in December 2019, these tiny (i.e. 65–125 nm) coronaviruses [1] traveled by humans across the globe in a short time thus changed our lives for good. Since its inception, COVID-19 disease has taken over 875K lives and infected 26.6M worldwide at the time of writing (on 6 September 2020) [2]. Finding a cure or effective treatment for COVID-19 is yet to be identified. As a result of its devastating consequences [3], governments have implemented serious measures such as stay at home orders, mandatory wearing masks in public, shutting down businesses and disrupting international travels. These extraordinary steps to contain this infectious disease have led to both health and economical disasters [4]. For instance, Australia may be facing its first ever recession in the last three decades [5]. To successfully overcome the COVID-19 crisis, adaptation to new norms and agile mindsets are recommended; however, some argue that agile and adaptative governance may not always go hand in hand in crisis response [6]. These negative side effects of pandemic require optimal strategies stemming from governments and ordinary people backed by science that can be swiftly tested and readjusted. Having these challenges in mind, I turned to experts to better understand how they evaluate the situation, how they cope with the pandemic, and how they think industries and businesses can thrive following/during the pandemic. Therefore, in this observational study, I interviewed experts [7] from academia, industry to gain their insights regarding the consequences of the pandemic and whether they plan to modify their strategies to achieve their goals.

37.2   Method

I interviewed six experts in different fields from industry and academia from April to July 2020[1]. Originally, I prepared some predefined questions (Table 37.1); however, the discussion was open for the interviewees to share their observations during the pandemic. I did not necessarily follow the questions in Table 37.1 as the discussion progressed. The main aim was to ask them whether they have changed their strategies following pandemic.

I produced word clouds of transcripts of all interviews. I first collected transcripts of all interviews from YouTube's free transcription tool embedded in each video. Then, a sentiment analysis was performed on the whole interviews using a simple online tool from `https://monkeylearn.com/`. Sentiment categories of positive, negative and neutral were done automatically on the transcripts of interviews. Finally, top 20 keywords from the interviews were extracted from a keyword extractor tool on MonkeyLearn website.

TABLE 37.1
Some predefined questions to ask participants during interviews. Not all the questions were asked during interviews.

#	Questions
1	How pandemic has changed your strategies in your own career and company?
2	Are you still adjusting to new ways of working (e.g. WFH, collaboration, etc.)? If yes, why and how?
3	What is your highlight of this period for you?
4	What are you learning now that you may apply in other unexpected events in the future?
5	What are our advantages/disadvantages in Australia regarding building industries considering pandemic?
6	Who would you like to hear about their strategy these days or as your role model?

37.3   Results

Interviews took over 3 hours with a mean and standard deviation of 32 ± 5 min for each. I observed that the interviewee's description of events were quite positive; however, using sentiment analysis, it was categorized "negative" (54.3% confidence) when all Australian participants were involved. Nevertheless, the sentiment analysis presented positive (96.2% confidence) when all participants' data was analyzed.

Among the top 20 keywords extracted from the transcripts using an online keyword extractor were the following words: "people"(197 times), time (81 times), "jobs" (64 times), "industry" (56 times), "strategy" (55 times), and "pandemic" (39 times).

Almost all participants were fine by working from home (WFH) which has also been recently confirmed in a large scale study in the US [8]. Academics in this study agreed that future directions of education could be hybrid combining face to face and in person trainings. CEOs agree that most

---

[1]All these interviews and their details are freely available on YouTube (`shorturl.at/clsxH`).

senior managers are quite busy during pandemic and consider it as a new opportunity even if one needs to look a bit harder to find them.

37.4 Discussion and Conclusion

In this observational study, I interviewed six experts in different fields regarding their professional and personal strategies during the pandemic. The interviewees agreed that the pandemic provides new opportunities despite health and economic challenges. For instance, these opportunities included being with family as a result of working from home and finding creative ways to adjust the business and return of cashflow during the pandemic. However, given a small sample size, I found that certain occupations (e.g. human performance and sense of balance) which deal with mind-body illustrated more positive (high confidence) category compared to interviewees from Australia when transcriptions were analyzed using sentiment analysis. These differences could be related to the type of questions I asked during the interviews and cannot be generalized. The pandemic arguably challenged most of our established methods (or strategies) of performing tasks. Work from home, online education, telemedicine and even online job interviews are widespread and acceptable, which may even be a new norm post-pandemic.

The top keywords extracted from the interviews referred to "people", "time", "industry" and "jobs" which may show the extent of concern individuals would have regarding job security in a timely manner. These findings indeed were interesting since the interviews were not necessarily about the job security. Though the findings require further scrutiny, such interviews and their analyses may provide a framework to explore how individuals' strategies can lead to prosperity post-pandemic [9]. Such understanding enables us to better choose our future endeavors and the values we appreciate. Collectively, this preliminary project reveals that we can develop agile strategies in a short time and be quite adaptive.

In conclusion, this preliminary study could pave the path toward more agile mindset to optimize our strategies in achieving our goals. Such an approach can be extended to larger scale decision making processes in a city, state, country or global challenges. Moreover, future studies can take advance of qualitative methods such as Interpretative Phenomenological Analysis to identify the underlying challenges everyone undergoes during the pandemic [10]. We need to develop these methods in advance to avoid the next global crisis affecting community resilience which may appear in a form of another pandemic or other disasters such a climate change.

Acknowledgement

I would like to sincerely thank all the guests of my program on YouTube Channel (shorturl.at/clsxH).

References

[1] Muhammad Adnan Shereen, Suliman Khan, Abeer Kazmi, Nadia Bashir, and Rabeea Siddique. Covid-19 infection: Origin, transmission, and characteristics of human coronaviruses. *Journal of Advanced Research*, 2020.

[2] Wikipedia. Covid-19 pandemic data, 2020. URL https://en.wikipedia.org/wiki/Template:COVID-19_pandemic_data.

[3] Maria Nicola, Zaid Alsafi, Catrin Sohrabi, Ahmed Kerwan, Ahmed Al-Jabir, Christos Iosifidis, Maliha Agha, and Riaz Agha. The socio-economic implications of the coronavirus and covid-19 pandemic: a review. *International Journal of Surgery*, 2020.

[4] Angel Carlos Bassols and Bassols Fj. The oil industry and its relation to the pandemic covid 19. *Archives of Petroleum & Environmental Biotechnology*, 5:164, 08 2020.

[5] Nassim Khadem. Australians are hurting from the coronavirus-led recession, but we fare better than most countries, 2020. URL https://www.abc.net.au/news/2020-06-05/australia-coronavirus-recession-compares-international-countries/12322260.

[6] Marijn Janssen and Haiko van der Voort. Agile and adaptive governance in crisis response: Lessons from the covid-19 pandemic. *International Journal of Information Management*, page 102180, 2020.

[7] H Mokhtarzadeh. Strategy interviews [internet], 2020. URL https://www.youtube.com/channel/UCeV5XhAkh_jcWmKylTIP38Q.

[8] E Bernstein, H Blunden, A Brodsky, W Sohn, and B Waber. The implications of working without an office, 2020. URL https://hbr.org/2020/07/the-implications-of-working-without-an-office.

[9] Ivan Hernandez, Daniel A Newman, and Gahyun Jeon. Twitter analysis: Methods for data management and a word count dictionary to measure city-level job satisfaction. 2016.

[10] Jonathan A Smith and Pnina Shinebourne. *Interpretative phenomenological analysis.* American Psychological Association, 2012.

38

COVID-19 Pandemic in Finland: Converting a Forced Digitalisation into an Opportunity

Kirsikka Riekkinen

COVID-19 pandemic challenged the Finnish society in terms of economic, institutional, and social aspects. Quick measures to support economic stability and institutional resilience were undertaken by the Finnish government. Private entrepreneurs could apply for funding to convert their products into digital format or develop digital platforms. The digitalisation of public services has been ongoing for years, but institutional change is slow and has tendency to resist the change. The sudden disruptive situation caused the change to speed up. The geographic location, sparsely populated country, and lack of digital skills especially among the oldest citizens have, however, brought challenges in the resilience of the society. While the preparedness for converting public and private services into digital format was high, the willingness or ability of citizens to use them have led to awareness of social resilience as part of recovering from the shock. For building and supporting the design of even better digital tools and services, the role of geographic data has become more important. Economic, institutional and social resilience rely heavily on this data, which emphasizes the importance of open and accessible data.

38.1 Many Dimensions of Resilience

Resilience overall is described as ability to recover from a shock. This spring has shown that resilience is needed on multi-level scale throughout our society. The complexity of the multiple levels can be simplified by dividing the problem into institutional, economic and social resilience [1, 2]. Institutional aspect of resilience during this pandemic covers the public administration and decision-making in a situation where the traditional in-person, paper-based administrative decisions have decreased their role in decision-making. Economic resilience in this situation is discussed and visible all over the world, and recovering from depression will be one of the key questions in the success of resilience after the pandemic. Social resilience, on its behalf, has roots on the cultural background of people. Will there be personal tragedies, how relationships between people are recovering, what happens to the most vulnerable members of society? Next, I will examine these aspects together with the use of geographic information in the Finnish context.

We have seen a sudden change in social and working life. In order to remain resilient, this has risen the need for digitalisation in all the dimensions of resilience. Due to several restrictions on social distances and still to keep the stones of public services of society rolling, the public administration has been forced to take a leap towards forced digitalisation and distant working. This has been enabled by temporary laws. The public administration has been slowly introducing different digital services for a long time, but their popularity amongst citizens has not been huge.

For example, electronic platform for property transactions was introduced already several years ago, but nevertheless, the vast majority of property transactions (97% in 2018, according to National Land Survey) has been done by paper so far. However, the digital services gain popularity, especially in commercial services. According to one of the two largest grocery sellers in Finland, the rate of online grocery shopping has risen by 500% during the pandemic. The economic support activities for digitalising services reached up to 30 000 companies. The regular ecommerce activities rose by 75% compared to previous year. And this all happened, even though there were no restrictions in opening times of physical shops. Digital services together with open access geodata have played a major role in economic resilience. Even though we have seen our economy declining, the government decided to invest in companies of every sizes to support the innovation of new digital services.

38.2   The Importance of Open Geographic Data and Social Inclusion

The topographic data in Finland provided by the National Land Survey is open, and it has been used in different new location based applications to provide new commercial services. At the same time the role of location data and maps has increased, especially due to changed consumer and customer behavior. Due to restrictions, restaurants were not allowed to serve food within their premises, but delivery services have gained interest. Online shopping for groceries has increased in average by 500% compared to last year. Half of these orders are delivered to home addresses, so we also have received new users for location information to find the route for delivery. From social resilience, the requirement for digitalisation is obvious. We see our relatives, friends and colleagues online. Social distancing has been the key in social relationships for the spring. There is a possibility to go beyond physical location, and having a glass of wine via Zoom does not seem such a silly idea anymore. But, again there are two sides of a coin: those who have already been in a risk to fall out of the society due to social distance, most likely do not have the possibility to use digital tools, and thus this situation increases social exclusion.

According to the Finnish experience, one key to resilience is trust towards decision-making bodies of the society. This requires the possibility to understand the data behind decisions restricting citizen's rights. We can say that we are going through times where open data plays a major role in both sustaining social peace and enhancing resilience, for example in terms of economic resilience, and maintaining trust towards decision-makers. It is crucial to maintain discussion about public decision-making, by opening the data behind the decisions for open access. But, the role of open geographic data could be even bigger in fighting the pandemic.

One of the globally most used strategy to stop the pandemic is the 'test, trace, isolate, support', and Finland makes no difference. The question of how to trace the exposed persons is urgent in this strategy. Ideas and openings of using geospatial data stored by mobile devices has been under discussion several times, and companies have started to develop such a method. But, we face the fundamental issue of person-related geographical data: who owns the data and can it be used for such purposes? Eventually, the question lies on public and private interests and rights. If the use of geographical data together with personal data is necessary to stop the pandemic, but it is violating basic human rights as restricting the freedom of a person, can we still use it? Coronavirus has proven to be transmitted in large crowds, and several countries including Finland, posed restrictions on number of people are allowed at the same place, same time. Geographical data could be used to track people's location and alert if too many are in a too small area. The fundamental question would lie on the legislation - there should be tools to take short-term legislation efficiently in to use, but the possibilities to ensure that this information is not used when it is no longer needed to stop the pandemic, is problematic.

For the large public, also professionals visualizing information of the pandemic on maps have had a major chance of influencing the mindset and behavior of people. GIS provides endless opportunities to steer people to different directions. Showing numbers on contagious people in different areas in dark red creates visions on people's minds. The fear of other people may be boosted by presenting most contagious areas on a map, when in reality the difference between areas might be small. This was evident when presenting number of confirmed infections in the capital, Helsinki. Maps can lie, and the responsibility for presenting the information not misleading is of utmost importance. Location information had also one totally new form or role during the past few months in Finland, and it was the distinction between 'us' and 'them', based on where people were living. We can say that the social dimension of location has had a totally new meaning.

38.3   Lessons Learnt from Finland

What have we learned during this spring and summer? People have changed their way of living forced by an external force to take a massive leap towards digitalisation. The society moved towards remote working, which will most likely to be the new normal from now on. This chance should be used to digitalise public administration and services, since citizens and other authorities are now much more ready to utilize these services. However, rapid digitalisation creates issues regarding for example data and privacy, especially regarding the location data. On the other hand, the meaning of open data in the society is getting more crucial to gain acceptance for the public decision-making processes. As a conclusion, we can say that eventually the battle against COVID-19 will end and it will leave marks to the society for good. We will be referring to these times as 'time before' and 'time after'. But what will remain, is the mindset of digitalisation, and also the mindset of how we all were in this together. Social distancing, with the help of tools of digitalisation, turned into social inclusion, supporting economic, institutional, and social resilience.

References

[1] Alberto Giacometti, Jukka Teräs, Liisa Perjo, Mari Wøien, Hjördis Sigurjonsdottir, Tuulia Rinne, A Giacometti, J Teräs, L Perjo, M Wøien, et al. Regional economic and social resilience: Conceptual debate and implications for nordic regions. Technical report, Discussion paper—Nordic Thematic Group for Innovative and Resilient Regions, 2018.

[2] Ron Martin, Peter Sunley, Ben Gardiner, and Peter Tyler. How regions react to recessions: Resilience and the role of economic structure. *Regional Studies*, 50(4):561–585, 2016.

39

What's the Future of Greek Cities in the Post-COVID-19 Period? New Perspectives on Urban Resilience and Sustainable Mobility

Efthimios Bakogiannis, Charalampos Kyriakidis and Chryssy Potsiou

COVID-19 would be recognized not only as a health crisis but also as a socio-economic emergency situation that brings to mind the concept of "urban resilience." Social distancing came into the forefront and many countries have been forced to adopt such measures immediately. Such early steps to contain the virus earlier than most European countries have been characterized as the key to Greece's success. People have been alienated from public space. Even now, during the second phase of the strategy against the COVID-19 pandemic, while the economic impacts are becoming obvious, the influence of public spaces still remains uncertain. However, decision makers have to schedule for the following day: an individualistic context came to the fore. Nevertheless, it is necessary to rebuilt communities' trust in public spaces in order to reconstitute future cities. To face such a challenge, a strategy combining urban resilience with sustainable mobility is going to be required. To gain this goal, case studies review analysis was implemented and best practices have been concentrated. Considerable emphasis has been placed on the intervention plan carried out by the Municipality of Athens, Greece. By implementing such a plan, there is hope that coronavirus might offer to modern societies an opportunity to radically reassess their values and the way they function.

39.1 Introduction: A Brief Review of the Pandemic

The disease COVID-19 outbreak is an on-going pandemic caused by the coronavirus SARS-CoV-2, first reported in Wuhan, the capital of Hubei Province, China on December 31, 2019 [1]. The novel coronavirus SARS-CoV-2 is now quickly spreading worldwide through a human-to-human transmission [2]. According to the John Hopkins University database [3], more than 10.5 million cases have been recorded in more than 215 countries around the world, by the end of June (30/06/2020). During this 6-month-period more than 512,000 deaths have been attributed to this virus infection.

Focusing on the epidemiological profile of COVID-19 during the early stages of the pandemic, the number of registered cases doubled in size every 7.4 days since the mean incubation period was 5.2 days [4]. It is obvious that the degree of transmission was great enough to maintain this rate of infection: according to Surveillances [5], until February 11, 2020, a total 44,672 cases were reported across China.

On January 30, 2020, the World Health Organization (WHO) declared this outbreak to be a global public health emergency [6] and declared it a pandemic on March 11, 2020 [7], as the virus spread to other countries like Thailand, Japan, Morocco, South Korea and Taiwan. The outbreak reached Europe, too: as of March 20, 2020, Italy has the second largest number of COVID-19 cases after China. That was the reason why, on March 8, 2020, the Italian Government introduced extraordinary mitigation measures to limit viral transmission by limiting social interactions [7, 8]. Other European countries, like Spain, France and Germany [6], appeared to be in a similar situation, "with a short time-lag of a couple of weeks" [7]. Thus, restrictive measures to limit viral diffusion were adopted. (Sweden and the UK preferred to follow a different strategy, earlier, based on the "heard immunity" model.) Similar measures were adopted in Greece where the first case was reported on February 26, 2020.

The measures put in place in Greece were strict; however, they also were among the most proactive in Europe and have been credited on a worldwide level for limiting the spread of the pandemic and kept the number of deaths among the lowest in Europe [9]. However, when the post-lockdown period was approaching the Greek Authorities faced a major dilema: which could be the best plan for the gradual lifting of the restrictive measures and restarting of business activity in the post-lockdown period? In response specific guidelines were adopted in order for shopping centers, recreational activities, schools and religious groups to function. Similar hygienic rules have been applied for hotels, cinemas, pools and gyms.

Nevertheless, another important issue had to be addressed: the way in which public space will have to re-open to the public again. Looking to the future, planners, academics and decision makers in Greece started to think about this topic and how this crisis will transform people's relationship with public space, as many others do, worldwide. The fruits of such discussions were some initial plans and interventions most of which have already started to be implemented. They focused on the Athens Metropolitan Area where the majority of the country's population is concentrated, with a large number of visiting foreigners. At the same time, the Ministry of Environment and Energy has published technical instructions to promote the creation of temporary pedestrian streets and cycle lanes, as well as the development of temporary traffic-calming zones (speed limit is reduced to 30 km/h).

This chapter focuses on the implementation works took place in Athens. They are presented and examined, taking into account similar decisions that other countries have taken. Finally, although there is a great uncertainty about the way COVID-19 pandemic will impact future urban planning and design approaches, an estimation of the results is considered.

39.2 Initial Ideas About an "Anti-social" Planning Policy: How Easy is to Combine such a Policy to the Sustainable Mobility Paradigm?

Public squares and streets consist of the main components of the public space of a city. They are spaces serving everyday needs [10] and are characterized by a symbolic function [11]. Both of those reasons urge people to concentrate on such spaces that are related to a high degree of psychological health of people [12], sociability [13] and democratic culture [14]. Taking all of the above into consideration, public squares and streets are mainly considered to be social spaces [15, 16].

Researchers whose studies focus on Greek cities [10, 17–20] agree to such an opinion. Nevertheless, after the lockdown period, a growing body of academics bemoans the decline and degradation of public spaces [21–24]. Honey-Rosés, et al. [25] and Scott [26] are interested in such a topic. Although the effects in other sectors seem to be more intense [27], Honey-Rosés, et al. [25] underline that, in some years, extensive changes are also expected in planning practice. According to the same authors [25] some interesting queries may be raised in the near future.

Some of the above questions (i.e. *Will our perceptions of public space change?; Will we experience infringements on civil liberties?; Do we need a new typology for public space?*) seem to be of a future concern. On the other hand, some others (i.e. *Will streets be redesigned?; Will green space planning need new designs, uses and practices?; What will happen to micro-mobility and mobility sharing?*) have already arisen during the lockdown period, not only abroad but also in Greece. Discussion about the principles for resilient cities [28] came again into the forefront. By examining those principles, it could be concluded that, resilient cities have aspects in common with compact cities. Indeed, both city planning models focus on transportation and environmental protection policies by promoting coherence and high-density building [29]. At this point a dispute has risen about whether high-building density is connected to social-distancing enforced by the protocols for the COVID-19 crisis management:

- How the compact city, based on small local residences, will manage to attract the people more to their homes – while until now it urged them to be in public spaces – in order to remain safe (to ensure that, social distancing –especially between individuals of sensitive groups or deceased – is necessary)?

- How the compact city, based on public means of transportation and sharing culture, will contribute to the protection of public health?

- Whether the practice of office workers to stay at home, performing their tasks from a distance from other workers during the crisis, will prove to be a preferred form of "distance employment" when the city returns to normal inter-social activity. If so, what will be the effect on commuting from the suburbs, traffic, parking, public transportation and other city services?

The above questions are being raised by the opponents of the urban density planning model. This oratory refers to the basic arguments against the adoption of the compact city, that namely it does not contribute to the development of adequate microclimate, does not permit the satisfactory solarisation, lighting and airing of buildings and considerably delimits the urban green in the urban fabric. However, those questions have been discussed in the past [17] and the compact city model has been evaluated as the most viable solution. Indeed, the European Union has sought to promote the compact city model since the 1990s [29].

The two new questions posed above have occupied urban planners all around the world. The answer to these refers to the answer of some of the questions posed by Honey-Rosés, et al. [25]. In particular:

- The small size of unattached houses does not seem to raise concerns regarding the virus dispersal in the cities, since it limits the direct association to individuals of the same household. The size of residences does not absolutely guarantee the observance of distances within the household but refers more to the layout of residences and the individuals' mentality. To the contrary, the small size of houses – usually entailing a narrow front - implies that adjoining residences' balconies will be close to each other and thus the neighbors will be able to communicate more easily among them. Such a thing is prevented in areas with spare housing. The communication between neighbors – so visibly passive [30, 31], as much as active - is the one that prompts Souvatzidou and Belavilas (in [32]) consideration of the balconies as substitutes for the city square; even future public squares, in case the pandemic persists.

- The compact city model is not based only on public transport; in terms of transportation, a city can be considered as a compact one when an ideal combination of sustainable means of transport (walking, cycling, scooters and public means of transport) is active. That is the reason why WHO [33] declares that there is a strong encouragement in order for cities to improve and upgrade their public space and citizens move on an easier and safer mode.

- Despite this, the establishment of a sharing culture is important for the promotion of the compact city; during a pandemic it can be expressed in different ways, such as sharing of public space while some walk, cycle or talk to others.

These are the key-points in order for public space to be reformed in the post-COVID-19 period; accordingly, an answer can be offered to some of the queries raised. Such directions can be underlined through a brief review of case studies around the world. Indeed, many cities have already completed a series of interventions in order to be quickly transformed into resilient and - at the same time - sustainability, as well. Some case studies are presented on the following section in order to be compared to the actions that have been implemented in Greece.

39.3   Case Studies: Combining resilient city strategy with compact city strategy

In many cities across the world various sorts of temporary measures have been quickly implemented in order to keep citizens as safe as possible by taking precautions to "flatten the curve." Those measures can be categorized into 2 main groups: (a) Enhance walking and (b) enhance cycling. More specifically:

(a) Enhance walking: In most of the cities, sidewalks tend to be crowded. Their width - if they exist - is not ideal while most of the time they are occupied by street vendors, trees and street equipment. People need more space on the streets. This need was obvious even before the COVID-19 era; now, it is a necessity, taking into account social distancing measures. In that condition cities must implement low cost and temporary interventions on streets in order to urge people to walk and stay outside. Actions that promote walking (Figure 39.1) include:

   (a1) Closing streets to private vehicles. Vienna, Austria has created nine temporary meeting zones by reallocating road space from motorized traffic to pedestrian traffic. Such an intervention was chosen to be implemented in neighborhoods where the population density is high enough while sidewalks are narrow and open spaces are limited. Moreover, 20 other streets have been fully pedestrianized [34].

   (a2) Extending existing sidewalks. The city of Hammersmith, London has temporarily widened the sidewalks in two busy streets providing city dwellers with social distancing. Apart from enabling pedestrians to pass each other while social distancing, through this intervention pedestrians are allowed to queue safely for essential supplies from pharmacies and food stores. The pavements have been widened by locating on the streets barriers, water-filled bollards and weighted cones. At the same time, signage has been put in place to inform not only drivers but also pedestrians of the new street design [35].

   (a3) removing crosswalk "beg buttons." The city of Des Moines, Iowa automated pedestrian walk signals at crosswalks so that pedestrians do not need to push the beg buttons. Currently, approximately 45% of the signaled crosswalks are automatic. They are mainly located at the city center and there consideration for expanding this measure to other areas of the city, as well [36].

FIGURE 39.1
Case studies worldwide. Source: a. [39]; b. [40]; c. [41]; d. [42]; e. [43]; f. [44]

(b) Enhance cycling: In many cities, cycling was not a popular means of transport until the lockdown period. Citizens tended to prefer private cars or public transport for various inner-city travels, although bicycle-friendly policies had already started to be applied (i.e. bike sharing schemes). After the COVID-19 outbreak such policies have been intensified in order to contribute to behavioral changes and the effective adoption of the bicycle, replacing a portion of public transport (and private car) trips with bicycles. The city of Bogota offers one example. Back in 1976, Ciclovia was introduced; it is about a program under which specific streets became car-free on Sundays and holidays for 7 hours per day. In that way a 585 km network of connected streets and bicycle lanes was developed thereby minimizing the construction costs. This initiative was extended to all days of the week, after the lockdown period [37]. Those streets are now the only way for citizens to move around the city while social distancing and exercising themselves. In spite of the fact that the interventions are not permanent, it turns out that such a measure seems to be one of the most resilient.

(c) A similar approach was applied in Budapest, where the use of public transport has been reduced by approximately 90% after the outbreak. Temporary bicycle lanes have been established on some important streets in order to provide citizens with an alternative and safe way to move around the city. Due to the fact the overall traffic is decreased, no significant traffic congestion is expected. Concerning the phases of the renovation, central locations are the priority [38]. Another action is related to bike sharing systems. Cities like New York and Chicago that have invested in bike sharing schemes and cycling infrastructure during recent years, have seen their systems surge in demand. To face the increased demand, new bicycles have been added. Moreover, the systems have been made entirely free for essential workers that had to move around the city.

Finally, it should be mentioned that another set of measures have been applied. It is related to public transport and contains measures like: (a) extending the timetable for the metro and tram lines, (b) increasing the number of itineraries, (c) promoting all-door bus boarding and (d) keeping stations and vehicles clean. However, we have not focused on such measures because they do not transform the form of urban space although they have a spatial footprint.

39.4 What's Happening in Greece? The Case Study of Athens

The management of public space preoccupied the General Secretariat of Civil Protection but also academics and urban planners in Greece. From the first weeks of lockdown, decisions were taken for the prohibition of access to public spaces. At first, the entrance and stay in the parks of Attica was forbidden. Typical are also the cases of the New Waterfront in Thessaloniki and the Waterfront (Argonauton Str.) in Volos. These prohibitions were the result of intense overcrowding of citizens. Nikiforidis (in [45]), referring to the case of Thessaloniki, underlined that overcrowding is not necessarily a result of citizen insubordination but is an element that designates the absence of public space. Gospodini [46] arrives at the same opinion, characterizing the decision for the closing of the waterfront in Volos as wrong. Since there is no central square, the streets are narrow with narrow sidewalks and pedestrian network is limited.

Although the authorities' intention was not the total prohibition of pedestrian movements but the prevention of congregation, the citizens' reaction was intense because of the deprivation of public space which is of vital importance for the smooth operation of the cities. Such decisions can be justified in periods of pandemics (lockdowns) and especially in any unprecedented situation in which the scientific community was unable to manage an unknown virus. However, their long-term extension is discouraged since, beyond the operating issues of the city, the connection of public space with factional disputes is unavoidable. Typical is the case of Agios Ioannis Sq. in a neighborhood of Athens that constituted the object of discussion for whether the specific square should be open to the public or the access to it should be prohibited.

Beyond the first - possibly unfortunate but effective - decisions for public space, the issue came again in to fore during the planning for the lifting of the restrictive measures. Taking into consideration the resumption of business activity and the normalization of city life, the question was whether measures could be taken quickly and effectively to restrict the spreading of COVID-19 without circumventing the role and operation of public space. In this context, the Transportation Engineers Association (SES) [47] was against the increase of automobiles that, in combination with walking and bicycling, was proposed as an ideal solution for moving around the cities by the infectious disease specialists team [48]. In parallel, it proposed [49] the immediate development of pedestrian and cycle networks in Greek cities, something that can take place with a series of interventions like those in cities abroad. Thus, beyond the temporary transformation of parts of road networks to spaces of exclusive pedestrian and cycle movement, the delimitation of parking, the widening of pavements and the liberation of pavements from obstacles, the SES [49] proposed the decrease of vehicle speed limit from 50 km/h to 30 km/h; the development of small parklets; the movement of pedestrians to be safe and overcrowding to be considerably limited, since the proposed socializing spaces will be of small size and capacity will be limited.

In this context, the Ministry of the Environment and Energy proposed a provision with which procedures have been quickly enacted for the temporary creation of cycle lanes and footpaths [50]. In Athens those directions were integrated in a uniform planning by the municipality of Athens for the city center, called "Great Walk" (Figure 39.2a).

It is an integrated plan of revival of the historic center that creates new paths for pedestrian and bicycle movement. These routes will connect the neighborhoods of the historic center of Athens as well as the archaeological areas, changing the image of the city. Through the interventions of this program, about 50,000 m2 will be devoted to pedestrians and cyclists. The total length of the course comes up to 6.8 km, while 1.9km of new bicycle paths are expected to be created in the center of Athens where the infrastructure is considerably limited today [51].

FIGURE 39.2
The interventions proposed in Athens. Source: a. [52]; b. [53]; c. [54]; d. [55]; e. [56]; f. [57]

As Figure 39.2 points out, the regeneration scheme includes 3 types of actions: a) closing streets to private vehicles; (b) extending the existing sidewalks; and (c) developing cycle-lanes. All of the three types of interventions have also been implemented in other cities abroad, as was mentioned in the previous section. More specifically, the regeneration scheme contains the following interventions:

- The redevelopment of Panepistimiou Str. The plan is based on closing three of the six traffic lanes. On that part of the street, a new cycle-lane has been developed. The pavement has also been extended. Concerning motor traffic, 2 car lanes and one bus lane have been preserved. In that way, two main squares of the city (Syntagma Sq. and Omonoia Sq.) have been connected by a green route and the "Trilogy of Buildings" (National Library-Central Building of the Kappodestrian University of Athens – Academy of Athens) has been vindicated. This intervention is also connected to another street redevelopment: It is about Patision Str. (from Omonoia Sq. to Egypt Sq.). On that part of Patision Str., an extension of the sidewalks and a new cycle-lane have been adopted (Figure 39.2d). The cycle-lane is going to end in Kifisia. According to the Minister of Environment and Energy this cycle-lane is one of the two additional interventions that will take place, apart from the "Great Walk of Athens." It should be underlined that such interventions are also proposed by the recent Regulatory Plan of Athens (2014) (Act No. 4277/2014). According to that plan, a whole cycling network is proposed to be developed. This provision compensates the absence of planning for cycling in the context of the General Development Plan for the Municipality of Athens which is old enough (1988) and obsolete.

- The redevelopment of Omonoia (Concord) Sq. was scheduled before the COVID-19 outbreak (Figure 39.2f). However, it is considered to be part of the "Great Walk of Athens" because: (a) it is spatially related to the interventions and (b) this scheme is an inspiration from many years ago (see below).

- The redevelopment of V. Olgas Ave. (Figure 39.2c) has been one of the works of great significance. It is about a narrow street that is characterized as an "avenue" due to its great importance; it is the street in front of the Zapeion Megaron. Until the COVID-19 outbreak it was a typical street for car-movement. A tram-line was also located within the street. After the interventions, the Kallimarmaron Stadium is well-connected to other important monuments such as the Parthenon, the Oden of Herodes Atticus, the Areopagus (Mars Hill) and the Museum of Acropolis. The intervention contains widening of the sidewalks and the development of a cycle-lane. The tram-line and one car-line have remained.

- The redevelopment of Herodes Atticus Str., Athenas Str., Ermou Str. and Metropoleos Str. includes the convertion from a road to a pedestrian street. However, specific cars of special purpose (ambulances, fire tracks, food supply tracks, hotel vans, taxis, etc.) and residents' cars are allowed on those streets.

- The redevelopment of Syntagma Sq. (Figure 39.2e) The plan is based on limiting car movements (in Stadiou Str.) to only three lanes. A bus-lane and a bus-stop-lane have also been developed. On the rest of the road space two elongated parklets have been developed. In that way, the sidewalks of the two blocks facing Stadiou Str. have been widened.

This plan is not a new inspiration. Many years ago (early 2000s), there was a proposal for the unification of archaeological sites of Athens. Through that idea, the previously separate archaeological sites of the historic center could be connected in order to create a large archaeological park enhancing the historic image of the city. A major part of the plan was implemented before the Olympic Games 2004. The most interesting intervention was the redevelopment of Dionysiou Areopagitou Str. which is now considered one of the best pedestrian routes in Europe. However, the regeneration scheme was not totally implemented. One part of a great significance was the one between the Temple of the Olympian Zeus and the Panathinaikon Stadion (V. Olgas Ave.). This part has been included into the "Great Walk" plan. Concerning Athenas Str., there was a prediction in the previous plan about a small scale pedestrianization (close to Omonoia Sq.). Through the "Great Walk" regeneration scheme, the whole length of Athens Str. has now been pedestrianized.

Moreover, the redevelopment of Ermou Str. was also proposed by Vlastos (in [58]), as an extension of the works took part before the Olympic Games 2004 although people - especially store owners - disagreed with that opinion. After a decade, this intervention has also been implemented (even partially due to the reactions of public).

Finally, the idea of pedestrianizing Panepistimiou Str. first appeared in 1983 by the Greek Ministry of Public Works, in the context of the Master Plan of Athens. However, no works were implemented until 2010s when the idea of a partial pedestrianization of Panepistimiou Str. came again to the forefront (Rethink Athens) (Figure 39.2b). In that context the tram line was proposed to be extended from Syntagma to Patissia, through Panepistimiou Str. A strong debate regarding this regeneration reached immense proportions and had a huge political and urban planning impact

[59]. However, the project was not implemented after the European Commission rejected the funding due to the economic crisis. Almost a decade after that, this is intervention has now been implemented.

It should be mentioned that, the "Great Walk" is also combined with other small-scale redevelopments that have been scheduled before the COVID-19 outbreak. Such interventions are the pedestrianization of the Historic Triangle of Athens and the redevelopment of some of the squares of the city center. The cost of the interventions (at the time, it is about a pilot implementation) was 2 million euros.

39.5   Brief Discussion

The "Great Walk" scheme manages to materialize interventions that for decades were not achieved. The concession of large areas of the city to pedestrians and cyclists took place with particularly quick procedures. As much the realization speed of the interventions as the turn to the prevailing concept for the city - from a car-centered point of view to a pedestrian-friendly one - are classified to the benefits of the action. To the benefits of the interventions we can factor in the financial benefits that result from the possibility of exploitation of a larger part of the pavements from the roadside establishments, without hindering pedestrians. In parallel, however, the positive effects extend to the social level since socializing is encouraged through the placement of benches. Some may be concerned considering that social contact could not coexist with social distancing. However, the one situation does not contradict the other. The instructions by the infectious disease specialists mention social contact by paying attention; it has not mentioned anything about isolation. Social contact by paying attention can be possibly adopted in large spaces where the benches are placed well apart and permit social distancing. Therefore, such a perspective advocates for the conservation of large open spaces that seem to constitute an advantage for a city, even during a pandemic. Honey-Roses, et al. [25] arrive at this opinion underlining the importance of existence of such spaces in the context of urban resilience.

The above benefits, however, were initially opposed by the opposition of the municipality of Athens. This part of the municipal authority, as well as by groups of citizens and architects, was not in favor of the redevelopment for the following reasons: (a) non-compliance of the provided procedures, since no consultation preceded them, (b) unsatisfactory aesthetic result, (c) insufficient urban planning considering the movement of individuals with restricted mobility, (d) non-viability in terms of environment since it creates congestions, and (e) cost of the project.

Most of these points (b-d) can be easily refuted since the interventions will become permanent in the second phase of the project, after the completion of which, a limited movement of motor vehicles (as a result, the total number of car trips within the city will be reduced; this is something that is considered a public health necessity for most people in America and elsewhere [60] is expected. Easier access by all users (pedestrians, cyclists, disabled, old people, etc.) is also expected.

Finally, it should be underlined that the case of Athens is not a typical one: although the planning policy has been implemented in order for the transmission of COVID-19 to be limited, it seems that the regeneration plan aims to something bigger than that. The ultimate goal is to promote useful interventions that upgrade the city's form and image by establishing permanent solutions to a series of urban and traffic planning problems.

39.6   Conclusions

In this chapter, a brief consideration of the effects derived from the COVID-19 outbreak in the cities and public spaces was attempted. The topic is particularly important as public space constitutes a field of expression of human life in the cities which historically were designed based on health criteria. Typical are the examples of the Renaissance and the post-industrial revolution period, as well as design practices proposed in the context of utopian idealism and modern movement. Cities evolve and the change of their form is not strange when public health is a major concern of the citizens.

In the post-lockdown era, a large number of cities have decided to change their form by suggesting interventions of great significance. Widening of pavements, closing streets to private vehicles, developing cycle-lanes and removing crosswalk "beg buttons" are only some of the mainstream strategies applied, worldwide. In Greece, discussion of those practices came to the fore when the need for restrictive measures for limiting the virus transmission became obvious.

In fact, the Municipality of Athens has immediately adopted a large-scale action: the "Great Walk of Athens" regeneration scheme.

It is a project that includes the concession of road space to pedestrians and cyclists by limiting motorized traffic in the historic city center. The action was accepted with mixed reactions by the authorities and the citizens. However, as mentioned, the positive effects are more than the negative ones. In support are the results from other countries where respective policies were adopted. Nevertheless, it could be said that the degree of positive feedback by the local public in such measures is related to two parameters: (a) the degree of the virus transmission as well as the number of recorded cases and (b) the mobility culture in each country that reflects its cultural identity. The low number of cases in Greece and the absence of sustainable mobility culture are the reasons why a negative climate was developed during the construction phase. However, the fact that the intervention proposed by the Municipality of Athens is in line with the principles of a sustainable, compact and resilient city, entails long term benefits for the city and its citizens. This is the reason why the permanence of the projects is encouraged despite the fact the implementation of the SUMP has not been completed.

It should be underlined that, although the "Great Walk of Athens" is a scheme of integrated measures of great significance, they are not the only ones that can be applied (i.e. crosswalk beg buttons have not been removed and bike sharing system has not been developed - the acquisition of bikes was subsidized, according to the Ministry of Energy and Environment decision). However, even those measures are superior to the corresponding ones that have been taken in cities of other countries where the outbreak was more intense. That proves that decision-makers in Athens were interested in acting as early as possible. On the other hand, no special interventions have been proposed in order for the cities to be safer in the post-lockdown era. The reason why no special interest have been expressed is probably related to the urban sprawl observed in most of them (e.g., buildings are located at ideal distances; building density is higher only in the center of cities). The good point is that many cities have already implemented SUMPs or have expressed interest in their consideration; some cities where many COVID cases have been reported fall into this category.

Taking all the above into consideration, it could be said that Athens is one of the cities across Europe where brave decisions have been taken. The whole format of the city center has been changed; a large pedestrianized space has now been developed that gives the opportunity for everybody to social distance and stay safe. After the COVID-19 outbreak, Athens has been considered as a resilient city. Nevertheless, this positive outcome could not have been attained had the National Technical University of Athens, other scientific organizations and local authorities not previously supported such studies. Hopefully, the ex-post evaluation will prove that through such actions cities can greatly benefit, not only for citizens to be protected from the pandemic but also for cities to be transformed into economic, compact and resilient urban cores.

References

[1] Wenjun Du, Shaolei Han, Qiang Li, and Zhongfa Zhang. Epidemic update of COVID-19 in Hubei Province compared with other regions in China. *International Journal of Infectious Diseases*, 95, 321-325, 2020.

[2] Robert Kruse. Therapeutic strategies in an outbreak scenario to treat the novel coronavirus originating in Wuhan, China. *F1000Research*, 9, 2020.

[3] John Hopkins University. COVID-19 Dashboard by the center for Systems Science and Engineering. 2020. URL https://gisanddata.maps.arcgis.com/apps/opsdashboard/index.html#/bda7594740fd40299423467b48e9ecf6. Accessed on 3 July 2020.

[4] Qun Li, Xuhua Guan, Peng Wu, Xiaoye Wang, Lei Zhou, Yeqing Tong, Ruiqi Ren, Kathy SM Leung, Eric HY Lau, Jessica Y Wong, et al. Early transmission dynamics in Wuhan, China, of novel coronavirus–infected pneumonia. *New England Journal of Medicine*, 382, 1199-1207, 2020.

[5] Vital Surveillances. The epidemiological characteristics of an outbreak of 2019 novel coronavirus diseases (COVID-19)—China, 2020. *China CDC Weekly*, 2(8):113–122, 2020.

[6] Zheng Ye, Yun Zhang, Yi Wang, Zixiang Huang, and Bin Song. Chest CT manifestations of new coronavirus disease 2019 (COVID-19): a pictorial review. *European radiology*, 30(3), 4381–4389, 2020.

[7] Andrea Saglietto, Fabrizio D'Ascenzo, Giuseppe Biondi Zoccai, and Gaetano Maria De Ferrari. COVID-19 in Europe: the Italian lesson. *Lancet*, 395(10230):1110–1111, 2020.

[8] Andrea Remuzzi and Giuseppe Remuzzi. Covid-19 and italy: what next? *The Lancet,* 7(5), 365-366, 2020.

[9] P. Tugwell and S. Nikas. Humbled Greeks show the world how to handle the virus outbreak. 2020. URL https://www.bloomberg.com/news/articles/2020-04-17/humbled-greeks-show-the-world-how-to-handle-the-virus-outbreak. Accessed on 7 July 2020.

[10] C Kyriakidis. The function of urban public space in relation to local parameters: Comparative study between Larisa and Nottingham. *Aeichoros*, 24:67–85, 2016.

[11] S. Radović. The politics of symbolis in city streets: Patterns of renaming the public space in post-Yugoslav countries. *Narodna Umjetnost,* 51(2), 117-132, 2014.

[12] Angela Curl, Catharine Ward Thompson, and Peter Aspinall. The effectiveness of "shared space" residential street interventions on self-reported activity levels and quality of life for older people. *Landscape and urban planning*, 139:117–125, 2015.

[13] Leila Mahmoudi Farahani, Mirjana Lozanovska, and Ali Soltani. The social life of commercial streets. In *8th Making Cities Livable Conference, Melbourne (VIC), Australia*, 2015.

[14] Ward Thompson. Urban open space in the 21st century. *Landscape and Urban Planning*, 60, 59–72, 2002.

[15] Osias Baptista Neto and Heloisa Maria Barbosa. Impacts of traffic calming interventions on urban vitality. *Urban design and planning*, 169(2):78–90, 2016.

[16] Maryam Lesan and Morten Gjerde. Management of business activities along streets; an often neglected aspect of urban design. In *Living and Learning: Research for a Better Built Environment: 49th International Conference of the Architectural Science Association 2015, Melbourne, Australia*, 2015.

[17] E. Bakogiannis, C. Kyriakidis, T. Papagerasimou, M. Siti, and C. Karolemeas. Research on the development potential of greenways for pedestrians and bicycles in medium sized-cities. The case of Drama. *International Conference on "Changing Cities IV": Spatial, Design, Landscape and Socioeconomic Dimensions, Chania, Greece*, 2019.

[18] E. Bakogiannis, C. Kyriakidis, M. Siti, and E. Kourmpa. Exploring the accessibility of landmarks in cities. The case study of the Stavros Niarchos Foundation Cultural Center. In: In A.M. Defner, P. Skayannis, P. Rodakinias, & E. Psatha (Eds), Modern questionings for planning and development. *University of Thessaly Press, pp. 1186-1197*, 2018.

[19] M. Andrakakou, P. Panagopoulos, Y. Paraskevopoulos, and S. Tsigdinos. Investigating the spatiotemporal footprint in central areas. Identification of centralities and human flows in Koukaki area of Athens. In 1th International Conference of the Hellenic Geographical Society: Innovative Geographies: Understanding and connecting our World. *(pp. n.r.). Lavrio, Greece: Hellenic Geographical Society*, 2018.

[20] Th Vlastos. Creating the "Public City". Public space in the 21st century digital world. 2016. URL https://drive.google.com/file/d/0B0NkroBRNMD9ekpUUExsakJJVDg/view. Accessed on 15 July 2020.

[21] P. Kyprianos. Coronavirus and public space: I Efimerida ton Syntakton. 2020. URL https://www.efsyn.gr/stiles/apopseis/239099_koronoios-kai-dimosios-horos. Accessed on 9 July 2020.

[22] S. Georgiou. Public space in the post-coronavirus era. *syntagma watch*, 2020. URL https://www.syntagmawatch.gr/trending-issues/o-dimosios-xoros-stin-meta-koronoio-epoxi/. Accessed on 6 July 2020.

[23] A. Karlantidis. What is the public space? *Parallaxi Magazine*, 2020. URL https://parallaximag.gr/parallax-view/poios-dimosios-choros. Accessed on 10 July 2020.

[24] K. Anesti. Professor Andreas Kourkoulas in Iefimerida: "Athens experiences conditions of amputation, during the coronavirus period". *iefimerida*, 2020. URL https://www.iefimerida.gr/ellada/koyrkoylas-athina-koronoios-akrotiriasmos. Accessed on 5 July 2020.

[25] Jordi Honey-Roses, Isabelle Anguelovski, Josep Bohigas, Vincent Chireh, Carolyn Daher, Cecil Konijnendijk, Jill Litt, Vrushti Mawani, Mike McCall, Arturo Orellana, et al. The impact of COVID-19 on public space: a review of the emerging questions. *OSF Preprints (pre-print/to be published)*, 2020. doi: 10.31219/osf.io/rf7xa.

[26] Mark Scott. Covid-19, Place-making and Health. *Planning Theory and Practice*, 1(6), *n.r*, 2020.

[27] Esteve Corbera, Isabelle Anguelovski, Jordi Honey-Rosés, and Isabel Ruiz-Mallén. Academia in the Time of COVID-19: Towards an Ethics of Care. *Planning Theory and Practice*, 21(2): 191–199, 2020.

[28] M. Evans. Resilient city-Definition and urban design principles: Building cities to be more resilient to physical, social and economic challenges. 2016. URL https://www.thebalance.com/resilient-city-definition-and-urban-design-principles-3157826. Accessed on 17 February 2017.

[29] E. Bakogiannis, C. Kyriakidis, M. Siti, T. Milioni, and C. Potsiou. Increasing urban resilience of Athens' Historic Center. FIG Working Week 2017: Surveying the world of tomorrow-From digitalization to augmented reality, 2017.

[30] Jan Gehl. Life Between Buildings: Using Public Space. *Washington, DC; London: Island Press*, 2006.

[31] William Hollingsworth Whyte et al. The social life of small urban spaces. *Conservation Foundation Washington, DC*, 1980.

[32] Monopoli Team. Does the balcony function as the new public square? 2020. URL https://www.monopoli.gr/2020/04/02/stin-poli/381192/einai-to-mpalkoni-i-nea-plateia/. Accessed on 2 April 2020.

[33] WHO. Moving around during the COVID-19 outbreak. 2020. URL http://www.euro.who.int/en/health-topics/health-emergencies/coronavirus-covid-19/novel-coronavirus-2019-ncov-technical-guidance/coronavirus-disease-covid-19-outbreak-technical-guidance-europe/moving-around-during-the-covid-19-outbreak. Accessed on 7 July 2020.

[34] Alan Rehfisch. Coronavirus (COVID-19): Remaking our streets. 2020. URL https://spice-spotlight.scot/2020/04/14/coronavirus-covid-19-remaking-our-streets/. Accessed on 6 July 2020.

[35] Mark Moran. London shopping street pavements to be widened to help social distancing. 2020. URL https://www.transportxtra.com/publications/parking-review/news/65206/london-shopping-street-pavements-to-be-widened-to-help-social-distancing/. Accessed on 9 July 2020.

[36] Maya Miller. Des Moines automates some crosswalks signals along MLK to reduce high-touch areas during COVID-19 pandemic. 2020. URL https://eu.desmoinesregister.com/story/news/local/des-moines/2020/05/28/des-moines-expands-automated-crosswalks-reduce-coronavirus-spread/5278406002/. Accessed on 8 July 2020.

[37] Olga Chepelianskaia. Urban Resilience: Learnings from COVID-19. 2020. URL https://www.resilience.org/stories/2020-05-12/urban-resilience-learnings-from-covid-19/. Accessed on 5 July 2020.

[38] D. Bencze. Temporary bike lanes will help traffic during the pandemic. 2020. URL https://koronavirus.budapest.hu/en/2020/04/06/temporary-bike-lanes-will-help-traffic-during-the-pandemic/. Accessed on 5 July 2020.

[39] J. Keesmaat. Picture on twiter. 2020. URL https://twitter.com/jen_keesmaat/status/1253664988167888896. Accessed on 16 July 2020.

[40] K. Johnson. Two more Leeds suburbs see social distancing barriers installed on busy roads. 2020. URL https://www.leeds-live.co.uk/news/leeds-news/two-more-leeds-suburbs-see-18363770. Accessed on 15 July 2020.

[41] A. Vaccaro. Share the road: Should cities close streets to make more room for walkers, runners? 2020. URL https://www.bostonglobe.com/2020/04/09/metro/share-road-should-cities-close-streets-make-more-room-walkers-runners/. Accessed on 15 July 2020.

[42] Vernon Matters Staff. Select no-touch crosswalks during COVID-19 response. 2020. URL https://vernonmatters.ca/2020/04/17/select-no-touch-crosswalks-during-covid-19-response/. Accessed on 15 July 2020.

[43] A. Schwedhelm, W. Li, L. Harms, and C. Adriazola-Steil. Biking provides a critical lifeline during the Coronavirus crisis. 2020. URL https://thecityfix.com/blog/coronavirus-biking-critical-in-cities-alejandro-schwedhelm-wei-li-lucas-harms-claudia-adriazola-steil/. Accessed on 15 July 2020.

[44] Associated Press. Covid-19 crisis: Berlin gets "pop-up" bike-lanes to boost cycling in pandemic. 2020. URL https://www.hindustantimes.com/world-news/covid-19-crisis-berlin-gets-pop-up-bike-lanes-to-boost-cycling-in-pandemic/story-4JXniei8HhyuSynE9rpJpL.html. Accessed on 5 July 2020.

[45] S. Ioannidis. The big cities after the pandemic: Kathimerini. 2020. URL https://www.kathimerini.gr/1071025/gallery/politismos/polh/oi-megales-poleis-meta-thn-epidhmia. Accessed on 4 July 2020.

[46] A. Gospodini. It was wrong to "close" the waterfront in Volos: MagnesiaNews. 2020. URL https://magnesianews.gr/volos/lathos-to-quot-kleisimo-quot-tis-paralias-toy-voloy-symfona-me-tin-kathigitria-poleodomias-toy-p-th-aspa-gospodini.html. Accessed on 6 July 2020.

[47] SES. Press release in relation to the gradual lifting of the restrictive measures due to the coronaviru. 2020. URL http://www.ses.gr/wp-content/uploads/2020/05/SES-212.pdf. Accessed on 6 July 2020.

[48] S. Tsiodras. Press conference. 2020. URL https://www.ethnos.gr/ellada/105178_tsiodras-aytes-einai-oi-epta-odigies-gia-na-min-kollisoyme-koronoio. Accessed on 10 July 2020.

[49] SES. Letter of SES to the Ministers of Infrastructure and Transportation, Interiors, Energy and Environment, Civil Protection and Crisis Management. 2020. URL https://www.smu.gr/2020/05/08/sygkoinoniologoi-zitoun-diktia-podilaton-pezon-logo-pandimias/. Accessed on 6 July 2020.

[50] Anon. Restriction on movements. How check-controls will be done-A detailed guide for the citizens: Newsroom. 2020. URL https://www.kathimerini.gr/1070385/article/epikairothta/ellada/apagoreysh-kykloforias-pws-8a-ginontai-oi-elegxoi---analytikos-odhgos-gia-toys-polites. Accessed on 5 July 2020.

[51] E. Bakogiannis, C. Kyriakidis, and C. Potsiou. The potential of Volunteered Geographic Information (VGI) to contribute in cycling infrastructure planning in Athens, Greece [Paper presentation]. FIG Commission 3 Annual Meeting and Workshop. *Cluj-Napoca, Romania*, 2019.

[52] Drive. The "Great Walk" of Athens: The center is pedestrianized. 2020. URL https://www.drive.gr/news/ellada/o-megalos-peripatos-tis-athinas-pezodromeitai-kentro. Accessed on 15 July 2020.

[53] G. Lialios and E. Karamanoli. Definite "NO" to the redevelopment of Panepistimiou St.: Kathimerini. 2015. URL https://www.kathimerini.gr/818146/article/epikairothta/ellada/oristiko-oxi-ste-sthn-anaplash--ths-panepisthmioy. Accessed on 15 July 2020.

[54] M. Vaularinos. The "Great Walk" and the great nagging. 2020. URL https://www.athensvoice.gr/politics/656050_o-megalos-peripatos-kai-i-megali-gkrinia. Accessed on 15 July 2020.

[55] Economy today. The "Great Walk" started to change Athens. 2020. URL https://economytoday.sigmalive.com/oikonomia/ellada/27231_o-megalos-peripatos-arhise-na-allazei-tin-athina-fotografies. Accessed on 15 July 2020.

[56] Skaitv. The "Great Walk": New view for the square – What has been changed: SKAI. 2020. URL https://www.skai.gr/news/environment/megalos-peripatos-nea-opsi-gia-tin-plateia-syntagmatos-ti-allakse. Accessed on 15 July 2020.

[57] Anon. The new Omonoia Sq. opens and a spectacular fountain now exists – Impressive timelapse video: Newsroom. 2020. URL https://www.iefimerida.gr/ellada/anoigei-nea-plateia-omonoias-entyposiako-sintribani. Accessed on 15 July 2020.

[58] G. Elafros. The whole center of Athens could be a "pedestrian street". 2009. URL https://www.kathimerini.gr/370382/article/epikairothta/ellada/olo-to-kentro-ths-a8hnas-enas-pezodromos.

[59] D. Kanellopoulou. Pedestrianizing the center of Athens: A brief history and queries: Athens Social Atlas. 2016. URL https://bit.ly/35kQ7Vo. Accessed on 10 July 2020.

[60] K. Wilson, C. MilNeil, and T. Snyder. COVID19 Legacy: The Death of the Avoidable Car Trip? 2020. URL https://usa.streetsblog.org/2020/03/23/covid19-legacy-the-death-of-the-avoidable-car-trip/. Accessed on 10 September 2020.

40

COVID-19 Pandemic Challenges and Impacts on the SDGs 2030: Indian Perspective

Saied Pirasteh, Hishmi Jamil Husain and Tammineni Rajitha

This chapter discusses the understanding of COVID-19 issues and its influences on Sustainable Development Goals (SDGs) 2030, particularly the Indian perspective. We require adopting interdisciplinary efforts and determining the challenges of social and education, economy, and health. COVID-19 global disaster has given us a big lesson on how transparent and reliable data with spatial information is efficient during an unexpected issue. Nevertheless, today, the world needs to work together on various aspects of disaster risk reduction, mitigation, and prevention. For example, it is strengthening regional cooperation in geospatial data sharing for mitigation of COVID-19 pandemics.

40.1 Introduction

The 2030 Agenda of Sustainable Development was launched in 2015 to foster a new 'Global Partnership' for sustainable development of the world. There are 17 SDGs with 169 targets and 232 indicators that demand the transformation of current systems for an equitable society and a healthy planet [1]. The achievement of SDGs requires strong political will and ambitious action by all stakeholders. The year 2020 remarkably shows the beginning of a decade of action to deliver the SDGs by 2030 [2]. It is a significant period for fulfilling the agenda, but in a very short period of time, with the unfortunate spread of the novel coronavirus, a global public health emergency happened, and the years of progress has been reversed. This global health crisis has changed the world as we know it. It has attacked societies at their core. It has affected not only human health but also the economy and social structures. The International Monetary Fund (IMF) has reassessed the prospect for growth for 2020 and 2021 and declared a recession period. It projects recovery in 2021 only if the world succeeds in containing the virus and take the necessary economic measures. In such an unprecedented situation, there is a tangible impact on all 17 goals. A global level impact has been summarized by the United Nations Department of Economic and Social Affairs (UNDESA) in the following infographic [3].

The authors believe that the work towards achieving SDGs begins with taking the SDGs from global to local. The first step is setting the national and subnational context of the 2030 agenda. Once the context is set, the goals and targets have to be adapted from national to local levels, and indicators have to identify, local means and structures of implementation have to design, and monitoring frameworks have to be created from national to local levels [4].

This chapter is an effort to document the impact of COVID-19 on the progress and status of the 17 sustainable development goals in India. The impact on each goal is evaluated in-depth based on the targets and indicators defined by India, using various reports by international agencies, newspaper reports and research publications.

40.2   COVID-19 Impact on SDGs

40.2.1   SDG-1

The goal-1 is No poverty and end poverty in all its forms everywhere. For India, there are a total of five national-level indicators that capture three out of the seven SDG targets for 2030 outlined under this goal [5]. In this study, we determined the local and global impact as follows:

The local impact of COVID-19 has been more disruptive to the urban workers who have lost their income sources than to the subsistence farmers. The subsistence farmers constitute the major percentage of the extreme poor in India, while urban workers majorly constitute the part of the population that has recently escaped from the 'extreme poverty'. The pandemic has pulled them back down, thus increasing the percentage of people living under extreme poverty in India. In addition to the above, IMF's World Economic Outlook Report 2020 has projected that India is likely to add 10 million to the poverty rolls this year and worldwide, more than 71 million [6].

The Mahatma Gandhi National Rural Employment Guarantee Act (MGNREGA) is a social refuge measure in India that aims to promise the 'right to work'. Under the MGNREGA system, the work dropped to 3.08 crore person-days in April in the aftermath of lockdown, which is 88.8% lower than April in the previous year [7]. Thus, leaving many people dependent on MGNREGA wages in rural areas with no income source. Therefore, the livelihoods of daily wage workers, migrant workers, agricultural labourers, fish workers, and others employed in the 'informal' sectors have been most severely affected. Overall, 4 million urban homeless people and 75 million inhabitants of informal settlements with no access to essential services such as water supply have suffered due to a lack of basic social protection measures [8].

In the global context, we determined that the first increase in global poverty as more than 71 million people worldwide are expected to exert back into extreme poverty [8]. Therefore, we will probably see the direct economic losses of $23.6 billion for the countries due to natural disasters.

Decreased labour income and poor job quality have disproportionately impacted the women and young workers more, creating disparities and has been exacerbated by the COVID-19 [9]. Therefore, the economies of the least developed countries are adversely affected. We can expect that 4 billion people not covered under any sort of social protection scheme have become exposed and are more vulnerable to the impact of COVID-19.

40.2.2   SDG-2

The goal-2 is Zero Hunger, which enhances end hunger, achieves food security and improved nutrition, and promote sustainable agriculture. For India, there are seven national-level indicators that capture three SDG targets for 2030 outlined under this goal. In this study, we determined the local and global impact as follows:

Almost in some countries, food security becomes one of the worst affected during these times of COVID-19 pandemic. The continued lockdowns across the country have affected labour and input availability for agricultural operations. This, coupled with the serious disruption in transport networks, has impacted food security [10, 11]. For example, in India, Punjab, Haryana, and Uttar Pradesh, the largest producer of wheat, faced a crisis at the time of harvest due to shortage of labour, transportation bottlenecks and unavailability of harvesting machines [12].

Besides, due to rumours regarding the association between poultry and COVID-19, it led to a loss of Rs. 22,500 CR to the poultry industry as many farmers destroyed their produce, and some sold at very low prices [13]. The demand for processed foods saw a huge surge, but due to a shortage of raw materials, manpower and exemption permissions, the production rate was low.

As reported in the Global Nutrition Report 2020, 37.9% of children under five years are stunted, and 20.8% are wasted in India, which is bound to increase with higher incidences of malnutrition [14]. Agriculture gross value added (GVA) is projected to grow by 2.5% in FY21 as compared to the average of 3.2% till 2017 due to the effect after the pandemic [15]. Bumper production of grain and horticulture output is estimated at 152.7 million tonnes and 313.35 million tonnes, respectively, even after the pandemic [16].

Considering the global impact, we estimated that 2 billion people worldwide are facing moderate food insecurity, and 700 million are facing severe food insecurity. This will be exacerbated by the pandemic, climate shock and the locust attacks as the yield and supply chain is disrupted [17].

Globally, in 2019, 47 million children were suffering from stunting and wasting due to acute malnourishment. This is projected to increase by 6.5 million more children due to constraints on nutrition services and limited accessibility. The food prices were adversely impacted throughout the world as COVID-19 disrupted the already fragile supply chains, which resulted in high price volatility for farmers and expensive essential commodities for consumers.

40.2.3 SDG-3

SDG-3 is focusing on good health and well-being. It ensures healthy lives and promotes well-being for all at all ages.

For India, there are a total of eight national-level indicators that capture five SDG targets for 2030 outlined under this goal.

We determined that the hospitals are overwhelmed with COVID-19 patients, and it is hampering the standard care required for other patients with acute or chronic ailments. The number of children affected by the COVID-19 pandemic is very less as compared to adults and the elderly, but the pandemic has severely impacted their growth and protection against infectious diseases, indirectly. As the household income will go down, the children, women and the elderly will become more vulnerable, and an increase in infant mortality rate (IMR) is imminent.

Besides, according to a UNICEF report, India is projected to give birth to 20 million babies, i.e. the highest number of births this year during the pandemic. With the majority of healthcare services redirected for pandemic control, neonatal mortality is set to rise [17].

Considering the global impact, with the overwhelming pressure on health systems, disrupted routine health services and constrained access to nutrition services, there will be an estimated 9.8 - 44.8% increase in under-5 deaths per month and an 8.3-38.6% increase in maternal deaths per month, over a period of six months in the 118 low- and middle-income countries.

However, there can be a 13% increase in TB related deaths worldwide, a 23% increase in malaria cases in Africa and a 100% increase in malaria-related deaths if the prevention and detection campaigns do not get back on track in the next six months [18, 19].

40.2.4 SDG-4

SDG-4 is delivering quality education, and it ensures inclusive and equitable quality education and promote lifelong learning opportunities for all.

For India, there are a total of nine national-level indicators that capture four SDG targets for 2030 outlined under this goal. The followings deliver the local and global impacts on SDG-4.

In India, there are more than 15 lakh schools and 50,000 higher education institutions which were closed due to the pandemic. It impacted millions of students as, along with education schools, also took care of the nutritional needs of the children. The inequality of access to the internet across India increased the digital divide, and even though classes were resumed through online mode, many children were left out of the fold. In addition to the above, access to technology in rural India and urban slums is highly gendered. According to a survey by Young Lives, 80% of the girls in rural areas have never accessed the internet, and 62% have never used a computer [18].

In the global context, according to a UNESCO report, the COVID-19 pandemic will negatively impact more than 290 million students from 22 countries due to the closure of schools. We predict that extended school closures will weaken the fundamentals of students, and it leads to loss of human capital as well as economic opportunities in the long run. Also, according to the World Bank, COVID-19 will deeply impact countries in where education may be grappling with high dropout or low learning outcomes rate. We found that several educational institutions had no choice but to embrace e-learning to sustain the momentum.

We have seen that in the last decade to now, encouraging to use e-learning has become more popular, and it witnessed an uptick due to ubiquitous internet connectivity, the proliferation of smartphones and significant advances in technology. Therefore, there will be a major shift in the curriculum and pedagogy in the post-COVID-19 era. For example, Climate Change Induced Disaster Management in Africa (CIDMA) has developed up-to-date courses in disaster management online courses. Many courses deliver by various institutions such as Coursera made it for free and learned online. For example, one of the courses is Do-It-Yourself Geo Apps, and it delivers how to use Web Application and to create Geo Application. Also, Southwest Jiaotong University (SWJTU) has planned to run MOOC courses, synchronous and asynchronous courses for students.

However, at least 500 million students globally are left out from the digital access to education. Such prolonged absence from school is associated with lower retention and graduation rates and worse learning outcomes, especially students from the disadvantaged section of society [9, 10].

40.2.5 SDG-5

SDG-5 is gender equality, and it stresses on achieving gender equality and empowering all women and girls.

The followings deliver the local and global impacts on SDG-5.

The local impact of COVID-19 under the lockdown, violence against women, has increased drastically. The domestic violence complaints in the period between March-May were at a 10-year high [19].

Perhaps post COVID-19 situations bring more and more behavioural and mental changes among women, particularly with huge post-traumatic stress. According to the Population Foundation of India, the disruption of routine health services, including pre- and post-natal health care, family planning and contraceptive supply, has put the health of women and girls at increased risk due to decreased access and taken away their control. The female labour force participation rate in India is 25 percent. 90% of working women are engaged in the informal sector or irregular formal sector, the majority of which is constituted by the hospitality and service sectors. The pandemic would force these women into more vulnerable jobs or result in their permanent exit from the market.

Finally, the pandemic has also disrupted the work of Self-Help Groups (SHGs), which had an important role in women empowerment. With only 46% of women having access to the mobile phone, digitized credit facilities will be out of reach for them [20].

Globally, we predict that 70% of the frontline healthcare workers are women putting them at greater risk from the pandemic [9–11]. The campaigns against female genital mutilation and child marriage have come to a halt due to the pandemic, which could severely affect the progress achieved till now. Therefore, due to the lockdown, the burden of unpaid household work and childcare is more than the pre-COVID-19 era, and it would have a long-term effect on women's health.

Besides, there are increased incidences of domestic violence against women during the pandemic lockdown. An estimated increase in 25-30% of reported cases has been seen in France, Argentina, Cyprus, and Singapore. And in many countries like Germany, Canada, Spain, the UK, the US and other countries, the demand for shelter homes by women has gone up [21].

40.2.6 SDG-6

SDG-6 is about clean water and sanitation, and it ensures the availability and sustainable management of water and sanitation for all.

For India, there are a total of seven national-level indicators that capture four SDG targets for 2030 outlined under this goal [5–10]. According to the above, we may provide the following local and global impacts on SDG-5.

Millions of Indians were already at risk due to the infectious diseases from unhygienic water and sanitation conditions. Therefore, we expect that water-borne diseases are more prevalent in rural Indian populations and urban slum dwellers because of inadequate hand washing and unclean water. Like these water-borne diseases, the coronavirus can also spread easily when clean water is not available.

As we can see in the world, the pandemic outbreak is projected to slow down investments in the water sector globally [22]. We estimated that the high-risk areas during the pandemic with the most chance of spread are the areas with low access, reliability, and the quality of water, sanitation, and hygiene (WASH). Moreover, industrial water demand will decrease by 27% due to the pandemic. This would result in reduced revenues to water utilities. There is a partial suspension of water billing and moratoriums on water service cut-offs in low-income countries globally.

40.2.7 SDG-7

The goal-7 serves for affordable and clean energy. It ensures access to affordable, reliable, sustainable, and modern energy for all.

For India, there are a total of two national-level indicators that capture one SDG target for 2030 outlined under this goal.

The impact of COVID-19 on SDG-7 estimates as (a) people without access to electricity declined from 1.2 billion to 789 million in 2018, but the world was lagging behind in achieving the targets by 2030 even before the pandemic, this is not expected to improve now with a constraint on funds. (b) There are millions of deaths due to a lack of clean cooking fuel. The progress in this sector is also stagnant since 2010 and is not expected to change. (c) The share of renewable energy is growing at a pace of 1.7 percent only. It is difficult to meet the target at this pace. (d) There is an urgent requirement to provide electricity for 1 billion people who are relying on health facilities without electricity. (e) Global energy investment is predicted to reduce by 20%, or $400 billion. (f) Global energy demand could fall by 6% in 2020, which would also cause a decrease in Global energy-related CO2 emissions by almost 8% in 2020, with coal demand also projected to fall by 8% [23].

40.2.8 SDG-8

The goal-8 is decent work and economic growth. It promotes sustained, inclusive and sustainable economic growth, full and productive employment and decent work for all.

For India, there are a total of seven national-level indicators that capture four SDG targets for 2030 outlined under this goal. We can determine the impacts of COVID-19 on SDG-8 as follows.

Locally, the economic impact of the pandemic has been disruptive, with the fourth-quarter growth of FY2020 has slipped to 3.1% according to the ministry of statistics. Research by State Bank of India estimates the contraction of gross domestic product (GDP) by 40% in the first quarter of FY21. Unemployment in India rose to 26% from 6.7% as a consequence of lockdown, i.e. at least 14 crore people lost employment.

The global impact of COVID-19 could increase the incidences of child labour and pose a serious threat to decent work for especially vulnerable women and men from the informal sector. With the reduction in working hours and economic decline due to the pandemic, labour productivity is expected to go down in 2020. It is estimated that the informal economy constitutes more than half of the workforce, amounting to approximately 1.6 billion workers who are vulnerable and severely affected.

40.2.9 SDG-9

The goal-9 is for industry, innovation, and infrastructure. We work together to build resilient infrastructure, promote inclusive and sustainable industrialization and foster innovation.

For India, there are a total of four national-level indicators that capture three SDG targets for 2030 outlined under this goal.

We can describe the local impacts of COVID-19 on SDG-9 as (a) standard & poor's (S&P) Bombay Stock Exchange (BSE) India Infrastructure Index lost 35% of its value during the initial months of the pandemic. That is to say, there is a demand cut in the transportation sector, power and industry, which would limit the growth with no clear recovery period insight [24]. Therefore, according to the government data, India's eight key industries in the infrastructure sector shrank 6.5% in March after the pandemic lockdown. The crude oil sector contracted 5.5%, natural gas 15.2%, refinery products 0.5%, fertilisers 11.9%, steel 13%, cement 24.7% and electricity 7.2% in the period of one month [25].

We estimate that the capital expenditure in the infrastructure segment would go down with limitations created due to pandemic for both private and government investments. India's monthly internet user base is estimated to reach 639 million, as reported by the ICUBETM report by Kantar. Currently is rural India, there being 264 million internet users, which is projected to reach 304 million in 2020 with students and housewives to adopting internet services. Some key elements that will drive the impact are Over The Top (OTT), hyperlocal services, social media, communication and online payments [26].

We have also seen that many industries and companies have focused on the development of new technologies and innovative devices and platforms. For example, GeoIME explored the innovative approaches toward reducing the number of inspections of vulnerability and risk estimation of buildings.

Globally 97% of people live within reach of a mobile signal, and 93% within reach of a mobile broadband signal. With the pandemic, there is an increased dependence on digital payments, e-learnings and many more, so the internet usage is bound to increase [9, 10].

40.2.10   SDG-10

The goal-10 focuses on the reduced inequalities. Everyone works on reducing inequality within and among countries.

For India, there are a total of nine national-level indicators that capture three SDG targets for 2030 outlined under this goal. We express the local and global impact as follows.

In India, the social distancing and lockdowns have led to the increase in income inequalities as the poorer segments of society who are engaged in informal sectors and other physical work for their livelihood are severely impacted as their work cannot be done remotely.

We observed that the educated white-collar employees working in Information Technology (IT) sector, finance and similar sectors had not faced many severe consequences as their work can be done remotely. Besides, the poorer segments have very few savings, which will be depleted by the end of this pandemic, and there is a lack of access to credit for them, which has put them in dire straits. Therefore, economists believe that due to the lockdown, there will be a widening in the gaps in access to quality education between high and low-income households. This will have far-reaching consequences in the future as the employment opportunities for low-income people reduce. Finally, the migrant labour community has suffered the brunt of the COVID-19 pandemic both economically and socially as they lost their livelihoods and forced to abandon the cities.

We also observed that globally the workers are receiving less share of what they help produce; with the pandemic, these workers have altogether lost employment, and with decreased production, their incomes have also contracted. Disabled people will be facing more challenges, be it the term of access to education, health care or the stigma attached. Finally, with the pandemic, there would be a reduction in the influx of money into developing and least developed countries from the developed nations of the world. This would turn back the progress achieved till now and widen the gap between the countries [9, 10].

40.2.11   SDG-11

The goal-11 provides sustainable cities and communities, and it makes cities and human settlements inclusive, safe, resilient, and sustainable.

For India, there are a total of five national-level indicators that capture two SDG targets for 2030 outlined under this goal. The impacts of the COVID-19 on SDG-11 can be considered for both local and global scales.

The air quality improved exponentially in Delhi, one of the most polluted cities in India. PM10 and PM2.5 concentrations in the air were reduced by half, NO2 and CO concentration also went down. In the transportation and industrial locations, the air quality improved as much as by 60% [27].

India has made special guidelines for dealing with the biomedical waste generated from dealing with the pandemic. App-based technologies are being used to monitor and streamline the disposal of waste [28]. In addition to the above, the population living in slums has decreased exponentially due to the large-scale migration back to rural areas after the pandemic shock. But this is a temporary change which is expected to change. However, the pandemic has pushed to rethink the current model of high-density habitation in cities. The high-density populations in metros like Mumbai and Delhi have created diseconomies and hampered the efficient dealing with the pandemic.

We predict that on a global scale, the people living in slums and informal settlements have suffered because of a lack of access to basic amenities like water, sanitation, waste management and similar challenges and issues. They are overcrowded and social distancing in such places is next to impossible in such a scenario; these places became hotspots of the pandemic. We have seen that the need for more public transport has arisen throughout the world to tackle the problem of overcrowding and address the need for social distancing. Therefore, the pandemic has pushed to rethink the urban cities. It has made clear that for better public health and mitigation of people's vulnerabilities, urban planning is crucial. Of the 150 countries having some kinds of urban plans, many are revisiting the plans to make them more sustainable.

Finally, we can say that air pollution is estimated to have caused 4.2 million premature deaths globally in 2016. With COVID-19 induced lockdowns, many of the cities saw a major drop in air and water pollutants as the factories were closed, and the automobiles decreased [9, 10].

40.2.12 SDG-12

Responsible consumption and production are goal-12. It ensures sustainable consumption and production patterns.

For India, there are seven national-level indicators that capture three SDG targets for 2030 outlined under this goal.

The domestic demand for steel has reduced in the range of 12% to 20% in FY 2020-21, showing a slowdown in the consumption of end products using steel. Fertilizer sales increased by 45% even amid the pandemic as there was no restriction on the fertilizer industry. Besides, with the experts suggesting hand wash as the most effective precaution against the pandemic, the water demand is predicted to go up by 20-25% as per household would need 100-200 liters more water [29].

A study by Jal Jan Jodo Abhiyan has found out that in the water scarce Bundelkhand region, per capita water usage has gone up by 60% after the pandemic as people are washing hands at least five times a day [30]. If this continues, it will prove difficult in the long run for the state to manage water supply for every household in the region.

Globally 13.8% of the food produced is lost during transport, storage, and processing, which amounts to $400 billion annually. It is highest in South Asia and Africa. With the pandemic disrupting already fragile supply chains this year, the losses of perishables are bound to be higher than in previous years.

40.2.13 SDG-13

The goal-13 is climate action, and it takes urgent action to combat climate change and its impacts.

For India, there are a total of four national-level indicators that capture two SDG targets for 2030 outlined under this goal.

The impacts of COVID-19 on climate action are determined. According to experts and newspaper reports, the lockdowns established as a precautionary measure against the pandemic has resulted in improvement of air and water quality across the globe. Also, the pandemic has exposed the vulnerabilities within our emergency response, governance, and early warning systems, which are important from the viewpoint of managing the disasters occurring due to climate change.

We observed that climate action had taken a backseat, and it is predicted to be slower than before as the focus and resources at state and national level have been redirected towards dealing with COVID-19 in India. We predicted that with the visible positive effects of lockdown on the environment, a stronger case for sustainability might be built with a greater push for alternative solutions like electric vehicles and rooftop solar power.

40.2.14   SDG-14

Goal-14 is for life below water, and it describes the conserve and sustainably use the oceans, seas, and marine resources for sustainable development.

For India, there are a total of five national-level indicators that capture four SDG targets for 2030 outlined under this goal.

We determined the impacts of COVID-19 to SDG-14 are not only reducing the economic activities but also much needed time for the water bodies to recuperate. However, the impacts are (a) the reduced human and economic activities have given much needed time for the water bodies to recuperate, the ponds, irrigation canals and lakes are many cleaners [31, 32].

In addition to the above, the pandemic crisis has adversely affected the livelihoods of small-scale fishermen as the global demand for seafood reduced, and the supply chain disruptions happened due to transport restrictions and limited market access. Therefore, a pandemic can increase the incidences of piracy, poaching and smuggling in the coastal regions, and illicit fishing might also increase with fewer resources to monitor the coastal areas. Also, industrial fishing will come down due to the fear induced by the pandemic, and it would prove beneficial to the artisanal fishers who have now reduced competition from the industrial fisheries [33].

Finally, there is a reduced use of chemical fertilizers and other human activities near the water bodies and in coastal regions, which has helped improve the quality of water by reducing the biochemical oxygen demand.

40.2.15   SDG-15

It is for life on land and describes how to protect, restore and promote sustainable use of terrestrial ecosystems, sustainably manage forests, combat desertification, and halt and reverse land degradation and halt biodiversity loss.

We have found that the impact of COVID-19 on many infectious diseases. These infectious diseases have been found to be of zoonotic origin, specifically transmitted from wildlife to human beings. The threat of such pandemic breaks increases with an increase in deforestation, habitat loss and illegal poaching.

For India, there are a total of five national-level indicators that capture five SDG targets for 2030 outlined under this goal.

40.2.16   SDG-16

Peace, justice, and strong institutions deliver in goal-16. It promotes peaceful and inclusive societies for sustainable development, provides access to justice for all and build effective, accountable, and inclusive institutions at all levels.

For India, there are a total of five national-level indicators that capture five SDG targets for 2030 outlined under this goal.

As we discussed in the previous sections, similar impacts almost have been seen in goal-16 as well. We describe the impacts as follows:

The pandemic has disrupted humanitarian aid flows, has limited the peace operations, and postponed or diverted the parties involved in the conflict from diplomacy. This might increase the unrest as conflicts arise within and among the countries.

We have also seen that there is already geopolitical friction created due to COVID-19 as the US has been blaming China for the novel coronavirus breakout, and China has been trying to gain favour by offering international aid to many countries. However, the authors do not believe this blame as it makes the current situation more complex to achieve the SDGs 2030, and these political frictions may create serious challenges and impacts on various collaborations, communications, and engagements.

Also, in some areas, there is also a chance of increased cooperation, as in the case of the UAE and Kuwait, who offered humanitarian aid to Iran. Moreover, China cooperated in providing humanitarian aids to several countries such as Iran, Italy, Argentina, Germany, and some African countries. The countries directly affected due to conflict have become vulnerable to the pandemic outbreak. Because their health systems are already broken, and the additional pressure of a global health crisis of this scale would put unprecedented demands on the system, which it is not capable of handling. For example, in Libya, during the war, most of the foreign medics had left the country, and in Venezuela, the political standoff had impacted the health system adversely.

40.2.17   SDG-17

Goal-17 encourages everyone to have a partnership for the above goals. It strengthens the means of implementation and revitalizes the global partnership for sustainable development.

Like the other SDGs, the impacts of COVID-19 have changed the nature of the collaborations. These impacts can be described as (a) remittances to low- and middle-income countries from international sources, which gave an economic lifeline for many poor households in these countries is projected to fall from \$554 Billion in 2019 to \$445 Billion in 2020. (b) Global foreign direct investments are expected to fall by 40% in 2020. (c) Net official development assistance from the member countries of the Development Assistance Committee (DAC) is expected to fall as the pandemic puts more pressure on the donor's aid budget. (d) There are instances where new partnerships have been forged. To develop a unified continent-wide strategy to deal with the pandemic and its impact, the African Union has established an Africa Taskforce for Coronavirus (AFTCOR). (e) The partnership between the African Union and the UN and has also been strengthened to deal with the pandemic outbreak [34]. (f) The European Union and the Member States have created 'Team Europe', which is helping the partner countries in dealing with COVID-19 through a comprehensive and decisive action to strengthen the healthcare, water and sanitation systems. Also, they collaborated to ensure fast and equitable access to safe, quality, effective and affordable tests, treatments and vaccines against coronavirus for the partner countries [35]. (g) WHO has initiated a Research and Development (R&D) Blueprint to accelerate the development of diagnostics, vaccines, and therapeutics for the fight against COVID-19. It has made a multinational coordinated research group for the purpose [36]. (h) In India, NITI Aayog CEO Amitabh Kant has reported the creation of empowered groups by the government, which constitute the NGOs, private sector and international aid agencies for tackling the COVID-19 crisis. The partnerships between these stakeholders are encouraged to lead an efficient fight against the pandemic [37].

40.3   Analysis and Interpretation

In the following diagram (Figure 40.1), the impact of the COVID-19 pandemic on sustainable goals has been mapped along with the interaction between different sustainable goals since each goal is affected by the progress of other goals (Table 40.1). The 17 sustainable development goals do not exist in isolation; there is a synergy among all goals. This synergy has been depicted through various linkages on the map. The analytical brainstorming and interpretational approach associated with some surveys attempted to define logical relationships among SDGs. We collected data and reports from various resources. We considered national and global level targets and indicators for SDGs. The SDGs targets and indicators are used as elements to interpret the relationships of 17 SDGs.

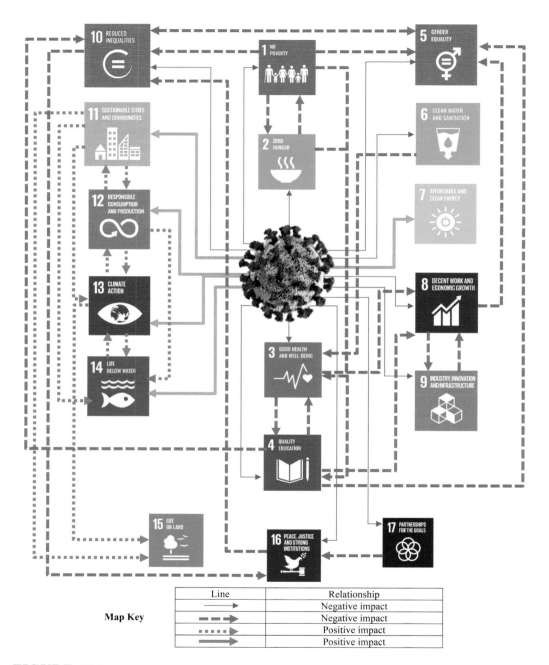

Line	Relationship
→	Negative impact
- - →	Negative impact
⋯⋯→	Positive impact
⟶	Positive impact

Map Key

FIGURE 40.1

Impact of COVID-19 pandemic on SDGs 2030

(Source: Created by qualitative analysis of collated information of the impact of COVID-19)

TABLE 40.1
Summary of COVID-19 impacts on SDGs for local and global scales

Goals	Local Impact	Global Impact	Impact on Other SDGs
1 - No Poverty	India is estimated to have 68% population below $3.2/day because of lack of livelihoods and disruption of the informal sector which involves 90% of the workforce	Global poverty is estimated to go up by 8.8%. Decreased labour income and poor job quality will push people into extreme poverty.	2,3,4,5,10
2 - Zero Hunger	ICDS Scheme, Mid-Day Meal Scheme have been compromised. Food supply chains have been disrupted—heavy post-harvest losses even with bumper production.	10,000 child deaths every month are recorded. Nutrition services have taken a hit. More than 2 billion are facing food insecurity.	1,3,4,5,8,10
3 - Good Health and Well-Being	Most adversely affected. Lack of sufficient healthcare workers and facilities. TB and HIV care would be drastically affected.	Estimated double-digit increase in child and maternal mortality, TB and HIV related deaths due to disruption of routine healthcare services.	1,2,4,5,8,10
4 - Quality Education	Unequal access to technology is predicted to cause a 20% drop out of girl students, disrupt the foundations of all students, and hurt their opportunities of better jobs.	Globally 290 million students will be impacted across 22 countries, and 397 million have lost out on food due to school closure. 500 million children and youth are not able to take the benefit of digital learning.	5,8,10
5 - Gender Equality	Increased domestic violence against women. Loss of livelihoods which could result in a permanent exit from the market. Healthcare and nutrition for women are also severely impacted.	25-30% increase in domestic abuse cases. The shutdown of prowoman campaigns. Increased stress and burden due to lockdowns	4,8,10
6 - Clean Water and Sanitation	The burden on the sanitation system and clean water availability is stretched in the cities. More than a crore people have migrated back to rural areas putting stress on sanitation in rural areas where although the toilets are built, they still need to be cleaned manually.	Capital expenditure on water and sanitation is expected to go down by 7% as the industrial demand has gone down, and the funds are directed for COVID-19 relief.	3
7 - Affordable and Clean energy	There is an urgency to provide electricity to 1 billion people who are dependent on healthcare facilities without electricity. There is an estimated reduction of 20% in energy investments and 6% reduction in global demand.		13
8 - Decent Work and Economic Growth	Economic growth has slipped to 3.2%, and unemployment has risen to 26%	Child labour is predicted to increase. Women might be pushed into dangerous jobs. The informal sector is adversely affected. Tourism and hospitality industry too.	5,9,10
9 - Industry, Innovation, and Infrastructure	Investments in infrastructure have gone down. The sector has shrunk by 6.5%. Eight key industries, i.e. crude oil, refinery, fertilizers, steel, cement electricity and natural gas, all have shrunk. Internet and mobile users are estimated to go up.	Globally there is a 6% decline in the manufacturing sector. Internet users are projected to go up. SMEs are projected to decline due to a lack of credit facilities.	8
10 - Reduced Inequalities	Inequalities are bound to increase with many blue-collar workers out of jobs while the white-collar workers work online to earn their livelihoods. With education also impacted the inequalities will further increase in the long run.	According to studies on previous pandemics, it has been observed that inequalities undoubtedly increase after such shock. The gap will widen between developed and developing and LDCs as funding are diverted or stopped in the wake of the pandemic.	5,16
11 - Sustainable Cities and Communities	Air quality has exponentially improved. New processes for BMW management have been streamlined. Rethinking of high-density city planning is triggered.	Air and water quality in the cities have improved. Many of the 150 countries are rethinking the city plans to make them more sustainable.	13,14,15
12 - Responsible Consumption and Production	Water demand is estimated to increase by 20-25%. Fertilizer demand has also spiked. Steel demand has gone down and estimated to further reduce by 20%. Consumption is majorly focused on essential commodities now.	Local sourcing and online working promoted due to the pandemic has reduced the demand for unsustainable fossil fuels and made a start towards responsible consumption	11,13,14
13 - Climate Action	6% reduction in global emissions. Vulnerabilities exposed; space has been created for designing of policies. For now, funds have been diverted to COVID-19 relief so climate action might be limited.		14,15
14 - Life Below Water	Water bodies are cleaner due to reduced human and industrial activity. Local fishermen are benefitting due to reduced industrial fishing. Water bodies and the fish stock got the recuperation time during the pandemic season		13
15 - Life on Land	No direct impact of Covid-19 but as a result of increased awareness about zoonotic diseases the laws against smuggling, protecting wildlife etc. might become stricter.		-
16 - Peace, Justice, And Strong Institutions	Internal conflicts have been put to rest for the time being as countries grapple with the pandemic. But International conflicts might increase due to increasing friction between US and China and unscrupulous politicians as the diplomacy efforts are restricted during these times.		11
17 - Partnerships for the Goals	All new partnerships are being forged for dealing with novel corona virus. In the process other goals are getting side-lined. But all the stakeholders the government, NGOs, private businesses, and international organizations are learning to work together.		16

40.4　Summary and Conclusion

We concluded that the pandemic had had severe impacts on the whole world, including India and the world. This is a public health crisis of unprecedented proportions that came as a shock and caught the world unprepared. By the end of 2020, 21 of the 169 SDGs targets would have matured, but the progress was already slow as the world was lagging behind in achieving the mentioned targets. This lethargic progress is further impacted by the sudden shock of the pandemic. It is expected that decades of progress in achieving the goals might be reversed because of this shock. The degree of impact might vary, but each and every single goal from the 17 SDGs has been affected either positively or negatively. All the goals are interconnected with the impact on one goal will have an impact on the other. Some goals like SDG 1, SDG 2, SDG 3, have seen a serious rollback in progress with more and more people losing livelihoods and slipping back into poverty, increased hunger crisis and insufficient healthcare system capacities. This has negatively impacted SDG 4, and in the long run, it will affect SDG 8 as the opportunities for decent work go down with a reduction in quality education opportunities. With the limited resources, capacities, and burgeoning crisis, the inequalities will increase for women and the poor, thus reversing the progress in SDG 5 and SDG 10. Some positive strides have been observed for SDG 7, SDG 11, SDG 12, SDG 13 and SDG 14 as the pandemic forced people to rethink the way cities were being developed and the lockdowns gave space for the environment to recuperate, the pressure on water life decreased as people become more conscious and responsible about their consumption and production. The pandemic also gave time to think and plan about the seriousness of the impending climate crisis. It brought to the forefront the weaknesses in current social, economic and governance systems of the world.

The COVID-19 experiences from various countries indicated that the more information we can access and analyze, the more effective nations we have. Therefore, it leads partners, including multilateral organizations and citizens, to explore and determine solutions for a disaster such as COVID-19 pandemic. This collaboration of partners requires several key components, such as existing and accessible geospatial information and the spatial data infrastructure (SDI) built. The geospatial information requires the integration of statistics and use it in various geography in a local, national, and global scale. We need technologies to demonstrate our geographic dimension on a global scale. It considers information that can be conveyed in a clearer and more useful manner than statistical data [38, 39]. In other words, we are fundamentally beyond the technologies and track platforms to enable visualization. This process relies on the people partnerships and the method of collaborations on how to build the ability to come together towards a shared purpose to remove barriers. However, the experiences of partnerships to data sharing of spatial information can also be considered to support COVID-19 response and recovery at this hard-pandemic situation and SDG2 2030.

We suggest empowering the implementation of geospatial technologies and methods such as Web App and Geo App. However, perhaps India requires speeding up to adopt these approaches. The adoption of spatial approaches such as Web App, Geo App, and smart mapping to spatial epidemiology, disease surveillance, and implementation of health policies in India has great potential for both success and efficacy. It is because India has a large population, ongoing public health challenges, and a growing economy with an emphasis on innovative technologies.

Acknowledgement

The authors thank the United Nations for providing information on the COVID-19 pandemic. We dedicate the chapter to people and families in the world who lost their beloved due to the COVID-19 pandemic disaster.

References

[1] SDG Indicators. Global indicator framework for the Sustainable Development Goals and targets of the 2030 Agenda for Sustainable Development. 2020. Retrieved on 27 July 2020.

[2] United Nations Sustainable Development Group. Finding transformative pathways in turbulent times. *The sustainable development goals report*, 2020. Retrieved on 27 July 2020.

[3] United Nations Sustainable Development Group. Shared Responsibility, Global Solidarity: Responding to the socio-economic impacts of COVID-19. 2020. Retrieved on 27 July 2020.

[4] United Nations High-Level Political Forum for Sustainable Development. The decade of action taking SDGs from Global to Local, India Voluntary National Review 2020. 2020. Retrieved on 27 July 2020.

[5] United Nations. SDG India: Index and Dashboard 2019-2020 Report1. 2020.

[6] Homi Kharas and Kristofer Hamel. The COVID-19 effect: Poverty headcount to rise the most in India. 10 million to be affected. 2020. 8 May 2020.

[7] Pallavi Nahata. Work Under MGNREGA Falls to Lowest in Five Years. 2020. URL https://www. bloombergquint.com/economy-finance/work-under-mgnrega-falls-to-lowest-in-five-years. 30 April, 2020.

[8] Shivani Chaudhry, Anagha Jaipal, and Aishwarya Ayushmaan. Housing and Land Rights Network. Human Rights Assessment and Compilation of State Relief Measures. 2020.

[9] United Nations. Sustainable development goals report 2020. 2020.

[10] United Nations. SDG India: Index and Dashboard 2019-2020 Report 2. 2020.

[11] Pramitha Elizabeth Pothan, Makiko Taguchi, and Guido Santini. Local food systems and COVID-19: A glimpse on India's responses. *FAO*, 2020. 22 April, 2020.

[12] URL https://www.news18.com/news/india/shortage-of-labour-and-machinery-during-covid-19-lockdown-worsens-indias-agrarian-crisis-2580143.html.

[13] URL https://smefutures.com/covid-19-rumours-fake-news-slaughter-poultry-industry-rs-22500-crore-lost-5-crore-jobs-at-stake/.

[14] URL https://www.newindianexpress.com/cities/delhi/2020/jun/29/malnutrition-among-children-the-unspoken-side-of-covid-19-pandemic-2162806.html.

[15] URL https://www.financialexpress.com/industry/agriculture-gva-growth-in-fy21-seen-at-2-5/1981655/.

[16] URL https://economictimes.indiatimes.com/news/economy/agriculture/record-grain-output-in-2020-horticulture-to-grow-too/articleshow/73684423.cms.

[17] UNICEF. Millions of pregnant mothers and babies born during COVID-19 pandemic threatened by strained health systems and disruptions in services. *UNICEF. Press Release*, 2020. URL https://www.unicef.org/rosa/press-releases/millions-pregnant-mothers-and-babies-born-during-covid-19-pandemic-threatened. 6 May, 2020.

[18] Rhiannon Moore and Lydia Marshall. Access to digital learning during COVID-19 closures: compounding educational inequality? 2020. Retrieved on 27 July 2020.

[19] URL https://www.thehindu.com/data/data-domestic-violence-complaints-at-a-10-year-high-during-covid-19-lockdown/article31885001.ece.

[20] Niaz M Asadullah and Kalyani Raghunathan. Tackling India's deepening gender inequality during COVID-19. 2020. URL https://blogs.lse.ac.uk/southasia/2020/07/08/tackling-indias-deepening-gender-inequality-during-covid-19/.

[21] United Nations Women. Policy Brief: The Impact of COVID-19 on Women. 2020.

[22] George Butler, Rogerio G. Pilotto, Youngki Hong, and Emelly Mutambatsere. The Impact of COVID-19 on the Water and Sanitation Sector. *International Finance Corporation (IFC)*, 2020.

[23] United Nations. Policy briefs in support of the high-level political forum 2020. Accelerating SDG7 achievement in the time of COVID-19. 2020.

[24] Pratik Sengupta. Infrastructure Sector and Investor Valuations Impact Amidst COVID-19. *International Finance Corporation (IFC)*, 2020. URL https://www.duffandphelps.com/about-us/news/infrastructure-sector-investor-valuations-impact-covid-19. 23 April 2020.

[25] URL https://www.deccanherald.com/business/business-news/coronavirus-impact-india-s-key-infrastructure-sector-output-contracts-in-march-831876.html.

[26] URL https://www.livemint.com/news/india/covid-19-to-push-india-s-monthly-active-internet-user-base-to-639-mln-kantar-11588758259831.html.

[27] Susanta Mahato, Swades Pal, and Krishna Gopal Ghosh. Effect of lockdown amid covid-19 pandemic on air quality of the megacity delhi, india. *Science of The Total Environment*, 730:139086, 2020.

[28] URL https://timesofindia.indiatimes.com/india/dealing-with-biomedical-waste-in-the-time-of-covid-19-presents-huge-challenge/articleshow/75905790.cms.

[29] URL https://www.downtoearth.org.in/blog/water/covid-19-outbreak-more-hand-washing-can-increase-india-s-water-woes-69900.

[30] URL https://economictimes.indiatimes.com/news/politics-and-nation/water-consumption-in-parched-bundelkhand-up-60-percent-due-to-covid-19-study/articleshow/75107081.cms?from=mdr.

[31] URL https://www.thehindu.com/sci-tech/energy-and-environment/lockdown-due-to-covid-19-how-our-waterbodies-are-cleaner/article31518267.ece.

[32] Ali P. Yunus, Yoshifumi Masago, and Yasuaki Hijioka. Covid-19 and surface water quality: Improved lake water quality during the lockdown. *Science of The Total Environment*, 731:139012, 2020.

[33] W. Saumweber, K. Luhr Amy, and Ty Lo.

[34] URL https://www.un.org/africarenewal/web-features/coronavirus/osaa/covid-19-strong-international-partnerships-key-bolstering-africa's-response.

[35] URL https://ec.europa.eu/international-partnerships/topics/eu-global-response-covid-19_en.

[36] WHO. Public statement for collaboration on COVID-19 vaccine development. 2020. URL https://www.who.int/news-room/detail/13-04-2020-public-statement-for-collaboration-on-covid-19-vaccine-development.

[37] URL https://indianexpress.com/article/opinion/columns/ngos-private-sector-international-organisations-fight-against-covid-amitabh-kant-6425547/.

[38] A. Laaribi and L. Peters. *GIS and the 2020 Census: Modernizing Official Statistics*. Esri Press, 2019.

[39] Saied Pirasteh and Masood Varshosaz. Geospatial information technologies in support of disaster risk reduction, mitigation and resilience: Challenges and recommendations. In A. Rajabifard, editor, *Sustainable Development Goals Connectivity Dilemma*, chapter 6, pages 93–105. CRC Press, 2019.

41

The Value of a Policy-Responsive Research Funding Model: The Geohealth Laboratory Collaboration in New Zealand

Malcolm Campbell, Jesse Wiki, Lukas Marek, Matthew Hobbs, Matthew Wilson and Simon Kingham

This chapter discusses the GeoHealth Laboratory (GHL) research model that is based on a relationship contract funding model between two parties, the University of Canterbury (UC) and the New Zealand Ministry of Health (MoH) around health geography, spatial epidemiology, and Geographical Information Systems (GIS). Further, the GHL seeks to produce high-quality research (i.e. journal articles) and policy-relevant outputs (e.g. in the form of plain English reports) in the fields of health and GIS. The chapter discusses the nature of the relationship and funding model, with examples of research from the annual research programme. We conclude by showing the importance of flexibility in research funding models, using emerging exemplars of research related to the COVID-19 response in New Zealand.

41.1   What Is the GeoHealth Laboratory?

The GeoHealth Laboratory (GHL) is a collective of researchers interested mainly in Quantitative Health and Medical Geography, based at the University of Canterbury (UC), New Zealand. The GHL began in 2005 as a strategic partnership between UC and the New Zealand Ministry of Health (MoH) [1] that provides a resource that is unique in the Southern Hemisphere. The aim of the collaboration is to build a strategic partnership between the two parties around health geography, spatial epidemiology, and Geographical Information Systems (GIS). It seeks to produce high-quality research (i.e. journal articles) and policy-relevant outputs (e.g. in the form of plain English reports) in the fields of health and GIS. The GHL programme has published across a range of topics including: inequity [2], inequity of mortality [3, 4], oral health [5, 6], social connection [7], obesity [8, 9] and natural disasters and health [10, 11] to highlight a few key themes. Researchers from the GHL also have a longstanding interest in policy relevant or responsive research. This includes using spatial microsimulation, a modelling technique, to understand the impacts on government health policy [12, 13] as well as in a NZ context to understand the social and spatial patterns in obesity [14]. The GHL also aims to increase research capability through a program of research degree scholarships, primarily through the Masters of Spatial Analysis for Public Health (MSAPH[1]) and

---

[1]https://www.canterbury.ac.nz/study/qualifications-and-courses/masters-degrees/master-of-spatial-analysis-for-public-health/

teaching, for example, a course entitled 'Spatial Analytics for Health'. This has resulted in a series of skilled graduates who are now employed throughout New Zealand and overseas[2].

41.2 The Funding Model

The nature of the relationship between UC and MoH means that the collaboration between the parties is funded[3] in advance, much like a research programme with several project outlines included as indicative components of the overarching programme. Subsequently, the precise detail of the research and scholarship projects are negotiated and co-designed by both academic staff and MoH staff (who act as a project stakeholder). An important aspect of the GHL model is that the projects are subject to change if circumstances require. This ability to change the direction of a research project provides flexibility, meaning that as research priorities change, so too can the research projects and the precise topics investigated. Enabling changes to projects, without changes to the whole programme, reduces the bureaucratic overhead in contracting and bidding for individual research projects, focusing instead on rapid delivery of timely results directly to policymakers. Thus, the funder of the research benefits from the transfer of effort from managing and administration of the bureaucratic overhead (for both parties) to the delivery of research outputs. The nature of the high level of trust in our collaboration and the built-in flexibility of the contract is a stark contrast to conventional funding routes. UC contributes a proportion of the time of two Directors (note in New Zealand, 40% of an academic's usual role is related to research, 40% to teaching and 20% to administration) and hosts the laboratory space in which the GHL. A key strength of the GHL is the critical mass of academic expertise in GIS and health. Moreover, being located within the multi-disciplinary Geospatial Research Institute (GRI) provides an opportunity to develop geospatial research in aligned areas for which health is an important factor, such as in the area of hazards research. Having a critical mass of academics and researchers with similar interests means that there is the possibility of securing additional funding and resources beyond the principal funding streams that come from MoH and UC. Historically the GHL funded has included a range of sources such as the Health Research Council (HRC), NZ Transport Agency (NZTA), Foundation for Research Science and Technology (FRST), The Cooperative Research Centre - Spatial Information (CRCSI), and Ministry of Health's Environmental Health Indicators Programme.

41.3 The Work Programme

The original work programme for 2019/20 consisted of six projects that were co-designed with stakeholders on the following topics: transient populations, major trauma injuries, alcohol-related harm, mental health, maternity and disability. However, with the need to support the Ministry's response to COVID-19 the work programme was reviewed to enable rapid delivery of outputs relating to data supply and the visualisation of COVID-19 cases (see Figure 41.1) as well as the identification of vulnerable populations based on demographic factors. Additionally, a project on population mobility was designed that utilises nationwide mobile phone data to analyse mobility patterns before, during and after national lockdown measures were implemented. This provides important information about the extent of population compliance to lockdown measures and how this varies during different periods of pandemic policy and alert levels[4], particularly by geographic area and socioeconomic status. The project also aims to allow for a better understanding of mobility patterns between places using a combination of traditional data sources such as Census travel data

---

[2]https://www.canterbury.ac.nz/science/research/geohealth/ (See "Former Postgraduate Students").
[3]The GeoHealth Laboratory is funded by the New Zealand Ministry of Health until June 2021.
[4]https://covid19.govt.nz/assets/resources/tables/COVID-19-alert-levels-summary.pdf

and the aforementioned mobile phone data. The results of the project are still emerging, however, we have reported the changing spatial patterns in mobility across NZ as well as the social and spatial differences that relate to the socio-economic position of neighbourhoods across NZ The ability to be flexible with projects provided significant advantages, ensuring the GHL work programme met the immediate and changing priorities of MoH.

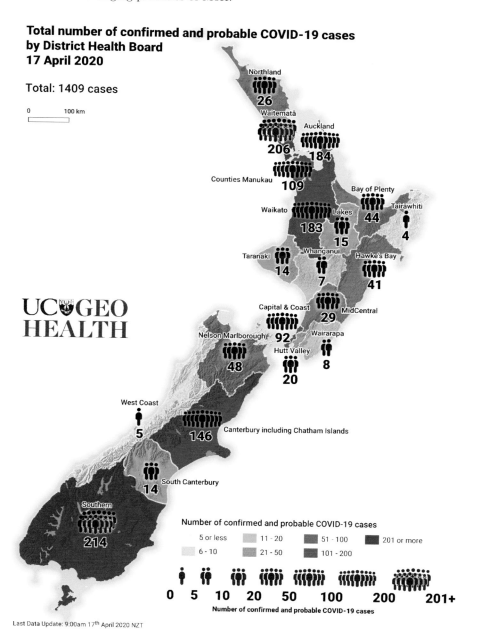

FIGURE 41.1

Spatial distribution of COVID-19 cases in New Zealand. 17 April 2020.

41.4   Conclusion

The key lessons learnt, from our observation and experience is that by utilising a relationship contract, rather than a project-based contract has particular advantages in times of significant disruption, especially when flexibility and responsiveness are required at short notice. Specifically, the ability to change projects which are valuable in the long term, but have no immediate urgency when compared to the rapid response needed for the COVID-19 pandemic. A project-based funding model is not as resilient or flexible to external events that require, or indeed that would benefit from a change in project scope. The GHL model mitigates this risk and allows the opportunity for research capacity to be redirected. Additionally, the GHL model is also more robust even when anticipated changes create a need for a change in projects and priorities. We would further argue that thinking about a relationship contract approach is particularly salient for those who contract and fund research due to the points discussed above. In a time of a pandemic, particularly in New Zealand, we have demonstrated that having skilled researchers and a flexible funding model produced an important contribution to national efforts to better understand and tackle COVID-19, thereby enhancing community resilience.

References

[1] Christopher Bowie, Paul Beere, Edward Griffin, Malcolm Campbell, and Simon Kingham. Variation in health and social equity in the spaces where we live: A review of previous literature from the geohealth laboratory. *New Zealand Sociology*, 28(3):164–191, 2013.

[2] Matthew Hobbs, Annabel Ahuriri-Driscoll, Lukas Marek, Malcolm Campbell, Melanie Tomintz, and Simon Kingham. Reducing health inequity for Māori people in New Zealand. *The Lancet*, 394(10209):1613–1614, 2019.

[3] Malcolm Campbell, Philippe Apparicio, and Peter Day. Geographic analysis of infant mortality in New Zealand, 1995–2008: an ethnicity perspective. *Australian and New Zealand Journal of Public Health*, 38(3): 221–226, 2014. doi: 10.1111/1753-6405.12222. URL https://onlinelibrary.wiley.com/doi/abs/10.1111/1753-6405.12222.

[4] M. Campbell, C. Bowie, S. Kingham, and J.P. McCarthy. Painting a picture of trans-tasman mortality. *Public Health*, 129(4):396–402, 2015. ISSN 0033-3506. doi: https://doi.org/10.1016/j.puhe.2015.01.015.

[5] Matthew Hobbs, Lukas Marek, Riana Clarke, John McCarthy, Melanie Tomintz, Alicia Wade, Malcolm Campbell, and Simon Kingham. Investigating the prevalence of non-fluoride toothpaste use in adults and children using nationally representative data from New Zealand: a cross-sectional study. *British Dental Journal*, 228(4):269–276, 2020. ISSN 1476-5373. doi: 10.1038/s41415-020-1304-5. URL https://doi.org/10.1038/s41415-020-1304-5.

[6] Matthew Hobbs, Alicia Wade, Peter Jones, Lukas Marek, Melanie Tomintz, Kanchan Sharma, John McCarthy, Barry Mattingley, Malcolm Campbell, and Simon Kingham. Area-level deprivation, childhood dental ambulatory sensitive hospitalizations and community water fluoridation: evidence from New Zealand. *International Journal of Epidemiology*, 49(3):908–916, 04 2020. ISSN 0300-5771. doi: 10.1093/ije/dyaa043. URL https://doi.org/10.1093/ije/dyaa043.

[7] Clémence Vannier, Malcolm Campbell, and Simon Kingham. Pathways to urban health and well-being: measuring and modelling of community services' in a medium size city. *Geospatial Health*, 15(1), June 2020. ISSN 1827-1987. doi: 10.4081/gh.2020.808. URL https://doi.org/10.4081/gh.2020.808.

[8] Matthew Hobbs, Melanie Tomintz, John McCarthy, Lukas Marek, Clémence Vannier, Malcolm Campbell, and Simon Kingham. Obesity risk in women of childbearing age in New Zealand: a nationally representative cross-sectional study. *International Journal of Public Health*, 64(4):625—635, May 2019. ISSN 1661-8556. doi: 10.1007/s00038-019-01239-8. URL https://doi.org/10.1007/s00038-019-01239-8.

[9] Jesse Wiki, Simon Kingham, and Malcolm Campbell. Accessibility to food retailers and socio-economic deprivation in urban New Zealand. *New Zealand Geographer*, 75(1):3–11, 2019. doi: 10.1111/nzg.12201. URL https://onlinelibrary.wiley.com/doi/abs/10.1111/nzg.12201.

[10] Daniel Hogg, Simon Kingham, Thomas M. Wilson, and Michael Ardagh. The effects of relocation and level of affectedness on mood and anxiety symptom treatments after the 2011 Christchurch earthquake. *Social Science & Medicine*, 152:18–26, 2016. ISSN 0277-9536. doi: https://doi.org/10.1016/j.socscimed.2016.01.025. URL http://www.sciencedirect.com/science/article/pii/S0277953616300259.

[11] Daniel Hogg, Simon Kingham, Thomas M. Wilson, and Michael Ardagh. Spatio-temporal variation of mood and anxiety symptom treatments in christchurch in the context of the 2010/11 canterbury earthquake sequence. *Spatial and Spatio-temporal Epidemiology*, 19:91–102, 2016. ISSN 1877-5845. doi: https://doi.org/10.1016/j.sste.2016.08.001. URL http://www.sciencedirect.com/science/article/pii/S1877584515300046.

[12] Malcolm Campbell and Dimitris Ballas. Simalba: A spatial microsimulation approach to the analysis of health inequalities. *Frontiers in Public Health*, 4:230, 2016. ISSN 2296-2565. doi: 10.3389/fpubh.2016.00230. URL https://www.frontiersin.org/article/10.3389/fpubh.2016.00230.

[13] Malcolm H Campbell. *Exploring the social and spatial inequalities of ill-health in Scotland: A spatial microsimulation approach.* PhD thesis, University of Sheffield, October 2011. URL http://etheses.whiterose.ac.uk/1942/.

[14] Alison F. Watkins. *Exploring the social and spatial context of adult obesity in Aotearoa New Zealand : a spatial microsimulation approach.* PhD thesis, University of Canterbury, 2017. URL https://ir.canterbury.ac.nz/handle/10092/15643.

42

Pandemic and the City: A Melbourne Perspective for Community Resilience

Mark Allan

Melbourne, Australia's most liveable city, has endured the nation's most severe lockdown measures as it plans for revitalisation. This chapter provides a snapshot of trends affecting generalised measures of liveability prior to and during COVID-19, and beyond. Collaboration between authorities and citizens is required for resilience and on-going adaptation.

42.1   Introduction

The coronavirus COVID-19 pandemic is a global crisis, it has taken lives and impacted the economies of developed and developing nations. Its impact on cities, in particular, has been unprecedented, requiring us to rethink ideas about sustainable built environments, urban proximity, density, and mobility. This paper presents some observations about Melbourne, a city with an enviable reputation for liveability and its response to COVID-19 and a future of co-existence with the pandemic.

Soon after the World Health Organisation's declaration of the COVID-19 pandemic in mid-March 2020, the Australian government implemented a program of financial support combined with travel restrictions, social distancing and other 'lockdown' measures. These restrictions generated considerable economic uncertainty and social anxiety in towns and cities across the country affecting households, government, and industry. By the end of June 2020 Australia's lockdown measures were showing comparative signs of success with some 7,008 people having recovered from the 7,767 reported cases of COVID-19 [1]. At about this time with states and territories reporting no new cases or small numbers restrictions began to be eased. In Melbourne, however, a second wave of COVID-19 emerged in July 2020 likely from a failure to adhere to hotel quarantine protocols. Community transmission of infection saw new daily case numbers rise from 15 to 20 in mid-June to over 600 by early August [2]. This led to stronger Stage 4 restrictions being introduced across metropolitan Melbourne for a six-week period on 2 August 2020, later extended. Server restrictions were also placed on movements between across state borders. During Stage 4 a curfew was put in place between the hours of 8pm and 5am requiring people to stay at home during these hours unless for work, medical care and caregiving. Face coverings were mandated when leaving home which was only allowed for permitted work, or to either exercise for up to one hour per day or for a sole member of each household to shop for food or essential items within a 5 kilometre radius of home. On 6 September 2020 'Victoria's Coronavirus (COVID-19) Roadmap to Reopening' was announced by the state's Premier. The 'Roadmap' sets out a four-step process to ease restrictions across Victoria staging expanded social interaction, and phasing in a return to the workplace, education, sport, recreation, ceremonies, and special occasions. The 'first step' is scheduled to commence on 13 September 2020 with the 'last step' targeting 'COVID Normal' after 23 November 2020 subject to 'trigger points and public health advice'.

42.2   Growth of Inner-City Melbourne

Melbourne is a global and liveable city known for its multicultural diversity and its cosmopolitan inner urban core. Recognised by the Economist Intelligence Unit as 'the world's most liveable city' for seven consecutive years (2010-17) and currently ranked number two, it has a legacy of leading international liveability rankings [3]. Melbourne's inner-city communities' express cultural diversity and creativity, home to major universities, hospitals, parks and gardens. The city hosts the nation's major sporting and entertainment events and its vibrant laneways and café culture draw international tourists and visitors. Melbourne is Australia's fastest growing city and its inner area is the nation's most densely populated area with 21,900 people per km^2. In 2018-19 Melbourne's population grew by 2.3% to 5 million people fuelled by net overseas migration it was forecast to grow to 7 million by 2030 outstripping Sydney as Australia's largest city [4]. The ABS forecast net overseas migration to Melbourne will fall by 85% over the next 12 months.

42.3   Reshaping Cities

As we look to Melbourne for some contemporary lessons of resilience it is worth remembering that epidemic diseases have plagued, shaped and reshaped cities for millennia. The City of London responding to the great plague of 1665 enacted municipal orders quarantining 'infected houses' mandating inspections, requiring extra cleaning of housing and streets, restricting assemblies at theatres, and implementing trade embargos [5]. Responses to a succession of epidemics has profoundly shaped cities, housing forms, human behaviours, communications, and urban living environments. The reality of co-existing with COVID-19 and a succession of future pandemics will challenge how we plan, design and manage people-centric cities, public spaces and spatial connections in the context of epidemiological measures to control the spread of infectious diseases.

42.4   Melbourne's Response to COVID-19

The lockdown measures introduced in response to the first and second waves of COVID-19 in March and July 2020 have severely impacted inner Melbourne's visitor economy, international education, and the services economy. Melbourne's population increase was immediately halted and the number of weekly payroll jobs in central Melbourne significantly reduced. The million daily visitors to Melbourne's Central Business District (CBD) reduced more than 30% as international students and professional service workers stayed home and retail premises and hospitality venues closed. Weekday road traffic levels across Melbourne were down and pedestrian movements around train stations in central Melbourne were down by up to 42% in July [6]. The Melbourne City Council reported the average number of pedestrians in Bourke Street mall dropped from an average of 25,000 to 6,476 per day with an estimated 1 in 3 shops closed or vacant. Vacancy rates for CBD offices typically at 5% rose sharply to 7.6% in March, with real estate agents reporting student accommodation occupancy-rate falls in inner Melbourne of between 20% and 50% [7]. The immediate response gave priority to health and wellbeing, emergency accommodation was provided to the homeless and city cleaning regimes increased. In addition to financial loans and grants to small business, economic stimulus projects are planned to include infrastructure, housing and construction and affordable housing. Inner Melbourne fast tracked approvals for 12 km of temporary cycling lanes and has committed to plant 150,000 trees, shrubs and grasses (an increase from the 3,000 planned) [8]. The importance of high-quality public realm and open spaces for people to safely exercise and enjoy fresh air has been underscored during the pandemic.

42.5 Impacts of COVID-19 on Central Melbourne's Liveability

The observations presented in Table 42.1 are grouped into categories using headings form the seven targets in the United Nations Sustainable Development Goal Number 11 (SDG 11) for 'Sustainable Cities and Communities'. The SDGs comprise 17 global goals with interrelated targets and indicators aimed at delivering globally sustainable development by 2030 [9]. Table 42.1 presents a 'snapshot' of trends affecting generalised measures of Inner Melbourne's liveability immediately prior to COVID-19, during and potential future responses. Movements are summarized by symbols, upward and downward 'arrows' or a neutral 'square' with traffic light colours green, red or amber indicating positive, negative or neutral impacts on liveability.

42.6 Planning to Co-Exist With COVID-19

The trends summarised in Table 42.1 reflect optimism in the people of Melbourne's resilience and capacity to respond to both the current and the future impacts of the COVID-19 health and economic crisis. Reduced housing demand will place negative downward pressure on property prices, however, this will ease rental costs and increase affordability in some locations. While intimate partner violence and social isolation has generated social hardship during the pandemic increased mainstream media attention has helped raise public awareness and prioritised the importance of good mental health and public policy. A reduction in traffic congestion is expected to continue with less commuting by those with the flexibility to work from home. Fewer public transport trips, capacity constraints and increased cleanliness will necessitate revised pricing, implementation of new technologies and changed operations likely to reduce future investment. The design and management of buildings and public spaces will see a greater emphasis on human health and wellbeing. Spaces will need to be adaptable and able to accommodate physical distancing as demand for flexible outdoor spaces increases. Digital communications will play a larger role in connecting people and maintaining social ties.

The short-term halt in Melbourne's rapid population growth in the view of Professor Giles-Corti of RMIT University provides an opportunity for the state's planners to recalibrate how Melbourne grows and to better integrate urban development and infrastructure provision for a more sustainable city [10]. This may also assist planners to implement urban policies embracing of 'local liveability' including '20-minute neighbourhood'. This concept prioritises local transport and jobs with high quality public realm connecting services so that people's daily needs are met within a 20-minute walk from their home [11].

The built environment has a key role in developing the health and wellbeing of communities and responding to impacts of climate change. During the COVID-19 pandemic communities in cities like Melbourne have rapidly embraced working from home, video conferencing for education and tele-medicine and increased online shopping. Rethinking our cities as healthy places will likely increase the cleanliness of public transport and change the way we move about the city and interact socially in terms of proximity and density. Delivery of urban strategies to reallocate road space to create wider footpaths and more bicycle lanes combined with increased tree planting and public space and other investments in the public realm offers real potential to improve the mental, physical and immunological health of communities.

TABLE 42.1
Inner Melbourne Liveability, Trends in Response to COVD-19

Legend:	▲ Positive upward	▪ Neutral	▲ Negative upward
	▼ Positive downward		▼ Negative downward

Category	Pre-COVID-19 Trends	2020 Response/Trends	2022+ Response/Trends
Safe, Affordable City (Refer SDG11 Target 11.1)	▲ Rapid population & housing demand ▼ Affordability ▲ Homelessness ▪ Real & perceived personal safety ▼ Access to services in car dependent low-density outer suburbs	▼ Population growth & migration halted ▲ Protection for tenants & economic stimulus ▲ Emergency homeless accommodation ▼ Vacancy rates ▲ Intimate partner violence	▼ Housing demand ▲ Supply of affordable & crisis housing ▲ Repurposing existing buildings for new uses ▼ Property prices/rents ▲ Safety, with metropolitan wide access to on-line health & other services
Mobility & Accessibility (Refer SDG11 Target 11.2)	▲ Overcrowded public transport (demand) ▲ Major projects including Melbourne Metro in construction ▲ Traffic congestion ▲ Bicycle culture	▼ International & national travel ▼ Reduced commuting, public transport trips & CBD pedestrians ▲ Local walking, cycling, home deliveries	▲ Private vehicle trips ▼ Commuting ▲ Bike paths ▲ Safer, cleaner public transport, touchless operations ▼ Investment in public transport
Land Use Efficiency (Refer SDG11 Target 11.3)	▲ Rapid expansion urban footprint ▲ Inner city café culture & online retail ▲ Medium density housing ▼ High-rise apartments ▼ High Street retail	▲ Temporary on-street bike paths ▼ Visits to retail, cafés & entertainment venues ▲ Construction hours ▲ CBD parking fines temporarily halted ▲ On-line retailing	▲ Reallocation of road space to wider footpaths & bike lanes ▲ Outdoor dining, retail pop-ups & markets ▲ Medium density housing aids 20-min n/hoods ▲ On-line services & retail
Cultural & Natural Heritage (Refer SDG11 Target 11.4)	▪ Australia's cultural & sporting capital ▲ Support Aboriginal reconciliation	▼ Visits to public buildings, libraries, galleries, public space ▲ On-line/virtual tours	▲ Virtual tours ▲ Technology supports social distancing & crowd management

TABLE 42.1
Continued - Inner Melbourne Liveability, Trends in Response to COVD-19

Legend:

| ▲ Positive upward | | ▲ Negative upward |
| ▼ Positive downward | ▪ Neutral | ▼ Negative downward |

Category	Pre-COVID-19 Trends	2020 Response/Trends	2022+ Response/Trends
Human Health & Wellbeing (Refer SDG11 Target 11.5)	▪ Liveability ▼ Youth mental health ▲ Health impacts of drug & alcohol, intimate partner violence ▲ Isolation &loneliness	▼ Jobs ▲ Employment benefits ▲ Working from home ▲ Restrictions on sports & entertainment ▲ Drug & alcohol use, intimate partner violence & isolation	▲ Workplace flexibility, home/office allows more leisure time/less commuting ▲ Technology to support social connections & physical distancing ▲ Mental, physical & immunological health & desire for social connection
Healthy Environment (Refer SDG11 Target 11.6)	▲ Value of green buildings & interest in well buildings ▼ Policy coordination	▼ Public health rules, physical distancing ▲ Increased on-street cleaning, cleaner air	▲ Urban resilience & 20-min neighbourhood ▲ Healthy buildings, better ventilation & materials
Sustainable public open spaces (Refer SDG11 Target 11.7)	▲ Demand for public space to support higher density housing ▲ Pressure on existing public spaces through high levels of usage ▲ Urban forest strategies	▼ Playgrounds & exercise equipment ▼ Use of parks & public open spaces, restricted street furniture ▲ Social distancing & short stay less than 15-minute visitation	▲ High quality, safe inclusive public space ▲ Digital tools to manage & for placemaking ▲ More trees planted ▲ Adaptable use of space at different times
City planning & urban policy (Refer SDG11 Targets 11.a, 11.b & 11.c)	▼ Planning system capacity to manage rapid urban growth ▼ Capacity to deliver infrastructure, transport, health, education	▲ Future city taskforces prepare action plans ▲ Whole of government approach ▲ Prioritised resilience projects ▲ Stimulus projects	▲ Focus on city planning (resilience/pandemics) ▲ SDGs framework for sustainability ▲ Community capacity building

Melbourne has experienced significant downturns in its visitor economy, international education sector and its services economy due to the pandemic, exacerbated by Victoria's second wave of COVID-19 and hard lockdown measures introduced in August 2020. The economic adversity forecast, and currently affecting Australia has hit hardest in Victoria and most severely in the state's capital city. Since mid-March 2020 when the pandemic emerged in Australia until late August 2020 payroll jobs fell 4.2 per cent nationally, in Victoria this figure was 7.9 per cent [12] resulting in significant hardship for many households. To date Victoria's response to COVID-19 has been based on health advice and statistical modelling adopting a policy of aggressive suppression to avoid restrictions being continuously lifted and reinstated.

The conditional phased easing of restrictions outlined in Victoria's 'Roadmap to Reopening',

September 2020, outlines public policy settings that balance human health priorities with the staged reopening of the state's economy. In addition to financial support for business and individuals, approvals for construction projects and delivery of national and state government services have been fast-tracked. Underpinning business and streamlining service delivery has also occurred at a local government level including plans for localised urban interventions and public realm improvements to revitalise city centres. In Melbourne streets, footpaths and parking bays are being converted for use as outdoor dining areas seating patrons at a safe distance as part of a staged return of people and strategies to revitalise the city.

Valuable lessons have had to been learnt quickly about how to plan, organise, and administer our city and safeguard citizens during a global pandemic. This awareness is important now and in the future as policies and action plans are developed to promote urban resilience to protect and improve human health and well-being. With Victoria now in economic recession, the outcomes of the serve lockdown will test the resilience and liveability of Melbourne as its capital. Just as Melbourne has responded to crises and economic downturns in the past, its social and physical infrastructure combined with the patience, optimism and creativity of its citizens, means it is well placed for a future that accepts and embraces reactivation and on-going adaptation.

References

[1] Australian Bureau of Statistics. 4940.0 - Household Impacts of COVID-19 Survey, 24-29 June 2020, 2020. URL https://www.abs.gov.au/ausstats/abs@.nsf/mf/4940.0. Retrieved July 20, 2020.

[2] Department of Health Victoria State Government and Human Services. Victorian coronavirus (COVID-19) data, 2020. URL https://www.dhhs.vic.gov.au/victorian-coronavirus-covid-19-data. Retrieved September 8, 2020.

[3] The Economist Intelligence Unit. Global Liveability Ranking. *The Economist*, 2020. URL https://www.eiu.com/topic/liveability. Retrieved July 20, 2020.

[4] Australian Bureau of Statistics. 3218.0 - Regional Population Growth, Australia, 2018-19, 2018. URL https://www.abs.gov.au/AUSSTATS/abs@.nsf/mf/3218.0. Retrieved July 20, 2020.

[5] Lukas Engelmann, John Henderson, and Christos Lynteris. *Plague and the City*. Taylor and Francis, 2018.

[6] Ashleigh McMillian. Pedestrians Clear out of CBD in Droves after Second Lockdown. *The Age*, 2020. URL https://bit.ly/3jW3DEo. Retrieved July 20, 2020.

[7] Max Opray. How Covid-19 will change cities. *The Saturday Paper*, 2020. URL https://bit.ly/3bEs8TV. Retrieved July 20, 2020.

[8] C40 Cities Climate Leadership Group. C40: Agenda for a Green and Just Recovery. 2020. URL https://www.c40.org/other/agenda-for-a-green-and-just-recovery. Retrieved July 20, 2020.

[9] United Nations. Habitat III Issue Papers 11 - Public Space, 2015.

[10] Jemimah Clegg. Melbourne's Slowing Population Growth Could Give Us Our Last Chance for Real Liveability. *Domain*, 2020. URL https://bit.ly/2GKE3Eh.

[11] Rory Shannon, James Mant, Marcus Dessewffy, and L Harrison. 20-minute neighbourhoods: Creating a more liveable melbourne. *Journal of Transportation and Health*, 14:100773, 2019.

[12] Australian Bureau of Statistics. Weekly Payroll Jobs and Wages in Australia, Week Ending 22 August 2020, 2020. URL https://bit.ly/35jNLHS. Retrieved September 8, 2020.

43

Spatial Modelling Concepts for Controlling COVID-19 Risk in Saudi Arabia

Hassan M. Khormi

Location and time are important in controlling diseases. This chapter aims to explain how the Saudi authorities implement GIS concepts in controlling the spatial risks of COVID-19. In Saudi Arabia, the impact of COVID-19 is still limited, as the total number of infections did not exceed 74,795 confirmed cases until 25 May 2020, of which 45,668 (61% out of the total cases) have recovered. This chapter shows regions with high risk and very low risks as well as spatial disease distribution in SA regions. Ar Riyad (17,656 cases), which includes the capital city of SA, Makkah (29,436), Almadinah (9,751), and Ash Sharqiyah (14,012) are the most impacted regions as they recorded most of the cases with 70,855 (95%) out of the all confirmed cases. Those spatial information must be presented on a different spatial scale, such as city, district, sub-district and house level. Many mobile-based map applications are developed by the Ministries of Health and Interior to, for example, provide insights about disease distributions, help people to find transport during the times of isolation, and show the locations of services, hospitals, etc. These applications are meant to help monitor the impact of the outbreak, manage it, communicate with the security and health services, and help allocate resources, which will help society and institutions to respond effectively.

43.1 Introduction

The incidence of COVID-19 started when the virus moved from animal to human populations [1]. The main mode of transmission is from the respiratory tract via droplets or indirectly via fomites and, to a lesser extent, via aerosols. This disease is considered by the World Health Organization (WHO) to be one of the most important and impactful globally. It has been recognized as the most prevalent viral disease in all places around the world [2]. Associations between the incidences and environmental, meteorological and socioeconomic conditions are not yet clearly understood [3]. That makes it difficult to model its risk spatially using GIS. The transmission patterns of the diseases are sensitive to social factors, such as population density, habits, practices, as well as customs and traditions giving rise to occasions and gatherings. This chapter aims to explain how the Saudi authorities implement GIS concepts in controlling the spatial risks of COVID-19. It also shows the current spatial distribution of the disease in Saudi Arabia (SA), with most infected groups according to their nationality, sex and age. Three key factors stand out when looking at COVID-19: human, space (location) and time. When a person gets infected, there is a person involved, and this determines the diseases one gets infected with. Then there is the location, the position on the earth's surface where the event occurred. This position can be accurately located using GPS.

The location can be used to extract environmental conditions and meteorological variables of areas related certain human practices and people gathering. Time of infection gives valuable information about when the infected person is active and his historical movements. Together with location, time allows one to develop a spatio-temporal picture of the event, and this aspect is extensively used in public health modelling [4].

43.2   GIS-based Mapping and Modelling

When we map or model a disease, we take into consideration that everything is related to everything else but near things are more related than distant things [5]. In other words, a person infected with COVID-19 or environmental and climatological conditions closer to an impacted community or disease occurrence should be more conducive to the survival, reproduction and transmission of the virus than conditions further away. This suggests that a study of the geographical location of pathogens and vectors, host interaction, environmental and climatological variables and proximity to human or animal victims is paramount in understanding disease patterns. Spatial analysis answers questions such as what types of habitat that contain the virus, how far the virus's host travels, what populations live in zones of high or low occurrences and what other regions have conditions similar to those where the hosts are currently found and should so be denoted as high-risk areas.

The accessibility of geo-referenced COVID-19 data is of significance in mapping the disease and linking it to environmental or social risk factors. The geographical spreading and seasonal behavior of the disease, as well as its transmission and abundance, are controlled by environmental (such as land use, land cover, elevation) and climatological variables (such as temperature, rainfall, degree days and humidity). Visual displays of quantitative data, such as cases of infections, on cartographic maps for understanding causes has a long history. The best-known example is that of Dr. John Snow and the cholera deaths of London in the mid-nineteenth century [6]. The visualization of spatial epidemiological data on a background of environmental or climatological layer enables one to discern patterns and correlations. Early disease mapping methods were mainly used for communicable diseases to identify sources of infection, rates of spread and general environmental variables present at those sites [7].

43.3   The Current Spatial Distribution of COVID-19 in Saudi Arabia (SA)

In Saudi Arabia, the impact of COVID-19 is still limited, as the total number of infections did not exceed 74,795 confirmed cases until 25 May 2020, of which 45,668 (61% out of the total cases) have recovered. The numbers indicate that males were more at risk of contracting the disease than females. Since the infection started spreading in the country, between 70 and 80% out of the total recorded cases were male. This is due to the culture of mobility and interaction between men compared with women and the fact that women are more likely to apply the culture of guarding against disease risks and to adhere to regulations and laws targeted at curtailing diseases. But another important reason is that most cases in the Kingdom were recorded between employees of certain companies. So cases involving non-Saudis are around 55% to 65% of the total recorded since the beginning of March 2020.

The majority of company employees in Saudi Arabia are males and are mostly citizens of East and Southeast Asia, Pakistan, Bangladesh, and some Arab countries, such as Egypt and Sudan. Some companies, especially those that did not observe the precautionary measures or who delayed in applying them in their premises, were more likely to see infections among their workers. Also, the educational and income levels of these employees are low, which required the health and municipal authorities to intervene and provide accommodation to achieve social distancing and create a better precautionary environment. The government decided to supply healthcare and COVID-19 testing for free to all non-Saudis. These steps have a significant impact on reducing the infection rate among workers.

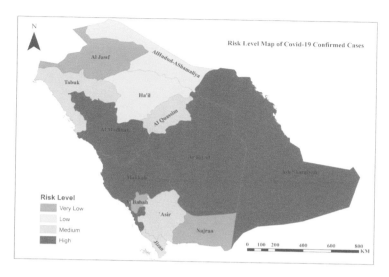

FIGURE 43.1

COVID-19 risk level and spatial distribution in SA regions (Data Source: Saudi Arabia Health Ministry)

Figure 43.1 shows regions with high risk and very low risks as well as spatial disease distribution in SA regions. Ar Riyad (17,656 cases), which includes the capital city of SA, Makkah (29,436), Almadinah (9,751), and Ash Sharqiyah (14,012) are the most impacted regions as they recorded most of the cases with 70,855 (95%) out of the all confirmed cases. The very low-risk areas are regions that recorded less than 150 cases. Those regions are Al Jawf (84 cases), Najran (147), and Al Baha (148). These numbers show the limited impact of COVID-19 across Saudi Arabia compared with other countries that registered similar numbers daily.

In SA, the deaths have not exceeded 400 since the emergence of the disease. The Makkah region obtained the highest rate of the deaths with 75%, followed by Almadinah (44 deaths), Ar Riyad (24), and Ash Sharqiyah (22). Most of the deaths were related to cases of people with underlying chronic medical conditions, such as diabetes, kidney failure, chronic lung disease, and deficient immune systems. Other regions recorded between zero and four cases of death. Once again, these figures show the minimal impact of the disease in Saudi Arabia compared with other countries around the world that recorded thousands of deaths in one day.

In general, the reason behind the limited negative impact of the disease in Saudi Arabia is the early measures taken by the authorities. That started with the formation of a higher committee headed by the Minister of Health and with the membership including a number of educational, research, service and security sector personnel to review international events related to the disease and assess the current conditions, make reference comparisons and gather experiences to address the disease, especially from countries that had already been ravaged by it.

At that time, the Saudi authorities began gradually isolating a number of the most affected neighbourhoods, then cities. Then they began closing international entry points and finally proceeded to completely isolating all Saudi regions. In all those steps and actions taken by the authorities, the geographical concepts were present, starting from determining the geographical location of the infected person, the relatives and friends of that person, the geographical locations of their movements, determining the boundaries of the closed neighbourhoods, setting a map to be used by the public, and determining on the maps the ports to be used for entering and exiting the isolated areas.

There is high awareness as to the use of GIS in all aspects of disease surveillance and system control. The Saudi Health Ministry developed many mobile applications and a GIS platform for uploading and illustrating locations and data of, for example, confirmed, active and recovered cases based on small and large geographical scales to present the events on house (point) (Figure 43.2A), sub-district, district, county, region and country (Figure 43.2B).

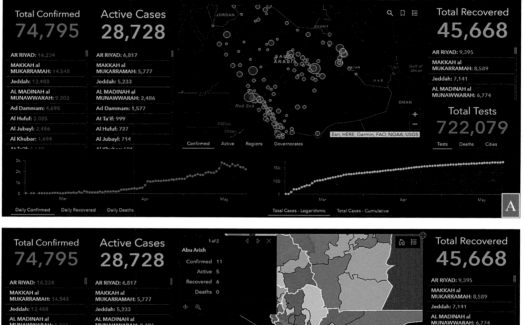

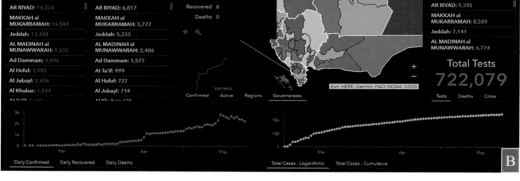

FIGURE 43.2
Interface of GIS platform developed by the Health Ministry to show daily spatial distribution and information of COVID-19 (https://covid19.moh.gov.sa/)

This GIS-based system can go far beyond the early studies on establishing correlates. So the main purpose can be enhanced to describe the geographical differences in disease occurrence for formulating aetiological hypotheses. Also, the system locates unusual high-risk hotspots to develop a preventive plan. Another purpose is to improve the reliability of disease risk models for allocating resources. Moreover, the system can undertake sophisticated spatial analyses of environmental features and disease rates, together with geostatistical analysis to statistically verify associations [8–10].

43.4 Conclusion

The spatial information must be presented on a different spatial scale, such as city, district, sub-district and house level. Many mobile-based map applications are developed by the Ministries of Health and Interior to, for example, provide insights about disease distributions, help people to find transport during the times of isolation, and show the locations of services, hospitals, etc. The main purpose of these applications is to help monitor the impact of the outbreak, manage it, communicate with the security and health services, and help allocate resources, which will help society and institutions to respond effectively. Accordingly, we summarize the aforementioned in this scientific paper to avoid the effects of the COVID-19 epidemic quickly. Immediate plans should be developed for the danger areas in your environment through several steps relying on GIS. The most important of these steps is to map the confirmed and active cases, deaths and retrieval operations to determine the whereabouts of the COVID-19 infections and to update the records continuously. Mapping the spatiotemporal distribution of the disease can reveal how the infection has spread over time and where you might want to target the interventions. Publishing a map of at-risk populations will provide information about how COVID-19 will unevenly affect some demographics, such as the elderly and those with chronic diseases as well as non-Saudi workers. Mapping social vulnerability, age and other factors also helps to monitor groups and areas at risk. It is important to map national capabilities and facility locations, such as a map of facilities, health providers, medical resources, equipment, goods and other services to understand and respond to the current and potential impacts of COVID-19. Interactive web maps, dashboard apps, story maps and historical tracking can be used to help quickly communicate with people about the national situation so everyone will be aware of all the procedures.

References

[1] Mackenzie, J. S., Smith, D. W. (2020) COVID-19: a novel zoonotic disease caused by a coronavirus from China: what we know and what we don't [published online ahead of print, 2020 Mar 17]. Microbiol Aust. 2020;MA20013. doi:10.1071/MA20013.

[2] WHO/2019-nCoV/Sci_Brief/Transmission_modes/2020.2

[3] Briz-Redón, Á., Serrano-Aroca, Á. (2020) A spatio-temporal analysis for exploring the effect of temperature on COVID-19 early evolution in Spain. Science of the Total Environment, Volume 728.

[4] Khormi, H., Kumar, L. (2015) Modeling interactions between vector-borne diseases and environment using GIS. CRC Press, Taylor and Fancies.

[5] Tobler, W. (1970) A computer movie simulating urban growth in the Detroit region". Economic Geography, 46(2): 234–240.

[6] Snow, J. (1855) On the mode of communication of cholera. London: John Churchill (2nd ed).

[7] Howe, G. M. (1989) Historical evolution of disease mapping in general and specifically of cancer mapping. Recent Results Cancer Research, 114: 1–21.

[8] Rytkonen, M. J. P. (2004) Not all maps are equal: GIS and spatial analysis in epidemiology. International Journal of Circumpolar Health, 63(1): 9–24.

[9] Lawson, A. B., Biggeri, A. B., Boehning, D., Lesaffre, E., Viel, J. F., Clark, A., Schlattmann, P., Divino, F. (2000) Disease mapping models: an empirical evaluation. Disease Mapping Collaborative Group. Stat Med, 19: 2217–2241.

[10] Lawson, A. B., Böhning, D., Biggeri, A., Lesaffre, E., Viel, J. F. (1999) Disease mapping and its uses. In: Lawson, A., Biggeri, A., Böhning, D., Lesaffre, E., Viel, J. F. and Bertollini, R. (eds.), Disease mapping and risk assessment for public health. West Sussex: John Wiley & Sons Ltd; 3–13.

44

COVID-19 in Spain and the Use of Geospatial Information

Carmen Femenia-Ribera and Gaspar Mora-Navarro

Spain declared a state of emergency on 14 March because of the serious situation due to COVID-19. Three months later there were more than 27,000 confirmed deaths due to the virus. During this period there were many initiatives using geospatial information to predict, follow, and detect infections, as well as control mobility. These measures were implemented by the central government, as well as regional governments and local councils. Most of these geospatial applications use open-access geospatial information that reuse public sector information and add value to this data. In this way, open data supports decision-making by the administration. Numerous thematic maps, spatial analyses, geoportals, websites, and mobile applications have recently appeared; and never have so many boundary maps have been published in the Spanish media. Geospatial information in Spain is likely to continue playing an important role as the pandemic evolves, and greater resilience is needed to address this and future challenges.

44.1   COVID-19 and the State of Emergency in Spain

Spain has been a member of the European Union since 1986 and is located in the southwest corner of Europe. The nation has an area of 505,944 km^2, 4,964 km of coastline, and a population of 46.5 million. Spain has the world's 15th largest economy (2019) in terms of gross domestic product according to the International Monetary Fund, and is the world's second most popular nation for tourist visits (2018) according to the World Tourism Organization.

Spain has a central government, 17 regional governments, and 2 largely self-governing cities on the Mediterranean coast in Africa. The nation is also divided into 50 provinces and there are 8,125 local councils.

For geographical information, the main national organisation is the National Geographic Institute (IGN) ("Instituto Geográfico Nacional, IGN," [1]). All of the national territory is mapped in digital format. Spain also has orthophotographs of the entire nation as part of the Aerial Photography National Plan (PNOA) ("Plan Nacional de Ortofotografía Aérea, PNOA," [2]). The Spanish Spatial Data Infrastructure (IDEE) ("Infraestructura de Datos Espaciales de España, IDEE," [3]) centralises the geographical information of the regional governments and local administrations in line with the European INSPIRE Directive. The regions also have their own cartographical institutes. Cadastral maps are made freely available through the Electronic Office of Cadastre (SEC) ("Sede Electrónica del Catastro, SEC," [4]) of the Directorate General for Cadastre (DGC) ("Dirección General del Catastro, DGC," [5]), as part of open data policies, and policies for the reuse of Spanish public sector information.

Spain was the country most affected by Covid-19 after China and Italy. The virus started to be noticed early in February, with the first cases in the Canary Islands towards the end of January. A state of emergency was declared on 14 March. At that moment, the central government assumed all relevant powers and residents were quarantined in their homes. On 14 March the number of infected people was 5,753, and there were already 136 deaths, according to the health ministry. Just three months later, on 14 June, the total number of notified cases was 244,109 and there had been 27,136 deaths. Madrid and Barcelona were the worst affected cities. Forty new cases of infections were notified on the last day of nationwide quarantine (14/6/2020) with 25 deaths in that week. At that moment, the virus was considered controlled in Spain, with only small localised infections remaining. The highest point of the infection curve was at the end of March and the beginning of April. On 1 April there were 930 deaths ("Enfermedad por nuevo coronavirus, COVID-19," [6]).

The state of emergency lasted just over three months (from 14 March to 21 June). At the end of the state of emergency, the central government returned powers to the regional governments. During this period, a four-stage plan for a transition to a new normality was introduced. Each stage lasted about two weeks. During these stages mobility was controlled to avoid the spread of the virus, and the borders between counties, regions, provinces, and local councils become very important – together with the associated geographical information ("Estado de alarma y Nueva normalidad. Medidas crisis sanitaria COVID-19," [7]).

44.2   Geospatial Information Use

Geospatial information has been fundamental from the first signals of infection. The regions sent daily numbers for infections, deaths, and recoveries for each province. That information could be seen on choropleth maps.

This type of map was also frequently used in the transition to a new normality, where the stage for each province was indicated. Each stage depended on the provincial sanitary conditions, and each stage meant different mobility restrictions. At the beginning, the areas of control were the individual hospital authority areas, but this idea was abandoned because it was too difficult for the police to control inter-regional mobility as the exact hospital areas boundaries were not well known.

The Spanish provinces were then used as the basic units for controlling mobility. However, the municipality boundaries were also used in stage 0 (started on 2 May). In stage 0, mobility was only allowed inside each municipality. People were allowed a daily walk within a one-kilometre radius from their homes. Numerous mobile applications showed a circle with a one-kilometre radius centred on the user's home. These applications were launched by both public and private organisations [8].

Many tools appeared that used geographical information to control mobility after quarantine, as well as track the contacts of infected people. These applications included mobile applications, geoportals, thematic maps (choropleths, point, heat maps, and so on); and were used at national, regional, and local levels. Many of these applications employed free and official open access digital map data.

Due to the seriousness of the pandemic, and the enormous importance of spatial data infrastructures in the management of the crisis, it was considered necessary to allow access for all resources that could be useful in fighting the pandemic. At a national level, there is a collection of open resources on Covid-19 in the IDEE website. In this collection, there is an index list of data published by international, national, and local administrations ("Infraestructura de Datos Espaciales de España, IDEE. Recursos abiertos sobre la COVID-19," [3]).

This information is mainly organised by regions. The geoportal of the Spanish Terrestrial Transport General Directorate shows maps of tourist accommodation, restaurants, shops, rest areas, and take-away restaurants near to main roads – all of which have been obliged to remain open. These maps facilitated the location of supplies for workforces and enabled the main national services to remain supplied ("Punto de Información de servicios de restauración," [9]). The Ministry for Ecological Transition and Demographic Challenge also published a map with open petrol stations.

Figure 44.1 shows an example of a regional COVID-19 geoportal. The geoportal monitors the pandemic situation in the region of Valencia. The geoportal has been developed by the Valencian Cartographic Institute (ICV) ("Institut Cartogràfic Valencià, ICV," [10]), using ESRI technology and open data from the regional health authority [11]. It shows the spatial distribution of the pandemic and information is updated daily. It was started on 11 April and initially showed the 24 sanitary boundaries within the region. Municipal boundaries were not initially included to avoid stigmatising any towns or cities. This information was later included when the pandemic came under more control.

FIGURE 44.1
Geoportal to Monitor the Pandemic in the Valencia Region. Source: [11]

Some cadastral offices worked with regional governments to map the location of strategic facilities such as public sport centres or schools.

Eurostat (the Statistical Office of the European Union) performed a spatial analysis to detect risk areas, using population data, combined with the European healthcare services dataset [12], transport networks, and cadastre addresses.

Universities performed spatial analyses to calculate, for example, the most vulnerable provinces (using the population density, risk population indices, and especially the layer of interest points, like hospitals, pharmacies, and supermarkets). Universities also made a predictive analyses.

There have also been many relevant mobile applications developed in both the private and public sectors, as well as by universities. Most of these applications use GNSS and the objective is mainly to help people to avoid crowds. The usefulness of these applications is conditioned by the number of users who install them and share their locations. Councils have developed applications to control access to public spaces and facilities, as well as beaches and pools. Some use drones and image analysis to automatically count people in open spaces. The main goal is to ensure the safety of tourists who mostly come to Spain looking for sunshine and sand. Private companies are developing these types of application and selling them to public administrations.

Telecommunication companies exceptionally made their customer mobility data available to the central government to control infections, despite the geolocation of user mobiles phones colliding with privacy policies. Currently there is an ongoing discussion about privacy rights in the Data Protection European Commission.

44.3   Conclusions

- Never before have so many boundaries maps been published in the Spanish media.

- Free and open access to geospatial data enables the development of many applications in private as well in public sectors – emphasising the value of geospatial data.

- Many ministries manage spatial information: including industry, health, transport, mobility, and ecological transition.

- Standardised geospatial information in the European framework enables spatial analysis using big data.

- User geolocation obtained from smartphones causes privacy problems that must be examined and clarified.

- Thematic maps, spatial analysis, geoportals, big data, GNSS, and drones are words linked to geospatial information that have frequently appeared in the media during this crisis.

- Geospatial data enables predictive analysis, tracking infected people, and statistical studies that support decision making by public administrations.

- Geospatial information in Spain is likely to continue playing an important role as the pandemic evolves.

- Updated and quality geospatial information is necessary to improve community resilience and respond to possible outbreaks and future crises.

References

[1] Instituto Geográfico Nacional (IGN). 2020. URL https://www.ign.es.

[2] Plan Nacional de Ortofotografía Aérea (PNOA). 2020. URL https://pnoa.ign.es/.

[3] Infraestructura de Datos Espaciales de España (IDEE). Recursos abiertos sobre la COVID-19. 2020. URL https://www.idee.es/web/guest/recursos-covid-19.

[4] Sede Electrónica del Catastro (SEC). 2020. URL http://www.sedecatastro.gob.es.

[5] Dirección General del Catastro (DGC). 2020. URL http://www.catastro.minhafp.es.

[6] COVID-19 Enfermedad por nuevo coronavirus. 2020. URL https://www.mscbs.gob.es/profesionales/saludPublica/ccayes/alertasActual/nCov-China/home.htm.

[7] Estado de alarma y Nueva normalidad. Medidas crisis sanitaria COVID-19. 2020. URL https://administracion.gob.es/pag_Home/atencionCiudadana/Nueva-normalidad-crisis-sanitaria.html#.XxWEOedS-Uk.

[8] IGN. Aplicación IGN conocer área radio 1 km. 2020. URL https://www.ign.es/resources/viewer/calculadora1km.html.

[9] Punto de Información de servicios de restauración. 2020. URL https://portalweb.fomento.es/VisorGeograficoDGTT/InformacionRestauracion.

[10] Punto de Información de servicios de restauraciónInstitut Cartogràfic Valencià (ICV). 2020. URL http://www.icv.gva.es/es.

[11] ICV. COVID-19 C. Valenciana: Monitoratge de la situació. 2020. URL https://experience.arcgis.com/experience/42474fe756ee4714b7d8fbb730134b92.

[12] Eurostat. Mapping healthcare services. 2020. URL https://ec.europa.eu/eurostat/web/products-eurostat-news/-/WDN-20200415-1?inheritRedirect=true&redirect=%2Feurostat%2Fweb%2Fcovid-19%2Fpopulation-health.

45

Lessons Learned from COVIDSafe: Understanding Conditions for Successful Implementation of Track and Trace Technologies

Nathaniel Carpenter and Anna Dabrowski

Digital track and trace works not just because of cutting edge technology, but because of public trust – a key condition for its utility. We have seen that trust is fundamental to other government COVID-19 tracking programs. This should be cultivated in Australia with engagement of experts and academics to provide a clear public message.

45.1 Introduction

As a consequence of the current COVID-19 pandemic, many national governments have retroactively deployed digital track and trace systems to support ongoing community health monitoring. In some contexts, contact tracing technologies have met with great success in monitoring the spread of the novel coronavirus, while in other spaces, there has been failure in regards to both implementation and uptake. This chapter focuses on the implementation of COVIDSafe, a track and trace technology designed for the Australian context. Building upon lessons learned from the successful implementation of contact tracing mechanisms in Asia, we argue that the success of contact tracing mechanisms depends not only on the quality of tracing technology, but on the cultural conditions of government and community that surround their enactment.

45.2 Do track and Trace Mechanisms Work?

Contact tracing technologies can provide communities with a method to contain the spread of communicable diseases by quickly identifying and notifying people who have come into contact with infected individuals [1]. Exposed individuals could then be informed, tested, and isolated, which would break the chain of further transmission. However, breaking the chain only works if individuals both use and trust the system while also adhering to self-isolating advice. It is also important to remember that track and trace mechanisms do not actually render individuals safe from the novel coronavirus. Although contact tracing should (in theory) support community awareness and protection, contact tracing alone does not offer inoculation like a vaccination might [2].

Effective uses of contact tracing tend to be found in East Asia, such as China, South Korea, Taiwan, Singapore and to a lesser extent, Japan [3, 4]. Yet the reason for the success of track and trace technologies in Asian nations may be cultural, as opposed to technological. In addition to developing technologies to monitor the population, many Asian nations have previous experience with epidemics such as MERS and SARS. Trust in government underpins civic duty and collectivist cultures, which often embrace compliance with government infection control mechanisms. Contact tracing applications in countries like South Korea are also mandated and invasive, yet extremely popular, and discussed widely by community members. In contrast, most western democracies have had little experience with modern infection control tracing techniques [5–7] which include adopting technology, implementing infrastructure, and streamlined data sharing agreements; let alone public awareness campaigns on contact tracing.

45.3   The Failures of COVIDSafe: Technology or User?

Despite the name, COVIDSafe has not succeeded in protecting the Australia public from COVID-19. However, the failures of this contact tracing mechanism can be attributed to several key factors that extend beyond the technological [8–10]. A lack of trust in government, coupled with a rushed response to developing the tool, has certainly led to a lack of public investment in the implementation of COVIDSafe. Mixed messages around the efficacy and safety of the tool has led to a belief of limited benefit, and individualistic culture has undermined Australia's efforts to implement their own track and trace mechanism successfully.

Inexperience in secure enactment of track and trace technology has also marred public perception of the efficacy of COVIDSafe. Australia lacks the experience of its Asian counterparts: even in May 2020, well after the novel coronavirus had developed into a pandemic, infrastructure was still not in place for the Australian government to act on notifications of infected individuals and their contacts. One major concern relates to data security [9]. In the case of COVIDSafe, if a user tests positive for COVID-19 and consents to their data being uploaded, the information is then held by the federal government on an Amazon Web Services server in Australia. Data from the app is stored on a user's device and transmitted in an encrypted form to the cloud-based server. Cloud based storage poses risks at the best of times [11]; unfortunately, Australia also has a long history of compromised data usage. Concerns around privacy render many members of the Australian public reticent to utilise basic health storage technologies, such as MyHealthRecord [12], let alone invasive track and trace technologies. Like financial data, spatial data is sensitive, identifiable information able to compromise an individual's identity and safety.

Although COVIDSafe does not access positioning information, it does ask for permission to collect information about accessing the phone network, which can be used as a form of location tracking. COVIDSafe uses Bluetooth to record anyone who is within range of the signal [10]. This concept does allow people to remain spatially anonymous; however, since most individuals' routines are fairly stable and most people have a physical contact group which tends to remain the same, it would not be difficult to infer locations and associations. Importantly, based on previous data security breaches [13], the Australian public is aware of vulnerability in data collection systems, and their ability to be exploited. Privacy implications remain murky. Evidence from the Australian public highlights issues with platforms and device error [9], often resulting in users uninstalling COVIDSafe. Another major issue is that individuals must upload their information through a rather complicated process; perhaps this is why individuals who test positive to COVID-19 fail to report.

45.4 Enhancing Implementation Through Education

There are many ways to enhance the utility of track and trace mechanisms, and success should not only be seen as culturally determined. For while South Korea and China have successfully employed contact tracing mechanisms [14], there have also been low levels of success in track and trace technologies in certain neighbouring contexts, such as Singapore. However, without public support of digitally enabled track-and-trace technologies, the purported digital inoculation will fall short of intended goals [15], be it low number of users such as seen in countries such as Singapore [16], or in an overall reduction in transmission rates [17].

Although it is crucial to improve user uptake, increasing awareness through broader education is also important, particularly to overcome a lack of community understanding as to the limits of contact tracing technology (see [18]). Awareness campaigns that raise knowledge and understanding are important tools for promoting change in social behaviours and norms; however, an important consideration is understanding the cultural context [19]. Raising awareness of track and trace processes is crucial, but assurances of data security and transparency are also necessary steps to building trust and overcoming public cynicism as to the utility of contact tracing tools. However, if governments fail to take into consideration that a country like Australia promotes a culture of self over community, it is unlikely that track and trace systems can ever succeed.

45.5 Lessons from Australia: Enhancing Contact Tracing

There are many reasons why track and trace mechanisms fail. In this chapter, we have reflected on the lessons learned from Australia, as evidenced in the example of Australia's COVIDSafe tool. While community hesitation and a lack of willingness to download the application can be attributed to an absence of trust towards the government, the manner of implementation is also of concern. A lack of public education and trust has failed to generate a meaningful awareness of what COVIDSafe can (and cannot do) in terms of providing protection for the Australian population. As a consequence, in order for COVIDSafe (or future track and trace technologies) to be successful, it is crucial for government efforts to focus on enhancing the capabilities of tracing technologies and providing an awareness which addresses community concerns. Increasing knowledge is the first step to behavioural change [15], however, being responsive and building trust will also help the Australian government to navigate the risks posed by this pandemic, and the next.

References

[1] Joel Hellewell, Sam Abbott, Amy Gimma, Nikos I Bosse, Christopher I Jarvis, Timothy W Russell, James D Munday, Adam J Kucharski, W John Edmunds, Fiona Sun, Stefan Flasche, Billy J Quilty, Nicholas Davies, Yang Liu, Samuel Clifford, Petra Klepac, Mark Jit, Charlie Diamond, Hamish Gibbs, Kevin van Zandvoort, Sebastian Funk, and Rosalind M Eggo. Feasibility of controlling COVID-19 outbreaks by isolation of cases and contacts. *The Lancet Global Health*, 8(4):e488–e496, 2020. ISSN 2214-109X. doi: https://doi.org/10.1016/S2214-109X(20)30074-7.

[2] Danielle Currie, Cindy Peng, David Lyle, Brydie Jameson, and Michael Frommer. Stemming the flow: How much can the Australian smartphone app help to control COVID-19? *Public Health Research & Practice*, 30(2), 2020. doi: 10.17061/phrp3022009.

[3] Kin On Kwok, Arthur Tang, Vivian W. I. Wei, Woo Hyun Park, Eng Kiong Yeoh, and Steven Riley. Epidemic Models of Contact Tracing: Systematic Review of Transmission Studies of Severe Acute Respiratory Syndrome and Middle East Respiratory Syndrome. *Computational and Structural Biotechnology Journal*, 17:186–194, Jan 2019. ISSN 2001-0370. doi: 10.1016/j.csbj.2019.01.003.

[4] Juhwan Oh, Jong-Koo Lee, Dan Schwarz, Hannah L. Ratcliffe, Jeffrey F. Markuns, and Lisa R. Hirschhorn. National Response to COVID-19 in the Republic of Korea and Lessons Learned for Other Countries. *Health Systems & Reform*, 6(1):e1753464, 2020. doi: 10.1080/23288604.2020.1753464.

[5] Sreeram Chaulia. Why East beats West in the war against coronavirus. 2020.

[6] Maria Savona. The Saga of the Covid-19 Contact Tracing Apps: Lessons for Data Governance. 2020.

[7] Max Fisher and Choe Sang-Hun. How South Korea Flattened the Curve. *The New York Times*, 2020.

[8] Kobi Leins, Chris Culnane, and Benjamin I. P. Rubinstein. Tracking, tracing, trust: contemplating mitigating the impact of COVID-19 through technological interventions. *The Medical Journal of Australia*, 213(1):6–8, 2020. doi: 10.5694/mja2.50669.

[9] Rae Thomas, Zoe Michaleff, Hannah Greenwood, Eman Abukmail, and Paul Glasziou. More than privacy: Australians' concerns and misconceptions about the COVIDSafe App: a short report. *medRxiv*, 2020. doi: 10.1101/2020.06.09.20126110.

[10] David Watts. COVIDSafe, Australia's Digital Contact Tracing App: The Legal Issues (May 2, 2020). *Australia's Digital Contact Tracing App*, 2020. doi: http://dx.doi.org/10.2139/ssrn.3591622.

[11] Justin Chan, Dean Foster, Shyam Gollakota, Eric Horvitz, Joseph Jaeger, Sham Kakade, Tadayoshi Kohno, John Langford, Jonathan Larson, Puneet Sharma, Sudheesh Singanamalla, Jacob Sunshine, and Stefano Tessaro. PACT: Privacy Sensitive Protocols and Mechanisms for Mobile Contact Tracing, 2020.

[12] Timothy Kariotis, Megan Prictor, Shanton Chang, and Kathleen Gray. Evaluating the Contextual Integrity of Australia's My Health Record. *Studies in health technology and informatics*, 265:213–218, Aug 2019. ISSN 0926-9630. doi: 10.3233/shti190166.

[13] Randike Gajanayake, Bill Lane, Tony Iannella, and Tony Sahama. Legal issues related to Accountable-eHealth systems in Australia. 2012. doi: https://doi.org/10.4225/75/5796f5b740a96.

[14] Vincent Chi-Chung Cheng, Josepha Wai-Ming Tai, Ng Lai-Ming, Jasper Chan, Sally Wong, Iris Li, Hon-Ping Chung, Wai-Kei Lo, Kwok-Yung Yuen, and Pak-Leung Ho. Extensive contact tracing and screening to control the spread of vancomycin-resistant Enterococcus faecium ST414 in Hong Kong. *Chinese Medical Journal*, 125(19):3450–3457, 2012. doi: 10.3760/cma.j.issn.0366-6999.2012.19.017.

[15] John Hawkins and Ben Freyens. Contact tracing apps: a behavioural economist's guide to improving uptake. *The Conversation*, 2020:1–7, April 2020.

[16] Lucy Simko, Ryan Calo, Franziska Roesner, and Tadayoshi Kohno. Covid-19 contact tracing and privacy: Studying opinion and preferences. *arXiv preprint arXiv:2005.06056*, 2020.

[17] Andrea Nuzzo, Can Ozan Tan, Ramesh Raskar, Daniel C. DeSimone, Suraj Kapa, and Rajiv Gupta. Universal Shelter-in-Place Versus Advanced Automated Contact Tracing and Targeted Isolation: A Case for 21st-Century Technologies for SARS-CoV-2 and Future Pandemics. *Mayo Clinic Proceedings*, 95(9):1898 – 1905, 2020. ISSN 0025-6196. doi: https://doi.org/10.1016/j.mayocp.2020.06.027.

[18] Leila Pfaeffli Dale, Lauren White, Marc Mitchell, and Guy Faulkner. Smartphone app uses loyalty point incentives and push notifications to encourage influenza vaccine uptake. *Vaccine*, 37(32):4594–4600, 2019. ISSN 0264-410X. doi: https://doi.org/10.1016/j.vaccine.2018.04.018. URL http://www.sciencedirect.com/science/article/pii/S0264410X18304870.

[19] Linda Brennan, Wayne Binney, Lukas Parker, Torgeir Aleti (né Watne), and Dang Nguyen. *Social Marketing and Behaviour Change: Models, Theory and Applications*, 11, 2014. ISBN 1782548157, 9781782548157. doi: 10.4337/9781782548157.

Sustainable Transport as a Key Pillar to Community Resilience During the COVID-19 Pandemic

Arturo Ardila-Gomez

As cities gradually exit COVID-19 quarantines, some are suggesting that public transport might increase contagion risk and that private cars should be considered the only safe alternative. This view, however, is based on perception rather than facts. Moreover, promoting widespread car use could actually impede recovery and come with a host of negative side effects, especially for the poor. This chapter uses the Three Cs framework—avoid closed and crowded spaces, and closed contact situations and in particular their overlap—to understand how sustainable transport can be resilient to the pandemic. To minimize the three Cs while preserving the economy the ideal is to have people work from home which applies only to workers who tele-commute. Yet for first responders, blue-collar, and informal workers getting to work is essential for generating income. Sustainable transport can provide efficient, dependable mobility that connects people to opportunities and be COVID-safe during this pandemic.

46.1   Introduction

As cities gradually exit COVID-19 quarantines and reopen their economies, some observers are suggesting that public transport might increase contagion risk [1] and that private cars [2] should be considered the only safe alternative. However, this stance is based on perception rather than facts. In addition, promoting widespread car use could actually impede recovery and come with a host of negative side effects, especially for the poor.

In this observation chapter I explain why sustainable transport — public transport, walking, and biking — must become an integral part of our response to the pandemic, and how we can make this happen in a safe, resilient way.

46.1.1   We Need to Keep People and Economies Moving

The International Labor Organization estimates that a whopping 1.6 billion people are at risk of losing their livelihoods [3]. Many of them are informal workers who do not have access to unemployment benefits or any other kind of social safety nets. Some 39 million people have already lost their jobs in the United States [4]. There is growing concern that many jobs lost to the pandemic will vanish forever [5], raising some significant questions about the future of the labor market, particularly in cities.

Furthermore, the ILO estimates that, globally, "more than 436 million enterprises [3] face high risks of serious disruption." Related, up to 580 million people could fall into poverty [6], as estimated by the United Nations University. There is also a high probability that the health crisis may contribute to a hunger pandemic [7] could push another 130 million people to the brink of starvation.

These numbers show how quarantine and shelter-at-home can hurt millions of people, particularly the poor. Now, imagine if these losses were permanent and the urban labor market collapsed. Poverty would skyrocket, middle classes would shrink, and tax revenue would plummet. To avoid this scenario, countries are anxious to reignite their economies while minimizing contagion risk, which remains a major preoccupation worldwide. Transport will be a key piece of the equation: we must find ways to connect people to jobs, and to connect them as safely and sustainably as possible. For example, 60 percent of the world's employed population work in the informal market [8]. Informally employed people typically must travel outside their homes to generate income [9].

46.2   Sustainable Transport and the Call for a Green Recovery

As the world grapples with the pandemic and its economic fallout, we cannot forget about the climate crisis that has been looming over the last few decades. While the measures to lower the spread of the virus have temporarily reduced greenhouse gas emissions [10], atmospheric carbon dioxide levels are the highest in human history [11]. Just in 2020, northern Siberia–above the Arctic Circle—experienced record-high temperatures [12] that can melt the permafrost and release even more GHG (greenhouse gas) into the atmosphere.

Clearly, decisionmakers at all levels must work toward a green recovery model that will help address the ongoing health, economic, and climate emergencies simultaneously. Moving toward sustainable transport will be a key part of that process: the transport sector already accounts for a quarter of energy-related emissions, and that number is poised to grow [13] much higher over the next decade. Low-carbon transport can significantly reduce overall emissions, and, concurrently, will help us build more competitive, more inclusive communities –and be COVID-safe. Transport is also key for community resilience, understood as the "measure of the sustained ability of a community to utilize available to respond, withstand, and recover from adverse situations," (RAND Corporation. N.d.) Sustainable transport is more resilient because it embeds redundancy: many buses provide service, bicycles and pedestrians can circumvent many obstacles. If the solution to the pandemic is to provide every adult in the planet with a car, then resiliency will go down because of the resulting gridlock. Worse, a planet with six billion cars will be very warm due to the huge cradle to grave and well to wheels emissions, regardless of the engine technology.

46.2.1   The Three Cs: Avoid Closed, Crowded, Close-Contact Situations

What exactly should sustainable transport look like in the context of COVID-19? What are the transport modes and solutions we should prioritize? And, importantly, how should we adapt existing systems to minimize health risks?

To answer this, I refer to the Three Cs framework: Closed spaces, Crowded spaces, and Close contact situations. According to the framework, the three Cs can drastically increase the risk of spreading the coronavirus, in particular where they overlap [14]. Japan developed this framework to help it contain the pandemic—quite successfully [15].

46.2.2   Managing Transport Demand Through Home-Based Work

The best way to minimize the three Cs while preserving the economy is to have people work from home—a situation that applies mostly to workers with access to digital technology. These workers—myself included—can hold virtual meetings, continue to read, and reply to emails, and can even make coffee and cook food at home. For a COVID-safe restart of economic activities, whoever can work from home should continue to do so: this will reduce transport demand and allow people who do need to travel to achieve proper physical distancing inside buses or metros, particularly during peak hours [16].

Whether home-based work is temporary or permanent is something that only the future will tell. But it is safe to say that the pandemic will have a lasting and dramatic impact on the way we manage office space [17]. However, it is important to note that not all workers are coping well with home-based work, as indicated by the troubling increase in domestic violence ([18] and [19]), stress [20], and depression [21].

46.3   Providing Safe Mobility to Those Who Need It

Yet home-based work is possible not only because of technology, but also because of the countless formal and informal workers who leave their homes every morning to keep supply chains running, deliver packages, and restock the shelves of our local markets. Add first responders who must also travel to work in order to keep us safe and healthy.

For those essential workers, the ability to get around is as important as ever—without a way to reach their jobs, most of them would likely lose their income and have no way to put food on the table. In the next sections, I analyze how we can use sustainable transport to provide safe, green, and efficient mobility for those who need it most, both during and after the pandemic. We will focus on public transport first, and then explore the potential of cycling and walking.

46.3.1   Safe Operation of Public Transport During a Pandemic

Many of those who must continue commuting rely on public transport systems, which are uniquely positioned to carry large volumes of passengers through urban areas. Even during a pandemic, public transport remains the backbone of sustainable mobility and essential to economic recovery.

There is growing evidence that public transport riders do not face higher infection risk than anyone else [22, 23]. While Hong Kong relies heavily on mass transit, it has registered few cases even as its mass transit system continues to operate [24]. Japan is also highly dependent on transit, yet researchers "did not trace any [infection] clusters to Japan's notoriously packed commuter trains... Riders are usually alone and not talking to other passengers. And lately, they are all wearing masks," [25]. A study in France found that of the 150 infection clusters that appeared after reopening the economy, none could be traced back to public transport [26]. Several authors rapidly and convincingly debunked attempts to blame the subway in New Your City for spreading the virus [27, 28]. For example, Manhattan had the highest density of subway lines but the lowest incidence of COVID-19 cases [29]. In contrast, areas with higher car use had higher contagion rates—some researchers found that it was cars that seeded the epidemic [30].

For the sake of public health, economic recovery, and environmental sustainability, we must keep the momentum going to preserve the appeal of public transport. As long as the virus is here, transport providers must adapt their operations to minimize the overlap of the three Cs: Closed and Crowded spaces, and Close contact situations. We need COVID-safe transit systems for staff and passengers.

Many transport systems have adopted stricter cleaning protocols with anti-viral chemicals or simply with soap and water because the virus "is no match for plain old soap [31]." Still, touching a surface such as a handle or a bar is not believed to be the primary way for the virus to spread [32]. Proper ventilation is critical ([23] and [33]). Transport companies should instruct their drivers to open windows systematically or keep the air-conditioning on. In Japan, for example, trains operate with the windows open to ensure proper ventilation [34]. However, the air conditioning cannot be in recirculation mode because air must circulate within the space [35] to prevent contagion.

As person-to-person [32] is the primary transmission means, then public transport users must do their part. They must not touch their faces [36], wear masks [37]—one of the most effective ways to prevent transmission [38]—and wash their hands with soap and water before and after using public transport [32].

Notice that this advice applies to everyone, not just public transport riders [32]. Indeed, car drivers should also wash their hands before and after using their private cars. The same goes for cyclists, who can sneeze or cough while riding their bike.

The proper physical distancing between riders is another critical requirement. The World Health Organization recommends people stay at least 1 meter [39] to minimize transmission risk. Masks could help reduce this distance [40] and are effective at preventing the spread of germs in public transport [41]. Still, there is a need to reduce occupancy rates and avoid crowding on transit vehicles. Public transport and particularly mass transit cannot operate initially at high occupancy rates due to regulations to reduce the risk of contagion. To make this possible, countries around the world have temporarily capped transit capacity: Colombia, for instance, announced that public transport can use only 35% of its capacity [42], while the UK (United Kingdom) set an even lower limit of just 10% [43]. Governments can increase these caps as the epidemic evolves [44], and scientists [45] gain knowledge on key epidemiological parameters [46]. Indeed, by September 2020 as the pandemic diminished, the Colombian government increased the maximum occupancy of mass transit to 50% by requiring improved ventilation and cleaning protocols [47].

46.3.1.1   Adapting Infrastructure and Resources

If cities are to decrease passenger density on public transport vehicles, they need to keep frequent service, which requires predictable speeds and traffic conditions. Easy to say but challenging to implement—especially in developing countries, where residents own fewer cars, but, paradoxically, tend to experience higher congestion levels [48]. The solution: "pop-up bus lanes" or bus priority lanes –implemented of course with proper road safety considerations [49] and proper traffic management measures. The New York Metropolitan Transit Authority, for example, has requested 97 km of new bus lanes in response to the pandemic [50].

But despite the best efforts of professionals across the sector, there is no denying that the COVID-19 crisis has dealt a massive blow to public transport. Demand nosedived almost overnight [51], leading to considerable financial distress for formal and informal public transport operators. The issue is complicated. The bottom line is that, if governments offer subsidies, they must set proper incentives to avoid service reductions and get operators committed to long-term improvements [52].

The current situation could have a profound impact on the way cities approach their transport policy [53], even once the virus subsides. The measures described in this chapter may have been taken hastily in the face of a global public health emergency. Nonetheless, these measures already challenge many deeply-rooted assumptions about urban transport [54]. Think of the space that private cars are supposedly entitled to in comparison to mass transit. Something as simple as a pop-up bus lane lets us envision what a transit-friendly city could look like: a greener, more inclusive place where the road belongs to everyone [55]. People at all income levels could get around quickly and efficiently.

Bolstering public transport will be instrumental if we are serious about putting sustainable mobility at the heart of the "new normal." Communities will be more resilient also because of the redundancy embedded in public transport and the efficient use of scarce resources such as road space. And even though the pandemic has dealt a significant blow to the sector, the lockdowns have also created unexpected opportunities to rethink sustainable transit vs. private cars.

46.3.2   Biking

Decisionmakers have quickly realized that bicycles could be a COVID-safe transport for residents to get around. Besides being an open-air form of transport, cycling also makes it easy to enforce physical distancing thanks to each bike's physical footprint and the additional gap that cyclists need to leave between each other to avoid collisions. Notice how bicycles naturally avoid the three Cs that increase the risk of infection, especially when they overlap: closed spaces, crowded spaces, and close-contact situations.

As a result, many cities in both developed and developing countries have been deploying pop-up bike lanes over the last few months, from Paris and London to Berlin, Milan [56], Bogotá, Mexico

City, Lima [57], and Wuhan. As part of this trend, new design guidelines help local governments implement simple changes to road infrastructure or signage, allowing for the creation of bike lanes at a low cost and in as little as ten days [58].

Although designed as a temporary solution, there is reason to believe that some bike lanes could become permanent. Public opinion is undoubtedly moving in the right direction: 56% of Londoners "want pavements to be permanently widened to make space for walking and 57% want to see new cycle lanes created and existing ones broadened" [59]. Further, with the right infrastructure, cycling can carry impressive volumes of passengers. In 2019, 583 km of permanent bike lanes in Bogotá absorbed 800,000 rides per day—about 6% of all trips, including walking and motorized [60].

46.3.3   Walking

Last but not least, walking is and will be a crucial pillar of urban mobility in developing countries [61], particularly for women [62] and the poor. People walk to access public transport, to shop, or even to commute to work. Walking brings many advantages to cities and their residents. Promoting pedestrian-friendly streets can make travel safer [63], reduce air pollution, improve public space, and create a more inclusive environment for all users [55], including children and people with disabilities.

Because they demand physical activity by users, public transit and active modes like walking or biking are also associated with tangible health benefits such as "lower Body Mass Index, lower waist circumference, less obesity, higher vitamin D, lower cholesterol and lower hepatic inflammation" [64].

The pandemic has made walking even more appealing because it is COVID-safe [65]. Pedestrians on a sidewalk can typically avoid the three Cs that increase the risk of infection. Sidewalks are open spaces. Pedestrians can usually avoid crowding and keep a safe distance of at least 1 meter. Moreover, pedestrians rarely engage strangers walking by, let alone closely. If needed, wearing masks can provide additional protection.

Yet pedestrians face significant challenges, including less-than-perfect infrastructure and competition with other transport modes. In developing countries, for instance, cars frequently park on the sidewalks, making it more challenging for pedestrians—as well as people on wheelchairs and children on strollers—to keep a safe distance.

Cities can take many concrete steps to enforce parking rules and, more generally, to expand the amount of space available to pedestrians. Some are converting road space into "pop-up sidewalks" for the benefit of pedestrians and bicycles [66]. Other cities are even creating "al fresco streets [54]" to allow retail and restaurants to set up shop outdoors. Al fresco streets are an innovative way to avoid the Three Cs and enjoy life in a safe, responsible manner.

These "road diets" [63] will hopefully continue after the pandemic so people everywhere can enjoy the advantages of walking. Road diets work if accompanied by solid traffic management so that car volumes do not lead to gridlock. Many cities are already taking this step and looking at long-term solutions to accommodate pedestrians [53].

46.3.4   A Window of Opportunity for Sustainable Transport

The pandemic has forced cities across the globe to take emergency measures that have created a window of opportunity to: Avoid unnecessary travel, Shift toward sustainable transport, and Improve transport infrastructure and services. This "Avoid-Shift-Improve" paradigm [67] is precisely what sustainable transport advocates like myself have been preaching over the last few decades to transform urban mobility. While many decisionmakers used to balk at this approach, the COVID-19 crisis has dramatically changed the transport conversation: people are now clearly seeing the value of sustainable transport, and the idea of reallocating space or resources toward public transit, cycling, and walking has become a lot more acceptable.

The challenge is to keep the momentum going to ensure cities do not move right back to auto-centric development as soon as the virus starts to subside. The transition to sustainable transport could significantly contribute to a green recovery [68] revive urban economies, and create 15 million jobs worldwide [69].

46.4   Conclusions

Sustainable transport—public transit, walking, and biking—can provide efficient, dependable mobility that connects people to opportunities [70] and be COVID-safe during this pandemic. Transport is indeed what sustains the agglomeration effects [71] that make urban economies so attractive and make the urban labor market work [70]. Sustainable transport is also paramount for achieving community resilience.

But relying on private cars alone will achieve negative results, partly because cars cannot absorb the large volumes of people transiting through busy urban centers every day. Private vehicles will weaken community resilience. Calls for one person per car to be COVID-safe will lead to gridlock and a very warm planet. Sustainable transport is highly relevant in developed and developing countries as this open letter for the European Union states: "As unemployment and lay-offs are expected to rise in the coming months, and family income will be under stress, walking, cycling and public transport will be the most affordable and equitable transport options, and they will be more necessary than ever" [72].

The window of opportunity for sustainable transport has opened. Public transport, biking and walking can create the conditions for a more robust, inclusive, and resilient recovery. Sustainable transport increases community resilience because of the more efficient use of resources, the redundancy embedded in public transport and the ease to navigate obstacles by buses, bicycles and pedestrians. Importantly, these sustainable transport options could also drastically reduce the greenhouse gas footprint of urban mobility—a key priority considering that, despite the temporary dip in emissions [10] induced by the pandemic, atmospheric carbon dioxide levels are at their highest in human history [11]. Promoters of sustainable transport need to become champions to implement sustainable transport and achieve a green recovery while also building a key pillar to community resilience.

References

[1] Rachel Schraer. Coronavirus: What's the risk on transport? *BBC News*, 2020. URL https://www.bbc.com/news/health-51736185.

[2] Tina Bellon. Empty trains, clogged roads: Americans get behind the wheel to avoid transit. *Reuters*, 2020. URL https://reut.rs/2yjXn7x.

[3] International Labor Organization (ILO). As job losses escalate, nearly half of global workforce at risk of losing livelihoods. 2020. URL https://www.ilo.org/global/about-the-ilo/newsroom/news/WCMS_743036/lang--en/index.htm.

[4] The Guardian. US unemployment rises by 2.4m despite easing of coronavirus lockdowns. 2020. URL https://www.theguardian.com/business/2020/may/21/us-unemployment-figures-jobs-lost-coronavirus.

[5] Patricia Cohen. Many Jobs May Vanish Forever as Layoffs Mount. *The New York Times*, 2020. URL https://www.nytimes.com/2020/05/21/business/economy/coronavirus-unemployment-claims.html.

[6] Andy Sumner, Chris Hoy, and Eduardo Ortiz-Juarez. Estimates of the impact of COVID-19 on global poverty. WIDER Working Paper 2020/43. *Helsinki: UNU-WIDER*, 2020.

[7] World Food Programme (WFP). Chief warns of hunger pandemic as COVID-19 spreads (Statement to UN Security Council). 2020. URL https://www.wfp.org/news/wfp-chief-warns-hunger-pandemic-covid-19-spreads-statement-un-security-council.

[8] International Labor Organization (ILO). More than 60 per cent of the world's employed population are in the informal economy. 2018. URL https://www.ilo.org/global/about-the-ilo/newsroom/news/WCMS_627189/lang--en/index.htm.

[9] Marketplace. Food Insecurity Goes Global under the Cloud of Covid-19, year = 2020. URL https://www.marketplace.org/shows/marketplace-morning-report/food-insecurity-goes-global-under-the-cloud-of-covid-19.

[10] Corinne Le Quéré, Robert B. Jackson, Matthew W. Jones, Adam J. P. Smith, Sam Abernethy, Robbie M. Andrew, Anthony J. De-Gol, David R. Willis, Yuli Shan, Josep G. Canadell, Pierre Friedlingstein, Felix Creutzig, and Glen P. Peters. Temporary reduction in daily global CO2 emissions during the COVID-19 forced confinement. *Nature Climate Change*, 10(7):647–653, Jul 2020. ISSN 1758-6798. doi: 10.1038/s41558-020-0797-x.

[11] Ishaan Tharoor. The World's Climate Catastrophe Worsens Amid the Pandemic. *The Washington Post*, 2020. URL https://www.washingtonpost.com/world/2020/06/29/worlds-climate-catastrophe-worsens-amid-pandemic/.

[12] Anton Troianovski. A Historic Heat Wave Roasts Siberia. *The New York Times*, 2020. URL https://www.nytimes.com/2020/06/25/world/europe/siberia-heat-wave-climate-change.html?referringSource=articleShare.

[13] Shiying Wang and Ge Mengpin. Everything You Need to Know About the Fastest-Growing Source of Global Emissions: Transport. 2019. URL https://www.wri.org/blog/2019/10/everything-you-need-know-about-fastest-growing-source-global-emissions-transport.

[14] Labor Ministry of Health and Welfare of Japan. Avoid the Three Cs. 2020. URL https://www.mhlw.go.jp/content/10900000/000619576.pdf.

[15] Taisuke Abiru. How Japan Responded to the COVID-19 Pandemic. 2020. URL https://valdaiclub.com/a/highlights/how-japan-has-responded-to-covid-19-pandemic/.

[16] Jarret Walker. The Collapse of Rush Hour: A Deep Dive. 2020. URL https://humantransit.org/2020/05/the-collapse-of-rush-hour-a-deep-dive.html.

[17] Soames Job. Can COVID-19 teach us something for the road safety epidemic? 2020. URL https://blogs.worldbank.org/transport/can-covid-19-teach-us-something-road-safety-epidemic.

[18] The Guardian. 'Calamitous': domestic violence set to soar by 20% during global lockdown. 2020. URL https://www.theguardian.com/global-development/2020/apr/28/calamitous-domestic-violence-set-to-soar-by-20-during-global-lockdown-coronavirus.

[19] Amanda Taub. A New Covid-19 Crisis: Domestic Abuse Rises Worldwide. *The New York Times*, 2020. URL https://www.nytimes.com/2020/04/06/world/coronavirus-domestic-violence.html.

[20] Center for Disease Control (CDC). Coping with Stress. 2020. URL https://www.cdc.gov/coronavirus/2019-ncov/daily-life-coping/managing-stress-anxiety.html.

[21] Healthline. What COVID-19 Is Doing to Our Mental Health. *Healthline*, 2020. URL https://www.healthline.com/health-news/what-covid-19-is-doing-to-our-mental-health.

[22] TUMInitiative. COVID19 transmission risks and infection rates in public transport BusTrolleybus - what do we know? 2020. URL https://twitter.com/TUMInitiative/status/1266662574453673985.

[23] Feargus O'Sullivan. In Japan and France, Riding Transit Looks Surprisingly Safe. *Bloomberg News*, 2020. URL https://www.bloomberg.com/news/articles/2020-06-09/japan-and-france-find-public-transit-seems-safe.

[24] Janette Sadik-Khan. Fear of Public Transit Got Ahead of the Evidence: Many have blamed subways and buses for coronavirus outbreaks, but a growing body of research suggests otherwise. *The Atlantic*, 2020. URL https://www.theatlantic.com/ideas/archive/2020/06/fear-transit-bad-cities/612979/?referringSource=articleShare.

[25] Dennis Normile. Japan ends its Covid-19 State of Emergency. *Science Magazine*, 2020. URL https://www.sciencemag.org/news/2020/05/japan-ends-its-covid-19-state-emergency.

[26] Nicolas Berrod. "Coronavirus : pourquoi aucun cluster n'a été détecté dans les transports." Le Parisien. 2020. URL https://www.leparisien.fr/societe/coronavirus-pourquoi-aucun-cluster-n-a-ete-detecte-dans-les-transports-05-06-2020-8330415.php.

[27] Aaron Gordon. It's Easy, But Wrong, to Blame the Subway for the Coronavirus Pandemic. *Motherboard:Thec by vice*, 2020. URL https://www.vice.com/amp/en_us/article/qjdy33/its-easy-but-wrong-to-blame-the-subway-for-the-coronavirus-pandemic.

[28] Jeffrey Harris. The Subways Seeded the Massive Coronavirus Epidemic in New York City. 2020. URL http://web.mit.edu/jeffrey/harris/HarrisJE_WP2_COVID19_NYC_13-Apr-2020.pdf.

[29] Alon Levy. The Subway is Probably not Why New York is a Disaster Zone. *Pedestrian Observations*, 2020. URL https://pedestrianobservations.com/2020/04/15/the-subway-is-probably-not-why-new-york-is-a-disaster-zone/.

[30] Salim Furth. Automobiles Seeded the Massive Coronavirus Epidemic in New York City. *Market Urbanism*, 2020. URL https://marketurbanism.com/2020/04/19/automobiles-seeded-the-massive-coronavirus-epidemic-in-new-york-city/.

[31] Palli Thordarson. The coronavirus is no match for plain, old soap — here's the science behind it. *Market Watch*, 2020. URL https://www.marketwatch.com/story/deadly-viruses-are-no-match-for-plain-old-soap-heres-the-science-behind-it-2020-03-08.

[32] CDC. How Covid Spreads. 2020. URL https://www.cdc.gov/coronavirus/2019-ncov/prevent-getting-sick/how-covid-spreads.html.

[33] Zeynep Tufecki. We Need to Talk About Ventilation: How is it that six months into a respiratory pandemic, we are still doing so little to mitigate airborne transmission? *The Atlantic*, 2020. URL https://www.theatlantic.com/health/archive/2020/07/why-arent-we-talking-more-about-airborne-transmission/614737/?referringSource=articleShare.

[34] Lucy Craft. Japan has long accepted COVID's airborne spread, and scientists say ventilation is key. *CBS News*, 2020. URL https://www.cbsnews.com/news/coronavirus-japan-has-long-accepted-covids-airborne-spread-and-scientists-say-ventilation-is-key/.

[35] Javier SALAS and MARIANO ZAFRA. Radiografía de tres brotes: así se contagiaron y así podemos evitarlo. *El Pais*, 2020. URL https://elpais.com/ciencia/2020-06-06/radiografia-de-tres-brotes-asi-se-contagiaron-y-asi-podemos-evitarlo.html.

[36] Stephen Benning, Brian Labus, and Kimberly Barchard. To fight coronavirus, here's a trick to stop touching your face so often. *Market Watch*, 2020. URL https://www.marketwatch.com/story/to-fight-coronavirus-heres-how-you-truly-can-stop-touching-your-face-so-often-2020-03-23.

[37] Renyi Zhang, Yixin Li, Annie Zhang, Yuang Wang, and Mario Molina. Identifying airborne transmission as the dominantroute for the spread of COVID-19. *Researchgate*, 2020. URL https://www.researchgate.net/publication/342128029_Identifying_airborne_transmission_as_the_dominant_route_for_the_spread_of_COVID-19.

[38] Derek Chu, Elie Akl, Stephanie Duda, Karla Solo, and et al. Physical distancing, face masks, and eye protection to prevent person-to-person transmission of SARS-CoV-2 and COVID-19: a systematic review and meta-analysis. *The Lancet*, 2020. URL https://www.thelancet.com/journals/lancet/article/PIIS0140-6736(20)31142-9/fulltext.

[39] World Health Organization. Coronavirus disease (COVID-19) advice for the public. 2020. URL https://www.who.int/emergencies/diseases/novel-coronavirus-2019/advice-for-public.

[40] Elena Polozova. So You're Going Outside: A Physics-Based Coronavirus Infection Risk Estimator for Leaving the House. *Medium*, 2020. URL https://medium.com/swlh/so-youre-going-outside-a-physics-based-coronavirus-infection-risk-estimator-for-leaving-the-house-d7dcae2746c0.

[41] Paul Edelstein and Ramakrishnan Lalita. Report on Face Masks for the General Public - An Update. DELVE Addendum MAS-TD1. Published 7 July 2020. *DELVE Addendum MAS-TD1*, 2020. URL http://rs-delve.github.io/addenda/2020/07/07/masks-update.html.

[42] El Heraldo. Transporte público debe operar a un 35% de su capacidad: Duque. *El Heraldo*, 2020. URL https://www.elheraldo.co/colombia/transporte-publico-debe-operar-un-35-de-su-capacidad-duque-719138.

[43] The Guardian. Back to work: capacity of transport network will be down by 90%. *The Guardian*, 2020. URL https://www.theguardian.com/world/2020/may/09/back-to-work-capacity-of-transport-network-will-be-down-by-90.

[44] CDC. Interpretation of Epidemic (Epi) Curves during Ongoing Outbreak Investigations. 2020. URL https://www.cdc.gov/foodsafety/outbreaks/investigating-outbreaks/epi-curves.html.

[45] Marti Makary. How to Reopen America Safely: Months ago, I called for a long lockdown. Now we must minimize collateral damage. *The New York Times*, 2020. URL https://www.nytimes.com/2020/05/14/opinion/reopen-america-coronavirus-lockdown.html?referringSource=articleShare.

[46] Gail Dutton. Multiple Studies Suggest COVID-19 Mortality Rate May Be Lower Than Expected. 2020. URL https://www.pharmalive.com/multiple-studies-suggest-covid-19-mortality-rate-may-be-lower-than-expected/.

[47] Ministerio de Salud de Colombia. Minsalud amplía al 50% de ocupación máxima en los sistemas de transporte masivo. 2020. URL https://www.minsalud.gov.co/Paginas/Minsalud-amplia-al-50-de-ocupacion-maxima-en-los-sistemas-de-transporte-masivo.aspx.

[48] Tom Traffic Index. 2020. URL https://www.tomtom.com/en_gb/traffic-index/.

[49] Nikolae Duduta, Claudia Adriazola-Steil, and et al. Traffic Safety on Bus Priority Systems. *EMBARQ - World Bank*, 2014. URL https://wrirosscities.org/sites/default/files/Traffic-Safety-Bus-Priority-Corridors-BRT-EMBARQ-World-Resources-Institute.pdf.

[50] Christina Goldbaum. Returning to Work on the Subway? Here's What You Need to Know. *The New York Times*, 2020. URL https://www.nytimes.com/2020/06/08/nyregion/mta-subway-riding-health-coronavirus.html?referringSource=articleShare.

[51] World Bank Group. World Bank Group Response to Covid-19. The Transport Sector: A Mobility Crisis. 2020. URL http://pubdocs.worldbank.org/en/375701590520360473/COVID-19-and-Transport-A-Mobility-Crisis.pdf.

[52] Georges Darido and Leonardo Canon. Protecting public transport from the coronavirus... and from financial collapse. *Transport for Development*, 2020. URL https://blogs.worldbank.org/transport/protecting-public-transport-coronavirus-and-financial-collapse.

[53] Somini Sengupta and Brad Plumer. How Cities Are Trying to Avert Gridlock After Coronavirus Lockdowns. *The New York Times*, 2020. URL https://www.nytimes.com/2020/06/26/climate/cities-cars-traffic-congestion.html?referringSource=articleShare.

[54] James Brasuell. NACTO Releases Pandemic Streets Design Guide. *Planetizen*, 2020. URL https://www.planetizen.com/node/109418?utm_source=newswire&utm_medium=email&utm_campaign=news-05282020&mc_cid=b2ec9d4bd2&mc_eid=6bed78ad1b.

[55] Justin Gillis and Heather Thompson. Take Back the Streets From the Automobile. *The New York Times*, 2020. URL https://www.nytimes.com/2020/06/20/opinion/pandemic-automobile-cities.html.

[56] Liz Alderman. Corona Cycleways' Become the New Post-Confinement Commute. *The New York Times*, 2020. URL https://www.nytimes.com/2020/06/12/business/paris-bicycles-commute-coronavirus.html?referringSource=articleShare.

[57] Deutsche Welle. Pandemia de coronavirus: ¿la oportunidad definitiva para la bicicleta en América Latina? 2020. URL https://www.dw.com/es/pandemia-de-coronavirus-la-oportunidad-definitiva-para-la-bicicleta-en-am%C3%A9rica-latina/a-53676128.

[58] Mobycon. Making Safe Space for Cycling in 10 Days. 2020. URL https://mobycon.com/wp-content/uploads/2020/05/FrKr-Berlin_Guide-EN.pdf.

[59] Thom Bawden. Coronavirus lockdown: Huge demand from the public for more and bigger cycle lanes. *inews*, 2020. URL https://inews.co.uk/news/coronavirus-lockdown-demand-britons-cycle-lanes-commuting-433665.

[60] Alcaldia Mayor de Bogota. Encuesta de Movilidad 2019. *Indicadores Preliminares*, 2019. URL http://ieu.unal.edu.co/images/Resultados_Preliminares_EncuestaMovilidad_2019.pdf.

[61] Sustainable Mobility for All. Global Mobility Report 2017. *Tracking Sector Performance*, 2017. URL https://sustainabledevelopment.un.org/content/documents/2643Global_Mobility_Report_2017.pdf.

[62] Karla Dominguez Gonzalez, Ana Luiza Machado, Bianca Bianchi Alves, Veronica Raffo, Sofia Guerrero, and Irene Portabales. Road diets: designing a safer street: Reconfigure traffic lanes and cars will slow down. *World Bank*, 2020. URL https://elibrary.worldbank.org/doi/abs/10.1596/33466.

[63] Carlos Waters. Road diets: designing a safer street. *Vox*, 2018. URL https://www.vox.com/2018/7/25/17593344/road-diets-lane-conversion-traffic-calming-explained-video.

[64] Álvaro Passi-Solar, Paula Margozzini, Andrea Cortinez-O'Ryan, Juan C Muñoz, and Jennifer S Mindell. Nutritional and metabolic benefits associated with active and public transport: Results from the Chilean National Health Survey, ENS 2016–2017. 17:100819, 2020. URL https://www.sciencedirect.com/science/article/pii/S2214140519301835?via%3Dihub.

[65] Lisa Weidenfeld. Yes, It's (Probably) Safe to Keep Going on Walks Outside. *Boston Magazine*, 2020. URL https://www.bostonmagazine.com/news/2020/04/03/walk-outside-coronavirus/.

[66] WSP. Walking and Cycling to Economic Recovery – Lessons. 2020. URL https://www.wsp.com/en-AU/insights/walking-and-cycling-to-economic-recovery?deliveryName=DM64561.

[67] Lee Schipper. Transport and CO2 Emissions: A New Framework for a New Challenge. 2009. URL https://www.mlit.go.jp/kokusai/MEET/documents/MEETFUM/S1-LeeSchipper.pdf.

[68] International Monetary Fund (IMF). Greening the Recovery. Special Series on Policies to Respond to Covid-19. 2020. URL https://www.imf.org/~/media/Files/Publications/covid19-special-notes/en-special-series-on-covid-19-greening-the-recovery.ashx.

[69] UN News. Post-pandemic 'green shift' in transport could create up to 15 million Jobs. *UN News*, 2020. URL https://news.un.org/en/story/2020/05/1064382.

[70] Alain Bertaud. Cities as Labor Markets. 2014. URL https://marroninstitute.nyu.edu/uploads/content/Cities_as_Labor_Markets.pdf.

[71] Thisse J. How Transport Costs Shape the Spatial Pattern of Economic Activity, OECD/ITF Joint Transport Research Centre Discussion Papers, No. 2009/13, OECD Publishing. *Paris*, 2009. URL https://doi.org/10.1787/5kmmr3j65tg0-en.

[72] Union Internationale des Transports Publics (UITP). The European exit strategy must include an integrated and sustainable approach to Urban Mobility. 2020. URL https://cms.uitp.org/wp/wp-content/uploads/2020/08/Letter_ExitStrategy_must_includeSustainableUrbanMobility.pdf.

Part V

The Future Direction

Preparing for the Next Pandemic: Geospatial Information for Enhanced Community Resilience

Greg Foliente, Daniel Paez and Abbas Rajabifard

This chapter presents a high-level synthesis of the knowledge and perspectives shared in the chapter contributions in the book. We suggest strategies to apply the geospatial and techno-social lessons learned to date. We also present proposals to develop new capabilities to build resilience in local communities and reproduce them worldwide, especially in preparation for the next pandemic or global crisis.

47.1   Introduction

Throughout human history, pandemics have caused major societal upheavals and impacts. While there have been a few global pandemic threats in the last twenty years, the emergence of SARS-CoV-2 in late 2019 and throughout 2020 and 2021 (i.e. the COVID-19 pandemic) has been one of the most significant disasters in the last 100 years. The extent of its impact to individuals, people groups, nations and the world will not be fully known for many years. Already, COVID-19 has set-back the UN's Sustainable Development Goals (SDGs) [1].

Even as we present and reflect on the technical and techno-social applications of geospatial information and the broader lessons in response to COVID-19 from around the world in the diverse chapter contributions in this book, the evolving global environmental and climate changes coupled with the increasing globalised settings in economics and trade, population growth, migration and movements, the potential for the next pandemic occurring in the not-so-distant future is not a far-fetched idea. We may not only have to deal with the continuing threat of the SARS-CoV-2 lingering on – despite the availability of a number of vaccines – but also with new equally if not more fatal viruses.

In this concluding chapter, we seek to bring together the knowledge and perspectives shared in the different chapters in the book. Our objective – beyond identifying common themes, differences or trends – is to synthesise and suggest a way forward to apply the geospatial knowledge shared and the techno-social lessons learned to date in this book into building community resilience worldwide, especially in preparation for the next pandemic. A well-considered and robust set of strategic and operational capabilities need to be in place long before the outset of a pandemic. We certainly will learn a lot more in the next few years about what worked and what did not work in the public health and wellbeing management of COVID-19. More data and research will surely follow, but this is still an opportune time to pause and take stock.

The rest of this chapter is organised in three parts. First, we summarise the key lessons learnt to date from the COVID-19 pandemic for the geospatial and allied industries from the chapter contributions in this book. Then we discuss some key considerations about an ideal or desired future. Finally, we present an overview of the core strategies that we can embark on today so that we can strengthen our capabilities against, and build community resilience in, future pandemics.

47.2   Key Lessons from COVID-19

> *"What we learn from history is that people don't learn from history."*
> American investor and philanthropist Warren Buffet (1930-).

The first affirmation to make is the critical importance of geospatial information, and the supporting technologies that underpin them and the software applications and web platforms that make them useful for a variety of stakeholders and decision-makers in managing COVID-19, as first outlined in Chapter 1. These are evident across the diverse contributions in this book. A wide range of geospatial and digital technologies has been featured, including remote sensing, drones and mobile applications. Countries in the Americas, Europe, Africa, Asia and Oceania are using maps and GIS dashboards as the key graphical interface to display data around COVID-19 infections, and to disseminate information. This will likely continue in planning and managing the logistics of vaccine distribution and guiding the recovery phase from COVID-19 and other disasters. But as noted by Kraak in Chapter 34, there are effective and ineffective ways of presenting data. Much more consideration needs be given to this.

Data and understanding what they mean (and what they do not say) are the foundations for sound decision making. This topic has many dimensions. Beyond geospatial information, many types of data needed to be sourced and analysed in a dynamic way, often in fast-changing situations. One of the early difficulties with COVID-19 was the scope of uncertainties in knowledge about its epidemiology. But the unprecedented scientific local and global collaboration amongst medical and public health researchers and with those in a wide range of disciplines across the physical and social sciences, including geospatial experts, system modellers, computing and data scientists and social scientists, have produced unprecedented COVID-19 related research. This book is an example of this cross-disciplinary effort.

The need for open data empowering open science has been raised by several authors. Both scientific research and the authorities' decision-making have been either aided or hindered by the availability of, or access to, data of appropriate quality and resolution. The latter is not just a challenge for small developing countries (e.g. in the Pacific Island Countries and Territories, Chapter 26) but also in developed countries (e.g. in the UK, Chapter 18). All types of information – quantitative and qualitative – and those obtained by surveys (e.g. Chapters 27 and 28) and social media feeds (Chapter 11) are especially important. These approaches allow understanding and monitoring of community resilience, engaging the public and understanding their attitudes, behaviours and actions.

Data need to be organised and managed via harmonised terms and definitions, and spatial data infrastructures (SDI) both at the local and national level, in land and in water (Chapter 9). The success of rapid tool developments to support the COVID-19 public health measures in Korea (Chapter 24), for example, has been partly credited to its national SDI. As noted in Chapter 1, the UN-GGIM's efforts to advance an Integrated Geospatial Information Framework (IGIF) across the globe are critical. Issues around core reference data, interoperability, common geographies, integration of statistics and geography, privacy and confidentiality and cybersecurity need to be addressed. Experiences during the pandemic, depicted in many parts of this book, tell us that when complex decisions are needed, there is no time to sign data custodian agreements or to integrate geospatial databases. In a number of case studies in this book, geospatial information effectively supported decision-making when the SDI was operational and not just conceived in a technical report.

Beyond data and technology, the critical role of leadership and governance cannot be overemphasised. In the web portal of endcoronavirus.org, the gallery of countries "winning" or "beating" COVID-19 includes both developed and developing countries, those that are technology-rich and those without much technology. In some ways, this affirms the importance of the first two of the three core themes of the UN-GGIM IGIF's strategic pathways: Governance, People and Technology. When informed by science and evidence, political leaders can manage COVID-19 using adaptive public health measures. Since the start of the pandemic, there have been multiple reports on how in many instances, government and institutions did not act in the multiple warnings around the need for stronger pandemic resilience at the local and regional levels. The lack of attention by some leaders to risks brought forward by the scientific community has not yielded the desired results.

It is hard to determine if the lack of attention to science was due to scientists not communicating results effectively or political leaders and authorities making decisions based on ideology. Either way, the lesson learnt is that community resilience building should be based on sound science and built on trust between the community and the authorities [2]. The more the authorities rely on science and evidence, the more chances the community will likely support the public health measures (Chapter 27). Cooperation, collaboration and trust across society are needed; in the end, human behaviour was key to the success of COVID-19 public health measures.

The COVID-19 pandemic has demonstrated that in a highly interconnected social, economic and natural environments, a highly contagious virus can become a global pandemic in no time. And from a safety perspective, nobody is out of the woods until everyone is out. It would not matter how strong a particular country is in its response to the pandemic. It requires its neighbours and the rest of the nations to be building resilience before normality can be returned to the natural, social and economic settings. New Zealand, Australia, Singapore and some other countries have had relatively effective responses to the pandemic with limited infections and a reduced number of deaths compared to the world's average. However, full epidemiological, social and economic recovery in these countries will not occur until the world achieves a lasting solution. Without a global solution, the risk of multiple re-infection waves will continue. Therefore, we have learnt from COVID-19 that community resilience is not an isolated concept for a particular community or group of people. Global crises such as climate change and the COVID-19 pandemic demand community and societal resilience that is built from broad stakeholder cooperation at the local, regional and national levels.

Still along the lines of high interconnectivity, cities – as a dense centre of human settlements and socio-economic activities – emerged as natural hot spots for COVID-19. Adapting from sustainability research, it can also be stated that, "Pandemics will be lost or won in cities". There are many considerations in managing the pandemic in urban centres (e.g. see Chapters 10, 17, 18, 28, 42 and 46), but we can only be successful beating a pandemic if we beat it in our urban centres.

Finally, COVID-19 has sped-up the digitalisation and online transformation of work and education, and in the process also highlighted societal inequalities. The most vulnerable groups of people and regions have been asymmetrically impacted not just health-wise, but also socially and economically [1]. Often, as in the case of people in informal settlements (e.g. Chapters 8 and 15), very little information is available about them even before the pandemic, making it difficult to monitor and support their situation during the pandemic. Recovery efforts, including economic stimulus measures, provide opportunity to re-set the social, economic and environmental conditions of the majority of a nation's populations, and thus make a major advance on many fronts across the SDGs. This requires strategic vision, leadership, political will and effective governance. Data and technology, in general, are just enablers.

Having come full circle, we acknowledge that there are many more lessons not listed in this chapter, and reaffirm the critical role of geospatial information and technologies in managing a pandemic. In the next section, we explore our desired future before the next pandemic and global crisis.

47.3   The Road Ahead: The Only Certainty in the Future is Change

"Prediction is very difficult, especially about the future."
Danish writer, artist and humourist Robert Storm Petersen (1882-1949).

In this section, we cast our future vision and aspirations on the basis of the observations and lessons discussed in the previous section. In other words, we will attempt to describe a desired future where the lessons are assumed to have been learnt and applied. As we do, it is worth noting that the authorities and our society, more broadly, need to face a future pandemic while facing other concurrent hazards and stresses. For example, in 2020 and 2021, we had to deal with the overlapping challenges and impacts of climate change and COVID-19; these included the wildfires and hurricanes in the US, and the tropical cyclones and flooding in the Asia-Pacific. Thus, we need to recognise also that this could be the new norm moving forward.

Following the structure of the previous section, we imagine a future where a multi-scale SDI is in place in most countries around the world. The maturity and adoption levels may be uneven across different countries but the core definitions and reference data are harmonised, with high interoperability and linkages with other data infrastructures and platforms. A diverse range and type of data contents can come from established and new sources – including those from new technologies and from the crowd – with trusted provenance and quality indicator and that protects individual and corporate privacy. The geospatial information of most data is preserved. The infrastructure and the contents are supported by sensible data governance regimes and appropriate cybersecurity measures. The supporting physical infrastructure is robust, in the face of an extreme event, and highly resilient in case of disruption. In other words, it is able to be made operational again swiftly; that is, a fail-safe system. Political appetite and societal expectations regarding cybersecurity risks and privacy – that vary from one country to another – could be a significant factor here. Putting these issues aside, the ultimate aim is to eventually realise the concept of a Digital Earth (Chapter 32).

With a solid data infrastructure in place and in operation, when the next global crisis occurs, new information can be readily managed and made widely available. New mobile and digital applications and solutions can be developed rapidly to meet the specific needs of a future crisis, allowing data to be used more effectively for a coordinated response and decision-making by different stakeholders, including the public. Information management protocols guide these stakeholders in an environment of information glut and where "infodemic" is widespread.

And so, as highlighted in the previous section, the most consequential factor remains the human factor, or the people's capabilities and ability to make sound decisions. This is a future that is challenging to describe because this is value-laden. What is a "sound decision" and who is even able to make this judgment? How do we shape critical thinking and innovation? What are acceptable and unacceptable moral values? Who decides? We can only generally hope that most people will aim for the "greater good".

Despite the above dilemma, identifying the critical role of human factors is important. From a top-down perspective, these are usually identified as vision, leadership and governance. From a bottom-up perspective, the complex nature of human behaviours and actions can lead to highly unpredictable emergent outcomes, which is a truly complex system. In an ideal future, we certainly hope that these behaviours are better understood and harnessed, again for the greater good, especially in times of crises.

In other words, we are describing herein a future where the UN-GGIM's aspirations for IGIF are in place in many countries around the world. In these aspirations, the performance settings for governance, technology and people are continually improving based on new knowledge and lessons from field experiences, including pandemics and other crises. In this future, the geospatial sector and allied industries and disciplines, collaborate widely and effectively to serve the needs of society and, in times of crisis, adapt our efforts to enable different stakeholders to manage the crisis and communities to bounce back better.

47.4   Strategies to Face the Next Crisis and Build Community Resilience

"The best way to predict the future is to invent it."
American computer scientist and pioneer Alan Kay (1940-).

The gap between lessons learned to date (present state) and our aspirations (future state) is how to get to the latter. Herein, we organise the strategies to fill this gap over time according to the general knowledge development and maturity curve in Figure 47.1. The main curve in this figure follows a Sigmoid (or simply, "S") curve. The concept being that new knowledge (early in time, left of the curve) grows and matures over time according to this curve, until such time that it is fully adopted and widely applied in industry or practice.

Knowledge topics in any area or discipline can be placed in this curve, according to its maturity. At the lowest levels of maturity are the topics that will typically be undertaken as PhD thesis projects in universities. Those at the middle may require a combination of research and development. Over time, some of these topics would have been developed into demonstration prototypes, field-tested and eventually deployed. Some of the knowledge may be adopted as industry guidelines, standards or regulations.

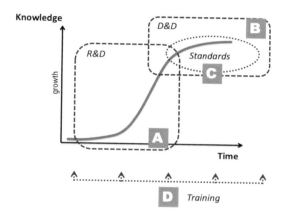

FIGURE 47.1
Knowledge development and maturity curve and the four strategic pathways to improved geospatial information capability in the future: (A) Research and development, (B) Demonstration and deployment, (C) Frameworks, standards and regulations, and (D) Training and human resource development.

The core strategies are, thus, organised as shown in Figure 47.1 and elaborated below.

A. Research and development

It was evident in this book and in the general COVID-19 literature that lack of knowledge, or epistemic uncertainty, hampered the early efforts to assess risks and manage the pandemic. Although the bulk of the research that needed to be undertaken about the virus and its epidemiology fall into the hands of experts in the medical and public health disciplines, it is clear now that interdisciplinary and transdisciplinary research collaborations have been significantly valuable. In other cases, questions raised by researchers from one discipline have led to collaborations and have enriched the understanding of key issues. For example, research by N.N. Taleb and his associates [3] on pandemic risk management based on the probability distribution's tail properties raised many salient points and helped identify common errors and fallacies when using point forecasts for fat- tailed variables like pandemic deaths. Together with the research gaps identified by various contributors in this book – across disciplines – it now seems that there are many more areas that demand deep research or serious research and development (R&D) efforts, especially where geospatial and temporal information are critical.

With even more data and improved insights about COVID-19 and its spread, impacts and control coming to fore in the next year or two, undertaking more quality research will consolidate and expand our knowledge further. Of special note, where geospatial information needs to have more prominent roles, for example, are in: network epidemiology, pandemic risk management, including perception vs. actual risk, community wellbeing, social attitudes and human behaviours and response (e.g., from public health measures to vaccines), economic and SDG impacts and recovery scenarios, balance of privacy and cybersecurity, amongst others. Some research will be about more fundamental science questions while others will be more applied. Research on addressing the methodological gaps in the use and analysis of qualitative and quantitative data, and developing new integrated approaches that take into account the spatio-temporal patterns in studying the impacts of the pandemic on urban residents' wellbeing, for example, will be worthwhile. Furthermore, R&D that support the full development of a Digital Earth, SDIs and interoperability standards, and strengthen data provenance and governance are needed.

B. Demonstration and deployment

For topics that are near the top of the knowledge S-curve in Figure 47.1, they need to be prototyped and/or their applications demonstrated. These efforts should have the goal of moving beyond proof of concepts and towards broader practical adoption and applications. In the past, pilots have not consolidated into operational applications in crisis response. For example, during the beginning of the COVID-19 pandemic, there was the idea that our tracking systems would be ideal to limit contact between healthy and infected people and help health authorities conduct better contact tracing and quarantine people. In a preliminary review of mobile phone applications used during the pandemic, we found that the role of geospatial technologies was very limited. We did not have proven technologies that could track individuals on a large scale. There were pilots but when they have been implemented on a rush during the pandemic, a limited contribution was provided.

Society will increasingly demand from the geospatial industry operational tools that can be embedded within community resilience systems. Current concepts of digital twins and the use of drones are spatial technologies that could not pass the "pilot" phase unless there is transdisciplinary collaborations and cooperation among practitioners in key areas such as standards and regulations. For the future, we cannot be afforded to be an industry of pilots, but we need to move into an industry of solutions. To be successful, the challenges of scaling and capital funding for technology commercialisation and/or deployment need to be addressed.

C. Frameworks, standards and regulations

There is an urgent need to develop and implement established knowledge as part of SDI frameworks and standards, and to consider relevant results from strategies A and B above for inclusion in future updates of these standards (Figure 47.1). Over time, issues around core reference data, interoperability, common geographies, integration of statistics and geography, privacy and confidentiality and cybersecurity need to be addressed. International harmonisation is key because the long-term or ultimate goal is to build the Digital Earth, country by country. Collaboration amongst UN-GGIM, the Open Geospatial Consortium (OGC) and ISO, together with national standards bodies, is vital. Broad support from the geospatial sector is needed.

Whether these frameworks and standards are initially voluntary or mandatory (or part of a regulatory regime or policy scheme) will depend on a country by country basis.

D. Training and human resource development

Across the knowledge life-cycle and maturity curve in Figure 47.1, we need to develop and implement intentional and flexible training, education and mentoring programs for personnel with different levels of capability and responsibilities in the geospatial sector and allied industries. Here we note that this is not just the role of academic institutions and professional organisations (Chapter 12) but it should be a collective goal and responsibility. After all, we have previously noted that, beyond data and technology, the critical role of leadership (at all levels) and governance cannot be overemphasised. Thus, a well-rounded program that goes beyond the technical and that fosters critical thinking and enhances collaboration and communication skills will be ideal. When the next pandemic strikes, a workforce with these attributes will be able to manage it effectively.

In all of the above, the practical challenge for the geospatial and allied sectors is to develop and deploy local resilience-enabling solutions but with global cooperation and harmonisation also in mind. Stronger partnerships and collaboration, even more than those demonstrated in the COVID-19 experience, in addressing a future pandemic will likely lead to successful outcomes. When a society's stakeholders join forces to address an existential crisis, pandemic or not, the greater good is served.

COVID-19 is a clear call to humanity to remind us to care beyond ourselves and about the need to work together to balance our interaction with the natural environment and to act – to save our common future. In this call, many people lost their lives during the COVID-19 pandemic. Their death will not be in vain if we learnt the lessons, particularly around working cooperatively to solve global crises, with a long-term perspective and more equitable societal outcomes in mind.

References

[1] United Nations. The Sustainable Development Goals Report 2020. United Nations Publications, New York, USA, 2020. URL https://unstats.un.org/sdgs/report/2020/The-Sustainable-Development-Goals-Report-2020.pdf

[2] R. McCrea, A. Walton, and R. Leonard. Developing a model of community wellbeing and resilience in response to change. Social Indicators Research, 129(1), 195-214, 2016. URL https://doi.org/10.1007/s11205-015-1099-y

[3] N.N. Taleb, Y. Bar-Yam and P. Cirillo. "On single point forecasts for fat-tailed variables." International Journal of Forecasting, October 2020. URL https://doi.org/10.1016/j.ijforecast.2020.08.008

Index

Note: Locators in *italics* represent figures and **bold** indicate tables in the text.